Read-Aloud Library
Vocabulary, Comprehension and Writing

Teacher Edition

Grade K

Terry Dodds
Fay Goodfellow
Rick Williams

 SRA

Columbus, OH

SRAonline.com

 SRA

Send all inquiries to this address:
SRA/McGraw-Hill
4400 Easton Commons
Columbus, OH 43219

ISBN: 978-0-07-612248-6
MHID: 07-612248-4

4 5 6 7 8 9 GLO 13 12 11

The *McGraw·Hill* Companies

Table of Contents

Introduction

Rationale for the Program

Long before children are able to speak using higher level vocabulary, they are able to understand and respond to sophisticated words. An extensive vocabulary is vital to a child's success in all aspects of language arts. It is important for beginning readers to develop higher level vocabulary on a verbal level long before they are able to read more difficult words. Higher level vocabulary is crucial to helping a beginning reader develop his or her reading comprehension skills.

In their book *Bringing Words to Life*, Beck, McKeown, and Kucan define three levels of vocabulary instruction by placing words into three tiers. Words in the first tier are words that do not require direct instruction. They are basic words that young children learn in their everyday lives. These are words like *house, tree,* and *car.* The second tier of words are those words that require explicit direct instruction. They are words that will allow children to expand their vocabulary into the world of mature speakers. Tier Two words enable children to become more precise and descriptive with their language. They are higher level words that are easy to explain in simple terms to young children. These are words like *curious, amazing,* and *starving.* Tier Three words are words that are best taught within a content area such as science, social studies, or literature. These are words like *metamorphosis, community,* and *plot.*

The SRA Read-Aloud Library: Vocabulary, Comprehension and Writing Teacher Edition combines two research-validated instructional approaches: Direct Instruction as designed by Siegfried Engelmann and robust vocabulary instruction as designed by Beck, McKeown, and Kucan. Vocabulary instruction in this program is explicit and developmental. It follows a tight instructional sequence that offers children an opportunity to interact with each word in a number of contexts, both literature-based and expository. Simple, easy to understand definitions are offered to the children. The conceptual framework for parts of speech are provided to children as words are categorized as naming, action, or describing words. The focus of this program is to provide children with instruction in Tier Two words and Tier Three words as related to literary analysis.

The SRA Read-Aloud Library: Vocabulary, Comprehension and Writing Teacher Edition provides you and your students a vocabulary development program that is trade book based. An important goal of this program is to provide children lessons that will instill a joy and enthusiasm for learning new words.

This multidimensional program offers the students literary works including folk tales, fairy tales, legends, and poetry, as well as social studies and science expository works.

In most lessons the children are presented with six Tier Two words each week. Four of the target words are words directly from the story. Two words each week are concept words. These concept words represent an abstract concept that can be applied to what is happening in the story. For example, children can understand the concept behind the word *desperate* as applied to *The Ant and the Grasshopper* as "wanting something very, very badly."

Program Components

A library of read-aloud trade books

A teacher edition that includes
- Explicit direct instruction lessons
- Activity Blackline Masters (BLMs)
- BLM folding expository books for independent reading (Lessons 16–25)
- Vocabulary Tally Sheet BLM
- Picture Vocabulary Card BLMs
- Quiz Answer Sheet BLM
- Weekly classroom center instructions
- A BLM homework program
- A glossary of all of the words taught in this program

Teaching the Lessons

The lessons for each trade book should take five days to teach. Lessons will take 30–45 minutes each day, depending on the length of the trade book. The preparation box provides an easy reference of the materials required for each day's lesson.

Lessons are designed to provide a thorough instructional sequence that uses the following conventions:

- What you say is printed in blue.
- (What you do is in parenthesis.)
- *Responses that are expected from children are written in black italics.*

For example:
(Show the illustration on pages 2 and 3.)

What do you think is happening? (Idea: *The grasshopper is going to play. The ant is getting ready to work.*)

A variety of formats for children's responses are offered:

- The question requires an answer that calls for the same response from all children. A hand or verbal signal can be used to get children to respond in unison. This provides children with an opportunity to become more actively involved in the lesson and to respond to more questions. For example: The name of a book or story is called the title. What is a title? *The name of a book or story.* What's another way of saying the name of a book or story? *Title.*
- If there are a number of possible responses to a question, the expected responses from children will be preceded by the word *Idea* or *Ideas.* These open-ended responses will produce a variety of answers. For example: What happened when Jack got home? (Ideas: *His mother threw the beans out; she sent him to bed without any supper.*)
- Some questions require a response based on the personal experiences of children. For these items the question is asked with no expected response listed. For example: Tell about a time when you were considerate.

Lessons follow a consistent pattern throughout

the program that provides explicit direct instruction as well as cumulative practice and review. Numerous encounters over time with the words enable children to incorporate them into their speaking vocabulary. Children participate in a number of activities that enable them to interact with the words in a variety of situations.

A typical week's sequence may be as follows:

Day 1: On the first day children are introduced to the book and learn the key elements of a book such as title, author, and illustrator. They participate in making predictions about what will happen in the story and share those predictions with their classmates. Children are invited to take a picture walk as they explore the possibilities of what is happening in the story. Children are offered the opportunity to formulate questions they may have about the story or the book. The story is read aloud to children with minimal interruptions. The four target vocabulary words and their meanings are introduced for the first time within the context of how they are used in the story. Words for the week are placed on the Vocabulary Tally Sheet. Finally, a Homework Sheet is given to the children to take home.

Day 2: The second day's lesson begins with the story being read aloud and then discussed. The questioning sequence in the story encourages children to become actively involved in responding to the story and to use higher level thinking skills. Children are encouraged throughout this discussion to use the target words in their discussion. Target vocabulary that was introduced on Day 1 is reviewed. One word each week is extended by teaching the children an alternate meaning for the word. The two concept or expanded target vocabulary words and their meanings are also taught to the children.

Day 3: Children are involved in a number of activities to allow them to practice using the new vocabulary words in a variety of ways, including retelling the story, playing word games, and completing an activity sheet.

Day 4: Literary analysis and cumulative review are provided in the fourth day of instruction.

Children play a verbal game that uses all of the new words in addition to words that have been taught in earlier lessons. Children also learn songs that help them recall the literary elements and patterns.

Day 4: Literary analysis and cumulative review are provided on the fourth day of instruction. The children play a verbal game that uses all of the new words in addition to words that have been taught in earlier lessons. The children also learn songs that help them recall the literary elements and patterns.

Day 5: On the last day children retell the story to a partner. An assessment is administered to measure for mastery of the new vocabulary as well as review items.

Children are allowed to choose a book that they would like you to read as a reward. Each week children are taught the routine for the learning center that they will work in the following week. The Super Words Center provides children with an opportunity to practice using the new vocabulary and to review vocabulary that has been taught in previous lessons. Words that are taught each week should be placed on a word wall and added to each week.

Using the Picture Vocabulary Cards

The Picture Vocabulary Cards for the week can be found at the top of the BLM for the homework program. These word cards should be copied and used in each day's lesson as well as in the Super Words Center at the end of each week.

You may wish to enlarge and laminate the cards for classroom use. The smaller size cards work well in the Super Words Center and may also be laminated for greater durability. You may find it useful to have a small pocket chart for displaying the words during the lessons.

Children are not expected to read the words on the Picture Vocabulary Cards. The words are for your information only. However, as children use the cards, some children will begin to read the words.

Using the Vocabulary Tally Sheet

The Vocabulary Tally Sheet (BLM A) provides you with a place to record the number of times each of the target words is used within a week. Each time you or children use the word, a tally mark should be placed on the Vocabulary Tally Sheet. It is important to model the use of the words in your everyday interactions with the children. This modeling is important for helping children incorporate the higher level words into their speaking vocabulary.

Using the Homework Program

Homework helpers can provide valuable practice and reinforcement that is important to the success of this vocabulary program. Each lesson provides you with a BLM Homework Sheet. The sheet gives the homework helper a simple weekly homework routine that can be used to reinforce the vocabulary words taught each week. The homework routine is consistent from week to week. Once the homework helper and the child know the routine, it remains the same throughout the program.

Copies of the Picture Vocabulary Cards are on the sheet as well as the word game that was played in class with those words that week.

You may wish to send a letter at the beginning of the program to introduce the homework helper to the homework routine. Another option is to have an information session to explain and demonstrate the homework routine.

It is important to explain to the homework helper that when the expected answer is preceded by the word *idea,* the child may not use the exact wording given. The homework helper should encourage the child to give an answer that is as close as possible to the idea. If the child makes a mistake, the homework helper should be instructed to tell the child the answer and to repeat the item at the end of the game.

Encourage the homework helper to make the homework routine fun and interactive. Remind him or her that children are not expected to read the words on the Picture Vocabulary

Cards. The words are for homework helper information only. However, as children use the cards, some children will begin to read the words.

The homework program can also be used at school as an intervention component if homework cannot be completed outside of the school day.

Playing the Word Games

The word games in this program offer children an opportunity to interact with the new vocabulary words and their meanings in a number of fun contexts. The games challenge children to use higher level thinking skills as they try to beat you at "word play."

The correction procedure for most of the games is the same. If children make an error, simply tell them or demonstrate the correct answer and then repeat the item at the end of the game.

The same game that is played in class that week is on the Homework Sheet for the homework helper to use. This provides further reinforcement of the vocabulary words and their meanings that were taught in that day's lesson.

The Show Me, Tell Me Game

In the Show Me, Tell Me Game, children are asked to show, through actions or facial expressions, what a vocabulary word means. They are then asked what the word is that they are "showing."

Today you will play the Show Me, Tell Me Game. I'll ask you to show me how to do something. If you show me, you will win one point. If you can't show me, I get the point.

Next I'll ask you to tell me. If you tell me, you will win one point. If you can't tell me, I get the point.

Whoopsy!

In the game *Whoopsy!* children are asked to discriminate between sentences that use the vocabulary word correctly or incorrectly. When they catch you making an error, they must provide a corrected version of the sentence to earn a point.

Today you will play *Whoopsy!* I'll say sentences using words we have learned. If the word doesn't fit in the sentence, you say "Whoopsy!" Then I'll ask you to say a sentence where the word fits. If you can do it, you get a point. If you can't do it, I get the point. If the word I use fits the sentence, don't say anything.

Chew the Fat

Chew the Fat develops children's listening and discrimination skills as they try to catch you using a vocabulary word incorrectly. They are then asked to finish the sentence starter with correct usage of the word.

Today you will play *Chew the Fat.* Remember that a long time ago, when people wanted to just sit and talk about things that were happening in their lives, they would say that they would sit and "chew the fat."

In this game, I will say some sentences with our vocabulary words in them. If I use the vocabulary word correctly, say "well done." If I use the word incorrectly, say "Chew the fat." That means that you want to talk about how I used the word. I'll say the beginning of the sentence again. If you can make the sentence end so that it makes sense, you'll get a point. If you can't, I get the point.

Tom Foolery

Tom Foolery develops children's listening and discrimination skills as they try to catch you making up a false meaning for words that have more than one meaning. They are then asked to finish the sentence starter with correct usage of the word.

Today I will teach you a new game called *Tom Foolery.* I will pretend to be Tom. Tom Foolery tries to trick students. Tom knows that some words have more than one meaning. He will tell you one meaning that will be correct. Then he will tell you another meaning that might be correct or it might be incorrect.

If you think the meaning is correct, don't say anything. If you think the meaning is incorrect, sing, "Tom Foolery." Then Tom will have to tell the truth and tell the correct meaning. Tom is sly enough that he may include some words that do not have two meanings. Be careful! He's tricky!

Hear, Say

Hear, Say is another game that develops children's listening and discrimination skills as they try to catch you making up "untruths" about how to use the vocabulary words. They are then asked to finish the sentence starter with correct usage of the word.

In *Hear, Say*, I will say some sentences with our vocabulary words in them. Some of the sentences I say will include hearsay—there might be some untruths and extra bits in them. If you think what I am saying is not true, say "Hear, Say!" That means you want to suggest a way to make the sentence truthful and not just hearsay. I'll say the beginning of the sentence again. If you can make the sentence end so that it makes sense, you'll get a point. If you can't, I get the point.

If I use the vocabulary word correctly and there are no untruths in what I say, say "That's the honest truth!" Be careful, though—if you say "That's the honest truth!" when there is hearsay in the sentence, I will get a point!

The Choosing Game

The Choosing Game challenges children to make choices by choosing the correct word from the two choices that are given. In the easier version of the game, children are shown the two Picture Vocabulary Cards and must make the correct choice.

Today you will play the Choosing Game. Let's think about the four words we have learned; decided, shouted, squeaked, and muttered. (Display the word cards.) I will say a sentence that has two of our words in it. You will have to choose which word is the correct word for that sentence.

What's My Word?

In this riddle game the children are given clues. It is their job to guess which word is being described.

Today you will play *What's My Word?* I'll give you three clues. After I give each clue, if you are sure you know my word you may make a guess. If you guess correctly, you will win one point. If you make a mistake, I get the point.

Using the Activity Sheet

A BLM Activity Sheet is provided each week. These sheets can be copied for individual children to use. Activity sheets give children practice with skills introduced in the program such as sequencing, matching, and beginning written expression.

Assessing Progress

Each week you should assess children's progress by playing the Happy Face Game. The Happy Face Game is a weekly assessment tool that tests the children's understanding of that week's words and provides some cumulative review. BLM B, the Happy Face Game Test Sheet, can be found in the Appendix.

A child must score 9 out of 10 to be at the mastery level. If a child does not achieve mastery, insert the missed words as additional items in the games for next week's lessons. Retest those children individually for the missed items before they take the next mastery test

Using the Super Words Classroom Center

At the end of each week children should be introduced to the Super Words Center activity. Children's participation in the Super Words Center will provide them with important hands-on practice as they interact conversationally with their peers using the new vocabulary.

Instructions for preparing each week's center are provided in the preparation box. The centers are designed to require a minimal amount of additional materials. Picture

Vocabulary Cards for the games should be copied and placed in plastic bags or containers. One set of materials will be needed for each pair of children who will be working at any given time in a center. For example, if four children will be working in the center, you will need two sets of cards.

A procedure for demonstrating the game is provided each week. It is important to demonstrate the use of the center before children are expected to use it independently.

Songs Found in the Program

Children delight in learning through music and songs. This program contains two cumulative songs that help children remember the literary elements and story patterns that they are learning during the literary analysis portion of each week's lessons.

The Story Song
By Rick Williams

(Sung to the tune of "Barnyard Song," also known as "Bought Me a Cat.")

Read me a book, and the book pleased me.
I read my book under yonder tree.
Book says, "I'm a story."
Read me a book, and the book pleased me.
I read my book under yonder tree.
Title says what its name is.
Book says, "I'm a story."

Read me a book, and the book pleased me.
I read my book under yonder tree.
Author says, "I'm who wrote it."
Title says what its name is.
Book says, "I'm a story."

Read me a book, and the book pleased me.
I read my book under yonder tree.
Illustrator draws the pictures.
Author says, "I'm who wrote it."
Title says what its name is.
Book says, "I'm a story."

Read me a book, and the book pleased me.
I read my book under yonder tree.
Characters make it happen.
Illustrator draws the pictures.
Author says, "I'm who wrote it."
Title says what its name is.
Book says, "I'm a story."

Read me a book, and the book pleased me.
I read my book under yonder tree.
Illustrations are the pictures.
Characters make it happen.
Illustrator draws the pictures.
Author says, "I'm who wrote it."
Title says what its name is.
Book says, "I'm a story."

Read me a book, and the book pleased me.
I read my book under yonder tree.
Setting tells where it happens.
Illustrations are the pictures.
Characters make it happen.
Illustrator draws the pictures.
Author says, "I'm who wrote it."
Title says what its name is.

The Poetry Song
By Rick Williams

(Sung to the tune of
"Row, Row, Row Your Boat.)

Rhyme, rhyme, rhyming words,
Making us a poem
Tell about where we like to live
Call it "Home, Sweet Home".

Rhyme, rhyme, rhyming words,
Making us a poem
Syllables tell us how many parts
Each of them will own.

Rhyme, rhyme, rhyming words,
Making us a poem
Something sweet that's sure to repeat
Patterns make it flow!

Rhyme, rhyme, rhyming words,
Making us a poem,
Rhythm's a pattern of strong and weak,
Feel it in your bones.

Rhyme, rhyme, rhyming words,
Making us a poem,
The refrain is the most familiar part,
Listen and you'll know!

Choose, choose, choose some lovely
words,
Quietly rehearse,
Take your time and polish your diamond,
Make a shapely verse!

Charts

On the following page are examples of simple charts that you will use for literary analysis activities. The lesson number(s) for each chart are specified above it.

Chart Graphics

Week 8

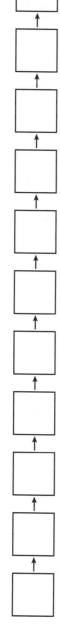

Week 9, 10

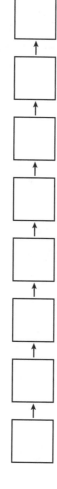

Week 11

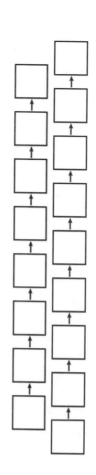

Week 12

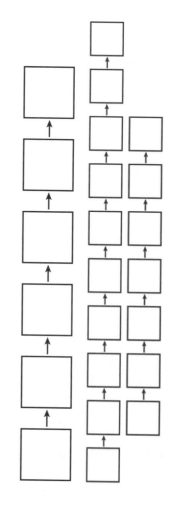

Chart Graphics

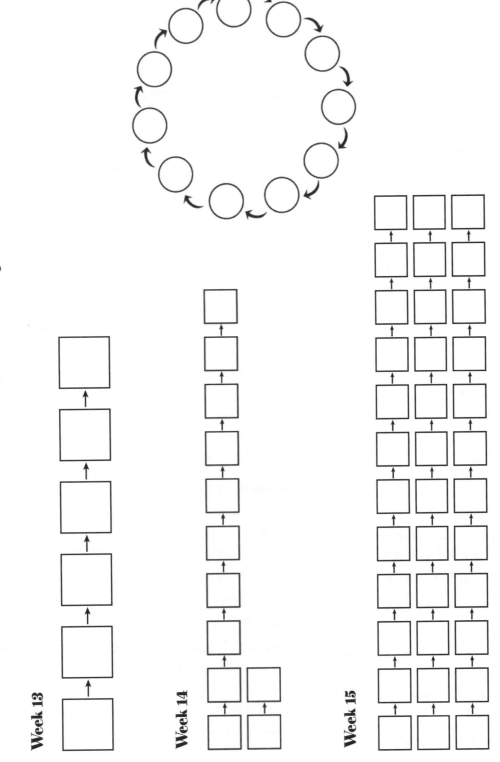

Week 13

Week 14

Week 15

Word List

accident something bad that happens that no one expects, and someone gets hurt

adventures dangerous or exciting journeys

allow give permission to do something

ambulance a truck made to carry sick or hurt people to the hospital

angry feeling mad at someone or something

annoy disturb and irritate

appear can be seen

appreciated thankful for what someone did

aquatic lives or grows on or in the water

arrive come to a place

attach to join or connect things

attractive nice to look at

awesome amazing and hard to believe

bare nothing is covering it

awkward 1. clumsy and have trouble getting your body parts to work together.
2. embarrassed and uncomfortable

bare nothing is covering it

beat the sounds that are in a rhythm

beware be careful

blossom 1. a flower that will turn into fruit.
2. grow or get better at things

bored tired because something is not interesting to you

bother 1. give someone trouble and disturb them. 2. take the trouble or trouble yourself

brave not afraid to do something that was hard

bullied frightened and picked on by people bigger than you

burrow dig down in the ground and make a tunnel or a hole

business a company that makes or sells things to earn money

calm 1. become less angry, upset, or excited. 2. not moving, or still

cave a large hole in the side of a hill or cliff or under the ground

chef a person who is a very skilled cook

chores jobs you have to do nearly every day

clues facts that help people solve a mystery or a puzzle

clumsy not good at actions with hands or feet

collect 1. find things in different places and put them together so you can use them 2. people get a large number of things that are the same in some way because they really like those things, and are interested in them

colony a large group of insects that live together

comfortably do something in a way that makes you feel cozy and relaxed

conceal to hide something

congratulations what people say when they want to tell you you've done a good job at something

considerate pays attention to what someone else needs, or wants, or wishes for

continued 1. kept on going. 2. lasted for a long time

corridor a long hallway

cottage a small house in the country or near the beach

coward a person who is not brave enough to face danger, pain , or something difficult

crept moved quietly and slowly

cross mad because someone did something you didn't like

curious 1. interested in something and want to know more about it. 2. unusual, or hard to understand

customers people who buy things in a store

damp a little bit wet or moist

dangerous not safe

dawn the time of day just before the sun rises

decided carefully thought about something and chose to do it

definitely for sure

delicious tastes very, very good

demanded asked for something using a very forceful voice

den 1. a home for some kinds of wild animals, such as foxes, skunks, and wolves. 2. a cozy, comfortable room in a house where people relax and do things they enjoy

desperate wanting something very, very badly

determined made up your mind about something and won't let anything stop you

devour eat quickly and hungrily

directions information that tells how to do something or how to get where you want to go

disagreeable unfriendly and unhelpful

disappears can't be seen anymore

disobedient does not do what he or she is told to do

disruptive caused a lot of trouble

disturb 1. interrupt a person or an animal and upset them. 2. bother or worry

doorbell a button you push to let someone know you are at the door

dormant plants have lost their leaves and are not growing but are still alive

emergency a serious problem that needs attention right away

enemies animals or people that want to hurt or harm each other

enormous really, really big

exclaimed said something loudly because you were surprised and excited

exhausted so tired you can hardly move

explore travel around so you can see what places are like

few some but not many

fine 1. good. 2. money paid as a punishment for doing something wrong

fire engine a truck that carries firefighters and their tools to a fire

firefighters people who fight fires

fire station the place where firefighters work when they're not fighting fires

fool 1. a person who can easily be tricked or made to look silly. 2. to trick someone

frontier the border between the part of the country where people have settled and the part where they have not moved to yet

frost white powdery ice that forms on things in freezing weather

frustrated feeling angry about not being able to do something after you have tried and tried

furious feeling very, very angry at someone or something

gathering picking up things and putting them together in a pile so you can use them later

generous happy to share what you have with others

gentle 1. do things in a kind, careful way. 2. soft or mild

genuine real, not fake

glimpse see something for only a second before it is gone

glorious wonderful

grains 1. wheat, oat or rice seeds 2. a hard, tiny piece of something.

harvest to gather crops so you can use them for food

hatch be born from an egg

helmet a hard hat that protects your head when you are doing sports or when you are doing something dangerous

helpful able to help others

hibernate spend the winter in a deep sleep

hose a long tube of rubber or plastic that a liquid such as water can go through

hover stay in one place in the air

human a person

ignore pay no attention to

imaginary something that is not real

imagination the part of your mind that lets you make pictures of imaginary things or of things that didn't really happen

immediately right away

impressions marks made by pressing down on something

insect a small animal that has three body parts and six legs

insisted used a very firm voice to say what you were going to do and wouldn't give in

journey a long trip to a place far away

kind 1. friendly, helpful, and considerate. 2. sort or type

kit a group of items that are kept together for a reason

law a rule people must follow

legend a story that explain how things came to be

limbs 1. the branches of a tree. 2. arms and legs

load 1. put things into or onto something. 2. what you can carry at one time

mailbox a place where cards and letters are left by a mail carrier

mail carrier a person who sorts and delivers mail to people and their houses

mail cart a wheeled wagon used to carry small loads of mail

mask 1. a covering for the face. 2. to cover or hide something

meadow a field where grass and flowers grow

metamorphosis the change some animals go through as they grow from an egg to an adult

migrate fly away to spend the winter somewhere else

mistake a thought or action that was wrong

muttered spoke in a very quiet voice so no one could hear

noble a good person who would share whatever he or she had with others

notion an idea

odor a smell

parade a group of people that march, ride, or drive together down a street

paramedics people who drive ambulances and help people who are sick or hurt

parents 1. animals that have babies. 2. a human mother and father

patient can wait without complaining or getting angry or upset

peacefully do something quietly and calmly

perfect exactly right

persistent keep on trying

pester bother and annoy someone and mean to do it

petals outer parts of a flower

pitch 1. suddenly move from side to side or end to end 2. throw or toss something

pleaded asked for something with all your heart, begged for something

police officers people who make sure others are safe and follow the laws

police station a place where police officers start their day and so some of their work

polite you do the right thing and act with your best manners and actions

post office a building where the mail is sorted and stamps are sold

precious very special and important

predator an animal that hunts other animals for food

prepare get ready for something to happen

present 1. a gift. 2. being somewhere. 3. (in the present) happening right now

prey 1. an animal that is hunted by another animal for food. 2. hunt and eat

probably almost for sure

proper like you should be

protect keep safe from danger or injury

reasons the facts that explain why you think what you do

remember you still have that thing or idea in your mind

rescue save someone from danger or death

resemble look similar to someone or something else

roared 1. shouted something in a very loud voice. 2. people or things moved very fast, and made a loud noise

rough 1. harsh; not gentle or kind. 2. not smooth; has dents or bumps on it.

rude showed bad manners

scrawl 1. writing that is careless and untidy. 2. write in a messy or untidy way

seasons the different parts of the year; winter, spring, summer, and autumn

sensitive able to smell, hear, taste, feel or see very well

severely speak in a voice that is harsh, not gentle

shed an animal's hair or skin falls or drops off

shouted 1. spoke in a very loud, angry voice. 2. said something very loudly because the person they were talking to was a long way away

siren a part of a police car, fire engine or ambulance that makes a loud, shrill sound

slimy soft, wet, and slippery

slithers moves by twisting and sliding along the ground

snuggle cuddle in a warm and comfortable spot, close to someone or something

soared flew quickly and easily, very high in the sky

special 1. not ordinary; better than usual. 2. a sale of certain things for lower prices

sprawled lay down with arms and legs spread out

spray 1. put water on something. 2. a liquid flying or falling in little drops

sprouted started to grow roots and leaves

squeaked spoke in a very high voice

stalks 1. long, thin stems that connect one part of a thing to another part. 2. follows an animal quietly in order to kill it, catch it, or observe it

starving so very, very hungry you think you might die

storage a safe place to keep things until you need them

stretcher a flat bed on which a sick or hurt person can be carried

successful doing well at something you want to do

surface 1. the outside of something. 2. to come up from below

taunted tried to hurt someone's feelings by teasing or making fun of them

tempting something makes you really want to have it

ticket 1. a piece of paper given to a driver who breaks the law. 2. a small card or piece of paper that shows you have paid for something

treats cares for someone who is sick or hurt

trespassing go on someone's property without asking them first

tunnel long, wide underground tube

uncooperative won't do anything to help anyone else or to make that person's life easier

wild 1. not tame; not looked after by people. 2. badly behaved or out of control

wilderness a place where no people live

winding 1. twisting and turning as it went along. 2. turning a key, a knob, or a handle to make something work

wise smart and able to make good choices

Preparation: You will need *The Ant and the Grasshopper* by Amy Palmer for each day's lesson.

Post a copy of the Vocabulary Tally Sheet, BLM A, with this week's Picture Vocabulary Cards attached.

Each child will need one copy of the Homework Sheet, BLM 1a.

DAY 1

Introduce Program

Today we are going to start a program that will help you learn to use hard words. We will work together to learn about books and the things that make up a story. We will have lots of fun reading books, learning songs, and playing games together. Let's get started!

Introduce the Book

The name of today's book is *The Ant and the Grasshopper.* The name of a book or a story is called the title. What is a title? *The name of a book or a story.* What's another word for the name of a book or a story? *Title.*

The title of this week's book is *The Ant and the Grasshopper.* What's the title of this week's book? *The Ant and the Grasshopper.*

This book was written by Amy Palmer. The person who writes a book or a story is called the author. What's another word for a person who writes a book or a story? *Author.* What is an author? *The person who writes a book or a story.* Who's the author of *The Ant and the Grasshopper?* *Amy Palmer.*

Pat Paris made the pictures for this book. Who made the pictures for *The Ant and the Grasshopper?* *Pat Paris.*

The cover of a book usually gives us some hints of what the book is about. Let's look at the front cover of *The Ant and the Grasshopper.* What do you see in the picture? (Ideas: *There are an ant and a grasshopper; the grasshopper is playing*

The Ant and the Grasshopper
author: Amy Palmer • illustrator: Pat Paris

🎯 Target Vocabulary

Tier II	Tier III
collect	title
pleaded	author
insisted	folk tales
prepare	
*desperate	
*considerate	

*Expanded Target Vocabulary Word

with a basketball; the ant is holding a rake; there is a strawberry plant.)

(Assign each child a partner.) Get ready to tell your partner what you think this story will be about. Use the information from the cover to help you.

(Ask the following questions, allowing sufficient time for children to share their predictions with their partners.)

- Whom do you think this story is about?
- What do you think the grasshopper will do?
- Where do you think the story happens?
- When do you think this story happens?
- Why do you think the ant is holding a rake?
- How do you think the grasshopper is feeling?
- How do you think the ant is feeling?
- Do you think this story is about real animals? Tell why or why not.

(Call on several children to share their predictions with the class.)

Take a Picture Walk

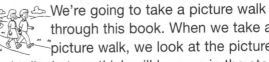

We're going to take a picture walk through this book. When we take a picture walk, we look at the pictures and tell what we think will happen in the story.

Page 3. (Point to the inset of the ant and the grasshopper.) Who do you think these creatures are? (Ideas: *The ant and the grasshopper.*)

(Point to the main illustration.) Where do you think this part of the story is happening? (Ideas: *At the beach; at a lake.*) What are people doing in the illustration? (Ideas: *Swimming; buying food; sitting in the sun; walking; eating.*) When do you think this part of the story happens? (Idea: *When it's nice; in the summer; when it's hot.*)

Page 4. What do you think is happening? (Ideas: *The grasshopper is going to play or sit in the sun; he is going to have a picnic; the ant is hauling some food; she is getting ready to work in her garden.*) Why do you think so? (Ideas: *The grasshopper has a mat, some toys, and a picnic basket; the ant has some gardening tools and food in the basket at the back of her bike.*)

Page 5. (Point to the thought balloon.) This is a thought balloon. It shows what the grasshopper is thinking about. What is the grasshopper thinking about? (Idea: *Eating popcorn.*)

(Point to the words *Beach Bum* on the grasshopper's shirt.) These words say "Beach Bum." A beach bum is someone who just likes to play and does not like to work. What do these words tell us about the grasshopper? (Idea: *He just wants to play; he does not want to work.*) What is the ant doing? (Ideas: *Carrying food—a strawberry, a tomato; she's on her way to work in her garden.*)

Page 6. When do you think this part of the story happens? (Ideas: *On a cold day, in the fall.*) Where do you think all of the people have gone? (Ideas: *Home; back to school and work.*) How do you think the grasshopper is feeling? (Ideas: *Sad; unhappy; worried; cold; lonesome.*)

Page 7. When do you think this part of the story happens? (Ideas: *On a cold day; in the winter; on a snowy day.*) How do you think the grasshopper is feeling? (Ideas: *Sad; unhappy; worried.*) What do you think is happening? (Ideas: *The grasshopper and the ant are talking; the grasshopper is at the ant's house; the grasshopper is asking for help.*)

Page 8. What do you think is happening here? (Ideas: *The grasshopper and the ant are getting food; the grasshopper and the ant are working together.*)

When do you think this part of the story happens? (Ideas: *When it's nice; in the summer, when it's hot.*)

 ## Read the Story Aloud
(Read story to children with minimal interruptions.)

Tomorrow we will read the story again, and I will ask you some questions.

(**Note:** If children have difficulty attending for an extended period of time, you may wish to present the next part of this day's lesson at another time of day.)

Present Target Vocabulary
◎⊶ Collect

In the story, the ant collected seeds, berries, beans, and corn. That means the ant found seeds, berries, beans, and corn in different places and put them together so she could use them. **Collect.** Say the word. *Collect.*

If you collect things, you find things in different places and put them together so you can use them. Say the word that means "to find things in different places and put them together so you can use them." *Collect.*

(Correct any incorrect responses, and repeat the item at the end of the sequence.)

Let's think about things you could collect. I'll name something. If you could collect that thing, say "collect." If not, don't say anything.

- Money dropped on the floor. *Collect.*
- Empty bottles to take back to the store. *Collect.*
- Houses on your street.
- A sunny day.
- Sidewalk.
- Wood for a fire. *Collect.*

What word means "to find things in different places and put them together so you can use them"? *Collect.*

◎⊶ Pleaded

In the story, when winter came, the grasshopper pleaded with the ant to help him. That means he really, really wanted the ant to help him, and he asked with all his heart. He begged the ant to help him. **Pleaded.** Say the word. *Pleaded.*

If someone pleaded for something, they asked for it with all their heart. They begged for it. Say the word that means "asked for something with all your heart; begged for something." *Pleaded.*

Let's think about some times when you might have pleaded for something. I'll name a time. If you might have pleaded at that time, say "pleaded." If not, don't say anything.

- It was bedtime, but you really, really wanted to stay up late to see a show on television. *Pleaded.*
- You were playing catch with your friend.
- Your mom packed your favorite lunch.
- You begged your mom to let your best friend sleep over. *Pleaded.*
- You rode your bike.
- You really, really wanted a puppy. *Pleaded.*

What word means "asked for something with all your heart; begged for something"? *Pleaded.*

◎← Insisted

In the story, when the grasshopper asked the ant to play, she insisted that she had to keep working. That means the ant used a very firm voice to say that she was going to keep working. She wouldn't give in about it or stop what she was doing. **Insisted.** Say the word. *Insisted.*

If you insisted, you used a very firm voice to say what you were going to do, and you wouldn't give in about it. Say the word that means "used a very firm voice to say what you were going to do and wouldn't give in about it." *Insisted.*

Let's think about times when someone might have insisted on something. I'll tell about a time. If you might have heard someone insist, say "insisted." If not, don't say anything.

- It was raining, and your mom wanted you to wear your coat to school. *Insisted.*
- Your friend wanted to play ball, but you really wanted to play tag. *Insisted.*
- The children were listening to a story.
- The boy said he had to be first in line. *Insisted.*
- Everyone laughed at the joke.
- The girl had a pet gerbil.

What word means "used a very firm voice to say what you were going to do and wouldn't give in about it"? *Insisted.*

◎← Prepare

At the end of the story, both the grasshopper and the ant worked together to prepare for winter. That means the ant and the grasshopper got ready for winter. **Prepare.** Say the word. *Prepare.*

If you prepare for something, you get ready for that thing to happen. Say the word that means "get ready for something to happen." *Prepare.*

Let's think about when people might prepare for something. If I say a time when someone was preparing for something, say "prepare." If not, don't say anything.

- Your dad cuts up vegetables for a salad. *Prepare.*
- Your sister studies hard for her math test. *Prepare.*
- Everyone runs outside to play.
- You brush your teeth, wash your face, and put on your pajamas. *Prepare.*
- You get ready to swing the bat and hit the ball. *Prepare.*
- Your teacher says "Good morning."

What word means "get ready for something to happen"? *Prepare.*

Present Vocabulary Tally Sheet

(Display the Vocabulary Tally Sheet. Explain to children that each time you or children use a new vocabulary word, you will put a mark by that word. Use the new vocabulary words throughout the week whenever an opportunity presents itself. Encourage children to do the same.)

Assign Homework

(Homework Sheet, BLM 1a: See the Introduction for homework instructions.)

DAY 2

Preparation: Picture Vocabulary Cards for *collect, pleaded, insisted, prepare.*

Read and Discuss Story

(Read story to children. Ask the following questions at the specified points in the story.)

Page 3. How did the grasshopper spend his day? (Ideas: *Watching people; walking along the boardwalk; lying on the beach in the sunshine.*) How did the ant spend her day? (Ideas: *Working and preparing for winter; collecting food for the winter.*)

Page 4. Why did the ant spend all her time collecting food? (Ideas: *So she would have enough food to eat in the wintertime.*)

Page 5. What is the grasshopper thinking about? (Idea: *The bag of popcorn that he ate.*) When you give someone advice you tell him or her what you think he or she should do. What advice did the ant give the grasshopper? (Idea: *That popcorn is good now but would not keep for winter.*) What do you think she wanted the grasshopper to do? (Idea: *Help her work.*) Did the grasshopper follow the ant's advice? *No.* What did he do? *He went to the beach.*

Page 6. How is the grasshopper feeling now? *Scared.* Why is he scared? (Idea: *Everyone has left and there is no food to eat.*) Who do you think he will go to for help? (Idea: *The ant.*)

Page 7. (Read to the end of the sentence: "Please give me something to eat.") Do you think the ant should share her food with the grasshopper? Tell why you think that. (Accept either response, as long as the child supports his or her answer with a reason. Ideas: *No, the grasshopper should have collected his own food when he had a chance. Yes, the ant had enough and she shouldn't let the grasshopper die.*)

Page 8. How did the story end? (Ideas: *The ant and the grasshopper both prepared for winter. The ant and the grasshopper both had time to play and have fun.*)

Review Vocabulary

(Display the Picture Vocabulary Cards. Point to each card as you say the word. Ask children to repeat each word after you.) These pictures show **collect, insisted, pleaded,** and **prepare.**

- What word means "asked for something with all your heart; begged for something"? *Pleaded.*
- What word means "find things in different places and put them together so you can use them"? *Collect.*
- What word means "get ready for something to happen"? *Prepare.*
- What word means "used a very firm voice to say what you were going to do and wouldn't give in"? *Insisted.*

Extend Vocabulary

 Collect

In *The Ant and the Grasshopper,* we learned that **collect** means "find things in different places and put them together so you can use them."

Here's a new way to use the word **collect.**

- **Janice will collect stamps.** Say the sentence.
- Ari and Rob collect rocks. Say the sentence.
- My mom collects spoons. Say the sentence.

In these sentences, collect tells about how people collect things for a hobby. The people get a large number of things that are the same in some way because they really like those things and are interested in them. They collect things as a hobby.

What kinds of things do you collect? (Call on several children. Encourage them to start their answers with the words "I collect …")

Present Expanded Target Vocabulary

⊙← Desperate

In the story, the grasshopper pleaded with the ant to share her food with him. He wanted food very, very badly. He was afraid he was going to die. Another way of saying the grasshopper wanted food very, very badly is to say he was desperate for food. When you are desperate, you want something very, very badly. **Desperate.** Say the word. *Desperate.*

If you are desperate, you want something very, very badly. Say the word that means "wanting something very, very badly." *Desperate.*

Let's think about when people might feel desperate. If I say a time when you or someone would feel desperate, say "desperate." If not, don't say anything.

- How you would feel if you really, really needed to go to the bathroom. *Desperate.*
- How your friend would feel if you invited him or her over to play.
- How you would feel if you lost your new coat and couldn't find it anywhere. *Desperate.*
- How you would feel if you really, really wanted a little kitten, but your mom and dad kept saying no. *Desperate.*
- How your teacher would feel if you were really good listeners.
- How your family would feel if they got a new house.

What word means "wanting something very, very badly"? *Desperate.*

◎⤙ Considerate

In the story, when the grasshopper came to the ant's door asking for food, the ant paid attention to what the grasshopper needed and said she would help him.

Another way of saying the ant paid attention to what the grasshopper needed is to say the ant was considerate. When someone pays attention to what someone else needs or wants or wishes for, the person is being considerate. **Considerate.** Say the word. *Considerate.*

If you are considerate, you pay attention to what someone else needs or wants or wishes for. Say the word that means "pays attention to what someone else needs or wants or wishes for." *Considerate.*

Let's think about things that someone might do that would be considerate. If I say something that would be considerate, say "considerate." If not, don't say anything.

- Does not push in line. *Considerate.*
- Uses a quiet voice in the library. *Considerate.*
- Grabs the crayons.
- Shares a book with a partner. *Considerate.*
- Colors on the table.
- Sets the table for supper. *Considerate.*

What word means "pays attention to what someone else needs or wants or wishes for"? *Considerate.*

Tell about a time when you were considerate. (Call on several children. Encourage children to start their answers with the words "I was considerate when …")

Preparation: Activity Sheet, BLM 1b.

Retell Story

Today I'll show you the pictures made for *The Ant and the Grasshopper*. As I show you the pictures, I'll call on one of you to tell the class that part of the story.

Tell me what happens at the **beginning** of the story. (Show the pictures on pages 2 and 3. Call on a child to tell what's happening.)

Tell me what happens in the **middle** of the story. (Show the pictures on pages 5–7. Call on a child to tell what's happening. Encourage use of the target words when appropriate. Model use as necessary.)

Tell me what happens at the **end** of the story. (Show the picture on page 8. Call on a child to tell what's happening.)

How do you think the grasshopper feels now? (Ideas: *Happy; prepared.*) Tell why you think so. (Idea: *He has time to play, but he also has food for the winter.*)

How do you think the ant feels now? (Ideas: *Happy; prepared.*) Tell why you think so. (Idea: *She has food for the winter, but she also has some time to play and have fun.*)

Introduce the Show Me, Tell Me Game

 Today you will learn to play a new game called Show Me, Tell Me. I'll ask you to show me how to do something. If you show me, you win one point. If you can't show me, I get the point.

Next I'll ask you to tell me. If you tell me, you win one point. If you can't tell me, I get the point.

Let's practice: My turn to show you how I would look if I **pleaded** for a cookie. (Show a pleading face.) What did I do? *Pleaded.*

Let's do one together. Show me how you would **collect** spilled crayons from the floor. (Pretend to collect spilled crayons with children.) What do we do? *We collect the crayons.*

 Now you're ready to play the game. (Draw a T-chart on the board for keeping score. Children earn one point for each correct answer. If they make an error, correct them as you normally would, and record one point for yourself. Repeat missed words at the end of the game.)

- Show me how you would **collect** books after we have read together. Tell me what you do. *Collect books.*
- Show me how you would look if you were **desperate** for a drink at the fountain. Tell me how you are feeling. *Desperate for a drink at the fountain.*
- Show me how you would **prepare** to go outside in the rain. Tell me what you do. *Prepare to go outside in the rain.*
- Show me how you would be **considerate** to your teacher when she is speaking. Tell me how you are acting. *Considerate.*
- Show me how you would **insist** on having a turn at a game. Tell me what you did. *Insisted on having a turn at the game.*

(Count the points and declare a winner.)
You did a great job of playing the Show Me, Tell Me game!

Complete the Activity Sheet

(Give each child a copy of the Activity Sheet, BLM 1b. Review the order of the story with children. Tell them to place the pictures in sequence to show beginning, middle, and end. Instruct children to color the pictures, cut them out, and paste or glue them in sequential order.)

DAY 4

Literary Analysis

Let's think about what we already know about how books are made.

- What do we call the name of a book? *Title.*
- What do we call the person who writes the story? *Author.*

Today we will learn a song that will help us remember some important things about books.

Listen while I sing the first verse of "The Story Song." (Sung to the tune of *Barnyard Song*. Also known as *Bought Me a Cat*.) (www.kididdles.com)

Read me a book and the book pleased me.
I read my book under yonder tree.
Book says, "I'm a story."

Read me a book and the book pleased me.
I read my book under yonder tree.
Title says what its name is.
Book says, "I'm a story."

Read me a book and the book pleased me.
I read my book under yonder tree.
Author says, "I'm who wrote it."
Title says what its name is.
Book says, "I'm a story."

Play Show Me, Tell Me Game (Cumulative Review)

Let's play the Show Me, Tell Me game you learned yesterday. I'll ask you to show me how to do something. If you show me, you win one point. If you can't show me, I get the point.

Next I'll ask you to tell me. If you tell me, you will win one point. If you can't tell me, I get the point.

 Now you're ready to play the game. (Draw a T-chart on the board for keeping score. Children earn one point for each correct answer. If they make an error, correct them as you normally would, and record one point for yourself. Repeat missed words at the end of the game.)

- Show me what you would do if you **pleaded** with me to let you go to play time early. Tell me what you did. *Pleaded.*
- Show me how you would look if you were **desperate** to answer a question your teacher had asked you. Tell me how you are feeling. *Desperate.*
- Show me how you would **collect** pencils that had fallen on the floor. Tell me what you do. *Collect pencils.*

- Show me how you would **insist** that someone be quiet in the library. Tell me what you did. *Insisted someone be quiet.*
- Show me how you would **prepare** to listen to a story. Tell me what you did. *Prepare to listen to a story.*
- Show me how you would be **considerate** to a classmate who had lost all of his pencils. Tell me how you are acting. *Considerate.*
- Show me how you would look if you were **desperate** to watch your favorite television show. Tell me how you were feeling. *Desperate.*
- Show me how you would **collect** seeds from the floor and put them in a cup. Tell me what you do. *Collect seeds.*
- Show me what you would do if you **collected** bottles to earn extra money. Tell me what you do. *Collect bottles.*
- Show me what you would do if you **prepared** your backpack for school. Tell what you do to your backpack. *Prepare it for school.*

DAY 5

Preparation: Happy Face Game Test Sheet, BLM B.

Learn About Folk Tales

Today you will learn about folk tales. What will you learn about? *Folk tales.*

A tale is another word for a story. What is a tale? *A story.* Folk are people who come from the same country and live the same kind of life. What are people who come from the same country and live the same kind of life? *Folk.* So a folk tale is a story told by people who come from the same country and live the same kind of life. What is a story told by people who come from the same country and live the same kind of life? *A folk tale.*

Long, long ago, most ordinary people in the world didn't know how to read. Could most ordinary people read? *No.* When people gathered together, they told stories to entertain themselves. How did people entertain themselves? *They told stories.*

Sometimes when parents told these stories to their children, they were trying to teach their children important things they needed to know. When parents told these stories to their children, what were they trying to teach them? (Idea: *Important things they needed to know.*)

The Ant and the Grasshopper is a folk tale. What kind of story is it? *A folk tale.*

Raise your hand if you enjoyed *The Ant and the Grasshopper.* (Pause.) Most of you enjoyed the story. That means you were entertained by the story.

When parents told this tale to their children, what do you think they were trying to teach them? (Ideas: *There is a time to work and there is a time to play; you need to be responsible for yourself; when you have a lot, you should put away something for when you have a little; it's important to share with others.*)

Assess Vocabulary

 (Give each child a copy of the Happy Face Game Test Sheet, BLM B.)

Today you're going to play the Happy Face Game. When you play the Happy Face Game, it shows me how well you know the hard words you are learning.

Before you can play the Happy Face Game, you must know about true and false.

If something is true it's right or correct. What word means "right" or "correct"? *True.* What does **true** mean? *Right or correct.*

I'll say some things. If I say something that is true, say "true." If not, don't say anything.

- You wear a shoe on your foot. *True.*
- You wear a hat on your hand.
- A dog has ears. *True.*
- A boy has ears. *True.*
- A table has ears.
- A table has legs. *True.*

What word means "right" or "correct"? *True.*

If something is false, it's wrong. What word means "wrong"? *False.* What does **false** mean? *Wrong.*

I'll say some things. If I say something that is false, say "false." If not, don't say anything.

- You wear a shoe on your head. *False.*
- A dog can sit.
- A dog can fly. *False.*
- A fish can swim.
- An elephant can fly. *False.*
- Girls have wings. *False.*

What word means "wrong"? *False.*

(Encourage children to do their own work and not to look at the work of others. Icons have been provided in front of numbers for children who do not yet recognize numerals.)

If I say something that is true, color in the happy face. What will you do if I say something that is true? *Color in the happy face.*

If I say something that is false, color in the sad face. What will you do if I say something that is false? *Color in the sad face.*

Listen carefully to each item that I say. Don't let me trick you!

Item 1: If you are **considerate,** you might help a friend. (*True.*)

Item 2: If your mom told you in a very firm voice that you had to wear your mittens to school, and she wouldn't give in about it, she **insisted** you wear your mittens. (*True.*)

Item 3: When you are hungry, you do **not** feel like eating. (*False.*)

Item 4: If you put on your raincoat before coming to school on a rainy day, you were **prepared.** (*True.*)

Item 5: If you gather things that belong together, you are **not collecting** them. (*False.*)

Item 6: If you helped a classmate with a problem, you would be **considerate.** (*True.*)

Item 7: If you really, really wanted something very badly, you might **plead.** (*True.*)

Item 8: When you are **desperate,** you want something very much. (*True.*)

Item 9: A book has an author and a title. (*True.*)

Item 10: Boys and girls usually have two arms and two legs. (*True.*)

You did a great job of playing the Happy Face Game!

(Score children's work later. A child must score 9 out of 10 to be at the mastery level. If a child does not achieve mastery, insert the missed words as additional items in the games for next week's lessons. Retest those children individually for the missed items before they take the next mastery test.)

Extensions

Read the Story as a Reward

(Display *The Ant and the Grasshopper* or alternate versions of the story. Allow children to choose which book they would like you to read to them as a reward for their hard work.)

(Read the story aloud for enjoyment with minimal interruptions.)

Preparation: Word containers for the Super Words Center.

Introduce the Super Words Center
(Place the new Picture Vocabulary Cards in the classroom center. Show children one of the word containers. If children need more guidance in how to work in the Super Words Center, role-play with two to three children as a demonstration.)

Let's think about how we work with our words in the Super Words Center.

You will work with a partner in the Super Words Center. Whom will you work with? *A partner.*

First you will draw a word out of the container. What do you do first? (Idea: *Draw a word out of the container.*)

Next you'll show your partner the picture and ask what word the picture shows. What do you do next? (Idea: *I show my partner the picture and ask what word the picture shows.*)

What do you do next? *Give my partner a turn.*

What do you do if your partner doesn't know the word? *Tell my partner the word.*

Week 2

Preparation: You will need *Jack and the Bean Stalk* by David Graham for each day's lesson.

Post a copy of the Vocabulary Tally Sheet, BLM A, with this week's Picture Vocabulary Cards attached.

Each child will need a copy of the Homework Sheet, BLM 2a.

DAY 1

Introduce Book

The name of this week's book is *Jack and the Bean Stalk.* The name of a book or a story is called the title. What's a title? *The name of a book or a story.* What's another word for the name of a book or a story? *Title.*

The title of this week's book is *Jack and the Bean Stalk.* What's the title of this week's book? *Jack and the Bean Stalk.*

This book was written by David Graham [gram]. The person who writes a book or a story is called the author. What's another word for the person who writes a book or a story? *Author.* What is an author? *The person who writes a book or a story.* Who's the author of *Jack and the Bean Stalk*? *David Graham.*

Pat Paris made the pictures for this book. Who made the pictures for *Jack and the Bean Stalk*? *Pat Paris.* The person who makes the pictures for a book or a story is called the illustrator. What's another word for the person who makes the pictures for a book or a story? *Illustrator.* What is an illustrator? *The person who makes the pictures for a book or a story.* Who's the illustrator of *Jack and the Bean Stalk*? *Pat Paris.*

The cover of a book usually gives us some hints of what the book is about. Let's look at the front cover of *Jack and the Bean Stalk.* What do you see in the picture? (Ideas: *There's a boy climbing up a big plant; he is up high; he's almost to the clouds; there's a house down below; there's a garden down below.*)

Jack and the Bean Stalk
author: David Graham • illustrator: Pat Paris

🎯 Target Vocabulary

Tier II	Tier III
cross	illustrator
crept	prediction
remember	folk tale
winding	
*brave	
*disobedient	

*Expanded Target Vocabulary Word

A stalk is the stem of a plant. What is a stalk? *The stem of a plant.* The plant in the picture is a bean plant. What kind of plant is it? *A bean plant.* So the stem the boy is climbing is called a bean stalk. What is the name of the stem the boy is climbing? *A bean stalk.* If you look carefully, you can see beans growing from the bean stalk. (Call on a child to come and point to the beans on the bean stalk.)

We have looked carefully at the cover of the book *Jack and the Bean Stalk.* Now we can make guesses about what the book is about. Our guesses are called predictions. What are guesses called? *Predictions.*

(Assign each child a partner.) Get ready to tell your partner your predictions about *Jack and the Bean Stalk.* That means you tell your partner your guesses about what you think this story will be about. Use the information from the cover to help you.

(Ask the following questions, allowing sufficient time for children to share their predictions with their partners.)

- Whom do you think this story is about?
- What do you think the boy will find at the top of the bean stalk?
- Where do you think the story happens?
- When do you think this story happens?
- Why do you think the boy is climbing the bean stalk?
- How long do you think it will take him to get to the top?

- Do you think this story is a true story? Tell why or why not.

(Call on several children to share their predictions with the class.)

Take a Picture Walk

 We're going to take a picture walk through this book. When we take a picture walk, we look at the pictures and tell what we think will happen in the story.

Page 1. What do you think is happening? (Ideas: *The woman is talking to the boy; the boy is feeding the cow; the woman is going to milk the cow.*) Why do you think so? (Ideas: *The woman has a pail; the boy has hay on the pitch fork.*)

Page 2. Where do you think the boy is going with the cow? What do you think the man is saying to the boy?

Page 3. What do you think is happening? Why do you think so? What's different about those beans? (Idea: *They're all different colors.*)

Page 4. Why do you think the cow is going with the man? Why do you think so? What do you think the boy is putting in his pocket?

Page 5. What do you think is happening? Why do you think so? How do you think the woman is feeling? How can you tell?

Pages 6–7. What do you think is happening? (Idea: *The boy is climbing the beanstalk and finding a castle.*)

Pages 8–9. Whom do you think the woman is? (Idea: *The lady who lives in the castle.*)

Do you see how big she is next to the boy? In stories like *Jack and the Bean Stalk,* a very big and strong person like this woman is called a giant. What do we call this woman? *A giant.*

Pages 10–11. What do you think is happening? (Idea: *The man is eating.*) This man is also very big and strong. What do we call him? *A giant.*

Pages 16–17. Where is the boy now? (Idea: *Back at the giant's castle.*)

Pages 18–19. What is different about the eggs the hen laid? (Idea: *They're made of gold.*)

Pages 20–21. What do you think is happening? (Ideas: *The boy has stolen the hen and is climbing down the bean stalk; he is chopping down the beanstalk with his ax.*)

Page 22. How does the story end? (Ideas: *The boy and his mother are drinking tea; they are wearing very fancy clothes.*)

It's your turn to ask me some questions. What would you like to know about the story? (Accept questions. If children tell about the pictures or the story instead of ask questions, prompt them to ask a question.) Ask me a question about who is in the story. Ask me a when question. Ask me a why question.

Read the Story Aloud

(Read story to children with minimal interruptions.)

Tomorrow we will read the story again, and I will ask you some questions. (If children have difficulty attending for an extended period of time, you may wish to present the next part of this day's lesson at another time of day.)

Present Target Vocabulary
Cross

In the story, the giant's wife said the giant was very cross with her. That means the giant was mad at her because she did something he didn't like. She gave Jack breakfast, and then he stole the giant's gold. Then everything she did made the giant mad. **Cross.** Say the word. *Cross.*

If you're cross with someone, you're mad because he or she did something you didn't like. Now everything he or she does makes you mad. Say the word that means "mad because someone did something you didn't like." *Cross.*

(Correct any incorrect responses, and repeat the item at the end of thie sequence.)

Let's think about things that might make you or someone else cross. I'll tell about something. If that thing could make someone cross, say "cross." If not, don't say anything.

- Someone stepped on your toe. *Cross.*
- Someone took something that belongs to you. *Cross.*
- Eating lunch.
- Someone fixed your bike for you.

- Someone took the book you wanted in the library. *Cross.*
- Saying "Hello!"

What word means "mad because someone did something you didn't like"? *Cross.*

⊙← Crept

In the story, when the giant fell asleep, Jack crept out of the big pot. That means he moved as quietly and slowly as he could. He didn't want to wake up the giant. **Crept.** Say the word. *Crept.*

Crept comes from the word **creep.** It means "did creep." **Crept** is a way of moving. **If you crept, you moved as quietly and slowly as you could.** Say the word that means "moved as quietly and slowly as you could." *Crept.*

(Call on a student.) Show me what you would look like if you crept to the door. (Pause.) Everyone, what did _____ do? _____ *crept to the door.* Everyone, show me how you would look if you crept around the room. (Pause.) Good, you crept around the room. I hardly knew you were moving.

Let's think about some times when a person or an animal might have crept. I'll tell about a time. If the person or the animal might have crept, say "crept." If not, don't say anything.

- When the lion was sleeping, the mouse wanted to get away quietly. *Crept.*
- Todd wanted to get to the finish line first.
- Dad burned his hand and wanted to get to the doctor's office.
- You wanted a cookie from the kitchen but mom already said "no." *Crept.*
- You wanted to surprise your teacher by coming into the classroom without her knowing. *Crept.*
- The cat wanted to get past the doghouse without the dog's hearing. *Crept.*

What word means "moved as quietly and slowly as you could?" *Crept.*

⊙← Remember

In the story, the author asked you to remember that Jack was really hungry because he didn't have any supper the night before. When you remember something, you keep that thing or

idea in your mind. **Remember.** Say the word. *Remember.*

If I knew I had oatmeal for breakfast yesterday, I would remember that I had it. Say the word that means you "still have a thing or an idea in your mind." *Remember.*

Let's think about things that you could remember. If I say something that you could remember, say "remember." If not, don't say anything.

- What you had for supper last night. *Remember.*
- The name of your teacher. *Remember.*
- The title of **every** book in the library.
- The names of **everyone** in our school.
- Where you can find a pencil in our classroom. *Remember.*
- Martin wanted to play catch with his brother.

What word means "still have a thing or idea in your mind"? *Remember.*

⊙← Winding

In the story, when Jack climbed up the bean stalk, he found another land in the sky and a road that went winding over the hills. That means the road was twisting and turning as it went from the bean stalk to the giant's house. **Winding.** Say the word. *Winding.*

If a road, river, or line of people was winding its way somewhere, it was twisting and turning as it went along. Say the word that means "twisting and turning as it went along." *Winding.*

Watch me. I'll use my hand to show a winding road. (Move your hand from side to side in a winding motion.) Use your hand to show a winding river. (Pause.) Good, you used your hand to show a winding river.

Let's think about some times when someone or something might be winding somewhere. I'll tell about a time. If I tell about a time when someone or something might be winding, say "winding." If not, don't say anything.

- We twisted and turned as we played "Follow the Leader." *Winding.*
- The road to the airport twisted and turned. *Winding.*

- We went straight outside for a fire drill.
- You had to walk around the trees, rocks, and streams in the forest. *Winding.*
- The baseball player ran to first base.
- You walked home as fast as you could.

What word means "twisting and turning as it went along"? *Winding.*

Present Vocabulary Tally Sheet
(See Lesson 1, page 3, for instructions.)

Assign Homework
(Homework Sheet, BLM 2a: See the Introduction for homework instructions.)

DAY 2

Preparation: Picture Vocabulary Cards for *cross, crept, remember, winding.*

Read and Discuss Story

 (Read story aloud to children. Ask the following questions at the specified points in the story. Encourage children to use target words in their answers.)

Page 1. Why do Jack and his mother have to sell the cow? (Ideas: *She doesn't give milk; they have no money for food.*)

Page 4. Why does Jack sell the cow to the funny little old man? (Idea: *So he can get the magic beans.*) Does Jack believe the beans are magic? *No.* Then why does he sell the cow for the beans? (Idea: *The man says that if the beans don't grow up to the sky he will give Jack his cow back.*) Do you think the funny little old man would really give the cow back? Tell why or why not.

Page 5. What happens when Jack gets home? (Ideas: *His mother throws the beans out; she sends him to bed without any supper.*)

Page 9. What good news does the giant woman give Jack? *She will give him some breakfast.* What bad news does she have? *Her husband likes to eat little boys.*

Page 10. Where does Jack hide? *In the oven.*

Page 11. (Read to the end of the sentence: "The giant said I smell fresh meat.") What do you think he smells? (Idea: *Jack.*)

Page 11. (Read to the end of the page.) What does the giant say after he says he smells fresh meat? *"Fe, Fi, Fo, Fum, I smell fresh meat and I must have some."* (Have children repeat the rhyme until they all can say it.) What does the giant's wife say he smells? *The sheep she cooked yesterday.* After the giant finishes his breakfast, what does he ask for? (Idea: *His gold.*)

Page 14. Do you think Jack should have taken the giant's gold? Tell why or why not. (Accept either response as long as children give a reason.)

Page 17. Where does Jack hide this time? *In a pot.*

Page 18. Everyone, say what the giant says when he smells fresh meat. *"Fe, Fi, Fo, Fum, I smell fresh meat and I must have some."* Name four places the giant's wife looks for Jack. (Ideas: *In the oven; behind the door; in the cupboard; under the table.*)

Page 19. After the giant finishes his breakfast, what does he ask for? (Idea: *His hen.*)

Page 20. What happens to the giant? (Ideas: *Jack kills him; he dies; he breaks his neck.*)

Page 21. How does the story end? (Ideas: *Jack's mother tells him that the giant had stolen the gold and magic hen from Jack's father; Jack, his mother, and the magic hen live happily ever after.*)

Review Vocabulary
(Display the Picture Vocabulary Cards. Point to each card as you say the word.) These pictures show **cross, crept, remember,** and **winding.**

- What word means "still have a thing or an idea in your mind"? *Remember.*
- What word means "moved as quietly and slowly as you could"? *Crept.*
- What word means "mad because someone did something you didn't like"? *Cross.*
- What word means "twisting and turning as it went along"? *Winding.*

Extend Vocabulary

 Winding

In *Jack and the Bean Stalk*, we learned that **winding** means "twisting and turning as it went along."

Here's a new way to use the word **winding**.

- Petey was **winding** up the car window. Say the sentence.
- Alice was **winding** up her mother's music box. Say the sentence.
- The little boy was **winding** up the toy rabbit and watching it hop. Say the sentence.

In these sentences, winding up means turning a key, a knob, or a handle to make something work. What might you turn when you're winding up a car window? (Idea: *A handle.*) What might you turn when you're winding up a music box? (Idea: *A key.*) What might you turn when you're winding up a toy rabbit? (Idea: *A key, a knob, or a handle.*)

Name something that needs winding up to make it work. (Call on several children.)

Present Expanded Target Vocabulary

Disobedient

In the story, Jack's mother told him to sell the cow. She wanted him to sell the cow to get money so they could buy some food. Jack didn't do what his mother told him to do. He traded the cow for some magic beans.

Another way of saying Jack didn't do what his mother told him to do is to say that Jack was disobedient. When Jack didn't do what he was told to do, he was disobedient. **Disobedient.** Say the word. *Disobedient.*

When a person does not do what he or she is told to do, he or she is disobedient. Say the word that means "does not do what he or she is told to do." *Disobedient.*

Let's think about things that would be disobedient. If I say something that would be disobedient, say "disobedient." If not, don't say anything.

- Not lining up when your teacher asked you to. *Disobedient.*
- Going to your friend's house when your aunt told you to come home. *Disobedient.*
- Lining up quietly when your teacher asked you to.
- Not looking both ways before you crossed the street after your mother told you to. *Disobedient.*
- Wearing a bicycle helmet when your dad told you to.
- Cleaning your room when your grandma told you to.

What word means "does not do what he or she is told to do"? *Disobedient.*

Tell about a time when you were disobedient. (Call on several children. Encourage them to start their answers with the words "I was disobedient when …")

Brave

In the middle of the story *Jack and the Bean Stalk*, Jack was not afraid to climb the bean stalk again, even though he knew it was hard. He knew that the giant ate little boys, but he was not afraid. Jack was very brave because he was not afraid to do something hard. Another way of saying Jack was not afraid to do something hard is to say Jack was brave. **Brave.** Say the word. *Brave.*

If you are brave, you are not afraid to do something, even though you know it is hard. Say the word that means "not afraid to do something hard." *Brave.*

Let's think about some times when people might be brave. If I say a time when someone would be brave, say "brave." If not, don't say anything.

- Going downstairs in the dark even though you were scared. *Brave.*
- Playing with your favorite toy.
- Not crying or yelling when you got a bee sting. *Brave.*
- Telling your teacher the truth when you did something you weren't supposed to do. *Brave.*
- Eating your lunch.
- Teaching your friend to play a game.

What word means "not afraid to do something hard"? *Brave.*

Preparation: Activity Sheet, BLM 2b.

Retell Story

Today I'll show you the pictures Pat Paris made for *Jack and the Bean Stalk.* As I show you the pictures, I'll call on one of you to tell the class that part of the story.

Tell me what happens at the **beginning** of the story. (Show the pictures on page 1. Call on a child to tell what's happening.)

Tell me what happens in the **middle** of the story. (Show the pictures on pages 2–20. Call on a child to tell what's happening. Encourage use of target words when appropriate. Model use as necessary.)

Tell me what happens at the **end** of the story. (Show the pictures on pages 21 and 22. Call on a child to tell what's happening.)

How do you think Jack and his mother feel now? (Ideas: *Happy; full—not hungry or starving; rich.*) Tell why you think so. (Ideas: *They're having tea; they're wearing fancy clothes; they're smiling.*)

Review the Show Me, Tell Me Game

Today you will play the Show Me, Tell Me Game. I'll ask you to show me how to do something. If you show me, you will win one point. If you can't show me, I get the point.

Next I'll ask you to tell me. If you tell me, you will win one point. If you can't tell me, I get the point.

Let's practice: My turn to show you how I would look if I felt **cross** because I had to stay very late after school. (Show a cross face.) How am I feeling? *Cross.*

Let's do one together. Show me how a dog would look if he **crept** past a mean person. (Creep with the children.) What did the dog do? *It crept.*

Now you're ready to play the game. (Draw a T-chart on the board for keeping score. Children earn one point for each correct answer. If they make an error, correct them as

you normally would, and record one point for yourself. Repeat missed words at the end of the game.)

- Show me what you would do if I asked you to stand up and you were **disobedient.** Tell me how you acted. *Disobedient.*
- Show me that you **remember** my name. Tell me what you do. *Remember your name.*
- Show me how you would walk a **winding** path in "Follow the Leader." Tell me what kind of path you walked. *Winding.*
- Show me how you would look if you were being **brave.** Tell me how you looked. *Brave.*
- Show me how you would look if you **crept** to get past a sleeping giant safely. Tell me what you did. *I crept.*
- Show me how your teacher looks when you forget to wipe your feet before coming inside on a yucky, mucky day. Tell me how your teacher looked. *Cross.*

(Count the points and declare a winner.) You did a great job of playing the Show Me, Tell Me Game!

Complete the Activity Sheet

(Give each child a copy of the Activity Sheet, BLM 2b. Review with children the order they will place the pictures to put them in sequence to show beginning, middle, and end. Instruct the children to color the pictures, cut them out, and paste or glue them in sequential order.)

Literary Analysis

Let's think about what we already know about how books are made.

- What do we call the name of the book? *Title.*
- What do we call the person who writes the story? *Author.*
- What do we call the person who draws the pictures? *Illustrator.*

Today we will sing a song that will help us remember some important things about books.

Listen while I sing the first verses of "The Story Song."

Read me a book and the book pleased me.
I read my book under yonder tree.
Book says, "I'm a story."

Read me a book and the book pleased me.
I read my book under yonder tree.
Title says what its name is.
Book says, "I'm a story."

Read me a book and the book pleased me.
I read my book under yonder tree.
Author says, "I'm who wrote it."
Title says what its name is.
Book says, "I'm a story."

Now we'll add a new verse that tells about the illustrator. What does the illustrator of a story do? *Draws the pictures.* Let's add that to the song by singing "Illustrator draws the pictures." What are we going to add to our song? *Illustrator draws the pictures.*

Read me a book and the book pleased me.
I read my book under yonder tree.
Illustrator draws the pictures.
Author says, "I'm who wrote it."
Title says what its name is.
Book says "I'm a story."

Now we'll sing the whole song. (Repeat the song, adding in the new verse. See the Introduction for the complete Story Song.)

Play Show Me, Tell Me Game (Cumulative Review)

Let's play the Show Me, Tell Me Game you learned last week. I'll ask you to show me how to do something. If you show me, you will win one point. If you can't show me, I get the point.

Next I'll ask you to tell me. If you tell me, you will win one point. If you can't tell me, I get the point.

Now you're ready to play the game. (Draw a T-chart on the board for keeping score. Children earn one point for each correct

answer. If they make an error, correct them as you normally would, and record one point for yourself. Repeat missed words at the end of the game.)

- Show me how you would look if I told you that recess was cancelled for the rest of the week. Tell me how you are looking. *Cross.*
- Show me what you would do if you were a kitten trying to sneak past a ferocious dog. Tell me what you did. *Crept.*
- Show me that you **remember** the name of our school. Tell me what you do. *Remember the name of our school.*
- Show me what you would do if I asked you to wave your hand and you were **disobedient.** Tell me how you acted. *Disobedient.*
- Show me how you would walk a path around trees, rocks, and streams in the forest. Tell me what kind of path you are walking. *A winding path.*
- Show me how you would turn a key to make a music box work. Tell me what you are doing to the music box. *Winding it up.*
- Show me how you would look when you are not afraid to read a hard book aloud. Tell me how you are looking. *Brave.*
- Show me what you would do if you **collected** crayons from the floor and put them in a tub. Tell me what you do. *Collect crayons.*
- Show me what you would do if you **prepared** to go out in the snow. Tell me what you do. *Prepare to go out in the snow.*

DAY 5

Preparation: Happy Face Game Test Sheet, BLM B.

Learn About Folk Tales

Today you will remember what you have learned about folk tales. What did you learn about? *Folk tales.*

A tale is another word for a story. What is a tale? *A story.* Folk are people who come from the same country and live the same kind of life. What are people who come from the same country and live the same kind of life? *Folk.* So a folk tale is a story told by people who come from the same country and live the same kind of life. What is a story told by people who come from the same country and live the same kind of life? *A folk tale.*

Long, long ago, most ordinary people in the world didn't know how to read. Could most ordinary people read? *No.* When people gathered together, they told stories to entertain themselves. How did people entertain themselves? *They told stories.*

Sometimes when parents told these stories to their children, they were trying to teach their children important things they needed to know. When parents told these stories to their children, what were they trying to teach them? (Idea: *Important things they needed to know.*)

Jack and the Bean Stalk is a folk tale. What kind of story is *Jack and the Bean Stalk*? *A folk tale.*

Raise your hand if you enjoyed *Jack and the Bean Stalk.* (Pause.) Most of you enjoyed the story. That means you were entertained by the story. Stories about ordinary people outsmarting giants are always entertaining, aren't they?

When parents told this tale to their children, what do you think they were they trying to teach them? (Ideas: *Children should look after their parents; bad things happen to people who do bad things.*) Today most parents look after their children, but long, long ago it was very different. Children were expected to look after their parents.

(**Note:** You may wish to discuss with children that Jack was really taking back from the giant what was his, as the giant had stolen the treasures from Jack's father.)

Assess Vocabulary

 (Give each child a copy of the Happy Face Game Test Sheet, BLM B.)

Today you're going to play the Happy Face Game. When you play the Happy Face Game, it shows me how well you know the hard words you are learning.

Before you can play the Happy Face Game, you must remember about true and false.

If something is true, it's right or correct. What word means "right" or "correct"? *True.* What does **true** mean? *Right or correct.* I'll say some things. If I say something that is true, say "true." If not, don't say anything.

- You have hair on your head. *True.*
- Dogs say, "Meow!"
- Airplanes fly. *True.*
- A room has a door. *True.*
- You walk on the ceiling.
- You blow your nose and wipe your feet. *True.*

What word means "right" or "correct"? *True.*

If something is false, it's wrong. What word means "wrong"? *False.* What does **false** mean? *Wrong.*

I'll say some things. If I say something that is false, say "false." If not, don't say anything.

- Books are good to eat. *False.*
- Chairs are for sitting on.
- Fish draw pictures. *False.*
- Vegetables are good for you.
- Cows can sing. *False.*
- You see with your stomach. *False.*

What word means "wrong"? *False.*

If I say something true, color in the happy face. What will you do if I say something that is true? *Color in the happy face.*

If I say something false, color in the sad face. What will you do if I say something that is false? *Color in the sad face.*

Listen carefully to each sentence that I say. Don't let me trick you!

Item 1: If you are **brave,** you will run away screaming. (*False.*)

Item 2: If you don't do what your teacher asks you to do you are being **disobedient.** (*True.*)

Item 3: If I ask you to say my name and you do, you **remember** my name. (*True.*)

Item 4: **Cross** means very happy. (*False.*)

Item 5: If you are turning the key on a music box you are **winding** up the music box. (*True.*)

Item 6: If a road is very straight with no curves, it is a **winding** road. (*False.*)

Item 7: **Crept** means that someone moved while making a lot of noise. (*False.*)

Item 8: If you are mean to other people and never pay attention to what other people want, you are **considerate.** (*False.*)

Item 9: If you threw marbles all over the room, you **collected** them. (*False.*)

Item 10: If you wear your rubber boots and take an umbrella on a rainy day, you are **prepared.** (*True.*)

You did a great job of playing the Happy Face Game!

(Score children's work. A child must score 9 out of 10 to be at the mastery level. If a child does not achieve mastery, insert the missed words as additional items in the games for next week's lessons. Retest those children individually for the missed items before they take the next mastery test.)

Extensions

Read a Story as a Reward

(Display *Jack and the Bean Stalk* and *The Ant and the Grasshopper* or display alternate versions of the stories. Allow children to choose which book they would like you to read to them as a reward for their hard work.)

(Read story aloud for enjoyment with minimal interruptions.)

 Introduce the Super Words Center
(Add the new Picture Vocabulary Cards to words from the previous week. Show children one of the word containers. If children need more guidance in how to work in the Super Words Center, role-play with two or three children as a demonstration.)

Let's think about how we work with our words in the Super Words Center.

You will work with a partner in the Super Words Center. Whom will you work with? *A partner.*

First you will draw a word out of the container. What do you do first? (Idea: *Draw a word out of the container.*)

Next you will show your partner the picture and ask what word the picture shows. What do you do next? (Idea: *I show my partner the picture and ask what word the picture shows.*)

What do you do next? *Give my partner a turn.*

What do you do if your partner doesn't know the word? *Tell my partner the word.*

Preparation: You will need *The Three Little Pigs* by Margot Zemach for each day's lesson.

Number the pages of the story to assist you in asking comprehension questions at appropriate points.

Post a copy of the Vocabulary Tally Sheet, BLM A, with this week's Picture Vocabulary Cards attached.

Each child will need one copy of the Homework Sheet, BLM 3a.

DAY 1

Introduce Book

This week's book is called *The Three Little Pigs.* Remember that the name of a book is called the title. What's the title of this week's book? *The Three Little Pigs.*

This book was written by Margot Zemach [mar-go zem-ack]. Remember that an author is the person who writes a book or a story. Who's the author of *The Three Little Pigs*? *Margot Zemach.*

Margot Zemach also made the pictures for this book. Remember that an illustrator is the person who makes the pictures for a book or a story. Who is the illustrator of *The Three Little Pigs*? *Margot Zemach.*

The cover of a book usually gives us some hints of what the book is about. Let's look at the front cover of *The Three Little Pigs.* What do you see in the illustration? (Ideas: *There are three pigs; one pig is looking at some flowers; one pig is smelling a turnip; one pig is sitting by a river—he is covered with mud; all the pigs are wearing clothes.*)

(Assign each child a partner.) Remember that when you make a prediction about something, you say what you think will happen. What do you do when you make a prediction? *You say what you think will happen.* Get ready to make some predictions to your partner about this book. Use the information from the cover to help you.

The Three Little Pigs
author: Margot Zemach • illustrator: Margot Zemach

Target Vocabulary

Tier II	Tier III
gathering	character
meadow	folk tale
roared	
angry	
*furious	
*delicious	

*Expanded Target Vocabulary Word

(Ask the following questions, allowing sufficient time for children to share their predictions with their partners.)

- Whom do you think this story is about?
- What do you think the pigs in the story will do?
- Where do you think the story happens?
- When do you think this story happens?
- Why do you think the pigs are doing what they are doing?
- How do you think the pigs are feeling?
- Do you think this story is about real pigs? Tell why or why not.

(Call on several children to share their predictions with the class.)

Take a Picture Walk

We're going to take a picture walk through this book. Remember that when we take a picture walk, we look at the pictures and tell what we think will happen in the story.

Pages 1–2. What do you think is happening? (Idea: *The little pigs are leaving home.*) Why do you think so? (Idea: *They are waving good-bye; they have a suitcase, a bag, and a box.*) How do you think the momma pig is feeling? *Sad.* Tell me why you think so. (Idea: *There's a tear on her cheek.*) Where do you think the little pigs are going?

Pages 3–4. What do you think is happening here? (Idea: *The little pig got some straw from the farmer and he is building a house.*)

Pages 5–6. What is happening to the little pig's house? (Idea: *The wolf is blowing it down.*) What do you think will happen to the little pig? (Ideas: *He'll run away; the wolf will catch him; the wolf will eat him.*)

Pages 7–8. What do you think is happening here? (Ideas: *The little pig got some sticks from the man; he is building a house.*)

Pages 9–10. What is happening to the little pig's house? (Idea: *The wolf is blowing it down.*) What do you think will happen to the little pig? (Ideas: *He'll run away; the wolf will catch him; the wolf will eat him.*)

Pages 11–12. What do you think is happening here? (Ideas: *The little pig got some bricks from the man; he is building a house.*)

Pages 15–16. What is happening to the little pig's house? (Idea: *Nothing.*) How do you think the wolf is feeling? (Ideas: *Angry; frustrated; mad.*)

Pages 25–26. What do you think is happening here? (Idea: *The wolf is going down the chimney.*) How do you think the little pig is feeling? (Ideas: *Scared; frightened.*)

Page 27. What do you think the pig is eating? (Idea: *The wolf.*) Tell why you think so. (Ideas: *There are bones on the floor; the wolf's tail is coming out of the pot; we don't see the wolf anymore.*)

It's your turn to ask me some questions. What would you like to know about the story? (Accept questions. If children tell about the pictures or the story instead of ask questions, prompt them to ask a question.) Ask me a question about who is in the story. Ask me a why question.

Read Story Aloud
(Read story to children with minimal interruptions.)

Tomorrow we will read the story again, and I will ask you some questions. (If children have difficulty attending for an extended period of time, you may wish to present the next part of this day's lesson at another time of day.)

Present Target Vocabulary
Gathering

In the story, the first little pig met a man who was gathering straw. That means the man was picking up bits of straw and putting them together in a pile so he can use them. **Gathering.** Say the word. *Gathering.*

If you are gathering things, you are picking them up and putting them together in a pile. Say the word that means "picking up things and putting them together in a pile." *Gathering.*

(Correct any incorrect responses, and repeat the item at the end of the sequence.)

Let's think about things that you could be gathering. I'll name something. If you could be gathering that thing, say "gathering." If not, don't say anything.

- Wood for a fire. *Gathering.*
- Toys on the floor. *Gathering.*
- Tall trees in the park.
- Stars in the sky.
- Buildings.
- Crayons to make a picture. *Gathering.*

What word means "picking up things and putting them together in a pile"? *Gathering.*

Meadow

In the story, the third little pig crossed the meadow to get to the apple tree. That means he crossed a field with grass and flowers growing in it. **Meadow.** Say the word. *Meadow.*

A meadow is a field where grass and flowers grow. Sometimes horses and cows are put in a meadow so they can eat the grass. Say the word that means "a field where grass and flowers grow." *Meadow.*

Let's think about things that you might see in a meadow. I'll name something. If you might see it in a meadow, say "meadow." If not, don't say anything.

- Grass. *Meadow.*
- Lots of trees.
- Cows. *Meadow.*
- Flowers. *Meadow.*
- A city.
- Horses. *Meadow.*

What word means "a field where grass and flowers grow"? *Meadow.*

◎—≪ Roared

In the story, the wolf was so angry that he roared at the third little pig. That means the wolf shouted at the little pig using a very loud voice. **Roared.** Say the word. *Roared.*

If someone roared, they shouted something in a very loud voice. Say the word that means "shouted something in a very loud voice." *Roared.*

Let's think about times when someone or something might have roared. I'll tell about a time. If someone or something might have roared, say "roared." If not, don't say anything.

- A lion was trapped under a net. *Roared.*
- A cat was being petted.
- The crowd saw the batter hit a home run. *Roared.*
- The tiger was mad. *Roared.*
- The children listened to the story.
- The man saw the car coming towards the little boy. *Roared.*

What word means "shouted something in a very loud voice"? *Roared.*

◎—≪ Angry

In the story, the wolf was angry when the little pig kept tricking him. That means the wolf was mad at the little pig. **Angry.** Say the word. *Angry.*

If you are angry, you are feeling mad at someone or something. Say the word that means "feeling mad at someone or something." *Angry.*

Let's think about when people might have felt angry. If I say a time when someone would have felt angry, say "angry." If not, don't say anything.

- Your mom fixed your favorite meal.
- Your sister got you into trouble. *Angry.*
- Someone took your new coat. *Angry.*
- Your little brother broke your game. *Angry.*
- You won a great prize.
- A girl hit her thumb with a hammer. *Angry.*

What word means "feeling mad at someone or something"? *Angry.*

Show me how your face would look if you felt angry when someone pushed you in line. Tell me how you are feeling. *Angry.*

Present Vocabulary Tally Sheet
(See Lesson 1, page 3, for instructions.)

Assign Homework
(Homework Sheet, BLM 3a. See the Introduction for homework instructions.)

DAY 2

Preparation: Picture Vocabulary Cards for *gathering, meadow, roared, angry.*

Read and Discuss the Story

(Read story to children. Ask the following questions at the specified points. Encourage them to use target words in their answers.)

Page 1. What does the momma pig tell her three little pigs? *"Build good, strong houses, and always watch out for the wolf. Now good-bye, my sons, good-bye."* Why do you think she tells her little pigs that? (Ideas: *So they would be safe; so the wolf won't catch them; they are leaving.*)

Page 3. What does the first little pig use to build his house? *Straw.* Do you think the straw house will be a good strong house? *No.* Tell why not.

Page 6. What happens when the wolf comes along? (Idea: *He blows the straw house down and eats the pig.*)

Page 7. What does the second little pig use to build his house? *Sticks.* Do you think the house made of sticks will be a good strong house? *No.* Tell why not.

Page 10. What happens when the wolf comes along? (Idea: *He blows down the house made of sticks and eats the pig.*)

Page 11. What does the third little pig use to build his house? *Bricks.* Do you think the brick house will be a good strong house? *Yes.* Tell why you think so.

Page 15. What happens when the wolf comes along? (Idea: *He can't blow down the brick house.*)

Page 18. (Point to a turnip.) The vegetable in this picture is called a turnip. What is this vegetable called? *A turnip.* Why do you think the wolf invites the pig to the turnip field? (Idea: *He is trying to trick him into coming out of his house.*)

Page 19. Does the wolf's trick work? *No.* Tell why not. (Idea: *The pig goes to the turnip field before the wolf comes.*) How do you think the wolf will feel? (If the children do not suggest "angry," say "If I were the wolf, I'd probably feel angry.")

Page 20. How does the wolf feel when he finds out that the pig has tricked him? *Very angry.* How does the wolf try to trick the pig next? (Idea: *He says he knows where the pig can get apples.*) Does the wolf's trick work? *No.* Tell why not. (Idea: *The pig goes to the apple tree before the wolf comes.*)

Page 22. How does the wolf try to trick the pig next? (Idea: *He says he will take the pig to the fair in town.*) Does the wolf's trick work? *No.* Tell why not.

Page 26. What happens to the wolf? (Idea: *He falls into the pot and is cooked.*)

Page 27. How does the story end? (Idea: *The pig has wolf soup for supper.*)

Review Vocabulary

(Display the Picture Vocabulary Cards. Point to each card as you say the word. Ask children to repeat each word after you.) These pictures show **gathering, meadow, roared,** and **angry.**

- What word means "a field where grass and flowers grow"? *Meadow.*
- What word means "picking up things and putting them together in a pile"? *Gathering.*
- What word means "shouted something in a very loud voice"? *Roared.*
- What word means "feeling mad at someone or something"? *Angry.*

Extend Vocabulary
◎⚫ Roared

In *The Three Little Pigs,* we learned that **roared** means "shouted something in a very loud voice."

Here's a new way to use the word **roared.**

- The plane **roared** down the runway. Say the sentence.
- The race car **roared** around the track. Say the sentence.

- The children **roared** around the house. Say the sentence.

In these sentences, roared tells how people or things moved and sounded. The people or things moved very fast and made a loud noise. They roared.

Present Expanded Target Vocabulary
◎⚫ Furious

In the story, the wolf wasn't able to catch the third little pig, so he became very, very angry. Another way of saying he was very, very angry is to say he was furious. When you are furious, you are very, very angry. **Furious.** Say the word. *Furious.*

If you are furious, you are feeling very, very angry at someone or something. Say the word that means "feeling very, very angry at someone or something." *Furious.*

Let's think about when people might feel furious. If I say a time when someone would feel furious, say "furious." If not, don't say anything.

- How my mother would feel if I spilled my juice on purpose. *Furious.*
- How you would feel if you got a new bicycle for your birthday.
- How your teacher would feel if nobody listened. *Furious.*
- How your friend would feel if you shared your toys.
- How you would feel if you always got blamed for things you didn't do. *Furious.*
- If you were the only one who had to clean up after everybody made a big mess. *Furious.*

What word means "feeling very, very angry"? *Furious.*

◎⚫ Delicious

In the story, when the wolf ate the first little pig, he said "Yumm-yum!" When he ate the second little pig, he said "Yumm-yum!" Do you think the wolf liked the way the little pigs tasted? *Yes.* The wolf thought the little pigs tasted very, very good.

Another way of saying the little pigs tasted very, very good is to say they were delicious. When something tastes delicious, it tastes very, very good. **Delicious.** Say the word. *Delicious.*

If something tastes delicious, it tastes very, very good. Say the word that means "tastes very, very good." *Delicious.*

Let's think about things that might taste delicious. If I say something that would taste delicious, say "delicious." If not, don't say anything.

- Ripe strawberries. *Delicious.*
- A red, juicy apple. *Delicious.*
- Sour lemons.
- A cold glass of milk. *Delicious.*
- A crunchy carrot. *Delicious.*
- Rotten grapes.

What word means "tastes very, very good"? *Delicious.*

At the end of the story, the third little pig eats wolf soup. He says "Yumm-yum!" He thought the wolf soup was … *Delicious.*

DAY 3

Preparation: Activity Sheet, BLM 3b.

Retell Story

Today I'll show you the pictures Margot Zemach made for *The Three Little Pigs.* As I show you the pictures, I'll call on one of you to tell the class that part of the story.

Tell me what happens at the **beginning** of the story. (Show the pictures on pages 1 and 2. Call on a child to tell what's happening.)

Tell me what happens in the **middle** of the story. (Show the pictures on pages 3–24. Call on a child to tell what's happening. Encourage use of target words when appropriate. Model use as necessary.)

Tell me what happens at the **end** of the story. (Show the pictures on pages 25–27. Call on a child to tell what's happening.)

How do you think the third little pig feels? (Ideas: *Happy; good; full; proud; safe.*)

Play the Show Me, Tell Me Game

Today you will play the Show Me, Tell Me Game. I'll ask you to show me how to do something. If you show me, you will win one point. If you can't show me, I get the point.

Next I'll ask you to tell me. If you tell me, you will win one point. If you can't tell me, I get the point.

Let's practice: My turn to show you how I would look if I felt **angry** because I had to stay very late after school. (Show an angry face.) How am I feeling? *Angry.*

Let's do one together. Show me how a race car would sound if it **roared.** (Roar like a race car with children.) What did the race car do? *It roared.*

Now you're ready to play the game. (Draw a T-chart on the board for keeping score. Children earn one point for each correct answer. If they make an error, correct them as you normally would, and record one point for yourself. Repeat missed words at the end of the game.)

- Show me how you would look if you were **gathering** your toys from the floor. Tell me what you're doing. *Gathering toys from the floor.*
- Show me how a lion would sound if it **roared.** Tell me what the lion did. *It roared.*
- Show me how your face would look if you felt **angry** when someone broke your favorite toy. Tell me how you are feeling. *Angry.*
- Show me how you would gather flowers in the **meadow.** Tell me where you gathered flowers. *In the meadow.*
- Show me how a vacuum cleaner would sound if it **roared.** Tell me what the vacuum clean did. *It roared.*

(Count the points and declare a winner.)
You did a great job of playing the Show Me, Tell Me Game!

Complete the Activity Sheet

(Give each child a copy of the Activity Sheet, BLM 3b. Review with children the order they will place the pictures to put them in sequence to show beginning, middle, and end.)

Preparation: Prepare two sheets of chart paper, each with a circle drawn in the middle. Fold the sheets of paper in half vertically to divide the circles in half. When you record children's responses, physical descriptors should be recorded on the left-hand side of each chart. Personality characteristics or actions should be recorded on the right-hand side.

Analyze Characters (Literary Analysis)

Let's think about what we already know about how books are made.

- What do we call the name of the book? *Title.*
- What do we call the person who writes the story? *Author.*
- What do we call the person who draws the pictures? *Illustrator.*

Let's sing the first verses of "The Story Song" to help us remember some important things about books. (See the Introduction for "The Story Song.")

Today we will learn more about how stories are made.

The characters in a story are the people or animals the story is about. What are the people or animals a story is about? *Characters.* Who are the characters in a story? *The people or animals the story is about.*

In *The Three Little Pigs,* are the characters people or animals? *Animals.*

Who are the characters in the story? (Ideas: *Momma pig; the first little pig; the second little pig; the third little pig; the wolf.*)

The most important characters in the story about the three little pigs are the third little pig and the wolf. Who are the most important characters in the story? *The third little pig; the wolf.* (Write *third little pig* in the middle of the circle on one of the charts; write *wolf* in the middle of the circle on the other sheet.)

Let's remember what we know about the third little pig. (Show children page 11.) What does the third little pig look like? (Call on several children. Record each child's response on the left-hand side of the pig chart.) (Ideas: *Long nose; blue pants; black jacket; wears a cap; has two toes.*)

(Show children page 12. Ask these questions. Call on several children. Record each child's response on the right-hand side of the chart.)

Do you think the third little pig is happy or sad? (Idea: *Happy.*) Tell why you think that. (Idea: *It looks like he's smiling.*) Do you think he likes to work hard or is lazy? (Idea: *Likes to work hard.*) Tell why you think that. (Idea: *Building a brick house by himself is hard.*)

(Show children page 18.) What does the third little pig like to eat? *Turnips.*

(Show children page 20.) What else does the third little pig like to eat? *Apples.* What else can you tell us about the third little pig? (Ideas: *He's smart; he likes to play tricks; he likes wolf soup.*)

(Follow a similar process to describe the wolf. Record responses on the second piece of chart paper.)

Today you have learned about the wolf and the third little pig. They are the two most important characters in *The Three Little Pigs.*

Now we'll learn a new verse to "The Story Song." Our sentence about characters will be "Characters make it happen."

Let's add that to the song by singing "Characters make it happen." What are we going to add to our song? *Characters make it happen.*

Read me a book and the book pleased me.
I read my book under yonder tree.
Characters make it happen.
Illustrator draws the pictures.
Author says "I'm who wrote it."
Title says what its name is.
Book says "I'm a story."

Now we'll sing the whole song.

Play Show Me, Tell Me Game (Cumulative Review)

Let's play the Show Me, Tell Me Game. I'll ask you to show me how to do something. If you show me, you will win one point. If you can't show me, I get the point.

Next I'll ask you to tell me. If you tell me, you will win one point. If you can't tell me, I get the point.

Now you're ready to play the game. (Draw a T-chart on the board for keeping score. Children earn one point for each correct answer. If they make an error, correct them as you normally would, and record one point for yourself. Repeat missed words at the end of the game.)

- Show me what you would do if you **pleaded** with me to let you go to recess early. Tell me what you did. *Pleaded.*
- Show me how you would look if you were very, very **angry.** Tell me how you are feeling. *Furious.*
- Show me how you would look if I told you to wave and you didn't. Tell me how you acted. *Disobedient.*
- Show me how a crowd would sound if it **roared.** Tell me what the crowd did. *It roared.*
- Show me with your hand how a **winding** road would look. Tell me what kind of road you showed me. *A winding road.*
- Show me how you would gather flowers in the **meadow.** Tell me where you gathered flowers. *In the meadow.*
- Show me how you would look if you ate something that was very **delicious.** Tell me how it tasted. *Delicious.*
- Show me how you would look if you were **cross** at your friend because she did something that you didn't like. Tell me how you are feeling. *Cross.*
- Show me how you would look if you were **angry** with your friend for not playing with you. Tell me how you are feeling. *Angry.*
- Show me how you would look if you were **desperate** to give the correct answer. Tell me how you are feeling. *Desperate.*

Preparation: Happy Face Game Test Sheet, BLM B.

Learn About Folk Tales

Today you will learn more about folk tales. What will you learn about? *Folk tales.*

A tale is another word for a story. What is a tale? *A story.* Folk are people who come from the same country and live the same kind of life. What are people who come from the same country and live the same kind of life? *Folk.* So a folk tale is a story told by people who come from the same country and live the same kind of life. What is a story told by people who come from the same country and live the same kind of life? *A folk tale.*

Long, long ago, most ordinary people in the world didn't know how to read. Could most ordinary people read? *No.* When people gathered together, they told stories to entertain themselves. How did people entertain themselves? *They told stories.*

Sometimes when parents told these stories to their children, they were trying to teach their children important things they needed to know. When parents told these stories to their children, what were they trying to teach them? (Idea: *Important things they needed to know.*)

The Three Little Pigs is a folk tale. What kind of story is *The Three Little Pigs*? *A folk tale.*

Raise your hand if you enjoyed *The Three Little Pigs.* (Pause.) Most of you enjoyed the story. That means you were entertained by the story.

When parents told this tale to their children, what do you think they were they trying to teach them? (Ideas: *If you're going to do a job, do it well; if you use your head you can save yourself from danger; the easiest way isn't always the best way.*)

Assess Vocabulary

 (Give each child a copy of the Happy Face Game Test Sheet, BLM B.)

Today you're going to play the Happy Face Game. When you play the Happy Face Game, it shows me how well you know the hard words you are learning.

If I say something that is true, color in the happy face. What will you do if I say something that is true? *Color in the happy face.*

If I say something that is false, color in the sad face. What will you do if I say something that is false? *Color in the sad face.*

Listen carefully to each item that I say. Don't let me trick you!

Item 1: If you are **furious,** you are very, very mad. (*True.*)

Item 2: If you were in a place with lots of tall trees, you would be in a **meadow.** (*False.*)

Item 3: A mouse who moved as loudly as it could past a sleeping cat **crept** past the cat. (*False.*)

Item 4: **Angry** means mad. (*True.*)

Item 5: If you are picking up your toys off the floor, you are **gathering** up your toys. (*True.*)

Item 6: If a lion **roared,** it made a very quiet sound. (*False.*)

Item 7: If you ate a meal that tasted good, you would say "That was **delicious**!" (*True.*)

Item 8: If your father **insisted** that you wear your mittens, he didn't really care that you wore them. (*False.*)

Item 9: When you **remember** someone's name, it means that you have kept that person's name in your mind. (*True.*)

Item 10: A firefighter who saves people's lives from fires is **brave.** (*True.*)

You did a great job of playing the Happy Face Game!

(Score children's work. A child must score 9 out of 10 to be at the mastery level. If a child does not achieve mastery, insert the missed words as additional items in the games for next week's lessons. Retest those children individually for the missed items before they take the next mastery test.)

Extensions

Read a Story as a Reward

(Display copies of the books that you have read since the beginning of the program or display alternate versions of *The Three Little Pigs.* Allow children to choose which book they would like you to read to them as a reward for their hard work.)

(Read the story aloud for enjoyment with minimal interruptions.)

Preparation: Word containers for the Super Words Center.

Introduce the Super Words Center

(Add the new Picture Vocabulary Cards to words from the previous two weeks. Show children one of the word containers. If children need more guidance in how to work in the Super Words Center, role-play with two or three children as a demonstration.)

Let's think about how we work with our words in the Super Words Center.

You will work with a partner in the Super Words Center. Whom will you work with? *A partner.*

First you will draw a word out of the container. What do you do first? (Idea: *Draw a word out of the container.*)

Next you will show your partner the picture and ask what word the picture shows. What do you do next? (Idea: *I show my partner the picture and ask what word the picture shows.*)

What do you do next? *Give my partner a turn.*

What do you do if your partner doesn't know the word? *Tell my partner the word.*

Preparation: You will need *The Little Red Hen* for each day's lesson.

- You will need *The Three Little Pigs* for Day 2.
- Number the pages of the story to assist you in asking questions at appropriate points.
- Post a copy of the Vocabulary Tally Sheet, BLM A, with this week's Picture Vocabulary Cards attached.
- Each child will need one copy of the Homework Sheet, BLM 4a.

DAY 1

Introduce Book

This week's book is called *The Little Red Hen*. What's the title? *The Little Red Hen.*

This book was written by Margot Zemach [mar-go zem-ack]. Who's the author of *The Little Red Hen*? *Margot Zemach.*

Margot Zemach also made the pictures for this book. Remember that an illustrator is the person who makes the pictures for a book or story. Who's the illustrator of *The Little Red Hen*? *Margot Zemach.*

The cover of a book usually gives us some hints of what the book is about. Let's look at the front cover of *The Little Red Hen*. What do you see in the illustration? (Ideas: *I see the little red hen; I see her three babies; the hen is wearing clothes; one baby has a hat.*)

(**Note:** If children do not use the word *chicks*, introduce the word, saying:) Baby chickens are called chicks. What are baby chickens called? *Chicks.* What are chicks? *Baby chickens.*

(Assign each child a partner.) Remember that when you make a prediction about something, you say what you think will happen. What do you do when you make a prediction? *You say what you think will happen.*

The Little Red Hen
author: Margot Zemach • illustrator: Margot Zemach

Target Vocabulary

Tier II	Tier III
cottage	character
harvest	folk tale
grains	
sprouted	
*determined	
*uncooperative	

*Expanded Target Vocabulary Word

Get ready to make some predictions to your partner about this book. Use the information from the cover to help you.

(Ask the following questions, allowing sufficient time for children to share their predictions with their partners.)

- Whom do you think this story is about?
- What do you think the hen in the story will do?
- Where do you think the story happens?
- When do you think this story happens?
- Why do you think the birds are doing what they are doing?
- How do you think the birds are feeling?
- Do you think this story is about real birds? Tell why or why not.

(Call on several children to share their predictions with the class.)

Take a Picture Walk

We're going to take a picture walk through this book. Remember that when we take a picture walk, we look at the pictures and tell what we think will happen in the story.

Page 1. Where do you think the chickens are? (Idea: *At home.*) Why do you think so? (Ideas: *I can see the lamp, the chairs, and the toys.*) What do you think is happening? (Ideas: *The chicks are playing; the hen is holding a towel.*) How do you think the hen is feeling? (Idea: *Happy.*) Tell me why you think so. (Idea: *It looks like she's smiling, talking, or singing.*)

Pages 2–3. What do you think is happening here? (Ideas: *The hen is talking to the goose, the cat, and the pig; the goose, the cat, and the pig look like they are walking away.*)

Pages 4–5. What do you think is happening here? (Idea: *The hen is planting some seeds.*)

Pages 6–7. What do you think is happening here? (Ideas: *The seeds have come up; the plants are growing.*)

Pages 8–9. What do you think the hen is saying to the other animals?

Pages 10–11. What is the hen doing? (Idea: *Cutting down the plants.*) What are the other animals doing? (Idea: *Watching the hen work.*) How do you think the hen is feeling? Why do you think so? (Accept any reasonable responses as long as children give a reason.)

Pages 12–13. What are the goose, the cat, and the pig doing? (Idea: *Playing cards.*) How do you think the hen is feeling now? (Idea: *Tired.*) Why do you think so? (Ideas: *She is wiping her head; she is sitting down.*)

Pages 14–15. Who is the only one working? *The hen.*

Pages 16–17. What are the goose, the cat, and the pig doing now? (Idea: *Sitting on a bench.*) What do you think the hen is saying to the other animals?

Pages 18–19. What is the hen doing? (Idea: *Pushing the wagon.*)

Pages 20–21. What are the goose, the cat, and the pig doing now? (Idea: *Playing cards.*) What do you think the hen is saying to the other animals?

Pages 22–23. What do you think is happening here? (Idea: *The hen is baking bread.*)

Pages 26–27. What do you think the hen is saying to the other animals?

Page 28. What do you think is happening here? (Idea: *The hen and her chicks are eating the bread she made.*)

It's your turn to ask me some questions. What would you like to know about the story? (Accept questions. If children tell about the pictures or the story instead of ask questions, prompt them

to ask a question.) Ask me a why question. Ask me a how question.

Read the Story Aloud
(Read story to children with minimal interruptions.)

Tomorrow we will read the story again, and I will ask you some questions. (If children have difficulty attending for an extended period of time, you may wish to present the next part of this day's lesson at another time of day.)

Present Target Vocabulary
 Cottage

In the story, the little red hen lived with her chicks in a small cottage. That means they lived in a small house. Cottages are often built in the country or near a beach. **Cottage.** Say the word. *Cottage.*

If you live in a cottage, you live in a small house in the country or near the beach. Say the word that means "a small house in the country or near the beach." *Cottage.*

(Correct any incorrect responses, and repeat the item at the end of the sequence.)

Let's think about cottages. I'll tell you something. If what I say could be about a cottage, you say "cottage." If not, don't say anything.

- A small family could live there. *Cottage.*
- It would have 100 rooms.
- It might be built near a beach. *Cottage.*
- It would have ten bathrooms.
- Fifty families could live there.
- Jack and his mother lived there before he climbed the bean stalk. *Cottage.*

What word means "a small house in the country or near the beach"? *Cottage.*

 Harvest

In the story, the little red hen asked the goose, the cat, and the pig to help her harvest the wheat. That means she asked them to help her gather the wheat from her garden. **Harvest.** Say the word. *Harvest.*

When you harvest something like wheat or potatoes, you gather those plants so you can use them for food. Plants that you gather for food are called crops. Say the word that means "to gather crops so you can use them for food." *Harvest.*

Let's think about things that you harvest. I'll name something. If you could harvest that thing, say "harvest." If not, don't say anything.

- Corn. *Harvest.*
- Pumpkins. *Harvest.*
- Jelly beans.
- Cars.
- Cows.
- Wheat. *Harvest.*

What word means "to gather crops so you can use them for food"? *Harvest.*

◎⫷ Grains

In the story, the little red hen collected the golden grains from the wheat and poured them into a large sack. That means the hen collected the seeds from the wheat. **Grains.** Say the word. *Grains.*

Grains are seeds of plants such as wheat, oats, or rice. Say the word that means "seeds of plants such as wheat, oats, or rice." *Grains.*

Let's think about things that are grains. I'll name something. If the thing I name is a grain, say "grains." If not, don't say anything.

- Rice. *Grains.*
- Wheat. *Grains.*
- Oats. *Grains.*
- Potatoes.
- Oranges.
- Green beans.

What word means "seeds of plants such as wheat, oats, or rice"? *Grains.*

◎⫷ Sprouted

In the story, the grains of wheat the little red hen planted sprouted. That means grains of wheat started to grow roots and leaves. **Sprouted.** Say the word. *Sprouted.*

If a seed sprouted, it started to grow roots and leaves. Say the word that means "started to grow roots and leaves." *Sprouted.*

Let's think about things that might sprout. I'll name something. If that thing sprouted, say "sprouted." If not, don't say anything.

- The bean seed grew roots and leaves. *Sprouted.*
- The carrot seed grew roots and leaves. *Sprouted.*
- The apple tree grew flowers.
- Pears were on the pear tree.
- The baby lamb was born.
- The potato grew new roots and leaves. *Sprouted.*

What word means "started to grow roots and leaves"? *Sprouted.*

Present Vocabulary Tally Sheet
(See Lesson 1, page 3, for instructions.)

Assign Homework
(Homework Sheet, BLM 4a: See the Introduction for homework instructions.)

DAY 2

Preparation: Picture Vocabulary Cards for *cottage, harvest, grains, sprouted.*

Read and Discuss Story

(Read story to children. Ask the following questions at the specified points in the story. Encourage children to use target words in their answers.)

Page 1. Where does the little red hen live? *In a cottage.* Is she a good mother to her little chicks? *Yes.* Tell why you think so. (Idea: *She works hard to feed her chicks.*)

Page 2. What does the little red hen find? *A few grains of wheat.* What does she ask her friends? *"Who will plant this wheat?"* What do her friends say? *"Not I."*

Page 4. Who plants the seeds? *The little red hen.*

Page 7. How do you think the hen and her chicks feel when they see the wheat has sprouted? (Ideas: *Happy; excited.*)

Page 9. What does she ask her friends? *"Who will harvest this wheat?"* What do her friends say? *"Not I."*

Page 11. Who harvests the wheat? *The little red hen.*

Page 12. (Read to the end of the first sentence: "At last the wheat was all cut down and it was time for it to be threshed.") When you thresh wheat, you separate the grains from the rest of the plant. What do you do when you separate the wheat grains from the rest of the plant? *You thresh the wheat.* What are you doing when you thresh wheat? *Separating the grains of wheat from the rest of the plant.*

Page 12. (Read to the end of the page.) What does she ask her friends? *"Who will thresh this wheat?"* What do her friends say? *"Not I."*

Page 15. Who threshes the wheat? *The little red hen.*

Page 17. What does she ask her friends? *"Who will take this wheat to the mill to be ground into flour?"* What do her friends say? *"Not I."*

Page 19. Who takes the wheat to the mill to be ground into flour? *The little red hen.*

Page 20. What does she ask her friends? *"Who will bake this flour into a lovely loaf of bread?"* What do her friends say? *"Not I."*

Page 23. Who bakes the flour into a lovely loaf of bread? *The little red hen.*

Page 25. What does she ask her friends? *"Who will eat this lovely loaf of bread?"* What do her friends say? *"I will!"*

Page 28. How does the story end? (Idea: *The little red hen and her chicks eat the bread.*)

We learned a word from *The Three Little Pigs* that might tell how the bread tasted. How do you think the bread tasted? *Delicious.*

Why didn't the little red hen share her bread with the goose, the cat, and the pig? (Idea: *They didn't help her when she asked them to.*) Do you think that was fair? *Yes.*

Predict what you think the goose, the cat, and the pig will do the next time the little red hen asks them for help.

Review Vocabulary

(Display the Picture Vocabulary Cards. Point to each card as you say the word. Ask children

to repeat each word after you.) These pictures show **cottage, harvest, grains,** and **sprouted.**

- What word means "seeds of plants such as wheat, oats, or rice"? *Grains.*
- What word means "started to grow roots and leaves"? *Sprouted.*
- What word means "to gather crops so you can use them for food"? *Harvest.*
- What word means "a small house in the country or near the beach"? *Cottage.*

Extend Vocabulary

◎← Grains

In *The Little Red Hen,* we learned that grains are the seeds of plants like rice, oats, or wheat.

Here's a new way to use the word **grain.**

- He had a **grain** of sand in his shoe. Say the sentence.
- There was only one **grain** of salt left in the salt shaker. Say the sentence.
- The ant carried a **grain** of sugar back to its nest. Say the sentence.

A grain of wheat, oats, and rice is a hard tiny seed. **In these sentences, grain means a hard, tiny piece of something.**

Present Expanded Target Vocabulary

◎← Determined

In the story, the little red hen never gave up when no one would help her. She just kept working and working and working. She really wanted to make her bread with wheat she had grown herself. She wouldn't let anything stop her.

Another way of saying she had made up her mind and wouldn't let anything stop her is to say she was determined. When you are determined, you know what you want to do, and you won't let anything stop you. **Determined.** Say the word. *Determined.*

If you are determined, you have made up your mind about something, and you won't let anything stop you. Say the word that means "you made up your mind about something and won't let anything stop you." *Determined.*

Let's think about when people might feel determined. If I say a time when someone would feel determined, say "determined." If not, don't say anything.

- How you would feel if you wanted to finish all of your work before going home. *Determined.*
- How you would feel at the beach on a warm Saturday.
- How you would feel if you wanted to save enough money for a new bike. *Determined.*
- How you and your mom would feel watching a video together.
- How you would feel if you wanted to be first in a race. *Determined.*
- How you would feel if everyone said you couldn't do something but you knew you could. *Determined.*

What word means "you made up your mind about something and you won't let anything stop you"? *Determined.*

◎— Uncooperative

In the story, the goose, the cat, and the pig wouldn't help the little red hen. Every time she asked them for help, they said no. They wouldn't do anything to help the little red hen.

Another way of saying the goose, the cat, and the pig wouldn't do anything to help the little red hen is to say they were uncooperative. When someone is uncooperative, they won't do anything to help anyone else. **Uncooperative.** Say the word. *Uncooperative.*

If someone is uncooperative, they won't do anything to help anyone else. Say the word that means "won't do anything to help anyone else." *Uncooperative.*

Let's think about times when someone might be uncooperative. If I tell about a time when someone is being uncooperative, say "uncooperative." If not, don't say anything.

- You drop all of your crayons on the floor and no one listens when you ask for help. *Uncooperative.*
- It's clean-up time, but the only person who will clean up is you. *Uncooperative.*
- Your friend helps you fix your bike.
- You are trying to move a bench, but no one will pick up the other end. *Uncooperative.*

- No one listens to your instructions. *Uncooperative.*
- Everyone plays well together.

What word means "won't do anything to help anyone else"? *Uncooperative.*

Tell about a time when you were uncooperative. (Call on several children. Encourage children to start their answers with the words "I was uncooperative when …")

(After each response, ask the child:) What might you have done to be more cooperative?

DAY 3

Preparation: Activity Sheet, BLM 4b.

Retell Story

Today I'll show you the pictures Margot Zemach made for *The Little Red Hen.* As I show you the pictures, I'll call on one of you to tell the class that part of the story.

Tell me what happens at the **beginning** of the story. (Show the pictures on pages 1–3. Call on a child to tell what's happening.)

Tell me what happens in the **middle** of the story. (Show the pictures on pages 4–25. Call on a child to tell what's happening. Encourage use of the target words when appropriate. Model use as necessary.)

Tell me what happens at the **end** of the story. (Show the pictures on pages 26–28. Call on a child to tell what's happening.)

How do you think the bread tasted? (Idea: *Delicious.*)

Play the Show Me, Tell Me Game

 Today you will play the Show Me, Tell Me Game. I'll ask you to show me how to do something. If you show me, you will win one point. If you can't show me, I get the point.

Next I'll ask you to tell me. If you tell me, you will win one point. If you can't tell me, I get the point.

Let's practice. My turn to show you how I would act if I was being **uncooperative.**

(Act out refusing to put away your books.) How am I acting? *Uncooperative.*

Let's do one together. Show me how you would **harvest** a field of carrots. (Stoop and pretend to pick carrots with children and put them in a bag.) What do we do? *Harvest carrots.*

Now you're ready to play the game. (Draw a T-chart on the board for keeping score. Children earn one point for each correct answer. If they make an error, correct them as you normally would, and record one point for yourself. Repeat missed words at the end of the game.)

- Show me how you would look if you were picking up **grains** of rice on the table. Tell me how you looked. *Like I was picking up grains of rice.*
- Show me how you would **sprout** if you were a tiny seed. Tell me what you did. *I sprouted.*
- Show me how you would **harvest** a great crop of apples. Tell me what you do. *Harvest apples.*
- Show me how you would look if you wanted to be the best at something. Tell me how you looked. *Determined.*
- Show me how you would be if I asked to you clean up and you did other things instead. Tell me how you acted. *Uncooperative.*

(Count the points and declare a winner.)
You did a great job of playing the Show Me, Tell Me Game.

Complete the Activity Sheet

 (Give each child a copy of the Activity Sheet, BLM 4b. Review with children the order they will place the pictures to put them in sequence to show beginning, middle, and end. Instruct children to color the pictures, cut them out, and paste or glue them into sequential order.)

Preparation: Prepare two sheets of chart paper, each with a circle drawn in the middle. Fold the sheets of paper in half vertically to divide the circles in half. When you record children's responses, physical descriptors should be recorded on the left-hand side of each chart. Personality characteristics or actions should be recorded on the right-hand side.

Analyze Characters (Literary Analysis)

Let's think about what we already know about how books are made.

- What do we call the name of the book? *Title.*
- What do we call the person who writes the story? *Author.*
- What do we call the person who draws the pictures? *Illustrator.*
- What are the people or animals a story is about? *Characters.*

Let's sing the verses of The Story Song to help us remember these important things about books. (See the Introduction for the complete Story Song.)

Today we will learn more about the characters in a story.

The characters in a story are the people or the animals the story is about. What are the people or the animals a story is about? *Characters.* Who are the characters in a story? *The people or the animals the story is about.*

In *The Little Red Hen,* are the characters people or animals? *Animals.*

Who are the characters in this story? (Ideas: *The little red hen; her chicks; the goose; the cat; the pig.*)

The most important characters in *The Little Red Hen* are the little red hen and her three friends. Who are the most important characters in the story? *The little red hen and her three friends.* (Write *little red hen* in the center of the circle on one of the charts; write *three friends* in the center of the circle on the other sheet.)

Let's remember what we know about the little red hen. (Show children pages 18–19.) What does the little red hen look like?

(Call on several children. Record each child's response on the left-hand side of the hen chart.) (Ideas: *Red feathers; wears hat; wears a dress; sometimes wears an apron; has a beak; uses her wings for hands.*)

(Show children pages 14–15. Ask these questions. Call on several children. Record each child's response on the right-hand side of the chart.) Do you think the little red hen works hard or is lazy? (Idea: *Works hard.*) Tell why you think that. (Idea: *She's threshing the wheat; she's the one who does all the work.*) What other things does she do that show you she works hard? (Ideas: *She plants the seeds; she harvests the wheat; she takes the flour to the mill; she makes the bread.*

(Show children pages 18–19.) We learned a new word that meant the little red hen really wanted to make her bread with wheat she had grown herself. She wouldn't let anything stop her. What word could we use to tell about the little red hen? She was … *Determined.*

(Show children page 28.) What does the little red hen like to eat? *Bread.* What else can you tell us about the little red hen? (Ideas: *She's a good mother; she likes to sing.*)

(Follow a similar process to describe the three friends. When describing the appearance of the three friends, write *goose, cat,* and *pig* as headings down the left-hand side of the chart paper. Record appropriate descriptive words under each heading.)

(When describing the personalities of the three friends, record words common to all the animals: *Lazy; likes to play cards; uncooperative; likes to sit in the sun; likes homemade bread.* Record responses on the right-hand side of the second piece of chart paper.)

Today you've learned about the little red hen and her three friends. They are the most important characters in the story *The Little Red Hen.*

Play Show Me, Tell Me Game (Cumulative Review)

Let's play the Show Me, Tell Me Game. I'll ask you to show me how to do something. If you show me, you will win one point. If you can't show me, I get the point.

Next I'll ask you to tell me. If you tell me, you will win one point. If you can't tell me, I get the point.

Now you're ready to play the game. (Draw a T-chart on the board for keeping score. Children earn one point for each correct answer. If they make an error, correct them as you normally would, and record one point for yourself. Repeat missed words at the end of the game.)

- Show me how you would look if you spent the weekend at a **cottage** at the beach. Tell me where you were. *I was at a cottage at the beach.*
- Show me what you do if you **harvest** corn. Tell me what you do. *Harvest corn.*
- Show me how you would look if you were gathering **grains** of salt on the table. Tell me what you're doing. *Gathering grains of salt.*
- Show me how a seed would look when it **sprouted.** Tell me what the seed did. *It sprouted.*
- Show me how you would look if you were **determined** to finish reading a book before recess. Tell me how you looked. *Determined.*
- Show me how it looks to be **uncooperative** when it's time to clean up. Tell me how you looked. *Uncooperative.*
- Show me how you would look if you were a farmer with a handful of **grains.** Tell me what you had in your hands. *Grains.*
- Show me what your face looks like when you feel **angry.** Tell me how you feel. *Angry.*
- Show me how you look when you are **gathering** workbooks and putting them away. Tell me what you are doing. *Gathering workbooks.*
- Show me how you would look if a lion **roared.** Tell me what happened. *The lion roared.*

Learn About Folk Tales

Today you will learn more about folk tales. What will you learn about? *Folk tales.*

What is a tale? *A story.* What are people who come from the same country and live the same kind of life? *Folk.* What is a story told by people who come from the same country and live the same kind of life? *A folk tale.*

Long, long ago, could most ordinary people read? *No.* How did people entertain themselves? *They told stories.*

Sometimes when parents told these stories to their children, they were trying to teach their children important things they needed to know. When parents told these stories to their children, what were they trying to teach them? (Idea: *Important things they needed to know.*)

The Little Red Hen is a folk tale. What kind of story is *The Little Red Hen*? *A folk tale.*

Raise your hand if you enjoyed *The Little Red Hen.* (Pause.) I can see most of you were entertained by the story.

When parents told this tale to their children, what do you think they were they trying to teach them? (Ideas: *You can't expect a reward if you don't help out; hard work pays off; if you work hard, you'll be rewarded.*) What other folk tale did we read where hard work was rewarded? (Idea: *The Three Little Pigs.*)

We have read four folk tales: *The Ant and the Grasshopper, Jack and the Bean Stalk, The Three Little Pigs,* and *The Little Red Hen.* Think about these stories. (Pause.) Which story was your favorite? Why did you like it best? (Call on several children. Encourage them to use the following frame to state their opinions. "I like the folk tale _____ the best because _____.")

Assess Vocabulary

(Give each child a copy of the Happy Face Game Test Sheet, BLM B.)

Today you're going to play the Happy Face Game. When you play the Happy Face Game, it shows me how well you know the hard words you are learning.

If I say something that is true, color in the happy face. What will you do if I say something that is true? *Color in the happy face.*

If I say something that is false, color in the sad face. What will you do if I say something that is false? *Color in the sad face.*

Listen carefully to each item that I say. Don't let me trick you!

Item 1: A **cottage** is a castle with 100 rooms. (*False.*)

Item 2: When you **harvest** vegetables, you **gather** them so that you can eat them. (*True.*)

Item 3: If you are **cross** with someone, you are happy about something he or she has done. (*False.*)

Item 4: If you are in a **meadow,** you are in a field with grass and flowers. (*True.*)

Item 5: When you are **determined,** you try hard. (*True.*)

Item 6: **Uncooperative** people always help. (*False.*)

Item 7: **Grains** of rice are the size of apples. (*False.*)

Item 8: You are **desperate** when you want something very, very badly. (*True.*)

Item 9: A **considerate** person pays attention to what someone else needs. (*True.*)

Item 10: When a seed starts to grow leaves and roots, we say that it **sprouted.** (*True.*)

You did a great job of playing the Happy Face Game!

(Score children's work. A child must score 9 out of 10 to be at the mastery level. If a child does not achieve mastery, insert the missed words as additional items in the games for next week's lessons. Retest those children individually for the missed items before they take the next mastery test.)

Extensions

Read a Story as a Reward

 (Display copies of the three books that you have read since the beginning of the program or display alternate versions of *The Little Red Hen.* Allow children to choose which book they would like you to read to them as a reward for their hard work.)

(Read the story aloud for enjoyment with minimal interruptions.)

Preparation: Word containers for the Super Words Center.

Introduce the Super Words Center

(Add the new Picture Vocabulary Cards to words from the previous two weeks.

Show children one of the word containers. If children need more guidance in how to work in the Super Words Center, role-play with two to three children as a demonstration.)

Let's think about how we work with our words in the Super Words Center.

You will work with a partner in the Super Words Center. Whom will you work with? *A partner.*

First you will draw a word out of the container. What do you do first? (Idea: *Draw a word out of the container.*)

Next you will show your partner the picture and ask what word the picture shows. What do you do next? (Idea: *I show my partner the picture and ask what word the picture shows.*)

What do you do next? *Give my partner a turn.*

What do you do if your partner doesn't know the word? *Tell my partner the word.*

Preparation: You will need *The Three Billy Goats Gruff* for each day's lesson.

Post a copy of the Vocabulary Tally Sheet, BLM A, with this week's Picture Vocabulary Cards attached.

Each child will need one copy of the Homework Sheet, BLM 5a.

DAY 1

Introduce Book

This week's book is called *The Three Billy Goats Gruff.* What's the title? *The Three Billy Goats Gruff.*

This book was written by Betty Jane Wagner. Who's the author of *The Three Billy Goats Gruff*? *Betty Jane Wagner.*

Shirley Cribb Breuel (Brew-al) made the pictures for this book. Who's the illustrator of *The Three Billy Goats Gruff*? *Shirley Cribb Breuel.*

The cover of a book usually gives us some hints of what the book is about. Let's look at the front cover of *The Three Billy Goats Gruff.* What do you see in the illustration? (Ideas: *Three goats; some mushrooms; a river; a frog; a bridge over the river.*)

(Assign each child a partner.) Remember that when you make a prediction about something, you say what you think will happen. Get ready to make some predictions to your partner about this book. Use the information from the cover to help you.

(Ask the following questions, allowing sufficient time for children to share their predictions with their partners.)

- Whom do you think this story is about?
- What do you think the goats in the story will do?
- Where do you think the story happens?
- When do you think this story happens?
- Why do you think the sign on the bridge says "Keep Off"?
- How do you think the goats are feeling?

The Three Billy Goats Gruff
author: Betty Jane Wagner • illustrator: Shirley Cribb Breuel

◎ Target Vocabulary

Tier II	Tier III
decided	character
shouted	fairy tale
squeaked	
muttered	
*starving	
*disagreeable	

*Expanded Target Vocabulary Word

- Do you think this story is about real goats? Tell why or why not.

(Call on individual children to share their predictions with the class.)

Take a Picture Walk

We're going to take a picture walk through this book. Remember that when we take a picture walk, we look at the pictures and tell what we think will happen in the story.

Page 3. Where do you think the goats are? (Idea: *Where no green plants grow.*) Why do you think so? (Ideas: *I can't see any leaves; there is no grass; I can see only mushrooms growing.*)

Pages 4–5. What do you notice about the land on the other side of the river? (Ideas: *There are lots of bushes; the grass is green.*)

Pages 6–7. What do you see under the bridge? (Idea: *A person with big eyes and a long nose sitting on a book; a frog with big eyes; a boat; a clock; a candle in a teacup; a lantern with a candle; a broken umbrella; a thing with N, S, E, and W.*) The thing with the N, S, E, and W is a weather vane. It turns with the wind to tell you which direction the wind is blowing. The letters stand for north, south, east, and west.

Pages 8–9. What do you think is happening here? (Ideas: *The goats are standing at the edge of the river.*)

Pages 10–11. What do you think the man is saying to the goat on the bridge? How do you think the man is feeling? (Idea: *Angry.*)

Pages 14–15. Where is the goat now? (Idea: *On the green side of the river.*)

Pages 16–17. What do you think the man is saying to the goat on the bridge? How do you think the man is feeling? (Idea: *Angry.*)

Pages 20–21. Where is the goat now? (Idea: *On the green side of the river.*)

Pages 22–23. What do you think the man is saying to the goat? How do you think the man is feeling? (Idea: *Angry.*)

Pages 26–27. Where is the goat now? (Idea: *On the bridge.*) What do you think the man is saying to the goat? How do you think the man is feeling? (Idea: *Angry.*)

Pages 28–29. How do you think the goat is feeling? How do you think the man is feeling?

Pages 30–31. What do you think is happening here? (Idea: *The man is falling into the river.*)

It's your turn to ask me some questions. What would you like to know about the story? (Accept questions. If children tell about the pictures or the story instead of ask questions, prompt them to ask a question.) Ask me a what question. Ask me a how question.

 Read the Story Aloud
(Read story to children with minimal interruptions.)

Tomorrow we will read the story again, and I will ask you some questions.

(If children have difficulty attending for an extended period of time, you may wish to present the next part of this day's lesson at another time of day.)

Present Target Vocabulary
◎— **Decided**

In the story, Big Billy Goat Gruff and Middle Billy Goat Gruff decided to send Little Billy Goat Gruff across the river. That means that after they thought about it, they chose to send Little Billy Goat Gruff across the river. They decided to send him across the river. **Decided.** Say the word. *Decided.*

If you've decided to do something, you've carefully thought about it, and then chose to do it. Say the word that means "carefully thought about something and then chose to do it." *Decided.*

(Correct any incorrect responses, and repeat the item at the end of the sequence.)

Let's think about things that you might decide to do. I'll name something. If you could decide to do that thing, say "decided." If not, don't say anything.

- The family thought about it and chose to move to Seattle. *Decided.*
- You thought about it and chose to buy flowers for Mother's Day. *Decided.*
- The sun is shining.
- It is hot outside.
- Dad thought about it and chose to buy a new lawn mower. *Decided.*
- You thought about it and chose to have fish for dinner. *Decided.*

What word means "carefully thought about something and chose to do it"? *Decided.*

◎— **Shouted**

In the story, the troll shouted at the billy goats when they tried to cross the bridge. That means he used a very loud voice to speak to the goats. He was angry at the goats for trying to cross his bridge. **Shouted.** Say the word. *Shouted.*

If you shouted at someone, you used a very loud voice to speak to them. You might have used a very loud voice because you were angry. Say the word that means "used a very loud, angry voice to speak to someone." *Shouted.*

Let's think about some times when you would have shouted at someone. I'll name a time. If you would have shouted, say "shouted." If not, don't say anything.

- Your friend dropped a heavy book on your toe. *Shouted.*
- Your little brother broke your favorite toy. *Shouted.*
- Your mom said, "Hi!"
- A car drove by.
- Your dog ate your hotdog. *Shouted.*

- Your friend tripped you and you scraped your knee. *Shouted.*

What word means "used a very loud, angry voice to speak to someone"? *Shouted.*

In *The Three Little Pigs,* we learned another word that means "spoke to someone in a very loud voice because they were angry." What was that word? *Roared.* That's right; **roared** and **shouted** mean the same thing. What two words mean the same thing? *Roared and shouted.*

◎–⊸ Squeaked

In the story, the troll shouted at Little Billy Goat Gruff, saying, "Who is that trip-trapping across my river bridge?" Little Billy Goat squeaked, "It is only I, Little Billy Goat Gruff." That means he used a very high voice to answer the troll's question. He was afraid of the troll. He used a voice that was like the sound a mouse makes. **Squeaked.** Say the word. *Squeaked.*

If you squeaked at someone, you used a very high voice to speak to them. You might have used a very high voice because you were afraid. Say the word that means "used a very high voice to speak to someone." *Squeaked.*

Let's think about some times when you would have squeaked at someone. I'll name a time. If you would have squeaked, say "squeaked." If not, don't say anything.

- You thought there was a creature under your bed. *Squeaked.*
- It was dark and you heard a noise downstairs. *Squeaked.*
- You walked to school.
- You helped to clean the yard.
- You called for help when the water got too deep. *Squeaked.*
- You did your homework.

What word means "used a very high voice to speak to someone"? *Squeaked.*

◎–⊸ Muttered

In the story, the troll muttered that he would wait for Little Billy Goat's brother to come so he could eat him. That means the troll spoke in a quiet voice so the goats couldn't hear him.

Usually when someone mutters, it means they are unhappy about something. **Muttered.** Say the word. *Muttered.*

If you muttered, you used a very quiet voice to speak. You were unhappy about something. Say the word that means "used a very quiet voice because they were unhappy about something." *Muttered.*

Let's think about some times when you would have muttered. I'll name a time. If you would have muttered, say "muttered." If not, don't say anything.

- Your mom told you that you had to clean your room before you could play. *Muttered.*
- Your dad said that you couldn't watch TV. *Muttered.*
- You saw a big dog.
- The stars came out.
- You could see the mountains in the distance.
- The babysitter told you to go to bed before it was time. *Muttered.*

What word means "used a very quiet voice because they were unhappy about something"? *Muttered.*

Shouted, squeaked, and **muttered** are three words that tell how people said something. What are three words that tell how people said something? *Shouted, squeaked, and muttered.*

(Mutter, "Oh, it's too early for me to go to bed. I don't want to go to bed right now.") Tell me if I shouted, squeaked, or muttered. *Muttered.*

(Shout, "Owwww! Please be careful where you step!") Tell me if I shouted, squeaked, or muttered. *Shouted.*

(Squeak, "Hello? Mom? Dad? Is somebody downstairs?") Tell me if I shouted, squeaked, or muttered. *Squeaked.*

Present Vocabulary Tally Sheet
(See Lesson 1, page 3, for instructions.)

Assign Homework
(Homework Sheet, BLM 5a: See the Introduction for homework instructions.)

Preparation: Picture Vocabulary Cards for *decided, shouted, squeaked, muttered.*

Read and Discuss Story

(Read story to children. Ask the following questions at the specified points in the story. Encourage the children to use target words in their answers.)

Page 4. Where do the goats live? (Idea: *On a hillside.*) What is wrong with their home? (Idea: *There is no grass.*) What has happened to all the grass on their side of the river? (Idea: *The goats have eaten it.*)

Page 6. Who lives under the bridge? *A troll.* A troll is a pretend man. Trolls are mean and ugly. They live under bridges and in caves. Are trolls real? *No.* That's right; trolls are only in stories. Where do trolls live? *Under bridges and in caves.*

Page 8. Who had to cross the bridge first? *Little Billy Goat Gruff.* How do you think he is feeling? (Ideas: *Scared; nervous; afraid.*)

Page 12. Predict what you think the troll will do.

Page 14. How do you think Little Billy Goat Gruff is feeling now that he is on the other side of the river? (Ideas: *Happy; glad.*)

Page 16. Who has to cross the bridge next? *Middle Billy Goat Gruff.* How do you think he is feeling? (Ideas: *Scared; nervous; afraid.*)

Page 18. Predict what you think the troll will do.

Page 20. How do you think Little Billy Goat Gruff is feeling now that he is on the other side of the river? (Ideas: *Happy; glad.*)

Page 22. Who has to cross the bridge next? *Big Billy Goat Gruff.* How do you think he is feeling? How do you think the troll is feeling? (Ideas: *Angry; furious.*)

Page 25. Predict what you think will happen.

Page 30. What happens to the troll? (Idea: *Big Billy Goat Gruff pushes him off the bridge; he pushes him into the water.*) How do you think Little Billy Goat Gruff is feeling now that he is on the other side of the river? (Ideas: *Happy; glad.*)

Page 32. How does the story end? (Idea: *The goats live happily ever after on the other side of the river; the troll is gone.*)

Lots of times, stories end with the words, "The End." This story ends with a little poem. Listen while I read the poem to you. "Snip, snap, snout—This tale's told out!" This little poem means the same thing as "The End."

Let's say the poem together that means "The End." *Snip, Snap, snout—This tale's told out!* (Repeat until children can say the poem on their own.)

Your turn. Say the poem that means "The End." *Snip, Snap, snout—This tale's told out!*

Review Vocabulary

(Display the Picture Vocabulary Cards. Point to each card as you say the word. Ask children to repeat each word after you.) These pictures show **decided, shouted, squeaked,** and **muttered.**

- What word means "used a very loud, angry voice to speak to someone"? *Shouted.*
- What word means "used a very high voice to speak to someone"? *Squeaked.*
- What word means "carefully thought about something and then chose to do it"? *Decided.*
- What word means "used a very quiet voice because they were unhappy about something"? *Muttered.*

Extend Vocabulary
 Shouted

In *The Three Billy Goats Gruff,* we learned that shouted means "used a very loud, angry voice to speak to someone."

Here's a new way to use the word **shouted.**

- Alisa **shouted** to her friend to come over. Say the sentence.
- The children **shouted** to the other team to come and play. Say the sentence.
- Her mom **shouted,** "Look both ways before you cross the street!" Say the sentence.

In these sentences, shouted means said something very loudly because the person they were talking to was far away.

Tell about some other times when you might have shouted to someone because they were far away. (Ideas: *You could call "Mommy!" if you hurt yourself and your mom was far away; you could yell, "Hey, Jacob, I'm over here!" if you wanted to tell your little brother where you were.*)

Present Expanded Target Vocabulary
◎⇤ Starving

At the beginning of the story, the three billy goats had no food on their side of the river. They were very, very hungry. Another way of saying they were very, very hungry is they were starving. **Starving.** Say the word. *Starving.*

If you are starving, you are so very, very hungry you think you might die. Say the word that means "so very, very hungry, you think you might die." *Starving.*

Let's think about when people might have been starving. If I say a time when someone would have been starving, say "starving." If not, don't say anything.

- You hadn't had breakfast, lunch, or dinner. There was no food in the refrigerator. *Starving.*
- You had been lost in the desert for three days and you couldn't find your way home. *Starving.*
- Your tummy was rumbling because you hadn't had anything to eat for a long, long time. *Starving.*
- You just finished a big dinner and you accidentally burped and said, "Excuse me!"
- You were walking to the store to buy more food for lunch.
- You had been sick for five days and couldn't eat. *Starving.*

What word means "so very, very hungry you think you might die"? *Starving.*

◎⇤ Disagreeable

In the story, the troll wouldn't let the goats cross his bridge even though he knew they were starving. He was unfriendly and unhelpful.

Another way of saying the troll was unfriendly and unhelpful is to say he was disagreeable. He wouldn't do anything to help the goats, and he shouted at them. **Disagreeable.** Say the word. *Disagreeable.*

If someone was disagreeable, they were unfriendly and unhelpful. Say the word that means "unfriendly and unhelpful." *Disagreeable.*

Let's think about times when someone might have been disagreeable. If I tell about a time when someone was being disagreeable, say "disagreeable." If not, don't say anything.

- Your aunt wasn't feeling well and had a bad headache. *Disagreeable.*
- You were unhappy because you had to do your schoolwork over again. *Disagreeable.*
- You got a new bike.
- You were enjoying playing with your friend.
- The class was acting up and wouldn't be quiet and the teacher was upset. *Disagreeable.*
- You found a quarter on your way home.

Last week we learned a word that means "won't do anything to help anyone else." Say the word that means "won't do anything to help anyone else." *Uncooperative.*

Disagreeable people are uncooperative and unfriendly. What word means "uncooperative and unfriendly"? *Disagreeable.*

Tell about a time when someone was disagreeable. (**Call on several children. Encourage children to start their answers with the words, "_____ was disagreeable when _____."**

After each response, ask the child:) What might _____ have done to be more cooperative and friendly? (**Accept reasonable responses.**)

DAY 3

Preparation: Activity Sheet, BLM 5b.

Retell Story

Today I'll show you the pictures Shirley Cribb Breuel made for *The Three Billy Goats Gruff*. As I show you the pictures, I'll call on one of you to tell the class that part of the story.

Tell me what happens at the **beginning** of the story. (**Show the pictures on pages 3–7. Call on a child to tell what's happening.**)

Tell me what happens in the **middle** of the story. (**Show the pictures on pages 8–29. Call on a** child to tell what's happening. Encourage use of the target words when appropriate. Model use as necessary.)

Tell me what happens at the **end** of the story. (Show the pictures on pages 30–32. Call on a child to tell what's happening.)

How do you think the grass tasted? (Idea: *Delicious.*)

Play the Whoopsy! Game

(Display the Picture Vocabulary Cards as you play this game.) Today you will play the *Whoopsy!* Game. I'll say sentences using words we have learned. If the word doesn't fit in the sentence, you say "Whoopsy!" Then I'll ask you to say a sentence where the word fits. If you can do it, you get a point. If you can't do it, I get the point. If the word I use fits the sentence, don't say anything.

Let's practice.

I **shouted** when … I didn't want anyone to hear what I said. *Whoopsy!*

Listen to the beginning of the sentence again. I **shouted** when. Say the beginning of the sentence. *I shouted when.* Can you finish the sentence so the word fits? (Idea: *I shouted when I wanted everyone to hear me.*)

Let's try another one. I was **starving** when … I had just finished my dinner. *Whoopsy!*

Listen to the beginning of the sentence again. I was **starving** when. Say the beginning of the sentence. *I was starving when.* Can you finish the sentence so the word fits? (Idea: *I was starving when I hadn't eaten all day.*)

Now you're ready to play the game. (Draw a T-chart on the board for keeping score. Children earn one point for each correct answer. If they make an error, correct them as you normally would, and record one point for yourself. Repeat missed words at the end of the game.)

- I was **disagreeable** when … I did everything my parents asked me to do. *Whoopsy!* Say the beginning of the sentence again. *I was disagreeable when.* Can you finish the sentence so the word fits? (Idea: *I was*

disagreeable when I didn't do what my parents asked me to do.)

- I **muttered** when … I wanted everyone to hear me. *Whoopsy!* Say the beginning of the sentence again. *I muttered when.* Can you finish the sentence so the word fits? (Idea: *I muttered when I didn't want anyone to hear me.*)

- The mouse **squeaked** when … it saw the cat.

- I **decided** what to do when … I couldn't make up my mind. *Whoopsy!* Say the beginning of the sentence again. *I decided what to do when.* Can you finish the sentence so the word fits? (Idea: *I decided what to do when I carefully thought about it and chose to do it.*)

- I **shouted** when … my friend told me a funny joke. *Whoopsy!* Say the beginning of the sentence again. *I shouted when.* Can you finish the sentence so the word fits? (Idea: *I shouted when my friend dropped a rock on my toe.*)

(Count the points and declare a winner.) You did a great job of playing *Whoopsy!*

Complete the Activity Sheet

Think about the characters in *The Three Billy Goats Gruff.* Who are those characters? (Ideas: *Big Billy Goat Gruff, Middle Billy Goat Gruff, Little Billy Goat Gruff.*)

(Give each child a copy of the Activity Sheet, BLM 5b.)

We're going to play a game called the Riddle Game. When you play the Riddle Game, I tell you some things that I know about a character. Your job is to guess who I'm talking about.

Let's play the riddle game. I'll give you some clues. Raise your hand when you think you can name the character who I am talking about.

- I live close by a river.
  I was very hungry.
  I have two brothers.
  I was the first one to cross the bridge.
  Who am I?

(Have children identify which character is the answer to the riddle: *Little Billy Goat Gruff.* Instruct children to color the picture, cut it out, and paste it underneath the riddle.)

(Repeat the process for these two riddles.)

- I live close by a river.
  I was very hungry.
  I shouted at someone.
  I didn't get anything to eat.
  Who am I? (*The troll.*)

- I was very hungry.
  I wanted to cross the river to the other side.
  I have two brothers.
  I knocked the troll into the water.
  Who am I? (*Big Billy Goat Gruff.*)

DAY 4

Preparation: Prepare two sheets of chart paper, each with a circle drawn in the middle. Fold the sheets of paper in half vertically to divide the circle in half. When you record children's responses, physical descriptors should be recorded on the left-hand side of each chart. Personality characteristics or actions should be recorded on the right-hand side.

Analyze Characters (Literary Analysis)

Let's think about what we already know about how books are made.

- What do we call the name of the book? *Title.*
- What do we call the person who writes the story? *Author.*
- What do we call the person who draws the pictures? *Illustrator.*
- What are the people or animals a story is about? *Characters.*

Let's sing The Story Song to help us remember these important things about books. (See the Introduction for the complete Story Song.)

Today we will learn more about the characters in a story.

The characters in a story are the people or animals the story is about. What are the people or the animals a story is about? *Characters.* Who are the characters in a story? *The people or the animals the story is about.*

In *The Three Billy Goats Gruff,* are the characters people or animals? (Ideas: *The goats are animals; the troll is a pretend man.*)

Who are the characters in the story? (Call on several children. Ideas: *Little Billy Goat Gruff; Middle Billy Goat Gruff; Big Billy Goat Gruff; the troll.*)

The most important characters in *The Three Billy Goats Gruff* are the goats and the troll. Who are the most important characters in the story? *The goats and the troll.* (Write *goats* in the circle on one of the charts; write *troll* in the circle on the other sheet.)

Let's remember what we know about the goats. (Show children the cover.) What do the goats look like? (Call on several children. Record each child's response on the left-hand side of the goat chart. Ideas: *White; have horns; have collars; have gold rings on their horns.*)

(Show children page 3. Ask these questions. Call on several children. Record each child's response on the right-hand side of the chart.) Do you think the goats are hungry or full? *Hungry.* Tell why you think that. (Ideas: *There's no grass to eat; their eyes are sad; they look skinny.*) We learned a new word that meant the goats were so hungry they thought they would die. What word could we use to tell about the goats? They were … *Starving.*

(Show children pages 18 and 19.) In Week 1 we learned a new word that meant Middle Billy Goat Gruff wanted food very, very badly. Say the word that means Middle Billy Goat Gruff wanted food very, very badly. He was … *Desperate.*

(Show children page 32.) What do the Billy Goats Gruff like to eat? *Grass.*

(Follow a similar process to describe the troll. Record responses on the second piece of chart paper.)

Today you have learned about the goats and the troll. They are the most important characters in the story *The Three Billy Goats Gruff.*

Play Whoopsy! (Cumulative Review)

Let's play *Whoopsy!* I'll say sentences using words we have learned. If the word doesn't fit in the sentence, you say "Whoopsy!"

Then I'll ask you to say a sentence where the word fits. If you can do it, you get a point. If you can't do it, I get the point. If the word I use fits the sentence, don't say anything.

T Now you're ready to play the game. (Draw a T-chart on the board for keeping score. Children earn one point for each correct answer. If they make an error, correct them as you normally would, and record one point for yourself. Repeat missed words at the end of the game.)

- I **decided** to go to the movies when … I didn't think about it or choose what to do. *Whoopsy!* Say the beginning of the sentence again. *I decided to go to the movies when.* Can you finish the sentence so the word fits? (Idea: *I decided to go to the movies when I thought about it and chose to go.*)
- The mouse **squeaked** as it ran across the kitchen floor.
- I **shouted** when … my brother helped me clean my room. *Whoopsy!* Say the beginning of the sentence again. *I shouted when.* Can you finish the sentence so the word fits? (Idea: *I shouted when my brother messed up my room.*)
- The boy **shouted** out to his friends when … he wanted them to hear him.
- The teacher was **cross** when … the children were working hard and being quiet. *Whoopsy!* Say the beginning of the sentence again. *The teacher was cross when.* Can you finish the sentence so the word fits? (Idea: *The teacher was cross when the children were acting up and wouldn't be quiet.*)
- I **muttered** under my breath when I broke my pencil for the third time.
- The animals were **starving** when … they had lots of food to eat. *Whoopsy!* Say the beginning of the sentence again. *The animals were starving when.* Can you finish the sentence so the word fits? (Idea: *The animals were starving when they had no food to eat.*)
- The boy was **brave** when … he ran away from the tiny mouse. *Whoopsy!* Say the beginning of the sentence again. *The boy was brave when.* Can you finish the sentence so the word fits? (Idea: *The boy was brave when he stayed to fight the dragon.*)

- The **cottage** at the lake had…one hundred rooms. *Whoopsy!* Say the beginning of the sentence again. *The cottage at the lake had.* Can you finish the sentence so the word fits? (Idea: *The cottage at the lake had only a few rooms.*)
- The boy was **disobedient** when…he did what his mother told him to do. *Whoopsy!* Say the beginning of the sentence again. *The boy was disobedient when.* Can you finish the sentence so the word fits? (Idea: *The boy was disobedient when he didn't do what his mother told him to do.*)

(Count the points and declare a winner.)
You did a great job of playing *Whoopsy!*

DAY 5

Preparation: A map or globe of the world. Happy Face Game Test Sheet, BLM B.

Learn About Fairy Tales

Today you will learn about a special kind of folk tale called a fairy tale. What will you learn about? *A fairy tale.*

Folk tales and fairy tales are both stories that were once told out loud. How are folk tales and fairy tales the same? (Idea: *They are both stories that were once told out loud.*)

But a fairy tale is a story that someone decided to write down in a book a long time ago. How is a fairy tale different from a folk tale? (Idea: *Someone decided to write it down in a book a long time ago.*)

The first people to write down the story *The Three Billy Goats Gruff* were two friends from Norway. Their names were Peter Christen Asbjornsen [as-be-yorn-sen] and Jorgen Moe [yore-gen mow].

(Locate Norway on the map or globe.) What country does the fairy tale *The Three Billy Goats Gruff* come from? *Norway.* The two friends first wrote down this story more than 150 years ago. When did they write down this story? (Idea: *More than 150 years ago.*) That's a very, very long time ago!

After Peter Christen Asbjornsen [as-be-yorn-sen] and Jorgen Moe [yore-gen mow] wrote down the story, many other people retold the story. (Point to the words *Retold by* on the cover.) Betty Jane Wagner retold the story in her own words, so she is known as the author of this version of the story. Who is the author of this version of the story? *Betty Jane Wagner.*

Fairy tales often begin with the same words. Listen while I read the first sentence of *The Three Billy Goats Gruff.* "Once upon a time there lived three billy goats." How does this fairy tale begin? *Once upon a time.*

Fairy tales often have good characters and evil characters. Who are the good characters in *The Three Billy Goats Gruff*? (Idea: *The three billy goats*.) Who is the evil character in *The Three Billy Goats Gruff*? (Idea: *The troll.*)

Fairy tales often have things that happen in threes. Tell about the things that happened in threes. (Ideas: *There were 3 billy goats; Little Billy Goat and Middle Billy Goat's feet went "trip-trap, trip-trap, trip-trap"; Big Billy Goat's feet went "tramp, tramp, tramp."*)

Let's remember three important things about fairy tales. How do fairy tales often begin? *Once upon a time.* What kinds of characters are often in fairy tales? *Good characters and evil characters.* What is the special number that is often in fairy tales? *Three.* Good remembering about fairy tales.

Assess Vocabulary

 (Give each child a copy of the Happy Face Game Test Sheet, BLM B.)

Today you're going to play the Happy Face Game. When you play the Happy Face Game, it shows me how well you know the hard words you are learning.

If I say something that is true, color in the happy face. What will you do if I say something that is true? *Color in the happy face.*

If I say something that is false, color in the sad face. What will you do if I say something that is false? *Color in the sad face.*

Listen carefully to each item that I say. Don't let me trick you!

Item 1: If you **shouted,** it means that you spoke in a very quiet voice. (*False.*)

Item 2: If you **squeaked,** it means that you spoke in a very high voice. (*True.*)

Item 3: If you were **starving,** you wouldn't be very hungry. (*False.*)

Item 4: **Decided** means the same as chose. (*True.*)

Item 5: If you are **determined** to ride a bicycle, you have made up your mind and will not let anything stop you. (*True.*)

Item 6: **Muttered** means to speak in a low voice that no one can hear. (*True.*)

Item 7: **Disagreeable** means happy and easy to get along with. (*False.*)

Item 8: When you **prepare,** you get ready to do something. (*True.*)

Item 9: **Pleaded** is the same as laughed. (*False.*)

Item 10: **Grains** of salt or sugar are very small. (*True.*)

You did a great job of playing the Happy Face Game!

(Score children's work. A child must score 9 out of 10 to be at the mastery level. If a child does not achieve mastery, insert the missed words as additional items in the games for next week's lessons. Retest those children individually for the missed items before they take the next mastery test.)

Extensions

Read a Story as a Reward

(Display copies of the books that you have read since the beginning of the program or display alternate versions of *The Three Billy Goats Gruff.* Allow children to choose which book they would like you to read aloud to them as a reward for their hard work.)

(Read the story aloud for enjoyment with minimal interruptions.)

<table>
<tr><td>

Preparation: Word containers for the Super Words Center.

</td></tr>
</table>

 ### Introduce the Super Words Center

(Add the new Picture Vocabulary Cards to the words from the previous weeks. Show the children one of the word containers. If children need more guidance in how to work in the Super Words Center, role-play with two to three children as a demonstration.)

Let's think about how we work with our words in the Super Words Center.

You will work with a partner in the Super Words Center. Whom will you work with? *A partner.*

Today I will teach you how to play a game called *What's New?*

First one partner will draw four Picture Vocabulary Cards out of the container and put them on the table so both partners can see. What do you do first? (Idea: *Draw four cards out of the container and put them on the table so both partners can see.*)

Next you will take turns looking at the cards and saying the words the pictures show. What do you do next? (Idea: *We take turns looking at the cards and saying the words the pictures show.*)

Next partner 2 looks away while partner 1 takes one of the four cards and places it back in the container. Then partner 1 draws a new card from the container and places it on the table with the other three. Watch while I show you what I mean. (Demonstrate this process with one child as your partner.) When you put down the new card, it's a good idea to mix the cards so they aren't in the same places any more. (Demonstrate this process as you go.)

Now partner 1 says, "What's New?" Partner 2 has to use his or her eyes and brain and say what new word card has been put down. If partner 2 is correct, they get a point. If partner 2 is not correct, partner 1 gets the point. (Demonstrate this process as you go.)

Next partner 2 has a turn to choose four different cards and the game starts again. What happens next? (Idea: *Partner 2 has a turn to choose four different cards and the game starts again.*)

Have fun playing *What's New?*

Preparation: You will need *Goldilocks and the Three Bears* for each day's lesson.

Number the pages of the story to assist you in asking questions at appropriate points.

Post a copy of the Vocabulary Tally Sheet, BLM A, with this week's Picture Vocabulary Cards attached.

Each child will need one copy of the Homework Sheet, BLM 6a.

🎯 Target Vocabulary

Tier II	Tier III
peacefully	character
comfortably	fairy tale
rough	
tempting	
*trespassing	
*enormous	

*Expanded Target Vocabulary Word

DAY 1

Introduce Book

This week's book is called *Goldilocks and the Three Bears.* What's the title? *Goldilocks and the Three Bears.*

This book was written by Jan Brett. Who's the author of *Goldilocks and the Three Bears? Jan Brett.*

Jan Brett also made the pictures for this book. Who's the illustrator of *Goldilocks and the Three Bears? Jan Brett.*

The cover of a book usually gives us some hints of what the book is about. Let's look at the front cover of *Goldilocks and the Three Bears.* What do you see in the picture? (Ideas: *A large father bear; a mother bear; and a baby bear going for a walk.*)

(Assign each child a partner.) Remember that when you make a prediction about something, you say what you think will happen. Get ready to make some predictions to your partner about this book. Use the information from the cover to help you.

(Ask the following questions, allowing sufficient time for children to share their predictions with their partners.)

- Whom do you think this story is about?
- What do you think they will do?
- Where do you think the story happens?
- When do you think the story happens?
- Why do you think they are going for a walk?

- How long do you think their walk will be?
- Do you think this story is about real bears? Tell why or why not.

(Call on several children to share their predictions with the class.)

Take a Picture Walk

(Encourage children to use target words in their answers.) We're going to take a picture walk through this book. Remember that when we take a picture walk, we look at the pictures and tell what we think will happen in the story.

Pages 1–2. Where does the story happen? (Ideas: *In a cottage in the woods.*) What are the bears doing? (Idea: *Playing together.*)

Pages 3–4. How do you think the bears feel here? (Ideas: *Happy; relaxed.*) What makes you think so? (Ideas: *The big bear looks like he's having a snack; the little bear is playing with a butterfly; there's a bit of a mess that looks like they've been playing.*) Jan Brett likes to put clues to her stories in the borders around her illustrations. What things do you see in the borders on these two pages? (Ideas: *Bowls; beds.*) Why do you think Jan Brett put these pictures in the borders? (Idea: *They will appear later in the story.*)

Pages 5–6. What are the bears doing on this page? (Ideas: *Mother and father bear are walking; baby bear is stuck on a tree trunk.*) Where do you think the bears might be going?

(Idea: *For a walk in the woods.*) What pictures has Jan Brett put in the borders of these pages? (Ideas: *A girl; animals.*)

Pages 7–8. What is Goldilocks doing in the first picture? (Idea: *Looking through the window of a little house.*) Whose house do you think it is? (Idea: *The bears' house.*) What clues tell you that this could be the bears' house? (Ideas: *There is a bear statue in front of the window; there is a bear carving around the window.*) Where is Goldilocks in the second picture? (Idea: *Inside the house.*) Do you think she is supposed to be in the house? *No.* Why? (Idea: *The bears are not home.*)

Pages 9–10. What is Goldilocks doing in this picture? (Idea: *Looking in a bowl/pot.*) There are more clues in the border. What are the three bears doing while the little girl is in their house? (Ideas: *Baby bear is playing with a beehive; the mother and father bear are walking together.*)

Pages 11–12. What is Goldilocks doing in the first picture? (Idea: *Sitting in a big chair.*) Does she look comfortable? *No.* What has happened in the second picture? (Idea: *The little girl has fallen on the floor.*) How do you think this happened? (Idea: *She sat on a chair and it broke.*)

Pages 13–14. Where is Goldilocks going in the first picture? (Idea: *Upstairs.*) How do you know? (Ideas: *She is facing the stairs and looking at them like that's where she wants to go.*) Where is Goldilocks in the second picture? (Ideas: *In the bedroom.*) Which bear do you think this bed belongs to? (Idea: *The big father bear.*)

Pages 15–16. Where are the bears? (Idea: *Back home.*) What are the bears doing? (Idea: *Looking in their bowls.*) Look in the border of these pages. What is Goldilocks doing while the bears are looking in their bowls? *Sleeping.* What do you think the bears are saying?

Pages 17–18. How is father bear feeling in this picture? (Ideas: *Mad; angry.*) What clues tell you that he is feeling that way? (Ideas: *His mouth is wide like he is shouting; he is jumping on his chair.*) What are mother bear and baby bear doing in the border pictures? (Ideas: *Mother bear*

is touching or straightening her cushion; Baby bear is looking at his broken chair.)

Pages 19–20. Where have the bears gone now? (Idea: *To their bedroom.*) What has happened to their beds? (Idea: *Their beds have been messed up.*) What do you think baby bear will find when he gets to his bed? (Idea: *Goldilocks.*)

Pages 21–22. What did baby bear find in his bed? *Goldilocks.* What do you think baby bear is thinking?

Pages 23–24. What are the bears looking at? (Idea: *Goldilocks.*)

Pages 25–26. How do you think Goldilocks is feeling? (Idea: *Scared.*) Where do you think she is going? (Ideas: *Away from the bears' house; home.*) In the second picture, what do you think the bears are looking at? (Idea: *Goldilocks running away.*) Do you think she'll come back? *No.*

Page 27. How do you think the bears are feeling in this picture? (Idea: *Happy.*) What clues tell you this? (Ideas: *They are hugging each other; they have little smiles on their faces.*)

It's your turn to ask me some questions. What would you like to know about the story? (Accept questions. If children tell about the pictures or the story instead of asking questions, prompt them to ask a question.) Ask me a what question. Ask me a when question.

Read the Story Aloud
(Read story aloud to children with minimal interruptions.)

Tomorrow we will read the story again, and I will ask you some questions.

(If children have difficulty attending for an extended period of time, you may wish to present the next part of this day's lesson at another time of day.)

Present Target Vocabulary
◎← Tempting

In the story, when Goldilocks smelled the sweet smell of the porridge, it was so tempting that she just helped herself. That means the porridge smelled so good she wanted to have it. **Tempting.** Say the word. *Tempting.*

If something is tempting you, it makes you really want to have it. Say the word that means "something makes you really want to have it." *Tempting.*

(Correct any incorrect responses, and repeat the item at the end of the sequence.)

Let's think about some things that might be tempting. I'll tell about something. If you think that thing would be tempting, say "tempting." If not, don't say anything.

- The smell of the warm cinnamon buns made Jessie really want to have one. *Tempting.*
- When David found out Auntie Susan was going on a camping trip and invited him to come, he really wanted to go. *Tempting.*
- Sarita wasn't at all interested in going to the movies.
- Steve tried his hardest to get the job done right.
- The pretty colors of the strawberries, apples, and oranges made everyone feel very hungry. *Tempting.*
- The coolness of the swimming pool made everyone want to jump right in. *Tempting.*

What word means "something makes you really want to have it"? *Tempting.*

◎← Comfortably

In the story, Goldilocks climbed into the little wee bear's bed, covered herself up comfortably, and fell fast asleep. That means she covered herself in a way that made her feel cozy and relaxed. **Comfortably.** Say the word. *Comfortably.*

When someone does something comfortably they do it in a way that makes them feel cozy and relaxed. Say the word that means "do something in a way that makes you feel cozy and relaxed." *Comfortably.*

Let's think about some things you could do comfortably. I'll tell about something someone is doing. If you think they are doing it comfortably, say "comfortably." If not don't say anything.

- Allen and his dad cuddled up on the sofa so Allen's father could read him a bedtime story. *Comfortably.*
- Jasmine just couldn't relax while she waited for the dentist to check her teeth.

- Estella and Grandpa relaxed in Grandpa's big chair while they watched TV. *Comfortably.*
- The children hid their heads under the covers when they heard the lightning.
- The children raced around playing a game of hide-and-seek.
- Lorenzo snuggled into his bed and pulled up his fuzzy blanket. *Comfortably.*

What word means "do something in a way that makes you feel cozy and relaxed"? *Comfortably.*

◎← Rough

In the story, the great, huge bear said in his great rough, gruff voice, "SOMEONE HAS BEEN EATING MY PORRIDGE!" That means his voice was harsh, not gentle or kind. **Rough.** Say the word. *Rough.*

Rough means harsh, not gentle or kind. Rough is the opposite of gentle or kind. What word means "harsh, not gentle or kind"? *Rough.*

Let's think about some times when someone might speak in a rough voice. I'll tell about a time. If you think the person would be using a rough voice, say "rough." If not, don't say anything.

- Your dad has already told you to put away your toys three times. Now he is telling you again. *Rough.*
- You are playing happily with your best friends.
- The bully is shouting at the children playing at the park. *Rough.*
- The sea lion is being bothered by the tourists. *Rough.*
- You've hurt your knee and the school nurse is putting a bandage on it.
- The mother bear is teaching her cubs to fish.

What word means "harsh, not gentle or kind"? *Rough.*

◎← Peacefully

In the story, Goldilocks was "sleeping peacefully, her long shiny braids spread across the pillow." That means she was sleeping quietly and calmly. **Peacefully.** Say the word. *Peacefully.*

When you do something peacefully, you do it quietly and calmly. Say the word that means "do something quietly and calmly." *Peacefully.*

Let's think about some times when someone might have done something peacefully. I'll tell you about a time. If you think someone would have done something peacefully, say "peacefully." If not, don't say anything.

- Stephan was sitting at his desk, quietly painting a picture of his pet guinea pig. *Peacefully.*
- Kim and Lee settled their disagreement quietly and without fighting. *Peacefully.*
- Everyone was running and shouting as they played tag.
- The girl and her mother were drifting along in their canoe, enjoying the sunny afternoon. *Peacefully.*
- The two sisters argued and fought all afternoon.
- The mother cat was curled up with her sleeping kittens in an old box. *Peacefully.*

What word means "do something quietly and calmly"? *Peacefully.*

Present Vocabulary Tally Sheet
(See Lesson 1, page 3, for instructions.)

Assign Homework
(Homework Sheet BLM 6a: See the Introduction for homework instructions.)

DAY 2

Preparation: Picture Vocabulary Cards for *tempting, comfortably, rough, peacefully.*

Read and Discuss Story

(Read story aloud to children. Ask the following questions at the specified points. Encourage them to use target words in their answers.)

Page 1. Where does this story take place? *In a house in a wood.* A wood is a place with lots of trees. What is a wood? *A place with lots of trees.* Who lives in the house in the wood? *Three bears.*

Page 2. What do the three bears look like? (Ideas: *There is a little, small, wee bear, a middle-sized bear, and a great, huge bear.*)

Page 4. What kind of bowl does the little, small, wee bear have? *A little, small, wee bowl.* What kind of chair does the medium-sized bear have? *A medium-sized chair.* What kind of bed did the great, huge bear have? *A great, huge bed.* Do you think these bears are real or imaginary? *Imaginary.* Why do you think so? (Idea: *Because bears don't live in houses or sleep in beds.*)

Page 5. Why do the bears go for a walk in the woods? (Idea: *Their porridge is too hot and they are waiting for it to cool.*)

Page 7. Who comes to the house while the bears are out for their walk? *Goldilocks.* What does she do first? (Idea: *Looks in at the window.*) What does she do next? (Idea: *Peeps in at the keyhole.*) I wonder what "peeped" means. I look at the picture and I see that Goldilocks is outside the house. The story says she "peeped in at the keyhole." A keyhole is very small. I think Goldilocks is trying to see if anyone is inside, so I think she looked in through the keyhole. "Peeped" must mean "looked through something very small." What word means "looked through something very small"? *Peeped.* What is the last thing Goldilocks does? (Idea: *Lifts the latch.*)

Page 8. Where is Goldilocks? *Inside the house.*

Page 9. Is Goldilocks happy to see the porridge? *Yes.* How do you know? (Ideas: *She is pleased. She helps herself to it.*)

Page 10. What is wrong with the great, huge bear's porridge? *It is too hot.* What is wrong with the middle-sized bear's porridge? *It is too cold.* Why does Goldilocks eat the porridge of the little, small, wee bear? *It is just right.*

Page 11. What does Goldilocks do after she eats the porridge? (Idea: *She sits in the chairs.*) Does Goldilocks like the great, huge chair? *No.* Why not? *It is too hard.* Does she like the medium-sized chair? *No.* Why not? *It is too soft.*

Page 12. Whose chair is just right for Goldilocks? (Idea: *The little, small, wee bear's chair.*) What happens while Goldilocks is sitting in that chair? *It breaks.*

Page 13. Where does Goldilocks go next? (Ideas: *Upstairs; to the bears' bedroom.*)

Read aloud page 14. What does Goldilocks do in the bedroom? (Idea: *She tries out all the beds.*) Which bed is just right for Goldilocks? (Idea: *The bed of the little, small, wee bear.*) Which bear do you think is the same size as Goldilocks? *The little, small, wee bear.* How do you know that? (Idea: *All of his things are just right for Goldilocks.*)

Page 15. Why do the bears decide to come home? (Idea: *They think their porridge should be cool.*) How does the great, huge bear know that someone had been at his porridge? (Idea: *The spoon is in his porridge.*)

Page 16. How is the little, small, wee bear's bowl different from the other two? (Idea: *The porridge is all gone.*) What has happened to the little, small, wee bear's porridge? (Idea: *Goldilocks ate it.*)

Page 18. How does the great, huge bear know that somebody had been sitting in his chair? (Idea: *The cushion is not on straight.*) What has Goldilocks done to the medium-sized bear's chair? (Idea: *Crumpled the cushions.*) What has happened to the little, small, wee bear's chair? (Idea: *Goldilocks has broken it.*)

Page 19. What does the great, huge bear say when he sees his pillow is out of place? Say it in a great, rough, gruff voice. *SOMEBODY HAS BEEN LYING IN MY BED!*

Page 20. What clue tells the middle-sized bear that someone has been lying in her bed? (Idea: *The blanket is out of place.*)

Page 21. What does the little, small, wee bear find in his bed? *Goldilocks.* What does he do? (Idea: *He stares at her and doesn't say anything.*)

Page 22. What does the little, small, wee bear say when he sees Goldilocks in his bed? Say it in a little, small, wee voice. *Somebody has been lying in my bed—and here she is!*

Page 23. Why doesn't Goldilocks wake up when she hears the great, rough, gruff voice and the middle voice? (Idea: *She thinks she is dreaming.*) What kind of voice does Goldilocks have? *A little, small, wee voice.* How do you know? (Idea: *The little, small, wee bear's voice is like her own.*)

Page 25. Where does Goldilocks run when she sees the bears? *To the window.*

Page 26. Why does Goldilocks jump out the window and run far away? (Idea: *She is afraid of the bears.*) Do you think Goldilocks will go into another house that isn't hers? (Idea: *No.*)

Page 27. What happens to Goldilocks after that? (Idea: *Nobody knows; the bears never saw her again.*)

Review Vocabulary

(Display the Picture Vocabulary Cards. Point to each card as you say the word. Ask children to repeat each word after you.) These pictures show **tempting, comfortably, rough,** and **peacefully.**

- What word means "do something quietly and calmly"? *Peacefully.*
- What word means "do something in a way that makes you feel cozy and relaxed"? *Comfortably.*
- What word means "harsh, not gentle or kind"? *Rough.*
- What word means "something makes you really want to have it"? *Tempting.*

Extend Vocabulary

◎← Rough

In *Goldilocks and the Three Bears,* we learned that **rough** can be used to tell about how people talk. When someone has a rough voice, it means that their voice is harsh, not gentle or kind.

Here's a new way to use the word **rough.**

- It was hard to ride my bike on the **rough** path. Say the sentence.
- When the wind blew hard the water was **rough.** Say the sentence.
- Wool sweaters feel **rough** on my skin. Say the sentence.

In these sentences, rough means not smooth. Something that is not smooth has dents or bumps on it. Tell about some other things that might feel rough. (Ideas: *Sandpaper; a bumpy road; the pavement on the playground.*)

Present Expanded Target Vocabulary

◎ Trespassing

Goldilocks went into the bears' house without asking them first. She was trespassing. **Trespassing.** Say the word. *Trespassing.*

If you are trespassing, you go on someone's property without asking them first. Say the word that means "go on someone's property without asking them first." *Trespassing.*

Let's think about some times when someone might have been trespassing. If I tell about a time when someone would have been trespassing, say "trespassing." If not, don't say anything.

- Joanie climbed over the neighbor's fence and picked apples from their apple tree without asking them first. *Trespassing.*
- The man took a shortcut across my grandma's field without asking her first. *Trespassing.*
- Our family had permission to camp by Mr. Johnston's lake.
- The sign on the tree said "Stay Out!" but the hunter went into the woods anyway. *Trespassing.*
- Mrs. Park invited all the children to come to her yard to watch the fireworks on the Fourth of July.
- There was a gate across the road, so we turned our car around and went back down the road.

What word means "go on someone's property without asking them first"? *Trespassing.*

◎ Enormous

In the story, the great, huge bear had a great huge bowl, and a great huge chair, and a great huge bed. That means he was really, really big, and all his things were really, really big. He and his things were **enormous.** Say the word. *Enormous.*

When something is enormous, it is really, really big. Say the word that means "really, really big." *Enormous.*

Let's think about some things that could be enormous. I'll name something. If you think that thing could be enormous, say "enormous." If not, don't say anything.

- A mountain. *Enormous.*
- A giant. *Enormous.*
- A furry mouse.
- The biggest tree in the world. *Enormous.*
- A grain of sand.
- A jet airplane. *Enormous.*

What describing word means "really, really big"? *Enormous.*

DAY 3

Preparation: Activity Sheet, BLM 6b.

Retell Story

Today I'll show you the pictures Jan Brett made for *Goldilocks and the Three Bears.* As I show you the pictures, I'll call on one of you to tell the class that part of the story.

Tell me what happens at the **beginning** of the story. (Show the pictures on pages 1–6. Call on a child to tell what's happening.)

Tell me what happens in the **middle** of the story. (Show the pictures on pages 7–24. Call on a child to tell what's happening. Encourage use of the target words when appropriate. Model use as necessary.)

Tell me what happens at the **end** of the story. (Show the pictures on pages 27–28. Call on a child to tell what's happening.)

Do you think the three bears will leave their door unlocked the next time they go for a walk? Tell why you think so. (Accept either answer as long as children support it.)

Play the Whoopsy! Game

(Display the Picture Vocabulary Cards as you play this game.) Today you will play the *Whoopsy! Game.* I'll say sentences using words we have learned. If the word doesn't fit in the sentence, you say "Whoopsy!" Then I'll ask you to say a sentence where the word fits. If you can do it, you get a point. If you can't do it, I get the point. If the word I use fits the sentence, don't say anything.

Let's practice:

The food on the table was very **tempting** because … it smelled terrible. *Whoopsy!* Listen to the beginning of the sentence again. The food on the table was very **tempting.** Say the beginning of the sentence. *The food on the table was very tempting.* Can you finish the sentence so the word fits? (Idea: *The food on the table was very tempting because it smelled delicious.*)

Let's try another one. My shoes fitted me **comfortably** when … they gave me blisters and pinched my toes. *Whoopsy!* Listen to the beginning of the sentence again. My shoes fitted me **comfortably** when. Say the beginning of the sentence. *My shoes fitted me comfortably when.* Can you finish the sentence so the word fits? (Idea: *My shoes fitted me comfortably when they didn't hurt my feet at all.*)

Now you're ready to play the game. (Draw a T-chart on the board for keeping score. Children earn one point for each correct answer. If they make an error, correct them as you normally would, and record one point for yourself. Repeat missed words at the end of the game.)

- The children were playing **peacefully** when … they were throwing puzzle pieces all around the room. *Whoopsy!* Say the beginning of the sentence again. *The children were playing peacefully when.* Can you finish the sentence? (Idea: *The children were playing peacefully when they worked together to finish the puzzle.*)
- The **tempting** smell of the apple pie made me want to … run away as fast as I could. *Whoopsy!* Say the beginning of the sentence again. *The tempting smell of the apple pie made me want to.* Can you finish the sentence? (Idea: *The tempting smell of the apple pie made me want to eat the pie right away.*)
- I was **trespassing** in the neighbor's yard when … I jumped the fence to get my ball back and I didn't have permission.
- The **enormous** dog was as big as … an ant. *Whoopsy!* Say the beginning of the sentence again. *The enormous dog was as big as.* Can you finish the sentence? (Idea: *The enormous dog was as big as a horse.*)

- The **rough** voice of the storekeeper sounded … gentle and kind. *Whoopsy!* Say the beginning of the sentence again. *The rough voice of the storekeeper sounded.* Can you finish the sentence? (Idea: *The rough voice of the storekeeper sounded harsh, not gentle or kind.*)

(Count the points and declare a winner.) You did a great job of playing *Whoopsy!*

Complete the Activity Sheet

 Think about the characters in the fairy tale *Goldilocks and the Three Bears.* Who are those characters? (Ideas: *Little, small, wee bear; middle-sized bear; great huge bear; and Goldilocks.*)

(Give each child a copy of the Activity Sheet, BLM 6b.)

We're going to play a game called the Riddle Game. When you play a riddle game, I tell you some things that I know about a character. Your job is to guess who I'm talking about.

Let's play the riddle game. I'll give you some clues. Raise your hand when you think you can name the character who I am talking about.

- I like porridge.
  I went upstairs in the house in the wood.
  I have brown fur.
  I found my pillow had been moved.
  Who am I?

(Have the children identify which character is the answer to the riddle. *Great, huge bear.* Instruct the children to color the correct picture, cut it out, and paste it underneath the riddle.)

(Repeat the process for these two riddles.)

- I went for a walk.
  I walked with my family.
  I saw someone had been sitting in my chair.
  My chair was broken.
  Who am I? (*Little, small, wee bear.*)
- I sat on a chair.
  I went upstairs in the house in the woods.
  I slept in a bed.
  I was trespassing.
  Who am I? (*Goldilocks.*)

Preparation: Prepare two sheets of chart paper, each with a circle drawn in the middle. Fold the sheets of paper in half vertically to divide the circle in half. When you record children's responses, physical descriptors should be recorded on the left-hand side of each chart. Personality characteristics or actions should be recorded on the right-hand side.

Analyze Characters (Literary Analysis)

Let's think about what we already know about how books are made.

- What do we call the name of the book? *Title.*
- What do we call the person who writes the story? *Author.*
- What do we call the person who draws the pictures? *Illustrator.*
- What do we call the people or animals a story is about? *Characters.*

Let's sing The Story Song to help us remember these important things about books.

(See the Introduction for the complete Story Song.)

Today we will learn more about the characters in a story.

Remember that the characters in a story are the people or animals the story is about. What are the people or animals a story is about? *Characters.* Who are the characters in a story? *The people or animals the story is about.*

In *Goldilocks and the Three Bears,* are the characters people or animals? *The bears are animals; Goldilocks is a girl—a person.*

Who are the characters in the story? (Ideas: *The little, small, wee bear; the middle-sized bear; the great, huge bear; Goldilocks.*)

The most important characters in *Goldilocks and the Three Bears* are the bears and Goldilocks. Who are the most important characters in the story? *The bears and Goldilocks.*

(Write *bears* in the circle on one of the charts; write *Goldilocks* in the circle on the other sheet.)

Let's remember what we know about the bears. (Show children the cover.) What do the bears look like? (Call on several children. Record each child's response on the left-hand side of the *bear* chart.) (Ideas: *Brown; furry; have claws; wear clothes.*)

(Show children pages 5 and 6. Ask these questions. Call on several children. Record each child's response on the right-hand side of the chart.) Do you think the bears are a happy family or an unhappy family? (Idea: *Happy.*) Tell why you think that. (Idea: *The father bear is playing with his son; the baby bear is turning somersaults; the mother bear looks like she's smiling.*)

(Show children pages 17 and 18.) In Week 2 we learned a new word that meant the great, huge bear was feeling very, very angry at someone or something. Say the word that means the great, huge bear was very, very angry at someone or something. He was … *Furious.*

(Follow a similar process to describe Goldilocks. Record responses on the second piece of chart paper.)

Today you have learned about the bears and Goldilocks. They are the most important characters in *Goldilocks and the Three Bears.*

Play Whoopsy! (Cumulative Review)

(Display the Picture Vocabulary Cards as you play this game.)

Let's play *Whoopsy!* I'll say sentences using words we have learned. If the word doesn't fit in the sentence, you say, "Whoopsy!" Then I'll ask you to say a sentence where the word fits. If you can do it, you get a point. If you can't do it, I get the point. If the word I use fits the sentence, don't say anything.

Now you're ready to play the game. (Draw a T-chart on the board for keeping score. Children earn one point for each correct answer. If they make an error, correct them as you normally would and record one point for yourself. Repeat missed words at the end of the game.)

- The man was **trespassing** when … he asked the farmer if he could cross his field. *Whoopsy!* Say the beginning of the sentence again. *The man was trespassing when.* Can you finish the sentence? (Idea: *The man was trespassing when he crossed the farmer's field without asking him first.*)
- Goldilocks was sleeping **comfortably** when … she had the covers pulled up around her nice and cozy.
- The cakes on the plate looked so **tempting** … I just couldn't eat them. *Whoopsy!* Say the beginning of the sentence again. *The cakes on the plate looked so tempting.* Can you finish the sentence? (Idea: *The cakes on the plate looked so tempting. I really wanted to eat them.*)
- The **rough** skin of the cantaloupe felt … as smooth as glass. *Whoopsy!* Say the beginning of the sentence again. *The rough skin of the cantaloupe felt.* Can you finish the sentence? (Idea: *The rough skin of the cantaloupe felt bumpy.*)
- The **rough** voice of the angry man … made me want to hide.
- The farmers were **harvesting** the corn when … they covered up the corn seed. *Whoopsy!* Say the beginning of the sentence again. *The farmers were harvesting the corn when.* Can you finish the sentence? (Idea: *The farmers were harvesting the corn when they picked the ears.*)
- The seeds **sprouted** when … they started to die. *Whoopsy!* Say the beginning of the sentence again. *The seeds sprouted when.* Can you finish the sentence? (Idea: *The seeds sprouted when they started to grow.*)
- The kittens were cuddling **peacefully** when … they were lying still and quiet next to their mother.
- The **enormous** box was as big as … a can of soup. *Whoopsy!* Say the beginning of the sentence again. *The enormous box was as big as.* Can you finish the sentence? (Idea: *The enormous box was as big as a refrigerator.*)
- A road is **winding** when … it goes straight. *Whoopsy!* Say the beginning of the sentence again. *A road is winding when.* Can you finish the sentence? (Idea: *A road is winding when it twists and turns.*)

(Count the points and declare a winner.) You did a great job of playing *Whoopsy!*

Preparation: A map or a globe of the world. Happy Face Game Test Sheet, BLM B.

Learn About Fairy Tales

Today you will learn more about a special kind of folk tale called a fairy tale. What will you learn about? *A fairy tale.*

Folk tales and fairy tales are both stories that were once told out loud. How are folk tales and fairy tales the same? (Idea: *They are both stories that were once told out loud.*) But a fairy tale is a story that someone decided to write down in a book a long time ago. How is a fairy tale different from a folk tale? (Idea: *Someone decided to write it down in a book a long time ago.*)

The first person to write down the story *Goldilocks and the Three Bears* was a man named Robert Southey. Robert Southey lived in England. (Locate England on the map or globe.) What country does the fairy tale *Goldilocks and the Three Bears* come from? *England.* Robert Southey wrote down this story more than 160 years ago. When did he write down this story? (Idea: *More than 160 years ago.*) That's a very, very long time ago!

After Robert Southey wrote down the story, many other people retold the story. (Point to the words *Retold by* on the cover.) Jan Brett retold the story in her own words, so she is known as the author of this version of the story. Who is the author? *Jan Brett.*

Fairy tales often begin with the same words. Listen while I read the first sentence of *Goldilocks and the Three Bears.* (Read aloud page 1.) How does this fairy tale begin? *Once upon a time.*

Fairy tales often have good characters and evil characters. Who are the good characters in *Goldilocks and the Three Bears*? (Idea: *The three bears.*) Who is the evil character in *Goldilocks and the Three Bears*? (Idea: *Goldilocks.*)

(**Note:** You may wish to discuss with children the point of view that Goldilocks was naughty rather than evil.)

Fairy tales often have things that happen in threes. Tell about the things that happened in threes. (Ideas: *There were three bears; three bowls; three chairs; three beds; there were nuts, honey, and berries in the porridge; Goldilocks tried three bowls of porridge, three chairs, and three beds; words repeated three times—"Somebody has been at my porridge"; "Somebody has been sitting in my chair"; "Somebody has been lying in my bed."*)

Let's remember three important things about fairy tales. How do fairy tales often begin? *Once upon a time.* What kinds of characters are often in fairy tales? *Good characters and evil characters.* What is the special number that is often in fairy tales? *Three.* Good remembering about fairy tales.

Assess Vocabulary

(Give each child a copy of the Happy Face Game Test Sheet, BLM B.) Today you're going to play the Happy Face Game. When you play the Happy Face Game, it shows me how well you know the hard words you are learning.

If I say something that is true, color in the happy face. What will you do if I say something that is true? *Color in the happy face.*

If I say something that is false, color in the sad face. What will you do if I say something that is false? *Color in the sad face.*

Listen carefully to each item that I say. Don't let me trick you!

Item 1: If you are sitting **comfortably,** you hurt all over. (*False.*)

Item 2: If you are **peacefully** playing, you are playing quietly and calmly. (*True.*)

Item 3: **Rough** means the same as smooth. (*False.*)

Item 4: A **rough** voice is harsh and unkind. (*True.*)

Item 5: If a house is **enormous,** it is really, really big. (*True.*)

Item 6: If someone invites you over to their house, you are **trespassing.** (*False.*)

Item 7: Ripe oranges picked from a tree are **tempting.** (*True.*)

Item 8: If something is **delicious,** it has a disagreeable taste. (*False.*)

Item 9: If you **crept** across the classroom, you ran as fast as you could and made lots of noise. (*False.*)

Item 10: If you chose to go swimming, you **decided** to go swimming. (*True.*)

You did a great job of playing the Happy Face Game!

(Score children's work at a later time. A child must score 9 out of 10 to be at the mastery level. If a child does not achieve mastery, insert the missed words as additional items in the games for next week's lessons. Retest those children individually for the missed items before they take the next mastery test.)

Extensions

Read a Story as a Reward

(Display copies of the books that you have read since the beginning of the program. Allow children to choose which book they would like you to read to them as a reward for their hard work.)

(Read the story aloud for enjoyment with minimal interruptions.)

Preparation: Word containers for the Super Words Center.

 Introduce the Super Words Center
(Add the new Picture Vocabulary Cards to words from the previous weeks. Show children one of the word containers. If children need more guidance in how to work in the Super Words Center, role-play with two to three children as a demonstration.)

Let's think about how we work with our words in the Super Words Center.

You will work with a partner in the Super Words Center. Whom will you work with? *A partner.*

Today I will teach you how to play a game called *What's New?*

First one partner will draw four Picture Vocabulary Cards out of the container and put them on the table so both partners can see. What do you do first? (Idea: *Draw four cards out of the container and put them on the table so both partners can see.*)

Next you will take turns looking at the cards and saying the words the pictures show. What do you do next? (Idea: *We take turns looking at the cards and saying the words the pictures show.*)

Next partner 2 looks away while partner 1 takes one of the four cards and places it back in the container. Then partner 1 draws a new card from the container and places it on the table with the other three. Watch while I show you what I mean. (Demonstrate this process with one child as your partner.) When you put down the new card, it's a good idea to mix the cards so they aren't in the same places any more. (Demonstrate this process as you go.)

Now partner 1 says, "What's new?" Partner 2 has to use his or her eyes and brain and say what new word card has been put down. If partner 2 is correct, they get a point. If partner 2 is not correct, partner 1 gets the point. (Demonstrate this process as you go.)

Next partner 2 has a turn to choose four different cards and the game starts again. What happens next? (Idea: *Partner 2 has a turn to choose four different cards and the game starts again.*)

Have fun playing *What's New?*

Preparation: You will need *The Princess and the Pea* for each day's lesson.

Post a copy of the Vocabulary Tally Sheet, BLM A, with this week's Picture Vocabulary Cards attached.

Each child will need one copy of the Homework Sheet, BLM 7a.

DAY 1

Introduce Book

This week's book is called *The Princess and the Pea*. What's the title? *The Princess and the Pea.*

This book was written by Susan Blackaby. Who's the author of *The Princess and the Pea*? *Susan Blackaby.*

Charlene DeLage [duh-lahj] made the pictures for this book. Who's the illustrator of *The Princess and the Pea*? *Charlene DeLage.*

The cover of a book usually gives us some hints of what the book is about. Let's look at the front cover of *The Princess and the Pea*. What do you see in the illustration? (Ideas: *There is a young girl lying on a tall stack of mattresses.*)

(Assign each child a partner.) Remember that when you make a prediction about something, you say what you think will happen. Get ready to make some predictions to your partner about this book. Use the information from the cover to help you.

(Ask the following questions, allowing sufficient time for children to share their predictions with their partners.)

- Whom do you think this story is about?
- What do you think the princess in the story will do?
- Where do you think the story happens?
- When do you think this story happens?
- Why do you think the princess is lying on so many mattresses?
- How do you think the princess is feeling?

The Princess and the Pea
author: Susan Blackaby • illustrator: Charlene DeLage

🎯 Target Vocabulary

Tier II	Tier III
noble	character
fine	fairy tale
wise	version
exclaimed	
*genuine	
*sensitive	

*Expanded Target Vocabulary Word

- Do you think this story is about a real princess? Tell why or why not.

(Call on several children to share their predictions with the class.)

Take a Picture Walk

We're going to take a picture walk through this book. Remember that when we take a picture walk, we look at the pictures and tell what we think will happen in the story.

Page 5. Who do you think these people are? (Idea: *A king, a prince, and a queen.*)

Page 6. Where is the prince in this illustration? (Ideas: *On the road.*) Where do you think he is going?

Page 7. What do you think the prince is thinking about?

Pages 8–9. Who do you think the men are? (Idea: *Guards.*) Who do you think these girls are? (Idea: *Princesses.*) What do you think the prince is saying to the princesses?

Page 10. Why do you think there's a map of the world on this page? (Idea: *To show how far the prince traveled.*) What do you think the line shows? (Idea: *All the places the prince has been.*)

Page 11. How do you think the prince is feeling? (Ideas: *Sad; upset.*) We learned a word in Week 1 that might tell how the prince is feeling. What word means "wanting something very, very badly"? *Desperate.* That's right. I think the prince might be feeling desperate.

Pages 12–13. What is happening in this illustration? (Ideas: *It's raining; a storm is coming.*)

Page 14. Who do you think is at the door of the castle? (Ideas: *A girl; a princess.*)

Page 15. What do you think the king is saying to the girl?

Page 16. What do you think the king and the girl are talking about? (Idea: *The storm; how wet she is.*) How do you think the guard is feeling? (Idea: *Surprised.*) What makes you think so? (Idea: *His mouth is round like he is saying, "Oh!"*) Do you think the king has ever had a late-night visitor like this before? *No.*

Page 17. What do you think the prince is asking the girl?

Pages 18–19. What do you think is happening here? (Ideas: *The king, the prince, and the girl are talking; the queen is thinking.*) What do you think the queen could be thinking about? (Ideas: *Who the strange girl is; how she got here at night; why she is all alone.*)

Page 20. What is the queen placing on the bed? (Idea: *A small pea.*)

Page 21. What is the queen doing here? (Idea: *Stacking up many mattresses.*) Why do you think she is doing that?

Page 22. What do you think the queen is saying to the girl? What is the girl doing? (Idea: *Curtsying to the queen.*) When a girl meets a king or a queen, she usually curtsies as a sign of respect. This is a curtsy. (Bend slightly at the knee, with one leg crossed behind the other, holding your skirt or the sides of your pants out to the sides.) Girls and women curtsy when they meet a king or a queen. What do girls and women do when they meet a king or a queen? *They curtsy.*

When a boy meets a king or a queen, he usually bows as a sign of respect. This is a bow. (Bend low from the waist, keeping your feet together and your hands at your sides.) Boys and men bow when they meet a king or a queen. What do boys and men do when they meet a king or a queen? *They bow.*

Page 23. What is the girl doing in this illustration? (Idea: *Getting into bed.*) What do you think the girl is thinking? (Ideas: *There are many mattresses on this bed; the bed should be really comfortable.*)

Page 24. When do you think this part of the story happens? (Idea: *In the morning.*) What do you think the king, queen, and girl are saying? (Ideas: *"Good morning"; "How did you sleep?"*)

Pages 26–27. What do you think the girl is telling the queen? (Children's answers should include ideas shown in the illustrations.)

Page 28. Why do you think the queen is smiling? (Idea: *She is thinking about the pea she put under the girl's mattresses.*)

Page 29. How do you think the prince and the girl feel in this illustration? (Idea: *Happy.*)

Page 30. What is happening in this illustration? (Idea: *The prince and the girl are getting married.*)

Page 31. What is being displayed on this pillow? (Idea: *The small pea.*)

It's your turn to ask me some questions. What would you like to know about the story? (Accept questions. If the children tell about the pictures or the story instead of ask questions, prompt them to ask a question.) Ask me a what question. Ask me a how question.

Read the Story Aloud
(Read story to children with minimal interruptions.)

Tomorrow we will read the story again, and I will ask you some questions.

(If children have difficulty attending for an extended period of time, you may wish to present the next part of this day's lesson at another time of day.)

Present Target Vocabulary
◎← Noble

In the story, "a noble king and wise queen had a son." That means the king was a good man who would share what he had with others. **Noble.** Say the word. *Noble.*

A person who is noble is a good person who would share whatever he or she had with

others. Say the word that tells about a good person who would share whatever he or she had with others. *Noble.*

(Correct any incorrect responses, and repeat the item at the end of the sequence.)

Let's think about some people who might be noble. If you think the person is noble, say "noble." If not, don't say anything.

- The woman worked for free at the soup kitchen, helping to feed the people who were homeless. *Noble.*
- The governor worked hard to make sure all the people in his state were happy and healthy. *Noble.*
- The king didn't care what happened to anyone else.
- The children went to school every day.
- The sixth-grade boy was good to the younger children, making sure they were safe and happy. *Noble.*
- Even though she was not rich, the old woman cared about her neighbors and helped them in every way she could. *Noble.*

What word tells about a good person who would share whatever he or she had with others? *Noble.*

 Fine

In the story, the prince was called "a fine young prince." That means he was a good person. **Fine.** Say the word. *Fine.*

When you say someone is fine you mean they are good. Say the word that means "good." *Fine.*

Let's think about some things that a fine person would have done. I'll tell about some things someone was doing. If you think they are things a fine person would have done, say "fine." If not, don't say anything.

- Armando was polite and considerate when he visited his grandparents. *Fine.*
- Jonah stomped his feet and screamed when he didn't get his own way.
- Zelina studied hard and did her homework. *Fine.*
- Eric threw his papers on the ground instead of putting them in the garbage can.

- Moira listened politely to her grandmother's stories even though she would rather have been outside playing tag. *Fine.*
- The children listened to their teacher, worked hard, and took turns. *Fine.*

What word means "good"? *Fine.*

 Wise

In the story, there was a wise queen. That means she was smart and made good choices. **Wise.** Say the word. *Wise.*

Wise means smart and able to make good choices. Foolish is the opposite of **wise.** What word means "smart and able to make good choices"? *Wise.*

Let's think about some times when someone might have been wise or made a wise decision. I'll tell about a time. If you think the person was smart and made a good choice, say "wise." If not, don't say anything.

- Charo looked both ways before crossing the street. *Wise.*
- Goldilocks went into the bears' house without their permission.
- Uncle Patrick always made good choices. *Wise.*
- The ant knew she needed to work hard collecting and storing food for the winter. *Wise.*
- The grasshopper never thought about tomorrow and played all day.
- The elder in the village told the old stories to the children so they could learn the right things to do. *Wise.*

What word means "smart and able to make good choices"? *Wise.*

 Exclaimed

In the story, the king exclaimed, "A princess!" That means he said the words "a princess" loudly because he was surprised and excited. **Exclaimed.** Say the word. *Exclaimed.*

If you exclaimed something, you said something loudly because you were surprised and excited. Say the word that means "said something loudly because you were surprised and excited." *Exclaimed.*

Let's think about some times when someone might have exclaimed something. I'll tell you what someone said. If you think that person would have said those words loudly because they were surprised or excited, say "exclaimed." If not, don't say anything.

- Oh! What a beautiful painting! *Exclaimed.*
- Please bring me the book.
- Somebody has been lying in my bed—and here she is! *Exclaimed.*
- Oh, come and see the green wheat growing! *Exclaimed.*
- What! Five beans for our cow! *Exclaimed.*
- Did you bring me a present?

What word means "said something loudly because you were surprised and excited"? *Exclaimed.*

Present Vocabulary Tally Sheet
(See Lesson 1, page 3, for instructions.)

Assign Homework
(Homework Sheet, BLM 7a: See the Introduction for homework instructions.)

DAY 2

Preparation: Picture Vocabulary Cards for *noble, fine, wise, exclaimed.*

Read and Discuss Story

(Read story to children. Ask the following questions at the specified points. Encourage them to use target words in their answers.)

Page 5. Who is in this family? (Idea: *A king, a queen, and a prince.*)

Page 6. What does the prince have to find? *A wife.*

Page 7. What kind of princess does the prince want to marry? *A real princess.* That's right, he wants to marry a real princess, not someone who is just pretending to be a princess.

Page 8. Why is the prince traveling to many places? (Idea: *To find a real princess to marry.*)

Page 9. What is wrong with the princesses the prince meets? (Ideas: *None of them are quite right; he can't tell if they are real princesses.*)

Page 10. Where does the prince look for a princess? *All over the world.* Does he find one? *No.*

Page 11. Why is the prince sad? (Idea: *He wants to marry a real princess, but he can't find one.*)

Page 12. When does this part of the story happen? (Ideas: *In the winter; at night; during a storm.*)

Page 13. What kind of night is it in this part of the story? (Ideas: *It is storming; there is thunder and lightning; it's raining.*)

Page 14. Who do you think is knocking at the castle gate? (Ideas: *A girl; a princess.*)

Page 15. Who is at the gate? *A princess.* Why does the king open the door quickly? (Idea: *The prince is looking for a princess to marry.*)

Page 16. What does the girl look like? (Ideas: *She is soaked and covered in mud; her hair looks like seaweed; water is pouring out of her shoes.*)

Page 17. Why does the prince ask the princess if she is a real princess? (Idea: *He is looking for a real princess; he wants to marry a real princess.*)

Page 18. Do you think the girl is a real princess? Tell why you think that.

Page 19. Does the queen believe the girl is a real princess? *No.* Predict what the queen will do to test if the girl is a real princess.

Page 20. What does the queen put in the bed? *A green pea.*

Page 21. (Read to the end of the first sentence.) What does the queen put on top of the pea? *Twenty mattresses.* (Read the rest of the page.) What does she put on top of the mattresses? *Twenty feather beds.* A feather bed is a mattress stuffed with feathers. What do you call a mattress stuffed with feathers? *A feather bed.*

Wow! Twenty mattresses and then twenty feather beds; that should sure be soft and comfortable! How do you think this will tell the queen if the girl is a real princess or not?

Page 22. How does the princess feel? (Idea: *Tired.*)

Page 23. Predict how you think the princess will sleep.

Page 24. When does this part of the story happen? (Idea: *The next morning.*) How do you know? (Idea: *They are having breakfast.*)

Page 25. Did the princess sleep well? *No.*

Page 26. Why didn't the princess sleep well? (Idea: *There was a bump in her bed.*)

Page 27. How does the princess describe the bump? (Idea: *It is hard as a rock and as large as an elephant.*)

Page 28. Why is the queen delighted to hear that the princess hadn't slept well? (Idea: *Only a real princess would have felt the pea; only a real princess would have such sensitive skin.*)

Page 29. Why is the prince thrilled? (Idea: *He has finally found a real princess to marry.*)

Page 30. What happens the next day? (Idea: *The prince and princess get married.*)

Page 31. Why would they display the pea in the royal hall? (Idea: *It proves the princess is a real princess.*)

Review Vocabulary

(Display the Picture Vocabulary Cards. Point to each card as you say the word. Ask children to repeat each word after you.) These pictures show **noble, fine, wise,** and **exclaimed.**

- What word means "said something loudly because you were surprised and excited"? *Exclaimed.*
- What word tells about a good person who would share whatever he or she had with others? *Noble.*
- What word means "good"? *Fine.*
- What word means "smart and able to make good choices"? *Wise.*

Extend Vocabulary

Fine

In *The Princess and the Pea,* we learned that **fine** means "good."

Here's a new way to use the word **fine.**

- The **fine** for speeding is $100.00. Say the sentence.
- The **fine** for parking without putting money in the meter is $35.00. Say the sentence.

- My mom **fines** me 25¢ for not making my bed in the morning. Say the sentence.

In these sentences, fine means money paid as a punishment for doing something wrong. What word means "money paid as a punishment for doing something wrong"? *Fine.*

Present Expanded Target Vocabulary

Genuine

The prince didn't want to marry "just any old princess." He wanted to find "a real princess." Another way of saying he wanted to find a real princess is to say he wanted to find a genuine princess. **Genuine.** Say the word. *Genuine.*

If something is genuine, it is real, not fake. Say the word that means "real, not fake." *Genuine.*

Let's think about some things that might be genuine. If I tell about something that is real, say "genuine." If I tell about something that is not real, say "fake."

- Inside his shoe there was a note that said the shoe was made of real leather. *Genuine.*
- The diamond was a real diamond. *Genuine.*
- The painter made a copy of the famous painting. *Fake.*
- The watch was made of real gold. *Genuine.*
- Instead of rubies, the bracelet was made of colored glass. *Fake.*
- The houses on the movie set only had the front wall. *Fake.*

What word means "real, not fake"? *Genuine.*

Sensitive

In the story, the princess felt the pea through twenty mattresses and twenty feather beds. Her skin was "black and blue all over." Her skin was very **sensitive.** Say the word. *Sensitive.*

We have five **senses.** How many senses do we have? *Five.* These five senses are smelling, hearing, tasting, feeling, and seeing. What are the five senses? *Smelling, hearing, tasting, feeling, seeing.* **If a person is sensitive, they are able to smell, hear, taste, feel, or see very well.** Say the word that means "able to smell, hear, taste, feel, or see very well." *Sensitive.*

Which sense was the real princess sensitive to? *Feeling.* If she could feel a tiny pea through all those mattresses and feather beds, her skin must have been very sensitive!

Let's think about some things that people could be sensitive to. I'll name a person and something they might be sensitive to. If you think that person could be sensitive to that thing, say "sensitive." Then tell what sense they would be using. If not, don't say anything.

- A teenager: loud music. *Sensitive—Hearing.*
- A baby: soft blankets. *Sensitive—Touching.*
- A deaf person: loud music.
- You: a colorful rainbow. *Sensitive—Seeing.*
- A blind person: a colorful rainbow.
- You: sweet cherries. *Sensitive—Tasting.*

What word means "able to smell, hear, taste, feel, or see very well"? *Sensitive.*

DAY 3

Preparation: Activity Sheet, BLM 7b.

Retell Story

Today I'll show you the pictures Charlene DeLage made for *The Princess and the Pea.* As I show you the pictures, I'll call on one of you to tell the class that part of the story.

Tell me what happens at the **beginning** of the story. (Show the pictures on pages 1–11. Call on a child to tell what's happening.)

Tell me what happens in the **middle** of the story. (Show the pictures on pages 12–29. Call on a child to tell what's happening. Encourage use of the target words when appropriate. Model use as necessary.)

Tell me what happens at the **end** of the story. (Show the pictures on pages 30 and 31. Call on a child to tell what's happening.)

Do you think this story is true or not true? Tell why you think so. (Accept either answer as long as children support their answer.)

Play the Whoopsy! Game

(Display the Picture Vocabulary Cards as you play this game.) Today you will play the *Whoopsy!* Game. I'll say sentences using words we have learned. If the word doesn't fit

in the sentence, you say, "Whoopsy!" Then I'll ask you to say a sentence where the word fits. If you can do it, you get a point. If you can't do it, I get the point. If the word I use fits the sentence, don't say anything.

Let's practice.

The **noble** queen … was mean and selfish. *Whoopsy!* Listen to the beginning of the sentence again. The **noble** queen. Say the beginning of the sentence. *The noble queen.* Can you finish the sentence so the word fits? (Idea: *The noble queen was a good person who would share what she had with others.*)

Let's try another one. The **wise** man … always told everyone the wrong answer. *Whoopsy!* Listen to the beginning of the sentence again. The **wise** man. Say the beginning of the sentence. *The wise man.* Can you finish the sentence so the word fits? (Idea: *The wise man always told everyone the right answer.*)

Now you're ready to play the game. (Draw a T-chart on the board for keeping score. Children earn one point for each correct answer. If they make an error, correct them as you normally would, and record one point for yourself. Repeat missed words at the end of the game.)

- Everyone said Paul was a **fine** young man when … he stole toys from the store. *Whoopsy!* Say the beginning of the sentence again. *Everyone said Paul was a fine young man when.* Can you finish the sentence? (Idea: *Everyone said Paul was a fine young man when he saved up to pay for the toys he wanted.*)
- That ring is **genuine** gold because … it is made of wood. *Whoopsy!* Say the beginning of the sentence again. *That ring is genuine gold because.* Can you finish the sentence? (Idea: *That ring is genuine gold because it is made of real gold.*)
- "What a beautiful day!" … Roger **exclaimed.**
- The driver was **fined** when … he went the speed limit. *Whoopsy!* Say the beginning of the sentence again. *The driver was fined when.* Can you finish the sentence? (Idea: *The driver was fined when he went too fast.*)

- The princess was **sensitive** because …
  she didn't feel the pea. *Whoopsy!* Say the
  beginning of the sentence again. *The princess
  was sensitive because.* Can you finish the
  sentence? (Idea: *The princess was sensitive
  because she felt the pea.*)

(Count the points and declare a winner.)
You did a great job of playing *Whoopsy!*

Complete the Activity Sheet

Think about the characters in the fairy
tale *The Princess and the Pea.* Who are
those characters? (Ideas: *The princess;
the king; the queen; the prince.*)

(Give each child a copy of the Activity Sheet,
BLM 7b.)

We're going to play a game called the Riddle
Game. When you play a riddle game, I tell you
some things that I know about a character. Your
job is to guess who I'm talking about.

Let's play the Riddle Game. I'll give you some
clues. Raise your hand when you think you can
name the character who I am talking about.

(Have the children identify which character is
the answer to the riddle. Instruct the children to
color the correct picture, cut it out, and paste it
under the riddle.)

- I am a person.
  I live in a castle.
  I wanted to find a real princess.
  I am the prince's mother.
  Who am I? (*The queen.*)

(Repeat the process for these two riddles.)

- I am a person.
  I live in a castle.
  I wanted to find a real princess.
  I am the prince's father.
  Who am I? (*The king.*)

- I am a person.
  I live in a castle.
  I am married.
  I married the prince.
  Who am I? (*The real princess.*)

Preparation: Prepare two sheets of
chart paper, each with a circle drawn
in the middle. Fold the sheets of paper
in half vertically to divide the circle in
half. When you record the children's
responses, physical descriptors should
be recorded on the left-hand side of
each chart. Personality characteristics or
actions should be recorded on the
right-hand side.

Analyze Characters
(Literary Analysis)

Let's think about what we already know about
how books are made.

- What do we call the name of the book? *Title.*
- What do we call the person who writes the
  story? *Author.*
- What do we call the person who draws the
  pictures? *Illustrator.*
- What do we call the people or animals a story
  is about? *Characters.*

Let's sing The Story Song to help us remember
these important things about books.

(See the Introduction for the complete story
song.)

Today we will learn more about the characters in
a story.

Remember that the characters in a story are
the people or animals the story is about. What
are the people or animals a story is about?
Characters. Who are the characters in a story?
The people or animals the story is about.

In *The Princess and the Pea,* are the characters
people or animals? *People.*

Who are the characters in the story? (Ideas: *The
king; the queen; the prince; the real princess.*)

The most important characters in *The Princess
and the Pea* are the prince and the princess.
Who are the most important characters in the
story? *The prince and the princess.* (Write *prince*
in the circle on one of the sheets of chart paper.)

Let's remember what we know about the prince. (Show children page 5.) What does the prince look like? (Call on several children. Record each child's response on the left-hand side of the prince chart. Ideas: *Blond hair; young; wears a special shirt.*) The special kind of shirt that the prince wears is called a tunic. What do you call the special shirt that the prince wears? *A tunic.*

(Show children pages 6–7.) In Week 4 we learned a new word that meant "made up his mind about something and wouldn't let anything stop him." Say the word that means "made up his mind about something and wouldn't let anything stop him." He was … *Determined.*

(Show children page 11. Ask these questions. Call on several children. Record each child's response on the right-hand side of the chart.) How do you think the prince is feeling? (Ideas: *Unhappy; desperate.*) Tell why you think so. (Idea: *He's holding his head; he's covering his eyes.*)

(Show children page 29.) How do you think the prince feels now? (Idea: *Happy; excited.*)

(Follow a similar process to describe the princess. Record responses on the second piece of chart paper.)

Today you have learned about the prince and the princess. They are the most important characters in the story *The Princess and the Pea.*

Play Whoopsy! (Cumulative Review)

Let's play *Whoopsy!* I'll say sentences using words we have learned. If the word doesn't fit in the sentence, you say "Whoopsy!" Then I'll ask you to say a sentence where the word fits. If you can do it, you get a point. If you can't do it, I get the point. If the word I use fits the sentence, don't say anything.

Now you're ready to play the game. (Draw a T-chart on the board for keeping score. Children earn one point for each correct answer. If they make an error, correct them as you normally would, and record one point for yourself. Repeat missed words at the end of the game.)

- Molly said that her couch was **genuine** leather because … it was not made of real leather. *Whoopsy!* Say the beginning of the sentence again. *Molly said that her couch was genuine leather because.* Can you finish the sentence? (Idea: *Molly said that her couch was genuine leather because it was made of real leather.*)
- Ed's skin was **sensitive** to the sun because … he never got sunburned. *Whoopsy!* Say the beginning of the sentence again. *Ed's skin was sensitive to the sun because.* Can you finish the sentence? (Idea: *Ed's skin was sensitive to the sun because he always got sunburned.*)
- When Paul received the **fine** for burning outdoors during fire season … the police paid him $500. *Whoopsy!* Say the beginning of the sentence again. *When Paul received the fine for burning outdoors during fire season.* Can you finish the sentence? (Idea: *When Paul received the fine for burning outdoors during fire season he paid the police $500.*)
- The **fine** young woman … studied hard at school and got good grades.
- The **noble** man helped … the rich people in his city. *Whoopsy!* Say the beginning of the sentence again. *The noble man helped.* Can you finish the sentence? (Idea: *The noble man helped the poor people in his city.*)
- In an emergency, a **wise** person … never knows what to do. *Whoopsy!* Say the beginning of the sentence again. *In an emergency, a wise person.* Can you finish the sentence? (Idea: *In an emergency, a wise person knows what to do.*)
- The girl **exclaimed** "How beautiful!" when … she saw the sunset.
- William was **uncooperative** when … he did what his father asked. *Whoopsy!* Say the beginning of the sentence again. *William was uncooperative when.* Can you finish the sentence? (Idea: *William was uncooperative when he didn't do what his father asked.*)
- Jason was **considerate** because … he never thought about what other people wanted. *Whoopsy!* Say the beginning of the sentence again. *Jason was considerate because.* Can you finish the sentence? (Idea: *Jason was*

considerate because he paid attention to what other people needed or wanted or wished for.)

- Rick **crept** along the sidewalk when … he ran as fast as he could go. *Whoopsy!* Say the beginning of the sentence again. *Rick crept along the sidewalk when.* Can you finish the sentence? (Idea: *Rick crept along the sidewalk when he moved slowly and quietly.*)

(Count the points and declare a winner.)
You did a great job of playing *Whoopsy!*

DAY 5

Preparation: A map or a globe of the world. Happy Face Game Test Sheet, BLM B.

Learn About Fairy Tales

Today you will learn more about a special kind of folk tale called a fairy tale. What will you learn about? *A fairy tale.*

Folk tales and fairy tales are both stories that were once told out loud. How are folk tales and fairy tales the same? (Idea: *They are both stories that were once told out loud.*) But a fairy tale is a story that someone decided to write down in a book a long time ago. How is a fairy tale different from a folk tale? (Idea: *Someone decided to write it down in a book a long time ago.*)

The Princess and the Pea was written by a man named Hans Christian Andersen. Hans Christian Andersen lived in Denmark. (Locate Denmark on the map or globe.) What country does the fairy tale *The Princess and the Pea* come from? *Denmark.* Hans Christian Andersen wrote this story in 1835. That was almost two hundred years ago. When did he write this story? (Idea: *Almost two hundred years ago.*) Wow! That is a very, very, long time ago!

After Hans Christian Andersen wrote the story, many other people retold the story. (Point to the words *Retold by* on the cover.) Susan Blackaby retold the story in her own words, so she is known as the author of this version of the story. Who is the author of this version of the story? *Susan Blackaby.*

Fairy tales often begin with the same words. Listen while I read the first sentence of *The Princess and the Pea.* "Once upon a time a noble king and a wise queen had a son." How does this fairy tale begin? *Once upon a time.*

Fairy tales often have good characters and evil characters. Who are the good characters in *The Princess and the Pea*? (Idea: *The king; the queen; the prince; the princess.*) Who is the evil character in *The Princess and the Pea*? (Idea: *There are no evil characters.*)

Fairy tales often have things that happen in threes. Tell about the things that happened in threes. (Ideas: *The princess said she slept "Bad, bad, bad!"*)

Fairy tales often have royal people and places. Royal people are kings, queens, princes, and princesses. Who are the royal people in *The Princess and the Pea*? (Idea: *The king; the queen; the prince; the princess.*)

Royal places are castles and palaces. What is the royal place in *The Princess and the Pea*? *A castle.*

Let's remember the important things about fairy tales. How do fairy tales often begin? *Once upon a time.* What kinds of characters are often in fairy tales? *Good characters and evil characters.* What is the special number that is often in fairy tales? *Three.* What kinds of people and places are often in fairy tales? (Idea: *Royal people and places.*) Good remembering about fairy tales.

Assess Vocabulary

 (Give each child a copy of the Happy Face Game Test Sheet, BLM B.)

Today you're going to play the Happy Face Game. When you play the Happy Face Game, it shows me how well you know the hard words you are learning.

If I say something that is true, color in the happy face. What will you do if I say something that is true? *Color in the happy face.*

If I say something that is false, color in the sad face. What will you do if I say something that is false? *Color in the sad face.*

Listen carefully to each item that I say. Don't let me trick you!

Item 1: If you are a **noble** person, you are a good person who would share whatever you had with others. (*True.*)

Item 2: If you **exclaimed** something, you said it quietly because you were surprised or excited. (*False.*)

Item 3: **Wise** means "smart and able to make good decisions." (*True.*)

Item 4: A **fine** is money you've paid because you did something wrong. (*True.*)

Item 5: A **fine** person is a bad person. (*False.*)

Item 6: If someone is **furious,** they are very, very happy. (*False.*)

Item 7: If something is **genuine,** it is not real. (*False.*)

Item 8: If you are **sensitive,** you are able to smell, hear, taste, feel, or see very well. (*True.*)

Item 9: If I **insisted** that you do something, I gave in easily about what you had to do. (*False.*)

Item 10: A **meadow** is a field where grass and flowers grow. (*True.*)

You did a great job of playing the Happy Face Game!

(Score children's work at a later time. A child must score of 9 out of 10 to be at the mastery level. If a child does not achieve mastery, insert the missed words as additional items in the games for next week's lessons. Retest those children individually for the missed items before they take the next mastery test.)

Extensions

Read a Story as a Reward

(Display copies of the books that you have read since the beginning of the program. Allow children to choose which book they would like you to read to them as a reward for their hard work.)

(Read the story aloud for enjoyment with minimal interruptions.)

Preparation: Word containers for the Super Words Center.

 Introduce the Super Words Center
(Add the new Picture Vocabulary Cards to words from the previous weeks. Show children one of the word containers. If children need more guidance in how to work in the Super Words Center, role-play with two to three children as a demonstration.)

Let's think about how we work with our words in the Super Words Center.

You will work with a partner in the Super Words Center. Whom will you work with? *A partner.*

Today I will teach you how to play a game called *What's New?*

First one partner will draw four Picture Vocabulary Cards out of the container and put them on the table so both partners can see. What do you do first? (Idea: *Draw four cards out of the container and put them on the table so both partners can see.*)

Next you will take turns looking at the cards and saying the words the pictures show. What do you do next? (Idea: *We take turns looking at the cards and saying the words the pictures show.*)

Next partner 2 looks away while partner 1 takes one of the four cards and places it back in the container. Then partner 1 draws a new card from the container and places it on the table with the other three. Watch while I show you what I mean. (Demonstrate this process with one child as your partner.) When you put down the new card, it's a good idea to mix the cards so they aren't in the same places any more. (Demonstrate this process as you go.)

Now partner 1 says "What's New?" Partner 2 has to use his or her eyes and brain and say what new word card has been put down. If partner 2 is correct, they get a point. If partner 2 is not correct, partner 1 gets the point. (Demonstrate this process as you go.)

Next partner 2 has a turn to choose four different cards and the game starts again. What happens next? (Idea: *Partner 2 has a turn to choose four different cards and the game starts again.*)

Have fun playing *What's New?*

Preparation: You will need *The Ugly Duckling* for each day's lesson.

Number the pages of the story to assist you in asking questions at appropriate points.

Post a copy of the Vocabulary Tally Sheet, BLM A, with this week's Picture Vocabulary Cards attached.

Each child will need one copy of the Homework Sheet, BLM 8a.

DAY 1

Introduce Book

This week's book is called *The Ugly Duckling*. What's the title? *The Ugly Duckling.*

This book was written by Jerry Pinkney. Who's the author of *The Ugly Duckling*? *Jerry Pinkney.*

Jerry Pinkney also made the pictures for this book. Who is the illustrator of *The Ugly Duckling*? *Jerry Pinkney.* The pictures an illustrator makes for a book are called the illustrations. What do you call the pictures an illustrator makes for a book? *Illustrations.* What are illustrations? *The pictures an illustrator makes for a book.*

The cover of a book usually gives us some hints of what the book is about. Let's look at the front cover of *The Ugly Duckling*. What do you see in the illustration? (Ideas: *A baby duck hatching from an egg; other broken eggs.*)

(Assign each child a partner.) Remember that when you make a prediction about something, you say what you think will happen. Get ready to make some predictions to your partner about this book. Use the information from the cover to help you.

(Ask the following questions, allowing sufficient time for children to share their predictions with their partners.)

Target Vocabulary

Tier II	Tier III
taunted	illustrations
awkward	setting (where)
exhausted	fairy tale
glorious	
*patient	
*bullied	

*Expanded Target Vocabulary Word

- Who are the characters in this story? (Whom do you think this story is about?)
- What do you think they will do?
- Where do you think the story happens?
- When do you think the story happens?
- Do you think this story is about a real duckling? Tell why or why not.

(Call on several children to share their predictions with the class.)

Take a Picture Walk

(Encourage children to use target words in their answers.) We're going to take a picture walk through this book. Remember that when we take a picture walk, we look at the pictures and tell what we think will happen in the story.

Pages 1–2. Where does the first part of the story happen? (Idea: *In the grass.*) What is the duck doing in the grass? (Ideas: *Looking at an egg; moving an egg.*)

Pages 3–4. What's happening in this picture? (Ideas: *The ducklings are hatching from their eggs.*) How many ducklings have hatched? *Five.*

Pages 5–6. What are the duck and the ducklings looking at? (Idea: *Another duckling.*) Why are they looking at the duckling? (Idea: *It looks different from the rest.*)

Pages 7–8. Who has come to see the new duckling? (Idea: *Another duck.*)

Pages 9–10. What are all the birds doing in this picture? (Ideas: *Flying away; splashing in the pond.*)

Pages 11–12. Uh-oh. Who has found the little duckling? *A dog.* What do you think the dog will do?

Pages 13–14. Where is the duckling now? (Idea: *In an old lady's house.*) How do you think the lady feels about the duckling being in her house? (Idea: *Angry.*) How do you know? (Idea: *She has an angry look on her face and is shaking her finger at the duckling.*)

Pages 15–16. Now where has the duckling gone? (Idea: *Under the water; in the pond.*) How do you know the duckling is under the water? (Ideas: *The color; there is a fish there too.*) Why do you think the duckling went under the water?

Pages 17–18. What time of the year is it in this picture? *Winter.* How do you know? (Idea: *There is snow on the ground.*)

Pages 19–20. Who is that in the water? (Idea: *The little duckling.*) What has happened to the duckling? (Idea: *He is frozen in the ice.*)

Pages 21–22. What is the man doing? (Idea: *Saving the duckling.*) Another word for saving is **rescuing.** We can say that the man is rescuing the duckling from the ice. What is the man doing to the duckling? *Rescuing it from the ice.*

Pages 23–24. Who has returned to the pond? (Idea: *The swans.*) What time of year do you think it is now? *Spring.* How do you know? (Ideas: *The swans have come back; the leaves are growing; there are butterflies.*)

Pages 25–26. What do you think the swans are doing in this picture? (Ideas: *Playing; swimming.*)

Pages 27–28. What are the swans and the other animals looking at? (Ideas: *The swans are looking at the beautiful swan; the beautiful swan is looking at its reflection in the water.*)

Pages 29–30. What are the children doing at the pond? (Idea: *Feeding the birds.* Point to the swan with its wings extended.) What do you think that swan is doing? (Idea: *Going after the food.*)

It's your turn to ask me some questions. What would you like to know about the story? (Accept questions. If children tell about the pictures or the story instead of ask questions, prompt them to ask a question.) Ask me a where question. Ask me a how question.

Read the Story Aloud
(Read story to children with minimal interruptions.)

Tomorrow we will read the story again, and I will ask you some questions.

(If children have difficulty attending for an extended period of time, you may wish to present the next part of this day's lesson at another time of day.)

Present Target Vocabulary
 Taunted

In the story, one of the ducks in the yard taunted, "Did you ever see anything as ugly as that?" That means the duck teased and made fun of the ugly duckling. The duck was trying to hurt the duckling's feelings. **Taunted.** Say the word. *Taunted.*

Taunted is an action word. It tells what someone did to someone else. What kind of word is **taunted?** *An action word.*

Taunted means tried to hurt someone's feelings by teasing or making fun of them. Say the word that means "tried to hurt someone's feelings by teasing or making fun of them." *Taunted.*

(Correct any incorrect responses, and repeat the item at the end of the sequence.)

Let's think about some times when someone might have taunted another person. If you think the person taunted the other person, say "taunted." If not, don't say anything.

- Billy said, "You're just a baby; you haven't taken the training wheels off your bicycle yet." *Taunted.*
- They teased and made fun of her about her strange clothes. *Taunted.*
- Zabra told Kyoko, "Your Japanese kimono is beautiful."
- "I really like the way you print your letters," Jodee said.

- Her brother said, "Can't you count to 100? What's the matter with you? I thought everybody could count to 100." *Taunted.*
- Her brother said, "You can count all the way to 50? Before you know it, you'll be able to count to 100."

What word means "tried to hurt someone's feelings by teasing or making fun of them"? *Taunted.*

◎◄ Awkward

In the story, the egg started to hatch. An awkward bird came out of the egg. That means the bird was clumsy and had trouble getting his body parts to work together. **Awkward.** Say the word. *Awkward.*

Awkward is a describing word. It tells more about someone or something. What kind of word is **awkward?** *A describing word.*

When you say you are awkward you mean you are clumsy and have trouble getting your body parts to work together. Say the word that means "clumsy and has trouble getting his or her body parts to work together." *Awkward.*

Let's think about some times when someone might be awkward. I'll tell about some things someone is doing. If you think the person is awkward, say "awkward." If not don't say anything.

- My brother is clumsy when he dances. His feet don't always move to the music the way he wants them to. *Awkward.*
- When I ride my bike, sometimes I turn the handlebars too far and then I think I'm going to tip over the bike. *Awkward.*
- Judy can stand on her hands for one whole minute, and she never falls over.
- When I first learned to dive off the diving board, I made a big huge splash when I hit the water. *Awkward.*
- Now when I dive, there's hardly any splash at all.
- I couldn't get my fingers to work together well enough to tie my shoelaces. *Awkward.*

What word means "clumsy and has trouble getting his or her body parts to work together"? *Awkward.*

◎◄ Exhausted

In the story, the duckling lay down in the cottage exhausted. That means he was so tired he could hardly move. **Exhausted.** Say the word. *Exhausted.*

Exhausted is a describing word. It tells more about someone or something. What kind of word is **exhausted?** *A describing word.*

Exhausted means so tired you can hardly move. What word means "so tired you can hardly move"? *Exhausted.*

Let's think about some times when someone might have felt exhausted. I'll tell about a time. If you think the person was exhausted, say "exhausted." If not, don't say anything.

- The boys went on a ten-mile hike, carrying their tents on their backs. *Exhausted.*
- Elena rode her bike to the end of her street.
- Pietro just woke up after a good night's sleep.
- The third little pig worked from morning until night to build his house of bricks. *Exhausted.*
- The little red hen planted the seeds, harvested the wheat, threshed it, took it to the mill to be ground into flour, and then baked the bread. *Exhausted.*
- The goose, the cat, and the pig did nothing to help the little red hen.

What word means "so tired you can hardly move"? *Exhausted.*

◎◄ Glorious

In the story, when the ugly duckling turned into the swan and first flew, he thought it felt glorious. That means it felt wonderful. **Glorious.** Say the word. *Glorious.*

Glorious is a describing word. It tells more about someone or something. What kind of word is **glorious?** *A describing word.*

If something is glorious, it is wonderful. Say the word that means "wonderful." *Glorious.*

Let's think about some things that might have been glorious. I'll tell you about something. If you think that thing could have been glorious, say "glorious." If not, don't say anything.

- Diving into a cool lake on a very hot day. *Glorious.*
- A double rainbow filled the sky. *Glorious.*
- Nothing interesting happened on Saturday.
- The sight of a huge flock of geese flying over your house with a rainbow behind them. *Glorious.*
- Tall beautiful mountains. *Glorious.*
- The children listened to the story.

What word means "wonderful"? *Glorious.*

Present Vocabulary Tally Sheet

(See Lesson 1, page 3, for instructions.)

Assign Homework

(Homework Sheet, BLM 8a: See the Introduction for homework instructions.)

DAY 2

Preparation: Picture Vocabulary Cards for *taunted, awkward, exhausted, glorious.*

Read and Discuss Story

(Read the story to children. Ask the following questions at the specified points. Encourage them to use target words in their answers.)

Now I'm going to read *The Ugly Duckling.* When I finish each part, I'll ask you some questions.

Page 2. Where does this story take place? (Idea: *Near a pond.*) When does this part of the story take place? (Idea: *In the summer.*) How many eggs is the duck sitting on? *Six.* How is the sixth egg different from the other five? (Idea: *It is bigger and has a funny shape.*) How does the duck treat the sixth egg? (Idea: *Just like the rest of the eggs.*)

Page 3. Has the duck ever laid eggs before? *No.* How does she feel about her eggs? (Idea: *Pleased and proud.*) How many eggs hatch? *Five.* Which egg is still left to hatch? (Idea: *The big egg.*)

Page 5. How is the sixth duckling different from the others? (Ideas: *It is much bigger; it has a long neck and a dull color.*)

Page 8. Why are the other ducks being so mean to the little duckling? (Idea: *Because they think he is so ugly.*) How does the duckling feel? *Sad.* How do you know? (Idea: *He "drooped" his head.*)

Page 9. How is the duckling treated? (Ideas: *Everybody is mean to him; everybody is bullying him; the other ducks chase and bite him; the hens peck at him; the little girl kicks him.*) What does the duckling do? (Idea: *He runs away.*) The duckling runs away to a dangerous place. What makes it dangerous? (Idea: *There are hunters there.*)

Page 11. What kind of dog chases after the duckling? *A hunting dog.* Why does the duckling think the dog ran off without hurting him? (Idea: *The duckling thinks he is too ugly even for a dog.*)

Page 13. Who dwells, or lives, in the small cottage? (Idea: *An old woman, her cat, and a hen.*) Why does the old woman decide to let the duckling stay? (Idea: *She thinks it will lay eggs.*)

Page 15. What does the duckling want most to do? *Swim.*

Page 18. What time of year is it when the leaves turn yellow and brown? (Ideas: *Autumn; fall.*) What is happening to the river? (Idea: *It is freezing; turning to ice.*) What does the duckling think of the birds in the sky? (Idea: *They are beautiful.*)

Page 19. What does the duckling do to keep the water from freezing? (Idea: *He swims around in circles.*) What does it mean that the duckling is "caught fast"? (Idea: *He is stuck in the ice.*)

Page 22. (Read the first sentence.) Good fortune is another way of saying good luck. What's another way of saying good luck? *Good fortune.* Why does the duckling fly out of the house? (Idea: *He thinks the children want to tease him and is scared.*)

Page 24. Who does the duckling see in the water? (Idea: *The beautiful birds that had been flying south the previous autumn.*)

Page 25. Did the duckling like flying? *Yes.*

Page 27. What kind of bird is the duckling? *A beautiful swan.*

Page 30. What makes the duckling so happy? (Idea: *He learns he is a beautiful swan.*) Do you think that if the swan goes back to his home the others will still tease him? *No.* Why not? (Idea: *They teased him because he was an ugly duckling and now he is a beautiful swan.*)

Review Vocabulary

(Display the Picture Vocabulary Cards. Point to each card as you say the word. Ask children to repeat each word after you.) These pictures show **taunted, awkward, exhausted,** and **glorious.**

- What word means "so tired you can hardly move"? *Exhausted.*
- What word means "wonderful"? *Glorious.*
- What word means "tried to hurt someone's feelings by teasing or making fun of them"? *Taunted.*
- What word means "clumsy and has trouble getting his or her body parts to work together"? *Awkward.*

Extend Vocabulary
◎← Awkward

In *The Ugly Duckling,* we learned that **awkward** means "clumsy and has trouble getting his or her body parts to work together."

Here's a new way to use the word **awkward.**

- I felt **awkward** when I called my teacher "Mom." Say the sentence.
- When the teacher asked who spilled the paint and no one said anything, we all felt **awkward.** Say the sentence.
- Many people feel **awkward** when they meet someone new. Say the sentence.

In these sentences, awkward means embarrassed and uncomfortable. Tell us about a time that you might have felt **awkward.** (Encourage children to use the frame "I felt awkward when …" as they share their experiences.)

Present Expanded Target Vocabulary
◎← Patient

All of the duck's eggs except one hatched. But the mother duck sat on the last egg for two whole days, afraid the egg would get too cold if she moved. The mother duck waited without complaining or getting angry or upset. The mother duck was being very patient, waiting for the last egg to hatch. **Patient.** Say the word. *Patient.*

Patient is a describing word. It tells more about someone or something. What kind of word is **patient?** *A describing word.*

If you are patient you can wait without complaining or getting angry or upset. Say the word that means "can wait without complaining or getting angry or upset." *Patient.*

Let's think about some times when a person or animal might have been patient. I'll tell about a time. If someone was being patient, say "patient." If not, don't say anything.

- The teacher waited quietly while the children found their crayons. *Patient.*
- The cat waited for hours until the mouse came out of its hole. *Patient.*
- Everyone waited while Colleen finished her drink. *Patient.*
- I couldn't wait to get my new bike, so I ran around in circles and yelled.
- Josea waited to have her turn to fly the kite. *Patient.*
- "I sure wish Saturday would come faster!"

What word means "can wait without complaining or getting angry or upset"? *Patient.*

◎← Bullied

In the story, the poor duckling was chased by everyone, even his brothers and sisters. The duckling was being **bullied** by everyone. Say the word. *Bullied.*

Bullied is an action word. It tells what everyone was doing. What kind of word is **bullied?** *An action word.*

If you are bullied, you are frightened and picked on by people bigger than you. Say the word that means "frightened and picked on by someone bigger than you." *Bullied.*

Let's think about some times when someone might have been bullied. I'll tell about a time. If someone was being bullied, say "bullied." If not, don't say anything.

- The big child pushed down the kindergarten child. *Bullied.*
- The big child and the kindergarten child were playground buddies.
- The big child called the little child a bad name. *Bullied.*
- The big children played "keep-away" with the little children's basketball. *Bullied.*
- The big boy made sure his little sister got home safely.
- The children teased the little boy and made him cry. *Bullied.*

What word means "frightened and picked on by someone bigger than you." *Bullied.*

(**Note:** You may wish to review the school's anti-bullying strategies with the children at this time.)

DAY 3

Preparation: Activity Sheet, BLM 8b.

Retell Story

Today I'll show you the pictures Jerry Pinkney made for *The Ugly Duckling.* As I show you the pictures, I'll call on one of you to tell the class that part of the story.

Tell me what happens at the **beginning** of the story. (Show the pictures on pages 1–6. Call on a child to tell what's happening.)

Tell me what happens in the **middle** of the story. (Show the pictures on pages 7–28. Call on a child to tell what's happening. Encourage use of the target words when appropriate. Model use as necessary.)

Tell me what happens at the **end** of the story. (Show the pictures on pages 29 and 30. Call on a child to tell what's happening.)

Do you think this story is true or not true? Tell why you think so. (Accept either answer as long as children support their answer.)

Play the Whoopsy! Game

(Display the Picture Vocabulary Cards as you play this game.)

Today you will play the *Whoopsy!* Game. I'll say sentences using words we have learned. If the word doesn't fit in the sentence, you say, "Whoopsy!" Then I'll ask you to say a sentence where the word fits. If you can do it, you get a point. If you can't do it, I get the point. If the word I use fits the sentence, don't say anything.

Let's practice:

The children **taunted** the little boy when … they told him he was a good batter at baseball. *Whoopsy!* Listen to the beginning of the sentence again. The children **taunted** the little boy when. Say the beginning of the sentence. *The children taunted the little boy when.* Can you finish the sentence so the word fits? (Idea: *The children taunted the little boy when they said he would never hit the ball.*)

Let's try another one. Melanie's mom was **patient** when … she told Melanie to hurry up and get ready for school. *Whoopsy!* Listen to the beginning of the sentence again. Melanie's mom was patient when. Say the beginning of the sentence. *Melanie's mom was patient when.* Can you finish the sentence so the word fits? (Idea: *Melanie's mom was patient when she waited quietly while Melanie put her books in her backpack.*)

Now you're ready to play the game. (Draw a T-chart on the board for keeping score. Children earn one point for each correct answer. If they make an error, correct them as you normally would, and record one point for yourself. Repeat missed words at the end of the game.)

- The older boys **bullied** the younger boys when … they helped them get their books. *Whoopsy!* Say the beginning of the sentence again. *The older boys bullied the younger boys when.* Can you finish the sentence? (Idea: *The older boys bullied the younger boys when they* *wouldn't let the younger boys get ready for class.*)

- Joanna was **awkward** when … she danced the Mexican Hat Dance with no mistakes. *Whoopsy!* Say the beginning of the sentence again. *Joanna was awkward when.* Can you finish the sentence? (Idea: *Joanna was awkward when she had trouble dancing the Mexican Hat Dance.*)
- Jamal felt **awkward** when … he had to introduce his parents to his teacher.
- The girls were **exhausted** after … they walked to the corner store that was nearby. *Whoopsy!* Say the beginning of the sentence again. *The girls were exhausted after.* Can you finish the sentence? (Idea: *The girls were exhausted after they walked ten miles up a hill.*)
- The swan felt a **glorious** feeling when … the other ducks bullied her. *Whoopsy!* Say the beginning of the sentence again. *The swan felt a glorious feeling when.* Can you finish the sentence? (Idea: *The swan felt a glorious feeling when she realized she was a beautiful swan.*)

(Count the points and declare a winner.) You did a great job of playing *Whoopsy!*

Complete the Activity Sheet

 Think about the characters in the fairy tale *The Ugly Duckling*. Who are those characters? (Ideas: *The duckling; the mother duck; the old woman; the cat; the hen; the man; the children; the swans.*)

(Give each child a copy of the Activity Sheet, BLM 8b.)

We're going to play a game called the Riddle Game. When you play a riddle game, I tell you some things that I know about a character. Your job is to guess who I'm talking about.

Let's play the Riddle Game. I'll give you some clues. Raise your hand when you think you can name the character who I am talking about.

(Have children identify which character is the answer to the riddle. Instruct children to color the correct picture, cut it out, and paste it under the riddle.)

- I am a bird.
  I can swim.
  I can fly.

I am white.
I am beautiful.
Who am I? (*The swan.*)

- I am a person.
  I let the ugly duckling come into my house.
  I saved the duckling from the ice.
  My two children frightened the duckling.
  Who am I? (*The man.*)
- I am a young bird.
  I can fly.
  I think that I am a duck.
  I was bullied by everyone.
  Who am I? (*The ugly duckling.*)

DAY 4

Preparation: Prepare a sheet of chart paper, landscape direction, titled *The Ugly Duckling*. Underneath the title, draw 11 boxes, connected by arrows.

See the Introduction for Week 8's chart.

Record children's responses by writing the words in the boxes.

Literary Analysis (Cumulative Review)

Let's think about what we already know about how books are made.

- What do we call the name of the book? *Title.*
- What do we call the person who writes the story? *Author.*
- What do we call the person who draws the pictures? *Illustrator.*
- What do we call the people or animals a story is about? *Characters.*
- What do we call the pictures the illustrator makes? *Illustrations.*

Let's sing The Story Song to help us remember these important things about books.

(See the Introduction for the complete story song.)

Today we will learn more about how stories are made.

The setting of a story tells two things. One thing the setting tells is where the story happens.

What is one thing the setting tells? *Where the story happens.*

Let's look at the pictures and talk about the story to figure out where *The Ugly Duckling* happens.

Pages 1–2. Where does the story begin? *In the grass near the pond.*

Pages 3–6. Where does the next part of the story happen? *In the nest.*

Pages 7–8. Where does the next part of the story happen? *In the farmyard.*

Pages 9–10. Where does the next part of the story happen? *In the marsh.*

Pages 11–12. Where does the next part of the story happen? *At the edge of the marsh.*

Pages 13–14. Where does the next part of the story happen? *In the cottage.*

(Note: If children respond, "In the house," say:**)** You're right, they are in a small house. We learned a word in Week 4 that means a small house in the country or near the beach. That word is **cottage. Cottage.** Say that word. *Cottage.* Where does this part of the story happen? *In the cottage.*

Pages 15–16. Where does the next part of the story happen? (Ideas: *In the water; under the water.*)

Pages 17–22. Where does the next part of the story happen? *At the river.*

Read the last paragraph on page 22. Where does the next part of the story happen? *At the man's house.*

Pages 23–30. Where does the next part of the story happen? *At the stream.*

The grass near the pond, the nest, the farmyard, the marsh, the edge of the marsh, the cottage, the water, the river, the man's house, and the stream are all in the country. So if we could use only one word to tell the setting of the story, we would use the word **country.** Where is the setting of *The Ugly Duckling*? *The country.*

Today you learned about one of the parts of the setting of *The Ugly Duckling*. You learned about where the story happened.

Now we'll learn a new verse to The Story Song. We'll sing, "Setting tells where it happens." (Repeat until children can say it with confidence.)

(See the Introduction for the complete Story Song.)

Read me a book and the book pleased me,
I read my book under yonder tree.
Setting tells where it happens.
Illustrations are the pictures.
Characters make it happen.
Illustrator draws the pictures.
Author says "I'm who wrote it."
Title says what its name is.
Book says "I'm a story."

Play Whoopsy! (Cumulative Review)

Let's play *Whoopsy!* I'll say sentences using words we have learned. If the word doesn't fit in the sentence, you say, "Whoopsy!" Then I'll ask you to say a sentence where the word fits. If you can do it, you get a point. If you can't do it, I get the point. If the word I use fits the sentence, don't say anything.

Now you're ready to play the game. (Draw a T-chart on the board for keeping score. Children earn one point for each correct answer. If they make an error, correct them as you normally would, and record one point for yourself. Repeat missed words at the end of the game.)

- The **awkward** skater ... performed a perfect spin. *Whoopsy!* Say the beginning of the sentence again. *The awkward skater.* Can you finish the sentence? (Idea: *The awkward skater fell when she tried to do her spin.*)
- The little boy was **bullied** when … the big child helped him fix his broken bike. *Whoopsy!* Say the beginning of the sentence again. *The little boy was bullied when.* Can you finish the sentence? (Idea: *The little boy was bullied when the big child broke his bike.*)
- The bullies **taunted** the children when … they told them how brave they were. *Whoopsy!* Say the beginning of the sentence again. *The bullies taunted the children when.* Can you finish the sentence? (Idea: *The bullies taunted the children when they called them bad names.*)

- The **exhausted** hikers wanted to … climb to the top of the mountain. *Whoopsy!* Say the beginning of the sentence again. *The exhausted hikers wanted to.* Can you finish the sentence? (Idea: *The exhausted hikers wanted to crawl into their sleeping bags and rest.*)
- The **glorious** sunset … had colors of purple, red, and orange.
- Camilla felt **awkward** when … she made her weekly visit to her grandmother. *Whoopsy!* Say the beginning of the sentence again. *Camilla felt awkward when.* Can you finish the sentence? (Idea: *Camilla felt awkward when she met her grandmother for the very first time.*)
- Her dad was **patient** when … he roared at everyone to hurry up and get in the car. *Whoopsy!* Say the beginning of the sentence again. *Her dad was patient when.* Can you finish the sentence? (Idea: *Her dad was patient when he listened to music while waiting for everyone to get ready.*)
- The **enormous** tree was … so tall that we couldn't see the top of it.
- The hikers were **trespassing** when … they got permission from the farmer to have a picnic by his pond. *Whoopsy!* Say the beginning of the sentence again. *The hikers were trespassing when.* Can you finish the sentence? (Idea: *The hikers were trespassing when they didn't get permission from the farmer to have a picnic by his pond.*)
- The princess rested **comfortably** when … she slept on the hard bed. *Whoopsy!* Say the beginning of the sentence again. *The princess rested comfortably when.* Can you finish the sentence? (Idea: *The princess rested comfortably when she slept on the soft bed.*)

(Count the points and declare a winner.) You did a great job of playing *Whoopsy!*

DAY 5

Preparation: A map or a globe of the world. Happy Face Game Test Sheet, BLM B.

Learn About Fairy Tales

Today you will learn more about a special kind of folk tale called a fairy tale. What will you learn about? *A fairy tale.*

Folk tales and fairy tales are both stories that were once told out loud. How are folk tales and fairy tales the same? (Idea: *They are both stories that were once told out loud.*) But a fairy tale is a story that someone decided to write down in a book a long time ago. How is a fairy tale different from a folk tale? (Idea: *Someone decided to write it down in a book a long time ago.*)

The Ugly Duckling was written by a man named Hans Christian Andersen. Hans Christian Andersen lived in Denmark. (**Locate Denmark on the map or globe.**) What country does *The Ugly Duckling* come from? *Denmark.* Hans Christian Andersen wrote this story in 1844. When did he write this story? (Idea: *In 1844.*) That was a very, very long time ago.

Hans Christian Andersen also wrote another fairy tale we've read. What was the title of that fairy tale? *The Princess and the Pea.* Hans Christian Andersen wrote *The Ugly Duckling* nine years **after** he wrote *The Princess and the Pea.* Which fairy tale did he write first? *The Princess and the Pea.*

After Hans Christian Andersen wrote the story, many other people retold the story. (**Point to the words** *Adapted by* **on the cover.**) Jerry Pinkney changed the story a little bit and wrote it in his own words, so he is known as the author of this version of the story. Who is the author of this version of the story? *Jerry Pinkney.*

Fairy tales often begin with the words "once upon a time." How do many fairy tales begin? *Once upon a time.* Listen while I read the first sentence of *The Ugly Duckling.* (**Read aloud the first sentence on page 2.**) How does this fairy tale begin? *It was summer.* Does this fairy tale begin with "once upon a time"? *No.* That's right. Remember that fairy tales often but don't always begin with the words "once upon time."

Fairy tales often have good characters and evil characters. Who are the good characters in *The Ugly Duckling*? (Idea: *The mother duck; the* ugly duckling; the man; the swan.) Who are the evil characters in *The Ugly Duckling*? (Idea: *The ducks in the farmyard; his brothers and sisters; the hens; the girl who fed them; the cat; the other swans.*)

Fairy tales often have things that happen in threes. Tell about the things that happened in threes. (Ideas: *The mother duck sat on the egg for three days after the other ducklings hatched; the ducks bit him, the hens pecked him, the girl who fed them kicked him aside; the duckling stayed with the woman for three weeks.*)

Fairy tales often have royal people and places. Royal people are kings, queens, princes, and princesses. Who are the royal people in *The Ugly Duckling*? (Idea: *There are none.*) Royal places are castles and palaces. What are the royal places in *The Ugly Duckling*? (Idea: *There are none.*) That's right. Remember that fairy tales often but don't always have royal people and places in them.

Let's remember the important things about fairy tales. How do fairy tales often begin? *Once upon a time.* What kinds of characters are often in fairy tales? *Good characters and evil characters.* What is the special number that is often in fairy tales? *Three.* What kinds of people and places are often in fairy tales? (Idea: *Royal people and places.*) Good remembering about fairy tales.

Assess Vocabulary

 (Give each child a copy of the Happy Face Game Test Sheet, BLM B.)

Today you're going to play the Happy Face Game. When you play the Happy Face Game, it shows me how well you know the hard words you are learning.

If I say something that is true, color in the happy face. What will you do if I say something that is true? *Color in the happy face.*

If I say something that is false, color in the sad face. What will you do if I say something that is false? *Color in the sad face.*

Listen carefully to each item that I say. Don't let me trick you!

Item 1: When someone **mutters,** they speak in a very loud voice because they are happy. (*False.*)

Item 2: Bullies often **taunt** people smaller than they are. (*True.*)

Item 3: Shy people sometimes feel **awkward** around people they do not know. (*True.*)

Item 4: If someone **bullied** you, they helped you when you fell down. (*False.*)

Item 5: An **awkward** person would have trouble balancing on a log at the beach. (*True.*)

Item 6: A **glorious** day would be a day when everything went wrong. (*False.*)

Item 7: If you are **patient,** you can wait without getting angry or upset. (*True.*)

Item 8: If something is **genuine,** it is real. (*True.*)

Item 9: Lions **squeak** and mice **roar.** (*False.*)

Item 10: If you are **exhausted,** you have lots of energy. (*False.*)

You did a great job of playing the Happy Face Game!

(Score children's work at a later time. A child must score 9 out of 10 to be at the mastery level. If a child does not achieve mastery, insert the missed words as additional items in the games for next week's lessons. Retest those children individually for the missed items before they take the next mastery test.)

Extensions
Read a Story as a Reward

 (Display copies of the books that you have read since the beginning of the program or other versions of *The Ugly Duckling*. Allow children to choose which book they would like you to read to them as a reward for their hard work.)

(Read the story aloud for enjoyment with minimal interruptions.)

Preparation: Word containers for the Super Words Center.

Introduce the Super Words Center
(Add the new Picture Vocabulary Cards to words from the previous weeks. Show children one of the word containers. If children

need more guidance in how to work in the Super Words Center, role-play with two to three children as a demonstration.)

Let's think about how we work with our words in the Super Words Center.

You will work with a partner in the Super Words Center. Whom will you work with? *A partner.*

Today I will teach you how to play a game called *What's New?*

First one partner will draw four Picture Vocabulary Cards out of the container and put them on the table so both partners can see. What do you do first? (Idea: *Draw four cards out of the container and put them on the table so both partners can see.*)

Next you will take turns looking at the cards and saying the words the pictures show. What do you do next? (Idea: *We take turns looking at the cards and saying the words the pictures show.*)

Next partner 2 looks away while partner 1 takes one of the four cards and places it back in the container. Then partner 1 draws a new card from the container and places it on the table with the other three. Watch while I show you what I mean. (Demonstrate this process with one child as your partner.)

When you put down the new card, it's a good idea to mix the cards so they aren't in the same places any more. (Demonstrate this process as you go.)

Now partner 1 says, "What's New?" Partner 2 has to use his or her eyes and brain and say what new word card has been put down. If partner 2 is correct, they get a point. If partner 2 is not correct, partner 1 gets the point. (Demonstrate this process as you go.)

Next partner 2 has a turn to choose four different cards and the game starts again. What happens next? (Idea: *Partner 2 has a turn to choose four different cards and the game starts again.*)

Have fun playing *What's New?*

Loon Lake

author: Jonathan London • illustrator: Susan Ford

Preparation: You will need *Loon Lake* for each day's lesson.

Number the pages of the story to assist you in asking questions at appropriate points.

Post a copy of the Vocabulary Tally Sheet, BLM A, with this week's Picture Vocabulary Cards attached.

Each child will need one copy of the Homework Sheet, BLM 9a.

DAY 1

Introduce Book

This week's book is called *Loon Lake.* What's the title? *Loon Lake.*

This book was written by Jonathan London. Who's the author of *Loon Lake*? *Jonathan London.*

Susan Ford made the pictures for this book. Who's the illustrator of *Loon Lake*? *Susan Ford.* Who made the illustrations for this book? *Susan Ford.*

The cover of a book usually gives us some hints of what the book is about. Let's look at the front cover of *Loon Lake.* What do you see in the illustration? (Ideas: *A man and a girl in a boat (canoe); two birds; a lake; some mountains; a sunrise or sunset.*)

(Assign each child a partner.) Remember that when you make a prediction about something, you say what you think will happen. Get ready to make some predictions to your partner about this book. Use the information from the cover to help you.

(Ask the following questions, allowing sufficient time for children to share their predictions with their partners.)

- Who are the characters in this story? (Who do you think this story is about?)
- What do you think made the waves on the water?
- Where do you think the story happens?

Target Vocabulary

Tier II	Tier III
precious	setting (where)
glimpse	legend
wild	realistic
slithers	
*legend	
*disappears	

*Expanded Target Vocabulary Word

- When do you think the story happens?
- Why do you think the people are wearing those red vests?
- How far out on the lake do you think the people are?
- Do you think this story is about real people? Tell why or why not.

(Call on several children to share their predictions with the class.)

Take a Picture Walk

(Encourage children to use target words in their answers.) We're going to take a picture walk through this book. Remember that when we take a picture walk, we look at the pictures and tell what we think will happen in the story.

Pages 1–2. Where do you think the illustrator was sitting when she painted this picture? (Idea: *High in the sky; in an airplane; in a helicopter.*) When an artist paints a picture and makes it look like she is painting it from high in the sky, we call that a bird's-eye view. What kind of painting is this? *A bird's eye view.* What things do you see in the sky? (Ideas: *A bird; a loon; clouds.*) What things do you see on the ground? (Ideas: *A tent; a canoe; a lake; lots of trees.*)

Pages 3–4. What do you think the man is pointing at? (Idea: *The loon.*) What do you think the girl is doing? (Idea: *Shouting; calling out.*) When do you think this part of the story happens? (Idea: *At sunrise; at sunset.*) Why do you think so?

Pages 5–6. When do you think this part of the story happens? (Idea: *At night.*) Why do you think so? (Idea: *The sky is dark; I see the moon.*)

(Turn back to pages 3 and 4 and show the illustration.) Now we know for sure when this part of the story happens. When does this part happen? (Idea: *At sunset.*)

Pages 7–8. What is happening here? (Idea: *Someone is throwing beads into the water; the beads are landing on the loon.*) What is painted on the side of the canoe? (Ideas: *A bird; a loon.*)

Pages 9–10. What do the people see? (Idea: *An animal; an otter.*) Why do you think the man has his finger in front of his mouth? (Ideas: *He is saying, "sh-sh-sh"; he's telling the girl to be quiet.*)

Pages 11–12. What is this animal doing? *Swimming.* What is the name of this animal? *A beaver.*

(**Note:** If children don't correctly name the beaver, say "We'll learn the name of this animal when we read the story.") Do you think this animal is swimming close to the edge of the water or out in the middle of the lake? *Close to the edge of the water.* Why do you think so? (Idea: *I can see water reeds and lily pads; I can see plants growing.*)

Pages 13–14. What is happening here? (Ideas: *The bird is going under the water; the bird is catching a fish.*)

Pages 15–16. What is different about this painting? (Idea: *We see on top of the water and under the water at the same time.*) When an artist paints a picture and makes it look like he or she has put a window in it so you can see above and below, we call that a cutaway view. What kind of painting is this illustration? *A cutaway view.* What things do you see above the water? (Ideas: *The man and the girl; the canoe; the top of the lake; the splash; the trees; the mountains; the stars and the moon.*) What things do you see below? (Ideas: *The bottom of the lake; sand or mud; the lower stems of the reeds; small plants; the loon swimming under the water.*)

Pages 17–18. What is the happening here? (Ideas: *The mother loon and her two babies are hiding in the reeds; the father loon is slapping his wings.*) What do you think the father loon is doing? (Ideas: *Trying to scare away the people in the canoe; protecting his family.*)

Page 19–20. What are the birds doing now? (Idea: *Swimming out of the reeds.*)

Pages 21–22. What are the birds doing? *Flying away.*

Pages 23–24. What are the girl and her father doing? (Ideas: *Toasting marshmallows; enjoying a bonfire.*) What do you think she is telling her father?

Pages 25–26. What is happening here? (Ideas: *The man is sleeping in the tent; it is raining; the girl is watching the rain.*) What do you think the girl is thinking about? (Ideas: *The loons; the rain; the canoe ride on the lake.*)

Let's talk about how Susan Ford made the illustrations for *Loon Lake*. There are lots of different ways to make illustrations for a book: the artist can paint them; the artist can draw them with a pen or pencil; the artist can make them with markers, crayons, pastels, or chalk; the artist can cut out different pieces of paper and glue them together. How do you think Susan Ford made her illustrations? (Ideas: *She used both pastels and paint to make her illustrations.*)

(Show the illustration on pages 21 and 22.) Which part of this illustration do you think was made with pastels? (Idea: *The trees; the shore.*) Which part of this illustration do you think was made with paint? (Idea: *The birds; the splashes.*) Susan Ford tried to make her pictures look as real as she could, so we say her illustrations are realistic. What kind of illustrations are they? *Realistic illustrations.*

It's your turn to ask me some questions. What would you like to know about the story? (Accept questions. If children tell about the pictures or the story instead of ask questions, prompt them to ask a question.) Ask me a why question. Ask me a how question.

Read the Story Aloud

(Read story to children with minimal interruptions.)

Tomorrow we will read the story again, and I will ask you some questions.

Present Target Vocabulary

Precious

In the Tsimshian [sim-shee-an] story "the old man gave Loon his precious shell necklace." That means the shell necklace was very special and important to the old man. **Precious.** Say the word. *Precious.*

Precious is a describing word. It tells more about the necklace. What kind of word is **precious?** *A describing word.*

If something is precious, it is very special and important to the person who owns it. Say the word that means "very special and important." *Precious.*

(Correct any incorrect responses, and repeat the item at the end of the sequence.)

Let's think about some things that might be precious to different people. I'll tell about something. If you think that thing is precious to the person, say "precious." If not, don't say anything.

- His violin is the most special thing he owns. *Precious.*
- Mom's wedding ring is very special to her. *Precious.*
- It is just an old piece of wood.
- That book isn't special—I have seven others just like it.
- The picture of her very first car is special to her. *Precious.*
- He knew he could have fresh vegetables again tomorrow if he wanted them.

What describing word means "very special and important"? *Precious.*

What is most precious to you? Why is that precious? (Call on several children. Encourage children to use this frame for their answers: "The thing that is most precious to me is _____, because _____.")

Glimpse

The girl telling the story says, "Now I glimpse him floating behind a screen of reeds." That means she sees the loon for only a short time as it floats behind the reeds. **Glimpse.** Say the word. *Glimpse.*

Glimpse is an action word. It tells what's happening. What kind of word is **glimpse?** *An action word.*

If you glimpse something, you see it for only a short time before it is gone. Say the word that means "see something for only a short time before it is gone." *Glimpse.*

Let's think about some times when you might glimpse something. I'll tell about a time. If you think you would glimpse something, say "glimpse." If not, don't say anything.

- As their car drove down the highway she saw a deer for only a short time before it jumped into the woods. *Glimpse.*
- The fish darted out from behind the weeds and then was quickly gone again. *Glimpse.*
- The moon could be seen for hours.
- He saw his friend in the busy airport terminal but only for a short time. *Glimpse.*
- Marietta stayed for a week, so they talked a lot.
- The raccoon peeked out from behind the tree for a short time and then ran quickly out of sight. *Glimpse.*

What action word means "see something for only a short time before it is gone"? *Glimpse.*

Wild

In the story, the girl hears the loon's wild wail. That means the girl hears a sound made by a wild bird, not a tame bird. **Wild.** Say the word. *Wild.*

Wild is a describing word. It tells what kind of bird. What kind of word is **wild?** *A describing word.*

If an animal is wild, it is not tame. A tame animal is looked after by people. A wild animal is not looked after by people. Say the word that means "not tame; not looked after by people." *Wild.*

Let's think about some animals. Some of these animals are usually wild. Some of these animals are usually tame. If the animal I name is usually wild, say "wild." If the animal I name is usually tame, say "tame."

- Tiger. *Wild.*
- Dog. *Tame.*
- Hummingbird. *Wild.*
- Salmon. *Wild.*
- House cat. *Tame.*
- Moose. *Wild.*

What describing word means "not tame; not looked after by people"? *Wild.*

◎⚊ Slithers

In the story, "Otter slithers out of the water and into low brush." That means Otter moves by twisting and sliding along the ground at the edge of the lake. **Slithers.** Say the word. *Slithers.*

Slithers is an action word. It tells about how things move. What kind of word is **slithers**? *An action word.*

If something slithers, it moves by twisting and sliding along the ground. Say the word that means "moves by twisting and sliding along the ground." *Slithers.*

Watch me. I'll use my hands to show **slithers.** (Hold out one hand flat, palm side down. Place your other hand on top of the first hand, and move the top hand from side to side, in a twisting, sliding motion.) Use your hands to show **slithers.** (Pause.) Good: you used your hands to show **slithers.**

Let's think about some animals that could slither. I'll name an animal. If you think that animal slithers when it moves, say "slithers." If not, don't say anything.

- Snake. *Slithers.*
- Horse.
- Lizard. *Slithers.*
- Cat.
- Eagle.
- Crocodile. *Slithers.*

What action word means "moves by twisting and sliding along the ground"? *Slithers.*

Assign Homework
(Homework Sheet, BLM 9a: See the Introduction for homework instructions.)

DAY 2

Preparation: Picture Vocabulary Cards for *precious, glimpse, wild, slithers.*

You may wish to play a recording of a loon's call for the children. Using the search words <u>sound of a loon</u>, you will find many Internet sites that have sound recordings you can play.

Read and Discuss Story

(Read story to children. Ask the following questions at the specified points. Encourage them to use target words in their answers.)

Page 1. What three names do the native people give to the loon? (Ideas: *Rain Bird; Rain Goose; Call-up-a-Storm.*) All these names have something to do with rain or a storm. Long ago, the native people probably thought the loon brought rain. What did they think the loon brought? *Rain.*

Page 4. When do they hear the loon's call? (Idea: *At sunset.*) What does the loon's call sound like? (Idea: *A crazy yodeling laugh.*)

(**Note:** You may wish to play a recording of a loon's call for children.) What happens when the girl tries to make the loon's laughing call? (Idea: *The loon laughs back.*)

Page 6. Why do they go out in their canoe? (Idea: *They want to see a loon up close.*)

Page 7. What is Papa doing? (Idea: *He's telling the girl a story about how Loon got his white necklace.*) Tell me the story that tells how the loon got his white necklace. (Ideas: *An old blind man asked the loon for help; the loon used his magic to help him see again; the old man gave the loon his shell necklace.*)

Page 10. What animal do they see? *An otter.*

Page 12. What animal do they see next? *A beaver.*

Page 14. What animal do they see next? *A loon.* Do they get a good look at the loon? *No.* Why not? (Idea: *It dives under the water before they get close.*)

Page 16. The story says, "He rests in a nest of stars on the still water." Is the loon really resting in a nest of stars? *No.* What does the author mean? (Idea: *The reflection of the stars on the water is all around the loon.*)

Page 18. What three things does the loon do to show that the people in the canoe are making him feel worried? (Idea: *He rears up, shakes his head, and flaps his wings.*) When a bird rears up, it lifts itself up to try to make it look bigger. (Point to the female bird in the reeds.) This loon is swimming calmly. (Point to the male loon.) This bird has reared up to make itself look bigger. How close to the loon do they paddle? *Thirty feet.*

(**Note:** Identify a distance of thirty feet for the students: that is, the length of your classroom; the length of their house; the height of a telephone pole; the distance from one side to the other on a two-lane road.)

Page 19. Why doesn't the girl shout out? (Idea: *She doesn't want to frighten the birds back into the reeds.*)

Page 22. How do loons get up in the air? (Idea: *They run on the water until they are going fast enough for their wings to lift them into the air.*) What are the splashes on the water from? (Idea: *Their feet.*)

Page 23. How does Papa know there will be rain tonight? (Idea: *He sees the dark cloud passing across the moon.*)

Page 26. Do you think the loons brought the rain? Tell why you think the way you do.

Review Vocabulary

(Display the Picture Vocabulary Cards. Point to each card as you say the word. Ask children to repeat each word after you.) These pictures show **precious, glimpse, wild,** and **slithers.**

- What word means "very special and important"? *Precious.*

- What word means "see something for only a short time before it is gone"? *Glimpse.*
- What word means "not tame; not looked after by people"? *Wild.*
- What word means "moves by twisting and sliding along the ground"? *Slithers.*

Extend Vocabulary

 Wild

In *Loon Lake* we learned that **wild** is a describing word that means "not tame; not looked after by people." Say the word that means "not tame; not looked after by people." *Wild.*

Raise your hand if you can tell us a sentence that uses **wild** as a describing word meaning "not tame; not looked after by people." (Call on several children. If they don't use several complete sentences, restate their examples as sentences. Have the class repeat the sentences.)

Here's a new way to use the word **wild.**

- The children ran **wild,** throwing paper airplanes everywhere. Say the sentence.
- The babysitter could not control the **wild** children. Say the sentence.
- When the teacher left the room the children went **wild.** Say the sentence.

In these sentences, wild is a describing word that means badly behaved or out of control. What action word means "badly behaved or out of control"? *Wild.*

Present Expanded Target Vocabulary
Legend

Loons have white feathers that go around their necks like a necklace. In *Loon Lake* Papa told the native story of how the loon got its white necklace. This kind of story that explains how something came to be is called a legend. **Legend.** Say the word. *Legend.*

Legend is a naming word. It names a kind of story. What kind of word is **legend?** *A naming word.*

A legend is a story that explains how something came to be. Say the word that means "a story that explains how something came to be." *Legend.*

I'll name some stories. If the story explains how something came to be, say "legend." If not, don't say anything.

- *How the Leopard Got Its Spots. Legend.*
- *Frog and Toad are Friends.*
- *Why Mosquitoes Buzz in People's Ears. Legend.*
- *How Music Came to Be. Legend.*
- *The Wind Blew.*
- *Cloudy, With a Chance of Meatballs.*

What naming word means "a story that explains how something came to be"? *Legend.*

◎⚬ Disappears

In *Loon Lake,* "Loon quick-dives quietly." He can't be seen anymore. He disappears. **Disappears.** Say the word. *Disappears.*

Disappears is an action word. It tells what happens. What kind of word is **disappears?** *An action word.*

When you disappear, you can't be seen anymore. Say the word that means "can't be seen anymore." *Disappears.* What word means "can't be seen anymore"? *Disappears.*

I'll tell about someone or something. If what I tell about disappears, say "disappears." If not, don't say anything.

- Melodie hides behind the tree. *Disappears.*
- Father comes around the corner of the barn.
- The seal slips below the surface of the ocean. *Disappears.*
- Thomson and his sister come up the driveway.
- The clouds leave the sky. *Disappears.*
- Zoe, Billie, and Gracie come inside for supper.

What action word means "can't be seen anymore"? *Disappears.*

DAY 3

Preparation: Activity Sheet, BLM 9b. Children will need crayons.

Retell the Story

Today I'll show you the pictures Susan Ford made for *Loon Lake.* As I show you the pictures, I'll call on one of you to tell the class that part of the story.

Tell me what happens at the **beginning** of the story. (Show the pictures on pages 1–4. Call on a child to tell what's happening.)

Tell me what happens in the **middle** of the story. (Show the pictures on pages 5–24. Call on a child to tell what's happening. Encourage use of the target words when appropriate. Model use as necessary.)

Tell me what happens at the **end** of the story. (Show the pictures on pages 25 and 26. Call on a child to tell what's happening.)

Play Chew the Fat

Today you will play a game called *Chew the Fat.* A long time ago, when people wanted to sit and talk about things that were happening in their lives, they would say they would sit and "chew the fat."

In this game, I will say some sentences with our vocabulary words in them. If I use the vocabulary word correctly, say "Well done!" If I use the word incorrectly, say "Chew the fat." That means that you want to talk about how I used the word. I'll say the beginning of the sentence again. If you can make the sentence end so that it makes sense, you'll get a point. If you can't, I get the point.

Let's practice: The book was **precious** to him because he didn't like the story. *Chew the fat.* Let's chew the fat. The first part of the sentence stays the same. I'll say the first part. The book was **precious** to him because. How can we finish the sentence so it makes sense? (Idea: *It was very special and he loved the story.*) Let's say the whole sentence together now. *The book was precious to him because it was very special and he loved the story.* I'm glad we chewed the fat!

Let's do another one together. Wally **glimpsed** the moon when it was high in the clear sky. *Chew the fat.* The first part of the sentence stays the same. I'll say the first part. Wally glimpsed the moon when. How can we finish the sentence so that it makes sense? (Idea: *It was low and behind some trees.*) Let's say the whole sentence now. *Wally glimpsed the moon when it was low and behind some trees.* I'm glad we chewed the fat!

Let's try one more. The **wild** parrot lives in the rainforests of Africa. *Well done!* I used the word **wild** correctly, so you said, "Well done!"

Now you're ready to play the game. (Draw a T-chart on the board for keeping score. Children earn one point for each correct answer. If children make an error, work with the children to construct a correct sentence. Record one point for yourself, and repeat the item at the end of the game.)

- Jillian **slithered** across the floor when … she pretended to be a kangaroo. *Chew the fat.* I'll say the first part of the sentence again. Jillian **slithered** across the floor when. Can you finish the sentence so it makes sense? (Idea: *She pretended to be a snake.*) Let's say the whole sentence together. *Jillian slithered across the floor when she pretended to be a snake.* Well done! I'm glad we chewed the fat!

- Jim **disappeared** because … he wanted everyone to see him. *Chew the fat.* I'll say the first part of the sentence again. Jim disappeared because. Can you finish the sentence so it makes sense? (Idea: *He didn't want anyone to see him.*) Let's say the whole sentence together. *Jim disappeared because he didn't want anyone to see him.* Well done! I'm glad we chewed the fat!

- The children were **wild** because everyone was shouting and jumping on the furniture. *Well done!*

- *How the Chipmunk Got Its Stripes* is a **legend** because … it's a story about a tame chipmunk. *Chew the fat.* I'll say the first part of the sentence again. *How the Chipmunk Got Its Stripes* is a **legend** because. Can you finish the sentence so it makes sense? (Idea: *It is a story that explains how something came to be.*) Let's say the whole sentence together. *How the Chipmunk Got Its Stripes is a legend because it explains how something came to be.* Well done!

- The musician's violin was **precious** to him because he had three more just like it. *Chew the fat.* I'll say the first part of the sentence again. The musician's violin was **precious** to him because. Can you finish the sentence so it makes sense? (Idea: *It was the only one he had.*) Let's say the whole sentence together. *The musician's violin was precious to him because it was the only one he had.* Well done!

(Count the points and declare a winner.) You did a great job of playing *Chew the Fat.*

Complete the Activity Sheet

(Reread the story on page 7 that the father told about the Loon's Necklace. Read aloud the retelling of the story on BLM 9b, saying "blank" as you reach each blank. Have children say the appropriate word to complete the sentence. Have them sound out and print the word on the line. When the story is complete, read it aloud, having the children chime in with the printed words. You may wish to have children draw and color a picture of the loon with its necklace on the back of the sheet.)

An old **man did** not **see**. He said, "Loon, please help **me see**."

The loon used his magic to fix the old man's eyes. "Thank you, Loon," the **man** said. He gave the loon his necklace **made** of shells. The white shells **at** the loon's neck turned into white feathers.

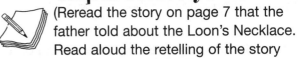

DAY 4

Preparation: Prepare a sheet of chart paper, landscape direction, titled *Loon Lake.* Underneath the title, draw 10 boxes connected by arrows.

See the Introduction for Week 9's chart.

Literary Analysis
(Cumulative Review)

Let's think about what we already know about how books are made.

- What do we call the name of the book? *Title.*
- What do we call the person who writes the story? *Author.*
- What do we call the person who draws the pictures? *Illustrator.*
- What do we call the people or animals a story is about? *Characters.*

- What do we call the pictures the illustrator makes? *Illustrations.*
- What is one thing the setting of a story tells? *Where a story happens.*

Let's sing The Story Song to help us remember these important things about books.

(See the Introduction for the complete Story Song.)

Today we will learn more about the setting of a story.

The setting of a story tells two things. One thing the setting tells is where the story happens. What is one thing the setting tells? *Where the story happens.*

Let's look at the pictures and talk about the story to figure out where *Loon Lake* happens. (Record children's responses by writing the words in the boxes on the chart paper that you prepared.)

Pages 1–2. Where does the story begin? (Idea: *At the lake.*)

Pages 3–4. Where does the next part of the story happen? (Idea: *On the shore.*)

Pages 5–6. Where does the next part of the story happen? (Ideas: *On the lake; in a canoe.*)

Pages 7–8. Where does the next part of the story happen? (Ideas: *On the lake; in a long boat.*)

Pages 9–10. Where does the next part of the story happen? (Ideas: *On the lake; near the shore.*)

Pages 11–20. Where does the next part of the story happen? (Ideas: *On the lake; in the reeds.*)

Pages 21–22. Where does the next part of the story happen? (Ideas: *On the lake; in the air.*)

Pages 23–24. Where does the next part of the story happen? (Idea: *At the campfire.*)

Pages 25–26. Where does the next part of the story happen? (Idea: *In the tent.*)

The shore, the canoe, the longboat, the reeds, and the campfire are all at Loon Lake. So, if we could use only two words to tell the setting of the story, we would use the words "Loon Lake." Where is the setting of the story *Loon Lake*? *At Loon Lake.* Isn't that interesting; the title of this story and the setting are the same. What is the title and the setting for this story? *Loon Lake.*

Today you learned about one of the parts of the setting of the story *Loon Lake.* You learned about where the story happened.

Play Chew the Fat (Cumulative Review)

Today you will play a game called *Chew the Fat.* Remember that a long time ago, when people wanted to sit and talk about things that were happening in their lives, they would say they would sit and "chew the fat." In this game, I will say some sentences with our vocabulary words in them. If I use the vocabulary word correctly, say "Well done!"

If I use the word incorrectly, say "Chew the fat." That means that you want to talk about how I used the word. I'll say the beginning of the sentence again. If you can make the sentence end so that it makes sense, you'll get a point. If you can't, I get the point.

Let's practice: The ring was **precious** because … it was ordinary and not very interesting to the king. *Chew the fat.* Let's chew the fat. The first part of the sentence stays the same. I'll say the first part. The ring was **precious** because. How can we finish the sentence so it makes sense? (Idea: *It was very special and important to the king.*) Let's say the whole sentence together now. *The ring was precious because it was very special and important to the king.* Well done! I'm glad we chewed the fat!

Let's do another one together. Piper caught a **glimpse** of the car as it was parked outside her apartment all day. *Chew the fat.* The first part of the sentence stays the same. I'll say the first part. Piper caught a **glimpse** of the car. How can we finish the sentence so that it makes sense? (Idea: *As it roared down the street.*) Let's say the whole sentence now. *Piper got a glimpse of the car as it roared down the street.* Well done! I'm glad we chewed the fat!

Now you're ready to play the game. (Draw a T-chart on the board for keeping score. Children earn one point for each correct answer. If children make an error, work with the children to construct a correct sentence. Record one point for yourself, and repeat the item at the end of the game.)

- Mark knew the deer was **wild** when … it walked up to him and let him pet it. *Chew the fat.* I'll say the first part of the sentence again. Mark knew the deer was **wild** when. Can you finish the sentence so it makes sense? (Idea: *It ran away when it saw him.*) Let's say the whole sentence together. *Mark knew the deer was wild when it ran away when it saw him.* Well done! I'm glad we chewed the fat!

- The lizard **slithered** because … it moved by twisting and sliding along the ground. *Well done!*

- *Why Raven is Black* is a **legend** because … it explains how the bird got its color. *Well done!*

- Aaron **disappeared** when … he closed his eyes. *Chew the fat.* I'll say the first part of the sentence again. Aaron **disappeared** when. Can you finish the sentence so it makes sense? (Idea: *He hid in the closet.*) Let's say the whole sentence together. *Aaron disappeared when he hid in the closet.* Well done! I'm glad we chewed the fat!

- The children were **wild** because … they were sitting politely eating the birthday cake. *Chew the fat.* I'll say the first part of the sentence again. The children were **wild** because. Can you finish the sentence so it makes sense? (Idea: *They were throwing birthday cake at each other.*) Let's say the whole sentence together. *The children were wild because they were throwing birthday cake at each other.* Well done!

- The grasshopper was **desperate** because … he had lots to eat. *Chew the fat.* I'll say the first part of the sentence again. The grasshopper was **desperate** because. Can you finish the sentence so it makes sense? (Idea: *He was starving.*) Let's say the whole sentence together. *The grasshopper was desperate because he was starving.* Well done! I'm glad we chewed the fat!

- The children were playing **peacefully** when … they played quietly and happily. *Well done!*

- The **rough** board was … smooth and even. *Chew the fat.* I'll say the first part of the sentence again. The **rough** board was. Can you finish the sentence so it makes sense? (Idea: *Bumpy and slivery.*) Let's say the whole sentence together. *The rough board was bumpy and slivery.* Well done! I'm glad we chewed the fat!

- The old man was **wise** because … he didn't know many answers. *Chew the fat.* I'll say the first part of the sentence again. The old man was **wise** because. Can you finish the sentence so it makes sense? (Idea: *He knew many answers.*) Let's say the whole sentence together. *The old man was wise because he know many answers.* Well done!

(Count the points and declare a winner.)
You did a great job of playing *Chew the Fat.*

DAY 5

Preparation: Happy Face Game Test Sheet, BLM B.

Learn About Legends

Today you will learn about a special kind of folk tale called a legend. What will you learn about? *A legend.*

Folk tales, fairy tales, and legends are all stories that were once told out loud. How are folk tales, fairy tales, and legends the same? (Idea: *They are all stories that were once told out loud.*) How is a fairy tale different from a folk tale? (Idea: *Someone decided to write it down in a book a long time ago.*) A legend is a special kind of folk tale that explains how something came to be. What does a legend explain? (Idea: *How something came to be.*)

Listen while I read the legend that Jonathan London included in *Loon Lake.* (Re-read page 7.) What does this legend explain? (Idea: *How the loon got the white feathers around its neck.*)

Different groups of people have different legends that explain how things around them came to be. This is a legend from the Tsimshian people. The Tsimshian people are the native people who first lived between the Nass and Skeena Rivers in British Columbia, Canada. (Locate northern British Columbia on the map or globe.)

What people does the legend The Loon's Necklace come from? *The Tsimshian.* No one knows when this legend was first told. Do we know when this legend was first told? *No.* But Jonathan London heard the story, and he wanted to include it in his book about Loon Lake.

Assess Vocabulary

 (Hold up a copy of the Happy Face Game Test Sheet, BLM B.)

Today you're going to play the Happy Face Game. When you play the Happy Face Game, it shows me how well you know the hard words you are learning.

If I say something that is true, color in the happy face. What will you do if I say something that is true? *Color in the happy face.*

If I say something that is false, color in the sad face. What will you do if I say something that is false? *Color in the sad face.*

Listen carefully to each item that I say. Don't let me trick you!

Item 1: A **precious** thing is important to you. (*True.*)

Item 2: Something that **disappears** goes out of sight. (*True.*)

Item 3: **Wild** can mean not tame <u>or</u> it can mean badly-behaved. (*True.*)

Item 4: A **legend** is a story that tells you how to make soup. (*False.*)

Item 5: A creature that **slithers** moves by hopping and bouncing. (*False.*)

Item 6: A **glimpse** is a quick look. (*True.*)

Item 7: When something is **tempting,** you do not want to have it. (*False.*)

Item 8: A person who is **patient** does <u>not</u> worry or feel upset when he or she has to wait. (*True.*)

Item 9: If something is **genuine,** it is not real. (*False.*)

Item 10: If you are **disagreeable,** you are **uncooperative.** (*True.*)

You did a great job of playing the Happy Face Game!

(Score children's work at a later time. A child must score 9 out of 10 to be at the mastery level. If a child does not achieve mastery, insert the missed words as additional items in the games for next week's lessons. Retest those children individually for the missed items before they take the next mastery test.)

Extensions

Read a Story as a Reward

(Display copies of several of the books that you have read since the beginning of the program or other legends. Allow children to choose which book they would like you to read to them as a reward for their hard work.)

(Read the story aloud for enjoyment with minimal interruptions.)

Preparation: Word containers for the Super Words Center. You may wish to remove some words from earlier lessons. Choose words children have mastered.

 Introduce the Super Words Center

(Add the new Picture Vocabulary Cards to words from the previous weeks. Show children one of the word containers. If children need more guidance in how to work in the Super Words Center, role-play with two to three children as a demonstration.)

Today let's review how to play the game called *What's Missing?*

Let's think about how we work with our words in the Super Words Center.

You will work with a partner in the Super Words Center. Whom will you work with? *A partner.*

First one partner will draw four word cards out of the container and put them on the table so both partners can see. What do you do first? (Idea: *Draw four cards out of the container and put them on the table so both partners can see.*)

Next you will take turns looking at the cards and saying the words the pictures show. What do you do next? (Idea: *We take turns looking at the cards and saying the words the pictures show.*)

Next partner 2 looks away while partner 1 takes one of the four cards and places it facedown on the table away from the other cards. Then partner 1 draws a new card from the container and places it on the table with the other three. Watch while I show you what I mean. **(Demonstrate this process with one child as your partner.)** When you put down the new card, it's a good idea to mix the cards so they aren't in the same places any more. **(Demonstrate this process as you go.)**

Now partner 1 says, "What's Missing?" Partner 2 has to use his or her eyes and brain and say what old card has been taken away. After partner 2 has guessed, turn over the facedown card. If partner 2 is correct, he or she gets a point. If partner 2 is not correct, partner 1 gets the point. **(Demonstrate this process as you go.)**

Next partner 2 has a turn to choose four different cards and the game starts again. What happens next? **(Idea:** *Partner 2 has a turn to choose four different cards and the game starts again.***)**

Have fun playing *What's Missing?*

Week 10

Preparation: You will need *Grandmother Spider Brings the Sun* for each day's lesson.

Number the pages of the story to assist you in asking questions at appropriate points.

Post a copy of the Vocabulary Tally Sheet, BLM A, with this week's Picture Vocabulary Cards attached.

Each child will need one copy of the Homework Sheet, BLM 10a.

Grandmother Spider Brings the Sun
author: Geri Keams • illustrator: James Bernardin

Target Vocabulary

Tier II	Tier III
calm	setting (where)
tunnel	legend
soared	
directions	
*journey	
*protect	

*Expanded Target Vocabulary Word

DAY 1

Introduce Book

This week's book is called *Grandmother Spider Brings the Sun.* What's the title? *Grandmother Spider Brings the Sun.*

This book was written by Geri Keams [keems]. Who's the author of *Grandmother Spider Brings the Sun? Geri Keams.*

James Bernardin [burn-ar-din] made the pictures for this book. Who's the illustrator of *Grandmother Spider Brings the Sun? James Bernardin.* Remember that the pictures an illustrator makes for a book are called the illustrations. What do you call the pictures an illustrator makes? *Illustrations.* What are illustrations? *The pictures an illustrator makes for a book.* Who made the illustrations for this book? *James Bernardin.*

The cover of a book usually gives us some hints of what the book is about. Let's look at the front cover of *Grandmother Spider Brings the Sun.* What do you see in the illustration? (Ideas: *Animals dancing in a circle around a spider with a pot; a wolf; a bear; a moose; a mountain goat; a fox; a raccoon; a cougar.*)

(Assign each child a partner.) Remember that when you make a prediction about something, you say what you think will happen. Get ready to make some predictions to your partner about this book. Use the information from the cover to help you.

(Ask the following questions, allowing sufficient time for children to share their predictions with their partners.)

- Who are the characters in this story? (Who do you think this story is about?)
- What do you think is in the pot?
- Where do you think the story happens?
- When do you think the story happens?
- Why do you think the animals are all dancing?
- How many animals do you see?
- Do you think this story is about real animals? Tell why or why not.

(Call on several children to share their predictions with the class.)

Take a Picture Walk

(Encourage children to use target words in their answers.) We're going to take a picture walk through this book. Remember that when we take a picture walk, we look at the pictures and tell what we think will happen in the story.

Pages 1–2. What animals do you see in this illustration? (Ideas: *Wolf; rabbit; rooster; wild pig; deer.*) Do you think the animals are afraid of the wolf? *No.* How do you know? (Idea: *They are running/walking toward the wolf, not away from it.*) What time is it at the beginning of this story? *Nighttime.*

Page 4. How do you think the wolf is feeling? (Ideas: *Angry; upset.*) Why do you think that?

(Idea: *His eyes are narrowed and his arms are crossed.*) What do you think the wolf is thinking about?

Page 5. This animal is a coyote. What kind of animal is this? *A coyote.* What do you think the coyote is thinking about? (Idea: *Playing a trick on someone; doing something mean.*) What makes you think that? (Idea: *The expression on his face; he looks kind of mean.*)

Page 7. (Point to the possum.) This animal is called a possum. What is the name of this animal? *Possum.* What is the possum doing? *Raising his hand.* What other animals are in this illustration? (Ideas: *Bear; deer; a type of wild cat; a beaver.*) The animals are all looking in the same direction. What do you think they're looking at?

Page 10. Where is Possum in this illustration? (Ideas: *Outside; in a meadow.*) When you squint, you squeeze your eyes almost shut, but you can still see. Show me how you squint. Why do you think Possum is squinting and hiding behind his tail?

Page 11. What is happening to Possum's tail? (Idea: *It is burning.*)

Page 14. Well, this is an interesting creature. What kind of animal do you think this is? (Idea: *A bird.*)

Pages 15–16. What is the bird doing? (Idea: *Flying through the cave.*) What is happening to the feathers on the bird's head? (Idea: *They're burning.*)

Page 17. What are the animals doing in this illustration? (Ideas: *Talking; arguing; having a meeting.*) What do you think they are saying?

Page 20. What animals do you see in this illustration? (Ideas: *Wolf; rabbit; mouse; spider.*) What are the animals looking at? (Idea: *A pot.*) What do you think is in the pot?

Page 21. Who seems to be carrying the pot? *A spider.* Where do you think the spider will take the pot?

Pages 23–24. What do you see in this illustration? (Ideas: *Creatures with weapons breathing fire.*)

(Point to the little pot in the lower right-hand corner of the illustration.) Here is the spider with

her pot. Do you think these creatures will notice her? *No.*

Page 26. What do you think is in the pot? (Idea: *Fire; a piece of the sun.*) Where do you think the spider is taking the fire? (Idea: *Back to the cave.*)

Page 27. Where have you seen this illustration before? *On the front cover.* Why do you think the animals are dancing around the spider? (Idea: *She brought fire to them.*)

It's your turn to ask me some questions. What would you like to know about the story? (Accept questions. If children tell about the pictures or story instead of ask questions, prompt them to ask a question.) Ask me a where question. Ask me a what question.

Read the Story Aloud
(Read story to children with minimal interruptions.)

Tomorrow we will read the story again, and I will ask you some questions.

(If children have difficulty attending for an extended period of time, you may wish to present the next part of this day's lesson at another time of day.)

Present Target Vocabulary

 Calm

In the story, Wolf got quite upset when Coyote said they should steal a piece of the sun. Coyote told Wolf to calm down. That means Coyote told Wolf to become less angry, upset, or excited. **Calm.** Say the word. *Calm.*

Calm is an action word. It tells what someone is doing. What kind of word is **calm?** *An action word.*

Calm means become less angry, upset, or excited. Say the word that means "become less angry, upset, or excited." *Calm.*

(Correct any incorrect responses, and repeat the item at the end of the sequence.)

Let's think about a time when someone might tell you to calm down. I'll tell about a time. If you think someone would tell you to calm down, say "calm down." If not, don't say anything.

- You are jumping on your bed and the babysitter comes into your bedroom. *Calm down.*
- You are sitting peacefully at the table playing a game of checkers with your brother.
- You can't wait to go to the fair. *Calm down.*
- You found your model airplane broken into hundreds of pieces. *Calm down.*
- You are at a restaurant and you are laughing and shouting with your friends. *Calm down.*
- You are sitting at your desk at school quietly drawing a picture.

What action word means "become less angry, upset, or excited"? *Calm.*

Tunnel

In the story, Possum said he could dig a tunnel. That means Possum thought he could dig a long, wide underground tube. **(Roll up a piece of paper into the shape of a tube.)** If this was underground so someone could travel through it, it would be a tunnel. **Tunnel.** Say the word. *Tunnel.*

Tunnel is a naming word. It names something. What kind of word is **tunnel?** *A naming word.*

A tunnel is a long, wide underground tube. Say the word that means "a long, wide underground tube." *Tunnel.*

Let's think about some things that might be tunnels. I'll name something. If you think it could be a tunnel, say "tunnel." If not, don't say anything.

- The gopher dug a long, wide underground tube to his den. *Tunnel.*
- The subway went from Yankee Stadium to Lexington Avenue. *Tunnel.*
- He traveled on the bus from San Francisco to Los Angeles.
- The miners dug deep into the mountain. *Tunnel.*
- The airplane flew high in the sky.
- The children walked to school every day.

What naming word means "a long, wide underground tube"? *Tunnel.*

 Soared

In the story, Buzzard jumped into the tunnel and soared through the darkness. That means he flew quickly and easily down the tunnel. **Soared.** Say the word. *Soared.*

Soared is an action word. It tells what something did. What kind of word is **soared?** *An action word.*

If something soared, it flew quickly and easily, very high in the sky. Say the word that means "flew quickly and easily, very high in the sky." *Soared.*

Let's think about some things that might have soared. I'll tell about something. If what I tell about soared, say "soared." If not, don't say anything.

- The eagle flew quickly and easily high over the forest. *Soared.*
- The airplane flew quickly and easily up through the clouds. *Soared.*
- The cougar ran quickly and easily through the forest.
- The loon flew just above the water of the lake.
- The seagulls flew quickly and easily, high above the ocean waves. *Soared.*
- The glider flew silently, high above the airfield. *Soared.*

What action word means "flew quickly and easily, very high in the sky"? *Soared.*

Directions

In the story, Wolf said he was tired of everyone asking him for directions. That means he didn't want anyone to ask him how to get where they wanted to go. **Directions.** Say the word. *Directions.*

Directions is a naming word. It names things. What kind of word is **directions?** *A naming word.*

Directions is information that tells how to do something or how to get where you want to go. Say the word that means "information that tells how to do something or how to get where you want to go." *Directions.*

Let's think about some things that could be directions. I'll tell you something. If I am giving you directions, say "directions." If not, don't say anything.

- Go south down Fifth Street for five blocks, then turn right and cross the street. Fairburn School is right there. *Directions.*
- In case of fire, break the glass and pull the handle. *Directions.*
- I love zucchini muffins.
- Take one pill twice a day until the rash is gone. *Directions.*
- Plant the seeds one inch deep, four inches apart. Water daily. *Directions.*
- I like to watch comedies on TV.

What naming word means "information that tells how to do something or how to get where you want to go"? *Directions.*

Present Vocabulary Tally Sheet
(See Lesson 1, page 3, for instructions.)

Assign Homework
(Homework Sheet, BLM 10a: See the Introduction for homework instructions.)

DAY 2

Preparation: Picture Vocabulary Cards for *calm, tunnel, soared, directions.*

Read and Discuss Story

 (Read story to children. Ask the following questions at the specified points. Encourage children to use target words in their answers.)

Page 2. When does this story happen? *A long time ago.* How is the world in the story different from our world? (Idea: *Half the world had sun and half didn't.*) In which part of the world do these animals live? (Idea: *The half with no sun.*) How is Wolf different from the other animals? (Idea: *He can see in the dark.*)

Page 3. Why does Wolf call all the animals together? (Ideas: *He is tired of the other animals bumping into him and asking for directions; he wants to solve the problem of having no sun.*)

How does Wolf think they should solve their problem? (Idea: *They should go to the other side of the world and ask for a piece of the sun.*)

Page 6. How does Coyote think they should solve their problem? (Idea: *He thinks they should sneak over and steal a piece of the sun.*) Whose plan do the animals decide to use? *Coyote's.*

Page 8. Who offers to go to the other side of the world? *Possum.* What is Possum's plan? (Idea: *He will dig a tunnel with his sharp claws. Then he will put a small piece of the sun in his big, bushy tail and carry it back home.*) Does Wolf like this idea? *Yes.*

Page 9. Show me how you make your eyes squinty. Is Possum able to get a piece of the sun? *Yes.* Where does he put it? *In his tail.*

Page 12. Why is Possum's tail on fire? (Idea: *The piece of the sun was very hot and set it on fire.*) What can you tell about the way possums look today from this story? (Ideas: *They have squinty eyes with dark rings around them and skinny tails.*) This part of the story explains how a possum's tail came to be skinny with no hair.

Page 13. Buzzard says he is going to hide the sun in his beautiful crown of feathers. Where is that on his body? *On his head.* What do you think is happening on top of his head? (Idea: *It is catching on fire.*)

Page 15. When Wolf looks at Buzzard's head he says Buzzard's bald. What does **bald** mean? (Idea: *It means he has no feathers left on top of his head.*) Why doesn't Buzzard like anyone to look at him? (Idea: *He thought he was the most beautiful creature when he had his crown of feathers. Now that he is bald, he does not think he is beautiful anymore.*) This part of the story explains how a buzzard's head came to have no hair.

Page 18. Who offers to go get the piece of sun next? *Grandmother Spider.* Why doesn't Wolf want Grandmother Spider to go? (Idea: *She is too old and too slow.*)

Page 19. Why does Grandmother Spider want to go to the other side of the world to get a piece of the sun? (Ideas: *She has done many things to help the animals and wants to do one more.*) Why do you think Grandmother Spider made the little clay bowl? (Idea: *To carry the piece of sun in.*) What lesson has Grandmother Spider learned from Possum and Buzzard? (Idea: *She learned that the sun is very hot and will burn, so she'll use a clay pot to carry it in.*)

Page 22. Who is protecting the sun? *The Sun Guards.*

Page 23. How is Grandmother Spider able to get past the Sun Guards? (Idea: *She is so tiny she is able to sneak past without them seeing her.*)

Page 25. What happens to the little piece of sun as Grandmother Spider carries it back to her side of the world? (Idea: *It grows bigger and bigger.*) Where does the sun go when the animals squeeze it out of the cave? (Idea: *It bounces up into the sky.*)

Page 28. What does the story tell us about spider webs today? (Idea: *The shape of the sun is in the center.*)

Review Vocabulary

(Display the Picture Vocabulary Cards. Point to each card as you say the word. Ask children to repeat each word after you.) These pictures show **calm, tunnel, directions,** and **soared.**

- What action word means "become less angry, upset, or excited"? *Calm.*
- What naming word means "a long, wide underground tube"? *Tunnel.*
- What naming word means "information that tells how to do something or how to get where you want to go"? *Directions.*
- What action word means "flew quickly and easily, very high in the sky"? *Soared.*

Extend Vocabulary

 Calm

In *Grandmother Spider Brings the Sun,* we learned that calm means "become less angry, upset, or excited."

Here's a new way to use the word **calm.**

- The water was **calm.** Say the sentence.
- We sailed into the **calm** waters of Roche Harbor. Say the sentence.
- Sunday was a clear and **calm** day. Say the sentence.

In these sentences, calm is a describing word that means not moving or still. What word means "not moving or still"? *Calm.*

Present Expanded Target Vocabulary
◎━ Journey

In the story, Possum, Buzzard, and Grandmother Spider all traveled a long, long way to get to the other side of the world. That means they each made a journey to the other side of the world. **Journey.** Say the word. *Journey.*

Journey is a naming word. It names a thing. What kind of word is **journey?** *A naming word.*

A journey is a long trip to a place far away. Say the word that means "a long trip to a place far away." *Journey.*

I'll tell about some things. If those things would be a journey, say "journey." If not, don't say anything.

- Christopher Columbus traveled across the Atlantic Ocean to reach America. *Journey.*
- The settlers traveled on foot from New York to Iowa. *Journey.*
- The dentist walked across the street to go from his home to his office.
- The children walked two blocks to school.
- The astronauts traveled all the way to the moon. *Journey.*
- The men paddled their canoes the full length of the Mississippi River. *Journey.*

What naming word means "a long trip to a place far away"? *Journey.*

◎━ Protect

In the story, Sun Guards stood in a tight circle around the sun. The Sun Guards were trying to protect the sun. **Protect.** Say the word. *Protect.*

Protect is an action word. It tells about what someone is doing. What kind of word is **protect?** *An action word.*

Protect means keep safe from danger or injury. Say the word that means "keep safe from danger or injury." *Protect.*

I'll tell about some people or animals. If those people or animals are being kept safe from danger or injury, say "protect." If not, don't say anything.

- I always wear my helmet when I ride my bicycle. *Protect.*
- Jackson went into the boat **without** a life jacket.
- Marcus wore knee pads and gloves when he was skateboarding. *Protect.*
- Damon wore a hat to keep the sun off his head. *Protect.*
- Dad forgot to wear his safety glasses when he was working on the car.
- The workmen didn't wear hard hats at the construction site.

What action word means "keep safe from danger or injury"? *Protect.*

DAY 3

Preparation: Activity Sheet, BLM 10b.

Retell Story

Today I'll show you the pictures James Bernardin made for *Grandmother Spider Brings the Sun.* As I show you the pictures, I'll call on one of you to tell the class that part of the story.

Tell me what happens at the **beginning** of the story. (Show the pictures on pages 1 and 2. Call on a child to tell what's happening.)

Tell me what happens in the **middle** of the story. (Show the pictures on pages 3–25. Call on a child to tell what's happening. Encourage use of the target words when appropriate. Model use as necessary.)

Tell me what happens at the **end** of the story. (Show the picture on page 27. Call on a child to tell what's happening.)

Play Chew the Fat

 Today you will play a game called *Chew the Fat.* A long time ago, when people wanted to sit and talk about things that were happening in their lives, they would say they would sit and "chew the fat."

In this game, I will say some sentences with our vocabulary words in them. If I use the vocabulary word correctly, say "Well done!" If I use the word incorrectly, say "Chew the fat."

That means you want to talk about how I used the word. I'll say the beginning of the sentence again. If you can make the sentence end so that it makes sense, you'll get a point. If you can't, I get the point.

Let's practice: I went on a **journey** when I walked from the kitchen to the living room. *Chew the fat.* Let's chew the fat. The first part of the sentence stays the same. I'll say the first part. I went on a **journey** when. How can we finish the sentence so it makes sense? (Idea: *I went across the country.*) Let's say the whole sentence together now. *I went on a journey when I went across the country.* Well done! I'm glad we chewed the fat!

Let's do another one together. I **calm** down when I get angry, upset, or excited. *Chew the fat.* The first part of the sentence stays the same. I'll say the first part. I **calm** down when. How can we finish the sentence so it makes sense? (Idea: *I become less angry, upset, or excited.*) Let's say the whole sentence now. *I calm down when I get less angry, upset, or excited.* Well done! I'm glad we chewed the fat!

Let's try one more. The ocean was **calm** when there were no waves. *Well done!* I used the word **calm** correctly, so you said, "Well done!"

Now you're ready to play the game. (Draw a T-chart on the board for keeping score. Children earn one point for each correct answer. If they make an error, correct them as you normally would, and record one point for yourself. Repeat missed words at the end of the game.)

- The robin was **protecting** its babies when … it flew away and left them alone. *Chew the fat.* I'll say the first part of the sentence again. The robin was **protecting** its babies when. Can you finish the sentence so it makes sense? (Idea: *It chased the other birds away from its nest.*) Let's say the whole sentence together. *The robin was protecting its babies when it chased the other birds away from its nest.* Well done! I'm glad we chewed the fat!

- The hawk **soared** when … it sat on its nest. *Chew the fat.* I'll say the first part of the sentence again. The hawk **soared** when. Can you finish the sentence so it makes sense? (Idea: *It flew high in the sky.*) Let's say the whole sentence together. *The hawk soared when it flew high in the sky.* Well done! I'm glad we chewed the fat!
- The leaves on the trees were still when … the wind was **calm.** *Well done!*
- I followed the **directions** for making bread when … I didn't read the recipe. *Chew the fat.* I'll say the first part of the sentence again. I followed the **directions** for making bread when. Can you finish the sentence so it makes sense? (Idea: *I did what the recipe told me to do.*) Let's say the whole sentence together. *I followed the directions for making bread when I did what the recipe told me to do.* Well done!
- My mother told me to **calm** down when I was waiting politely for the party to begin. *Chew the fat.* I'll say the first part of the sentence again. My mother told me to **calm** down when. Can you finish the sentence so it makes sense? (Idea: *I couldn't be still waiting for the party to begin.*) Let's say the whole sentence together. *My mother told me to calm down when I couldn't be still waiting for the party to begin.* Well done!

(Count the points and declare a winner.) You did a great job of playing *Chew the Fat.*

Complete the Activity Sheet

 (Reread the story on pages 8–12 about Possum going to steal the sun. Read aloud the rebus story on BLM 10b, saying "blank" each time you come to a line. Call on children to fill in the blank with the appropriate word.)

(Give each child a copy of the Activity Sheet, BLM 10b. Reread the rebus story, having children point to the rebus picture that would fit in the blank. Have children cut out the rebus pictures and glue them in the appropriate spaces. They may then read their rebus story to their partner.)

(**Note:** If children require more assistance, complete this activity as a guided activity.)

Completed Rebus:

> Why Possum Has a Skinny Tail
> Possum said, "I will get the sun." He dug a tunnel with his sharp claws. He went to the other side of the world.
> Possum put some of the sun in his tail and ran and ran. His tail got on fire. The animals put out the fire, but his tail got all skinny.
> And possums have had skinny tails ever since.

DAY 4

Preparation: Prepare a sheet of chart paper, landscape direction, titled *Grandmother Spider Brings the Sun.* Underneath the title, draw 10 boxes connected by arrows.

See the Introduction for Week 10's chart.

Literary Analysis (Cumulative Review)

Let's think about what we already know about how books are made.

- What do we call the name of the book? *Title.*
- What do we call the person who writes the story? *Author.*
- What do we call the person who draws the pictures? *Illustrator.*
- What do we call the people or animals a story is about? *Characters.*
- What do we call the pictures the illustrator makes? *Illustrations.*
- What is one thing the setting of a story tells? *Where a story happens.*

Let's sing The Story Song to help us remember these important things about books.

(See the Introduction for the complete Story Song.)

Today we will learn more about the setting of a story.

The setting of a story tells two things. One thing the setting tells is where the story happens. What is one thing the setting tells? *Where the story happens.*

Let's look at the pictures and talk about the story to figure out where *Grandmother Spider Brings the Sun* happens. (Record children's responses by writing the words in the boxes on the chart paper that you prepared.)

Pages 1–2. Where did the story begin? (Idea: *On the dark side of the world.*)

Pages 4–7. Where did the next part of the story happen? (Idea: *In the cave.*)

Page 10. Where did the next part of the story happen? (Idea: *On the sunny side of the world.*)

Page 11. Where did the next part of the story happen? (Idea: *In the tunnel.*)

Page 14. Where did the next part of the story happen? (Idea: *In the cave.*)

Pages 15–16. Where did the next part of the story happen? (Idea: *In the tunnel.*)

Pages 17–20. Where did the next part of the story happen? (Idea: *In the cave.*)

Pages 21–24. Where did the next part of the story happen? (Idea: *On the sunny side of the world.*)

Page 26. Where did the next part of the story happen? (Idea: *In the tunnel.*)

Page 27. Where did the next part of the story happen? (Idea: *Outside the cave.*)

The dark side of the world, the cave, the tunnel, the sunny side of the world, and outside the cave are all in the world. So, if we could use only one word to tell the setting of the story, we would use the word **world**. Where is the setting of *Grandmother Spider Brings the Sun*? *In the world.*

Today you learned about part of the setting of *Grandmother Spider Brings the Sun.* You learned about where the story happened.

Play Chew the Fat (Cumulative Review)

Today you will play a game called *Chew the Fat.* Remember that a long time ago, when people wanted to sit and talk about things that were happening in their lives, they would say they would sit and "chew the fat." In this game, I will say some sentences with our vocabulary words in them. If I use the vocabulary word correctly, say "Well done!"

If I use the word incorrectly, say "Chew the fat." That means you want to talk about how I used the word. I'll say the beginning of the sentence again. If you can make the sentence end so it makes sense, you'll get a point. If you can't, I get the point.

Let's practice: We knew the wind was **calm** when the branches on the trees were breaking off. *Chew the fat.* Let's chew the fat. The first part of the sentence stays the same. I'll say the first part. We knew the wind was **calm** when. How can we finish the sentence so it makes sense? (Idea: *The branches on the trees didn't move.*) Let's say the whole sentence together now. *We knew the wind was calm when the branches on the trees didn't move. Well done!* I'm glad we chewed the fat!

Let's do another one together. The guards **protected** the gold when they let someone steal it. *Chew the fat.* The first part of the sentence stays the same. I'll say the first part. The guards **protected** the gold when. How can we finish the sentence so that it makes sense? (Idea: *They didn't let anyone steal it.*) Let's say the whole sentence now. *The guards protected the gold when they didn't let anyone steal it.* Well done! I'm glad we chewed the fat!

Now you're ready to play the game. (Draw a T-chart on the board for keeping score. Children earn one point for each correct answer. If they make an error, correct them as you normally would, and record one point for yourself. Repeat missed words at the end of the game.)

- Mark knew the woman was **wise** when she told him silly answers. *Chew the fat.* I'll say the first part of the sentence again. Mark knew the woman was **wise** when. Can you finish the sentence so it makes sense? (Idea: *She told him the smart answers.*) Let's say the whole sentence together. *Mark knew the woman was wise when she told him smart answers.* Well done! I'm glad we chewed the fat!

- The **journey** lasted a long, long time because we traveled so far. *Well done!*
- He followed the **directions** when he did what the paper told him to do. *Well done!*
- The airplane **soared** when it rolled down the runway. *Chew the fat.* I'll say the first part of the sentence again. The airplane **soared.** Can you finish the sentence so it makes sense? (Idea: *When it flew high in the sky.*) Let's say the whole sentence together. *The airplane soared when it flew high in the sky.* Well done! I'm glad we chewed the fat!
- They got a **glimpse** of the rocket as it sat on the launching pad. *Chew the fat.* I'll say the first part of the sentence again. They got a **glimpse** of the rocket as it. Can you finish the sentence so it makes sense? (Idea: *Blasted off into space.*) Let's say the whole sentence together. *They got a glimpse of the rocket as it blasted off into space.* Well done!
- The ring was **precious** to him because he didn't like it at all. *Chew the fat.* I'll say the first part of the sentence again. The ring was **precious** to him because. Can you finish the sentence so it makes sense? (Idea: *He liked it more than anything else he owned.*) Let's say the whole sentence together. *The ring was precious to him because he liked it more than anything else he owned.* Well done! I'm glad we chewed the fat!
- The **tunnel** was built under the river. *Well done!*
- The lizard was **wild** because it let me feed it. *Chew the fat.* I'll say the first part of the sentence again. The lizard was **wild** because. Can you finish the sentence so it makes sense? (Idea: *It ran away when it saw me.*) Let's say the whole sentence together. *The lizard was wild because it ran away when it saw me.* Well done! I'm glad we chewed the fat!

- The **grains** of sand were the size of tennis balls. *Chew the fat.* I'll say the first part of the sentence again. The **grains** of sand were. Can you finish the sentence so it makes sense? (Idea: *The size of pencil dots.*) Let's say the whole sentence together. *The grains of sand were the size of pencil dots.* Well done!

(Count the points and declare a winner.) You did a great job of playing *Chew the Fat.*

DAY 5
A map or a globe of the world. Each child will need a copy of the Happy Face Game Test Sheet, BLM B.

Learn About Legends

Today you will learn more about a special kind of folk tale called a legend. What will you learn about? *A legend.*

Folk tales, fairy tales, and legends are all stories that were once told out loud. How are folk tales, fairy tales, and legends the same? (Idea: *They are all stories that were once told out loud.*) A legend is a special kind of folk tale that explains how something came to be. What does a legend explain? (Idea: *How something came to be.*)

Yesterday we retold one of the legends from *Grandmother Spider Brings the Sun* as a rebus story. What does that legend explain? (Idea: *How the possum got its skinny tail with no hair.*)

Listen while I read another legend that Geri Keams included in *Grandmother Spider Brings the Sun.* (Reread pages 13–15, beginning with the third paragraph.) What does this legend explain? (Ideas: *Why buzzards are bald; why buzzards stay away from people.*)

Listen while I read a third legend that Geri Keams included in *Grandmother Spider Brings the Sun.* (Reread page 25–28.) What does this legend explain? (Ideas: *Why there is the shape of a sun in the center of a spider web.*)

Different groups of people have different legends that explain how things around them came to be. The legends in *Grandmother Spider Brings the Sun* come from the Cherokee people. The Cherokee people are the native people who first lived in the area of the United States that included parts of Virginia, Kentucky, Tennessee, North Carolina, South Carolina, Georgia, and Alabama. **(Locate these areas on the map or globe.)** Today many Cherokee people live in Oklahoma. **(Locate this area on the map or globe.)** What people do the legends in *Grandmother Spider Brings the Sun* come from? *The Cherokee.* No one knows when these legends were first told. Do we know when these legends were first told? *No.* But Geri Keams heard these stories, and she wanted to include them in her book.

Assess Vocabulary

 (Hold up a copy of the Happy Face Game Test Sheet, BLM B.)

Today you're going to play the Happy Face Game. When you play the Happy Face Game, it shows me how well you know the hard words you are learning.

If I say something that is true, color in the happy face. What will you do if I say something that is true? *Color in the happy face.*

If I say something that is false, color in the sad face. What will you do if I say something that is false? *Color in the sad face.*

Listen carefully to each item that I say. Don't let me trick you!

Item 1: A **calm** day is a day with no wind. (*True.*)

Item 2: If you are in a **tunnel,** you are in a long wide tube under the ground. (*True.*)

Item 3: Erin **exclaimed** if she said something loudly because she was excited. (*True.*)

Item 4: If someone tells you to **calm down,** they want you to be really noisy. (*False.*)

Item 5: An animal that **soared** would probably have been a bird. (*True.*)

Item 6: **Directions** help you find your way somewhere. (*True.*)

Item 7: A **journey** is a very short trip. (*False.*)

Item 8: If your mom is driving the speed limit, the police will stop her and make her pay a **fine.** (*False.*)

Item 9: A **noble** person is a person who would share whatever he or she had with others. (*True.*)

Item 10: **Grains** of sand are **enormous.** (*False.*)

You did a great job of playing the Happy Face Game!

(Score children's work at a later time. A child must score 9 out of 10 to be at the mastery level. If a child does not achieve mastery, insert the missed words as additional items in the games for next week's lessons. Retest those children individually for the missed items before they take the next mastery test.)

Extensions

Read a Story as a Reward

 (Display copies of several books that you have read since the beginning of the program or other legends. Allow children to choose which book they would like you to read to them as a reward for their hard work.)

(Read the story aloud for enjoyment with minimal interruptions.)

> **Preparation:** Word containers for the Super Words Center. You may wish to remove some words from earlier lessons. Choose words children have mastered.

Introduce the Super Words Center

(Add the new Picture Vocabulary Cards to words from the previous weeks. Show children one of the word containers. If children need more guidance in how to work in the Super Words Center, role-play with two to three children as a demonstration.)

Let's review how to play the game called *What's Missing?*

Let's think about how we work with our words in the Super Words Center.

You will work with a partner in the Super Words Center. Whom will you work with? *A partner.*

First one partner will draw four word cards out of the container and put them on the table so both partners can see. What do you do first? (Idea: *Draw four cards out of the container and put them on the table so both partners can see.*)

Next you will take turns looking at the cards and saying the words the pictures show. What do you do next? (Idea: *We take turns looking at the cards and saying the words the pictures show.*)

Next partner 2 looks away while partner 1 takes one of the four cards and places it facedown on the table away from the other cards. Then partner 1 draws a new card from the container and places it on the table with the other three. Watch while I show you what I mean. (Demonstrate this process with one child as your partner.) When you put down the new card, it's a good idea to mix the cards so they aren't in the same places any more. (Demonstrate this process as you go.)

Now partner 1 says, "What's Missing?" Partner 2 has to use his or her eyes and brain and say what old card has been taken away. After partner 2 has guessed, turn over the facedown card. If partner 2 is correct, he or she gets a point. If partner 2 is not correct, partner 1 gets the point. (Demonstrate this process as you go.)

Next partner 2 has a turn to choose four different cards and the game starts again. What happens next? (Idea: *Partner 2 has a turn to choose four different cards and the game starts again.*)

Have fun playing *What's Missing?*

Preparation: You will need *The Story of Johnny Appleseed* for each day's lesson.

Number the pages of the story to assist you in asking the comprehension questions at the appropriate points in the story.

Post a copy of the Vocabulary Tally Sheet, BLM A, with this week's Picture Vocabulary Cards attached.

Each child will need one copy of the Homework Sheet, BLM 11a.

DAY 1

Introduce Book

This week's book is called *The Story of Johnny Appleseed.* What's the title? *The Story of Johnny Appleseed.*

This book was written by Aliki [Ah-leek-ee]. Who's the author of *The Story of Johnny Appleseed*? *Aliki.*

Aliki also made the pictures for this book. Who is the illustrator of *The Story of Johnny Appleseed*? *Aliki.* Who made the illustrations for this book? *Aliki.*

The cover of a book usually gives us some hints of what the book is about. Let's look at the front cover of *The Story of Johnny Appleseed.* What do you see in the illustration? (Ideas*: A man eating an apple*; *the man is carrying a big backpack and a smaller pouch; his clothes look old and torn.*)

Get ready to make some predictions to your partner about this book. Use the information from the cover to help you.

(Assign each child a partner. Ask the following questions, allowing sufficient time for children to share their predictions with their partners.)

- Whom do you think this story is about?
- What do you think the man is carrying in his pouch?
- Where do you think the story happens?

The Story of Johnny Appleseed
author: Aliki • illustrator: Aliki

Target Vocabulary

Tier II	Tier III
gentle	setting (when)
frontier	legend
dangerous	
adventures	
*imagination	
*appreciated	

*Expanded Target Vocabulary Word

- When do you think the story happens?
- Why do you think the man is smiling?
- How heavy do you think the backpack is?
- Do you think this story is about a real person? Tell why or why not.

(Call on several children to share their predictions with the class.)

Take a Picture Walk

(Encourage children to use target words in their answers.) We're going to take a picture walk through this book. Remember that when we take a picture walk, we look at the pictures and tell what we think will happen in the story.

Pages 1–2. Where is this man? (Idea: *In a forest; in the woods.*) How do you think the man is feeling? (Idea: *Happy.*) How can you tell he is happy? (Idea: *He is smiling; he has picked a flower.*) Why do you think the man is barefoot?

Pages 3–4. What is the man doing in this illustration? (Idea: *Feeding the animals.*) The man looks very peaceful in this illustration. **Peaceful** means that he is calm and quiet and enjoying what he is doing. How does the man look? *Peaceful.*

Pages 5–6. What places are shown in this illustration? (Ideas: *Farms; the ocean.*) How can you tell that's an ocean and not a river or lake? (Idea: *There are large ships on it.*)

Pages 7–8. Do you think this story takes place now or a long time ago? *A long time ago.* What clues tell you that this story takes place a long time ago? (Idea: *There are covered wagons instead of cars.*)

Page 9. What do you think is in the bag the man is giving to the woman?

Page 10. What is happening here? (Idea: *The men are building a fence; one woman is planting seeds; the other woman is raking.*)

Pages 11–12. What do you think the man is telling the children about? Do the children seem to like what the man is telling them? *Yes.* How do you know? (Ideas: *They are watching him and smiling; they look like they are listening carefully.*)

Pages 13–14. What time is it in this illustration? *Nighttime.* Where is the man now? (Idea: *In the woods; in a forest.*) Does the man seem peaceful in this illustration? *Yes.* What clues show you that he is peaceful? (Ideas: *He is kneeling down; he is calmly feeding the animals; he has a small smile on his face.*)

Pages 15–16. What is happening in this illustration? (Idea: *The bear cubs are jumping on the man.*) Does the man seem to be afraid of the bear and her cubs? *No.*

Pages 17–18. Who has the man met in this illustration? (Idea: *Native Americans.*) The people who lived in the United States before people came here from other countries are called Native Americans. What do we call the people who lived in the United States before people came here from other countries? *Native Americans.* What do you think the man is giving to these Native Americans?

Pages 19–20. What is the man doing here? (Idea: *Keeping the groups of people apart.*) How do the two groups of men look? (Idea: *Angry.*) Do you think the man feels peaceful here? *No.* Why not? (Ideas: *The people don't look very calm or happy.*)

Pages 21–22. Where is the man in this illustration? (Idea: *In an apple orchard; in a place that has lots of apple trees.*) Do you think he's happy to be there? *Yes.* What makes you think that? (Ideas: *He has his arms open and looks like he is running towards the children.*) Who do you think these other people are?

Pages 23–24. What season is it in this illustration? *Winter.* What do you think the man is thinking?

Pages 25–26. What is happening here? (Ideas: *The man fell down; he got sick; he died.*)

Pages 27–28. Who is taking care of the man? *The Native Americans.* Do you think the man will get better?

Pages 29–30. What is happening here? (Ideas: *The man is better and is leaving the Native Americans.*)

Page 31. What kind of tree is this? (Idea: *An apple tree.*)

It's your turn to ask me some questions. What would you like to know about the story? (Accept questions. If children tell about the pictures or the story instead of ask questions, prompt them to ask a question.) Ask me a what question. Ask me a who question.

 Read the Book Aloud
(Read the story to children with minimal interruptions.)

Tomorrow we will read the story again, and I will ask you some questions.

Present Target Vocabulary
◎← *Gentle*

In the story, we learned that John Chapman was a brave and gentle man. That means he was a man who did things in a kind, careful way. **Gentle.** Say the word. *Gentle.*

Gentle is a describing word. It tells more about someone. What kind of word is **gentle?** *A describing word.*

If someone is gentle, they do things in a kind, careful way. Say the word that means "do things in a kind, careful way." *Gentle.*

Let's think about some times when someone might be gentle. I'll tell about a time. If someone is being gentle, say "gentle." If not, don't say anything.

- I carefully held my new baby brother. *Gentle.*
- The tiny kitten was shivering as I petted her. *Gentle.*
- My friend was scared, so I spoke to him quietly and put my arm around him. *Gentle.*

- I hugged the new puppy so hard that it squealed.
- Mom pounded the nail into the floor.
- I shook my dad softly to wake him up. *Gentle.*

What describing word means "do things in a kind, careful way"? *Gentle.*

◎⟜ Frontier

In the story, "John Chapman lived on the frontier, in Massachusetts, where the country had been settled." That means he lived on the border between the part of the country where people had settled and the part where they had not moved to yet. **Frontier.** Say the word. *Frontier.*

Frontier is a naming word. It names a place. What kind of word is **frontier?** *A naming word.*

The frontier is the border between the part of the country where people have settled and the part where they have not moved to yet. Say the word that means "the border between the part of the country where people have settled and the part where they have not moved to yet." *Frontier.*

Let's think about some places that might have been called a frontier. I'll tell about a place. If you think it could have been a frontier, say "frontier." If not, don't say anything.

- His great-grandparents had traveled west to Ohio so they could buy land. *Frontier.*
- They lived in New York City.
- Near the border of China and Mongolia there were not many people. *Frontier.*
- The soldiers were given land in Virginia where not many people lived. *Frontier.*
- Shanghai was the biggest city in China.
- Her family lived in a small house on a busy street.

What naming word means "the border between the part of the country where people have settled and the part where they have not moved to yet"? *Frontier.*

◎⟜ Dangerous

In the story, "the pioneers made the long and dangerous journey though the wilderness." That means the journey was not safe.

Dangerous is a describing word. It tells more about something. What kind of word is **dangerous?** *A describing word.*

When something is dangerous, it is not safe. Say the word that means "not safe." *Dangerous.*

Let's think about some things that could be dangerous. I'll name something. If you think that thing is dangerous, say "dangerous." If not, don't say anything.

- Riding your bicycle without holding on to the handlebars. *Dangerous.*
- An angry bear. *Dangerous.*
- Wearing a lifejacket in a boat.
- Riding in a car with no seatbelt. *Dangerous.*
- Walking on the sidewalk.
- Playing near the edge of a cliff. *Dangerous.*

What describing word means "not safe"? *Dangerous.*

◎⟜ Adventures

In the story, the children liked to listen to stories of Johnny Appleseed's adventures. That means they liked to hear stories about his dangerous and exciting journeys. **Adventures.** Say the word. *Adventures.*

Adventures is a naming word. It names things. What kind of word is **adventures?** *A naming word.*

Adventures are dangerous or exciting journeys. Say the word that means "dangerous or exciting journeys." *Adventures.*

Let's think about some adventures. I'll tell about something. If what I tell about is an adventure, say "adventure." If not, don't say anything.

- Rick sailed around the world alone. *Adventure.*
- Joshua went to school.
- Neil Armstrong traveled to the moon. *Adventure.*
- Edmund Hillary climbed to the top of Mt. Everest, the tallest mountain in the world. *Adventure.*
- The children played with their new puppy.
- David Livingstone spent twenty-one years exploring the jungles of Africa. *Adventure.*

What naming word means "dangerous or exciting journeys"? *Adventures.*

(See Lesson 1, page 3, for instructions.)

Assign Homework

(Homework Sheet, BLM 11a: See the Introduction for homework instructions.)

DAY 2

Preparation: Picture Vocabulary Cards for *gentle, frontier, dangerous, adventures.*

Read and Discuss Story

(Read story to children. Ask the following questions at the specified points. Encourage children to use target words in their answers.)

Page 1. Who is this story about? (Idea: *John Chapman.*) What kinds of things does John Chapman enjoy doing? (Idea: *He enjoys being out-of-doors; walking in the woods; thinking.*)

Page 3. What does John think he can do with the seeds from his apple? (Idea: *He can plant them and they will grow into trees.*)

Page 6. Why do you think the people are leaving to travel west?

Page 8. What is different about the way John Chapman travels? (Ideas: *He travels in his bare feet; he carries no weapons.*) What does John Chapman bring with him as he travels west? (Idea: *A sack of apple seeds and a pot for cooking.*)

Page 9. Why do people start calling John Chapman Johnny Appleseed? (Idea: *Because he plants apple seeds and also gives apple seeds to everyone he meets.*)

Page 10. What are the pioneer families doing? (Ideas: *Clearing the land; building new homes.*) How does Johnny Appleseed help them? (Ideas: *He helps clear the land and build the houses; he gives them seeds to plant for apple trees.*)

Page 12. Why do the children especially love Johnny Appleseed? (Idea: *He tells them stories about his adventures.*)

Page 13. Is it dangerous for Johnny to sleep in the woods? *No.* Why not? (Idea: *The animals are his friends.*)

Page 16. How do you think Johnny Appleseed feels when he sees the bear cubs running toward him? (Idea: *Calm.*) Why do you think he is calm? (Idea: *He knows the animals are his friends and has no reason to be afraid.*)

Page 18. What word does the author use for Native Americans? *Indians.* Why are the Native Americans nice to Johnny Appleseed but not to other white men? (Ideas: *Johnny Appleseed is kind to them; other white men chase them out of their homes.*)

Page 20. Why does Johnny Appleseed want to make peace between the pioneers and the Native Americans? (Ideas: *He does not like fighting; he thinks all men should live together like brothers.*)

Page 21. (Read to "cider mills.") A cider mill is a place where they use apples to make cider or juice. What do we call a place where they use apples to make cider? *A cider mill.* (Read to the end of the page.) How does Johnny Appleseed get more seeds when he runs out? (Ideas: *People save them for him; he collects them from the cider mills.*) How do there get to be so many apple trees? (Ideas: *Johnny Appleseed travels around the country planting apple seeds; he gives sacks of apple seeds to people who plant them.*)

Page 23. Why is Johnny afraid his trees might die? (Idea: *Trees need the warm spring weather to grow.*)

Page 26. How do you think Johnny Appleseed becomes sick?

Page 27. Do you think the Native Americans would have helped Johnny Appleseed if he had not been kind to them? *No.* Why not? (Idea: *They don't like white men because the white men keep chasing them out of their homes.*)

Page 29. How do you think Johnny Appleseed feels when he sees that spring has finally arrived? (Ideas: *Happy; excited; relieved.*) What do you think Johnny Appleseed will do next? (Idea: *Continue traveling around planting apple trees.*)

Page 31. What kind of person is Johnny Appleseed? (Ideas: *Kind; gentle; peaceful; generous.*) What is the gift that Johnny Appleseed left for us? *Apple trees.*

Review Vocabulary

(Display the Picture Vocabulary Cards. Point to each card as you say the word. Ask children to repeat each word after you.) These pictures show **gentle, frontier, dangerous,** and **adventures.**

- What naming word means "dangerous or exciting journeys"? *Adventures.*
- What describing word means "do things in a kind, careful way"? *Gentle.*
- What describing word means "not safe"? *Dangerous.*
- What naming word means "the border between the part of the country where people have settled and the part where they have not moved to yet"? *Frontier.*

Extend Vocabulary

 Gentle

In *The Story of Johnny Appleseed* we learned that **gentle** means "do things in a kind, careful way."

Here's a new way to use the word **gentle.**

- A **gentle** breeze blew through the leaves. Say the sentence.
- The mother used a **gentle** soap to bathe the baby. Say the sentence.
- Her **gentle** touch calmed the injured animal. Say the sentence.

In these sentences, gentle is a describing word that means soft or mild. What word means "soft or mild"? *Gentle.*

Present Expanded Target Vocabulary

Imagination

In the story, John thought if he "gathered seeds and planted them [the] land would soon be filled with apple trees." He used his mind to create pictures of things that hadn't happened yet. **Imagination.** Say the word. *Imagination.*

Imagination is a naming word. It names a part of your mind. What kind of word is **imagination?** *A naming word.*

Your imagination is the part of your mind that lets you make pictures of things that are not real or that haven't happened yet. Say the word that means "the part of your mind that lets you make pictures of things that are not real or that haven't happened yet." *Imagination.*

(Correct any incorrect responses, and repeat the item at the end of the sequence.)

Let's think about some things that might come from someone's imagination. I'll tell about something. If you think it comes from someone's imagination, say "imagination." If not, don't say anything.

- A horse with wings. *Imagination.*
- A bean stalk that could grow to the clouds. *Imagination.*
- A wonderful world called Middle Earth where hobbits live. *Imagination.*
- An ordinary house.
- Lunch with talking cows and pigs. *Imagination.*
- A street with nothing special about it.

What naming word means "the part of your mind that lets you make pictures of things that are not real or haven't happened yet"? *Imagination.*

Appreciated

In the story, Johnny Appleseed was kind to the Native Americans and gave them seeds and herbs that they used as medicine. Later, these Native Americans gave Johnny medicine and took care of him when he was sick. The Native Americans appreciated Johnny for giving them seeds and herbs. Johnny appreciated the Native Americans for taking care of him when he was sick. **Appreciated.** Say the word. *Appreciated.*

Appreciated is an action word. It tells what people did. What kind of word is **appreciated?** *An action word.*

If you appreciated something someone did for you, you are thankful for what they did. Say the word that means "thankful for what someone did for you." *Appreciated.*

Let's think about some times when someone might have appreciated what someone else did. I'll tell about a time. If you think someone would have appreciated what that person did, say "appreciated." If not, don't say anything.

- Tanis washed the kitchen floor for her mother without being asked. *Appreciated.*
- Geordie tracked mud all over the kitchen floor.
- Bill read stories to his little brother when he was sick. *Appreciated.*
- Everyone was quiet on Saturday morning so Daddy could sleep a little later. *Appreciated.*
- The children were sitting quietly at their desks ready for their lesson when the teacher came in. *Appreciated.*
- Adam didn't make his bed in the morning.

What action word means "thankful for what someone did for you"? *Appreciated.*

DAY 3

Preparation: Activity Sheet, BLM 11b.

Retell Story

Today I'll show you the pictures Aliki made for *The Story of Johnny Appleseed.* As I show you the pictures, I'll call on one of you to tell the class that part of the story.

Tell me what happens at the **beginning** of the story. (Show the pictures on pages 1–4. Call on a child to tell what's happening.)

Tell me what happens in the **middle** of the story. (Show the pictures on pages 5–30. Call on a child to tell what's happening. Encourage use of the target words when appropriate. Model use as necessary.)

Tell me what happens at the **end** of the story. (Show the picture on page 31. Call on a child to tell what's happening.)

Play Chew the Fat

Today you will play a game called *Chew the Fat.* A long time ago, when people wanted to sit and talk about things that were happening in their lives, they would say they would sit and "chew the fat."

In this game, I will say some sentences with our vocabulary words in them. If I use the vocabulary word correctly, say, "Well done!" If I use the word incorrectly, say, "Chew the fat." That means that you want to talk about how I used the word.

I'll say the beginning of the sentence again. If you can make the sentence end so that it makes sense, you'll get a point. If you can't, I get the point.

Let's practice: The **gentle** giant was mean to everyone. *Chew the fat.* Let's chew the fat. The first part of the sentence stays the same. I'll say the first part. The **gentle** giant. How can we finish the sentence so it makes sense? (Idea: *Was kind to everyone.*) Let's say the whole sentence together now. *The gentle giant was kind to everyone.* Well done! I'm glad we chewed the fat!

Let's do another one together. It is **dangerous** to wear your helmet when you ride your bicycle. *Chew the fat.* The first part of the sentence stays the same. I'll say the first part. It is **dangerous** to. How can we finish the sentence so it makes sense? (Idea: *Not wear your helmet when you ride your bicycle.*) Let's say the whole sentence now. *It is dangerous to not wear your helmet when you ride your bicycle.* Well done! I'm glad we chewed the fat!

Let's try one more. The farmers lived on the **frontier** when they lived between the empty prairies and the city. *Well done!* I used the word **frontier** correctly, so you said, "Well done!"

Now you're ready to play the game. (Draw a T-chart on the board for keeping score. Children earn one point for each correct answer. If they make an error, correct them as you normally would, and record one point for yourself. Repeat missed words at the end of the game.)

- The family had many **adventures** when … they stayed inside their house. *Chew the fat.* I'll say the first part of the sentence again. The family had many **adventures** when. Can you finish the sentence so it makes sense? (Idea: *They traveled around the world.*) Let's say the whole sentence together. *The family had many adventures when they traveled around the world.* Well done! I'm glad we chewed the fat!
- The **gentle** breeze … broke branches off the trees. *Chew the fat.* I'll say the first part of the sentence again. The **gentle** breeze. Can you finish the sentence so it makes sense? (Idea: *Moved the leaves a little bit.*) Let's say the whole sentence together. *The gentle breeze*

moved the leaves a little bit. Well done! I'm glad we chewed the fat!

- David Livingstone had many **adventures** when he spent twenty-one years exploring the jungles of Africa. *Well done!*
- A person with **imagination** … cannot make pictures in her mind that have not happened yet. *Chew the fat.* I'll say the first part of the sentence again. A person with **imagination.** Can you finish the sentence so it makes sense? (Idea: *Can make pictures in her mind of things that haven't happened yet.*) Let's say the whole sentence together. *A person with imagination can make pictures in her mind of things that haven't happened yet.* Well done!
- My parents **appreciate** it when … I don't pick up my toys. *Chew the fat.* I'll say the first part of the sentence again. My parents **appreciate** it when. Can you finish the sentence so it makes sense? (Idea: *I pick up my toys.*) Let's say the whole sentence together. *My parents appreciate it when I pick up my toys.* Well done!

(Count the points and declare a winner.) You did a great job of playing *Chew the Fat.*

Complete the Activity Sheet

(Give each child a copy of the Activity Sheet, BLM 11b. Read the retelling of the story, saying "blank" as you reach each blank. Have children say the appropriate word to complete the sentence. Have them sound out and print the word on the line. When the story is complete, read the story, having children chime in with the printed words. You may wish to have the children draw and color a picture of Johnny Appleseed or an apple tree on the bottom of the sheet.)

Johnny Appleseed was a real **man.** He had bare **feet.** He wore a pot **on** his head.

He had a sack of apple **seeds.** He planted **seeds.** He gave away **seeds.** We **can** still **see** many of **his** apple **trees** today.

Preparation: Prepare a sheet of chart paper, landscape direction, titled *The Story of Johnny Appleseed.* Underneath the title, draw 8 boxes connected by arrows.

Underneath the 8 boxes, draw 9 boxes connected by arrows.

See the Introduction for Week 11's chart.

Literary Analysis (Cumulative Review)

Let's think about what we already know about how books are made.

- What do we call the name of the book? *Title.*
- What do we call the person who writes the story? *Author.*
- What do we call the person who draws the pictures? *Illustrator.*
- What do we call the people or animals a story is about? *Characters.*
- What do we call the pictures the illustrator makes? *Illustrations.*
- What is one thing the setting of a story tells? *Where a story happens.*

Let's sing The Story Song to help us remember these important things about books.

(See the Introduction for the complete Story Song.)

Today we will learn more about how stories are made.

The setting of a story tells two things. One thing the setting tells is where the story happens. What is one thing the setting tells? *Where the story happens.* The second thing the setting tells is when the story happens. What is the second thing the setting tells? *When the story happens.*

Let's look at the pictures and talk about the story to figure out where *The Story of Johnny Appleseed* happens.

(Follow the procedure established in Lessons 8, 9, and 10 to identify <u>where</u> the story happens. Record responses in the first row of boxes. (Ideas: *In the forest; on the frontier; in the wilderness; at the pioneers' homes; in the* woods; at the Indian village; in the apple orchard; at the Indian village; near an old apple tree.)

(Record responses in the second row of boxes.) Now let's think about when this story happens.

Page 1. (Read the sentence, "Many years ago when America was a new country, there lived a brave and gentle man named John Chapman.") When does the story begin? (Idea: *Many years ago.*)

Page 3. (Read the sentences, "One day after a long walk, John sat under a tree to rest. He felt the warm sun on his back and the fresh grass tickling his toes." Turn to pages 5 and 6.) When does this part of the story happen? (Idea: *In the summer.*)

Pages 13–14. When does this part of the story happen? (Idea: *At night.*)

Page 16. (Read the sentence, "One day, as Johnny was eating lunch, he heard a noise, and three little bear cubs ran from behind a tree.") When does this part of the story happen? (Idea: *One day; at lunchtime.*)

Page 21. (Read the sentence, "Many years passed.") When does this part of the story happen? (Idea: *Many years later.*)

Pages 23–24. When does this part of the story happen? (Idea: *In the winter.*)

Pages 29–30. (Read the sentence, "And one day, Johnny Appleseed opened his eyes." Show the illustration on page 30, pointing to the trees.) When did this part of the story happen? (Idea: *One day in the spring.*)

Page 31. (Read the sentence, "We can still see them today.") When does the end of the story happen? (Idea: *Today.*)

(Point to the words as you say each time.) *Many years ago, in the summer, at night, one day at lunchtime, many years later, in the winter, one day in spring.* (Draw a line underneath these 8 boxes.) These things all happened when Johnny Appleseed was having his adventures. Another way of saying when Johnny Appleseed was having his adventures is in the past. When does this part of the story happen? *In the past.* (Write *in the past* underneath the line.)

The ending of the story happened much, much later. (Draw a line under today.) The ending of the story happens today; right now. Another way of saying right now is **in the present.** When does the ending of the story happen? *In the present.* (Write *in the present* underneath the line.)

When is the setting of *The Story of Johnny Appleseed*? (Idea: *Both in the past and in the present.*) You were great detectives! You used the clues and figured out when the story happened.

Today you learned about both of the parts of the setting of *The Story of Johnny Appleseed.* You learned about where and when the story happened.

Now, we'll learn a new verse to The Story Song. This time, though, we'll just change the verse we already sing about setting so that it tells both when and where. Instead of singing *Setting tells when it happened,* we'll sing, *Setting tells when and where.* We can use one verse to tell about both of the things that setting tells about.

(See the Introduction for the complete Story Song.)

Play Chew the Fat (Cumulative Review)

Today you will play a game called *Chew the Fat.* Remember that a long time ago, when people wanted to sit and talk about things that were happening in their lives, they would say they would sit and "chew the fat." In this game, I will say some sentences with our vocabulary words in them. If I use the vocabulary word correctly, say, "Well done!"

If I use the word incorrectly, say, "Chew the fat." That means that you want to talk about how I used the word. I'll say the beginning of the sentence again. If you can make the sentence end so that it makes sense, you'll get a point. If you can't, I get the point.

Let's practice: The principal **appreciated** it when the children tracked mud into the school. *Chew the fat.* Let's chew the fat. The first part of the sentence stays the same. I'll say the first part. The principal **appreciated** it when. How can we finish the sentence so it makes sense? (Idea: *The children wiped their muddy feet at the door.*) Let's say the whole sentence together now. *The principal appreciated it when the children wiped their muddy feet at the door.* Well done! I'm glad we chewed the fat!

Let's do another one together. Elsa went on an **adventure** when she watched a movie about Africa. *Chew the fat.* The first part of the sentence stays the same. I'll say the first part. Elsa went on an **adventure** when. How can we finish the sentence so that it makes sense? (Idea: *She went to Africa.*) Let's say the whole sentence now. *Elsa went on an adventure when she went to Africa.* Well done! I'm glad we chewed the fat!

Now you're ready to play the game. (Draw a T-chart on the board for keeping score. Children earn one point for each correct answer. If they make an error, correct them as you normally would, and record one point for yourself. Repeat missed words at the end of the game.)

- Alan knew he was on the **frontier** when he saw buildings all around him. *Chew the fat.* I'll say the first part of the sentence again. Alan knew he was on the **frontier** when. Can you finish the sentence so it makes sense? (Idea: *He saw buildings behind him and forests ahead of him.*) Let's say the whole sentence together. *Alan knew he was on the frontier when he saw buildings behind him and forests ahead of him.* Well done! I'm glad we chewed the fat!
- The **journey** lasted a long, long time. *Well done!*
- The twins were **gentle** with their dolls when they threw them down on the floor. *Chew the fat.* I'll say the first part of the sentence again. The twins were **gentle** with their dolls when. Can you finish the sentence so it makes sense? (Idea: *They set them carefully on the bed.*) Let's say the whole sentence together. *The twins were gentle with their dolls when they set them carefully on the bed.* Well done! I'm glad we chewed the fat!
- The audience used its **imagination** to pretend the play was taking place under the sea. *Well done!*

- The dancer was **awkward** when he moved gracefully across the floor. *Chew the fat.* I'll say the first part of the sentence again. The dancer was **awkward** when. Can you finish the sentence so it makes sense? (Idea: *He kept falling down.*) Let's say the whole sentence together. *The dancer was awkward when he kept falling down.* Well done!
- The big child **bullied** the little children when she pushed them gently on the swings. *Chew the fat.* I'll say the first part of the sentence again. The big child **bullied** the little children when she. Can you finish the sentence so it makes sense? (Idea: *Pushed them too hard on the swings.*) Let's say the whole sentence together. *The big child bullied the little children when she pushed them too hard on the swings.* Well done! I'm glad we chewed the fat!
- It is **dangerous** to carry scissors with the points up. *Well done!*
- The workers were **exhausted** when they worked for only one hour. *Chew the fat.* I'll say the first part of the sentence again. The workers were **exhausted** when. Can you finish the sentence so it makes sense? (Idea: *They worked hard all day.*) Let's say the whole sentence together. *The workers were exhausted when they worked hard all day.* Well done! I'm glad we chewed the fat!
- The scouts were **gathering** wood for the fire when they left the sticks in the woods. *Chew the fat.* I'll say the first part of the sentence again. The scouts were **gathering** wood for the fire when. Can you finish the sentence so it makes sense? (Idea: *They were picking up sticks and putting them in a pile.*) Let's say the whole sentence together. *The scouts were gathering wood for the fire when they were picking up sticks and putting them in a pile.* Well done! I'm glad we chewed the fat!

(Count the points and declare a winner.) You did a great job of playing *Chew the Fat.*

Learn About Legends

Today you will learn more about a special kind of folk tale called a legend. What will you learn about? *A legend.*

Folk tales, fairy tales, and legends are all stories that were once told out loud. How are folk tales, fairy tales, and legends the same? (Idea: *They are all stories that were once told out loud.*) A legend is a special kind of folk tale that explains how something came to be. What does a legend explain? (Idea: *How something came to be.*)

In *Loon Lake,* we read a legend about the loon. What did that legend explain? (Idea: *How the loon got its necklace of white feathers.*)

In *Grandmother Spider Brings the Sun,* we read a legend about a possum. What did this legend explain? (Idea: *How the possum got its skinny tail.*)

We also read a legend about a buzzard. What did this legend explain? (Ideas: *Why buzzards are bald; why buzzards stay away from people.*)

We also read a legend about a spider's web. What did this legend explain? (Ideas: *Why there is the shape of a sun in the center of a spider web.*)

Different groups of people have different legends that explain how things around them came to be. The legend of the loon's necklace comes from the Tsimshian people. The legends in *Grandmother Spider Brings the Sun* come from the Cherokee people. No one knows when these legends were first told. Do we know when these legends were first told? *No.*

The Story of Johnny Appleseed is an American legend. What does it explain? (Idea: *Why there are apple trees growing all across the United States.*)

Johnny Appleseed was a real person. His name was John Chapman. Was Johnny Appleseed

a real person? *Yes.* What was his name? *John Chapman.*

As more and more people told the story of Johnny Appleseed, they added fantastic details to make the story more fun to tell. After a while, people couldn't remember which things were true and which things were made up from the storytellers' imaginations. Because we don't know anymore which parts of the story are true and which parts are made up from the storytellers' imaginations, we call this kind of legend a tall tale. What kind of legend is Johnny Appleseed? *A tall tale.*

Which parts of this tall tale do you think are true? Which parts of this tall tale do you think are made up from the storytellers' imaginations?

Assess Vocabulary

 (Give each child a copy of the Happy Face Game Test Sheet, BLM B.)

Today you're going to play the Happy Face Game. When you play the Happy Face Game, it shows me how well you know the hard words you are learning.

If I say something that is true, color in the happy face. What will you do if I say something that is true? *Color in the happy face.*

If I say something that is false, color in the sad face. What will you do if I say something that is false? *Color in the sad face.*

Listen carefully to each item that I say. Don't let me trick you!

Item 1: The **frontier** is the border between the part of the country where people have settled and the part where they have not moved to yet. (*True.*)

Item 2: When something is **dangerous,** it is safe. (*False.*)

Item 3: **Gentle** can mean soft or mild and also to do things in a kind and careful way. (*True.*)

Item 4: A flying banana is something from your **imagination.** (*True.*)

Item 5: **Adventures** are dangerous or exciting journeys. (*True.*)

Item 6: If you **appreciated** what someone did for you, you wish they hadn't done it. (*False.*)

Item 7: A **noble** person would share whatever she had with you. (*True.*)

Item 8: If you are **sensitive,** you might be able to smell things very well. (*True.*)

Item 9: If something is **tempting,** you really want to have it. (*True.*)

Item 10: If you are **trespassing,** someone has allowed you to go on their property. (*False.*)

You did a great job of playing the Happy Face Game!

(Score children's work at a later time. A child must score 9 out of 10 to be at the mastery level. If a child does not achieve mastery, insert the missed words as additional items in the games for next week's lessons. Retest those children individually for the missed items before they take the next mastery test.)

Extensions

Read a Story as a Reward

 (Display copies of several books that you have read since the beginning of the program or other legends that are tall tales. Allow children to choose which book they would like you to read to them as a reward for their hard work.)

(Read the story aloud for enjoyment with minimal interruptions.)

Preparation: Word containers for the Super Words Center. You may wish to remove some words from earlier lessons. Choose words children have mastered.

Introduce the Super Words Center

(Add the new Picture Vocabulary Cards to words from the previous weeks. Show children one of the word containers. If children need more guidance in how to work in the Super Words Center, role-play with two to three children as a demonstration.)

Let's review how to play the game called *What's Missing?*

Let's think about how we work with our words in the Super Words Center.

You will work with a partner in the Super Words Center. Whom will you work with? *A partner.*

First one partner will draw four word cards out of the container and put them on the table so both partners can see. What do you do first? (Idea: *Draw four cards out of the container and put them on the table so both partners can see.*)

Next you will take turns looking at the cards and saying the words the pictures show. What do you do next? (Idea: *We take turns looking at the cards and saying the words the pictures show.*)

Next partner 2 looks away while partner 1 takes one of the four cards and places it facedown on the table away from the other cards. Then partner 1 draws a new card from the container and places it on the table with the other three. Watch while I show you what I mean. (Demonstrate this process with one child as your partner.) When you put down the new card, it's a good idea to mix the cards so they aren't in the same places any more. (Demonstrate this process as you go.)

Now partner 1 says, "What's Missing?" Partner 2 has to use his or her eyes and brain and say what old card has been taken away. After partner 2 has guessed, turn over the facedown card. If partner 2 is correct, he or she gets a point. If partner 2 is not correct, partner 1 gets the point. (Demonstrate this process as you go.)

Next partner 2 has a turn to choose four different cards and the game starts again. What happens next? (Idea: *Partner 2 has a turn to choose four different cards and the game starts again.*)

Have fun playing *What's Missing?*

Preparation: You will need *The Apple Pie Tree* for each day's lesson.

Number the pages of the story to assist you in asking questions at appropriate points.

Post a copy of the Vocabulary Tally Sheet, BLM A, with this week's Picture Vocabulary Cards attached.

Each child will need one copy of the Homework Sheet, BLM 12a.

DAY 1

Introduce Book

This week's book is called *The Apple Pie Tree*. What's the title? *The Apple Pie Tree.*

This book was written by Zoe [**zoh**-ee] Hall. Who's the author of *The Apple Pie Tree*? *Zoe Hall.*

Shari Halpern made the pictures for this book. Who's the illustrator of *The Apple Pie Tree*? *Shari Halpern.* Who made the illustrations for this book? *Shari Halpern.*

The cover of a book usually gives us some hints of what the book is about. (Open the book so children can see the front and back covers at the same time.) Let's look at the cover of *The Apple Pie Tree*. What do you see in the illustration?

(Ideas: *A tree; branches; leaves; apples; two robins; a nest; a butterfly; a bee.*)

(Assign each child a partner.) Get ready to make some predictions to your partner about this book. Use the information from the cover to help you.

(Ask the following questions, allowing sufficient time for children to share their predictions with their partners.)

- Who are the characters in this story? (Who do you think this story is about?)
- What do you think the story is about?
- Where do you think the story happens?

Target Vocabulary

Tier II	Tier III
bare	setting (when)
appear	pattern
blossom	linear
petals	collage
*seasons	
*present	

*Expanded Target Vocabulary Word

- When do you think the story happens?
- Why do you think the robins built the nest?
- How many apples are on the tree?
- Do you think this story is about real things? Tell why or why not.

(Call on several children to share their predictions with the class.)

Take a Picture Walk

(Encourage children to use target words in their answers.) We're going to take a picture walk through this book. Remember that when we take a picture walk, we look at the pictures and tell what we think will happen in the story.

Page 1. What do you see in this illustration? (Idea: *An apple; a big container with something white in it: flour; a small container with something white in it: sugar; two brown sticks; a rectangle of something yellow: butter.*)

(**Note:** It isn't necessary for children to identify the ingredients, although some may do so based on the title.)

Pages 2–3. What do you think is happening here? (Idea: *The children are looking out the window at the tree; the tree has no leaves.*)

Pages 4–5. Where are the children? (Idea: *Outside.*) How is the tree different? (Idea: *It has leaves.*) What else do you see in the tree? (Ideas: *Two robins; a nest.*) What are the birds doing? (Idea: *Building the nest.*) Why do you think so? (Idea: *One robin has a twig in its mouth.*)

Pages 6–7. How is the tree different? (Idea: *It has flowers.*) How is the robin's nest different? (Ideas: *It's bigger; it has three eggs in it.*)

Pages 8–9. How is the tree different? (Idea: *The flowers are bigger; the flowers have opened.*) How is the robin's nest different? (Idea: *It has three baby birds in it.*) What is the big robin doing? (Idea: *Feeding her babies, giving worms to the babies.*)

Pages 10–11. How is the tree different? (Idea: *The flowers are even bigger.*) How are the baby birds different? (Ideas: *They have brown feathers on their heads, they have red breasts.*) What do you see on two of the flowers? *Bees.*

Pages 12–13. What is happening here? (Ideas: *The flowers are floating to the ground; the robins are flying; the cat is chasing the flowers.*)

Pages 14–15. What is happening here? (Ideas: *It's raining; the wind is blowing; the birds are all in the nest.*) How is the tree different? (Idea: *There are no flowers.*)

Pages 16–17. How is the tree different? (Idea: *There are little green and brown round things on it; there are tiny apples on it.*) What are the robins doing? *Flying.*

Pages 18–19. What are the children doing? (Ideas: *Playing in the sprinkler; playing in the water.*) How is the tree different? (Idea: *The apples are bigger.*) How are the baby birds different? (Idea: *They are bigger.*)

Pages 20–21. How is the tree different? (Ideas: *It's full of leaves; the apples are bigger; some of the apples are red.*) Where are the baby birds? (Ideas: *Gone; they're not there.*) What are the deer doing? *Eating the apples.*

Pages 22–23. What is happening here? (Ideas: *Someone is picking an apple; the person is on a ladder.*)

Pages 24–25. What is happening here? (Ideas: *They are making a pie; the girl is sprinkling something on the apples; the little boy is holding a piece of apple peel.*)

Pages 26–27. What do you see in this illustration? (Ideas: *An apple pie; a whole apple; an apple core; some pieces of apple peel.*)

Pages 28–29. What is happening here? (Ideas: *The children are eating the pie.*)

Let's talk about how Shari Halpern made the illustrations for *The Apple Pie Tree.*

There are lots of different ways to make illustrations for a book: the artist can paint them; draw them with a pen or pencil; make them with markers, crayons, pastels, or chalk; cut out different pieces of paper and glue them together. How do you think Shari Halpern made her illustrations? (Idea: *She cut out different pieces of paper and glued them together.*)

Pages 2–3. Sometimes Shari Halpern used plain paper in her illustrations. Which part of the illustration do you think was made from plain paper? (Ideas: *The blue walls; the faces; the green parts of the eyes.*)

Sometimes Shari Halpern used paper that already had a pattern on it. Which part of the illustration do you think was made from that kind of paper? (Idea: *The curtain.*)

Sometimes Shari Halpern painted paper to get the exact colors she wanted. Which part of the illustration do you think was made from painted paper? (Ideas: *The tree; the ground; the children's hair.*)

When an artist makes an illustration by cutting out different pieces of paper and gluing them together, we say the artist made a collage. What do you call an illustration that is made by cutting out different pieces of paper and gluing them together? *A collage.*

Shari Halpern made her illustrations by cutting out different pieces of paper and gluing them together, so we say her illustrations are collages. What kind of illustrations did Shari Halpern make for *The Apple Pie Tree*? *Collages.*

It's your turn to ask me some questions. What would you like to know about the story? (Accept questions. If children tell about the pictures or the story instead of ask questions, prompt them to ask a question.) Ask me a why question. Ask me a when question.

Read the Book Aloud
(Read the story to children with minimal interruptions.)

Tomorrow we will read the story again, and I will ask you some questions.

Present Target Vocabulary

◎— Bare

In the story, the apple tree was bare in the winter. That means the branches are not covered with leaves. **Bare.** Say the word. *Bare.*

Bare is a describing word. It tells more about the tree. What kind of word is **bare?** *A describing word.*

If something is bare, nothing is covering it. Say the word that means "nothing is covering it." *Bare.*

(Correct any incorrect responses, and repeat the item at the end of the sequence.)

Let's think about some things that might have been bare. I'll tell about something. If you think that thing is bare, say "bare." If not, don't say anything.

- She had no shoes or socks on her feet. *Bare.*
- John was wearing overalls and a heavy coat.
- There were no pictures on the walls. *Bare.*
- The rock was covered with moss.
- When the family moved, their house was empty. *Bare.*
- All of the leaves had fallen off the tree. *Bare.*

What describing word means "nothing is covering it"? *Bare.*

◎— Appear

In the story, flower buds appeared on the branches. That means buds could be seen on the branches. **Appear.** Say the word. *Appear.*

Appear is an action word. It tells what happens. What kind of word is **appear?** *An action word.*

When things appear, they can be seen. Say the word that means "can be seen." *Appear.* What word means "can be seen"? *Appear.*

We learned a word in Week 9 that means things can't be seen anymore. That word is **disappear.** Say the word **disappear.** *Disappear.*

Appear and **disappear** are opposites. What kind of words are **appear** and **disappear?** *Opposites.*

What word is the opposite of **appear?** *Disappear.* What word is the opposite of **disappear?** *Appear.*

I'll tell about someone or something. If what I tell about appears, say "appear." If what I tell about disappears, say "disappear."

- The sun goes down. *Disappear.*
- Uncle Josh drives up in his new car. *Appear.*
- The otter swims past us and then, "Sploot!" He is gone! *Disappear.*
- When my mom makes spaghetti, I eat my plateful really fast. *Disappear.*
- My puppy, Dexter, runs up and jumps on me. *Appear.*
- Joe and Amy suddenly fall into a deep hole. *Disappear.*

What action word means "can be seen"? *Appear.* What action word means "can't be seen anymore"? *Disappear.*

◎— Blossom

In the story, the tree was covered in blossoms. That means the tree was covered with flowers that will turn into fruit. **Blossom.** Say the word. *Blossom.*

Blossom is a naming word. It names the things covering the tree. What kind of word is **blossom?** *A naming word.*

A blossom is a flower that will grow into fruit. Say the word that means "a flower that will grow into fruit." *Blossom.*

Let's think about some things that might blossom. If the thing I name might blossom, say "blossom." If not, don't say anything.

- Cherry tree. *Blossom.*
- Broom.
- Pear tree. *Blossom.*
- Blackberry bush. *Blossom.*
- Apple tree. *Blossom.*
- Car.

What naming word means "a flower that will turn into fruit"? *Blossom.*

◎ Petals

In the story, breezes made the petals fall. (Draw a simple flower with petals on the board. Point to the petals.) That means these outer parts of the flower fell to the ground. **Petals.** Say the word. *Petals.*

Petals is a naming word. It names a part of a flower. What kind of word is **petals?** *A naming word.*

Petals are the outer parts of a flower. Say the word that means "the outer parts of a flower." *Petals.*

Let's think about petals. I'll name something. If what I say could have petals, say "petals." If not, don't say anything.

- Cherry blossom. *Petals.*
- A clock.
- Rose. *Petals.*
- A table.
- Your uncle Jim.
- Water lily. *Petals.*

What naming word means "the outer parts of a flower"? *Petals.*

Introduce the Vocabulary Tally Sheet
(See Lesson 1, page 3, for instructions.)

Assign Homework
(Homework Sheet, BLM 12a: See the Introduction for homework instructions.)

DAY 2

Preparation: Picture Vocabulary Cards for *bare, appear, blossom, petals.* You may want to have a cinnamon stick available.

Read and Discuss Story

(Read story to children. Ask the following questions at specified points. Encourage children to use target words in their answers.)

Page 1. What do you think is the answer to the question? *Apples.* (Point to the illustration.) These are the things you need to make something. We call the things that you need to make something ingredients. What word means "the things you need to make something"? *Ingredients.* That's right, all these things are the ingredients you need to make apple pie. Let's name these ingredients. (Ideas: *Apples; flour; sugar; butter; cinnamon.*)

(**Note:** You may wish to show children a cinnamon stick and let them smell it.)

Page 2. When does this part of the story happen? *In winter.* What does the tree look like in winter? (Ideas: *Bare; brown; it has no leaves.*)

Page 4. When does this part of the story happen? *In spring.* What does the tree look like in spring? (Ideas: *It is getting leaves.*) What else happens to this tree in spring? (Idea: *Robins build a nest in it.*)

Page 7. What else happens to the tree in spring? *Buds appear.* What do the robins do? (Ideas: *Lay eggs in their nest; guard the eggs.*)

Pages 8–9. What else happens in the spring? (Idea: *The flower buds open; the baby robins hatch.*)

Page 11. What else happens in spring? (Idea: *The tree is covered with blossoms; the baby robins start to get their feathers.*)

Page 12. What else happens in spring? (Idea: *The breezes blow; the petals fall; the little birds learn to fly.*)

Page 14. What protects the birds on stormy, rainy days? (Idea: *The tree.*)

Page 17. What happens to the blossoms? (Idea: *They turn into small green apples.*)

Pages 18–19. When does this part of the story happen? *In summer.* What happens to the apples in summer? (Idea: *They get bigger.*) What happens to the baby robins in summer? (Idea: *They've grown up.*)

Page 21. What else happens in summer? (Idea: *The apples grow bigger; the branches bend down.*)

Page 22. When does this part of the story happen? *In autumn.* What happens to the apples in autumn? (Idea: *Someone picks them.*)

Pages 24–26. What do they make from the apples? *Apple pie.*

Pages 27–28. What do the children like about the apple pie? (Ideas: *It smells so good; it tastes delicious.*)

At the end of the story the children say, "There's nothing as good as an apple pie you grew yourself." Raise your hand if you think that is true. (Pause.) Raise your hand if you think that is false. (Pause.)

Review Vocabulary

(Display the Picture Vocabulary Cards. Point to each card as you say the word. Ask children to repeat each word after you.) These pictures show **bare, appear, blossoms,** and **petals.**

- What word means "the outer parts of a flower"? *Petals.*
- What word means "nothing is covering it"? *Bare.*
- What word means "flowers that will turn into fruit"? *Blossoms.*
- What word means "can be seen"? *Appear.*

Extend Vocabulary
◎—◄ Blossom

In *The Apple Pie Tree,* we learned that **blossom** is a naming word that means "a flower that will turn into fruit." Say the word that means "a flower that will turn into fruit." *Blossom.*

Raise your hand if you can tell us a sentence that uses **blossom** as a naming word that means "a flower that will turn into fruit." (Call on several children. If they don't use complete sentences, restate their examples as sentences. Have the class repeat the sentences.)

Here's a new way to use the word **blossom.**

- Teresa **blossomed** into a wonderful singer. Say the sentence.
- Leo the Late Bloomer took a long time to **blossom.** Say the sentence.
- The class **blossomed** as excellent readers. Say the sentence.

In these sentences, blossom is an action word that means grow or get better at things. What action word means "grow or get better at things"? *Blossom.*

Raise your hand if you can tell us a sentence that uses **blossom** as an action word that

means "grow or get better at things." (Call on several children. If they don't use complete sentences, restate their examples as sentences. Have the class repeat the sentences.)

Present Expanded Target Vocabulary
◎—◄ Seasons

In *The Apple Pie Tree,* we learned about what happened to the tree in winter, spring, summer, and autumn. Winter, spring, summer, and autumn are four parts of the year. We call these parts the seasons. **Seasons.** Say the word. *Seasons.*

Seasons is a naming word. It names the parts of the year. What kind of word is **seasons?** *A naming word.*

The seasons are the four parts of the year: winter, spring, summer, and autumn. Say the word that means "the four parts of the year: winter, spring, summer, and autumn." *Seasons.*

I'll name some activities. If that activity happens in winter, say "winter." If that activity happens in spring, say "spring." If that activity happens in summer, say "summer." If that activity happens in autumn, say "autumn." (Note: If these activities happen in other seasons in your area, accept those responses.)

- Throwing snowballs. *Winter.*
- Leaves change color and fall off the trees. *Autumn.*
- Snow melts and water runs down the street. *Spring.*
- Bears sleep for a long, long time (hibernate). *Winter.*
- You wear shorts, t-shirts, and sunscreen. *Summer.*
- People burn big piles of dead leaves and enjoy pumpkins and other squashes. *Autumn.*

What naming word means "the different parts of the year: winter, spring, summer, and autumn"? *Seasons.*

◎—◄ Present

The story *The Apple Pie Tree* was written so it is happening right now. (Read aloud pages 8–14.) When a story is written so it is happening right now, the story is written in the present. **Present.** Say the word. *Present.*

Present is a naming word. It names a time. What kind of word is **present**? *A naming word.*

When things happen in the present, they are happening right now. Say the words that mean "happening right now." *In the present.*

I'll tell about something. If what I tell about is happening right now, say "in the present." If not, don't say anything.

- (Clap your hands and keep clapping them.)
- I am clapping right now. *In the present.*
- I was clapping.
- I am teaching you a lesson right now. *In the present.*
- Your hearts are beating and you are paying attention to me with your eyes, ears, and brains. *In the present.*
- The dog is barking right now. *In the present.*

What words mean "happening right now"? *In the present.*

Raise your hand if you can tell us a sentence about something that is in the present— happening right now. (Call on several children. If they don't use complete sentences, restate their examples as sentences. Have the class repeat the sentences.)

DAY 3

Preparation: Activity Sheet, BLM 12b. Children will need crayons.

Retell the Story

Today I'll show you the pictures Shari Halpern made for *The Apple Pie Tree.* As I show you the pictures, I'll call on one of you to tell the class that part of the story.

Tell me what happens in the winter. (Show the pictures on pages 2 and 3. Call on a child to tell what's happening. Encourage use of the target words when appropriate. Model use as necessary.)

Tell me what happens in the spring. (Show the pictures on pages 4–7. Call on a child to tell what's happening. Encourage use of the

target words when appropriate. Model use as necessary.)

Tell me what happens in the summer. (Show the pictures on pages 18–21. Call on a child to tell what's happening. Encourage use of the target words when appropriate. Model use as necessary.)

Tell me what happens in the autumn. (Show the pictures on pages 22–29. Call on a child to tell what's happening.)

Collect or prepare word cards for all of the words used since the beginning of the program that have dual meanings as taught in the lessons. Have these cards in your teaching area where children can see them in a pocket chart, on a chalkboard ledge, or in some obvious location. These words are *awkward, blossom, calm, collect, fine, gentle, grains, roared, rough, shouted, wild, winding.*

Play Tom Foolery

Today we will play *Tom Foolery.* I will pretend to be Tom. Tom Foolery has a reputation of trying to trick students. Tom knows that some words have more than one meaning. He will tell you one meaning that will be correct. Then he will tell you another meaning that might be correct or might be incorrect.

If you think the meaning is correct, don't say anything. If you think the meaning is incorrect, sing, "Tom Foolery." Then Tom will have to tell the truth and tell the correct meaning. Tom is sly enough that he may include some words that do <u>not</u> have two meanings. Be careful! He's tricky!

Let's practice: If something is **bare,** nothing is covering it. **Bare** also means a big container made with wood or metal. *Tom Foolery!* Oh, you're right. I was thinking of **barrel,** not **bare.**

When we play *Tom Foolery,* Tom will keep score. If you catch him being tricky, you will get one point. If you don't catch him, Tom gets the point. Watch out! Tom might try to give himself extra points while you're not looking!

Now you're ready to play the game. (Draw a T-chart on the board for keeping score. Children earn one point for each correct answer. If they make an error, correct them as you normally would, and record one point for yourself. Repeat missed words at the end of the game.)

- If you are **gentle,** you do things in a kind, careful way. A **gentle** is also something you put in soup. *Tom Foolery!* Oh, you're right. I must have been thinking of **lentil** instead of **gentle.**
- **Seasons** are the four different times of the year. You also call **"Season!"** (sea's in), when the tide comes in at the beach. *Tom Foolery!* Oh, you're right. We only know the one meaning for **seasons.**
- Sometimes you have to pay a **fine** if you do something wrong.
- When you **appear,** you come into sight. **Appear** is also two of something. *Tom Foolery!* Oh, you're right. I was thinking of **a pair.** I wear **a pair** of mittens when it gets cold.
- **Petals** are the outside parts on a flower. **Petals** are also where you put your feet to make your bike move. *Tom Foolery!* Oh, you're right. I'm thinking of **pedals,** not **petals.**

(Count the points and declare a winner.) You did a great job of playing *Tom Foolery!*

Complete the Activity Sheet

(Review with children the name of the seasons, starting with winter.)

(Give each child a copy of the Activity Sheet, BLM 12b. Children will place the pictures in the sequence of the seasons, starting with winter. Have children copy the words *winter, spring, summer,* and *autumn* under the appropriate pictures.)

DAY 4

Preparation: Prepare a sheet of chart paper, landscape direction, titled *The Apple Pie Tree.* Underneath the title, draw 6 boxes connected by arrows.

See the Introduction for Week 12's chart.

Let's think about what we already know about how books are made.

- What do we call the name of the book? *Title.*
- What do we call the person who writes the story? *Author.*
- What do we call the person who draws the pictures? *Illustrator.*
- What do we call the people or animals a story is about? *Characters.*
- What do we call the pictures the illustrator makes? *Illustrations.*
- What is one thing the setting of a story tells? *Where a story happens.*
- What is the second thing the setting of a story tells? *When a story happens.*

Let's sing the first [number] verses of The Story Song to help us remember these important things about books. (At this point it is unnecessary to sing the whole song. Choose which verses you would like children to sing. Include *setting* as it is a relatively new concept. See the Introduction for the complete Story Song.)

Today we will learn more about the setting of a story.

The setting of a story tells two things. One thing the setting tells is where the story happens. What is one thing the setting tells? *Where the story happens.* The second thing the setting tells is when the story happens. What is the second thing the setting tells? *When the story happens.*

Now let's think about when this story happens.

(Record responses in the row of boxes.)

Pages 2–3. (Read the last sentence on page 2.) When does the story begin? (Idea: *In the winter.*)

Pages 4–5. (Read the first sentence on page 4.) When does this part of the story happen? (Idea: *In the spring.*)

Pages 12–13. Look at the illustrations. When does the next part of the story happen? (Idea: *On a windy day.*)

Pages 14–15. Look at the illustrations. When does the next part of the story happen? (Idea: *On a rainy day.*)

Pages 18–19. (Read the first sentence on page 18.) When does the next part of the story happen? (Idea: *In the summer.*)

Pages 22–23. (Read the first sentence on page 22.) When does this part of the story happen? (Idea: *In autumn.*)

The story starts in the winter. (Draw a line underneath the first box. Write *winter* under the line.)

In the spring, on a windy day, and on a rainy day. All these things happen in the spring. (Draw a line underneath these three boxes. Write *spring* underneath the second line.)

The next part of the story happens in the summer. (Draw a line underneath the fifth box. Write *summer* under the line.)

The ending of the story happens in the autumn. (Draw a line underneath the last box. Write *autumn* underneath the last line.)

Winter, spring, summer, autumn. These seasons happen in one year. When is the setting of *The Apple Pie Tree*? (Idea: *One year.*) You were great detectives! You used the clues and figured out when the story happened.

Today you learned about **when** *The Apple Pie Tree* happened.

Play Tom Foolery (Cumulative Review)

Today we will play *Tom Foolery.* I will pretend to be Tom. You know that Tom has a reputation for trying to trick students. Tom knows that some words have more than one meaning. He will tell you one meaning that will be correct. Then he will tell you another meaning that might be correct or might be incorrect.

If you think the meaning is correct, don't say anything. If you think the meaning is incorrect, sing, "Tom Foolery." Then Tom will have to tell the truth and tell the correct meaning. Tom is sly enough that he may include some words that do <u>not</u> have two meanings. Be careful! He's tricky!

Let's practice: **Season** is a word that tells about times of the year. If I give you a **season,** I am explaining why I did something. *Tom Foolery!* Oh, you're right. I suppose I must have been thinking of **reason** and not **season.** We only know one meaning.

When we play *Tom Foolery*, Tom will keep score. If you catch him being tricky, you will get one point. If you don't catch him, Tom gets the point. Watch out! Tom might try to give himself extra points while you're not looking!

Now you're ready to play the game. (Draw a T-chart on the board for keeping score. Children earn one point for each correct answer. If they make an error, correct them as you normally would, and record one point for yourself. Repeat missed words at the end of the game.)

- **Calm** is how you feel when you are not angry, upset, or excited. **Calm** is also the name of a sea creature you dig at the seashore. *Tom Foolery!* Oh, you are very hard to fool. The sea creature you dig at the seashore is a **clam.**
- **Awkward** means "you have trouble getting your body parts to work together." It also means "embarrassed and uncomfortable."
- When you **appear,** you come into sight. **Appear** is also a wooden sidewalk that juts out into a lake. *Tom Foolery!* Oh, you're right. I was thinking of something called **a pier.** (Print *appear* and *a pier* on the board to demonstrate the difference.) Those words sound the same, but they mean different things.
- **Present** can mean that you are here right now. **Present** also means "nice or pleasing." *Tom Foolery!* Oh, you're right. I must be thinking of **pleasant** and not **present.** Another meaning for **present** is "a gift."
- If a table is **bare,** nothing is covering it. If a tree has no leaves left on it, the tree is **bare.**

- **Blossom** means "a flower that will turn into fruit." **Blossom** is also a kind of fluffy candy you get at a fair. *Tom Foolery!* Oh, you're right. I guess I was thinking of candy **floss.** Another meaning for **blossom** is "to grow and get better at things."
- **Imagination** means "the part of your mind that lets you make pictures of things that are not real or that haven't happened yet." Unicorns, dragons, and space aliens all come from people's **imaginations.**
- **Roared** means "shouted something in a very loud voice." It also means "cooking meat in the oven." *Tom Foolery!* Oh, you're right. I was thinking of **roasted.** The other meaning for **roared** means moved "very fast and made a loud noise."
- **Petals** are the outside parts on a flower. **Petals** are also things like steel, and iron and aluminum. *Tom Foolery!* Oh, you're right. I'm thinking of **metals,** not **petals.**

(Count the points and declare a winner.) You did a great job of playing *Tom Foolery!*

DAY 5

Preparation: Prepare a sheet of chart paper, landscape direction, titled *The Apple Pie Tree.* Underneath the title, draw a row of 10 boxes connected by arrows. Underneath the first row of boxes, draw a second row of 7 boxes connected by arrows. The first box in the second row is underneath the second box in the first row.

See the Introduction for Week 12's chart.

Record children's responses by writing the underlined words in the boxes.

Each child will need a copy of the Happy Face Game Test Sheet, BLM B.

Introduce Linear Story Pattern

A pattern is an action or something that repeats in a certain way.

Watch me. I'll clap a pattern. (Clap *slow, slow, quick, quick, quick* twice.) Clap the pattern with me. (Clap the pattern with children until all children are clapping the pattern.) I'll clap the pattern once more. (Clap *slow, slow, quick, quick, quick* twice.) Now it's your turn to clap the pattern by yourself. (Pause.) You just repeated a clapping pattern.

Watch me. I'll draw a pattern. (Draw a circle, box, circle, box pattern on the board in a horizontal line.) Say the pattern with me. (Say *circle, box, circle, box* with children.) I'll add to my pattern. (Add a circle.) Now tell me what comes next in my pattern. *Box.* (Extend the pattern for two or three more repeats.) You just added on to a drawing pattern.

When authors write stories, they sometimes write in patterns.

Let's see if we can figure out the pattern for *The Apple Pie Tree.* First let's think only about the apple tree, not the robins. You tell me what happens in the story, and I'll write it down.

Pages 2–3. What does the apple tree look like in winter? (Idea: *It is <u>bare</u>; it has <u>no leaves</u>.*)

Pages 4–5. Then what happens? (Idea: *It gets <u>leaves</u>.*)

Pages 6–7. Then what happens? (Idea: *It gets <u>buds</u>.*)

Pages 8–9. Then what happens? (Idea: *The <u>buds</u> <u>open</u>.*)

Pages 10–11. Then what happens? (Idea: *The <u>bees</u> come to the <u>blossoms</u>.*)

Pages 12–13. Then what happens? (Idea: *The <u>petals fall</u>.*)

Pages 14–15. Then what happens? (Idea: *It <u>rains</u>.*)

Pages 16–21. Then what happens? (Idea: *Small green <u>apples</u> <u>grow</u>.*)

Pages 22–23. Then what happens? (Idea: *They <u>pick</u> the <u>apples</u>.*)

Pages 24 to 29. Then what happens? (Idea: *They <u>make</u> the <u>pie</u>.*)

(Point to the story map that is on the chart paper. Draw a line under the story map.) Look at the shape of the story of the apple tree. It's a line. This story starts and ends at a different time, so this story has a **linear** pattern. What kind of a story has a pattern that starts and ends at a different time? *A linear story.*

Now let's think only about the robins, not the apple tree. You tell me what happens in the story, and I'll write it down.

Pages 4–5. What do the robins do first? (Idea: _Build a nest_.)

Pages 6–7. Then what happens? (Idea: _They guard their eggs_.)

Read pages 8–9. Then what happens? (Idea: _The baby robins hatch_.)

Read page 11. Then what happens? (Idea: _The baby robins grow feathers_.)

Pages 12–13. Then what happens? (Idea: _The baby robins learn to fly_.)

Pages 14–15. Then what happens? (Idea: _The robins are safe in their nest_.)

Read page 19. Then what happens? (Idea: _The little robins have grown up_.)

(Point to the story map that is on the chart paper. Draw a line under the story map.) Look at the shape of the story of the robins. It's a line. This story starts and ends at a different time, so this story has a **linear** pattern. What kind of a story has a pattern that starts and ends at a different time? _A linear story._

So this story has a two linear patterns: one for the apple tree and one for the robins.

Assess Vocabulary

 (Hold up a copy of the Happy Face Game Test Sheet, BLM B.)

Today you're going to play the Happy Face Game. When you play the Happy Face game, it shows me how well you know the hard words you are learning.

If I say something that is true, color in the happy face. What will you do if I say something that is true? _Color in the happy face._

If I say something that is false, color in the sad face. What will you do if I say something that is false? _Color in the sad face._

Listen carefully to each item that I say. Don't let me trick you!

Item 1: A **bare** tree has no leaves. (_True._)

Item 2: A **blossom** is a flower that turns into fruit. (_True._)

Item 3: There are seven **seasons**: Monday, Tuesday, Wednesday, Thursday, Friday, Saturday, and Sunday. (_False._)

Item 4: In the **present** means that something is happening right now. (_True._)

Item 5: When you **appear,** people can't see you. (_False._)

Item 6: **Blossom** means to get better at doing things. (_True._)

Item 7: A rainbow is **glorious** because it is very beautiful and wonderful to look at. (_True._)

Item 8: A **legend** is a story that explains how something came to be. (_True._)

Item 9: If you **soared,** you raced around on the ground and made a lot of noise. (_False._)

Item 10: Children who are **disobedient** are **disagreeable.** (_True._)

You did a great job of playing the Happy Face Game!

(Score children's work at a later time. A child must score 9 out of 10 to be at the mastery level. If a child does not achieve mastery, insert the missed words as additional items in the games for next week's lessons. Retest those children individually for the missed items before they take the next mastery test.)

Extensions
Read a Story as a Reward

(Display copies of several books that you have read since the beginning of the program. Allow children to choose which book they would like you to read to them as a reward for their hard work.)

(Read the story aloud for enjoyment with minimal interruptions.)

Preparation: Word containers for the Super Words Center. You may wish to remove some words from earlier lessons. Choose words children have mastered. You will need 2 copies of each card that remains in the word containers.

Introduce the Super Words Center
(Add the new Picture Vocabulary Cards to words from the previous weeks. Show children one of the word containers. If children need more guidance in how to work in the Super Words Center, role-play with two to three children as a demonstration.)

I will teach you how to play a new game today called *Go Fish.*

Let's think about how we work with our words in the Super Words Center.

You will work with a partner in the Super Words Center. Whom will you work with? *A partner.*

First you and your partner will each draw six word cards out of the container and hold them so your partner cannot see them. What do you do first? (Idea: *Draw six cards out of the container and hold them so my partner cannot see them.*)

Next you will look at the cards in your hand and lay down any cards that you have two of. You will tell your partner the word the pictures show. What do you do next? (Idea: *Lay down any cards that I have two of, and tell my partner the word the pictures show.*)

Then your partner has a chance to lay down any cards he or she has two of, and tell the word the pictures show. What does your partner do? (Idea: *Lay down any cards that he or she has two of, and tell the word the pictures show.*)

Next you will ask your partner for a card that you have only one of by saying the word the picture shows. If your partner has that card, he or she will give it to you. If your partner gives you the card, you will lay down the two cards. What does your partner do if they have the card you ask for? (Idea: *Give me the card.*) What will you do if your partner gives you a card? (Idea: *Lay down the two cards that are the same.*)

If your partner does not have the card you ask for, your partner will say "Go Fish." What will your partner do if he or she doesn't have the card you ask for? (Idea: *Say "Go Fish."*) If your partner says "Go Fish," you must choose another card from the word container. What will you do if your partner says "Go Fish"? (Idea: *Choose a card from the word container.*)

Then it's your partner's turn.

Watch while I show you what I mean. (Demonstrate this process with one child as your partner.)

When one partner has no cards left in his or her hand, the game is over. Each person gets one point for each pair of cards they have laid down. The winner is the person with the most points. Who wins the game? (Idea: *The person with the most points.*)

Have fun playing *Go Fish!*

WHEN WE GO CAMPING

Week 13

Preparation: You will need *When We Go Camping* for each day's lesson.

Number the pages of the story to assist you in asking questions at appropriate points.

Post a copy of the Vocabulary Tally Sheet, BLM A, with this week's Picture Vocabulary Cards attached.

Each child will need one copy of the Homework Sheet, BLM 13a.

DAY 1

Introduce Book

This week's book is called *When We Go Camping*. What's the title? *When We Go Camping.*

This book was written by Margriet Ruurs. [margreet rew-urss] Who's the author of *When We Go Camping*? *Margriet Ruurs.*

Andrew Kiss made the pictures for this book. Who's the illustrator of *When We Go Camping*? *Andrew Kiss.* Who made the illustrations for this book? *Andrew Kiss.*

The cover of a book usually gives us some hints of what the book is about. Let's look at the front cover of *When We Go Camping*. What do you see in the illustration? (Ideas: *Two people in a tent; a boy and a girl in a tent; two children in a tent; a canoe; a campfire; some food cooking; a moose; a squirrel; trees; birds flying; a mountain.*)

(Assign each child a partner.) Get ready to make some predictions to your partner about this book. Use the information from the cover to help you.

(Ask the following questions, allowing sufficient time for children to share their predictions with their partners.)

- Who are the characters in this story? (Who do you think this story is about?)
- What kind of birds do you think are flying?
- Where do you think the story happens?
- When do you think the story happens?

When We Go Camping
author: Margriet Ruurs • illustrator: Andrew Kiss

Target Vocabulary

Tier II	Tier III
snuggle	setting (when)
explore	pattern
disturb	(explaining)
odor	realistic
*wilderness	
*reasons	

*Expanded Target Vocabulary Word

- Why do you think the children are being so still?
- How far away from the children do you think the moose is?
- Do you think this story is about real people and animals? Tell why or why not.

(Call on several children to share their predictions with the class.)

Take a Picture Walk

(**Note:** There are many different wild animals in the illustrations. Do not expect children to find all the animals during this picture walk. If children locate animals but do not know what the animals are, briefly respond with the name of the animal. Encourage children to use target words in their answers.)

We're going to take a picture walk through this book. Remember that when we take a picture walk, we look at the pictures and tell what we think will happen in the story.

Title page. What other story have we read that has a setting nearly the same as *When We Go Camping*? *Loon Lake.* I wonder if there will be a loon in this story.

Page 1. Where else did you see this illustration? (Idea: *On the cover.*) What are the children watching? (Idea: *An animal; a moose.*) When do you think this part of the story happens? Why do you think so?

Pages 3–4. What are the children doing? (Idea: *Pulling the canoe into the water.*) What do you think they are going to do? (Idea: *Go canoeing; go fishing.*) What makes you think so? (Ideas: *They're pulling the canoe into the water; there's a fishing rod beside the boat; there's a box of hooks.*) What animals do you see? (Ideas: *Loons; a blue heron; a rabbit; a squirrel.*)

Pages 5–6. What other people do you see? (Ideas: *A father; a man; a mother; a woman.*) Who is the one fishing? *The man.* What is the woman doing? (Ideas: *Sitting on a log; drinking coffee; watching the children; enjoying the view.*) What animals do you see? (Ideas: *Ducks; a blue heron; a loon; a deer; a crow; a squirrel.*)

Pages 7–8. What is happening here? (Ideas: *The boy is pulling on a rope; he is lifting a cooler off the ground; the woman is cooking something over the fire; the girl is washing; the man is chopping wood.*) What animals do you see? (Ideas: *A bear; a marmot; a rabbit; a woodpecker; a squirrel.*)

Pages 9–10. What are the children looking at? (Idea: *A tree stump; a tree that has been cut down; a tree.*) What animal do you think cut down the tree? *A beaver.* What animals do you see? (Ideas: *A skunk; a deer; a woodpecker; a raccoon; a porcupine; a frog; a squirrel.*)

Pages 11–12. What do you think is happening? (Ideas: *They're going on a hike; they're going for a walk in the woods.* Point to the meadow.) What do you call a field where grass and flowers grow? *A meadow.* What animals do you see in the meadow? (Ideas: *Elk; a hawk; a squirrel.*)

Pages 13–14. What is happening here? (Ideas: *The girl is looking at a frog; the boy is watching a robin pull a worm out of the ground.*) What other animals do you see? (Ideas: *A blue jay; a butterfly; a squirrel.*)

Pages 15–16. Where does this part of the story happen? (Idea: *At the lake.*) What are the children doing? (Idea: *Playing in the water with sticks.*) What do you think they are looking for? (Ideas: *Fish; water bugs; frogs; tadpoles.*) What animals do you see? (Ideas: *A deer; a red-winged blackbird; a loon; a squirrel.*)

Pages 17–18. What are the children doing? (Idea: *Swimming.*) How do you think the water feels? (Ideas: *Cold; refreshing.*) What is the father doing? (Ideas: *Looking across the lake; holding a camera.*) What do you think he is trying to get a picture of? What animals do you see? (Ideas: *A bird—a killdeer; a squirrel.*)

Pages 19–20. What are the people doing? (Idea: *Gathering berries.*) What animals do you see? (Ideas: *A beaver; a crow; a squirrel.*)

Pages 21–22. What is happening here? (Ideas: *They are cooking dinner; the mom is putting a fish in a pan; the children are adding sticks to the fire.*) What animals do you see? (Ideas: *A fish; a squirrel.*)

Pages 23–24. When do you think this part of the story happens? (Ideas: *At sunset; in the evening.*) What animals do you see? (Ideas: *An otter; a bald eagle; an owl; a squirrel.*)

Pages 25–26. What is happening here? (Ideas: *They're having a campfire; they're toasting marshmallows.*) What animals do you see? (Ideas: *Raccoons; a fox; an owl; a squirrel.*)

In what season do you think this story happens? (Idea: *Summer.*) Why do you think so? (Ideas: *The family is on vacation; the children are swimming in the lake; the grass is green and the flowers are blooming; many people go camping in the summer.*)

Let's talk about how Andrew Kiss made the illustrations for *When We Go Camping*. There are lots of different ways to make illustrations for a book: the artist can paint them; draw them with a pen or pencil; make them with markers, crayons, pastels, or chalk; cut out different pieces of paper and glue them together.

How do you think Andrew Kiss made his illustrations? (Idea: *He painted them.*) That's right; Andrew Kiss used oil paints to paint the pictures for *When We Go Camping*.

(**Note:** If you have tubes of oil paint available, you may wish to show them to children and model how different pigments are mixed to get different colors.)

Andrew Kiss tried to make his pictures look as real as he could, so we say his illustrations are realistic. What kind of illustrations did Andrew Kiss make for *When We Go Camping*? *Realistic illustrations.*

Pages 17–18. Andrew Kiss also did something special for children who like to look especially carefully at his illustrations. Raise your hand if you found something special in his paintings that we haven't talked about. **(Call on several children. If no one has noticed the hidden pictures, point to the fish in the lake.)** What do you think this is? **(Ideas:** *A fish; a trout.***)** Does it look like a real fish? *No.* That's right; the shape of the fish is hidden in the ripples on the lake. There are hidden animals in each of Andrew Kiss's illustrations. We'll try to find more of them later this week.

It's your turn to ask me some questions. What would you like to know about the story? **(Accept questions. If children tell about the pictures or the story instead of ask questions, prompt them to ask a question.)** Ask me a what question. Ask me a where question.

Read the Book Aloud
(Read the story to children with minimal interruptions.)

Tomorrow we will read the story again, and I will ask you some questions.

Present Target Vocabulary
◎╼ Snuggle

In the story the child says, "I snuggle into my sleeping bag, then roll over and quietly peek outside." That means the child cuddles in a warm and comfortable spot, close by someone or something. **Snuggle.** Say the word. *Snuggle.*

Snuggle is an action word. It tells what someone is doing. What kind of word is **snuggle?** *An action word.*

If someone snuggles somewhere, they cuddle in a warm and comfortable spot, close to someone or something. Say the word that means "cuddle in a warm and comfortable spot, close to someone or something." *Snuggle.*

(Correct any incorrect responses and repeat the item at the end of the sequence.)

Let's think about some times when you might snuggle. I'll tell about a time. If you think that

someone is snuggling, say "snuggle." If not, don't say anything.

- The boy and his dog were cuddling close to each other in front of the fireplace. *Snuggle.*
- Tamsin cuddled up close to her mom in the cold room. *Snuggle.*
- It was so hot that Jack and Jill stayed well apart.
- Marfa said, "Please move away—you're too close!"
- Belinda curled up in her dad's lap and listened to music. *Snuggled.*
- Nasser cuddled his kitten and they fell asleep together. *Snuggled.*

What action word means "cuddle in a warm and comfortable spot, close to someone or something"? *Snuggle.*

◎╼ Explore

In the story, the children went out in their canoe to explore the lake. That means they traveled around the lake so they could find out what the lake was like. **Explore.** Say the word. *Explore.*

Explore is an action word. It tells what is happening. What kind of word is **explore?** *An action word.*

When you go exploring, you travel around so you can find out what places are like. Say the word that means "travel around so you can find out what places are like." *Explore.*

I'll tell about someone. If that person is exploring, say "explore." If not, don't say anything.

- Julie and Justin travel though the jungles of Africa to see what is there. *Explore.*
- Mr. Pfister was so scared of the cave that he stood still and wouldn't move.
- When the kids got under the porch, they traveled around to see what it was like down there. *Explore.*
- Mr. Columbus wanted to find out what places were like, so he sailed his ships. *Explore.*
- Binford knew that the river was dangerous, so he didn't go canoeing with the others.
- Lewis and Clark were curious about where they could go if they journeyed down the rivers. *Explore.*

What action word means "travel around so you can see what places are like"? *Explore.*

What places would you like to explore? Why? (Call on several children. Encourage them to start their answers with the words, "I would like to explore _____ because _____.")

⌖= Disturb

In the story, the sound of a twig snapping disturbs the elk and they disappear. That means the sound interrupts the elk and upsets them. **Disturb.** Say the word. *Disturb.*

Disturb is an action word. It tells what is happening. What kind of word is **disturb?** *An action word.*

If you disturb a person or an animal, you interrupt what they are doing and upset them. What word means "interrupt what a person or animal is doing and upset them"? *Disturb.*

Let's think about some times when a person or an animal might be disturbed. If the person or animal is interrupted and upset, say "disturb." If not, don't say anything.

- Lorenzo tried to speak to his brother when his brother was on the telephone. *Disturb.*
- Marco shook Polo's shoulder to get his attention. *Disturb.*
- Sara left her mom alone when she was concentrating on sewing.
- Lewis kept interrupting Clark while he was searching for the trail. *Disturb.*
- I kept quiet when my dad was fixing the window I broke.
- The mama bear stood up, grunted, and growled when we woke her up. *Disturb.*

What action word means "interrupt a person or an animal and upset them"? *Disturb.*

⌖= Odor

In the story, the child says "I can smell the musky odor that tells me that a bear has been here to eat berries too." That means the child recognizes the bear's smell. **Odor.** Say the word. *Odor.*

Odor is a naming word. It names a thing. What kind of word is **odor?** *A naming word.*

An odor is a smell. Say the word that means "a smell." *Odor.*

Let's think about when you might smell an odor. I'll tell about something. If you think you might smell an odor, say "odor." If not, don't say anything.

- Mom was making popcorn. *Odor.*
- The skunk was frightened and sprayed. *Odor.*
- The peach pie was cooling on the windowsill. *Odor.*
- When I broke my nose, I couldn't smell a thing!
- The ice had no smell at all.
- Wow! That turkey smells delicious! *Odor.*

What naming word means "a smell"? *Odor.*

Introduce the Vocabulary Tally Sheet
(See Lesson 1, page 3, for instructions.)

Assign Homework
(Homework Sheet, BLM 13a: See the Introduction for homework instructions.)

DAY 2

Preparation: Picture Vocabulary Cards for *snuggle, explore, disturb, odor.*

Read and Discuss Story

(Read story to children. Ask the following questions at the specified points. Encourage them to use target words in their answers.)

Page 2. What does the person who is telling the story love to do? *Go camping.* When does the story begin? (Idea: *Early in the morning.*) What words from the story let you know it is cold early in the morning? (Ideas: *My nose is cold; my breath forms a little cloud.*) What do the children do when they first wake up? (Ideas: *Snuggle into their sleeping bags; peek outside.*)

Pages 3–4. What do the children hear as they push their canoe into the water? (Ideas: *The sound of chickadees; chickadees singing.*) What are they going to do? (Idea: *Explore; travel around the lake so they can see what it is like.*)

Pages 5–6. We experience the world around us using our five senses. Those senses are sight, hearing, touch, taste, and smell. What are the five senses? *Sight, hearing, touch, taste, and* *smell.* (Repeat the senses with children until they can say them confidently without assistance.) What three senses does this part of the story tell about? (Ideas: *Sight—mountaintops on the far shore; circles in the lake from their paddles; sound—the loon's laugh; touch—the feel of the water against the paddles.*)

Page 7. What are three of the things they do when they go camping? (Ideas: *Catch trout; chop wood; make a fire.*)

Page 8. Why does the boy hoist their food high up in a tree? (Idea: *To keep the bears away.*)

Page 9. Who cut down the tree? *The beavers.* Why did the beavers cut down the tree? *For their lodge.* A lodge is a home for a beaver. (Point to the lodge in the lake.) This is a beaver lodge. What is this? *A beaver lodge.*

Page 10. Why do you think the woodpecker will soon have to find a new place to hammer for insects? (Idea: *The beaver is cutting down the tree; the beaver will soon take the tree out to its lodge.*)

Pages 11–12. What did they think the sound was at first? *A cougar.* What was the sound? (Idea: *Elk, eating grass.*) What scares the elk away? (Idea: *A twig snapping; a twig breaking; someone stepped on a twig.*)

Page 13. What things does the person wonder about? (Ideas: *Does a butterfly like butter; why is a dragonfly called a dragonfly.*) What things in nature do you wonder about?

Page 14. Where do you think the robin's babies are? (Idea: *In their nest; in a nest in a tree.*) We had to read this far in the story before we knew for sure who is telling the story. Who is looking at the robin? *The boy.* So who would say, "Come look! The robin wants a worm to feed her babies." *The boy.* So who is telling the story? *The boy.*

Pages 15–16. Remember that we experience the world around us using our five senses. What are those senses? *Sight, hearing, touch, taste, and smell.* What three senses does this part of the story tell about? (Ideas: *Sight—water bugs gliding across the top of the water; sound—frogs croaking; touch—mud squishing between their toes.*)

Pages 17–18. Are the children enjoying the water in the lake? *Yes.* Why isn't the father swimming? (Idea: *He thinks the water is freezing cold.*)

Pages 19–20. What kinds of berries are the children gathering? (Ideas: *Raspberries; saskatoons; blackberries.*) What four senses does this part of the story tell about? (Ideas: *Sight—red raspberries; purple saskatoons; touch—soft raspberries; warm saskatoons; taste—sweet blackberries; smell—musky odor of the bear.*) What do you think the musky odor of a bear is like? (Idea: *A stinky wet dog; wet sheep; sweaty horse.*)

Pages 21–22. Why do you think cooking when you're camping is more fun that cooking at home? (Ideas: *You cook over a campfire; you cook different kinds of foods.*)

Pages 23–24. What two senses does this part of the story tell about? (Ideas: *Sight—shadows on the lake; an eagle gliding in the sky; sound—a howl hooting.*) Why do you think an eagle gliding is like a kite without a string? (Ideas: *An eagle gliding doesn't move its wings; it just floats in the wind like a kite.*)

Page 26. What kinds of things does the story say the family does around the campfire? (Ideas: *Snuggle close to each other; tell scary tales.*) What sounds do they hear as they fall asleep? (Ideas: *Crickets; frogs; the waves on the shore.*)

Where are the children at the beginning of the story? (Idea: *In their tent.*) Where are the children at the end of the story? (Idea: *In their tent.*)

The children start and end the story in the same place. So the pattern of *When We Go Camping* is a circle story. What is the pattern of *When We Go Camping*? *A circle story.*

Review Vocabulary

(Display the Picture Vocabulary Cards. Point to each card as you say the word. Ask children to repeat each word after you.) These pictures show **snuggle, explore, disturb,** and **odor.**

- What word means "a smell"? *Odor.*
- What word means "cuddle in a warm and comfortable spot, close to someone or something"? *Snuggle.*

- What word means "interrupt a person or an animal and upset them"? *Disturb.*
- What word means "travel around so you can see what places are like"? *Explore.*

Extend Vocabulary
 Disturb

In *When We go Camping,* we learned that **disturb** means "interrupt a person or an animal and upset them." Say the word that means "interrupt a person or an animal and upset them." *Disturb.*

Raise your hand if you can tell us a sentence that uses **disturb** as an action word meaning "interrupt a person or an animal and upset them." (Call on several children. If they don't use complete sentences, restate their examples as sentences. Have the class repeat the sentences.)

Here's a new way to use the word **disturb.**

- It **disturbs** me when I see someone who is homeless and hungry. Say the sentence.
- It **disturbs** me when I see a dog left in a car on a hot day. Say the sentence.
- It **disturbs** me when I see people driving too fast. Say the sentence.

In these sentences, disturbs is an action word that means bothers or worries. What action word means "bothers or worries"? *Disturbs.*

Raise your hand if you can tell us a sentence that uses **disturb** as an action word meaning "bothers or worries." (Call on several children. Encourage them to start their answers with the words "It disturbs me when _____." If they don't use complete sentences, restate their examples as sentences. Have the class repeat the sentences.)

Present Expanded Target Vocabulary
 Wilderness

In *When We Go Camping,* the family goes to a place where there are no people. We call this place a wilderness. A wilderness can be a desert, where there is lots of sand or rocks, or a forest, where there are lots of trees and many different kinds of animals. **Wilderness.** Say the word. *Wilderness.*

Wilderness is a naming word. It names a place. What kind of word is **wilderness?** *A naming word.*

A wilderness is a place where no people live. Say the word that means "a place where no people live." *Wilderness.*

I'll tell about some places. If that place is a wilderness, say "wilderness." If not, don't say anything.

- High in the mountains. *Wilderness.*
- At the North Pole. *Wilderness.*
- At a busy beach in the middle of the summer.
- In the middle of a crater on the moon. *Wilderness.*
- In the desert. *Wilderness.*
- At your house.

What naming word means "a place where no people live"? *Wilderness.*

 Reasons

When We Go Camping starts with the sentence "I love to go camping!" Then the person telling the story tells why he loves to go camping. He tells about the chickadees, the squirrels, and the loons. He tells about seeing an elk and watching a robin hunt for worms. He tells about splashing in the lake and picking wild berries. All the things he tells about are the reasons he loves to go camping. **Reasons.** Say the word. *Reasons.*

Reasons is a naming word. It names things. What kind of word is **reasons?** *A naming word.*

Reasons are the facts that explain why you think what you do. Say the word that means "the facts that explain why you think what you do." *Reasons.*

I'm going to tell you something I think. Here's what I think: I think the children in this class are getting smarter every day. Now I'll tell you something more. If what I tell about is a reason I think that children in this class are getting smarter every day, say "reason." If not, don't say anything.

- You have learned how to sit quietly and listen to a story. *Reason.*
- You can't count to a million.
- You can count forward and backward to ten. *Reason.*
- You haven't fixed the computer so that it works faster.
- You say kind things to each other when you do smart things. *Reason.*

- You remember to say, "Good morning!" when you come to class. *Reason.*

What words means "the facts that explain why you think what you do"? *Reasons.*

Raise your hand if you can tell us another reason I might think the children in this class are getting smarter every day. (Call on several children. Encourage them to use this frame for their answers: "The reason I think the children in this class are getting smarter is _____." If they don't use complete sentences, restate their examples as sentences. Have the class repeat the sentences.)

DAY 3

Preparation: Activity Sheet, BLM 13b. Each child will need one crayon.

Retell the Story

Today I'll show you the pictures Andrew Kiss made for *When We Go Camping.* As I show you the pictures, I'll call on one of you to tell the class that part of the story.

Tell me what happens at the **beginning** of the story. (Show the pictures on page 1. Call on a child to tell what's happening.)

Tell me what happens in the **middle** of the story. (Show the pictures on pages 3–24. Call on a child to tell what's happening. Encourage use of the target words when appropriate.)

Tell me what happens at the **end** of the story. (Show the pictures on page 25. Call on a child to tell what's happening.)

Collect or prepare word cards for all words with dual meanings. Display them prominently in a pocket chart, on a chalkboard ledge, or another obvious location. These words are *awkward, blossom, calm, collect, disturb, fine, gentle, grains, roared, rough, shouted, wild, winding.*

Play Tom Foolery

Today we will play *Tom Foolery.* I will pretend to be Tom. Tom Foolery has a reputation of trying to trick students. Tom knows that some words have more than one meaning. He will tell you one meaning that will be correct. Then he will tell you another meaning that might be correct or might be incorrect.

If you think the meaning is correct, don't say anything. If you think the meaning is incorrect, sing, "Tom Foolery." Then Tom will have to tell the truth and tell the correct meaning. Tom is sly enough that he may include some words that do <u>not</u> have two meanings. Be careful! He's tricky!

Let's practice. Something that **slithers** moves by twisting and sliding on the ground. **Slithers** are also what you get in your fingers when you handle rough wood without gloves on. *Tom Foolery!* Oh, you're right. I must have been thinking about **slivers** and not **slithers.** I hate it when I get a **slither.** I mean, **sliver.**

Let's do another one together. **Odor** means "a smell." It is also what the judge says when people are noisy in court. *Tom Foolery!* Oh, you're right. I was thinking of the word **order.** The judge says, "Order in the court!"

When we play *Tom Foolery,* Tom will keep score. If you catch him being tricky, you will get one point. If you don't catch him, Tom gets the point. Watch out! Tom might try to give himself extra points while you're not looking!

Now you're ready to play the game. (Draw a T-chart on the board for keeping score. Children earn one point for each correct answer. If they make an error, correct them as you normally would, and record one point for yourself. Repeat missed words at the end of the game.)

- When you **snuggle,** you cuddle in a warm and comfortable spot, close to your father or your puppy. **Snuggle** is also what you do when you have trouble doing something. *Tom Foolery!* Oh, you're right. I must have been thinking of **struggle** instead of **snuggle.**

- **Explore** means "travel around so you can see what places are like." You also **explore** when you say something loudly when you are excited. *Tom Foolery!* Oh, you're right. I was thinking of **exclaim.** We only know the first meaning for **explore.**

- The **wilderness** is a place where wild animals live. No people live in the **wilderness.** In the **wilderness** of Alaska there are lots of trees.
- **Reasons** are the facts that explain why we do something. The four **reasons** are also winter, spring, summer, and autumn. *Tom Foolery!* Oh, you're right. I was thinking of **seasons,** not **reasons.**
- If something is **rough,** it is not smooth. **Rough** also tells how my voice sounds if it is not gentle or kind.

(Count the points and declare a winner.) You did a great job of playing *Tom Foolery!*

Complete the Activity Sheet

(Discuss with children the idea of going camping. Use these questions to help get the discussion started.) Have you ever been camping? Did you enjoy it? Would you like to go camping? What do you think would be the best thing about going camping? What do you think you would not like about going camping?

(Give each child a copy of the Activity Sheet, BLM 13b.) Today our class will use our crayons to make a graph to show if we would like to go camping or not.

Touch under the words in front of the first line of boxes. Those words say, "I would like to go camping." What do those words say? *I would like to go camping.*

Touch under the words in front of the second line of boxes. Those words say, "I would not like to go camping." What do those words say? *I would not like to go camping.*

(Call on children one at a time. Ask each child the question, "Would you like to go camping?" The child should respond with either of the two sentences. If the child responds "I would like to go camping," the class colors in one box on the line after that sentence. If the child responds "I would not like to go camping," the class colors in one box on the line after that sentence.)

(After each child has had a turn to respond, help the class draw some conclusions from the graphs: most children would like/would not like to go camping; nearly all children would like/would not like to go camping; (number of children) would like/would not like to go camping.)

DAY 4

Preparation: Prepare a sheet of chart paper, landscape direction, titled *When We Go Camping.* Underneath the title, draw 6 boxes connected by arrows.

See the Introduction for Week 13's chart.

Let's think about what we already know about how books are made.

- What do we call the name of the book? *Title.*
- What do we call the person who writes the story? *Author.*
- What do we call the person who draws the pictures? *Illustrator.*
- What are the people or animals a story is about? *Characters.*
- What do we call the pictures the illustrator makes? *Illustrations.*
- What is one thing the setting of a story tells? *Where a story happens.*
- What is the second thing the setting of a story tells? *When a story happens.*

Let's sing the first [number] verses of The Story Song to help us remember these important things about books. (At this point it is unnecessary to sing the whole song. Choose which verses you would like children to sing. Include *setting* as it is a relatively new concept. See the Introduction for the complete story song.)

Today we will learn more about the setting of a story.

The setting of a story tells two things. One thing the setting tells is where the story happens. What is one thing the setting tells? *Where the story happens.* The second thing the setting tells in when the story happens. What is the second thing the setting tells? *When the story happens.*

Now let's think about when this story happens.

(Record underlined responses in the row of boxes.)

Pages 2–3. (Read the sentence, "When I wake up in our tent, it is still early.") When does the story begin? (Idea: *In the morning*.)

Pages 7–8. Look at the illustrations. When does this part of the story happen? (Idea: *At breakfast time*.) What clues tell you it's breakfast time? (Ideas: *The woman is cooking breakfast; the girl is washing her face.*)

Pages 17–18. (Read the sentence, "When we get hot, we splash and swim in the lake to cool off, even though grown-ups think the water is freezing cold!") When does this part of the story happen? (Idea: *In the afternoon*.) What clues tell you it's afternoon? (Idea: *They are hot, and the hottest part of the day is the afternoon.*)

Pages 21–22. (Read the sentence, "We are proud of the trout we caught for supper.") When does this part of the story happen? (Idea: *At supper time*.)

Pages 23–24. (Read the sentence, "When the sun sets, long shadows reach across the lake.") When does this part of the story happen? (Idea: *At sunset*.)

Pages 25–26. (Read the sentence, "When stars wink from up high and sparks fly into the night sky, orange flames dance away the darkness.") When does this part of the story happen? (Idea: *At night*.)

The story starts in the morning. Then it happens at breakfast time, in the afternoon, at supper time, at sunset, and at night. All these things happen in one day. (Draw a line underneath all the boxes. Write *one day* underneath the line.)

In what season do you think this story happens? (Idea: *Summer*.) Why do you think this story happens in the summer? (Ideas: *The family is on vacation; the day is hot enough for swimming; the berries are ripe; they are wearing summer clothes.*)

(Add *in the summer* after *one day*.)

When is the setting of *When We Go Camping*? (Idea: *One day in the summer*.) You were great detectives! You used the clues and figured out when the story happened.

Today you learned about when *When We Go Camping* happened.

Play Tom Foolery (Cumulative Review)

Today we will play *Tom Foolery*. I will pretend to be Tom. You know that Tom has a reputation for trying to trick students. Tom knows that some words have more than one meaning. He will tell you one meaning that will be correct. Then he will tell you another meaning that might be correct or might be incorrect.

If you think the meaning is correct, don't say anything. If you think the meaning is incorrect, sing, "Tom Foolery." Then Tom will have to tell the truth and tell the correct meaning. Tom is sly enough that he may include some words that do <u>not</u> have two meanings. Be careful! He's tricky!

Let's practice. **Glimpse** means "to see something just for a short time." **Glimpse** also means "more than one glimp." *Tom Foolery!* Oh, you're right. I made up that second meaning. That's why my name is Tom Foolery!

Let's do another one together. **Shouted** means that you yelled when you were mad. **Shouted** also means that you sang a song using your best singing voice. *Tom Foolery!* Oh, you're right. **Shouted** means that you called to someone in a loud voice to get their attention.

When we play *Tom Foolery,* Tom will keep score. If you catch him being tricky, you will get one point. If you don't catch him, Tom gets the point. Watch out! Tom might try to give himself extra points while you're not looking!

Now you're ready to play the game. (Draw a T-chart on the board for keeping score. Children earn one point for each correct answer. If they make an error, correct them as you normally would, and record one point for yourself. Repeat missed words at the end of the game.

- If something **disturbs** you, it bothers or worries you. **Disturb** also means "to pass out papers to everyone." *Tom Foolery!* Oh, you are very hard to fool. When you pass out papers to everyone, you **distribute** the papers.
- I like to **snuggle** up with my mom, my dad, and my favorite blanket. I also like to **snuggle** them in the air, throwing them up and catching them again, one after the other. *Tom Foolery!* I must have been thinking of **juggle**. I can't even lift my mom and dad, much less throw them up in the air!
- **Odor** is a smell.
- **Explore** can mean "travel to different places so you can find out what they are like." **Explore** can also mean "say something loudly because you are surprised or excited." *Tom Foolery!* Oh, you're right. I must be thinking of **exclaim** and not **explore**.
- The **wilderness** is a place where no people live. There are no cities in the **wilderness**.
- **Reasons** are the facts that explain why you think what you do. **Reasons** are also dried grapes. *Tom Foolery!* Oh, you're right. I guess I was thinking of **raisins**. The **reason** I like **raisins** is because they are sweet.
- **Collected** means "to gather things together so you can use them." **Collected** also means "to get a red pencil and mark student homework." *Tom Foolery!* Oh, you're right. I must have been thinking of **corrected**. **Collected** means "to get a large number of things that are the same in some way because you really like those things."
- A **wild** duck is a duck that is not tame. A **wild** party is a party where everyone is well-behaved. *Tom Foolery!* Oh, you're right. A **wild** party is a party where people wouldn't be well-behaved, isn't it?

(Count the points and declare a winner.) You did a great job of playing *Tom Foolery!*

Preparation: Prepare a sheet of chart paper, portrait direction, titled *When We Go Camping*.

See the Introduction for Week 13's chart.

Record children's responses by writing the underlined words in the boxes.

Each child will need a copy of the Happy Face Game Test Sheet, BLM B.

Introduce Explaining Story Pattern

When authors write stories, they sometimes write in patterns. Let's see if we can figure out the pattern for this story. You tell me what happens in the story, and I'll write it down.

(Read the first sentence from page 1.) What is the first sentence of the story? *I love to go camping!* The first sentence of this story tells what the boy thinks. What does the first sentence tell? *What the boy thinks.*

(Read the rest of page 1.) What reasons does the boy give to explain why he likes camping? (Number the responses as a list. Ideas:
   1. *Wakes up early*;
   2. *in a tent*;
   3. can *snuggle* in his *sleeping bag*;
   4. he can *peek outside*.)

(Read pages 3–4.) What new reason does the boy give to explain why he likes camping? (Continue to number the responses as you add them to the list. Idea: 5. *We can explore*.)

(Read pages 5–6.) What new reasons does the boy give to explain why he likes camping? (Ideas:
   6. *We can paddle our canoe*;
   7. *see the mountains*;
   8. *hear the loons*.)

(Continue this procedure until you have reread all the story except the last paragraph and compiled a list of all the reasons the boy likes to go camping. Your list will be similar to this one:
   9. catch trout
   10. chop wood
   11. make a fire
   12. hoist food

13. <u>see tree beavers cut down</u>
14. <u>see elk</u>
15. <u>wonder about butterfly</u>; <u>dragonfly</u>
16. <u>see robin catch worms</u>
17. <u>watch waterbugs</u>
18. <u>hear frogs croak</u>
19. <u>squish mud between toes</u>
20. <u>splash</u>, <u>swim in the lake</u>
21. <u>pick and eat berries</u>
22. <u>cook on a campfire</u>
23. <u>catch a trout</u>
24. <u>hear owls</u>
25. <u>see the eagle</u>
26. <u>sit around the campfire</u>
27. <u>tell scary tales</u>)

The last paragraph uses different words to tell how much the boy likes camping. (Read the last paragraph of the story. Show pages 26 and 27.) What words does the boy use to tell us how much he likes camping? *I dream of camping.*

(Point to the chart.) What does the boy do first? (Idea: *He tells what he thinks.*) What does the boy do next? (Idea: *He tells all the reasons he thinks that.*) What does the boy do last? (Idea: *He tells what he thinks using different words from his first words.*)

When the boy tells his story, his reasons tell more about why he likes camping so we can understand better.

Explained is a word that means "told more about something so that someone could understand it." What word means "told more about something so that someone could understand it"? *Explained.* That's right, the boy explained why he liked to go camping, so this story is an explaining story. What kind of story is *When We Go Camping*? *An explaining story.*

This story starts by telling what the boy thinks. Then it gives the reasons he thinks that. It ends by using different words that tell what the boy thinks. This pattern is an explaining pattern. What kind of a story has a pattern that starts by telling what you think, gives reasons you think that, and ends by using different words to tell what you think? *An explaining story.*

Assess Vocabulary

 (Hold up a copy of the Happy Face Game Test Sheet, BLM B.)

Today you're going to play the Happy Face Game. When you play the Happy Face Game, it shows me how well you know the hard words you are learning.

If I say something that is true, color in the happy face. What will you do if I say something that is true? *Color in the happy face.*

If I say something that is false, color in the sad face. What will you do if I say something that is false? *Color in the sad face.*

Listen carefully to each item that I say. Don't let me trick you!

Item 1: **Wilderness** is where lots of people live. (*False.*)

Item 2: An **odor** is something you can smell. (*True.*)

Item 3: The **seasons** are winter, spring, summer, and autumn. (*True.*)

Item 4: People who **explore** don't like to travel. (*False.*)

Item 5: **Reasons** are facts that tell why you think the way you do. (*True.*)

Item 6: Something that is **precious** is very special and important to the person who owns it. (*True.*)

Item 7: When you cuddle up to someone, you **snuggle** with them. (*True.*)

Item 8: If you are **disturbed,** it can mean that something is bothering you. (*True.*)

Item 9: If a group of children are **taunting** a wild animal, they are standing still and quiet as they watch it. (*False.*)

Item 10: If you are **starving,** you are so hungry you think you will die. (*True.*)

You did a great job of playing the Happy Face Game!

(Score children's work at a later time. A child must score 9 out of 10 to be at the mastery level. If a child does not achieve mastery, insert the missed words as additional items in the games for next week's lessons. Retest those children individually for the missed items before they take the next mastery test.)

Extensions

Read a Story as a Reward

 (Display copies of several books that you have read since the beginning of the program. Allow children to choose which book they would like you to read to them as a reward for their hard work.)

(Read the story aloud for enjoyment with minimal interruptions.)

Preparation: Word containers for the Super Words Center. You may wish to remove some words from earlier lessons. Choose words children have mastered. See the Introduction for instructions on how to set up and use the Super Words Center.

Introduce the Super Words Center

(Add the new Picture Vocabulary Cards to words from the previous weeks. Show children one of the word containers. If children need more guidance in how to work in the Super Words Center, role-play with two to three children as a demonstration.)

I will teach you how to play a new game today called *Go Fish.*

Let's think about how we work with our words in the Super Words Center.

You will work with a partner in the Super Words Center. Whom will you work with? *A partner.*

First you and your partner will each draw six word cards out of the container and hold them so your partner cannot see them. What do you do first? (Idea: *Draw six cards out of the container and hold them so my partner cannot see them.*)

Next you will look at the cards in your hand and lay down any cards that you have two of. You will tell your partner the word the pictures show. What do you do next? (Idea: *Lay down any cards that I have two of, and tell my partner the word the pictures show.*)

Then your partner has a chance to lay down any cards he or she has two of, and tell the word the pictures show. What does your partner do? (Idea: *Lay down any cards that he or she has two of, and tell the word the pictures show.*)

Next you will ask your partner for a card that you have only one of by saying the word the picture shows. If your partner has that card, he or she will give it to you. If your partner gives you the card, you will lay down the two cards. What does your partner do if he or she has the card you ask for? (Idea: *Give you the card.*) What will you do if your partner gives you a card? (Idea: *Lay down the two cards that are the same.*)

If your partner does not have the card you ask for, your partner will say "Go Fish." What will your partner do if he or she doesn't have the card you ask for? (Idea: *Say "Go Fish."*) If your partner says "Go Fish," you must choose another card from the word container. What will you do if your partner says "Go Fish"? (Idea: *Choose a card from the word container.*)

Then it's your partner's turn.

Watch while I show you what I mean. **(Demonstrate this process with one child as your partner.)**

When one partner has no cards left in his or her hand, the game is over. Each person gets 1 point for each pair of cards they have laid down. The winner is the person with the most points. Who wins the game? (Idea: *The person with the most points.*)

Have fun playing *Go Fish*!

TIME TO SLEEP

Time to Sleep
author: Denise Fleming • illustrator: Denise Fleming

Preparation: You will need *Time to Sleep* for each day's lesson.

Number the pages of the story to assist you in asking questions at the appropriate points.

Post a copy of the Vocabulary Tally Sheet, BLM A, with this week's Picture Vocabulary Cards attached.

Each child will need one copy of the Homework Sheet, BLM 14a.

🎯 Target Vocabulary

Tier II	Tier III
cave	setting
den	(where, when)
burrow	pattern
frost	(circle)
*hibernate	
*migrate	

*Expanded Target Vocabulary Word

DAY 1

Introduce Book

This week's book is called *Time to Sleep*. What's the title? *Time to Sleep.*

This book was written by Denise Fleming. Who's the author of *Time to Sleep*? *Denise Fleming.*

Denise Fleming also made the pictures for this book. Who's the illustrator of *Time to Sleep*? *Denise Fleming.* Who made the illustrations for this book? *Denise Fleming.*

The cover of a book usually gives us some hints of what the book is about. Let's look at the front cover of *Time to Sleep.* What do you see in the illustration? (Ideas: *A bear sleeping; the head and front paws of a bear; leaves that are orange and red.*)

(Assign each child a partner.) Get ready to make some predictions to your partner about this book. Use the information from the cover to help you.

(Ask the following questions, allowing sufficient time for children to share their predictions with their partners.)

• Who is the main character in this story? (Who do you think this story is about?)
• What is the bear doing?
• Where do you think the story happens?
• When do you think the story happens?
• Why do you think the bear is sleeping?

• How many leaves do you see?
• Do you think this story is about real animals? Tell why or why not.

(Call on several children to share their predictions with the class.)

Take a Picture Walk

(Encourage children to use target words in their answers.) We're going to take a picture walk through this book. Remember that when we take a picture walk, we look at the pictures and tell what we think will happen in the story.

Pages 1–2. What season do you think it is when the story begins? (Idea: *Autumn; fall.*) Why do you think so? (Ideas: *There is orange, red, brown and yellow in the illustration; I see the autumn colors.*) What is the bear doing? (Idea: *Sniffing.*)

Pages 3–6. What is the bear doing? (Ideas: *Sniffing something on the ground; looking at something on the ground; looking at a snail; talking to a snail.*)

Pages 7–8. Who do you see? (Ideas: *The snail and the skunk.*) What is the skunk doing? (Ideas: *Digging in the ground; looking at the snail; talking to the snail.*)

Pages 9–10. Who do you see? *The skunk.* What is the skunk doing? (Ideas: *Looking up in the tree; sniffing the air.*)

Pages 11–12. Who do you see? (Ideas: *The skunk; the turtle.*) What is the skunk doing?

(Idea: *Looking at the turtle.*) What is the turtle doing? (Idea: *Walking away from the skunk.*)

Pages 13–14. Who do you see? (Ideas: *The skunk; the turtle.*) What is the skunk doing? (Idea: *Talking to the turtle.*) What is the turtle doing? (Idea: *Talking to the skunk.*)

Pages 15–16. What is happening here? (Ideas: *The turtle is climbing a hill.*)

Pages 17–18. Who do you see? (Idea: *An animal; a woodchuck.*) What is the animal doing? (Idea: *Looking down the hill.*)

(Note: If the children do not identify the animal as a woodchuck, it is not necessary to name the animal.)

Pages 19–20. What is the animal doing? (Idea: *Standing up on its back legs.*) Who else do you see? (Idea: *A ladybug.*)

Pages 21–22. What is the animal doing? (Ideas: *Looking at the ladybug; talking to the ladybug.*)

Pages 23–24. Where is the ladybug going? (Ideas: *To a cave.*) What other animals do you see? (Idea: *Geese.*)

Pages 25–26. Who do you see? (Idea: *The bear.*) Who is sitting on the bear's nose? (Idea: *The ladybug.*) What do you think the bear and the ladybug are doing? (Idea: *Talking.*)

Pages 27–28. Who do you see? (Idea: *The bear.*) What is the bear doing? (Idea: *Sleeping.*)

Page 29. What do you see? (Ideas: *Nighttime; snow falling; a tree; lots of words.*) Where do you think all the animals are?

Let's talk about how Denise Fleming made the illustrations for *Time to Sleep.* There are lots of different ways to make illustrations for a book: the artist can paint them; draw them with a pen or pencil; make them with markers, crayons, pastels, or chalk; or cut out different pieces of paper and glue them together.

How do you think Denise Fleming made her illustrations? (Idea: *She cut out different pieces of paper and glued them together to make a picture.*) You are almost right. Denise Fleming used stencils and made her own paper to fill in those stencils to make these pictures. She calls her illustrations "pulp paintings."

(Note: You may wish to make a stencil of a leaf and use it to explain how Denise Fleming made rag pulp, colored it, and then used it to fill in the stencils. As this is a very complicated process, we would suggest that you use only one stencil and one color to explain the process. If you want your students to experiment with papermaking, look at the information on the web that explains Denise Fleming's process of forcing cotton pulp through hand-cut stencils to make the distinctive art in her books. Use the search words Denise Fleming paper making to find out more about her technique.)

It's your turn to ask me some questions. What would you like to know about the story? (Accept questions. If children tell about the pictures or the story instead of ask questions, prompt them to ask a question.) Ask me a how question. Ask me a why question.

 Read the Story Aloud
(Read the story to children with minimal interruptions.)

Tomorrow we will read the story again, and I will ask you some questions.

Present Target Vocabulary
Cave

In the story, Bear says, "It is time to crawl into my cave and sleep." That means it was time for the bear to crawl into a large hole and sleep. **Cave.** Say the word. *Cave.*

Cave is a naming word. It names a place. What kind of word is **cave?** *A naming word.*

A cave is a large hole in the side of a hill or mountain. Say the word that means "a large hole in the side of a hill or mountain." *Cave.*

(Correct any incorrect responses, and repeat the item at the end of the sequence.)

Let's think about some places that might be caves. I'll tell about some places. If you think the place I'm telling about is a cave, say "cave." If not, don't say anything.

- The explorers squeezed past the rocks and went into the large hole in the side of the mountain. *Cave.*
- The hikers put on their safety equipment and carefully climbed down into the big hole. *Cave.*

- The girls walked down the street and past the school.
- As the boys peered into the large hole in the side of the hill, they caught a glimpse of two shining eyes. *Cave.*
- There were no holes in the hills or mountains.
- The bears lived in a hole in the mountain. *Cave.*

What naming word means "a large hole in the side of a hill or mountain"? *Cave.*

 Den

In the story, Snail told Skunk, "It is time for you to curl up in your den and sleep." That means it was time for the skunk to go into its home and sleep. **Den.** Say the word. *Den.*

Den is a naming word. It names a place. What kind of word is **den?** *A naming word.*

A den is a home for some kinds of wild animals, such as bears, foxes, skunks, and wolves. Say the word that means "a home for some kinds of wild animals, such as foxes, skunks, and wolves." *Den.*

Let's think about some places that might be dens. I'll tell about some places. If you think the place I'm telling about is a den, say "den." If not, don't say anything.

- The fox dug a hole in the ground so she would have a place to have her babies. *Den.*
- The eagle built a nest high in a tree.
- The bear found a cave in the side of a hill, where it could live for the winter. *Den.*
- The wolf lived in its home most of the time. *Den.*
- Henry lived in an apartment on 54th Street.
- The skunk went into its home for a nice nap. *Den.*

What naming word means "a home for some kinds of wild animals, such as bears, foxes, skunks, and wolves"? *Den.*

 Burrow

In the story, Turtle told Woodchuck, "It is time for you to burrow down and sleep." That means it was time for the woodchuck to dig down, make a tunnel or a hole, and sleep. **Burrow.** Say the word. *Burrow.*

Burrow is an action word. It tells about what an animal is doing. What kind of word is **burrow?** *An action word.*

When animals burrow down into the ground, they dig down in the ground and make a tunnel or a hole. Say the word that means "dig down in the ground and make a tunnel or a hole." *Burrow.*

Let's think about some times when animals might burrow. I'll tell about what an animal is doing. If you think the animal is burrowing, say "burrow." If not, don't say anything.

- The gopher dug a hole in the farmer's field. *Burrow.*
- The fish swam upstream.
- A chipmunk dug a hole in the park. *Burrow.*
- A mole was living in a tunnel under my mom's front lawn. *Burrow.*
- The frog lived in a pond.
- The ground was so rocky that gophers and chipmunks couldn't build homes there.

What action word means "dig down in the ground and make a tunnel or a hole"? *Burrow.*

 Frost

In the story, Snail said, "This morning there was frost on the grass." That means the grass was white because it had been very cold the night before. **Frost.** Say the word. *Frost.*

Frost is a naming word. It names a thing. What kind of word is **frost?** *A naming word.*

Frost is white powdery ice that forms on things in freezing weather. What word means "white powdery ice that forms on things in freezing weather"? *Frost.*

Let's think about some times when there might be frost. I'll tell you about a time. If you think you would see frost, say "frost." If not, don't say anything.

- After the winter storm, white powdery ice covered the outside of the windows. *Frost.*
- It rained in the night.
- It was so hot that everyone was sweating.
- I slipped on the white powdery ice that was on the sidewalk. *Frost.*

- The trees were covered with thick layers of white, powdery ice. They looked like they were made of sugar. *Frost.*
- The white powder on my face was flour because I had been baking.

What naming word means "white powdery ice that forms on things in freezing weather"? *Frost.*

Introduce the Vocabulary Tally Sheet
(See Lesson 1, page 3, for instructions.)

Assign Homework
(Homework Sheet, BLM 14a: See the Introduction for homework instructions.)

DAY 2

Preparation: Picture Vocabulary Cards for *cave, den, burrow, frost.*

Read and Discuss Story

(Read story to children. Ask the following questions at the specified points in the story. Encourage children to use target words in their answers.)

Page 2. What does Bear smell? *Winter.* What does Bear want to do? (Idea: *Crawl into her cave and sleep.*) What must Bear do before she goes to sleep? (Idea: *Tell Snail winter is in the air.*)

Page 4. What does Bear tell Snail? (Ideas: *Winter is in the air; it is time to seal your shell and sleep.*)

Page 6. What does Snail say? (Ideas: *You are right; it is time to sleep; this morning there was frost on the grass; I must tell Skunk.*)

Page 7. What does Snail tell Skunk? (Ideas: *Winter is on its way; it is time for you to curl up in your den and sleep.*)

Page 9. What does Skunk say? (Ideas: *I will sleep; I must tell Turtle.*)

Page 12. What does Skunk tell Turtle? (Ideas: *I have news; winter is on its way.*)

Page 14. What does Turtle say? (Ideas: *The days have been growing shorter; it is time to sleep; I must tell Woodchuck.*)

Page 15. What does Turtle tell Woodchuck? (Ideas: *Winter is on its way; it is time for you to burrow down and sleep.*)

Page 17. What does Woodchuck say? (Ideas: *My skin is so tight I could not eat another bite; I am ready to sleep; I must tell Ladybug.*)

Pages 19–22. What does Woodchuck tell Ladybug? (Ideas: *Winter is on its way; the leaves are falling from the trees; it is time for you to slip under a log and sleep.*) What does Ladybug say? (Idea: *I must tell Bear.*)

Page 23. What does Ladybug tell Bear? (Ideas: *Wake up; the sky is full of geese honking goodbye; winter is on its way.*)

Page 25. What else does Ladybug tell Bear? (Idea: *It is time to crawl into your cave and sleep.*) What does Bear tell Ladybug? (Ideas: *I am in my cave; I was asleep.*) What does Ladybug say? (Ideas: *I am so sorry; please go back to sleep.*) It looks like the ladybug disturbed the bear's sleep.

Page 29. What is everyone saying? (Idea: *Good night.*) What do you think everyone is doing at the end of the story? (Idea: *Going to sleep.*)

Review Vocabulary
(Display the Picture Vocabulary Cards. Point to each card as you say the word. Ask children to repeat each word after you.) These pictures show **cave, den, burrow,** and **frost.**

- What word means "a home for some kinds of wild animals, such as bears, foxes, skunks, and wolves"? *Den.*
- What word means "a large hole in the side of a hill or mountain"? *Cave.*
- What word means "white powdery ice that forms on things in freezing weather"? *Frost.*
- What word means "dig down in the ground and make a tunnel or a hole"? *Burrow.*

Extend Vocabulary

 Den

In *Time to Sleep,* we learned that **den** means "a home for some kinds of wild animals, such as bears, foxes, skunks, and wolves." Say the word that means "a home for some kinds of wild animals, such as bears, foxes, skunks, and wolves." *Den.*

Raise your hand if you can tell us a sentence that uses **den** as a naming word meaning "a home for some kinds of wild animals, such as bears, foxes, skunks, and wolves." (Call on several children. If they don't use complete sentences, restate their examples as sentences. Have the class repeat the sentences.)

Here's a new way to use the word **den.**

- Some people have their television in their **den.** Say the sentence.
- The Johnson family keeps their board games in the **den.** Say the sentence.
- Leroy's dad likes to read in the **den.** Say the sentence.

In these sentences, den is a naming word that means a cozy, comfortable room in a house where people relax and do things they enjoy. What naming word means "a cozy, comfortable room in a house where people relax and do things they enjoy"? *Den.*

Raise your hand if you can tell us a sentence that uses **den** as a naming word meaning "a cozy, comfortable room in a house where people relax and do things they enjoy." (Call on several children. If they don't use complete sentences, restate their examples as sentences. Have the class repeat the sentences.)

Present Expanded Target Vocabulary
◎━ Hibernate

In *Time to Sleep,* the bear, the snail, the skunk, the turtle, the woodchuck, and the ladybug were all getting ready to sleep because winter was coming. Another way of saying the animals were going to sleep for the winter is to say the animals were going to hibernate for the winter. **Hibernate.** Say the word. *Hibernate.*

Hibernate is an action word. It tells what animals do. What kind of word is **hibernate?** *An action word.*

When animals hibernate they spend the winter in a deep sleep. Say the word that means "spend the winter in a deep sleep." *Hibernate.*

I'll tell about some animals. If that animal is hibernating, say "hibernate." If not don't say anything.

- The bear slept all winter. *Hibernate.*
- The mouse raced across the snow looking for seeds.
- The squirrel slept in the hollow tree all winter. *Hibernate.*
- In the winter, the raccoon slept for a long, long time. *Hibernate.*
- The brown bat slept in a cave all winter. *Hibernate.*
- Your dog runs and plays in the snow.

What action word means "spend the winter in a deep sleep"? *Hibernate.*

◎━ Migrate

In *Time to Sleep,* Ladybug said, "The sky is full of geese, honking good-bye." The geese were flying away to spend the winter somewhere else. Another way of saying the geese were flying away to spend the winter somewhere else is to say the geese were migrating. **Migrate.** Say the word. *Migrate.*

Migrate is an action word. It tells what some animals do. What kind of word is **migrate?** *An action word.*

When birds and insects migrate they fly away to spend the winter somewhere else. Say the word that means "fly away to spend the winter somewhere else." *Migrate.*

I'll tell about some animals. If that animal is migrating, say "migrate." If that animal is hibernating, say "hibernate."

- The ducks flew south for the winter. *Migrate.*
- The turtle slept all winter at the bottom of the pond. *Hibernate.*
- The Monarch butterflies flew from Michigan to Mexico. *Migrate.*
- As they always did, the swallows came back to Capistrano. *Migrate.*
- The frog slept at the bottom of the pond all winter. *Hibernate.*
- The Canada Geese flew south for the winter with their loud honking call. *Migrate.*

What action word means "fly away to spend the winter somewhere else"? *Migrate.*

Preparation: Activity Sheet, BLM 14b. Each child will need a pencil and their crayons.

You may wish to have available a nonfiction book of different animals to assist children with their drawings.

Retell the Story

Today I'll show you the pictures Denise Fleming made for *Time to Sleep.* As I show you the pictures, I'll call on one of you to tell the class that part of the story.

Tell me what happens at the **beginning** of the story. (Show the pictures on pages 1 and 2. Call on a child to tell what's happening.)

Tell me what happens in the **middle** of the story. (Show the pictures on pages 3–28. Call on a child to tell what's happening. Encourage use of the target words when appropriate. Model use as necessary.)

Tell me what happens at the **end** of the story. (Show the pictures on page 29. Call on a child to tell what's happening.)

Prepare Picture Vocabulary Cards for all words with dual meanings. Display them prominently in a pocket chart, on a chalkboard ledge, or another obvious location. These words are: *awkward, blossom, calm, collect, den, disturb, fine, gentle, grains, roared, rough, shouted, wild, winding.*

Play Tom Foolery

Today we will play *Tom Foolery.* I will pretend to be Tom. Tom Foolery has a reputation of trying to trick students. Tom knows that some words have more than one meaning. He will tell you one meaning that will be correct. Then he will tell you another meaning that might be correct or might be incorrect.

If you think the meaning is correct, don't say anything. If you think the meaning is incorrect, sing, "Tom Foolery." Then Tom will have to tell the truth and tell the correct meaning. Tom is sly enough that he may include some words that do <u>not</u> have two meanings. Be careful! He's tricky!

Let's practice. **Fine** can be money paid as a punishment for doing something wrong. It can also tell about a person who is disagreeable and uncooperative. *Tom Foolery!* Oh, you're right. The other meaning for **fine** is "good." You would call a good person a fine person.

Let's do another one together. **Grains** are things like wheat, and oats, and rice. **Grains** are also dirty marks on your clothes that are hard to get out. *Tom Foolery!* Oh, you're right. I was thinking of **stains.** Grass stains on your pants are particularly hard to get out.

When we play *Tom Foolery,* Tom will keep score. If you catch him being tricky, you will get one point. If you don't catch him, Tom gets the point. Watch out! Tom might try to give himself extra points while you're not looking!

Now you're ready to play the game. (Draw a T-chart on the board for keeping score. Children earn one point for each correct answer. If they make an error, correct them as you normally would, and record one point for yourself. Repeat missed words at the end of the game.)

- A **den** is a home for wild animals like bears and beavers. **Den** is also the number that comes after nine. *Tom Foolery!* Oh, you're right. I must have been thinking of **ten** instead of **den.**
- A **cave** is a large hole in the side of a hill or mountain. A **cave** can also be a young cow or bull. *Tom Foolery!* Oh, you're right. I was thinking of **calf.** We only know the first meaning for **cave.**
- On cold mornings, **frost** sometimes appears on the grass. **Frost** can also be found on car windows on really cold mornings.
- Many animals **burrow** down in the ground to make a tunnel or hole. Sometimes your parents may go to the bank to **burrow** money.

Tom Foolery! Oh, you're right. I was thinking of **borrow.** You go to the bank to **borrow** money.

- A **den** can be a cozy room in your house where you relax and do things you enjoy. A **den** can also be a bang on your aunt's car. *Tom Foolery!* Oh, you're right. I was thinking of **dent.** The old car has so many **dents** it looks like a golf ball.

(Count the points and declare a winner.) You did a great job of playing *Tom Foolery!*

Complete the Activity Sheet

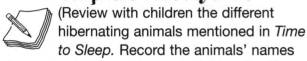

(Review with children the different hibernating animals mentioned in *Time to Sleep.* Record the animals' names on the chart paper as they are identified. (Ideas: *Bear; snail; skunk; turtle; woodchuck; ladybug.*)

(Have children suggest other animals that hibernate. Record them on the chart paper. **Note:** You need to record at least one more animal than the number of children in your class. Here are the names of some other animals that hibernate: badger; black bear; brown bat; chipmunk; echidna; frog; Gila monster; grizzly bear; groundhog; hamster; hedgehog; lizard; lemur; marmot; opossum; raccoon; squirrel; toad; wasp. Many insects also hibernate over the winter.)

(Give each child a copy of the Activity Sheet, BLM 14b.) Today we will make a class book of animals that spend the winter in a deep sleep. What word means "spend the winter in a deep sleep"? *Hibernate.* Touch under the words at the bottom of the page. Those words say "Blank says, 'It's time to sleep.'" What do those words say? *Blank says, "It's time to sleep."*

Print the name of the animal you have chosen on the blank. Then you can draw and color a picture of your animal in the space above the sentence.

(Make a cover titled *Animals that Hibernate* and fasten the pages together into a class book.)

Preparation: Prepare a sheet of chart paper, landscape direction, titled *Time to Sleep.* Underneath the title, draw 10 boxes connected by arrows.

Underneath the 10 boxes, draw 2 boxes connected by arrows.

See the Introduction for Week 14's chart.

Literary Analysis (Cumulative Review)

Let's think about what we already know about how books are made.

- What do we call the name of the book? *Title.*
- What do we call the person who writes the story? *Author.*
- What do we call the person who draws the pictures? *Illustrator.*
- What are the people or animals a story is about? *Characters.*
- What do we call the pictures the illustrator makes? *Illustrations.*
- What is one thing the setting of a story tells? *Where a story happens.*

Let's sing the first [number] verses of The Story Song to help us remember these important things about books. (At this point it is unnecessary to sing the whole song. Choose which verses you would like the children to sing. Include *setting* as it is a relatively new concept. See the Introduction for the complete Story Song.)

Today we will learn more about the setting of a story.

The setting of a story tells two things. One thing the setting tells is where the story happens. What is one thing the setting tells? *Where the story happens.* The second thing the setting tells is when the story happens. What is the second thing the setting tells? *When the story happens.*

Let's look at the pictures and talk about the story to figure out where *Time to Sleep* happens.

(Follow the procedure established in Lessons 8, 9, and 10 to identify <u>where</u> the story happens. Record responses in the first row of boxes.

Ideas: *In the forest; in the grass; on a leaf; near a rock; in the forest; on the grass; on Woodchuck's hill; at the maple tree; in Bear's cave; near Bear's cave.*)

In the forest, in the grass, on a leaf, near a rock, in the forest, on the grass, on Woodchuck's hill, at the maple tree, in Bear's cave, and near Bear's cave are all in the wilderness. So, if we could only use one word to tell the setting of the story, we would use the word **wilderness.** Where is the setting of *Time to Sleep*? *In the wilderness.*

(Record responses in the second row of boxes.) Now let's think about when this story happens. I'm going to show you all the illustrations in this story. Then I'm going to ask you how many days it took for the story to happen. (**Slowly turn the pages without commenting.**) How many days does it take for this story to happen? (**Idea:** *One day.*) How do you know it takes one day for this story to happen? (**Idea:** *It is daytime—light—all through the story until the last page when it is nighttime—dark.*)

(Show pages 1, 2, 9 and 10.) In what season does the story happen? (**Idea:** *Autumn.*) How do you know it is autumn? (**Ideas:** *The leaves are colored red, orange, and yellow; the leaves are falling from the trees.*)

So when is the setting of *Time to Sleep*? (**Idea:** *One day in autumn.*)

You were great detectives! You used the clues and figured out both of the parts of the setting of *Time to Sleep.* You figured out where and when the story happened.

Play Tom Foolery (Cumulative Review)

Today we will play *Tom Foolery.* I will pretend to be Tom. You know that Tom has a reputation for trying to trick students. Tom knows that some words have more than one meaning. He will tell you one meaning that will be correct. Then he will tell you another meaning that might be correct or might be incorrect.

If you think the meaning is correct, don't say anything. If you think the meaning is incorrect, sing, "Tom Foolery." Then Tom will have to tell

the truth and tell the correct meaning. Tom is sly enough that he may include some words that do <u>not</u> have two meanings. Be careful! He's tricky!

Let's practice. A **legend** is a story that tells how something came to be. When you climb a mountain, a **legend** is a place where you can stop and rest your feet. *Tom Foolery!* Oh, you're right. I'm thinking about **ledge,** not **legend.** They aren't the same at all!

Let's do another one together. **Disappears** means that something or someone goes out of sight. **Disappears** also means a certain kind of ears that you can show or not show, depending on how you feel. *Tom Foolery!* Oh, you're right. We only know the first meaning. I would sure like to have a pair of "disapp ears," though.

When we play *Tom Foolery,* Tom will keep score. If you catch him being tricky, you will get one point. If you don't catch him, Tom gets the point. Watch out! Tom might try to give himself extra points while you're not looking!

Now you're ready to play the game. (Draw a T-chart on the board for keeping score. Children earn one point for each correct answer. If they make an error, correct them as you normally would, and record one point for yourself. Repeat missed words at the end of the game.)

- Gophers **burrow** down in the ground to make their dens. A **burrow** is also a long, narrow ditch made in the ground so you can plant seeds. *Tom Foolery!* I must have been thinking of **furrow.** But **furrows** and a gopher that **burrows** can both be found in a field, so I was close!
- A **cave** is a large hole in the side of a hill or mountain. Some people like to explore **caves.**
- **Frost** is a white powdery ice that forms on things in freezing weather. **Frost** also tells where you finished in a race if you beat everyone else. *Tom Foolery!* Oh, you are very hard to fool. If you beat everyone in a race, you come in **first.**
- Animals that spend the winter in a deep sleep **hibernate.** The **hibernates** are also the highest mountains in the world. *Tom Foolery!* Oh, you're right. I must be thinking of **Himalayas** and not **hibernate.** Do you think

there are any animals that **hibernate** in the **Himalayas?**

- A **den** is a place in your home where you might play games or read a book. A **den** is also a home for wild animals such as skunks and wolves.
- **Roared** means that someone shouted something in a loud voice. **Roared** also means that you have nothing to do and you don't like to feel that way. *Tom Foolery!* Oh, you're right. I must have been thinking of **bored. Roared** also means that people or things moved very fast and made a loud noise.
- When birds and insects **migrate,** they fly away to spend the winter somewhere else. Some animals like reindeer **migrate** to find food.
- A **winding** road twists and turns as it goes along. **Winding** is also what you do when you complain all the time in a really annoying voice. *Tom Foolery!* Oh, you're right. I'm thinking of **whining.** (Say in a whining voice:) I just hate it when people whine, whine, whine.

(Count the points and declare a winner.) You did a great job of playing *Tom Foolery!*

DAY 5

Preparation: Prepare a sheet of chart paper, portrait direction, titled *Time to Sleep.* Underneath the title, make a circle of 11 circles connected by arrows.

See the Introduction for Week 14's chart.

Record children's responses by writing the underlined words in the boxes.

Each child will need a copy of the Happy Face Game Test Sheet, BLM B.

Introduce Circle Story Pattern

When authors write stories, they sometimes write in patterns. Let's see if we can figure out the pattern for this story. You tell me what happened in the story, and I'll write it down.

Pages 1–2. What animal starts the story? *Bear.* What does Bear want to do? (Idea: *Sleep.*) Who is Bear going to talk to before she goes to sleep? *Snail.*

Pages 3–6. Who is Bear talking to? <u>Snail</u>. What does Snail want to do? (Idea: *Sleep.*) Who is Snail going to talk to before Snail goes to sleep? *Skunk.*

Pages 7–10. Who is Snail talking to? <u>Skunk</u>. What does Skunk want to do? (Idea: *Sleep.*) Who is Skunk going to talk to before Skunk goes to sleep? *Turtle.*

Pages 11–14. Who is Skunk talking to? <u>Turtle</u>. What does Turtle want to do? (Idea: *Sleep.*) Who is Turtle going to talk to before Turtle goes to sleep? *Woodchuck.*

Pages 15–18. Who is Turtle talking to? <u>Woodchuck</u>. What does Woodchuck want to do? (Idea: *Sleep.*) Who is Woodchuck going to talk to before Woodchuck goes to sleep? *Ladybug.*

Pages 19–22. Who is Woodchuck talking to? <u>Ladybug</u>. What does Ladybug want to do? (Idea: *Sleep.*) Who is Ladybug going to talk to before Ladybug goes to sleep? *Bear.*

Pages 23–28. Who is Ladybug talking to? *Bear.* (Point to the first circle with *Bear* written in it.) What does Bear want to do? (Idea: *Sleep.*)

(Point to the story map that is on the chart paper.) Look at the shape of this story. It's a circle. This story starts and ends with the same animal at the same place so this story has a **circle** pattern. What kind of a story has a pattern that starts and ends at the same place? *A circle story.*

Assess Vocabulary

 (Give each child a copy of the Happy Face Game Test Sheet, BLM B.)

Today you're going to play the Happy Face Game. When you play the Happy Face Game, it shows me how well you know the hard words you are learning.

If I say something that is true, color in the happy face. What will you do if I say something that is true? *Color in the happy face.*

If I say something that is false, color in the sad face. What will you do if I say something that is false? *Color in the sad face.*

Listen carefully to each item that I say. Don't let me trick you!

Item 1: A **cave** is a small hole that even an ant couldn't fit into. (*False.*)

Item 2: **Migrate** means to go to another place for part of the year. (*True.*)

Item 3: **Frost** is a white, powdery cake that you cook for dinner. (*False.*)

Item 4: A gopher or chipmunk might **burrow.** (*True.*)

Item 5: **Den** is another word for a comfortable room in a house. (*True.*)

Item 6: When animals **hibernate,** they sleep for weeks and weeks. (*True.*)

Item 7: You **mutter** to yourself if you don't want anyone else to hear what you are saying. (*True.*)

Item 8: If you **crept** across the classroom, you moved as quietly and as slowly as you could. (*True.*)

Item 9: **Pleaded** means begged. (*True.*)

Item 10: When seeds **sprout** they die. (*False.*)

You did a great job of playing the Happy Face Game!

(Score children's work at a later time. A child must score 9 out of 10 to be at the mastery level. If a child does not achieve mastery, insert the missed words as additional items in the games for next week's lessons. Retest those children individually for the missed items before they take the next mastery test.)

Extensions

Read a Story as a Reward

(Display copies of several of the books that you have read since the beginning of the program. Allow children to choose which book they would like you to read to them as a reward for their hard work.)

(Read the story aloud for enjoyment with minimal interruptions.)

Preparation: Word containers for the Super Words Center. You may wish to remove some words from earlier lessons. Choose words children have mastered. See the Introduction for instructions on how to set up and use Super Words Center.

Introduce the Super Words Center

(Add the new Picture Vocabulary Cards to the words from the previous weeks. Show children one of the word containers. If children need more guidance in how to work in the Super Words Center, role-play with two to three children as a demonstration.)

Let's review how we play the game called *Go Fish.*

Let's think about how we work with our words in the Super Words Center.

You will work with a partner in the Super Words Center. Whom will you work with? *A partner.*

First you and your partner will each draw six word cards out of the container and hold them so your partner cannot see them. What do you do first? (Idea: *Draw six cards out of the container and hold them so my partner cannot see them.*)

Next you will look at the cards in your hand and lay down any cards that you have two of. You will tell your partner the word the pictures show. What do you do next? (Idea: *Lay down any cards that I have two of, and tell my partner the word the pictures show.*)

Then your partner has a chance to lay down any cards he or she has two of, and tell the word the pictures show. What does your partner do? (Idea: *Lay down any cards that he or she has two of, and tell the word the pictures show.*)

Next you will ask your partner for a card that you have only one of by saying the word the picture shows. If your partner has that card, he or she will give it to you. If your partner gives you the card, you will lay down the two cards. What does your partner do if they have the card you ask for? (Idea: *Give you the card.*) What will you do if your partner gives you a card? (Idea: *Lay down the two cards that are the same.*)

If your partner does not have the card you ask for, your partner will say, "Go Fish." What will your partner do if he or she doesn't have the card you ask for? (Idea: *Say "Go Fish."*) If your partner says "Go Fish," you must choose another card from the word container. What will you do if your partner says "Go Fish"? (Idea: *Choose a card from the word container.*)

Then it's your partner's turn.

Watch while I show you what I mean. (Demonstrate this process with one child as your partner.)

When one partner has no cards left in his or her hand, the game is over. Each person gets 1 point for each pair of cards they have laid down. The winner is the person with the most points. Who wins the game? (Idea: *The person with the most points.*)

Have fun playing *Go Fish*!

Preparation: You will need *The First Day of Winter* for each day's lesson.

Number the pages of the story to assist you in asking questions at appropriate points.

Post the Vocabulary Tally Sheet, BLM A, with this week's Picture Vocabulary Cards attached.

Each child will need the Homework Sheet, BLM 15a.

The First Day of Winter
author: Consie Powell • illustrator: Consie Powell

Target Vocabulary

Tier II	Tier III
limbs	setting
chores	(where, when)
awesome	pattern
devour	(counting)
*impressions	cutaway view
*dormant	mixed media

*Expanded Target Vocabulary Word

(Ask the following questions, allowing sufficient time for children to share their predictions with their partners.)

- Who are the main characters in this story? (Who do you think this story is about?)
- What are the children doing?
- Where do you think the story happens?
- When do you think the story happens?
- Why do you think the rabbit is hiding?
- How far do you think it is to the house?
- Do you think this story is about real people? Tell why or why not.

(Call on several children to share their predictions with the class.)

DAY 1

Introduce Book

This week's book is called *The First Day of Winter*. What's the title? *The First Day of Winter.*

This book was written by Consie Powell. Who's the author of *The First Day of Winter*? *Consie Powell.*

Consie Powell also made the pictures for this book. Who's the illustrator of *The First Day of Winter*? *Consie Powell.* Who made the illustrations for this book? *Consie Powell.*

The cover of a book usually gives us some hints of what the book is about. Let's look at the front cover of *The First Day of Winter.* What do you see in the illustration? (Ideas: *Three children playing in the snow; one has a snowball; one is catching snowflakes on his tongue; one is catching snowflakes on her mittens; a white rabbit is hiding in a bush; two birds are sitting on branches; there are snowflakes; there's a tree.*)

(Assign each child a partner.) Remember that when you make a prediction about something, you say what you think will happen. Get ready to make some predictions to your partner about this book. Use the information from the cover to help you.

Take a Picture Walk

(Encourage children to use target words in their answers.) We're going to take a picture walk through this book. Remember that when we take a picture walk, we look at the pictures and tell what we think will happen in the story.

Page 1. What season do you think it is when the story begins? (Idea: *Winter.*) Why do you think so? (Ideas: *There's snow on the ground; I see snowshoes, a toboggan, a snow shovel; some of the trees have no leaves; the people are putting on warm coats, boots, hats, and mittens.*) Where do you think the family is going? (Idea: *Outside to play in the snow.*)

Pages 2–3. This illustration has two parts: a background that shows an outdoor scene, and an oval that shows a close-up. First tell me about the background scene. What do you see? (Ideas: *A green tree covered with snow; a bird on a branch; some trees with no leaves; snow; a fence.*) Now tell me about the close-up in the oval. What is happening in this part of the illustration? (Idea: *A child is hiding under a branch of the green tree.*)

Pages 4–5. This illustration has two parts: a background that shows an outdoor scene, and an oval that shows a close-up. First tell me about the background scene. What do you see? (Ideas: *Lots of snow; a bird; a crow; an animal sliding down into the water.*) Now tell me about the close-up in the oval. What is happening in this part of the illustration? (Idea: *Two children are sliding down the snowy hill on big inner tubes.*)

Pages 6–7. This illustration has two parts: a background that shows an outdoor scene, and an oval that shows a close-up. First tell me about the background scene. What do you see? (Ideas: *Snow; trees; bushes; grasses; funny marks in the snow.*) What do you think made the funny marks in the snow? Now tell me about the close-up in the oval. What is happening in this part of the illustration? (Idea: *The children are making snow angels; the children are making marks in the snow.*)

Pages 8–9. First tell me about the background scene. What is different about this illustration? (Idea: *We can see on top of the water and under the water at the same time.*) When an artist makes an illustration that looks like they have put a window in so you can see above and below, we call that a cut-away view. What kind of illustration is this? *A cut-away view.*

What things do you see above the water? (Ideas: *Snow; the tops of some water plants.*) What things do you see below? (Ideas: *A turtle; some bugs; a beaver; some fish; some sticks; some rocks; some dirt or sand.*) What other story did we read that had a cut-away view? (Idea: *Loon Lake.*) Now tell me about the close-up in the oval. What is happening in this part of the illustration? (Idea: *Four children are skating; one boy has a hockey stick.*) Where do you think the children are skating? (Idea: *On the frozen pond.*)

Pages 10–11. First tell me about the background scene. What is different about this illustration? (Idea: *We can see on top of the snow and under the snow at the same time.*) What kind of illustration is this? *A cut-away view.* What things do you see above the snow? (Ideas: *Bare branches; birds.*) What things do you see below? (Ideas: *A chipmunk; some voles; some other animals; some snakes; a frog.*)

(**Note:** If children don't correctly name the animals, tell them that they will learn the names of the animals when you read the story aloud to them.)

Now tell me about the close-up in the oval. What is happening in this part of the illustration? (Idea: *Five people are inside their house; two children are doing a jigsaw puzzle; a boy is playing with his dog; the man is reading the paper; the woman is toasting marshmallows; the cat is sleeping on the couch.*)

Pages 12–13. First tell me about the background scene. What do you see? (Ideas: *Snow; house; trees; branches; snowflakes.*) Now tell me about the close-up in the oval. Where have we seen this illustration before? (Idea: *On the front cover.*) What are the children doing? (Idea: *Playing in the snow.*)

Pages 14–15. First tell me about the background scene. What do you see? (Ideas: *Snow; lots of trees and bushes; the leaves on the trees all look dead; some trees have seeds.*) Now tell me about the close-up in the oval. What is happening in this part of the illustration? (Idea: *The people are carrying wood; the dog is playing with a stick.*) Why do you suppose they have so much wood stacked in the shed? (Idea: *They need it to keep their house warm in the winter.*)

Pages 16–17. First tell me about the background scene. What do you see? (Ideas: *Snow; lots of trees and bushes; animals walking on the snow; animals sitting on the snow; a squirrel coming down a tree.*) Now tell me about the close-up in the oval. What is happening in this part of the illustration? (Idea: *Everyone is wearing snowshoes; they are going for a walk in the snow.*) Where do you think they might be going?

Pages 18–19. First tell me about the background scene. What is different about this illustration? (Idea: *We can see on top of the snow and under the snow at the same time; we can see inside the trees.*) What kind of illustration is this? *A cut-away view.* What things do you see above the snow? (Ideas: *Trees; bushes; plants.*) What things do you see below? (Ideas: *Ants; insects; bugs.*) What things do you see in the cut-away view of the trees? (Ideas: *Butterflies; ladybugs; insects; bugs.*) Now tell me about the close-up in the oval. What is happening in this part of the illustration? (Idea: *They are building a snow fort; they are making snowballs.*)

Pages 20–21. First tell me about the background scene. What do you see? (Ideas: *Snow; trees; the pond; lots of footprints.*) Now tell me about the close-up in the oval. What is happening in this part of the illustration? (Ideas: *The boy is shoveling snow; one girl is playing with the dog; the other girl is looking at the footprints in the snow.*)

Pages 22–23. First tell me about the background scene. What do you see? (Ideas: *A birdfeeder; some bread in a bag; lots of birds.*) Now tell me about the close-up in the oval. What is happening in this part of the illustration? (Ideas: *The girl is watching the birds eating seeds at the bird feeder.*)

Pages 24–25. First tell me about the background scene. What do you see? (Ideas: *Snow; trees; lots of birds and animals; they're all eating something.*) Now tell me about the close-up in the oval. What is happening in this part of the illustration? (Ideas: *Two people are making cookies; some people are eating cookies.*)

There are lots of different ways to make illustrations for a book: the artist can paint them; draw them with a pen or pencil; make them with markers, crayons, pastels, or chalk; or cut out different pieces of paper and glue them together.

Let's see if we can figure out how Consie Powell made the illustrations for *The First Day of Winter.*

Page 9. What do you think Consie Powell used to draw the people? (Ideas: *Ink; a pen.*) How do you know she didn't use a pencil? (Idea: *The lines are dark, not light like a pencil.*) Consie

Powell doesn't use a pen to draw the lines—she likes to use a small brush dipped in ink. That way, her lines can change from narrow to wide and back again if she wants.

(Point to the lines used to draw the snow.) Here she wanted a thick line. (Point to the lines used to draw the children.) And here she wanted a thin line. (Point to the line in the mud beneath the beaver.) Here she wanted a line that started thin, got thicker, and then got thin again. She could do that with a brush but not with a pen.

What do you think Consie Powell used to color the water and the mud? (Idea: *Watercolors.*) That's right: she mixed lots of water and a little color and painted these big areas, being careful to stay inside the lines. When an artist uses a lot of water and a little paint to cover a large area on an illustration, we say she put a wash on the painting.

(Point to the crosshatching on the mud at the bottom of the pond and the lines on the beaver.) What do you think Consie Powell used to add shading and details to her drawings? (Idea: *Pencil crayons.*)

(Point to the bushes at the top of the oval.) If you look carefully here, you can see many different colors of pencil lines that she used to draw the bushes.

On this page, Consie Powell used three different things to make her illustrations: ink, watercolors, and pencil crayons. When an artist uses different things to make an illustration, we say she used mixed media. What kind of illustrations did Consie use in *The First Day of Winter*? *Mixed media.*

It's your turn to ask me some questions. What would you like to know about the story? (Accept questions. If children tell about the pictures or the story instead of ask questions, prompt them to ask a question.) Ask me a how question. Ask me a why question.

 Read the Story Aloud
(Read the story to children with minimal interruptions.)

Tomorrow we will read the story again, and I will ask you some questions.

Present Target Vocabulary

 Limbs

In the story, it says "We'll hide and seek beneath the limbs of one big old fir tree." That means we'll play hide and seek under the branches of the tree. **Limbs.** Say the word. *Limbs.*

Limbs is a naming word. It names things. What kind of word is **limbs?** *A naming word.*

Limbs are the branches of a tree. Say the word that means "the branches of a tree." *Limbs.*

(Correct any incorrect responses, and repeat the item at the end of the sequence.)

Let's think about some things that might be limbs. I'll name some things. If you think the things I'm naming are limbs, say "limbs." If not, don't say anything.

- There was a robin's nest in the branches of the tree. *Limbs.*
- The heavy snow bent the branches of the tree low. *Limbs.*
- The part of the tree that grows underground was strong and healthy.
- The branches of the trees were hidden by the leaves. *Limbs.*
- The leaves of the trees needed water.
- The man had a sore back, so he had trouble sleeping.

What naming word means "the branches of a tree"? *Limbs.*

 Chores

In the story, on the seventh day of winter, the family completed their chores. That means they finished all the jobs they had to do. **Chores.** Say the word. *Chores.*

Chores is a naming word. It names things. What kind of word is **chores?** *A naming word.*

Chores are the jobs you have to do nearly every day. Say the word that means "jobs you have to do nearly every day." *Chores.*

Let's think about some things that might be chores. I'll tell about something. If you think I'm telling about a chore, say "chore." If not, don't say anything.

- Setting the table for dinner. *Chore.*
- Playing with your best friend.
- Putting dirty clothes into the clothes hamper. *Chore.*
- Getting a present for your birthday.
- Picking up toys. *Chore.*
- Feeding the cat. *Chore.*

What naming word means "jobs you have to do nearly every day"? *Chores.*

 Awesome

In the story, the evening grosbeaks devoured all the seed "with awesome speed." That means the people were amazed by how fast the birds could eat the seeds. They could hardly believe their eyes. **Awesome.** Say the word. *Awesome.*

Awesome is a describing word. It tells more about a naming word. What kind of word is **awesome?** *A describing word.*

If something is awesome, it is amazing and hard to believe. Say the word that means "amazing and hard to believe." *Awesome.*

Let's think about some things that might be awesome. I'll tell about something. If you think I am telling about something that is awesome, say "awesome." If not, don't say anything.

- The mountain was so high I could hardly believe my eyes. *Awesome.*
- The sight of a hundred elephants charging across the plains in Africa was amazing. *Awesome.*
- It was just another ordinary day as I walked to school.
- The sound of Niagara Falls pouring over the cliffs was amazing! *Awesome.*
- My bedroom is painted pale blue.
- I like to eat yogurt and fruit for lunch.

What describing word means "amazing and hard to believe"? *Awesome.*

 Devour

In the story, "eleven evening grosbeaks devour all our seed." That means they eat all the seeds quickly and hungrily. **Devour.** Say the word. *Devour.*

Devour is an action word. It tells what happens. What kind of word is **devour?** *An action word.*

When you devour something, you eat quickly and hungrily. What word means "eat quickly and hungrily"? *Devour.*

Let's think about some times when someone might devour something. I'll tell you about a time. If you think you would see someone devouring something, say "devour." If not, don't say anything.

- The children ate the bucket of ice cream quickly and hungrily. *Devour.*
- Jojuan didn't have much appetite for the food on his plate.
- The lion hungrily ate the gazelle as soon as it had killed it. *Devour.*
- The cat refused to eat the food in its dish.
- The monkeys gobbled down the whole bunch of bananas. *Devour.*
- The rescued boys quickly ate everything they were given. *Devour.*

What action word means "eat quickly and hungrily"? *Devour.*

Present Vocabulary Tally Sheet
(See Lesson 1, page 3, for instructions.)

Assign Homework
(Homework Sheet, BLM 15a: See the Introduction for homework instructions.)

DAY 2

Preparation: Picture Vocabulary Cards for *limbs, chores, awesome, devour.*

Read and Discuss Story
(Note: This book is long and complex. You may wish to read parts of it throughout the day rather than in one sitting. Read story aloud to children. Ask the following questions at the specified points. Encourage them to use target words in their answers.)

Page 1. What two things are special about the twenty-first of December? (Ideas: *It's the shortest day of the year; it's the first day of winter.*) What are we invited to do? (Idea: *Go outside and have fun.*) What do we need to

remember to do? (Idea: *Look around.*) Why should we look around? (Idea: *There are lots of things happening that we might not notice.*)

Page 2. What will we do on the first day of winter? (Idea: *Play hide and seek underneath the big old fir tree.*) How many children do you see? *One.*

Page 3. (Call on a child to come forward and touch the tree. Read the words written on the oval.) What two important facts did we learn about the fir tree? (Idea: *It has waxy needles and a cone shape.*) The leaves on a fir tree are called needles. What do we call the leaves on a fir tree? *Needles.* How many fir trees are nearby? *One.*

Page 4. What will we do on the second day of winter? (Idea: *Go sliding on tubes.*) How many children do you see? *Two.*

Page 5. (Call on a child to come forward and touch the slider with fur. Call on a child to come forward and touch the slider with feathers. Read the words written on the oval.) What animal is the slider with fur? *An otter.* What animal is the slider with feathers? *A raven.* How many animal sliders do you see? *Two.*

Let's try to figure out the main idea found on pages 4 and 5. The main idea is the reason this part was written. What is the main idea? *The reason this part was written.* When Consie Powell wrote these words and made these illustrations, what do you think she wanted us to know? (Idea: *Both animals and people slide on the snow.*) That's right: so the main idea found on pages 4 and 5 is *both animals and people slide on the snow.* What is the main idea found on pages 4 and 5? *Both animals and people slide on the snow.*

Page 6. What will we do on the third day of winter? (Idea: *Make snow angels.*) How many children have left their marks on the snow? *Three.*

Page 7. (Call on a child to come forward and touch the three sets of marks in the snow. Read the words written on the oval.) Which marks show where an owl caught a mouse? (Call on a student to touch the marks.) Why do you think this shows where an owl caught a mouse?

(Ideas: *I can see the mouse footprints leading up to the marks, then they disappear; I can see where the wings of the owl hit the snow.*) Which marks show where a ruffed grouse left a snow burrow? (Call on a child to touch the marks.) Why do you think this shows where a ruffed grouse left a snow burrow? (Ideas: *I can see inside the burrow; I can see where the footprints and wing marks are.*) Which marks show where pine siskins searched for seeds? (Call on a child to touch the marks.) Why do you think this shows where pine siskins searched for seeds? (Ideas: *I can see some seeds; I can see where the footprints and wing marks are.*) How many places do you see where animals have left their marks in the snow? *Three.*

Let's try to figure out the main idea found on pages 6 and 7. Remember that the main idea is the reason this part was written. What is the main idea? *The reason this part was written.* When Consie Powell wrote these words and made these illustrations, what do you think she wanted us to know? (Ideas: *Both animals and people leave their marks on the snow; both people and animals can make marks in the snow.*) That's right; so the main idea found on pages 6 and 7 is *both animals and people leave their marks on the snow.* What is the main idea found on pages 6 and 7? *Both animals and people leave their marks on the snow.*

Page 8. What will we do on the fourth day of winter? (Idea: *Go skating on the ice.*) How many children are skating? *Four.*

Page 9. (Call on a child to come forward and touch the four kinds of animals under the ice. Read the words written on the oval.) Where are the prowling dragonfly nymphs? (Call on a child to touch the two nymphs.) Where is the snapping turtle? (Call on a child to touch the snapping turtle.) Where is the beaver? (Call on a child to touch the beaver.) Where are the blue gills? (Call on a child to touch the blue gills.)

Let's try to figure out the main idea found on pages 8 and 9. Remember that the main idea is the reason this part was written. What is the main idea? *The reason this part was written.*

When Consie Powell wrote these words and made these illustrations, what do you think she wanted us to know? (Idea: *In winter, people play on the ice, but animals live underneath the ice.*) That's right: so the main idea found on pages 8 and 9 is *people play on the ice, but animals live under the ice.* What is the main idea found on pages 8 and 9? *People play on the ice, but animals live under the ice.*

(Continue with this established procedure to read each of the remaining pages, counting the items and identifying the main ideas.)

Fifth day: *Both people and animals stay inside when it is really cold.*
Sixth day: *Children are different and snowflakes are different.*
Seventh day: *Many different trees lose their leaves in the winter.*
Eighth day: *Both people and animals can walk on top of the snow because of the shape of their feet.*
Ninth day: *Both people and animals find protection from the cold.*
Tenth day: *Both animals and people make footprints in the snow.*
Eleventh day: *We can help feed the birds that stay all winter.*
Twelfth day: *Both people and animals need food.*)

Let's remember what Consie Powell tells us to do when we read the story. What do we need to remember to do? (Idea: *Look around.*) Why did she want us to look around? (Idea: *There are lots of things happening that we might not notice.*)

When Consie Powell wrote the words and made the illustrations for *The First Day of Winter,* what do you think she wanted us to know? (Idea: *If we look carefully, we'll notice people and animals doing lots of things in the winter.*) That's right: so the main idea of *The First Day of Winter* is *if we look carefully we'll notice people and animals doing lots of things in the winter.* What is the main idea of *The First Day of Winter*? (Idea: *If we look carefully, we'll notice people and animals doing lots of things in the winter.*)

Review Vocabulary

(Display the Picture Vocabulary Cards. Point to each card as you say the word. Ask the children to repeat each word after you.) These pictures show **chores, limbs, awesome,** and **devour.**

- What word means "jobs you have to do nearly every day"? *Chores.*
- What word means "eat quickly and hungrily"? *Devour.*
- What word means "amazing and hard to believe"? *Awesome.*
- What word means "the branches of a tree"? *Limbs.*

Extend Vocabulary

 Limbs

In *The First Day of Winter,* we learned that **limbs** mean "the branches of a tree." Say the word that means "the branches of a tree." *Limbs.*

Raise your hand if you can tell us a sentence that uses **limbs** as a naming word meaning "the branches of a tree." (Call on several children. If they don't use complete sentences, restate their examples as sentences. Have the class repeat the sentences.)

Here's a new way to use the word **limbs.**

- His **limbs** were stiff and sore after he finished his exercises. Say the sentence.
- The baby's **limbs** grew longer and stronger. Say the sentence.
- If we didn't have **limbs,** we couldn't move or pick things up. Say the sentence.

In these sentences, limbs is a naming word that means arms and legs. What naming word means "arms and legs"? *Limbs.*

Raise your hand if you can tell us a sentence that uses **limbs** as a naming word meaning "arms and legs." (Call on several children. If they don't use complete sentences, restate their examples as sentences. Have the class repeat the sentences.)

Present Expanded Target Vocabulary

Impressions

In *The First Day of Winter,* the people and the animals left marks in the snow. Another way of saying the people and animals left marks in the

snow is to say they left impressions in the snow. **Impressions.** Say the word. *Impressions.*

Impressions is a naming word. It names things. What kind of word is **impressions?** *A naming word.*

Impressions are marks made by pressing down on something. Say the word that means "marks made by pressing down on something." *Impressions.*

I'll tell about a person or an animal. If that person or animal made marks by pressing down on something, say "impressions." If not don't say anything.

- Our feet made marks in the wet sand. *Impressions.*
- You could not see any marks on the smooth wood floor.
- We knew a deer had been in our garden because we could see its footprints in the dirt. *Impressions.*
- In the winter, the hooves of the moose left marks in the snow. *Impressions.*
- There were marks on the couch where people had been sitting. *Impressions.*
- She made her bed carefully so all the blankets were smooth.

What naming word means "marks made by pressing down on something"? *Impressions.*

Dormant

In *The First Day of Winter,* there were no leaves on many of the trees. The trees were not growing but they were still alive. Another way of saying the trees were not growing but they were still alive is to say the trees were dormant. **Dormant.** Say the word. *Dormant.*

Dormant is a describing word. It tells more about something. What kind of word is **dormant?** *A describing word.*

Dormant means plants have lost their leaves and are not growing but are still alive. Say the word that means "plants have lost their leaves and are not growing but are still alive." *Dormant.*

I'll tell about some plants. If that plant is dormant, say "dormant." If not, don't say anything.

- In the winter the birch tree loses its leaves and stops growing. *Dormant.*
- In the winter the lawns turned brown and stopped growing, but the grass was still alive. *Dormant.*
- The lawns were lush and green.
- If there is no rain, some trees will lose their leaves and stop growing. *Dormant.*
- The jungle was thick with huge trees and long green vines.

What describing word means "plants have lost their leaves and are not growing but are still alive"? *Dormant.*

DAY 3

Preparation: Prepare a sheet of chart paper titled *Winter Activities.*

Activity Sheet, BLM 15b.

Each child will need a pencil and crayons.

Retell the Story

Today I'll show you the pictures Consie Powell made for *The First Day of Winter.* As I show you the pictures, I'll call on one of you to tell the class that part of the story.

Tell me what happens at the **beginning** of the story. (Show the pictures on page 1. Call on a child to tell what's happening.)

Tell me what happens in the **middle** of the story. (Show the pictures on pages 2–23. Call on a child to tell what's happening. Encourage use of the target words when appropriate. Model use as necessary.)

Tell me what happens at the **end** of the story. (Show the pictures on pages 24 and 25. Call on a child to tell what's happening.)

Prepare Picture Vocabulary Cards for all words with dual meanings as taught in the lessons. Display them prominently in a pocket chart, on a chalkboard ledge, or in another obvious location. These words are: *awkward, blossom, calm, collect, den, disturb, fine, gentle, grains, limbs, roared, rough, shouted, wild, winding*

Play Tom Foolery

Today we will play *Tom Foolery.* I will pretend to be Tom. Tom Foolery has a reputation of trying to trick students. Tom knows that some words have more than one meaning. He will tell you one meaning that will be correct. Then he will tell you another meaning that might be correct or might be incorrect.

If you think the meaning is correct, don't say anything. If you think the meaning is incorrect, sing, "Tom Foolery." Then Tom will have to tell the truth and tell the correct meaning. Tom is sly enough that he may include some words that do <u>not</u> have two meanings. Be careful! He's tricky!

Let's practice. **Roared** means that someone shouted something in a loud voice. **Roared** also means that you made a snorting and snuffling sound while you were sleeping. *Tom Foolery!* Oh, you're right. Snorting and snuffling when you sleep is **snored.** The other meaning for **roared** is "when a person or thing goes by fast and makes a lot of noise."

When we play *Tom Foolery,* Tom will keep score. If you catch him being tricky, you will get one point. If you don't catch him, Tom gets the point. Watch out! Tom might try to give himself extra points while you're not looking!

Now you're ready to play the game. (Draw a T-chart on the board for keeping score. Children earn one point for each correct answer. If they make an error, correct them as you normally would, and record one point for yourself. Repeat missed words at the end of the game.)

- **Limbs** are the branches of a tree. **Limbs** are also baby sheep. *Tom Foolery!* Oh, you're right. I must have been thinking of **lambs** instead of **limbs**.
- **Awesome** means amazing and hard to believe. **Awesome** is also a season we sometimes call "fall." *Tom Foolery!* Oh, you're right. I was thinking of **autumn**. We only know the first meaning for **awesome**.
- If you eat quickly and hungrily you **devour** your food. People often **devour** their favorite foods.
- **Chores** are the jobs you have to do nearly every day. **Chores** are also the places you go to buy things. *Tom Foolery!* Oh, you're hard to fool. I was thinking of **stores**. We only know the first meaning for **chores**.
- **Limbs** are your arms and legs. **Limbs** are also the branches on trees.

(Count the points and declare a winner.) You did a great job of playing *Tom Foolery!*

Complete the Activity Sheet

(Review with children the different winter activities mentioned in the text. Record the activities on the chart paper as they are identified. Ideas: *Snow tubing; making snow angels; skating; playing in the snow; stacking wood; snowshoeing; building a fort; having a snowball fight.* Have children suggest other winter activities. Record them on the chart paper.)

(**Note:** You need to record at least one more activity than the number of children in your class.)

(Give each child a copy of the Activity Sheet, BLM 15b. Each child will select and initial a winter activity from the chart. They will then print the name of the activity on their Activity Sheet and draw an illustration to accompany it. If children are not yet able to copy the words, scribe it for them while they work on their illustrations. Make a cover titled *Winter Fun* and fasten the pages together into a class book.)

DAY 4

Preparation: Prepare a sheet of chart paper, landscape direction, titled *The First Day of Winter.* Underneath the title, draw three rows of 12 boxes each, connected by arrows.

See the Introduction for Week 15's chart.

Literary Analysis (Cumulative Review)

Let's think about what we already know about how books are made.

- What do we call the name of a book? *Title.*
- What do we call the person who writes a story? *Author.*
- What do we call the person who draws pictures for a story? *Illustrator.*
- What do we call the people or animals a story is about? *Characters.*
- What do we call the pictures the illustrator makes? *Illustrations.*
- What is one thing the setting of a story tells? *Where a story happens.*

Let's sing the first verses of "The Story Song" to help us remember these important things about books. (At this point it is unnecessary to sing the whole song. Choose which verses you would like children to sing. Include *setting* as it is a relatively new concept. See the Introduction for the complete Story Song.)

Today we will learn more about the setting of a story.

The setting of a story tells two things. One thing the setting tells is where the story happens. What is one thing the setting tells? *Where the story happens.* The second thing the setting tells is when the story happens. What is the second thing the setting tells? *When the story happens.*

Let's look at the pictures and talk about the story to figure out where the story *The First Day of Winter* happens.

(Follow the procedure established in Lessons 8–10 to identify where the story happens. Repeat the process twice, starting on pages 2 and 3, once for the full page illustrations, and once for the insets. Record responses in the first two rows of boxes.)

(Full Page Illustrations—Ideas: _In the yard_; _by the stream_; _on the hill_; _under the pond_; _under the snow_; _in the yard_; _in the woods_; _on the snow_, _inside the plants_, _on the snow_, _at the bird feeder_,)

(Oval Close-up Illustrations—Ideas: _Under a tree branch_; _on a hill_; _in the snow_; _on the pond_; _in the den_; _outside_; _near the woodshed_; _on the trail_; _in the snow fort_; _near the steps_; _in the window_; _in the kitchen_.)

In the yard, by the stream, on the hill, under the pond, under the snow, in the yard, in the woods, on the snow, inside the plants, and at the bird feeder are all outdoors. So if we could use only one word to tell the setting of this part of the story, we would use the word "outdoors." Where is the setting of this part of _The First Day of Winter_? _Outdoors._

Under a tree branch, on a hill, in the snow, on the pond, in the den, outside, near the woodshed, on the trail, in the snow fort, near the steps, in the window, and in the kitchen are all at the cabin. So if we could only use a few words to tell the setting of this part of the story, we would use the words "at the cabin." Where is the setting of this part of _The First Day of Winter_? _At the cabin._

(Record responses in the third row of boxes.)
Now let's think about when this story happens. I'm going to read you parts of this story. Then I'm going to ask you when this story happens.

Page 2. (Read the first line of text:) On the first day of winter. The first day of winter is December 21st. When is the first day of winter? _December 21st._ So when does this story begin? _December 21$\underline{^{st}}$._

Page 4. (Read the first line of text:) On the second day of winter. The first day of winter is December 21st. When is the second day of winter? _December 22nd._ So when does this part of the story happen? _December 22$\underline{^{nd}}$._

(Repeat this process, identifying the twelve days of winter as December 21st to January 1st.)

When does the story _The First Day of Winter_ happen? _December 21st to January 1st._

So when is the setting of _The First Day of Winter_? _December 21st to January 1st._

You were great detectives! You used the clues and figured out where and when the story happens.

Play Tom Foolery (Cumulative Review)

Today we will play _Tom Foolery_. I will pretend to be Tom. You know that Tom has a reputation for trying to trick students. Tom knows that some words have more than one meaning. He will tell you one meaning that will be correct. Then he will tell you another meaning that might be correct or might be incorrect.

If you think the meaning is correct, don't say anything. If you think the meaning is incorrect, sing, "Tom Foolery." Then Tom will have to tell the truth and tell the correct meaning. Tom is sly enough that he may include some words that do not have two meanings. Be careful! He's tricky!

Let's practice. **Wild** means that a creature is not tame. **Wild** also means that it is quite warm and pleasant outdoors. _Tom Foolery!_ Oh, you're right. I must have been thinking of **mild**. All of you know that another meaning for **wild** is "badly behaved."

Let's do another one together. Something that is **precious** is something that is very important to you. Also, someone can put **precious** on you when they try hard to make you do something. _Tom Foolery!_ Oh, you're right. I guess I was thinking of **pressure**. **Precious** is something that is special or important to you.

When we play _Tom Foolery_, Tom will keep score. If you catch him being tricky, you will get one point. If you don't catch him, Tom gets the point. Watch out! Tom might try to give himself extra points while you're not looking!

Now you're ready to play the game. (Draw a T-chart on the board for keeping score. Children earn one point for each correct answer. If they make an error, correct them as you normally would, and record one point for yourself. Repeat missed words at the end of the game.)

- Trees have **limbs.** People have **limbs.**
- **Devour** means to eat quickly and hungrily. A **devour** is also a different road you have to take if your road can't be used. *Tom Foolery!* I must have been thinking of **detour. Devour** only means to eat quickly and hungrily.
- If something is **awesome,** it is amazing and hard to believe. If something is **awesome,** it is also very bad or terrible. *Tom Foolery!* I was thinking of **awful.** I was **awful,** but you were **awesome!**
- **Chores** are the jobs you have to do nearly every day. **Chores** are also a kind of candy that you can chew on nearly every day. *Tom Foolery!* Oh, you are very hard to fool. I just made up the candy.
- **Impressions** are marks you make by pressing down on something. You could make **impressions** with your hands, your feet, or your head if you wanted to.
- **Gentle** means that you touch things or people very softly. **Gentle** also means the opposite of lady. *Tom Foolery!* Oh, you're right. I was thinking of **gentleman.** The opposite of **lady** is **gentleman.**
- **Shouted** means that you yelled at someone when you were mad. **Shouted** also means that you didn't believe what someone told you. *Tom Foolery!* Oh, you're right. **Shouted** also means you called to someone in a loud voice. I think that I was thinking about **doubted.**
- If a plant is **dormant,** it has lost its leaves and is not growing, but it is still alive. A **dormant** is also what you wipe your muddy feet on before you come in the house. *Tom Foolery!* Oh, you're right. I guess I was thinking of **doormat.** There's only one meaning for **dormant.**

(Count the points and declare a winner.) You did a great job of playing *Tom Foolery!*

Preparation: Prepare a sheet of chart paper, portrait direction, titled *The First Day of Winter.* Underneath the title, make 12 boxes connected by arrows. Leave room to write underneath the boxes.

See the Introduction for Week 15's chart.

Record children's responses by writing the ordinal words in the boxes and the examples underneath.

Happy Face Game Test Sheet, BLM B.

Introduce Counting Story Pattern

When authors write stories, they sometimes write in patterns. Let's see if we can figure out the pattern for this story. You tell me what happened in the story, and I'll write it down.

(Read the first verse of the rhyme from page 2, and show the illustrations on pages 2 and 3.) When does the story begin? *On the first day of winter.* What important things come in ones? (Idea: *One child, one nearby fir tree.*)

(Read the second verse of the rhyme from page 4, and show the illustrations on pages 4 and 5.) When does this part of the story happen? *On the second day of winter.* What important things come in twos? (Idea: *Two sliding children; two sliding animals; two snow tubes.*)

(Read the third verse of the rhyme from page 6, and show the illustrations on pages 6 and 7.) When does this part of the story happen? *On the third day of winter.* What important things come in threes? (Idea: *Three children playing; three snow angels; three impressions in the snow.*)

(Follow the established procedure, recording the ordinals to twelfth and examples that are found on the corresponding pages.)

(Point to the story map that is on the chart paper.) Listen while I read from our story map. First, second, third, fourth … twelfth. One child; one nearby fir tree; two sliding children; two sliding animals; two snow tubes; three children playing; three snow angels; three impressions in the snow. Raise your hand if you know what the pattern is for the story *The First Day of Winter.* (Ideas: *A number pattern; a counting pattern.*)

This story has a **counting pattern.** A story with a counting pattern is called a **counting story.** What kind of a story has numbers that go up in order? *A counting story.*

Assess Vocabulary

 (Give each child a copy of the Happy Face Game Test Sheet, BLM B.)

Today you're going to play the Happy Face Game. This shows me how well you know the hard words you are learning.

If I say something that is true, color in the happy face. What will you do if I say something that is true? *Color in the happy face.*

If I say something that is false, color in the sad face. What will you do if I say something that is false? *Color in the sad face.*

Listen carefully to each item that I say. Don't let me trick you!

Item 1: **Limbs** is another word for arms and legs. (*True.*)

Item 2: **Devour** means to eat hungrily and quickly. (*True.*)

Item 3: **Impressions** in the sand at the beach could be footprints or handprints. (*True.*)

Item 4: A **dormant** plant is one that still has all of its leaves but is dead. (*False.*)

Item 5: The most amazing thing that you have ever done could be called **awesome.** (*True.*)

Item 6: **Chores** are usually made of wood and you walk on them. (*False.*)

Item 7: Branches of a tree are also called **limbs.** (*True.*)

Item 8: Birds that **hibernate** fly away to spend the winter somewhere else. (*False.*)

Item 9: One kind of animal that **slithers** is a snake. (*True.*)

Item 10: The outside parts of a flower are called **metals.** (*False.*)

You did a great job of playing the Happy Face Game!

(Score children's work at a later time. A child must score 9 out of 10 to be at the mastery level. If a child does not achieve mastery, insert the missed words as additional items in the games for next week's lessons. Retest those children individually for the missed items before they take the next mastery test.)

Extensions

Read a Story as a Reward

(Display copies of several books that you have read since the beginning of the program. Allow children to choose which book they would like you to read to them as a reward for their hard work.)

(Read the story aloud for enjoyment with minimal interruptions.)

> **Preparation:** Word containers for the Super Words Center. You may wish to remove some words from earlier lessons. Choose words children have mastered. See the Introduction for instructions on how to set up and use Super Words Center.

Introduce the Super Words Center

 (Add the new Picture Vocabulary Cards to words from the previous weeks. Show children one of the word containers. If children need more guidance in how to work in the Super Words Center, play with two to three children as a demonstration.)

Let's review how to play the game called *Go Fish.*

Let's think about how we work with our words in the Super Words Center.

You will work with a partner in the Super Words Center. Whom will you work with? *A partner.*

First you and your partner will each draw six word cards out of the container and hold them so your partner cannot see them. What do you do first? (Idea: *Draw six cards out of the container and hold them so my partner cannot see them.*)

Next you will look at the cards in your hand and lay down any cards that you have two of. You will tell your partner the word the pictures show. What do you do next? (Idea: *Lay down any cards that I have two of and tell my partner the word the pictures show.*)

Then your partner has a chance to lay down any cards he or she has two of, and tell the word the pictures show. What does your partner do? (Idea: *Lay down any cards that he or she has two of, and tell the word the pictures show.*)

Next you will ask your partner for a card that you have only one of, by saying the word the picture shows. If your partner has that card, he or she will give it to you. If your partner gives you the card, you will lay down the two cards. What does your partner do if they have the card you ask for? (Idea: *Give me the card.*) What will you do if your partner gives you a card? (Idea: *Lay down the two cards that are the same.*)

If your partner does not have the card you ask for, your partner will say "Go Fish." What will your partner do if he or she doesn't have the card you ask for? (Idea: *Say "Go Fish."*) If your partner says "Go Fish," you must choose another card from the word container. What will you do if your partner says "Go Fish"? (Idea: *Choose a card from the word container.*)

Then it's your partner's turn.

Watch while I show you what I mean. (Demonstrate this process with one child as your partner.)

When one partner has no cards left in his or her hand, the game is over. Each person gets 1 point for each pair of cards they have laid down. The winner is the person with the most points. Who wins the game? (Idea: *The person with the most points.*) Have fun playing *Go Fish!*

The Eensy-Weensy Spider
author: Mary Ann Hoberman • illustrator: Nadine Bernard Westcott

Preparation: You will need a copy of *The Eensy-Weensy Spider* for each day's lesson.

Number each *right-hand* page of the story (except for the page of music) to assist you in asking questions at appropriate points. Also number the large two-page illustration at the end of the story.

Post a copy of the Vocabulary Tally Sheet, BLM A, with this week's Picture Vocabulary Cards attached.

Each child will need one copy of the Homework Sheet, BLM 16a.

DAY 1

Introduce Book

This week's book is called *The Eensy-Weensy Spider.* What's the title? *The Eensy-Weensy Spider.*

This book is made from a song that some of us know. Mary Ann Hoberman [**hoe**-ber-mun] added new words. She is the author of the parts of the song that we don't already know. Who's the author of the parts of *The Eensy-Weensy Spider* we don't know? *Mary Ann Hoberman.*

Nadine Bernard Westcott [nuh-**deen** ber-**nard west**-cott] made the pictures for this book. Who is the illustrator of *The Eensy-Weensy Spider*? *Nadine Bernard Westcott.* Who made the illustrations for this book? *Nadine Bernard Westcott.*

The cover of a book usually gives us some hints of what the book is about. Let's look at the front cover of *The Eensy-Weensy Spider.* What do you see in the illustration? (Ideas: *A spider being washed out of a drainpipe; a spider wearing a hat with flowers.*)

(Assign each child a partner.) Get ready to make some predictions to your partner about this book. Use the information from the cover to help you.

Target Vocabulary

Tier II	Tier III
polite	rhyme
continued	poem
allow	syllable
few	
*clumsy	
*rescue	

*Expanded Target Vocabulary Word

(Ask the following questions, allowing sufficient time for children to share their predictions with their partners.)

- Who is the character in this story? (Who do you think this story is about?)
- What do you think the spider will do?
- Where do you think the story happens?
- When do you think the story happens?
- In what season of the year do you think the story happens?
- What color is the spider in this story?
- Do you think this story is about a real spider? Tell why or why not.

(Call on several children to share their predictions with the class.)

Take a Picture Walk

(Encourage children to use target words in their answers.) We're going to take a picture walk through this book. Remember that when we take a picture walk, we look at the pictures and tell what we think will happen in the story.

(Printed music.) What can you tell me about the lines, black dots, and words on this page? (Ideas: *It's the music for the song; it shows what to do when you sing the song.*) What can you see on the rest of the page? (Idea: *There are pictures of bugs.*) We'll sing the song with the actions when I read the story to you.

Pages 1–2. What is the spider doing in the big picture? (Idea: *Climbing up the drainpipe.*) What else is happening? (Ideas: *It is raining; water is coming out of the pipe.*) What is happening in the small picture? (Ideas: *The rain stopped; the spider is drying off; the water stopped coming out of the spout; the sun came out.*)

Pages 3–4. What is the spider doing in the large picture? (Ideas: *Lying in a hammock; singing; lying in a garden.*) What is the spider doing in the small picture? (Idea: *Skipping out to play.*)

Pages 5–6. What is the spider doing in the large picture? (Ideas: *Hugging a baby bug; going for a walk in a garden playground.*) What is the spider doing in the small picture? (Idea: *Speaking to the mother bug.*) What might a real spider do if it met a baby bug? (Ideas: *Catch it in a web; eat it for lunch; devour it.*)

Pages 7–8. What is the spider doing in the large picture? (Ideas: *Being caught in the rain; getting wet.*) What is the spider doing in the small picture? (Idea: *Drying off and walking.*) If the bird in the large picture really saw a spider in the garden, what do you think would happen? (Idea: *The bird might eat the spider; it would devour the spider.*)

Pages 9–10. What is the spider doing in the large picture? (Idea: *Swimming in the frog's pool.*) The word that the frog is saying is "Out!" The frog is saying it in a loud voice called a shout. Can you shout "Out!"? *Out!* Why do you think the frog doesn't want spiders in his pool? What is the spider doing in the small picture? (Idea: *Swimming in the pool with the frog.*) They are both feeling pretty good in this picture. How can you tell they are feeling happier? (Idea: *They are smiling in the picture.*)

Pages 11–12. What is the spider doing in the large picture? (Ideas: *Trying to walk; trying to walk with the other bugs.*) Those bugs are doing something odd for bugs. What is it? (Idea: *Walking and playing instruments.*) Some of the instruments are made from interesting things. What are they? (Idea: *Flowers and leaves.*) What is the spider doing in the small picture? (Idea: *Falling down.*)

Pages 13–14. What is the spider doing in the large picture? I'll give you a hint—look carefully at her knees. (Ideas: *Crying; she fell and scraped*

her knees when she walked with the other bugs.*) What is the spider doing in the small picture? (Idea: *Eating cookies with her mom with bandages on her knees.*)

Pages 15–16. What is the spider doing in the large picture? (Ideas: *She fell into a stream; she might hit a big rock.*) Tell about how the other bugs are feeling. (Ideas: *Upset; scared; the dragonfly is shouting for help and waving his legs.*) What is the spider doing in the small picture? (Idea: *Getting saved from the water.*)

Pages 17–18. What is the spider doing in the large picture? (Idea: *Shopping for shoes.*) Who else is in the picture? (Idea: *Other bugs who are shopping for shoes.*) What is the spider doing in the small picture? (Idea: *Trying on shoes.*) Let's count the shoes that the spider is going to buy. (Count aloud with the children.) How many shoes will she buy? *Six.*

Pages 19–20. What is the spider doing in the large picture? (Idea: *Walking in a dark place.*) Can you see someone helping the spider? (Idea: *Yes, there is a lighted caterpillar walking with her.*) Look carefully at the dark shadows the illustrator made. What do they look like? (Idea: *They look like scary faces but they're not really.*) What is the spider doing in the small picture? (Idea: *Saying good-bye to the light worm.*)

Pages 21–22. What is the spider doing in the large picture? (Idea: *Falling asleep while she eats.*) The mother spider has some nice lamps in her room. What are they? (Idea: *They are lightning bugs.*) What is the spider doing in the small picture? (Idea: *Her mom is carrying her to bed, and she's asleep already.*)

Pages 23–24. What is the spider doing in the large picture? (Ideas: *Sleeping; hanging in a hammock that's a web.*) What is the spider doing in the small picture? (Idea: *Climbing up the drainpipe again.*)

(Two-page illustration at end of story.) Does this picture remind you of anything you have seen before? (Ideas: *It's all the bugs that have been in the story; it's the same picture as the one at the beginning of the story.*) (Turn back to the illustration with the music, and compare the two illustrations.) The story begins and ends with the same illustration, doesn't it? I wonder how many of these bugs you can name. (Touch under each bug, and ask students to say what bug they think it is. There are butterflies, dragonflies, lightning bugs, caterpillars, bees, and others.)

It's your turn to ask me some questions. What would you like to know about the story? (Accept questions. If children tell about the pictures or the story instead of ask questions, prompt them to ask a question.) Ask me a what question. Ask me a how question.

Read the Story Aloud
(Read the story to children with minimal interruptions.)

Tomorrow we will read the story again, and I will ask you some questions.

Present the Target Vocabulary

◎⚬ Polite

In the story, the mama spider hugged the baby bug too tightly when she only meant to be polite. That means that she meant to do the right thing and act with her best manners and actions. **Polite.** Say the word. *Polite.*

Polite is a describing word. It tells about how a person behaves. It means doing the right thing and acting with our best manners and actions. What kind of word is **polite?** *A describing word.*

If you are polite, you do the right thing and act with your best manners and actions. Say the word that means "to do the right thing and act with your best manners and actions." *Polite.*

(Correct any incorrect responses, and repeat the item at the end of the sequence.)

Let's think about some situations where people might be polite. I'll tell about some situations. If the person or animal is polite in the situation, say "polite." If the person or animal is impolite, say "impolite." **Impolite** is the opposite of **polite.** What word is the opposite of **polite?** *Impolite.*

- The boy held the door open for the elderly lady. *Polite.*
- Gerald let Harold go ahead of him to see the whales. *Polite.*
- Faith and Hope yelled at each other in the restaurant. *Impolite.*

- Jillian **taunted** her little sister. *Impolite.*
- Mrs. Dodds spoke nicely, even when she was very angry. *Polite.*
- The spider hugged the baby bug too tightly. *Impolite.*

What describing word means "to do the right thing and act with your best manners and actions"? *Polite.*

I'm going to say two words. Each word has two parts. Tell me how the words I say are like the word **polite. Tonight. Alright.** Listen again. **Tonight. Alright.** How are those two words like the word **polite?** (Ideas: *They sound like polite; they rhyme; they have two parts.*)

(**Note:** Your goal is to draw from the children the two ideas of rhyme and syllables.)

When words sound alike, we sometimes say they rhyme. What do we sometimes call it when words sound alike? *Rhyme.* **Polite, tonight,** and **alright** all rhyme. Tell me some other words that rhyme with **polite.** (Ideas: *Bite, sight, flight, might, kite, tight, fight.*)

Polite, tonight, and **alright** have two parts. Word parts are called syllables. What do we call word parts? *Syllables.* **Po** and **lite** are the two syllables in **polite.** What are the two syllables in **polite?** *Po and lite.* (Repeat process for *tonight* and *alright.*)

◎⚬ Continued

In the story, after it rained in the garden, the spider continued on her walk. That means the spider kept going. **Continued.** Say the word. *Continued.*

Continued is an action word. It tells what someone or something did. What kind of word is **continued?** *An action word.*

If you continued eating your lunch, you kept on eating your lunch. If you continued on your 10-mile run, you kept going. Say the action word that means "kept going." *Continued.*

Let's think about some times when someone might have continued. I'll tell about a time. If someone continued, say "continued." If not, don't say anything.

- The cat picked up her kitten in her mouth and kept going toward shelter. *Continued.*

- After lunch, Bob kept going towards home. *Continued.*
- The family stopped and put up their tent.
- After the rain, the spider kept going on her walk. *Continued.*
- After chewing her food well and swallowing, Alison kept eating her dinner. *Continued.*
- When the motor broke, the car stopped and wouldn't start again.

What naming word means "kept going"? *Continued.*

Sometimes, it is hard to find words that sound the same. **Continued** is one of those words, so we'll go on to the next word.

 Allow

In the story, the frog allowed the spider to swim in his pool. That means the frog gave permission for the spider to swim in the pool. **Allow.** Say the word. *Allow.*

Allow is an action word. It tells how someone gives permission for something to happen. What kind of word is **allow**? *An action word.*

If you allow someone to do something, you give permission for them to do that thing. Say the word that means "give permission to do something." *Allow.*

Let's think about some times when you might allow someone to do something. I'll tell about a time. If someone is allowed, say "allow." If not, don't say anything.

- I let my baby brother hold my new kitten. *Allow.*
- My friend asked whether he could use my crayons, and I said yes. *Allow.*
- Mrs. Johnson said, "Get out of our pool!"
- The teacher told her student that he could use her pencil. *Allow.*
- The mirror fell off the table and broke in a shower of tiny pieces.
- Mom said it was okay to have a banana before dinner. *Allow.*

What action word means "to give permission to do something"? *Allow.*

I'm going to say two words. Each word has two parts. Tell me how the words I say are like the word **allow. Somehow. Meow.** Listen again.

Somehow. Meow. How are those two words like the word **allow**? (Ideas: *They sound like allow; they rhyme; they have two parts.*)

(Note: Your goal is to draw from the children the two ideas of rhyme and syllables.)

When words sound alike, we sometimes say they rhyme. What do we sometimes call it when words sound alike? *Rhyme.* **Allow, somehow,** and **meow** all rhyme. Tell me some other words that rhyme with **allow.** (Ideas: *Bow, cow, how, now, pow.*)

Allow, somehow, and **meow** have two parts. Word parts are called syllables. What do we call word parts? *Syllables.* **Al** and **low** are the two syllables in allow. What are the two syllables in **allow?** *Al and low.* (Repeat process for *some-how* and *me-ow.*)

 Few

In the story, the mother spider only had a few bandages for her daughter's knees. Few is another way of saying some but not many. **Few.** Say the word. *Few.*

Few is a describing word. It tells about how many things there are. What kind of word is **few?** *A describing word.*

If you had a few peanuts, it would mean that you had some but not many. Say the word that means "some but not many." *Few.*

Let's think about some times when you might have a few things. I'll tell about a time. If you think it would be a time when a person has a few things, say "few." If you think the person had many things, say "many." Many is the opposite of few. What word is the opposite of few? *Many.*

- Ronald had only four marbles in his marble sack. *Few.*
- Reginald had so many marbles that they were spilling out of his sack and onto the ground. *Many.*
- I had some cookies but not enough to make me full. *Few.*
- Only three lifeguards watched over a thousand people on the beach. *Few.*
- When we spilled the beans, it seemed like there were beans everywhere. *Many.*
- When Elizabeth sang like a bird, lots of people were impressed. *Many.*

What describing word means "some but not many"? *Few.*

I'm going to say two words. Each word has one part. Tell me how the words I say are like the word **few. New. Grew.** Listen again. **New. Grew.** How are those two words like the word **few?** (Ideas: *They sound like few; they rhyme; they have one part.*)

(**Note:** Your continued goal is to draw from children the two ideas of rhyme and syllables.)

When words sound alike, we sometimes say they rhyme. What do we sometimes call it when words sound alike? *Rhyme.* **Few, new,** and **grew** all rhyme. Tell me some other words that rhyme with **few.** (Ideas: *Dew, hue, Lou, mew, pew, flew.*)

Few, new, and **grew** have one part. Word parts are called syllables. What do we call word parts? *Syllables.* There is only one syllable in **few—few.** What is the one syllable in **few?** *Few.* (Repeat process for *new* and *grew*.)

Introduce the Vocabulary Tally Sheet
(See Lesson 1, page 3, for instructions.)

Assign Homework
(Homework Sheet, BLM 16a. See the Introduction for homework instructions.)

DAY 2

Preparation: Picture Vocabulary Cards for *polite, continued, allow, few.*

You will need a piece of chart paper titled "Our Favorite Shoe Colors."

Read and Discuss Story
(Encourage children to use previously taught target words in their answers.)

Today I will read the story of *The Eensy-Weensy Spider.* First, though, let's sing the part that you know. (Teach children the actions on the inside cover, and sing the first verse with them.) *The Eensy-Weensy Spider* can be sung as a song, just like the part we just sang together. Partly because the words rhyme, the story is a poem with many verses.

A verse is a part of a poem. What is a verse? *Part of a poem.*

(Read or sing the story to children. As the story is in the form of a song, singing is the most appropriate form of delivery. Ask the following questions at the specified points. Encourage them to use target words in their answers.)

Pages 1–2. The spider was washed out of the waterspout and then went right back up again. What do you know about the spider? (Ideas: *She doesn't give up; she tries again; she's determined.*)

Pages 3–4. What kind of bed does the spider sleep in? (Idea: *It looks like it is made of a web.*) There is something interesting about the big picture and the small picture on each page. Can you tell what it is? Listen while you hear this verse again. (Read or sing the verse again. By use of gestures, indicate that the large picture shows what happens at the beginning of the verse while the small picture shows what happens at the end of the verse.) Can you tell about what the large picture tells and what the small picture tells? (Ideas: *The large picture tells about waking up, and the small picture tells about skipping out to play; the large picture tells what happens first, and the small picture tells what happens last.*)

Pages 5–6. What is the playground made of? (Ideas: *Flowers for merry-go-rounds, leaves and vines for swings, a big bent leaf for a slide, and a sardine can for a sandbox.*) Everyone in the large picture is happy except for one. Who is unhappy? (Idea: *The mother bug.*) Why do you think she is unhappy? (Idea: *She is afraid the spider is hugging her baby too tightly.*)

Pages 7–8. Do you suppose that a few drops of rain fell on the spider or many drops? Look at the large picture to help you. (Idea: *A few.*) Would a few drops of rain give *you* a bath? Why would the spider get all wet from a few raindrops? (Idea: *The spider is small and we're big so it takes less rain to get the spider all wet.*)

Pages 9–10. If the spider went swimming to get cool, what do you know about the day? (Idea: *It was a warm day and she was hot.*) What word did the spider use that was a polite word? (Idea: *Please.*)

Pages 11–12. What is a parade? (Idea: *It's a big lineup of people, bands, floats, and other things that go by while people watch.*) What was the spider's problem? (Ideas: *She couldn't march so she skinned her knees. She had too many legs to march well.*)

Pages 13–14. If the mother spider only had a few bandages, how many did she have? (Idea: *Some, but not many.*) A spider has eight legs. Why does she only need six bandages? (Ideas: *Maybe she didn't scrape all of her knees. She uses two of her legs for arms and they didn't get skinned.*) If you look carefully, you will see some words in the web at the top of the large picture. Those words say, "Home, Sweet Home." What things can you see in the large picture that makes it seem like home? (Ideas: *Mother Spider is making tea; there is bread and jam and cookies; there is soap and a rubber ducky for the bathtub; there are hooks for a scarf and a hat.*)

Pages 15–16. This verse of the story and song tells about helping. Who helped in this verse? (Ideas: *The beetle helped with his legs, the other bugs helped by holding onto the beetle so he wouldn't fall in.*) Look at the bugs and the fish in the large picture. There is something about the way they are drawn that lets you know they are upset. What can you see? (Ideas: *Their mouths are open like they are yelling, "Help!" Their eyes are bugging out like they are scared.*) Can you see the lines the illustrator has drawn beside the beetle's legs in the large picture? Those lines show that the beetle's legs are moving. The beetle was very quick to help the spider.

Pages 17–18. I absolutely love this large picture because it shows joy and delight. What do you think is joyful and delightful about this picture? (Ideas: *Everyone is happy because they are trying on shoes that they like; everyone is happy because no matter how many feet they have, there are shoes to fit them.*) The spider chose red shoes like Dorothy's ruby shoes in a story called *The Wizard of Oz*. If you could choose a color of shoes—wait, *Choose, Shoes!*—what can you tell about those words? (Ideas: *They rhyme; they have one part or syllable each.*) If you could

choose your favorite color of shoes, what would it be? (Call on individual children to state their favorite color of shoes. Record this information on the class chart.)

Pages 19–20. Have you noticed that the spider gets some help in each verse? Who helps the spider in this verse? (Idea: *The glowworm.*) Why shouldn't the spider be outside alone when it is dark? (Ideas: *It's not safe to be out after dark; you shouldn't be by yourself outside after dark.*)

Pages 21–22. In this verse, the author says that the eensy-weensy spider had a "heavy head." What did the author mean by that? (Idea: *It means that she was very sleepy.*) Isn't that an interesting thing to say instead of saying "The spider was sleepy"? Show me how you would look if *your* head were heavy. (Observe children, and comment on heavy-headed actions that demonstrate the idea of sleepiness like: eyelids fluttering; head dipping and rising again; a sleepy expression.)

Pages 23–24. What letter does the spider have above her head in the large picture? (Touch under the three *z*s.) *Z*. The *z*s are meant to show the sound that the spider is making when she is sleeping. She's not saying "zeeeee," though. Zeee is the letter's name. Instead, she's making the *sound* that we learned for the letter *z*.

It sounds like this: /z/. (Make the /z/ sound.) Let's make that sound together. *Zzzzzzzzzzz.* Now let's make the sound softly and quietly, just like your breathing when you sleep. *Zzzzz. Zzzzz. Zzzzz.*

Pages 24 and 2. Look at the small picture on page 24. Now look at the large picture on page 2. Look again. What is different about the spider on page 24? (Show the pictures in alternation a few times.) (Idea: *She has yellow rubber boots and an umbrella.*) The spider will be ready for the rain now with her yellow boots and yellow umbrella!

Review Vocabulary

(Display the Picture Vocabulary Cards. Point to each card as you say the word. Ask children to repeat each word after you.) These pictures show **continued, polite, allow,** and **few.**

- What word tells about doing the right thing and acting with your best manners and actions? *Polite.*

- What action word means "kept going"? *Continued.*
- What word means "give permission to do something"? *Allow.*
- What word means "some but not many"? *Few.*

Extend Vocabulary
◎← Continued

In *The Eensy-Weensy Spider,* we learned that **continued** means "kept going." Say the word that means "kept going." *Continued.*

Raise your hand if you can tell us a sentence that uses **continued** as an action word meaning "kept going." (Call on several children. If they don't use complete sentences, restate their examples as sentences. Have the class repeat the sentences.)

Here's a new way to use the word **continued.**

- The meteor shower continued for weeks. Say the sentence.
- Mrs. Lucas continued as the principal for twelve years. Say the sentence.
- I continued as the coach of my team for fifteen years. Say the sentence.

In these sentences, continued is an action word that means lasted for a long time. What word means "lasted for a long time"? *Continued.*

Raise your hand if you can tell us a sentence that uses **continued** as a describing word that means "lasted for a long time." (Call on several children. If they don't use complete sentences, restate their examples as sentences. Have the class repeat the sentences.)

Present the Expanded Target Vocabulary
◎← Clumsy

In the story, we saw the spider trip over her own feet while trying to march in a parade. She couldn't march like the other bugs. When you are awkward and have trouble doing action things with your feet or your hands, you might be clumsy. **Clumsy.** Say the word. *Clumsy.*

Clumsy is a describing word. It tells about when you are not good at actions with your hands or feet. What kind of word is **clumsy?** *A describing word.*

Clumsy means you are not good at actions with your hands or feet. Say the word that means "you are not good at actions with your hands or feet." *Clumsy.*

I'll tell about some people or animals. If those people or animals are clumsy, say "clumsy." If not, don't say anything.

- The spider tripped over her own feet in the parade. *Clumsy.*
- Rochester always had trouble picking up books with his hands. *Clumsy.*
- The baby couldn't walk three steps without falling. *Clumsy.*
- Sue skated better than anyone else on her team.
- The hippopotamus tripped and fell. Splat! *Clumsy.*
- Tom ran smoothly, evenly, and faster than his friend Jerry.

What describing word means "not good at actions with your hands or feet"? *Clumsy.* **Clumsy** is not an easy word to find a rhyme for unless you like to spend time with your Mumsey-wumsey.

◎← Rescue

In the story, the spider clumsily fell into a brook because she forgot to look. The beetle stuck out a helping leg or two and rescued the spider. That means that the beetle saved the spider from danger or death. **Rescue.** Say the word. *Rescue.*

Rescue is an action word. It tells what someone does. It means to save someone from danger. What kind of word is **rescue?** *An action word.* **Rescue** is an action word because, to save someone from danger, you have to *do* something to help.

Rescue means to save someone from danger. Say the word that means "to save someone from danger." *Rescue.*

I'll name some things that people or animals might do. If the things I name are a rescue, say "rescue." If not, say, "Call 9-1-1!" The phone number 9-1-1 is what you call if someone needs to be rescued and you can't help.

- The mother cat picked up her kitten and took her away from the busy road. *Rescue.*

- The beetle saved the spider from drowning in the brook. *Rescue.*
- Mr. Layzeepants, from Paris, France, saw the puppy in the fast-moving stream but couldn't save it. *Call 9-1-1!*
- Horace saw the dangerous accident happen and the first thing he did was call 9-1-1 to get help. *Rescue.*
- Everyone stood around while the mountain climber hung from his torn rope. *Call 9-1-1!*
- The five of us dug dirt and rocks away from the boy's face after the cave-in. *Rescue.*

What action word means "to save someone from danger"? *Rescue.*

DAY 3

Preparation: Activity Sheet, BLM 16b. Each child will need crayons.

Retell the Story

Today I'll show you the pictures Nadine Bernard Westcott made for *The Eensy-Weensy Spider.* As I show you the pictures, I'll call on one of you to tell the class that part of the story.

Tell me what happens at the **beginning** of the story. (Show the pictures on page 1. Call on a child to tell what's happening.)

Tell me what happens in the **middle** of the story. (Show the pictures on pages 2–11. Call on a child to tell what's happening. Encourage use of the target words when appropriate. Model use as necessary.)

Tell me what happens at the **end** of the story. (Show the pictures on page 12. Call on a child to tell what's happening.)

Would you agree that the spider had many helpers in this story and song? *Yes.* Name some of the helpers the spider had. Tell how each helper helped. (Ideas: *The mother spider helped the spider when she scraped her knees; the beetle helped when the spider fell in the brook; the salesman helped to find some good shoes; the glowworm helped the spider to find her way in the dark.*) Of all the helpers in the story, who helped the most? (Idea: *The mother spider helped the most.*)

Tell about the ways your family helps you every day. (Ideas: *Helps me to get ready for school; makes my lunch; makes me feel better if I'm hurt or sad.*)

Play Hear, Say!

Today you will learn a game called *Hear, Say!* Hearsay is a naming word that tells about stories and ideas you might be told about people or things. Usually hearsay is a mixture of truth and untruth.

One person hears something about someone else. They tell another person what they think they heard. Then that next person tells what they think they heard the first person say.

Along the way, new bits sometimes get mixed in until the story isn't much like it was when it started out. Right now, before we play *Hear, Say!* we are going to play a game called *Pass it On.* *Pass it On* explains what hearsay can be like.

(Arrange children in a circle. Ask a child to whisper a short sentence of his or her choice in your ear. Then have the child take a seat in the circle and whisper the sentence into the ear of the child on his or her left. That child then whispers the sentence to the next child, and so on. When the sentence has gone all the way around the circle, ask the last child to tell what he or she heard. Invariably, it will have little in common with the original sentence! Explain to children that this is what hearsay does to communication.)

In *Hear, Say!* I will use target words in sentence. Some of the sentences I say might have some untruths or extra information in them. If you think what I am saying is not all true, say "Hear, Say!" That means you want to suggest a way to make the sentence truthful and not just hearsay. I'll say the beginning of the sentence again. If you can make the sentence end so it is true, you'll get a point. If you can't, I get the point.

If I use the vocabulary word correctly and there are no untruths in what I say, say "That's the honest truth!" Be careful, though. If you say, "That's the honest truth!" when there is hearsay in the sentence, I will get a point!

Let's practice. A **polite** girl is one who … does the right thing, has four legs, and talks like a parrot. *Hear, Say!* Well, that's what *I* heard. The first part of the sentence stays the same. I'll say the first part. A **polite** girl is one who. How can we finish the sentence so it doesn't have hearsay in it? (Idea: *Does the right thing and acts with her best manners and actions.*) Let's say the whole sentence together now. *A polite girl is one who does the right thing and acts with her best manners and actions.* That's the honest truth!

Let's do another one together. If you **allow** someone to do something, you give them … persimmons, pomegranates, or parsnips to do it. *Hear, Say!* Well, that's what *I* heard. The first part of the sentence stays the same. I'll say the first part. If you **allow** someone to do something, you. How can we finish the sentence so it doesn't have hearsay in it? (Idea: *Give them permission to do it.*) Let's say the whole sentence together now. *If you allow someone to do something, you give them permission to do it.* That's the honest truth!

Now you're ready to play the game. (Draw a T-chart on the board for keeping score. Children earn one point for each correct answer. If they make an error, correct them as you normally would, and record one point for yourself. Repeat missed words at the end of the game.)

- Everyone knows that "a **few** cookies" means … enough to fill all of your pockets, your backpack, both hands, and your little brother's lunch box, but not many. *Hear, Say!* Well, that's what *I* heard. I'll say the first part of the sentence again. Everyone knows that "a **few** cookies" means. How can we finish the sentence so it doesn't have hearsay in it? (Idea: *Some cookies, but not many.*) Let's say the whole sentence together. *Everyone knows that "a few cookies" means some cookies, but not many.* That's the honest truth!
- After a long, hard hike, Jim **continued** on his way by … sitting, unpacking his tent, and spending the night. *Hear, Say!* Well, that's what *I* heard. I'll say the first part of the sentence again. After a long, hard hike, Jim **continued** on his way by. How can we finish

the sentence so it doesn't have hearsay in it? (Idea: *Keeping going.*) Let's say the whole sentence together. *After a long, hard hike, Jim continued on his way by keeping going.* That's the honest truth!
- Orville was **clumsy** because … he was not good at actions with his hands and feet. *That's the honest truth!*
- The brothers **rescued** the swimmer by … pulling him out of the deep water and then pushing him back in and giving him a rock to hold. *Hear, Say!* Well, that's what *I* heard. I'll say the first part of the sentence again. The brothers **rescued** the swimmer by. How can we finish the sentence so it doesn't have hearsay in it? (Idea: *Pulling him out of the deep water and up onto the shore.*) Let's say the whole sentence together. *The brothers rescued the swimmer by pulling him out of the deep water and up onto the shore.* That's the honest truth!
- Bob **continued** as the coach of his team … for a couple of minutes until he got bored or grew a beard—I can't remember which. *Hear, Say!* Well, that's what *I* heard. I'll say the first part of the sentence again. Bob **continued** as the coach of his team. How can we finish the sentence so it doesn't have hearsay in it? (Idea: *For a very long time.*) Let's say the whole sentence together. *Bob continued as the coach of his team for a very long time.* That's the honest truth!

(Count the points, and declare a winner.) You did a great job of playing *Hear, Say!*

Complete the Activity Sheet
(Show the pictures on page 9 of *The Eensy-Weensy Spider.*)

(Display the class chart.) Earlier you told me what your favorite color of shoes is. Today we will make a poem about shoes and you can draw and color a pair that you would like to wear. (Give each child a copy of the Activity Sheet, BLM 16b.) I will read the poem. It says:

I like shoes.
I like <u>blank</u> shoes.
These are shoes that I would choose.
I like <u>blank</u> shoes.

That sounds funny, doesn't it? When I said "blank" that means there is a space for you to print your favorite color of shoes. I'll read the poem again with *my* favorite color of shoes.

(Touch the blank spaces on the page as you read. Add your own favorite color.)

I like shoes.
I like <u>red</u> shoes.
These are shoes that I would choose.
I like <u>red</u> shoes.

I told you this is a shoe poem. You should hear some words that rhyme in this poem. What words rhyme in this poem? **(Idea:** *Shoes and choose.***)**

Your job is to fill the blank spaces with your favorite color. Then draw a pair of shoes that you would like to wear.

DAY 4

Preparation: Prepare a sheet of chart paper with the heading "Poetry." Below the heading, print a numbered list as follows:

1. Rhyme (draw a human ear beside this word)
2. Poem _____**rhyme**
   _____**rhyme**
   _____**rhyme**
   _____**rhyme**
3. Syllable: How many parts?

Literary Analysis

You know that *The Eensy-Weensy Spider* is a story and song because it tells a story but it can be sung like a song. It sounds like a song because it has words in it that **rhyme. (Point to the word rhyme on the chart.)** Say this word. *Rhyme.*

(Touch the ear beside the word rhyme.) The ear reminds you that rhyme means "sounds like." When words sound alike, we say that they rhyme. You are already getting good at hearing rhyming words.

Look at the next word on the chart. **(Touch under the word.)** This word is **poem.** A poem is like a song because it includes words that rhyme. Listen to this poem. Raise your hand when you hear words that rhyme and be ready to tell about them.

Humpty-Dumpty sat on a **wall,**
Humpty-Dumpty had a great **fall. (Repeat this brief passage.)**

What are the rhyming words in this poem? *Wall and fall.*

Listen to another poem. Raise your hand when you hear words that rhyme and be ready to tell about them.

Twinkle, twinkle, little **star,**
How I wonder what you **are.**

What are the rhyming words in this poem? *Star and are.*

Look beside the word **poem** on the chart. You can see the empty lines of words. The word at the end of each line says **rhyme.** A poem can look like that—four lines with words that rhyme at the end of each line.

Look at the last word on the chart. I'm going to say it in a funny way. Listen: **syl-la-ble.** Say that word in that funny way. *Syl-la-ble.* Let's figure out how many parts we heard when we said **syl-la-ble.**

(Count out the syllables on yours fingers with children.) Listen again, and let's count on our fingers each time we hear a new part. **Syl-la-ble.** Say it again. *Syl-la-ble.* How many parts did we hear? *Three.*

Syllable is just a fancy way of saying "how many parts." I wrote "How many parts?" next to the word **syllable** to help you remember. What does the word **syllable** mean? *How many parts.*

We're going to learn to sing a song that helps us to remember the words we need to know about poems. It's called "The Poetry Song." I'll sing the first verse for you **(The tune for this song is** *Row, Row, Row Your Boat.***):**

Rhyme, rhyme, rhyming words,
Making us a poem
Tell about where we like to live
Call it "Home, Sweet Home."

Sing the first verse about rhyming words with me now:

Rhyme, rhyme, rhyming words,
Making us a poem
Tell about where we like to live
Call it "Home, Sweet Home."

There is a verse about syllables too. I'll sing the second verse for you:

Rhyme, rhyme, rhyming words,
Making us a poem
Syllables tell us how many parts
Each of them will own.

Sing the second verse with me now:

Rhyme, rhyme, rhyming words,
Making us a poem
Syllables tell us how many parts
Each of them will own.

Now let's sing both of the verses we know:

Rhyme, rhyme, rhyming words,
Making us a poem
Tell about where we like to live
Call it "Home, Sweet Home."

Rhyme, rhyme, rhyming words,
Making us a poem
Syllables tell us how many sounds
Each of them will own.

That was fun. We'll learn more verses for "The Poetry Song" as we learn more about poetry.

(See the Introduction for the complete Poetry Song.)

Play Hear, Say! (Cumulative Review)

Today, you will play *Hear, Say!* again. Hearsay is a naming word that names stories and ideas you might be told about people or things. Usually, hearsay is a mixture of truth and untruth.

One person hears something about someone else. They tell another person what they think they heard. Then that next person tells what they think they heard the first person say.

Along the way, new bits sometimes get mixed in until the story isn't much like it was when it started out.

In *Hear, Say!* I will use target words in sentences. Some of the sentences I say might have some untruths or extra information in them. If you think what I am saying is not all true, say "Hear, Say!" That means you want to suggest a way to make the sentence truthful and not just hearsay. I'll say the beginning of the sentence again. If you can make the sentence end so it is true, you'll get a point. If you can't, I get the point.

If I use the vocabulary word correctly and there are no untruths in what I say, then say "That's the honest truth!" Be careful, though. If you say "that's the honest truth" when there is hearsay in the sentence, I will get a point!

Let's practice: If you **rescue** someone, you … save them from a manger and a ranger. *Hear, Say!* Well, that's what *I* heard. The first part of the sentence stays the same. I'll say the first part. If you **rescue** someone, you. How can we finish the sentence so it doesn't have hearsay in it? **(Idea: *Save them from danger.*)** Let's say the whole sentence together now. *If you rescue someone, you save them from danger.* That's the honest truth! I'm glad we removed the hearsay!

Let's do another one together. Mr. Ford **continued** in his job as principal … for a few minutes until he was bored. *Hear, Say!* Well, that's what *I* heard. The first part of the sentence stays the same. I'll say the first part. Mr. Ford **continued** in his job as principal. How can we finish the sentence so it doesn't have hearsay in it? (Idea: *For a very long time.*) Let's say the whole sentence now. *Mr. Ford continued in his job as principal for a very long time.* That's the honest truth!

Now you're ready to play the game. (Draw a T-chart on the board for keeping score. Children earn one point for each correct answer. If they make an error, correct them as you normally would, and record one point for yourself. Repeat missed words at the end of the game.)

- Jill knew that the word **allow** meant … to do whatever she wanted as long as she had persuasion. *Hear, Say!* Well, that's what *I* heard. I'll say the first part of the sentence again. Jill knew that the word **allow** meant. How can we finish the sentence so it doesn't have hearsay in it? (Idea: *To give permission to do something.*) Let's say the whole sentence together. *Jill knew that the word allow meant to give permission to do something.* That's the honest truth! I'm glad we examined the hearsay!
- When Rover **continued** his walk in the forest … he just kept going. *That's the honest truth!*
- George was called **clumsy** because … he had trouble doing actions with his hands or feet. *That's the honest truth!*
- Richard said that a **few** chocolate almonds meant … four buckets overflowing with them. *Hear, Say!* Well, that's what *I* heard. I'll say the first part of the sentence again. Richard said that a **few** chocolate almonds meant. How can we finish the sentence so it doesn't have hearsay in it? (Idea: *Some, but not many.*) Let's say the whole sentence together. *Richard said that a few chocolate almonds meant some, but not many.* I'm glad we got rid of the hearsay!
- Charlotte was **polite** when … she stamped her foot, wailed, and pouted in the corner. *Hear, Say!* Well, that's what *I* heard. I'll say the first part of the sentence again. Charlotte was **polite** when. How can we finish the sentence

so it doesn't have hearsay in it? (Idea: *She did the right thing and acted with her best actions and manners.*) Let's say the whole sentence together. *Charlotte was polite when she did the right thing and acted with her best actions and manners.*) That's the honest truth!

- When I **allow** you to use my eraser … I am dangerous and uncooperative. *Hear, Say!* Well, that's what *I* heard. I'll say the first part of the sentence again. When I allow you to use my eraser. How can we finish the sentence so it doesn't have hearsay in it? (Idea: *I give permission for you to use it.*) Let's say the whole sentence together. *When I allow you to use my eraser, I give permission for you to use it.* That's the honest truth!
- If you **prepare** to play baseball … you get your bat, ball, and glove ready to play with. *That's the honest truth!*
- If you are **desperate** for a drink of water … you really, really want and need a drink of water. *That's the honest truth!*
- A **cross** person is one who … always has a smile, speaks nicely, and is happy, happy, happy. *Hear, Say!* Well, that's what *I* heard. I'll say the first part of the sentence again. A **cross** person is one who. How can we finish the sentence so it doesn't have hearsay in it? (Idea: *Is mad and has a frown and an angry voice.*) Let's say the whole sentence together. *A cross person is one who is mad and has a frown and an angry voice.* I'm glad we cleared up the hearsay!
- I knew there were only a **few** words on the list because there were … all of the words in the world that started with *A* and about four thousand other ones. *Hear, Say!* Well, that's what *I* heard. I'll say the first part of the sentence again. I knew that there were only a **few** words on the list because there were. How can we finish the sentence so it doesn't have hearsay in it? (Idea: *Some, but not many.*) Let's say the whole sentence together. *I knew that there were only a few words on the list because there were some, but not many.* That's the honest truth!

(Count the points and declare a winner.) You did a great job of playing *Hear, Say!*

Preparation: Happy Face Game Test Sheet, BLM B.

Retell Story to a Partner

(Assign each child a partner, and ask the partners to take turns telling part of the story each time you turn to a new set of pages. Encourage children to use target words when appropriate.)

Tell me what happened at the **beginning** of the story. (Show the pictures on pages 1 and 2.)

Tell me what happened in the **middle** of the story. (Show the pictures on pages 3–22.)

Tell me what happened at the **end** of the story. (Show the pictures on pages 23 and 24.)

Assess Vocabulary

 (Give each child a copy of the Happy Face Game Test Sheet, BLM B.)

Today you're going to play the Happy Face Game. When you play the Happy Face Game, it shows me how well you know the hard words you are learning.

If I say something that is true, color in the happy face. What will you do if I say something that is true? *Color in the happy face.*

If I say something that is false, color in the sad face. What will you do if I say something that is false? *Color in the sad face.*

Listen carefully to each item that I say. Don't let me trick you!

Item 1: A **polite** person does the right things and acts with his or her best manners and actions. (*True.*)

Item 2: When you **rescue** someone, you save them from danger. (*True.*)

Item 3: **Continued** means to stop and wait. (*False.*)

Item 4: A **few** is the same as more than you could ever count in your life. (*False.*)

Item 5: If you **allow** someone to do something, you give him or her permission to do that thing. (*True.*)

Item 6: A **clumsy** person could have trouble doing actions with his or her hands or feet. (*True.*)

Item 7: A person who **continued** in a job was in that job for a long time. (*True.*)

Item 8: If you were on the **frontier,** you would see lots of houses and high buildings. (*False.*)

Item 9: If someone **appreciated** what you did for them, they would be mad at you and not say thank you. (*False.*)

Item 10: **Adventures** are dangerous or exciting **journeys**. (*True.*)

You did a great job of playing the Happy Face Game!

(Score children's work. A child must score 9 out of 10 to be at the mastery level. If a child does not achieve mastery, insert the missed words as additional items in the games in next week's lessons. Retest those children individually for the missed items before they take the next mastery test.)

Extensions

Read a Story as a Reward

(Display copies of several books that you have read since the beginning of the program or other poetry books that children might enjoy. Allow children to choose which book they would like you to read to them as a reward for their hard work.)

(Read the story aloud for enjoyment with minimal interruptions.)

Preparation: Word containers for the Super Words Center. You may wish to remove some words from earlier lessons. Choose words children have mastered. See the Introduction for instructions on how to set up and use Super Words Center.

You will need to include the 10 onion cards supplied as BLM C with the vocabulary cards for this lesson. The object of the game is to collect the greatest number of onion cards before the play time is over.

Introduce the Super Words Center

(Add the new Picture Vocabulary Cards to words from the previous weeks. Show children one of the word containers. If children need more guidance in how to work in the Super Words Center, role-play with two to three children as a demonstration.)

You will play a game called *Hold the Onions!* in the Super Words Center.

Let's think about how we work with our words in the Super Words Center.

You will work with a partner in the Super Words Center. Whom will you work with? *A partner.*

First you will draw five word cards out of the container. What do you do first? (Idea: *Draw five word cards out of the container.*) Don't show your partner the word cards. Your partner should then draw five word cards for himself or herself from the container so each of you has five cards.

(Show an onion card.) You may have chosen one or more onion cards when you chose your five cards. Keep them! Your goal is to collect as many onion cards as you can before the center time is over.

Next you discard a card by placing it faceup between you and your partner. You must tell your partner what word the card means. Then you may draw another card from the container. Remember that it is your goal to find as many onion cards as possible.

(Demonstrate this part of the game.) Then your partner takes a turn to discard, name, and draw another card.

When the center time is over, lay down your five cards so you can see each other's cards. Whoever has the greatest number of onion cards is the winner of *Hold the Onions!*

Have fun playing *Hold the Onions!*

Preparation:
You will need *Shoo Fly!* for each day's lesson.

Number each right-hand page, starting with the title page that shows the mouse peering out of his hole in the baseboard, to assist you in asking comprehension questions at appropriate points. The final page contains music and all thirteen verses.

Post a copy of the Vocabulary Tally Sheet, BLM A, with this week's Picture Vocabulary Cards attached. Each child will need one copy of the homework sheet, BLM 17a.

You will need a blank sheet of chart paper.

DAY 1

Introduce Book

This week's book is called *Shoo Fly!* What's the title? *Shoo Fly!*

This book is made from a song that some of us know. It was added to by Iza Trapani. [**Eye**-za Tra-**paa**-nee] She is the author of some of the parts of the song. Who's the author of some of the parts of *Shoo Fly!* *Iza Trapani.*

We don't know who wrote the first verse of this song. It was written so long ago that people have forgotten who wrote it. The author of the first verse is unknown. Iza Trapani made the rest of the verses that tell the story.

Iza Trapani also made the pictures for this book. Who is the illustrator of *Shoo Fly!* *Iza Trapani.* Who made the illustrations for this book? *Iza Trapani.*

The cover of a book usually gives us some hints of what the book is about. Let's look at the front cover of *Shoo Fly!* What do you see in the illustration? (Ideas: *A mouse is blowing bubbles; there is a fly in one of the bubbles; the mouse looks angry.*)

(Assign each child a partner.) Get ready to make some predictions to your partner about this book. Use the information from the cover to help you.

Shoo Fly!
author: Iza Trapani • illustrator: Iza Trapani

Target Vocabulary

Tier II	Tier III
bother	verse
pester	pattern
annoy	
immediately	
*frustrated	
*persistent	

*Expanded Target Vocabulary Word

(Ask the following questions, allowing sufficient time for children to share their predictions with their partners.)

- Who is the character in this story? (Who do you think this story is about?)
- What do you think the mouse will do?
- Where do you think the story happens?
- When do you think the story happens?
- In what season of the year do you think the story happens?
- Do you think this story is about a real mouse? Tell why or why not.

(Call on several children to share their predictions with the class.)

Take a Picture Walk

(Encourage children to use target words in their answers.) We're going to take a picture walk through this book. Remember that when we take a picture walk, we look at the pictures and tell what we think will happen in the story.

Page 1. What is the mouse doing in this picture? (Idea: *Looking out of his hole.*) Look at the mouse's face. What do you think he is thinking right now? (Ideas: *He's looking for something; he's scared of something; he's not coming out all the way.*)

Pages 2–3. What is the mouse doing now? (Ideas: *He has come out of his hole; he looks happy.*) What else do you see that looks like it might cause a problem? (Idea: *A fly is flying towards him.*)

Pages 4–5. What are the fly and the mouse doing in the smaller picture? (Ideas: *The mouse is angry; the mouse is trying to hide under a blanket; the fly is pulling the blanket to get at the mouse.*) What is the mouse doing in the larger picture? (Idea: *He's blowing bubbles.*) That picture should make you think of the cover of this story. What do you think will happen? (Idea: *The fly is going to get inside the bubbles.*)

(Note: For pages 6–31, make a list on chart paper with the page number and a "Yes" or a "No," telling whether the fly is seen in that picture. The children will find the resulting pattern to be of interest. You may also draw their attention to the recurring pattern of the song, for example, the *Shoo Fly!* verse appears when the fly is on the page. Keep this chart because you will add to it in a subsequent lesson.)

Pages 6–7. What is happening here? (Ideas: *The mouse is angry; the mouse is trying to catch the fly in a net.*)

Page 8–9. What is the mouse doing here? (Ideas: *The mouse is playing and turning somersaults.*) Can you see the fly anywhere? *No.*

Pages 10–11. There are two small pictures and one large picture on this page. (Indicate each picture by touching under it.) What's happening in this picture? (Idea: *The mouse is jumping to catch the fly but he trips over a block.*) What's happening in the bottom left picture? (Idea: *The mouse is jumping through the stacking rings to catch the fly.*) What's happening in the large picture on the right? (Idea: *The mouse is stuck in the rings, and the fly is squeezing his nose.*)

Pages 12–13. You will have to look carefully to find the mouse in this picture. Can you see him? (If necessary, help children locate the mouse in the basket of yarn.) What is the mouse doing now? (Idea: *He is reading a book.*) Can you see the fly anywhere? *No.*

Pages 14–15. What has happened now? (Ideas: *The fly came; the mouse got angry and tried to catch the fly, but he got tied up in the wool.*)

Pages 16–17. What has the mouse decided to do in these pictures? (Idea: *He has decided to hide outside in a flowerpot.*) Use sharp eyes now—can you see the fly? *No.*

Pages 18–19. What is happening in this picture? (Idea: *The mouse is trying to catch the fly, but he is getting caught in the old glove.*) Is the mouse having much success in getting rid of the fly? *No.*

Pages 20–21. What is happening in the smaller picture? (Ideas: *The mouse is going across the sink; the sink is full of dishes, and the mouse is using them like stepping-stones.*) What is the mouse doing in the larger picture? (Idea: *He's eating cheese.*) Can you see the fly anywhere? *No.*

Pages 22–23. What is happening now? (Ideas: *The mouse is really angry; the mouse is trying to soak the fly; the fly has an umbrella so he won't get wet.*)

Pages 24–25. What is happening now? (Ideas: *The mouse looks like he is going to take a nap; the mouse is watching for the fly.*) Can you see the fly anywhere? *No.*

Pages 26–27. What is happening now? (Idea: *The mouse would like to bat the fly with the honey dipper but he's stuck in the honey himself.*)

Pages 28–29. What is happening now? (Ideas: *The mouse is going back into his hole; the mouse gave up trying to catch the fly.*) Can you see the fly in the picture? *No.* How do you suppose the mouse is feeling after working so hard to avoid that fly? (Ideas: *Tired, sad, exhausted.*)

Pages 30–31. What is happening now? (Ideas: *The mouse's mom and dad are tucking him in; the mouse is smiling and happy.*)

(Music.) What is happening in the picture at the top of the page? (Ideas: *The fly has parents too; the fly's parents are tucking him in to bed.*) How do you suppose the fly feels after spending a day bothering the mouse? (Ideas: *He's probably tired too; he looks like he feels happy.*)

(Printed music.) What can you tell me about the lines, black dots, and words on this page? (Ideas: *It's the music for the song; it shows what to do when you sing the song.*)

It's your turn to ask me some questions. What would you like to know about the story? (Accept questions. If children tell about the pictures or the story instead of ask questions, prompt them to ask a question.) Ask me a what question. Ask me a how question.

Read the Story Aloud
(Read or sing the story to children with minimal interruptions.)

Tomorrow we will read the story again, and I will ask you some questions.

Present the Target Vocabulary
 Bother

In the story, I sang or read "Shoo, fly, don't bother me." The mouse was always being bothered by the fly, and you could tell that he became angry and distracted with that fly buzzing around. **Bother.** Say the word. *Bother.*

Bother is an action word that tells how someone acts toward someone else. What kind of word is **bother?** *An action word.*

If you bother someone, you give them trouble and disturb them. Say the word that means "you give someone trouble and disturb them." *Bother.*

(Correct any incorrect responses, and repeat the item at the end of the sequence.)

You might not mean to bother someone. The fly didn't mean to bother the mouse—it was only doing what flies do. You might bother your mom by playing too loudly in the kitchen. You don't mean to, but you might.

Let's think about some situations when people might bother someone else. I'll tell about some situations. If the person or animal is bothering another person or animal in the situation, say "bother." If not, don't say anything.

- The boy was playing too loudly in the kitchen and he disturbed his mom. *Bother.*
- The fly kept on buzzing around the mouse's ears. *Bother.*
- Harold and Gerald sat quietly in the room together.
- The loud trucks rumbling by gave me trouble and distracted me from my work. *Bother.*
- Mosquitoes kept trying to bite me while I was trying to go to sleep. *Bother.*
- The fly's parents tucked him into bed nicely.

What action word means "to give someone else trouble and disturb them"? *Bother.*

I'm going to say two words. Each word has two parts, or syllables. Tell me how the words I say are alike. **Bother. Father.** Listen again. **Bother. Father.** How are those two words alike? (**Ideas:** *They rhyme. They have two parts.*)

(**Note:** Your goal is to draw from children the two ideas of rhyme and syllables.)

When words sound alike, we sometimes say they rhyme. What do we sometimes call it when words sound alike? *Rhyme.* **Bother** and **father** rhyme. Tell me some other words that rhyme with bother.

Bother and **father** have two parts. Word parts are called syllables. What do we call word parts? *Syllables.* **Both** and **er** are the two syllables in **bother.** What are the two syllables in **bother?** *Both and er.* (Repeat process for *fa-ther.*)

 Annoy

In the story, the mouse tells the fly to stop annoying him. **Annoy.** Say the word. *Annoy.*

Annoy is an action word. It tells what someone or something does. What kind of word is annoy? *An action word.*

If you annoy someone, you disturb them and irritate them. Say the action word that means "disturb and irritate." *Annoy.*

Let's think about some times when someone might have annoyed someone else. I'll tell about a time. If someone was annoyed, say "annoyed." If not, don't say anything.

- The mouse was disturbed and irritated when the fly kept bothering him. *Annoyed.*
- Bobby was ripping the Velcro straps on his gym shoes over and over so I couldn't think any more. Riiiiiip! Riiiiiip! Riiiiiip! *Annoyed.*
- The three brothers got along well and enjoyed each other's company.
- I was disturbed and irritated when the tap kept dripping while I was trying to sleep. Blip! … Blip! … Blip! *Annoyed.*
- The kitten jumped on her mother and chewed her ears while her mother was trying to rest. *Annoyed.*
- The principal saw that all the children were doing their best.

What action word means to "disturb and irritate" someone? *Annoy*.

I'm going to say two words. Each word has two parts, or syllables. Tell me how the words I say are alike. **Annoy** and **employ**. Listen again. **Annoy. Employ.** How are those two words alike? (Ideas: *They rhyme. They have two parts.*)

(**Note:** Your goal is to draw from children the two ideas of rhyme and syllables.)

When words sound alike, we sometimes say they rhyme. What do we sometimes call it when words sound alike? *Rhyme.* **Annoy** and **employ** rhyme. Tell me some other words that rhyme with annoy. (Ideas: *Boy, coy, decoy, joy, koi, poi, Roy, toy.*)

Annoy and **employ** have two parts. Word parts are called syllables. What do we call word parts? *Syllables.* **An** and **noy** are the two syllables in **annoy.** What are the two syllables in **annoy?** *An and noy.* (Repeat process for *em-ploy.*)

◎◄ Pester

I have waited until now to talk to you about the three words **bother, annoy,** and **pester.** These three words are alike in many ways. Think of them like the different shades of a color that you know, like navy blue, sky blue, and baby blue. These three words are similar but different enough that they can add spice to a story and make it more interesting to read or listen to.

Pester. Close to the end of the story, the mouse sprays water on the fly to make him go away because the fly has been bothering and annoying the mouse all day. **Pester.** Say the word. *Pester.*

Pester is an action word. It tells what someone does. It means that someone bothers and annoys someone without stopping and means to do it. What kind of word is **pester?** *An action word.*

If you pester someone, you bother and annoy someone, and you mean to do it. Say the word that means "to bother and annoy someone, and mean to do it." *Pester.*

Now you can see what I mean about **bother, annoy,** and **pester** being similar. **Pester** comes last in the book because it is the worst of the three.

Let's think about some times when you might pester someone. I'll tell about a time. If someone is pestered, say "pester." If not, don't say anything.

- Raoul made mean faces and silly sounds, and he kept on doing it because he knew it made me mad. *Pester.*
- He poked me with a pencil over and over and called me names too; and he wouldn't stop. *Pester.*
- My teacher asked me to show my work to the class.
- Judy's little sister kept jumping on the bed and yelling, "Bouncy, bouncy, bouncy!" while Judy was trying to rest. *Pester.*
- The lion curled up in the corner and had a long nap.
- The fly wouldn't leave the mouse alone and kept bothering and annoying him all through the day. *Pester.*

What action word means "to bother and annoy someone and mean to do it"? *Pester.*

I'm going to say two words. Each word has two parts. Tell me how the words I say are like the word **pester. Fester. Tester.** Listen again. **Fester. Tester.** How are those two words like the word **pester?** (Ideas: *They sound like pester. They rhyme. They have two parts.*)

(**Note:** Your goal is to draw from children the two ideas of rhyme and syllables.)

When words sound alike, we sometimes say they rhyme. What do we sometimes call it when words sound alike? *Rhyme.* **Pester** and **fester** rhyme. Tell me some other words that rhyme with **pester.** (Ideas: *Jester, Lester.*)

Pester and **fester** have two parts. Word parts are called syllables. What do we call word parts? *Syllables.* **Pest** and **er** are the two syllables in **pester.** What are the two syllables in **pester?** *Pest and er.* (Repeat process for *fest-er.*)

◎◄ Immediately

In the story, the mouse tries to catch the fly but he gets caught in an old gardening glove. The mouse wants the fly to leave immediately. **Immediately** is another way of saying right away. **Immediately.** Say the word. *Immediately.*

Immediately is a describing word. It tells about when something should be done. What kind of word is **immediately**? *A describing word.*

If I told you to leave the classroom immediately, I would mean that you should leave right away. Say the word that means "right away." *Immediately.*

Let's think about some times when you have to, or should, do things immediately. I'll tell about a time. If you think it would be a time when a person should have, or had to, do something immediately, say "immediately." If you think the person didn't have to do it immediately, say "no rush." **No rush** could be the opposite of **immediately.**

- Billie had to stop the ball right away before it rolled into the creek. *Immediately.*
- When my sister Sara broke her arm, I knew I had to get help right away. *Immediately.*
- There was lots of time before the bell rang, so I took my time walking back to the school door. *No rush.*
- "The house is on fire! Call 9-1-1!" yelled Nancy-Belle. *Immediately.*
- After a long, hard day with a pestering fly, the mouse went to bed right away. *Immediately.*
- There was no hurry to mow the lawn because it grew so slowly. *No rush.*

What describing word tells that something should be done "right away"? *Immediately.*

I'm going to say two words. Tell me how the words I say are alike. **Immediately. Quickly.** Listen again. **Immediately. Quickly.** How are these two words alike? (Idea: *They have the same endings; they sound alike.*)

When words sound alike, we sometimes say that they rhyme. What do we sometimes call it when words sound alike? *Rhyme.* **Immediately** and **quickly** don't rhyme, but they have the same ending. Tell me some other words that have the same ending as **immediately.** (Ideas: *Happily, carefully, sadly.*)

Present Vocabulary Tally Sheet
(See Lesson 1, page 3, for instructions.)

Assign Homework
(Homework Sheet, BLM 17a. See the Introduction for homework instructions.)

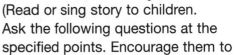

DAY 2

Preparation: Picture Vocabulary Cards for *bother, annoy, pester, immediately.*

Prepare a sheet of chart paper that lists the pages of the story vertically.

Read and Discuss Story
(Read or sing story to children. Ask the following questions at the specified points. Encourage them to use target words in their answers.)

Today I will read or sing the story *Shoo Fly!* First, though, let's sing the part that many people know. The *Shoo Fly!* story can be sung as a song, just like the part we just sang together. This story is also a poem with many verses.

Page 6. This is the beginning of the song and of the story. I'll read and sing this verse again. Count and be ready to tell me how many times I sing or say, "Shoo fly, don't bother me." How many times? *Three.* What is the rhyme for "me" at the end of the verse? *Somebody.*

A **verse** is a group of sentences that go together in a song or poem. Often there are four sentences in a verse, just like this one. This verse begins with the words "Shoo, fly." I'll draw a fly beside page 6 on the chart. (Draw a fly next to page 6.)

Page 9. I'll sing the first two sentences again. What words rhyme? *Away and play.* Now listen to the last two sentences. What two words rhyme? *Scram and clam.* Does this verse begin with "Shoo, fly"? *No.* We'll leave the space beside page 9 blank.

Page 10. I'll read or sing the first two sentences again. Listen and get ready to tell me what words rhyme. What two words rhyme? *Me and tea.* Now listen to the last two sentences. What words rhyme? *Me and be.* Does this verse begin with "Shoo, fly"? *Yes.* Let's add a fly to the chart. (Draw a fly next to page 10.)

Page 12. I'll read or sing the first two sentences again. What words rhyme? *Nook and book.* Now listen to the last two sentences. What words rhyme? *Spot and not.* Does this verse begin with "Shoo, fly"? *No.* We'll leave the space blank beside page 12.

Page 15. I'll read or sing the first two sentences again. What words rhyme? *Me and Tennessee.* Now listen to the last two sentences. What words rhyme? *Three and me.* Does this verse begin with "Shoo, fly"? *Yes.* Let's add a fly to the chart. (Draw a fly next to page 15.)

Page 16. I'll read or sing the first two sentences again. What words rhyme? *Outside and hide.* Now listen to the last two sentences. What words rhyme? *Work and berserk.* If you go berserk, it means that you go pretty crazy with anger. Does this verse begin with "Shoo, fly"? *No.* We'll leave the space beside page 16 blank.

Page 18. Tell how the mouse looks like he's crazy with anger in this picture. (Ideas: *He's clawing at the air and jumping; he's shouting and his face looks mad; he's trying to claw his way through an old glove to get the fly.*)

I think the mouse has really gone berserk! I'll read or sing the first two sentences again. What words have the same ending? *Me and immediately.* Now listen to the last two sentences. What words rhyme? *Me and company.* Does this verse begin with "Shoo, fly"? *Yes.* Let's add a fly next to page 18.)

Page 20. I'll read or sing the first two sentences again. What words rhyme? *Hunch and lunch.* Now listen to the last two sentences. What words rhyme? *Clear and ear.* Does this verse begin with "Shoo, fly"? *No.* We'll leave the space blank beside page 20.

Page 23. I'll read or sing the first two sentences again. What words have the same ending? *Me and family.* Now listen to the last two sentences. What words rhyme? *Tree and me.* Does this verse begin with "Shoo, fly"? *Yes.* Let's add a fly to the chart. (Draw a fly next to page 23.)

Page 24. I'll read or sing the first two sentences of this verse again. What words rhyme? *Rest and guest.* Now listen to the last two sentences. What words rhyme? *Nap and snap.* Does this verse begin with "Shoo, fly"? *No.* We'll leave the space blank beside page 24.

Page 26. I'll read or sing the first two sentences again. What words rhyme? *Me and flee.* Now listen to the last two sentences. What words rhyme? *Sea and Waikiki.* Does this verse begin with "Shoo, fly"? *Yes.* Let's add a fly to the chart. (Draw a fly next to page 26.)

Page 28. I'll read or sing the first two sentences again. What words rhyme? *Doubt and out.* Now listen to the last two sentences. What words rhyme? *Eyes and flies.* Does this verse begin with "Shoo, fly"? *No.* We'll leave the space blank beside page 28 .

Page 31. I'll read or sing the first two sentences again. What words rhyme? *Me and me.* Now listen to the last two sentences. What words have the same ending? *Me and somebody.* Does this verse begin with "Shoo, fly"? *Yes.* Let's add a fly to the chart. (Draw a fly next to page 31.)

Let's look at our chart. I'll touch beside the page numbers. If there is a fly on that line, say "fly." If there is no fly, say "no fly." (Read through the list once with children responding. Then, do it again while keeping a steady beat by snapping your fingers for "fly" and patting your leg for "no fly" to generate a rhythmic pattern. Repeat this, and invite children to join in with the actions.)

We have a **pattern** on our chart. We say, "fly," "no fly," "fly," "no fly," over and over again all the way through the chart. When we do the actions, we go snap, pat, snap, pat, over and over. Let's make another pattern by choosing two colors. (Look for or create other patterns with shapes, sizes, colors, and actions as you see fit.)

Review Vocabulary
(Display the Picture Vocabulary Cards. Point to each card as you say the word. Ask children to repeat each word after you.) These pictures show **bother, annoy, pester,** and **immediately.**

- What action word means "to give someone trouble and disturb them"? *Bother.*

- What action word means "to disturb someone and irritate them"? *Annoy.*
- What action word means "to bother and annoy someone and mean to do it"? *Pester.*
- What word means "right away"? *Immediately.*

Extend Vocabulary

 Bother

In *Shoo Fly!* we learned that if you **bother** someone you give them trouble and disturb them. Say the action word that means "to give someone trouble and disturb them." *Bother.*

Raise your hand if you can tell us a sentence that uses **bother** as an action word meaning "to give someone trouble and disturb them." (Call on several children. If they don't use complete sentences, restate their examples as sentences. Have the class repeat the sentences.)

Here's a new way to use the word **bother.**

- Please don't **bother** to call me back. Say the sentence.
- I hope you didn't **bother** to say, "Thank you," to that rude man. Say the sentence.
- I wish you wouldn't **bother** to return the favor. Say the sentence.

In these sentences, bother is an action word that means take the trouble or trouble yourself. What word means "take the trouble or trouble yourself"? *Bother.*

Raise your hand if you can tell us a sentence that uses **bother** as an action word meaning "take the trouble or trouble yourself." (Call on several children. If they don't use complete sentences, restate their examples as sentences. Have the class repeat the sentences.)

Present the Expanded Target Vocabulary

 Frustrated

In the story, the mouse tried to catch the fly because the fly was pestering him. The mouse couldn't catch the fly. When he tried and tried but still couldn't catch the fly, he became **frustrated. Frustrated.** Say the word. *Frustrated.*

Frustrated is a naming word. It tells how someone feels when they are not able to do something after they have tried and tried. What kind of word is **frustrated?** *A naming word.*

Frustrated means feeling angry about not being able to do something after you have tried and tried. Say the word that means "feeling angry about not being able to do something after you have tried and tried." *Frustrated.*

I'll tell about some people or animals. If those people or animals are frustrated, say "frustrated." If not, don't say anything.

- The mouse tried and tried to catch the fly, but he couldn't. *Frustrated.*
- The spider tried and tried to march in the parade, but she got angry because her feet wouldn't work. *Frustrated.*
- The fly was able to pester the mouse again and again. He was happy.
- The mouse's parents were glad that he came home safely.
- Jimmy tried and tried to print his name carefully, but he became angry when he couldn't. *Frustrated.*
- I became angry after I tried and tried to fix my car and it still wouldn't go. *Frustrated.*

What naming word means "feeling angry about not being able to do something after you have tried and tried"? *Frustrated.*

 Persistent

In the story, the mouse tried to catch the fly until he became frustrated and tired. Then he just gave up. Did the fly ever give up? *No.* No, the fly kept on trying and trying and trying. **Persistent.** Say the word. *Persistent.*

Persistent is a describing word. It tells about someone who keeps trying. What kind of word is **persistent?** *A describing word.*

I'll name some situations when people or animals might be persistent. If the people or animals are persistent, say "persistent." If not, don't say anything.

- The fly kept trying to pester the mouse. *Persistent.*
- The mountain climber kept trying to reach the top. *Persistent.*
- The work was too hard, so Thomas gave up and went home.
- Edna and Ed kept trying to speak a new language. *Persistent.*

- Shawntanna tried skipping once but gave up when she couldn't do it.
- We all kept trying to find words that rhyme with "oranges." *Persistent.*

What describing word tells about "someone who keeps on trying"? *Persistent.*

DAY 3

Preparation: Activity Sheet, BLM 17b. Each child will need crayons.

Retell Story

Today I'll show you the pictures Iza Trapani made for *Shoo Fly!* As I show you the pictures, I'll call on one of you to tell the class that part of the story.

Tell me what happens at the **beginning** of the story. (Show the picture on page 6.)

Tell me what happens in the **middle** of the story. (Show the pictures on pages 8–27. Encourage use of the target words when appropriate. Model use as necessary.)

Tell me what happens at the **end** of the story. (Show the pictures on pages 28–31.)

Play Hear, Say

Today you will play *Hear, Say!* Hearsay is a naming word that tells about stories and ideas you might be told about people or things. Usually, the hearsay is a mixture of truth and untruth.

One person hears something about someone else. They tell another person what they think they heard. Then that next person tells what they think they heard the first person say.

Along the way, new bits sometimes get mixed in until the story isn't much like it was when it started out. To help you remember about hearsay, we are going to play the game *Pass It On* again. *Pass It On* explains what hearsay can be like.

(Arrange children in a circle. Ask a child to whisper a short sentence of his or her choice in your ear. Then have the child take a seat in the circle and whisper the sentence into the ear of the child on his or her left. That child then whispers the sentence to the next child, and so on. When the sentence has gone all the way around the circle, ask the last child to tell what he or she heard. Invariably, it will have little in common with the original sentence! Explain to children that this is what hearsay does to communication.)

In *Hear, Say!* I will use target words in sentences. Some of the sentences I say might have some untruths or extra information in them. If you think what I am saying is not all true, say "Hear, Say!" That means you want to suggest a way to make the sentence truthful and not just hearsay. I'll say the beginning of the sentence again. If you can make the sentence end so it is true, you'll get a point. If you can't, I get the point.

If I use the vocabulary word correctly and there are no untruths in what I say, say "That's the honest truth!" Be careful, though. If you say "That's the honest truth!" when there is hearsay in the sentence, I will get a point!

Let's practice: If you **bother** someone … you give them trouble by being very quiet and not disturbing them. *Hear, Say!* Well, that's what *I* heard. The first part of the sentence stays the same. I'll say the first part. If you **bother** someone. How can we finish the sentence so it doesn't have hearsay in it? (Idea: *You give them trouble by disturbing them.*) Let's say the whole sentence together now. *If you bother someone, you give them trouble by disturbing them.* That's the honest truth! I'm glad we bumped the hearsay!

Let's do another one together. When you **annoy** your mom … you destroy and elevate her. *Hear, Say!* Well, that's what *I* heard. The first part of the sentence stays the same. I'll say the first part. When you **annoy** your mom. How can we finish the sentence so it doesn't have hearsay in it? (Idea: *You disturb and irritate her.*) Let's say the whole sentence together now. *If you annoy your mom, you disturb and irritate her.* That's the honest truth! I'm glad we lumped the hearsay!

Now you're ready to play the game. (Draw a T-chart on the board for keeping score. Children earn one point for each correct answer. If they make an error, correct them as you normally would, and record one point for yourself. Repeat missed words at the end of the game.)

- **Pester** means to … bother and annoy someone and *not* mean to do it. *Hear, Say!* Well, that's what *I* heard. I'll say the first part of the sentence again. **Pester** means to. (Idea: *Bother and annoy someone and mean to do it.*) Let's say the whole sentence together. *Pester means to bother and annoy someone and mean to do it.* That's the honest truth! I'm glad we dumped the hearsay!

- Bob's mom said, "Take out the garbage **immediately**," so … he waited a couple of days before he did it. *Hear, Say!* Well, that's what *I* heard. I'll say the first part of the sentence again. Bob's mom said, "Take out the garbage **immediately**," so. (Idea: *He took it out right away.*) Let's say the whole sentence together. *Bob's mom said, "Take out the garbage immediately," so he took it out right away.* I'm glad we jumped the hearsay!

- Mary Beth didn't **bother** to call back because … she didn't want to take the time. *That's the honest truth!*

- You could tell that the mouse was **frustrated** because … he didn't try to catch the fly and got happier. *Hear, Say!* Well, that's what *I* heard. I'll say the first part of the sentence again. You could tell that the mouse was **frustrated** because. (Idea: *He tried to catch the fly and got angry.*) Let's say the whole sentence together. *You could tell that the mouse was frustrated because he tried to catch the fly and got angry.* That's the honest truth! I'm glad we galumped the hearsay!

- Nan was very **persistent** because … she tried to swim once and gave up. *Hear, Say!* Well, that's what *I* heard. I'll say the first part of the sentence again. Nan was very **persistent** because. (Idea: *She kept trying to swim.*) Let's say the whole sentence together. *Nan was very persistent because she kept on trying to swim.* That's the honest truth! I'm glad we pumped the hearsay.

(Count the points and declare a winner.) You did a great job of playing *Hear, Say!*

Complete the Activity Sheet
(Show children the picture on page 31.)

Today, we will make a poem about belonging that's just like the song *Shoo Fly!* (Give each child a copy of the Activity Sheet, BLM 17b.) I will read the poem. It says:

Shoo fly don't bother me,
Shoo fly don't bother me,
Shoo fly don't bother me,
(blank) *belongs to somebody.*

That sounds funny, doesn't it? When I said "blank," that means there is a space for you to print your name. I'll read or sing the poem again with *my* name in the blank space. (Touch the blank space on the page as you read, and add your own name.)

Your job is to fill in the blank space with your name. Then draw a picture of yourself with the person or people that *you* belong to.

DAY 4

Preparation: Use the "Poetry" chart you prepared for *The Eensy-Weensy Spider.* Add <u>verse</u> and <u>pattern</u> to the list as follows:

1. Rhyme (draw a human ear beside this word)
2. Poem _____**rhyme**
   _____**rhyme**
   _____**rhyme**
   _____**rhyme**
3. Syllable: How many parts?
4. Verse: 4 sentences (see 2.)
5. Pattern: Repeat. For example, *red, blue, red, blue.*

Literary Analysis
You know that *Shoo Fly!* is a story and song because it tells a story but it can be sung like a song. It sounds like a song because it has words in it that rhyme, like **vine, fine, mine,** and **pine.** A poem is like a song because it has rhyming

words in it. You also know that **syllable** is a fancy word that means "how many parts."

Many of the poems you will read or hear have groups of sentences that belong together. Often, there are four sentences in each group. Each group of four sentences is called a **verse.** What do we call a group of sentences that belongs together in a poem? *A verse.*

The poem you wrote about who you belong to had four sentences in the verse. (**Point to item 4 on the chart.**) On our poetry chart, number 4 says, "Verse: 4 sentences." Then it says, "See 2." Look at item 2 now. How many sentences do you see in item 2? *Four.* "See 2" helps you to remember about 4 sentences in a verse.

Listen carefully. When you have figured out what I am doing, raise your hand to tell me using words. (**Create a two-part pattern, keeping a steady beat by clapping and then touching your head—clap, touch, clap, touch. Invite children to join in once they have figured out what you are doing.**) Use your words now. What did we do? (Idea: *We made the pattern clap, touch, clap, touch.*) (Try two or three different movement patterns like step, clap, step, clap and touch hips, touch toes.)

You did a good job of figuring out what **pattern** I was doing. When we make a pattern, we pick two or more actions or words or colors or shapes and we **repeat** them. That means we do them over and over and over again. Say the word that means "do two or more things over and over and over again." *Repeat.*

What words repeat in "The Poetry Song"? (If children are unsure, sing the first two verses to remind them.) *Rhyme, rhyme, rhyming words, making us a poem.*

The first two sentences of each verse in "The Poetry Song" are the same each time. The last two sentences are *different* every time. That's a pattern. (**Point to item 5 on the chart.**) Look at item 5. How have I given you a reminder about pattern? (Idea: *You printed red, blue, red, blue and you used the right colors to do it.*) Do the colors red and blue repeat over and over? *Yes.* I did that to help you remember about patterns.

Let's sing the first two verses of "The Poetry Song" before I teach you some new verses.

(The tune for this song is *Row, Row, Row Your Boat.*)

Rhyme, rhyme, rhyming words,
Making us a poem
Tell about where we like to live
Call it "Home, Sweet Home."

Rhyme, rhyme, rhyming words,
Making us a poem
Syllables tell us how many parts
Each of them will own.

Today we learned about verses and patterns. I'll sing the verse that tells about verses.

Rhyme, rhyme, rhyming words,
Making us a poem
Sentences four make a verse you'll adore
Then you'll take it home!

Get ready to sing the verse about verses with me:

Rhyme, rhyme, rhyming words,
Making us a poem
Sentences four make a verse you'll adore
Then you'll take it home!

Now we'll add the verse about patterns. Listen while I sing it:

Rhyme, rhyme, rhyming words,
Making us a poem
Something sweet that's sure to repeat
Patterns make it flow!

Now let's sing that verse together:

Rhyme, rhyme, rhyming words,
Making us a poem
Something sweet that's sure to repeat
Patterns make it flow!

Now let's sing all that we've learned together:

(See the Introduction for the complete Poetry Song.)

That was fun. We'll learn more verses of "The Poetry Song" as we learn more about poetry.

Play Hear, Say! (Cumulative Review)

Today you will play *Hear, Say!* again. Hearsay is a naming word that tells about stories and ideas you might be told about people or things. Usually, the hearsay is a mixture of truth and untruth.

One person hears something about someone else. They tell another person what they think they heard. Then that next person tells what they think they heard the first person say.

Along the way, new bits sometimes get mixed in until the story isn't much like it was when it started out.

In *Hear, Say!* I will use target words in sentences. Some of the sentences I say might have some untruths or extra information in them. If you think what I am saying is not all true, say "Hear, Say!" That means you want to suggest a way to make the sentence truthful and not just hearsay. I'll say the beginning of the sentence again. If you can make the sentence end so it is true, you'll get a point. If you can't, I get the point.

If I use the vocabulary word correctly and there are no untruths in what I say, say "That's the honest truth!" Be careful, though. If you say "That's the honest truth!" when there is hearsay in the sentence, I will get a point!

Let's practice: If you are **persistent,** you … keep frying. *Hear, Say!* Well, that's what *I* heard. The first part of the sentence stays the same. I'll say

the first part. If you are **persistent,** you. How can we finish the sentence so it doesn't have hearsay in it? (Idea: *Keep trying.*) Let's say the whole sentence together. *If you are persistent, you keep trying.* That's the honest truth! I'm glad we erased the hearsay!

Let's do another one together. Hartley was **frustrated** when…he was able to skate the very first time and he was happy about it. *Hear, Say!* Well, that's what *I* heard. The first part of the sentence stays the same. I'll say the first part. Hartley was **frustrated** when. How can we finish the sentence so it doesn't have hearsay in it? (Idea: *He wasn't able to skate after trying and trying.*) Let's say the whole sentence together. *Hartley was frustrated when he wasn't able to skate after trying and trying.* That's the honest truth! I'm glad we uncased the hearsay!

Now you're ready to play the game. (Draw a T-chart on the board for keeping score. Children earn one point for each correct answer. If they make an error, correct them as you normally would, and record one point for yourself. Repeat the missed words at the end of the game.)

- Rafe wanted to **bother** his father so … he found a way to give him rubble and inspect him. *Hear, Say!* Well, that's what *I* heard. I'll say the first part of the sentence again. Rafe wanted to **bother** his father so. How can we finish the sentence so it doesn't have hearsay in it? (Idea: *He found a way to give him trouble and distract him.*) Let's say the whole sentence together. *Rafe wanted to bother his father, so he found a way to give him trouble and distract him.* That's the honest truth! I'm glad we chased away the hearsay!

- Joseph didn't **bother** to bring the cat inside because … he didn't want to take the time to do it. *That's the honest truth!*

- Lester **pestered** his sister, Hester, by … bothering her and annoying her and really meaning to do it. *That's the honest truth!*

- Lloyd **annoyed** his mom by … making so much noise that she was herbed and implicated. *Hear, Say!* Well, that's what *I* heard. I'll say the first part of the sentence again. Lloyd **annoyed** his mom by. (Idea:

Read-Aloud Library Teacher Edition **181**

Making so much noise that she was disturbed and irritated.) Let's say the whole sentence together. *Lloyd annoyed his mom by making so much noise that she was disturbed and irritated.* I'm glad we faced the hearsay!

- Sissy was **disobedient** when … she did everything her mom told her to do. *Hear, Say!* Well, that's what *I* heard. I'll say the first part of the sentence again. Sissy was **disobedient** when. (Idea: *She didn't do everything her mom told her to do.*) Let's say the whole sentence together. *Sissy was disobedient when she didn't do everything her mom told her to do.* That's the honest truth! I'm glad we unlaced the hearsay!

- I knew there was a **meadow** outside my window because … when I looked out, I could see the water stretching off into the distance. *Hear, Say!* Well, that's what *I* heard. I'll say the first part of the sentence again. I knew there was a **meadow** outside my window because. (Idea: *When I looked out I could see the grass and the flowers.*) Let's say the whole sentence together. *I knew there was a meadow outside my window because when I looked out I could see the grass and flowers.* That's the honest truth! I'm glad we refaced the hearsay!

- Food that is **delicious** … tastes really, really good. *That's the honest truth!*

- **Gathering** something up means … collecting things and putting them in one place. *That's the honest truth!*

- If I don't **bother** to clean the chalkboard … I go to great trouble to get it perfectly clean. *Hear, Say!* Well, that's what *I* heard. I'll say the first part of the sentence again. If I don't bother to clean the chalkboard. (Idea: *I don't trouble myself to get it clean.*) Let's say the whole sentence together. *If I don't bother to clean the chalkboard, I don't trouble myself to get it clean.* I'm glad we paced the hearsay!

(Count the points and declare a winner.) You did a great job of playing *Hear, Say!*

Retell Story to a Partner

(Assign each child a partner, and ask the partners to take turns telling part of the story each time you turn to a new set of pages. Encourage children to use target vocabulary when appropriate.)

Assess Vocabulary

 (Give each child a copy of the Happy Face Game Test Sheet, BLM B.)

Today you're going to play the Happy Face Game. When you play the Happy Face Game, it shows me how well you know the hard words you are learning.

If I say something that is true, color in the happy face. What will you do if I say something that is true? *Color in the happy face.*

If I say something that is false, color in the sad face. What will you do if I say something that is false? *Color in the sad face.*

Listen carefully to each item that I say. Don't let me trick you!

Item 1: If you are **bothered,** you are given trouble and you are disturbed. (*True.*)

Item 2: A **frustrated** person has tried and tried and was still unable to do what he or she wanted to do. (*True.*)

Item 3: **Annoy** means to disturb and irritate someone. (*True.*)

Item 4: A **persistent** person is one who gives up right away. (*False.*)

Item 5: If you don't **bother** to wash, you don't trouble yourself to be clean. (*True.*)

Item 6: If you **pester** someone, you bother and annoy them and you really mean to do it. (*True.*)

Item 7: Something that is happening right now is happening in the **present.** (*True.*)

Item 8: **Blossoms** and leaves are the same thing. (*False.*)

Item 9: If you didn't **bother** to do your homework, you didn't take the trouble to do it. (*True.*)

Item 10: If a tree is **bare** it is covered with leaves. (*False.*)

You did a great job of playing the Happy Face Game!

(Score children's work. A child must score 9 out of 10 to be at the mastery level. If a child does not achieve mastery, insert the missed words as additional items in the games in next week's lessons. Retest those children individually for the missed items before they take the next mastery test.)

Extensions

Read a Story as a Reward

 (Display copies of the books that you have read since the beginning of the program or display other poetry books. Allow children to choose which book they would like you to read to them as a reward for their hard work.)

(Read the story aloud for enjoyment with minimal interruptions.)

Preparation: Word containers for the Super Words Center. You will need to include the 10 onion cards supplied as BLM C.

Introduce the Super Words Center

(Add the new Picture Vocabulary Cards to the words from the previous weeks. Show children one of the word containers. If children need more guidance in how to work in the Super Words Center, role-play with two to three children as a demonstration.)

Let's review how to play the *Hold the Onions!* game.

Let's think about how we work with our words in the Super Words Center.

You will work with a partner in the Super Words Center. Whom will you work with? *A partner.*

First you will draw five word cards out of the container. What do you do first? (Idea: *Draw five word cards out of the container.*) Don't show your partner the word cards. Your partner should then draw five word cards for himself or herself from the container so each of you has five cards.

(Show an onion card.) You may have chosen one or more onion cards when you chose your five cards. Keep them! Your goal is to collect as many onion cards as you can before the center time is over.

Next you discard a card by placing it faceup between you and your partner. You must tell your partner what word is shown on the card. Then you may draw another card from the container. Remember that it is your goal to find as many onion cards as possible.

(Demonstrate this part of the game.) Then your partner takes a turn to discard, name, and draw another card.

When the center time is over, lay down your five cards so you can see each other's cards. Whoever has the greatest number of onion cards is the winner of *Hold the Onions!*

Have fun playing *Hold the Onions!*

Dinosaur Days

author: Linda Manning • illustrator: Vlasta van Kampen

Preparation: You will need *Dinosaur Days* for each day's lesson.

Number the pages of the story to assist you in asking the comprehension questions at the appropriate points in the story.

Post a copy of the Vocabulary Tally Sheet, BLM A, with this week's Picture Vocabulary Cards attached.

Each child will need one copy of the Homework Sheet, BLM 18a.

Target Vocabulary

Tier II	Tier III
scrawl	fantasy
chef	rhyme
severely	rhythm
sprawled	beat
*imaginary	
*disruptive	

*Expanded Target Vocabulary Word

- When do you think the story happens?
- Why do you think the dinosaur is sliding down the post?
- How did it get its nails polished?
- Do you think the characters in this story are real? Tell why or why not.

(Call on several children to share their predictions with the class.)

Take a Picture Walk

(Encourage children to use previously taught target words in their answers.) We are going to take a picture walk through this book. Remember that when we take a picture walk, we look at the pictures and tell what we think will happen in the story.

Pages 1–2. Where is the dinosaur? *In the kitchen.* What is it doing? **Ideas:** *Drinking juice; sitting on the toast.* How would you be feeling if you were the girl? What number do you see on the girl's shirt? *One.*

Pages 3–4. What is happening here? (Idea: *The dinosaur is tied to the post; the little girl is touching its tongue.*)

Pages 5–6. Where is the dinosaur? *In the girl's bedroom.* What is it doing? *Coloring on her ceiling.* How would you be feeling if you were the girl? What number do you see on the girl's shirt? *Two.*

Pages 7–8. What is happening here? (Idea: *The girl is sitting on the dinosaur's tail; she is touching the dinosaur's toes; the dinosaur is writing twos on the floor.*)

DAY 1

Introduce Book

Today's book is called *Dinosaur Days.* What's the title? *Dinosaur Days.* This book was written by Linda Manning. Who's the author of *Dinosaur Days*? *Linda Manning.*

Vlasta van Kampen [vlast-uh van CAMP-en] made the pictures for this book. Who's the illustrator of *Dinosaur Days*? *Vlasta van Kampen.* Who made the illustrations for this book? *Vlasta van Kampen.*

The cover of a book usually gives us some hints of what the book is about. Let's look at the front cover of *Dinosaur Days.* What do you see in the illustration? (Ideas: *A dinosaur sliding down a post; a little girl; the dinosaur has a flower in its mouth; it's wearing a necklace; it has purple nail polish on its claws.*)

(Assign each child a partner.)

Get ready to make some predictions to your partner about this book. Use the information from the book's cover to help you.

(Ask the following questions, allowing sufficient time for children to share their predictions with their partners.)

- Who are the characters in this story? (Whom do you think this story is about?)
- What is the child doing?
- Where do you think the story happens?

Pages 9–10. Where is the dinosaur? *In the living room*. What is it doing? *Sitting on the chair, making muddy footprints on everything.* How would you be feeling if you were the girl? (Point to the calendar.) What number do you see on the calendar? *Three.*

Pages 11–12. What is happening here? (Idea: *The girl is standing on the dinosaur's back; she is drying it off with a towel; there are threes everywhere.*)

Pages 13–14. Where is the dinosaur? *Outside.* What is it doing? *Hanging on to a pole.* Where is the girl? *Up the tree.* What is she doing? (Idea: *Pulling numbers up into the tree.*) How would you be feeling if you were the girl? What numbers do you see hanging from the tree? *Fours.*

Pages 15–16. What is happening here? (Idea: *The girl and the dinosaur are skipping.*)

Pages 17–18. Where is the dinosaur? *In the bathroom.* What is it doing? *Flying around; squeezing the toothpaste.* What is the girl doing? (Idea: *Brushing her teeth.*) How would you be feeling if you were the girl? What number do you see? *Five.*

Pages 19–20. What is happening here? (Idea: *The dinosaur is sitting on the sink; the girl is squeezing out the toothpaste.*)

Pages 21–22. Where is the dinosaur? (Ideas: *In the laundry room; near the washer.*) What is it doing? *Knocking over the soap; spilling the water.* How do you think the girl is feeling? What number do you see? *Six.*

Pages 23–24. What is happening here? (Idea: *The girl is telling the dinosaur to be good; she's pointing her finger at him; he's hiding his face.*)

Pages 25–26. Where are the dinosaurs? (Ideas: *Outside.*) What are they doing? *Having a party.* (Point to the dinosaur with the chef's hat.) What is this dinosaur doing? (Ideas: *Barbecuing; cooking hamburgers and hotdogs.*) What is the girl doing? *Eating a hamburger.* How do you think the girl is feeling? What number do you see? *Seven.*

Pages 27–28. What is happening here? *Everyone is sleeping.*

It's your turn to ask me some questions. What would you like to know about this story? (Accept questions. If children tell about the pictures or the story instead of ask questions, prompt them to ask a question.) Ask me a why question. Ask me a how question.

Read the Story Aloud
(Read story to children with minimal interruptions.)

Tomorrow we will read the story again and I will ask you some questions.

(If children have difficulty attending for an extended period of time, you may wish to present the next part of this day's lesson at another time of day.)

Present Target Vocabulary

Scrawl

In the story, the girl taught the dinosaur how to write his name in dinosaur scrawl. That means writing that was careless and untidy. Another word for scrawl is scribble. **Scrawl.** Say the word. *Scrawl.*

Scrawl is a naming word. It names a kind of writing. What kind of word is **scrawl?** *A naming word.*

If someone's writing is a scrawl it is careless and untidy. It doesn't look like writing; it looks like a scribble. Say the word that means "writing that is careless and untidy." *Scrawl.*

Watch me. I'll write my name in my best writing. (Print your name slowly, forming each letter carefully.) Now I'll write my name in scrawl. (Scribble your name so it is not completely legible. Point to the first name.) This is my best writing. (Point to the second name.) This is a scrawl.

(Correct any incorrect responses and repeat the item at the end of the sequence.)

Let's think about some writing that might be a scrawl. I'll tell about some writing. If you think the writing I'm telling about is a scrawl, say "scrawl." If not, don't say anything.

- Dr. Chen signed his name really fast so that it was messy. *Scrawl.*
- The two-year-old boy used a crayon to write his name all over the wall. *Scrawl.*

- She didn't care how her printing looked. *Scrawl.*
- He took the time to write his name neatly.
- You would almost say that Vonette scribbled her name. *Scrawl.*
- My teacher has the neatest writing I have ever seen.

What naming word means "writing that is careless and untidy"? *Scrawl.*

◎◄ Chef

In the story, a fancy chef dinosaur took over the yard to cook hot dogs and burgers. A chef is a very skilled cook. **Chef.** Say the word. *Chef.*

Chef is a naming word. It names a person. What kind of word is **chef?** *A naming word.*

If you are a chef you are very good at cooking. You are a very skilled cook. Say the word that means "a very skilled cook." *Chef.*

Let's think about some situations where a chef might cook a meal. I'll tell about a situation. If you think the situation I'm telling about would need a chef, say "chef." If not, don't say anything.

- The restaurant needed someone who could cook fancy meals. *Chef.*
- The school cafeteria needed a skilled cook to prepare meals for the children. *Chef.*
- The family wanted a very special meal cooked for the holiday. *Chef.*
- Meralee is just learning how to cook.
- Paul needed a special cook to prepare a meal for his friends. *Chef.*
- Molly and her family went camping. They quickly made sandwiches to eat.

What naming word means "a person who is a very skilled cook"? *Chef.*

◎◄ Severely

In the story, the girl said quite severely, "don't do that again!" That means she spoke to him with a harsh voice. She did not say the words gently. **Severely.** Say the word. *Severely.*

Severely is a describing word. It tells about how someone says something. What kind of word is **severely?** *A describing word.*

If you speak severely, you speak in a voice that is harsh, not gentle. Say the word that means you "speak in a voice that is harsh, not gentle." *Severely.*

Let's think about some times when someone might speak severely. I'll tell about a time. If you think the person I'm telling about would speak severely, say "severely." If not, don't say anything.

- The puppy would never listen. Its owner spoke to it. *Severely.*
- Your friend invites you to play at his house.
- The guard at the pool yelled, "Do not run on the pool deck!" *Severely.*
- Ginnie whispered to her baby brother.
- Aunt Cary shouted at us to close the gate when we let the chickens out. *Severely.*
- Mom told us how to behave in a quiet voice.

What describing word means "speak in a voice that is harsh, not gentle"? *Severely.*

◎◄ Sprawled

At the end of the story, all the dinosaurs sprawled in a heap under the tree. That means they were lying down with their legs spread out. **Sprawled.** Say the word. *Sprawled.*

Sprawled is an action word. It tells how someone did something. What kind of word is **sprawled?** *An action word.*

If someone sprawled out, they sat or lay down with their arms and legs spread out. Say the word that means "sat or lay down with arms and legs spread out." *Sprawled.*

Watch me. I'll sit carefully on my chair. (Sit with your feet flat on the floor, hands folded on your lap. Then stand up.) What did I do? *You sat carefully on your chair.*

Now I'll sprawl on my chair. (Slide forward on your chair so only your upper back touches the back of the chair. Stretch your legs out in different directions. Put one arm over the back of the chair, and hang your other arm over the side of your chair. Then stand up.) What did I do? *You sprawled on your chair.*

I'll quietly ask someone to do some actions in our classroom. Your job is to watch what he or she does. If he or she sprawls, you say "sprawled." If he or she doesn't sprawl, don't say anything. (Whisper an instruction to a selected child to perform.)

- (Sprawl at a desk.) *Sprawled.*
- (Sit nicely in a chair.)
- (Sprawl on a table.) *Sprawled.*
- (Sprawl on the floor.) *Sprawled.*
- (Sit nicely at the Super Words Center.)
- (Sit nicely at your desk.)

What action word means "sat or lay down with arms and legs spread out"? *Sprawled.*

Introduce the Vocabulary Tally Sheet
(See Lesson 1, page 3, for instructions.)

Assign Homework
(Homework Sheet, BLM 18a. See the Introduction for homework instructions.)

DAY 2

Preparation: Picture Vocabulary Cards for *scrawl, chef, severely, sprawled.*

Read and Discuss Story
(Read or sing story to children. Ask the following questions at the specified points. Encourage children to use target words in their answers.)

Now I'm going to read *Dinosaur Days*. When I finish each part, I'll ask you some questions. This story is written as a poem.

Sometimes when poets write poems they use rhyming words. Words that rhyme sound alike. **Hat** and **cat** rhyme. What's another word that rhymes with **hat** and **cat?** (Ideas: *Bat, sat, chat, that.*)

The words **tan** and **man** rhyme. What's another word that rhymes with **tan** and **man?** (Ideas: *Can, Dan, fan, Nan.*)

The words **win** and **tin** rhyme. What's another word that rhymes with **win** and **tin?** (Ideas: *Chin, fin, kin, thin.*)

You did a great job of rhyming. You would make great poets. Listen carefully as I read the story. See whether you can hear the words that rhyme.

(**Note:** Before beginning the story, explain to the children that in this book the author talks to the reader; she asks children what they would do if they found themselves face to face with some unusual dinosaurs. The illustrator draws pictures to answer the question and show what one girl did when faced with that problem.)

Pages 2–5. When did the story begin? *On Monday.* This dinosaur is an Apatosaurus. [a pat o **sore** us] What's the problem? (Ideas: *The Apatosaurus slurped up the orange juice and squished flat the toast.*)

What did the girl do to solve the problem? (Idea: *She tamed him and taught him to lie by a post.*)

What two words rhyme in this part of the poem? *Toast and post.* (If children have difficulty finding the rhyming words, reread the two lines that rhyme. Then ask them to tell you the two words that rhyme.)

Pages 6–8. When did this part of the story happen? *On Tuesday.* This dinosaur is a Stegosaurus. [steg uh **sore** us] What's the problem? (Ideas: *The stegosaurus drew on the ceiling and messed up the clothes.*) What did the girl do to solve the problem? (Idea: *She caught her and held her by two ticklish toes.*)

What two words rhyme in this part of the poem? *Clothes and toes.* (If children have difficulty finding the rhyming words, reread the two lines that rhyme. Then, ask them to tell you the two words that rhyme.)

(Repeat process for pages 9–24, identifying the dinosaurs and the rhyming words:

Wednesday—Ankylosaurus [an keel o **sore** us]; chair and care

Thursday—Hadrosaurus [had ro **sore** us]; rose and hose

Friday—Pteranodon [ter **an** o don]; wall and scrawl

Saturday—Triceratops [try **sair** ah tops]; drain and again

Sunday—Tyrannosaurus Rex [tie ran uh **sore** us rex]; popping and toppings; around and round.)

Page 28. How does the story end? (Idea: *All of the dinosaurs fell asleep.*)

What two words rhyme in this part of the poem?

Heap and *asleep*. (If children have difficulty finding the rhyming words, reread the two lines that rhyme. Then ask them to tell you the two words that rhyme.)

Review Vocabulary

(Display the Picture Vocabulary Cards. Point to each card as you say the word. Ask the children to repeat each word after you.) These pictures show **scrawl, chef, severely,** and **sprawled.**

- What naming word means "a very skilled cook"? *Chef.*
- What action word means "lay down with arms and legs spread out"? *Sprawled.*
- What describing word means "speak in a voice that is harsh, not gentle"? *Severely.*
- What naming word means "writing that is careless and untidy"? *Scrawl.*

Extend Vocabulary

 Scrawl

In *Dinosaur Days,* we learned that **scrawl** was a naming word that means "writing that is careless and untidy."

Here's a new way to use the word **scrawl.**

- He **scrawled** his name at the end of the letter. Say the sentence.
- They **scrawled** on the paper with their markers. Say the sentence.
- He **scrawled** his name on the bag. Say the sentence.

In these sentences, **scrawl** is an action word. **When you scrawl on something, you write on it in a messy or untidy way.** What do you do when you scrawl on something? *You write on it in a messy or untidy way.*

Present the Expanded Target Vocabulary

Imaginary

In the story, the dinosaurs lived when real dinosaurs didn't live. They went places real dinosaurs couldn't go. They did things real dinosaurs couldn't do. These dinosaurs were not real dinosaurs. They were imaginary dinosaurs. **Imaginary.** Say the word. *Imaginary.*

Imaginary is a describing word. It tells about how things are. What kind of word is **imaginary?** *A describing word.*

If something is imaginary, it is not real. What word means "something that is not real"? *Imaginary.*

Let's think about some things that could be imaginary. I'll name something. If it could tell about something that is imaginary, say "imaginary." If it tells about something that is real, say "real."

- Pigs that can build houses of brick. *Imaginary.*
- A girl that gets a kite for her birthday. *Real.*
- Goats that eat grass. *Real.*
- Trolls that live under bridges. *Imaginary.*
- A hen that makes bread. *Imaginary.*
- People that make stone soup. *Real.*

What describing word means "things that are not real?" *Imaginary.*

Disruptive

In the story, the dinosaurs caused a lot of trouble in the girl's house. Nothing happened the way it should. The dinosaurs were very disruptive. **Disruptive.** Say the word. *Disruptive.*

Disruptive is a describing word. It tells about someone's actions. What kind of word is **disruptive?** *A describing word.*

When someone is disruptive, they cause a lot of trouble. The opposite of disruptive is well-behaved. Say the word that means "someone caused a lot of trouble." *Disruptive.*

Let's think about some people who might do something that is disruptive. I'll tell about someone. If that person is being disruptive, say "disruptive." If that person is not being disruptive, say "well-behaved."

- Kyle didn't yell when he got upset. *Well-behaved.*
- The baby hit and kicked and screamed when it didn't get its way. *Disruptive.*
- The children wouldn't be quiet when the substitute teacher came. *Disruptive.*
- All of us sat quietly and read while we waited. *Well-behaved.*
- None of the children cried or shouted when the lights went out. *Well-behaved.*
- The bullies made the little kids scared. *Disruptive.*

What describing word means "caused a lot of trouble"? *Disruptive.*

Tell about a time when you or someone you know was disruptive. (Call on several children. Encourage children to start their answers with the words "I was disruptive when _____" or "_____ was disruptive when." After each response, ask the child:) What might you have done to be well behaved?

DAY 3

Preparation: Activity Sheet, BLM 18b.

Retell Story

Today I'll show you the pictures Vlasta Van Kampen made for the story *Dinosaur Days.* As I show you the pictures, I'll call on one of the children to tell the class about that part of the story.

Pages 1–4. (Call on a child to tell what's happening. Encourage use of target words when appropriate. If there is opportunity on a page for a child to use one of the target words, and he or she doesn't, model using the word. Repeat this procedure to the end of page 26.)

Pages 27–28. (Chime read the end of the story, with the children chiming in with the days of the week.)

Listen while I read part of this story to you again. (Read any one verse.) This story is written as a poem. How is this story written? *As a poem.*

Play Hear, Say

Today you will play *Hear, Say!* Remember that hearsay is a naming word that tells about stories and ideas you might be told about people or things. Usually, the hearsay is a mixture of truth and untruth.

One person hears something about someone else. They tell another person what they think they heard. Then that next person tells what they think they heard the first person say.

Along the way, new bits sometimes get mixed in until the story isn't much like it was when it started out.

In *Hear, Say!* I will say some sentences with our vocabulary words in them. Some of the sentences I say will include hearsay—there might be some untruths and extra bits in them. If you think what I am saying is not true, say "Hear, Say!" That means you want to suggest a way to make the sentence truthful and not just hearsay. I'll say the beginning of the sentence again. If you can make the sentence end so that it makes sense, you'll get a point. If you can't, I get the point.

If I use the vocabulary word correctly and there are no untruths in what I say, say "That's the honest truth!" Be careful, though—if you say "That's the honest truth!" when there is hearsay in the sentence, I will get a point!

Let's practice: If a person is a **chef,** he … would not be a very good cook. *Hear, Say!* Well, that's what I hear … The first part of the sentence stays the same. I'll say the first part. If a person is a **chef,** he. How can we finish the sentence so it doesn't have hearsay in it? (Idea: *Would be a very good cook.*) Let's say the whole sentence together. *If a person is a chef, he would be a very good cook.* That's the honest truth! I'm glad we clipped the hearsay!

Let's do another one together. If the children were **disruptive** … they were quiet and well behaved. *Hear, Say!* Well, that's what I heard. The first part of the sentence stays the same. I'll say the first part. If the children were **disruptive.** How can we finish the sentence so it doesn't have hearsay in it? (Idea: *They were noisy and badly behaved.*) Let's say the whole sentence together. *If the children were disruptive, they were noisy and badly behaved.* That's the honest truth! I'm glad we dipped the hearsay!

Now you're ready to play the game. (Draw a T-chart on the board for keeping score. Children earn one point for each correct answer. If they make an error, correct them as you normally would and record one point for yourself. Repeat missed words at the end of the game.)

- A **scrawl** is … neat and tidy writing. *Hear, Say!* Well, that's what I heard. I'll say the first part of the sentence again. A **scrawl** is. How can we finish the sentence so it makes sense? (Idea: *Messy and untidy writing.*) Let's say the whole sentence together. *A scrawl is messy and untidy writing.* That's the honest truth! I'm glad we chipped the hearsay!

- An **imaginary** story is … not make-believe. *Hear, Say!* Well, that's what I heard. I'll say the first part of the sentence again. An **imaginary** story is. How can we finish the sentence so it makes sense? (Idea: *Make-believe.*) Let's say the whole sentence together. *An imaginary story is make-believe.* I'm glad we nipped the hearsay!

- If someone spoke to you in a voice that was harsh and not gentle, they spoke to you **severely.** *That's the honest truth!*

- The boy **sprawled** on the chair when … he sat up tall with his hands folded on his lap. *Hear, Say!* Well, that's what I heard. I'll say the first part of the sentence again. The boy **sprawled** when. How can we finish the sentence so it makes sense? (Idea: *He sat with his legs spread out and his hand over the back of the chair.*) Let's say the whole sentence together. *The boy sprawled on the chair when he sat with his legs spread out and his hand over the back of the chair.* That's the honest truth! I'm glad we flipped the hearsay!

- Mary **scrawled** her name when … she printed it neatly. *Hear, Say!* Well, that's what I heard. I'll say the first part of the sentence again. Mary **scrawled** her name when. How can we finish the sentence so it makes sense? (Idea: *She scribbled it.*) Let's say the whole sentence together. *Mary scrawled her name when she scribbled it.* That's the honest truth! I'm glad we zipped the hearsay.

(Count the points, and declare a winner.) You did a great job of playing *Hear, Say!*

Complete the Activity Sheet

In *Dinosaur Days* things happened on each day of the week. Say the days of the week, starting with Monday. (Repeat until firm.)

(Give each child a copy of the Activity Sheet BLM 18b.) My turn. I'll read the first item on the sheet. On Monday, blank came. (Chime read with the students the first item on the sheet. Say "blank" when you get to the line. Have children

decide which dinosaur came that day. Have them cut out the picture of that dinosaur and glue it on the line. Children who are able to copy words may copy each word beside the picture.)

(Repeat this process for the remaining items.)

Literary Analysis

You know that *Dinosaur Days* is a poem because it has words in it that rhyme like **post** and **toast**.

Another thing that poets do to make their poems more interesting is to use rhythm. When you mix short, long, and longer sounds together, you get something called **rhythm.** The sounds that are in a rhythm are called the beat. What do we call the sounds that are in a rhythm? *The beat.* All the words we say when we speak have rhythm in them. So do our names.

Listen to some short words with one beat:

cat

dog

hat

Now listen to some longer words with two beats:

ice-cream

rockstar

(long, long: that is the same time for each syllable)

Now listen to some longer words with <u>three</u> beats (stress the first syllable):

blueberries

hamburgers

(long, short-short)

Now listen to the short and long sounds in these groups of words:

Pizza, **chips**, and **ice**-cream

Big ba**lon**ey **sand**wich

(short-short, short-short, long, long)

It's the rhythm in a poem that makes the words sound interesting. Imagine if we all just spoke in long sounds. (Speak the words in a monotone, holding each syllable for the same amount of time.) **Big. Ba. Lo. Ney. Sand. Wich.** It's pretty boring and it's hard to listen to. Rhythm makes words sound bouncy and light, the way they should! (Select a few lines from the poem to read using a monotone voice without rhythm. Read the same lines using rhythm, beat, and voice inflection. Discuss the differences with the children.)

Let's sing the verses of "The Poetry Song" before I teach you a new verse. (The tune for this song is *Row, Row, Row Your Boat*):

(See the Introduction for the complete Poetry Song.)

Here's a new verse that tells about rhythm. Listen while I sing it for you:

> *Rhyme, rhyme, rhyming words,*
> *Making us a poem,*
> *Rhythm's a pattern of strong and weak,*
> *Feel it in your bones.*

Now sing the new verse with me:

> *Rhyme, rhyme, rhyming words,*
> *Making us a poem,*
> *Rhythm's a pattern of strong and weak,*
> *Feel it in your bones.*

Now let's sing all the verses of The Poetry Song together.

That was fun. We'll learn more verses of The Poetry Song as we learn more about poetry.

Play Hear, Say! (Cumulative Review)

Today you will play *Hear, Say!* again. Hearsay is a naming word that tells about stories and ideas you might be told about people or things. Usually, hearsay is a mixture of truth and untruth. One person hears something about someone else. They tell another person what they think they heard. Then that next person tells what they think they heard the first person say. Along the way, new bits sometimes get mixed in until the story isn't much like it was when it started out.

In *Hear, Say,* I will say some sentences with our vocabulary words in them. Some of the sentences I say will include hearsay—there might be some untruths and extra bits in them. If you think what I am saying is not true, say "Hear, Say!" That means you want to suggest a way to make the sentence truthful and not just hearsay. I'll say the beginning of the sentence again. If you can make the sentence end so that it makes sense, you'll get a point. If you can't, I get the point.

If I use the vocabulary word correctly and there are no untruths in what I say, say "That's the honest truth!" Be careful, though—if you say "That's the honest truth!" when there is hearsay in the sentence, I will get a point!

Let's practice: If you are **disruptive,** you … are sitting quietly. *Hear, Say!* Well, that's what I heard. The first part of the sentence stays the same. I'll say the first part If you are **disruptive,** you. How can we finish the sentence so it makes sense? (Idea: *Are noisy and running around.*) Let's say the whole sentence together now. *If you are disruptive, you are noisy and running around.* That's the honest truth! I'm glad we caught the hearsay!

Let's do another one together. The **imaginary** story told about … things that were true. *Hear, Say!* Well, that's what I heard. The first part of the sentence stays the same. I'll say the first part. The **imaginary** story told about. How can we finish the sentence so that it makes sense? (Idea: *Things that were not true.*) Let's say the whole sentence together. *The imaginary story told about things that were not true.* That's the honest truth! I'm glad we got the hearsay!

Now you're ready to play the game. (Draw a T-chart on the board for keeping score. Children earn one point for each correct answer. If they make an error, correct them as you normally would and record one point for yourself. Repeat missed words at the end of the game.)

- When grandfather spoke to us **severely,** he spoke in a … quiet, gentle voice. *Hear, Say!* Well, that's what I heard. I'll say the first part of the sentence again. When grandfather spoke to us **severely,** he spoke in a. How can we finish the sentence so that it makes sense? (Idea: *A harsh voice.*) Let's say the whole sentence together. *When grandfather spoke to us severely, he spoke in a harsh voice.* That's the honest truth! I'm glad we brought the hearsay!

- Something that is happening in the **present** is … happening now. *That's the honest truth!*
- Another word for **scrawl** is … scribble. *That's the honest truth!*
- A **bare** tree … is covered with leaves. *Hear, Say!* Well, that's what I heard. I'll say the first part of the sentence again. A **bare** tree. How can we finish the sentence so it makes sense? (Idea: *Has no leaves.*) Let's say the whole sentence together. *A bare tree has no leaves.* I'm glad we taught the hearsay!
- The meal the **chef** prepared … tasted terrible. *Hear, Say!* Well, that's what I heard. I'll say the first part of the sentence again. The meal the **chef** prepared. How can we finish the sentence so it makes sense? (Idea: *Tasted great.*) Let's say the whole sentence together. *The meal the chef prepared tasted great.* That's the honest truth! I'm glad we bought the hearsay!
- The kitten lay **sprawled** out … when it was curled up in a ball. *Hear, Say!* Well, that's what I heard. I'll say the first part of the sentence again. The kitten lay **sprawled** out. How can we finish the senence so it makes sense? (Idea: *When it lay with its legs spread out.*) Let's say the whole sentence together. *The kitten lay sprawled out when it lay with its legs spread out.* That's the honest truth! I'm glad we fought the hearsay!
- The snake … **slithered** across the grass. *That's the honest truth!*
- The **wise** teacher … taught her students to think carefully before they speak. *That's the honest truth!*
- The sign on the yard said, "No **Trespassing**." That means … the people want you to come in their yard. *Hear, Say!* Well, that's what I heard. I'll say the first part of the sentence again. The sign on the yard said, "No **Trespassing**." That means. How can we finish the sentence so it makes sense? (Idea: *You should not go in that yard.*) Let's say the sentences together. *The sign on the yard said,*

"No Trespassing." That means you should not go in that yard. That's the honest truth!

(Count the points and declare a winner.) You did a great job of playing *Hear, Say!*

DAY 5

Preparation: Happy Face Game Test Sheet, BLM B.

Retell the Story to a Partner

(Assign each child a partner.) Today I'll show you the pictures Vlasta van Kampen made for *Dinosaur Days.* As I show you the pictures, you and your partner will take turns telling part of the story. (The partners should take turns telling part of the story each time the day of the week changes.)

Tell what happened on Monday. (Show the pictures on pages 1–4.)

Tell what happened on Tuesday. (Show the pictures on pages 5–8. Ask the partners to take turns telling what's happening. Encourage the children to include the target words when appropriate. Repeat this procedure until you finish page 26.)

Tell me what happened at the end of the story. (Show the pictures on pages 27–28. Chime read the end of the story, with the children chiming in with as much of the story as they can remember.)

Are the dinosaurs in this story real or imaginary? *Imaginary.*

Assess Vocabulary

 (Give each child a copy of the Happy Face Game Test Sheet, BLM B.)

Today you're going to play the Happy Face Game. When you play the Happy Face Game, it shows me how well you know the hard words you are learning.

If I say something that is true, color in the happy face. What will you do if I say something that is true? *Color in the happy face.*

If I say something that is false, color in the sad face. What will you do if I say something that is false? *Color in the sad face.*

Listen carefully to each item that I say. Don't let me trick you!

Item 1: **Scrawl** means to print very neatly. (*False.*)

Item 2: If students are **disruptive,** they are making trouble in the classroom. (*True.*)

Item 3: A **chef** is not a very good cook. (*False.*)

Item 4: If you are **sprawled** on the floor, your arms and legs are everywhere and it looks like you just fell where you were. (*True.*)

Item 5: If your teacher speaks **severely,** he is speaking quietly and nicely. (*False.*)

Item 6: **Imaginary** animals are not real. (*True.*)

Item 7: There no tall buildings in the **wilderness.** (*True.*)

Item 8: When birds **migrate** they slowly walk to a colder place. (*False.*)

Item 9: A **rough** road is smooth with no bumps or holes. (*False.*)

Item 10: If the name on the book was a **scrawl** is would **not** be neat and easy to read. (*True.*)

You did a great job of playing the Happy Face Game!

(Score children's work. A child must score 9 out of 10 to be at the mastery level. If a child does not achieve mastery, insert the missed words as additional items in the games in next week's lessons. Retest those children individually for the missed items before they take the next mastery test.)

Extensions

Read a Story as a Reward

(Display copies of several of the books that you have read since the beginning of the program or other books of poetry. Allow children to choose which book they would like you to read to them as a reward for their hard work.)

(Read the story aloud for enjoyment with minimal interruptions.)

Preparation: Word containers for the Super Words Center. You will need to include the 10 onion cards, BLM C, with the Picture Vocabulary Cards for this lesson. The object of the game is to collect the greatest number of onion cards before the play time is over.

Introduce the Super Words Center

(Add the new Picture Vocabulary Cards to the words from the previous weeks. Show children one of the word containers. If children need more guidance in how to work in the Super Words Center, role-play with two to three children as a demonstration.)

Let's review how to play the *Hold the Onions!* game.

Let's think about how we work with our words in the Super Words Center.

You will work with a partner in the Super Words Center. Whom will you work with? *A partner.*

First you will draw five word cards out of the container. What do you do first? (Idea: *Draw five word cards out of the container.*) Don't show your partner the word cards. Your partner should then draw five word cards for himself or herself from the container so each of you has five cards.

(Show an onion card.) You may have chosen one or more onion cards when you chose your five cards. Keep them! Your goal is to collect as many onion cards as you can before the center time is over.

Next you discard a card by placing it faceup between you and your partner. You must tell your partner what word the card means. Then you may draw another card from the container. Remember that it is your goal to find as many onion cards as possible. (Demonstrate this part of the game.) Then your partner takes a turn to discard, name, and draw another card.

When the center time is over, lay DOWN your five cards so you can see each other's cards. Whoever has the greatest number of onion cards is the winner of *Hold the Onions!*

Have fun playing *Hold the Onions!*

One Monkey Too Many

author: Jackie French Koller • illustrator: Lynn Munsinger

Preparation: You will need a copy of *One Monkey Too Many* for each day's lesson. Number the pages of the story to assist you in asking comprehension questions at appropriate points in the story.

Post a copy of the Vocabulary Tally Sheet, BLM A, with this week's Picture Vocabulary Cards attached.

Each child will need one copy of the Homework Sheet, BLM 19a.

Target Vocabulary

Tier II	Tier III
arrive	verse
demanded	refrain
rude	period
pitch	exclamation mark
*ignore	
*accident	

*Expanded Target Vocabulary Word

DAY 1

Introduce Book

This week's book is called *One Monkey Too Many*. What's the title of this week's book? *One Monkey Too Many.*

This book was written by Jackie French Koller [**Call**-er]. Who's the author of *One Monkey Too Many*? *Jackie French Koller.*

Lynn Munsinger made the pictures for this book. Who is the illustrator of *One Monkey Too Many*? *Lynn Munsinger.* Who made the illustrations for this book? *Lynn Munsinger.*

The cover of a book usually gives us some hints of what the book is about. Let's look at the front cover of *One Monkey Too Many*. What do you see in the illustration? (Ideas: *One monkey is lying in bed; the other monkeys are making a big mess; they are being noisy and messy.*)

(Assign each child a partner.) Get ready to make some predictions to your partner about this book. Use the information from the cover to help you.

(Ask the following questions, allowing sufficient time for children to share their predictions with their partners.)

- Who are the characters in this story?
- What do you think will happen if the mother monkey sees what the monkeys have done?
- Where do you think the story happens?
- When do you think the story happens?

- Why do you think the monkey in the bed looks so content?
- Do you think this story is about real monkeys? Tell why or why not.

(Call on several children to share their predictions with the class.)

Take a Picture Walk

(Encourage children to use target words in their answers.) We are going to take a picture walk through this book. Remember that when we take a picture walk, we look at the pictures and tell what we think will happen in the story.

Page 1. What do you think the bear is doing? (Idea: *Selling a bike to the monkey with the yellow shirt.*) Who is hiding behind the bear? (Ideas: *Another monkey; a monkey with a red cap.*) What do you think the monkey with the yellow shirt is going to do? (Idea: *Ride the bike.*) What do you think the monkey with the red shirt is going to do?

Pages 2–3. What did the monkey with the red cap do? (Idea: *He jumped on the back of the bike.*) What are the monkeys doing now? (Ideas: *They're both riding on the bike.*) Are they enjoying themselves? *Yes.* How can you tell? (Idea: *It looks like they're laughing.*) I think those monkeys are monkeying around.

Pages 4–5. Uh-oh, what's happening now? (Ideas: *The bike is wobbling; the monkeys are falling off.*) That bit of monkey business didn't turn out too well, did it?

Page 6. What do you think the tiger has been doing? *Playing golf.* What do you call this vehicle? *A golf cart.* What do you think the tiger is saying to the two monkeys? (Ideas: *Do you like my golf cart? Would you like a ride?*) Who is hiding behind the tiger? (Ideas: *Another monkey; a girl monkey; a monkey with a pink ribbon.*) What do you think the two monkeys are going to do? (Idea: *Climb into the golf cart.*) What do you think the monkey with the pink ribbon is going to do?

Page 7. What did the monkey with the pink ribbon do? (Idea: *She jumped in the golf cart.*)

Page 8. What are the monkeys doing now? (Ideas: *They're all riding in the golf cart.*) Are they enjoying themselves? *Yes.* How can you tell? (Idea: *It looks like they're smiling.*) I think those monkeys are monkeying around.

Page 9. Uh-oh, what's happening now? (Ideas: *The golf cart is tipping; the golf cart is driving into the water; the monkeys have fallen off.*) That bit of monkey business didn't turn out too well, did it?

Page 10. What do you think the goat is saying to the three monkeys? (Ideas: *Would you like a ride in my canoe? Would you like to go canoeing?*) Who is hiding in the tree? (Ideas: *Another monkey; a monkey in a blue striped t-shirt.*) What do you think the three monkeys are going to do? (Idea: *Climb into the canoe.*) What do you think the monkey with the blue striped t-shirt is going to do?

Page 11. What is the monkey with the blue striped t-shirt doing? (Idea: *Jumping into the canoe.*)

Page 12. What are the monkeys doing now? (Ideas: *They're all riding in the canoe; they're paddling the canoe down the river.*) Are they enjoying themselves? *Yes.* How can you tell? (Ideas: *They are all paddling; they look content.*) I think those monkeys are monkeying around.

Page 13. Uh-oh, what's happening now? (Ideas: *The canoe has gone over a waterfall; the monkeys have fallen out of the canoe; the monkeys are falling.*) That bit of monkey business didn't turn out too well, did it?

(Repeat this established procedure for the next two sections of the book: pages 14–17 and pages 18–21.)

Pages 22–23. Who do you think the woman is? How many monkeys do you see? *Six.* Where do you think the woman is going?

Pages 24–25. Let's count the monkeys. (Touch the monkeys and count out loud with children.) How many monkeys do you see? *Seven.* What do you think will happen next? (Ideas: *They'll be monkeying around; they'll be up to more monkey business.*)

Pages 26–27. What are the monkeys doing? (Ideas: *Coloring in the book, doing all the things we've seen in the book.*)

Page 28. What are these monkeys doing? (Idea: *Monkeying around.*) I guess monkeys must do what monkeys must do!

It's your turn to ask me some questions. What would you like to know about the story? (Accept questions. If children tell about the story instead of ask questions, prompt them to ask a question.) Ask me a who question. Ask me a how question.

Read the Story Aloud
(Read the story to children with minimal interruptions.)

Tomorrow we will read the story again, and I will ask you some questions.

Present the Target Vocabulary
Arrive

In the story, the bellman says, "This bed is for five. I cannot allow any more to arrive." **Arrive.** Say the word. *Arrive.*

Arrive is an action word. It tells what someone does. What kind of word is **arrive?** *An action word.*

If you arrive, you come to a place. Say the action word that means "come to a place." *Arrive.*

(Correct any incorrect responses, and repeat the item at the end of the sequence.)

Let's think about some times when someone might arrive. I'll tell about a time. If someone or something arrived, say "arrived." If not, don't say anything.

- All my friends came to my birthday party. *Arrived.*
- My dad came home at 6:00 P.M. *Arrived.*
- The jaguar never left the jungle.
- The airplane landed at the airport on time. *Arrived.*
- I waited and waited, but my friend never came.
- The fire engine roared to the fire and quickly put it out. *Arrived.*

What action word means "come to a place"? *Arrive.*

Demanded

In the story, "one monkey too many demanded to eat." **Demanded.** Say the word. *Demanded.*

Demanded is an action word. It tells what someone did. What kind of word is **demanded?** *An action word.*

If you demanded something you asked for something using a very forceful voice. Say the action word that means "asked for something using a very forceful voice." *Demanded.*

Let's think about some times when someone might have demanded something. I'll tell about a time. If someone demanded something, say "demanded." If not, don't say anything.

- Karl went to the store and very forcefully asked the clerk to replace the broken toy. *Demanded.*
- When I found my bananas were rotten, I asked for a refund with a forceful voice. *Demanded.*
- When Billy hurt my arm, I forcefully asked him to apologize. *Demanded.*
- After the man helped me collect my marbles, I thanked him politely.
- I saw the pretty painting my friend had made and said, "Wow, that's great!"
- Our mom forcefully asked us to stop making so much noise. *Demanded.*

What action word means "asked for something using a very forceful voice"? *Demanded.*

I'll say some words with three parts. Be ready to tell me how they are the same as the word **demanded. Commanded. Two-handed.** Listen

again. **Commanded. Two-handed.** How are those words the same as demanded? (Ideas: *They each have three parts; they sound the same; they rhyme.*)

Rude

In the story, "Drinks spilled and plates tumbled and monkeys got rude." That means they did things that showed bad manners. They did things that were not polite. **Rude.** Say the word. *Rude.*

Rude is a describing word. It tells about a way of acting or talking. What kind of word is **rude?** *A describing word.*

If you are rude, you do or say things that show bad manners. You do or say things that are not polite. Say the word that means "do or say things that show bad manners; are not polite." *Rude.*

Let's think about some times when someone might be rude. I'll tell about a time. If you think the person I'm telling about is rude, say "rude." If not, don't say anything.

- Zach kept interrupting the teacher when she was talking to the class. *Rude.*
- When it was Colleen's turn to listen, she talked instead. *Rude.*
- Vinnie stuck out his tongue and made a noise. *Rude.*
- Fern crept across the room so she wouldn't be heard.
- Faith forgot to say thank you when she got a present. *Rude.*
- Greg and his brother waited until the speaker finished his speech to ask a question.

What describing word means "do or say things that show bad manners; are not polite"? *Rude.*

I'm going to say two words. Each word has one part. Tell me how the words I say are like the word **rude. Glued. Stewed.** Listen again. **Glued. Stewed.** How are those two words like the word **rude?** (Ideas: *They sound like rude. They rhyme. They have one part or syllable.*)

Pitch

In the story, the bike "started to wobble. It started to **pitch." Pitch.** Say the word. *Pitch.*

Pitch is an action word. It tells what something does. What kind of word is **pitch**? *An action word.*

If a bicycle or a boat starts to pitch, it suddenly moves from side-to-side or end-to-end. Imagine this book is a boat. Watch me make it **pitch** from side-to-side. (Hold the book out, flat and level; then rock it from side-to-side.) Now watch me make it pitch from end-to-end. (Hold the book out, flat and level; then rock it from end-to-end.) Say the word that means "suddenly move from side-to-side or end-to-end." *Pitch.*

Let's think about some times when something might pitch. I'll tell about a time. If you think it would be a time when something might pitch, say "pitch."

- The waves were huge and the boat was moving from end-to-end. *Pitch.*
- Up and down went the airplane's nose. Everyone began to feel ill. *Pitch.*
- The ship floated on calm, smooth water.
- The bike rocked and swayed as Henry rode over the bumpy patch. *Pitch.*
- The car moved from end-to-end as it went over the speed bumps. *Pitch.*
- The path was so smooth that my scooter seemed like it was gliding along.

What action word means "move suddenly from side-to-side or end-to-end"? *Pitch.*

I'm going to say two words. Each word has one part. Tell me how the words I say are like the word **pitch. Glitch. Snitch.** Listen again. **Glitch. Snitch.** How are those two words like the word **pitch**? (Ideas: *They sound like pitch. They rhyme. They have one part or syllable.*)

Present Vocabulary Tally Sheet
(See Lesson 1, page 3, for instructions.)

Assign Homework
(Homework Sheet, BLM 19a. See the Introduction for homework instructions.)

Preparation: Picture Vocabulary Cards for *arrive, demanded, rude, pitch.*

Read and Discuss Story

Today I will read the story *One Monkey Too Many* to you. Partly because the words rhyme, the story is a poem with many verses.

(Read story to children. Ask the following questions at the specified points. Encourage them to use target words in their answers.)

Page 1. This bike is designed for how many monkeys? *One.* I'll read this verse again. Listen carefully and be ready to tell me the rhyme for "one" in this verse. What word rhymes with one? *Fun.*

Remember that a **verse** is a group of sentences that go together in a poem or song. What do we call a group of sentences that go together in a poem or song? *A verse.* Often there are four sentences in a verse, just like this one.

Jackie Koller helps us to know how many sentences there are by using symbols at the end of her sentences. Those symbols say, "Stop. This is the end of a sentence." Watch and see if you can see the stop symbols. (Read the verse again, tracking with your finger under the words as you go. Point out the periods and say, "Stop. This is the end of a sentence." when you arrive at them.) The little dot at the end of a sentence is called a **period.** It says, "Stop."

Page 2. The poem says the monkeys wheeled off down the pike. Pike is another word for road. What is another word for road? *Pike.*

I'll read the first sentence of this verse again. "One monkey too many jumped onto the bike." Listen to tell me what word rhymes with "bike." "One monkey too many wheeled off down the pike." What word rhymes with bike? *Pike.* Watch and see if you can see the stop symbols. (Read and track as above. You may ask children to call out "Period" or "Stop" as you wish.)

Page 3. I'll read the first two sentences of this verse again. "Hooray!" the two shouted. "We're having such fun." Listen to tell me what word rhymes with "fun." "This bike is far better for two than for one." What word rhymes with fun? *One.* Watch and see if you can see the stop symbols. (Repeat the process for finding the "stop" symbols. When you get to the end of the verse point out the exclamation mark.) The straight line with the period under it at the end of the third sentence is called an **exclamation mark.** It says, "Stop!" too, but it also tells you to say that sentence more loudly. Let's read that sentence together loudly. *This bike is far better for two than for one!*

Pages 4–5. I'll read the first two sentences of this verse again. "It started to wobble. It started to pitch." Listen to tell me what word rhymes with "pitch." "One monkey too many crashed into the ditch." What word rhymes with pitch? *Ditch.* Watch and see if you can see the stop symbols. (Repeat the process for finding the "stop" symbols.)

Page 6. Who did the monkeys meet next? *The golfer.* I'll read this verse again. Listen to tell me what words rhyme. What words rhyme? *Two and you.* Watch and see if you can see the stop symbols. (Repeat the process for finding the "stop" symbols.)

Page 7. What happened when the monkeys climbed into the golf cart? (Idea: *Another monkey jumped in, too.*) I'll read this verse again. Listen to tell me what words rhyme. What words rhyme? *Between and green.* Watch and see if you can see the stop symbols. (Repeat the process for finding the "stop" symbols.)

Page 8. Are those three monkeys having fun? *Yes.* I'll read this verse again. Listen to tell me what words rhyme. What words rhyme? *Glee and three.* Watch and see if you can see the stop symbols. (Repeat the process for finding the "stop" symbols.)

Page 9. Are those three monkeys having fun? (Idea: *Not any more.*) I'll read this verse again. Listen to tell me what words rhyme. What words rhyme? *Brake and lake.* Watch and see if you can see the stop symbols. (Repeat the process for finding the "stop" symbols.)

(Repeat this established procedure for the remaining pages, checking for understanding and identifying rhyming words and stop symbols.)

The monkeys in this story were always up to monkey business. They were always monkeying around. That means they were always getting into trouble. Sometimes we use those two expressions to talk about children who are getting into trouble. If you were getting into trouble, what might your mom and dad insist that you do? (Ideas: *Stop monkeying around; stop that monkey business!*) And they'd say it really loud, so their sentences would have to end with what mark? (Idea: *An exclamation mark.*)

Review Vocabulary

(Display the Picture Vocabulary Cards. Point to each card as you say the word. Ask children to repeat each word after you.) These pictures show **arrive, rude, demanded,** and **pitch.**

- What word means "come to a place"? *Arrive.*
- What word means "showed bad manners"? *Rude.*
- What word means "asked for something using a very forceful voice"? *Demanded.*
- What word means "suddenly move from side-to-side or end-to-end"? *Pitch.*

Extend Vocabulary

 Pitch

In *One Monkey Too Many,* we learned that pitch is an action word meaning "suddenly move from side-to-side or end-to-end."

Raise your hand if you can tell us a sentence that uses pitch as an action word meaning "suddenly moves from side-to-side or end-to-end." (Call on several children. If they don't use complete sentences, restate their examples as sentences. Have the class repeat the sentences.)

Here's a new way to use the word **pitch.**

- Pitch me that ball. Say the sentence.
- My grandpa likes to pitch horseshoes. Say the sentence.
- Nolan Ryan can pitch a baseball at over 100 miles per hour. Say the sentence.

In these sentences, pitch is an action word that means throw or toss something. What action word means "throw or toss something"? *Pitch.*

Raise your hand if you can tell us a sentence that uses pitch as an action word meaning "throw or toss something." (Call on several children. If they don't use complete sentences, restate their examples as sentences. Have the class repeat the sentences.)

Present the Expanded Target Vocabulary
 Ignore

In *One Monkey Too Many,* the monkeys paid no attention to what the biker, the golfer, the boatman, the waiter, the bellman, and the author told them. The monkeys **ignored** all these characters. **Ignore.** Say the word. *Ignore.*

Ignore is an action word. It tells what someone does. What kind of word is **ignore?** *An action word.*

If you ignore someone, you pay no attention to them. Say the word that means "pay no attention to." *Ignore.*

I'll tell about some people. If you think those people are ignoring someone or something, say "ignore." If not, don't say anything.

- Amy paid no attention when the dog scratched at the door to get out. *Ignore.*
- When kids called out without raising their hands, Mrs. Goodfellow didn't pay attention to them. *Ignore.*
- Every time the baby made a peep, her mom jumped up to find out what she wanted.
- If your ankle hurts a little when you're walking, just forget about it and enjoy the walk. *Ignore.*
- It was loud in the swimming pool, but it was so much fun that I didn't pay attention to it. *Ignore.*
- My dog barks every time someone drives by the house. I don't pay attention to him any more. *Ignore.*

What action word means "pay no attention to"? *Ignore.*

Accident

In the story, the monkeys had a lot of **accidents** because they didn't listen. That means something bad happened that no one expected, and they got hurt. **Accident.** Say the word. *Accident.*

Accident is a naming word. It names a thing. What kind of word is **accident?** *A naming word.*

An accident is something bad that happens that no one expects, and someone gets hurt. Say the word that means "something bad that happens that no one expects, and someone gets hurt." *Accident.*

Let's think some things that might be accidents. I'll tell about something that happened. If you think what happened was an accident, say "accident." If not, don't say anything.

- When she bumped into the curb, Sophie fell off her bike and hurt her knee. *Accident.*
- Colleen said that Joshua made a face at her.
- When Hansel spilled his glass of milk, it spilled on the floor and Gretel slipped in the puddle. *Accident.*
- Damon handed the paper to Lou.
- "Amanda splattered me with paint on purpose!" exclaimed April.
- Jack fell off the beanstalk and broke the giant's golden harp. *Accident.*

What naming word means "something bad that happens that no one expects, and someone gets hurt"? *Accident.*

DAY 3

Preparation: Activity Sheet, BLM 19b. Each child will need crayons.

Retell Story
Today I'll show you the pictures Lynn Munsinger made for *One Monkey Too Many.* As I show you the pictures, I'll call on one of you to tell the class that part of the story.

Tell me what happens at the **beginning** of the story. (Show the picture on page 1.)

Tell me what happens in the **middle** of the story. (Show the pictures on pages 2–21. Call on a child to tell what's happening. Encourage use of the target words when appropriate. Model use as necessary.)

Tell me what happens at the **end** of the story. (Show the pictures on pages 22–28.)

Play Hear, Say!

 Today you will play *Hear, Say!* In *Hear, Say!* I will use target words in sentences. Some of the sentences I say might have some untruths or extra information in them. If you think what I am saying is not all true, say *Hear, Say!* That means you want to suggest a way to make the sentence truthful and not just hearsay. I'll say the beginning of the sentence again. If you can make the sentence end so it is true, you'll get a point. If you can't, I get the point.

If I use the vocabulary word correctly and there are no untruths in what I say, say "That's the honest truth!" Be careful, though. If you say "That's the honest truth!" when there is hearsay in the sentence, I will get a point!

Let's practice. When someone **arrives,** they … jump through a space and shout, "I'm alive!" *Hear, Say!* Well, that's what *I* heard. The first part of the sentence stays the same. I'll say the first part. When someone **arrives,** they. How can we finish the sentence so it doesn't have hearsay in it? (Idea: *Come to a place.*) Let's say the whole sentence together. *When someone arrives, they come to a place.* That's the honest truth! I'm glad we stopped the hearsay!

Let's do another one together. When your mom spoke with a forceful voice, she … **frustrated** that you listen to her. *Hear, Say!* Well, that's what *I* heard. The first part of the sentence stays the same. I'll say the first part. When your mom spoke with a forceful voice, she. How can we finish the sentence so it doesn't have hearsay in it? (Idea: *Demanded that you listen to her.*) Let's say the whole sentence together. *When your mom spoke with a forceful voice, she demanded that you listen to her.* That's the honest truth! I'm glad we chopped the hearsay!

Now you're ready to play the game. (Draw a T-chart on the board for keeping score. Children earn one point for each correct answer. If they make an error, correct them as

you normally would and record one point for yourself. Repeat missed words at the end of the game.)

- A **rude** person … shows mad planners. *Hear, Say!* Well, that's what *I* heard. I'll say the first part of the sentence again. A **rude** person. How can we finish this sentence so it doesn't have hearsay in it? (Idea: *Shows bad manners.*) Let's say the whole sentence together. *A rude person shows bad manners.* That's the honest truth! I'm glad we lopped the hearsay!
- If the waves are huge, the boat will … snitch. *Hear, Say!* Well, that's what *I* heard. I'll say the first part of the sentence again. If the waves are huge, the boat will. How can we end this sentence so it doesn't have hearsay in it? *Pitch.* Let's say the whole sentence together. *If the waves are huge, the boat will pitch.* That's the honest truth! I'm glad we popped the hearsay!
- If you ignore someone … you pay them no attention. *That's the honest truth!*
- A bad thing that happens that no one planned is … a **pester.** *Hear, Say!* Well, that's what *I* heard. I'll say the first part of the sentence again. A bad thing that happens that no one planned is. How can we finish this sentence so it doesn't have hearsay in it? *An accident.* Let's say the whole sentence together. *A bad thing that happens that no one planned is an accident.* That's the honest truth! I'm glad we copped the hearsay!
- Suzie threw the baseball and made a good … glitch. *Hear, Say!* Well, that's what *I* heard. I'll say the first part of the sentence again. Suzie threw the baseball and made a good. How can we finish this sentence so it doesn't have hearsay in it? *Pitch.* Let's say the whole sentence together. *Suzie threw the baseball and made a good pitch.* That's the honest truth! I'm glad we stopped the hearsay.

(Count the points and declare a winner.) You did a great job of playing *Hear, Say!*

Preparation: Use the "Poetry" chart you prepared for *The Eensy-Weensy Spider.* Add <u>rhythm</u> and <u>refrain</u> to the list as follows:

6. Rhythm: Loooooong and short, **STRONG** and weak sounds that make words bounce around a beat.

7. Refrain:
Different **Same** Different Different
Different **Same** Different Different
Different **Same** Different Different
Different **Same** Different Different

Literary Analysis

You know that *One Monkey Too Many* is a poem because it has rhyming words in it. It has verses that look like they are four sentences long. The rhyming words make a pattern in the sentences.

In *One Monkey Too Many* there are verses that are different and verses that sound almost the same. The "almost the same" verses keep coming back over and over and over again. The "almost the same" verse is the part that you know the best. You start to say it every time it comes around. Listen while I read the poem again. Say the "almost the same" verse with me when we come to it. (Read from the beginning of the poem. The refrain (almost the same) is the *One monkey too many* part. As you read, point to the same/different pattern that is on the chart. This pattern repeats in a four-verse sequence throughout the book.)

The "almost the same" verse that keeps coming back with the words "One monkey too many" has a special name. It is called a **refrain.** Say the word **refrain.** *Refrain.* The word refrain means "comes back." What does the word **refrain** mean? *Comes back.*

(You can reinforce the concept of a refrain by singing or playing a few songs that contain refrains. Some popular choices might be *Looby Loo* (the refrain being *Here we go Looby Loo, here we go Looby light...*), *This Old Man* (the refrain being *With a knick-knack, paddy-whack,*

give the dog a bone ...), and B-I-N-G-O (the refrain being *B-I-N-G-O, B-I-N-G-O, B-I-N-G-O and Bingo was his name-o!*)

Let's sing the verses of "The Poetry Song" before I teach you a new verse. (The tune for this song is *Row, Row, Row Your Boat.* Sing the verses that have been previously introduced, as found in Day 4 of Lesson 18.)

Here's a new verse that tells about a refrain. Listen while I sing it for you:

Rhyme, rhyme, rhyming words,
Making us a poem,
The refrain is the most familiar part,
Listen and you'll know!

Now sing the new verse with me:

Rhyme, rhyme, rhyming words,
Making us a poem,
The refrain is the most familiar part,
Listen and you'll know!

Now let's sing all that we have learned together. (See the Introduction for the complete "The Poetry Song.")

That was fun. We'll learn one more verse of "The Poetry Song" as we learn more about poetry.

Complete Activity Booklet

(Use BLM 19c to make a take-home-and-share book using a similar pattern as *One Monkey Too Many.* Read the poem aloud. Have children illustrate the booklet. They are not expected to be able to read it independently. When the book is sent home, include a note asking someone to read the book to the child.)

Play Hear, Say! (Cumulative Review)

Today you will play *Hear, Say!* again. I will use target words in sentences. Some of the sentences I say might have some untruths or extra information in them. If you think what I am saying is not all true, say "Hear, Say!" That means you want to suggest a way to make the sentence truthful and not just hearsay. I'll say the beginning of the sentence again. If you can make the sentence end so it is true, you'll get a point. If you can't, I get the point.

If I use the vocabulary word correctly and there are no untruths in what I say, say "That's the honest truth!" Be careful, though. If you say "That's the honest truth!" when there is hearsay in the sentence, I will get a point!

Let's practice. A **rude** person … has sad banners. *Hear, Say!* Well, that's what *I* heard. The first part of the sentence stays the same. A **rude** person has. How can we finish the sentence so it doesn't have hearsay in it? (Idea: *Bad manners.*) Let's say the whole sentence together now. *A rude person has bad manners.* That's the honest truth! I'm glad we noted the hearsay!

Let's do another one together. When you **ignore** someone, you … stand at attention. *Hear, Say!* Well, that's what *I* heard. The first part of the sentence stays the same. I'll say the first part. When you **ignore** someone. How can we finish the sentence so it doesn't have hearsay in it? (Idea: *You pay them no attention.*) Let's say the whole sentence now. *When you ignore someone, you pay them no attention.* That's the honest truth!

Now you're ready to play the game. (Draw a T-chart on the board for keeping score. Children earn one point for each correct answer. If they make an error, correct them as you normally would and record one point for yourself. Repeat missed words at the end of the game.)

- When you **arrive,** you … hide in a den. *Hear, Say!* Well, that's what *I* heard. I'll say the first part of the sentence again. When you **arrive,** you. How can we finish the sentence so it doesn't have hearsay in it? (Idea: *Come to a place.*) Let's say the whole sentence together. *When you arrive, you come to a place.* That's the honest truth! I'm glad we boated the hearsay!
- If the road is very bumpy, your car might start to … **pitch.** *That's the honest truth!*

- An **accident** is … something bad that happens that no one planned. *That's the honest truth!*
- Amir made a good **pitch** when … he blew the baseball to the batter. *Hear, Say!* Well, that's what *I* heard. I'll say the first part of the sentence again. Amir made a good **pitch** when. How can we finish this sentence so it doesn't have hearsay in it? (Idea: *He threw the baseball to the batter.*) Let's say the whole sentence together. *Amir made a good pitch when he threw the baseball to the batter.* I'm glad we gloated the hearsay!
- When dad **demanded** that we stop shouting … he used a cross voice. *Hear, Say!* Well, that's what *I* heard. I'll say the first part of the sentence again. When dad **demanded** that we stop shouting. How can we finish this sentence so it doesn't have hearsay in it? (Idea: *He used a forceful voice.*) Let's say the whole sentence together. *When dad demanded that we stop shouting, he used a forceful voice.* That's the honest truth!
- Bob **shouted,** using … a cloud moist. *Hear, Say!* Well, that's what *I* heard. I'll say the first part of the sentence again. Bob **shouted,** using. How can we finish this sentence do it doesn't have hearsay in it? (Idea: *A loud voice.*) Let's say the whole sentence together. *Bob shouted, using a loud voice.* That's the honest truth!
- Brian used a quiet voice when … he **muttered** to himself. *That's the honest truth!*

(Count the points and declare a winner.) You did a great job of playing *Hear, Say!*

DAY 5

Preparation: Happy Face Game Test Sheet, BLM B.

Retell Story to a Partner
(Assign each child a partner, and ask the partners to take turns telling part of the story each time you turn to a new set of pages. Encourage children to use target words when appropriate.)

Tell what happens at the **beginning** of the story. (Show the picture on page 1.)

Tell what happens in the **middle** of the story. (Show the pictures on pages 2–21.)

Tell what happens at the **end** of the story. (Show the pictures on pages 22–28.)

Assess Vocabulary

 (Give each child a copy of the Happy Face Game Test Sheet, BLM B.)

Today you're going to play the Happy Face Game. When you play the Happy Face game it shows me how well you know the hard words you are learning. (Use the same procedure for giving directions that has been used in previous lessons.)

Listen carefully to each item that I say. Don't let me trick you!

Item 1: A **rude** person has bad manners. (*True.*)

Item 2: A boat will **pitch** when the waves are large. (*True.*)

Item 3: When you **demand** something, you use a quiet and gentle voice. (*False.*)

Item 4: When a train **arrives,** it comes to a place. (*True.*)

Item 5: When Hester made a good **pitch,** she threw the ball well. (*True.*)

Item 6: Dogs have **sensitive** noses. This means that they can smell very well. (*True.*)

Item 7: The outer parts of a flower are called **petals.** (*True.*)

Item 8: **Ignoring** someone means paying them no attention. (*True.*)

Item 9: An **accident** is something you plan for. (*False.*)

Item 10: If a mouse **squeaked,** it made a very soft, low noise. (*False.*)

You did a great job of playing the Happy Face Game!

(Score children's work. A child must score 9 out of 10 to be at the mastery level. If a child does not achieve mastery, insert the missed words as additional items in the games in next week's lessons. Retest those children individually for the missed items before they take the next mastery test.)

Extensions

Read a Story as a Reward

 (Display copies of the books you have read since the beginning of the program or other books of poetry. Allow children to choose which book they would like you to read to them as a reward for their hard work.)

(Read the story aloud for enjoyment with minimal interruptions.)

Preparation: Word containers for the Super Words Center. You will need to include the 10 onion cards, BLM C.

Introduce the Super Words Center

(Add the new Picture Vocabulary Cards to words from the previous weeks. Show children one of the word containers. If children need more guidance in how to work in the Super Word Center, role-play with two to three children as a demonstration. Follow the same procedure that is found in Lesson 18.)

My Shadow

author: Robert Louis Stevenson • illustrator: Glenna Lang

Preparation: You will need a copy of *My Shadow* for each day's lesson.

Number the pages to assist you in asking comprehension questions at appropriate points in the story.

Post a copy of the Vocabulary Tally Sheet, BLM A, with this week's Picture Vocabulary Cards attached.

Each child will need one copy of the Homework Sheet, BLM 20a.

🎯 Target Vocabulary

Tier II	Tier III
proper	concrete poem
notion	diamante
fool	
coward	
*curious	
*dawn	

*Expanded Target Vocabulary Word

DAY 1

Introduce Book

This week's book is called *My Shadow.* What's the title of this week's book? *My Shadow.*

This book is a poem that was written more than one hundred years ago by the famous poet Robert Louis Stevenson. Robert Louis Stevenson first published this poem in a book of poetry called *A Child's Garden of Verses*. Who's the author of *My Shadow*? *Robert Louis Stevenson.*

Glenna Lang made the pictures for this book. Who is the illustrator of *My Shadow*? *Glenna Lang.* Who made the illustrations for this book? *Glenna Lang.*

The cover of a book usually gives us some hints of what the book is about. Let's look at the front cover of *My Shadow.* What do you see in the illustration? (Ideas: *A child standing by a bush, the child's shadow, a rabbit, two squirrels, two trees, the sky, stars.*)

(Assign each child a partner.) Get ready to make some predictions to your partner about this book. Use the information from the cover to help you.

(Ask the following questions, allowing sufficient time for children to share their predictions with their partners.)

- Who is the character in this story? (Who do you think this story is about?)

- What do you think the child will do?
- Where do you think the story happens?
- When do you think the story happens?
- In what season do you think the story happens?
- Do you think this story is about a real child? Tell why or why not.

(Call on several children to share their predictions with the class.)

Take a Picture Walk

(Encourage children to use target words in their answers.) We're going to take a picture walk through this book. Remember that when we take a picture walk we look at the pictures and tell what we think will happen in the story.

Page 1. Look at the child and the way she is painted. Is there much detail in this illustration? How do you know? (Idea: *No. The child is just patches of color. You can only see the shape of her hair, not what her hair really looks like.*) What shape is her shadow? (Idea: *It is the same shape as she is.*)

Page 2. What is happening now? (Idea: *The girl is sitting and emptying sand out of her shoe.*) What shape is her shadow, small and short or long and skinny? *Small and short.*

Page 3. What is the girl doing now? *Brushing her teeth.* What does her shadow look like? (Ideas: *It looks just like her and is doing what she is doing.*)

Pages 4–5. What time of day is it? How do you know? (Ideas: *It's bedtime because it's dark outside and she's getting into bed; she's wearing pajamas.*)

Pages 6–7. What is happening now? (Ideas: *The girl is sleeping; the girl is dreaming.*) Why doesn't she have a shadow? (Idea: *She doesn't have a shadow because there's no light.*)

Page 8–9. This is a strange picture. The sky is still dark and the girl is walking in her pajamas behind some ducks. What do you think is happening? (Idea: *She must be dreaming about her shadow.*) What shape is her shadow now? (Idea: *It's long and skinny.*)

Pages 10–11. This is still the dream, I think. What shadows can you see in this picture? (Ideas: *The girl; the ducks; the rabbits; a tree.*) Isn't that interesting? You know that there is a tree where the girl is but you can't see it—only its shadow!

Pages 12–13. Why is the girl's shadow so tall? (Idea: *She's reaching up to touch a branch—that makes her shadow taller.*) Do the ducks have shadows? Why not? (Idea: *No. They're in the shade of the tree, so no light can fall on them to give them shadows.*)

Pages 14–15. What has happened to the girl's shadow now? (Idea: *It has gotten very small.*) But the other shadows are long and skinny. Why is her shadow small? Here's a hint: look what she is sitting under! (Idea: *She is sitting under the light and that makes her shadow small.*)

Pages 16–17. On page 16, the girl's shadow looks like her. On page 17, it looks different. Why do you think it looks different? (Ideas: *Her shadow is on a bush; the leaves make her shadow into a different shape.*) What does her shadow make her look like? (Idea: *A big gorilla.*)

Pages 18–19. She's still dreaming. Now her shadow looks like a puddle that she's stepping into.

Pages 20–21. What shadows can you see in this picture? (Ideas: *The girl; the rabbit; the trees; the house; some rocks.*)

Pages 22–23. What is happening now? (Idea: *It's morning and the girl is waking up.*)

Pages 24–25. What is happening now? (Ideas: *She's going out to play with her toy rabbit and bear.*) Look at the sky. At what time of day do you see those colors in the sky? (Ideas: *Early in the morning; at dawn.*) Is her shadow in the picture with her? *No.*

Pages 26–27. What is she doing now? (Idea: *She's sitting and looking at flowers with her rabbit and bear.*) Can you see her shadow? *No.*

Page 28. This is the end of the story. Can you find the shadow? Where is it? (Ideas: *It's inside the house; on the bed.*)

Read the Story Aloud
(Read the story to children with minimal interruptions.)

Tomorrow we will read the story again and I will ask you some questions.

Present the Target Vocabulary
Proper

In the story, the child says that her shadow is "not at all like **proper** children." **Proper.** Say the word. *Proper.*

Proper is a describing word that tells about how someone should be. What kind of word is **proper?** *A describing word.*

If you are **proper,** you are like you should be. Say the word that means "you are like you should be." *Proper.*

(Correct any incorrect responses and repeat the item at the end of the sequence.)

Let's think about some situations when someone might be described as proper. I'll tell about some situations. If the person or animal is proper in the situation, say "proper." If not, don't say anything.

- The little boy grew up, just like children should. *Proper.*
- John had two eyes, two ears, a nose, and a mouth—just like most human boys. *Proper.*
- The cow looked just like it should with four legs and a tail. *Proper.*
- The fish didn't look like any other fish I'd ever seen. It had twelve eyes and six ears!
- The shadow grew too fast—not like children usually do.
- The new baby had ten fingers and ten toes—just like she should. *Proper.*

What describing word means "someone who is just like he or she should be"? *Proper.*

I'm going to say two words. Each word has two parts or syllables. Tell me how the words I say are like the word **proper. Chopper. Hopper.** Listen again. **Chopper. Hopper.** How are those two words like the word **proper?** (Ideas: *They rhyme. They have two parts or syllables.*)

ⓒ◄ Notion

In the story, the child says that her shadow "hasn't got a **notion** of how children ought to play." **Notion.** Say the word. *Notion.*

Notion is a naming word. It means the same as idea. What kind of word is **notion?** *A naming word.*

If you have a notion, you have an idea about something. If you haven't any notion, you haven't any idea about something. Say the naming word that means "an idea about something." *Notion.*

Let's think about some times when someone might have a notion. I'll tell about a time. If someone has a notion, say "notion." If not, don't say anything.

- Tom had the idea that his sister was unhappy. *Notion.*
- I had the idea that my children needed to act politely. *Notion.*
- Marika didn't have any idea what the time was.
- Jordyn had an idea that swimming would be fun. *Notion.*
- Sally never even thought about her little sister.
- The storeowner had the idea that he should put flowers in the window. *Notion.*

What naming word means "an idea about something"? *Notion.*

I'll say some words with two parts or syllables. Be ready to tell me how they are the same as the word **notion. Ocean. Lotion.** Listen again. **Ocean. Lotion.** How are those words the same as **notion?** (Ideas: *They each have two parts or syllables; they sound the same; they rhyme.*)

ⓒ◄ Fool

In the story, the child says that her shadow "can only make a **fool** of [her] in every sort of way."

Fool. Say the word. *Fool.*

Fool is a naming word. It names a person who is silly or foolish. What kind of word is **fool?** *A naming word.*

If someone makes a fool of you, they make you look silly. Say the word that means you "look silly." *Fool.*

Let's think about some times when you might look silly. I'll tell about a time. If the thing that happens makes a person or animal look silly, say "fool." If not, don't say anything.

- Mary put a silly cap on my head. *Fool.*
- Sam told me to shout, "I'm a do-do bird!" at the top of my lungs. I did, but I felt silly about it afterwards. *Fool.*
- I wore my best suit to the meeting and I felt good about it.
- Joseph pulled my chair away as I was going to sit down and I sat on the floor, looking silly. *Fool.*
- Kali smiled at her new teacher and said, "Hello!"
- When Alvin bent over, the seat of his pants tore and he felt silly and embarrassed. *Fool.*

What naming word means you "look silly"? *Fool.*

I'm going to say two words. Each word has one part or syllable. Tell me how the words I say are like the word **fool. Tool. School.** Listen again. **Tool. School.** How are those two words like the word **fool?** (Ideas: *They sound like fool; they rhyme; they have one part or syllable.*)

ⓒ◄ Coward

In the story, the girl calls her shadow a **coward** because it sticks so close to her. **Coward.** Say the word. *Coward.*

Coward is a naming word. It tells about a person who is fearful or timid. What kind of word is **coward?** *A naming word.*

A coward is a person who is more fearful or timid than others. Say the word that means "more fearful or timid than others." *Coward.*

I'll tell about a time. If you think it would be a time when a person or animal would be a coward, say "coward." If not, don't say anything.

- When Rolf heard the rumbling in the tunnel, he was fearful and timid. *Coward.*
- There was thunder and lighting and we kept playing cards except for Julio, who hid under the bed. *Coward.*
- The enormous lion was fearful of a tiny little mouse! *Coward.*
- Piper was brave when the lights went out.
- The growling dog didn't scare Franklin.
- The door slammed with a "BANG!" and I was so afraid that I hid in the closet. *Coward.*

What naming word tells about "a person who is more fearful or timid than others"? *Coward.*

I'm going to say two words. Each word has two parts or syllables. Tell me how the words I say are like the word **coward. Flowered. Showered.** Listen again. **Flowered. Showered.** How are those two words like the word **coward?** (Ideas: *They sound like coward; they rhyme; they have two parts.*)

Present Vocabulary Tally Sheet
(See Lesson 1, page 3, for instructions.)

Assign Homework
(Homework Sheet, BLM 20a. See the Introduction for homework instructions.)

DAY 2

Preparation: Picture Vocabulary Cards for *proper, notion, fool, coward.* Prepare two sheets of chart paper titled "Action Words" and "Describing Words."

You will need two sheets of chart paper and two different colored felt pens for recording. The charts should be titled "Action Words" and "Describing Words." These charts will be used to create a modified "Diamante" (diamond) poem about shadows.

Note: Normally, a diamante poem has 7 lines and a more complex language structure. This modified version will be easier for young children and will still produce the desired shape.

Read and Discuss Story
(Encourage children to use target words in their answers.)

Today I will read *My Shadow* to you. (Read the poem to children twice. The first time through, do not stop so that they can enjoy the mood and feeling of the poetry. Ask the following questions at the specified points in the poem the second time through.)

Pages 1–2. What is the use of a shadow? Is there one? (Ideas: *No, it has no use; yes, it shows us where the light is coming from; yes, it helps us to know what time it is.*)

(Point to the class charts.) We're going to make lists of words. (Point to the chart titled "Action Words.") This chart is for action words. What kind of words will I list on this chart? *Action words.* Action words tell about things the shadows do. What do action words tell about? *Things the shadows do.*

(Point to the chart titled "Describing Words.") This chart is for describing words. What kind of words will I list on this chart? *Describing words.* Describing words tell about what the shadows look like. What do describing words tell about? *What the shadows look like.*

Let's look at the pictures on pages 1 and 2 and choose some words to tell about shadows. (Ideas: Actions: *Moving, sitting, standing.* Describing words: *Tall, small, round, short, dark.*)

Pages 3–5. At the sink, is the light coming from above the girl or from beside the girl? *From beside the girl.* Where is the light coming from when the girl is climbing into bed? *From behind the girl.* Look carefully at the white goose. It has an electrical cord going into it. It must be a lamp.

Let's look at the pictures on pages 3, 4, and 5 and choose some words to tell about shadows. (Ideas: Actions: *Copying, jumping.* Describing words: *Smooth, inky, dark.*)

(Continue this process throughout the story, adding words to each chart as you go. You needn't generate words for each page—just when there is something interesting and/or different to record.)

Pages 6–7. This is when the girl's dream begins.

Pages 8–11. If proper children grow rather slowly, how does a shadow grow? (Idea: *Quickly.*) Yes, because a shadow grows "not at all like proper children." Quickly is the opposite of slowly.

Pages 12–15. Can you see what she means about her shadow growing or shrinking quickly? Look at the shadow under her and then the shadows of the trees. Tell about those shadows. (Ideas: *Her shadow is small; the trees have long shadows.*) Where is the light that lights the girl coming from? *From above.* Where is the light that lights the trees coming from? *From behind.* The size of a shadow depends on where the light is coming from.

Pages 16–17. How is the shadow making a fool of the girl? (Idea: *The bush's leaves make her shadow look like a gorilla shadow.*)

Read pages 18–21. You can see that the girl's shadow starts at her feet. She tells us that it sticks to her. She means that it stays with her almost all the time as though it is afraid.

Pages 22–26. Why is there no shadow in these pictures? Listen to the words again for a hint. (Read the pages again. Idea: *There's no sun so there can't be a shadow.*)

Pages 27–28. When you look at the picture on page 28, what do you know has happened to the light? (Idea: *The sun is up because there is a shadow now.*) Is the shadow really fast asleep in bed? *No.* Why would the girl think that? (Idea: *Because when she looks into her room, the sun is behind her and it makes a shadow on the bed.*)

It's your turn to ask me some questions. What would you like to know about the poem? (Accept questions from children. If children tell about the pictures or the poem instead of ask questions, prompt them to ask a question.) Ask me a how question. Ask me a why question.

Review Vocabulary

(Display the Picture Vocabulary Cards. Point to each card as you say the word. Ask children to repeat each word after you.) These pictures show **notion, proper, fool,** and **coward.**

- What word means you are "just like you should be"? *Proper.*
- What naming word means "an idea about something"? *Notion.*
- What word means you "look silly"? *Fool.*
- What naming word means you are "more fearful or timid than others"? *Coward.*

Extend Vocabulary
 Fool

Fool is a naming word that names you when you are made to look silly. Raise your hand if you can tell us a sentence that uses the word **fool** as a naming word that means "you are made to look silly or foolish." (Call on individual children. If children do not use complete sentences, restate their examples as sentences. Have the class repeat the sentences.)

Here's a new way to use the word **fool.**

- I decided to **fool** my dad. I played a trick on him! Say the sentence.
- Uncle Dave **fooled** me by making me think I'd forgotten to put on my pants. Say the sentence.
- Judy **fooled** Johnny by telling him to come for supper when it wasn't suppertime. Say the sentence.

In these sentences, **fool** is an action word that means trick. What action word means "trick"? *Fool.*

Raise your hand if you can tell us a sentence that uses fool as an action word meaning "trick." (Call on several children. If they don't use complete sentences, restate their examples as sentences. Have the class repeat the sentences.)

Present the Expanded Target Vocabulary
Curious

In the story the girl wanted to know more about her shadow. She was **curious. Curious.** Say the word. *Curious.*

Curious is a describing word. It tells about when you want to know more about a thing. What kind of word is **curious?** *A describing word.*

Curious means that you want to know more about a thing. If you are **curious** about your shadow, you want to know more about it.

I'll tell about some people or animals. If those people or animals are curious, say "curious." If not, don't say anything.

- Nathan wanted to know more about his shadow. *Curious.*
- Johnson wanted to know more about how airplanes fly. *Curious.*
- Sandy knew enough about cats—she didn't want to know any more.
- Frederic wanted to know more about how to play the guitar. *Curious.*
- The Queen wanted to know more about the country she was visiting. *Curious.*
- I know enough about the word **curious.** I don't want to know any more!

What describing word means "wanting to know more about a thing"? *Curious.*

How was the girl in the story curious? (Idea: *She wanted to know more about her shadow.*)

I'll say a word. Listen to how many parts or syllables that word has. Tell me how it is the same as **curious.** Listen. **Furious.** How many parts? *Three.* How is **furious** like **curious?** (Ideas: *They rhyme; they sound the same; they both have three parts or syllables.*)

 Dawn

In the story, the girl went out before the sun was up to learn more about her shadow. **Dawn.** Say the word. *Dawn.*

Dawn is a naming word. It names the very first part of the day when it is just getting light outside. What kind of word is **dawn?** *A naming word.*

Dawn means the very first part of the day when it is just getting light outside. Say the word that names the "very first part of the day when it is just getting light outside." *Dawn.*

I'll name some situations where something might happen at dawn. If the situation happens at dawn, say "dawn." If not, don't say anything.

- It was very early in the morning and just starting to get light. *Dawn.*
- The girl in the story got up early, before the sun was up, and found dew on the flowers. *Dawn.*

- The sun was high overhead and it was blistering hot outside.
- Roosters always crow at dawn and my rooster was crowing very loudly. *Dawn.*
- When Morgan woke up in the tent, it was just starting to be light outside and the air was cold and clear. *Dawn.*
- The sun was setting in the west and all of the clouds were orange and yellow. It was the end of a great day.

What naming word means "the very first part of the day when it is just getting light outside"? *Dawn.*

I'll say two words. Tell me how many parts or syllables they have. Then tell me how they are the same as the word **dawn. Fawn. Lawn.** Listen again. **Fawn. Lawn.** How many parts or syllables? *One.* How are they the same as **dawn?** (Idea: *They have one part or syllable, they sound the same; they rhyme.*)

Retell Story

Today I'll show you the pictures Glenna Lang made for *My Shadow.* As I show you the pictures, I'll call on one of you to tell the class that part of the poem.

(Show the pictures on pages 1–28. Call on children to tell what's happening. Encourage children to use target words when appropriate. Model using target words as necessary.)

Play Hear, Say!

 Today you will play *Hear, Say!* I will use target words in sentences. Some of the sentences I say might have some untruths or extra information in them. If you think what I am saying is not all true, say "Hear, Say!" That means you want to suggest a way to make the sentence truthful and not just hearsay. I'll say the beginning of the sentence again. If you can make the sentence end so it is true, you'll get a point. If you can't, I get the point.

If I use the vocabulary word correctly and there are no untruths in what I say, say "That's the honest truth!" Be careful, though. If you say "That's the honest truth!" when there is hearsay in the sentence, I will get a point!

Let's practice. If you are a **proper** child, you … have three eyes. *Hear, Say!* Well, that's what *I* heard. The first part of the sentence stays the same. I'll say the first part. If you are a **proper** child, you. How can we finish the sentence so it doesn't have hearsay in it? (Idea: *You have two eyes.*) Let's say the whole sentence together now. *If you are a proper child, you have two eyes.* That's the honest truth! I'm glad we nipped the hearsay!

Let's do another one together. If you had a **notion** about a game to play, you … had no idea about what to do. *Hear, Say!* Well, that's what *I* heard. The first part of the sentence stays the same. I'll say the first part. If you had a **notion** about a game to play, you. How can we finish the sentence so it doesn't have hearsay in it? (Idea: *Had an idea about what to do.*) Let's say the whole sentence together now. *If you had a notion about a game to play, you had an idea about what to do.* That's the honest truth! I'm glad we dipped the hearsay!

[T] Now, you're ready to play the game. (Draw a T-chart on the board for keeping score. Children earn one point for each correct answer. If they make an error, correct them as you normally would and record one point for yourself. Repeat missed words at the end of the game.)

- When your friend made you look silly, you … cooked like a tool. *Hear, Say!* Well, that's what *I* heard. I'll say the first part of the sentence again. When your friend made you look silly, you. How can we finish this sentence so it doesn't have hearsay in it? (Idea: *Looked like a fool.*) Let's say the whole sentence together. *When your friend made you look silly, you looked like a fool.* That's the honest truth! I'm glad we tipped the hearsay!
- A **coward** is a person who … is more tearful than others. *Hear, Say!* Well, that's what *I* heard. I'll say the first part of the sentence again. A **coward** is a person who. How can

we finish this sentence so it doesn't have hearsay in it? (Idea: *Is more fearful than others.*) Let's say the whole sentence together. *A coward is a person who is more fearful than others.* I'm glad we zipped the hearsay!

- When Bob played a trick on us … he **fooled** us. *That's the honest truth!*
- I was **curious,** so I … didn't want to know any more about elephants. *Hear, Say!* Well, that's what *I* heard. I'll say the first part of the sentence again. I was curious so I. How can we finish this sentence so it doesn't have hearsay in it? (Idea: *Wanted to know more about elephants.*) Let's say the whole sentence together. *I was curious so I wanted to know more about elephants.* That's the honest truth! I'm glad we flipped the hearsay!
- I knew it was **dawn** because … it was getting dark and it was late at night. *Hear, Say!* Well, that's what *I* heard. I'll say the first part of the sentence again. I knew it was **dawn** because. How can we finish this sentence so it doesn't have hearsay in it? (Idea: *It was early and just starting to get light.*) Let's say the whole sentence together. *I knew it was dawn because it was early and just starting to get light.* That's the honest truth! I'm glad we tripped the hearsay.

(Count the points and declare a winner.) You did a great job of playing *Hear, Say!*

DAY 4

Preparation: Activity Sheet, BLM 20b. *Trees* poem, BLM 20c. Use the "Poetry" chart you added to in Lesson 19. Add Concrete poem/diamante/diamond to the list as follows:

Concrete poem/Diamante/Diamond: The words make a shape.

Prepare a sheet of chart paper with the diamante pattern.

Literary Analysis

When I was reading the story to you and asking questions, we made lists of action words and describing words about shadows. We are going to use those words to make a poem about shadows.

This poem is unusual, because it has no rhyming words. Instead of rhyming, we choose words that we like the <u>sound</u> of. Then we make them into a <u>shape</u>! Yes, a <u>shape</u>! I'll share a poem with you right now that has a shape but no rhyming words. **(Show children the** *Trees* **poem printed on BLM 20c. Ask them what shape it is in before you begin. Then read the poem.)**

(Draw the shape of a diamond around the poem.) What shape is this poem? *A diamond.* A diamond-shaped poem has a special name. It is called a "Diamante Poem." What is a diamond-shaped poem called? *A diamante poem.*

Today you will make a poem about shadows using the action words and describing words that we wrote on our charts. Your poem will be in the shape of a diamond.

Let's sing the verses of "The Poetry Song" before I teach you a new verse. **(The tune for this song is** *Row, Row, Row Your Boat.* **Sing the verses that have been previously introduced, as found in Day 4 of Lesson 19.)**

Here's a new verse that tells about a diamond-shaped poem. This is the very last verse of our poetry song. A diamante poem doesn't have rhyming words so I have changed the words of the verse. Listen carefully while I sing it for you:

Choose, choose some lovely words,
Quietly rehearse,
Take your time and polish your diamond,
Make a shapely verse!

Now sing the new verse with me:

Choose, choose some lovely words,
Quietly rehearse,
Take your time and polish your diamond,
Make a shapely verse!

Now let's sing all that we've learned together. (See the Introduction for the complete "The Poetry Song".)

That was fun. That was the last verse of "The Poetry Song." Now that you've learned so much about poetry, we'll go on to learn many other things!

Complete the Activity Sheet

 (Display the charts that were generated on Day 3. Display the pattern chart for a diamante poem as found below:

Shadows

Describing word　　Describing word

Action word　　Action word　　Action word

Describing word　　Describing word

Shadows

Have children choose words from the lists to fill in the spaces. Have them do this in sequence and monitor carefully—<u>only</u> put up the describing words while they're working on describing words. <u>Only</u> put up action words while they're working on action words. Model writing a "Shadows" poem with the children before sending them to work on their own with your assistance. A finished poem may look like this:

Shadows

Blobby　　Skinny

Jumping　　Climbing　　Falling

Small　　Huge

Shadows

You may wish to accompany this poem with life-size child "shadows." Place each child, in turn, in front of a strong light source like an overhead or slide projector. Trace each child's shadow onto a child-size sheet of dark (black or navy) paper taped to the wall behind the child. The children may adopt different poses like reaching over their heads, jumping, squatting, sitting, running, standing, and so on. Cut out the "shadows" and make a hallway or gym display with the "Shadows" poems affixed to them. A striking display!)

Today we will write a diamante poem about shadows. Touch the empty space at the very bottom of your page. The sentence says, "My Shadow Poem by." The empty space is for your name. Print your name in the empty space at the bottom of the page.

(Guide the children through the process of choosing describing and action words to complete the pattern of a diamante poem. Numbering the words on the charts prior to the children writing makes it easier for you to help them when they ask "Which word is X?" You can tell them to find the "number 3 word" and print it in the space.)

Play Hear, Say! (Cumulative Review)

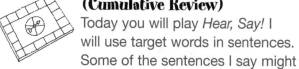 Today you will play *Hear, Say!* I will use target words in sentences. Some of the sentences I say might have some untruths or extra information in them. If you think what I am saying is not all true, say "Hear, Say!" That means you want to suggest a way to make the sentence truthful and not just hearsay. I'll say the beginning of the sentence again. If you can make the sentence end so it is true, you'll get a point. If you can't, I get the point.

If I use the vocabulary word correctly and there are no untruths in what I say, say "That's the honest truth!" Be careful, though. If you say "That's the honest truth!" when there is hearsay in the sentence, I will get a point!

Let's practice. At **dawn** … it is just starting to fight. *Hear, Say!* Well, that's what *I* heard. The first part of the sentence stays the same. I'll say the first part. At **dawn.** How can we finish the sentence so it doesn't have hearsay in it? (Idea: *It is just getting light.*) Let's say the whole sentence together now. *At dawn, it is just getting light.* That's the honest truth! I'm glad we caught the hearsay!

Let's do another one together. Jeff was **curious,** so he … wanted to know less and less about trucks. *Hear, Say!* Well, that's what *I* heard. The first part of the sentence stays the same. I'll say the first part. Jeff was **curious,** so he. How can we finish the sentence so it doesn't have hearsay in it? (Idea: *Wanted to learn more and more about trucks.*) Let's say the whole sentence now. *Jeff was curious, so he wanted to learn more and more about trucks.* That's the honest truth! I'm glad we got the hearsay!

Now you're ready to play the game. (Draw a T-chart on the board for keeping score. Children earn one point for each correct answer. If they make an error, correct them as you normally would and record one point for yourself. Repeat missed words at the end of the game.)

- Jennifer was more timid and fearful than others, so she was … flowered. *Hear, Say!* Well, that's what *I* heard. I'll say the first part of the sentence again. Jennifer was more timid and fearful than others, so she was. How can we finish the sentence so that it doesn't have hearsay in it? (Idea: *A coward.*) Let's say the whole sentence together. *Jennifer was more timid and fearful than others, so she was a coward.* That's the honest truth! I'm glad we brought the hearsay!

- If you **fool** me, it means that … you play a trick on me. *That's the honest truth!*

- A **notion** is the same as … a direction. *Hear, Say!* Well, that's what *I* heard. I'll say the first part of the sentence again. A **notion** is the same as. How can we finish this sentence so it doesn't have hearsay in it? (Idea: *An idea.*) Let's say the whole sentence together. *A notion is the same as an idea.* I'm glad we taught the hearsay!

- If you are made to look silly … you feel like a pool. *Hear, Say!* Well, that's what *I* heard. I'll say the first part of the sentence again. If you are made to look silly. How can we finish this sentence so it doesn't have hearsay in it? (Idea: *You feel like a fool.*) Let's say the whole sentence together. *If you are made to look silly, you feel like a fool.* That's the honest truth! I'm glad we bought the hearsay!

- If you live without fighting or fear … you live preciously. *Hear, Say!* Well, that's what *I* heard. I'll say the first part of the sentence again. If you live without fighting or fear. How can we finish this sentence so it doesn't have hearsay in it? (Idea: *You live peacefully.*) Let's say the whole sentence together. *If you live without fighting or fear, you live peacefully.* That's the honest truth! I'm glad we fought the hearsay!
- A **rough** board is … bumpy and uneven to touch. *That's the honest truth!*
- When you want to know more about a thing … you are furious. *Hear, Say!* Well, that's what *I* heard. I'll say the first part of the sentence again. When you want to know more about a thing. How can we finish this sentence so it doesn't have hearsay in it? (Idea: *You are curious.*) Let's say the whole sentence together. *When you want to know more about a thing you are curious.* That's the honest truth!

(Count the points and declare a winner.) You did a great job of playing *Hear, Say!*

DAY 5

Preparation: Happy Face Game Test Sheet, BLM B.

Retell Story to a Partner

(Assign each child a partner and ask the partners to take turns telling part of the poem each time you turn to a new set of pages. Encourage children to use target words when appropriate.)

Tell me what happens at the **beginning** of the poem. (Show the pictures on page 1.)

Tell me what happens in the **middle** of the poem. (Show the pictures on pages 2–26.)

Tell me what happens at the **end** of the poem. (Show the pictures on pages 27 and 28.)

Assess Vocabulary

(Give each child a copy of the Happy Face Game Test Sheet, BLM B.)

Today you're going to play the Happy Face Game. When you play the Happy Face Game it shows me how well you know the hard words

you are learning. (Use the same procedure for giving directions that has been used in previous lessons.)

Listen carefully to each item that I say. Don't let me trick you!

Item 1: A **coward** is timid and more fearful than others. (*True.*)

Item 2: A **proper** child is like he or she should be. (*True.*)

Item 3: A **fool** is a person who is made to look very smart and handsome. (*False.*)

Item 4: If you are **curious,** you want to know more about a thing. (*True.*)

Item 5: At **dawn,** it is getting dark and windy. (*False.*)

Item 6: When you **fool** someone, you play a trick on them. (*True.*)

Item 7: A **notion** and an idea are the same thing. (*True.*)

Item 8: An airplane is leaving the airport when it **arrives.** (*False.*)

Item 9: Something that is **glorious** is not wonderful. (*False.*)

Item 10: An **accident** is something bad that happens that no one expects, and someone gets hurt. (*True.*)

You did a great job of playing the Happy Face Game!

(Score children's work. A child must score 9 out of 10 to be at the mastery level. If a child does not achieve mastery, insert the missed words as additional items in the games in next week's lessons. Retest those children individually for the missed items before they take the next mastery test.)

Extensions

Read a Story as a Reward

 (Display copies of the books that you have read since the beginning of the program or other books of poetry. Allow children to choose which book they would like you to read to them as a reward for their hard work.)

(Read the story aloud for enjoyment with minimal interruptions.)

Introduce the Super Words Center

(Add the new Picture Vocabulary Cards to words from the previous weeks. Show children one of the word containers. If children need more guidance in how to work in the Super Word Center, role-play with two to three children as a demonstration. Follow the same procedure that is found in Lesson 18.)

Preparation: You will need *A Day with Firefighters* for each day's lesson.

Post a copy of the Vocabulary Tally Sheet, BLM A, with this week's Picture Vocabulary Cards attached.

Each child will need one copy of the Homework Sheet, BLM 21a.

DAY 1

Introduce Series

For the next five weeks, we will be reading books about different kinds of workers. We will learn about five different workers: firefighters, a mail carrier, paramedics, police officers, and a grocery store owner. What workers will we read about? (Ideas: *Firefighters; a mail carrier; paramedics; police officers; a grocery store owner.*)

All these books are true. When an author writes books about things that are true, those books are called nonfiction books. What kind of books are about true things? *Nonfiction books.*

Introduce Book

This week's book is called *A Day with Firefighters.* What's the title of this week's book? *A Day with Firefighters.*

This book was written by Jan Kottke [kott-key]. Who's the author of *A Day with Firefighters*? *Jan Kottke.*

The pictures for this book were taken with a camera. They are called photographs. What do you call pictures taken with a camera? *Photographs.* What kind of illustrations does *A Day with Firefighters* have? *Photographs.*

The cover of a book usually gives us some hints of what the book is about. Let's look at the front cover of *A Day with Firefighters.* What do you see in the photograph? (Ideas: *Six firefighters; a fire engine; a fire station; the firefighters have special clothes.*)

A Day With Firefighters
author: Jan Kottke

🎯 Target Vocabulary

Tier II	Tier III
firefighters	nonfiction
fire station	photograph
fire engine	
spray	
hose	
siren	
helmet	

*Expanded Target Vocabulary Word

Take a Picture Walk

(Encourage children to use target words in their answers.) We're going to take a picture walk through this book. When we take a picture walk through a nonfiction book, we look carefully at the pictures and think about what we see.

Page 5. Who do you think the men are? (Idea: *Firefighters.*) Where are they standing? (Ideas: *In front of a fire station; in front of a fire engine.*) How many firefighters are there? *Six.*

Page 7. Why do you think the man is sliding down the pole? (Ideas: *To get down faster; because the fire alarm rang; because there's a fire somewhere; because he's in a hurry.*) What do you think the firefighter is pointing to on the computer? (Ideas: *A map; where the fire is; how to get to where the fire is.*) What do you think the firefighter standing near the fire engine is going to do? (Idea: *Drive the fire engine.*)

Page 9. Let's think about what clothes the firefighters wear. Tell me the clothes you see. (Ideas: *Helmets; jackets; pants; boots.*)

Page 11. Where is the firefighter going? (Idea: *Into the fire engine.*) Why do you think the firefighter is getting into the fire engine? (Ideas: *The firefighters are going to a fire; the firefighters are having a practice.*) Why do you think there are yellow stripes on the firefighter's jacket? (Idea: *So he can be seen when it's smoky; so he can be seen at night; for safety.*)

Page 13. Why do you think the photograph looks like that? (Idea: *The fire engine is going really fast.*) Who do you think is riding in the fire engine? *The firefighters.* How fast do you think the fire engine is going? (Ideas: *Really fast; very fast.*)

Page 15. How would you feel if you were the firefighter at the top of the ladder? What is the firefighter spraying on the fire? *Water.* What do you think is making all the smoke? (Idea: *The fire.*)

Page 17. Who is in the picture? *A firefighter.* Where is the firefighter? (Ideas: *At the top of the ladder; in the middle of the smoke; at the fire.*) Why is the firefighter spraying water on the fire? (Idea: *To put out the fire.*)

Page 19. Where do you think the firefighters are now? (Idea: *Back at the fire station.*) How do you think the firefighters are feeling? (Ideas: *Happy; relieved; tired; smoky; sweaty.*) Tell why they are feeling this way. (Idea: *They have just returned from fighting a fire.*)

Page 21. Who do you think the women are? Why do you think the woman is shaking the firefighter's hand? (Ideas: *They are proud of the fireman; he put out the fire in their house; they want to say thank you.*)

Read the Book Aloud
(Read the story to children with minimal interruptions.)

Tomorrow we will read the book again, and I will ask you some questions.

Present the Target Vocabulary
 Firefighters

This book tells about firefighters. That means it tells about people who fight fires. **Firefighters.** Say the word. *Firefighters.*

Firefighters is a naming word. It names a group of people. What kind of word is **firefighters?** *A naming word.*

Firefighters are people who fight fires. Say the word that means "people who fight fires." *Firefighters.*

(Correct any incorrect responses, and repeat the item at the end of the sequence.)

Let's think some things that firefighters might do. I'll tell about some things. If these things are what firefighters do when they are at work, say "firefighters." If not, don't say anything."

- The people poured water on the burning house. *Firefighters.*
- The people rode in the fire engine to the fire. *Firefighters.*
- The people sang songs on the stage.
- The people sold bread in a bakery.
- The people climbed a ladder to get the hose closer to the fire. *Firefighters.*
- The people picked tomatoes in the field.

What naming word means "people who fight fires"? *Firefighters.*

 Fire station

In the book, when firefighters were not fighting fires, they worked at the fire station. **Fire station.** Say the words. *Fire station.*

Fire station is a group of naming words. They name a place. What kind of group of words is **fire station?** *Naming words.*

The fire station is the place where firefighters work when they're not fighting fires. Say the group of words that mean "the place where firefighters work when they're not fighting fires." *Fire station.*

Let's think about some places that might be fire stations. If the place I name is where firefighters work when they're not fighting fires, say "fire station." If not, don't say anything.

- This is where firefighters dry out their hoses. *Fire station.*
- This is where firefighters answer the telephone. *Fire station.*
- This is where people sell groceries.
- This is where firefighters put on their heavy boots. *Fire station.*
- This is where children go to swim.
- This is where firefighters slide down poles. *Fire station.*

What group of naming words means "the place where firefighters work when they're not fighting fires"? *Fire station.*

Fire engine

In the book, firefighters rode in a large truck to a fire. This truck carried the firefighters and their tools. **Fire engine.** Say the words. *Fire engine.*

Fire engine is a group of naming words. They name a thing. What kind of group of words is **fire engine?** *Naming words.*

A fire engine is a truck that carries firefighters and their tools to a fire. Say the group of words that means "a truck that carries firefighters and their tools to a fire." *Fire engine.*

Let's think about some people and things you might see on a fire engine. If the person or thing I name is usually carried on a fire engine, say "fire engine." If not, don't say anything.

- People who fight fires. *Fire engine.*
- Hoses. *Fire engine.*
- Ladders. *Fire engine.*
- Your teacher.
- Books.
- Doctor.

What group of naming words means "a truck that carries firefighters and their tools to a fire"? *Fire engine.*

Spray

In the book, the firefighter uses the hose to spray water on the fire. That means the firefighter put water on the fire. **Spray.** Say the word. *Spray.*

Spray is an action word. It tells what someone does. What kind of word is **spray?** *An action word.*

When you spray something, you put water on it. Say the word that means "put water on something." *Spray.*

Let's think about some times when you might spray someone or something. I'll tell about a time. If you think you would spray it, say "spray." If not, don't say anything.

- You put water on the dishes to rinse off the food. *Spray.*
- You put water on the thirsty plants. *Spray.*
- You covered the paper with drawings.
- You stood under the shower to get the soap out of your hair. *Spray.*

- You rode your bike down the street.
- You had spaghetti for supper.

What action word means "put water on something"? *Spray.*

Present Vocabulary Tally Sheet
(See Lesson 1, page 3, for instructions.)

Assign Homework
(Homework Sheet, BLM 21a. See the Introduction for homework instructions.)

DAY 2

Preparation: Picture Vocabulary Cards for *firefighters, fire station, fire engine,* and *spray.*

Read and Discuss Story

(Read story to children. Ask the following questions at the specified points. Encourage them to use target words in their answers.)

Page 4. Where do the firefighters work? (Idea: *At the fire station.*) Where else do you think firefighters would work? (Ideas: *At a fire in a building; at a forest fire; at a school when there's a fire drill.*)

Page 6. How do the firefighters know when there's a fire somewhere? (Idea: *A bell rings in the fire station.*) What do you think the firefighters were doing before the bell rang? (Ideas: *Resting; studying; practicing fire fighting; cleaning the station; polishing the fire engines.*)

Page 8. How do you think each firefighter knows where to find his clothes? (Idea: *There are numbers above the cubbies.*) Why do you think the coats have yellow stripes? (Idea: *So the firefighters are easier to see when it's dark or smoky.*) What else do you think would be special about a firefighter's coat? (Ideas: *They'd probably be waterproof; the heat wouldn't go through them; they'd be made of really strong material.*) Why do you think a helmet is an important part of a firefighter's outfit? (Ideas: *To protect the firefighter from parts of buildings that are falling; to hold a light; so other firefighters can tell who the firefighter is.*)

Page 10. Do you think this firefighter is the driver? *No.* Why not? (Idea: *He is getting in the passenger door.*) What might this firefighter do on the way to the fire? (Ideas: *Give directions; watch for cars, people.*) Where do you think the rest of the firefighters will ride? (Ideas: *One in the driver's seat; others in a back seat; on the back of the fire engine.*)

Page 12. What are two tools firefighters use to warn people get out of the way? (Ideas: *Flashing red lights; a siren.*)

Pages 14–16. Why do you think the firefighter climbed the ladder to spray the water on the fire? (Ideas: *The building was too tall to spray the water on the fire from the ground; to get the water in the right place.*) Why else might a firefighter climb a ladder at a fire? (Idea: *To rescue people trapped in the fire.*)

Page 18. How are the firefighters feeling? (Idea: *Tired; exhausted; happy.*) Why would they be exhausted? (Ideas: *It's hard work fighting a fire; they've climbed the ladders; they've carried hoses; they've put out the fire.*) Why would they be happy? (Ideas: *The fire is out; everyone is safe; no one was hurt.*)

Page 20. Why do the firefighters like what they do? (Idea: *They like helping people.*)

Let's think about *A Day with Firefighters*. What is this book about? (Idea: *Firefighters.*) The main idea of a nonfiction book is the most important thing we learn when we read it. What do we call the most important thing we learn when we read a nonfiction book? *The main idea.*

What do you think is the most important thing we learned when we read *A Day with Firefighters*? (Idea: *Firefighters work hard to help people.*)

(Note: At first, children will probably give details relating to the story—firefighters climb ladders; they spray water on fires; they put out fires. If children give these responses, ask leading questions such as:) Do you think that's easy to do? Why do you think firefighters do these things? So what is the main idea of the book *A Day with Firefighters*?

Review Vocabulary

(Display the Picture Vocabulary Cards. Point to each card as you say the word. Ask children to repeat each word after you.) These pictures show **firefighters, fire station, fire engine,** and **spray.**

- What word means "put water on something"? *Spray.*
- What group of words means "a truck that carries firefighters and their tools to a fire"? *Fire engine.*
- What word means "people who fight fires"? *Firefighters.*
- What group of words means "a place where firefighters work when they're not fighting fires"? *Fire station.*

Extend Vocabulary

◎⟶ Spray

In *A Day with Firefighters*, we learned that **spray** means "put water on something." Say the word that means "put water on something." *Spray.*

Raise your hand if you can tell us a sentence that uses **spray** as an action word meaning "put water on something." (Call on several children. If they don't use complete sentences, restate their examples as sentences. Have the class repeat the sentences.)

Here's a new way to use the word **spray.**

- The **spray** from the waterfall got us all wet. Say the sentence.
- She put a **spray** of oil in the pan. Say the sentence.
- Her grandma always uses hair **spray.** Say the sentence.

In these sentences, spray is a naming word that means a liquid flying or falling in little drops.

What word means "a liquid flying or falling in little drops"? *Spray.*

Raise your hand if you can tell us a sentence that uses **spray** as a naming word meaning "a liquid flying or falling in little drops." (Call on several children. If they don't use complete sentences, restate their examples as sentences. Have the class repeat the sentences.)

Present Target Vocabulary

 Hose

In the book, the firefighter used a hose to spray water on the fire. **Hose.** Say the word. *Hose.*

Hose is a naming word. It names a thing. What kind of word is **hose?** *A naming word.*

A hose is a long tube of rubber or plastic that a liquid such as water can go through. What word means "a long tube of rubber or plastic that a liquid such as water can go through"? *Hose.*

I'll tell about some times when someone might use a hose. If the person would use a hose, say "hose." If not, don't say anything.

- Estella watered her vegetable garden. *Hose.*
- Bob cooked dinner for his family.
- The mechanic told me I needed a new tube for the radiator in my car. *Hose.*
- The fireman wanted to spray water on the fire. *Hose.*
- Amy watered the baskets of flowers. *Hose.*
- Melanie played with her friends.

What naming word means "a long tube of rubber or plastic that a liquid such as water can go through"? *Hose.*

 Siren

In the book, the siren warns cars to move out of the way. **Siren.** Say the word. *Siren.*

Siren is a naming word. It names a thing. What kind of word is **siren?** *A naming word.*

A siren is a part of a police car, fire engine, or ambulance that makes a loud, shrill sound. Say the word that means "a part of a police car, fire engine, or ambulance that makes a loud, shrill sound." *Siren.*

Let's think about some times when someone might hear a siren. I'll tell about a time. If you think that person would hear a siren, say "siren." If not, don't say anything.

- The fire engine is rushing to a fire. *Siren.*
- The painters are painting the new house.
- The police car needs to get to the accident quickly and safely. *Siren.*
- The baker has just taken the hot muffins out of the oven.

- The ambulance wants the cars to move over. *Siren.*
- The doctor listened to Emil's heartbeat.

What naming word means "a part of a police car, fire engine, or ambulance that makes a loud, shrill sound"? *Siren.*

Helmet

In the book, the firefighter put on his helmet. That means he put on a hard hat to protect his head. **Helmet.** Say the word. *Helmet.*

Helmet is a naming word. It names a thing. What kind of word is **helmet?** *A naming word.*

A helmet is a hard hat that protects your head when you are doing sports or when you are doing something dangerous. Say the word that means "a hard hat that protects your head when you are doing sports or when you are doing something dangerous." *Helmet.*

Let's think about some times when someone might wear a helmet. I'll tell about a time. If you think that person should be wearing a helmet, say "helmet." If not, don't say anything.

- You are riding your bicycle. *Helmet.*
- A carpenter is working on a very tall apartment building. *Helmet.*
- Your mother is cooking dinner.
- The fireman is climbing up the ladder at a fire. *Helmet.*
- Your teacher is talking to the class.
- You are up to bat on your baseball team. *Helmet.*

What naming word means "a hard hat that protects your head when you are doing sports or when you are doing something dangerous"? *Helmet.*

Preparation: Prepare a sheet of chart paper with a web and *Firefighters* in the center circle. Record children's responses by recording the underlined words (and any other relevant information identified during the discussion) on the web. Draw lines to indicate connections between the various parts of the web. A sample web is provided in the Appendix.

Make Connections (Build a Web)

Today I'll show you the photographs taken for *A Day with Firefighters*. As I show you the pictures, I'll call on several of you to tell more about firefighters.

Tell me what you know about where firefighters work when they are not fighting fires. What do you call the place where firefighters work when they're not fighting fires? *A fire station.* (Add a circle to the web for fire station.)

Pages 5–8. What things might be at a fire station? (Ideas: *Firefighters; fire engine; firefighters' clothes.*) (Add circles to the web for each answer.)

(Point to the fire station circle.) What else would you see at the fire station? (Ideas: A *computer; a bell; a pole; a notice board; boots; a clothes rack.* Encourage children to include target words when appropriate. Model use as necessary.)

(Repeat this process for *fire engine* and *clothes,* showing the appropriate photographs in the book.)

Pages 7–11. Tell me more about the work firefighters do. (Add a *work* circle to the web.) What things do firefighters do when they're at work at the fire station? (Ideas: *Slide down the pole; put on their helmets; put on their boots; put on their coats; get in the fire engine.*)

Pages 13–17. What things do firefighters do when they're at a fire? (Ideas: *Climb the ladder; spray the water; hold the hose; put out the fire.*)

Play the Choosing Game

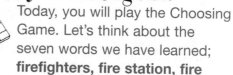

Today, you will play the Choosing Game. Let's think about the seven words we have learned; **firefighters, fire station, fire engine, spray, hose, siren,** and **helmet.**

(Display Picture Vocabulary Cards.) I will say a sentence that has two target words in it. You will have to choose the correct word for the sentence. Let's practice. (Display the word cards for the two words in each sentence as you say the sentence.)

- People who fight fires are called **firefighters** or **fire engines**? *Firefighters.*
- When firefighters put out a fire they spray water with a **siren** or a **hose**? *A hose.*
- A fire engine has a **helmet** or a **hose**? *A hose.*

If you tell me the correct answer, you will win one point. If you can't tell me the correct answer, I get the point.

Now you're ready to play the game. (Draw a T-chart on the board for keeping score. Children earn one point for each correct answer. If they make an error, correct them as you normally would, and record one point for yourself. Repeat missed words at the end of the game. Display the Picture Vocabulary Cards for the two words in each sentence as you say the sentence.)

- If a firefighter got ready to go to a fire, would he ride on a **fire engine** or a **hose**? *A fire engine.*
- Would a **hose** or a **siren** warn people to get out of the way? *A siren.*
- Which is a place: a **fire station** or a **fire engine**? *A fire station.*
- If firefighters went into a burning building, would they wear a **hose** or a **helmet**? *A helmet.*
- If firefighters went into a burning building, would they carry a **hose** or a **helmet**? *A hose.*

(Count the points and declare a winner.) You did a great job of playing the Choosing Game.

Preparation: Photocopy and assemble *Firefighters* Booklet.

Introduce Firefighters Booklet

(Give each child a copy of the *Firefighters* Booklet.) My turn to read the title of the booklet. Touch under each word as I read it. Firefighters. What is the title? *Firefighters.*

(Hold up the booklet.) Open the booklet to page 1. (Point to the picture.) Who is this? *A firefighter.* Touch the words under the picture in your booklet. My turn to read the words. You touch each word as I read it. This is a firefighter. Let's read the words together. *This is a firefighter.* Your turn. Read the words by yourselves. *This is a firefighter.*

(Repeat the procedure for the remaining pages in the booklet.)

(**Note:** On pages 4 and 5 children should identify the words printed by each item.)

(Assign each child a partner. Allow sufficient time for each child to read the booklet to his or her partner. Circulate as children are reading, offering praise and assistance.)

(Children should color the illustrations in their *Firefighter* booklets.)

Play the Choosing Game (Cumulative Review)

Let's play the Choosing Game. I will say a sentence that has two target words in it. You will have to choose the correct word for that sentence. (Display the Picture Vocabulary Cards for *firefighters, fire station, fire engine, spray, hose, siren,* and *helmet.* Display the two words in each sentence as you say the sentence.)

Now you're ready to play the Choosing Game. (Draw a T-chart on the board for keeping score. Children earn one point for each correct answer. If they make an error, correct them as you normally would, and record one point for yourself. Repeat missed words at the end of the game.)

- If a person fought fires would she be a **firefighter** or a **fire station**? *A firefighter.*

- If you went to the place where firefighters work when they're not fighting fires would you be at a **fire engine** or a **fire station**? *A fire station.*
- If you stood near a waterfall would you feel the **siren** or the **spray**? *The spray.*
- Would a firefighter ride on a **fire engine** or a **siren**? *A fire engine.*
- Would a firefighter wear a **hose** or a **helmet**? *A helmet.*
- Which would make a loud, shrill sound: a **helmet** or a **siren**? *A siren.*
- What would protect your head: a **hose** or a **helmet**? *A helmet.*
- If you used a squirt bottle to put water on your plants, would you **spray** them or **hose** them? *Spray them.*

Now you will have to listen very carefully, because I'm not going to show you the word cards. (This part of the game includes review words collected from previous lessons.)

- Is a firefighter's job **dangerous** or **delicious**? *Dangerous.*
- After fighting a fire would a firefighter be **migrated** or **exhausted**? *Exhausted.*
- Would smoke from a fire have an **odor** or a **calm**? *An odor.*
- Would firefighters go to a fire **sprouted** or **immediately**? *Immediately.*
- Would a helmet **protect** or **taunt** a firefighter? *Protect.*
- Would it be **awkward** or **polite** to hold a firefighter's hose? *Awkward.*
- Would a person trapped in a burning building be **dormant** or **desperate**? *Desperate.*
- Would you think the spray from a beautiful waterfall was **awesome** or **disagreeable**? *Awesome.*

(Tally the points and declare a winner.) You did a great job of playing the Choosing Game.

Preparation: Prepare a sheet of chart paper titled *Reading Goals.*

Happy Face Game Test Sheet, BLM B.

Read the Firefighters Booklet

(Assign each child a partner.) Today you'll read your booklet about firefighters to your partner. (Allow sufficient time for each child to read the booklet to his or her partner. Circulate as children read, offering praise and assistance.)

(Have children look at the back of their *Firefighters* booklet.) This part of the book is for people who can help you find other books to read. It tells those people about other books that are like *A Day with Firefighters*. It also tells them about a place where you can find other books. Where are some places that you could go to find other books about firefighters or other workers in our community? (Ideas: *To the school library; to the public library; to a bookstore.*)

(You may wish to read aloud and discuss the information on the back cover.)

There's one more important thing on the back cover of your book. Touch the box that is at the bottom of the page. The words above the box say "My reading goal." What do the words say? *My reading goal.*

(Display the chart titled *Reading Goals.*) A goal is something that you want to succeed at doing. What is a goal? *Something that you want to succeed at doing.* A reading goal is something that you want to succeed at doing with your reading. I might decide that my goal is to read the book aloud to someone with just a little bit of help. (Record goal on the chart.) I might decide that my goal is to read the book with only a few mistakes. (Record goal on the chart.)

What are some other reading goals that someone might have when they read their book? (Accept reasonable responses. Help children put their ideas into goal statements. Add to the list of goal statements on the chart. Ask children to choose a goal and to copy it into the box. Children may also make up an original goal that is not on the list. If children are unable to copy the goals or to write a goal of their own, you or a helper may wish to scribe their goal statements for them before the booklets are sent home.)

Assess Vocabulary

 (Give each child a copy of the Happy Face Game Test Sheet, BLM B.)

Today, you're going to play the Happy Face Game. When you play the Happy Face Game, it shows me how well you know the hard words you are learning.

If I say something that is true, color in the happy face. What will you do if I say something that is true? *Color in the happy face.*

If I say something that is false, color in the sad face. What will you do if I say something that is false? *Color in the sad face.*

Listen carefully to each item that I say. Don't let me trick you!

Item 1: If you are a **firefighter,** you put out fires. (*True.*)

Item 2: A **siren** sprays water. (*False.*)

Item 3: You wear a **helmet** on your feet. (*False.*)

Item 4: A **hose** carries water. (*True.*)

Item 5: Firefighters are brave because they do **dangerous** jobs. (*True.*)

Item 6: A **fire engine** has a siren and carries hoses to a fire. (*True.*)

Item 7: You would find a **cave** in a **cottage.** (*False.*)

Item 8: A **den** is a comfortable room in a house. (*True.*)

Item 9: Another word for your arms and legs is **limbs.** (*True.*)

Item 10: It would be unusual to see a fire engine in a **fire station.** (*False.*)

You did a great job of playing the Happy Face game!

(Score children's work. A child must score 9 out of 10 to be at the mastery level. If a child does not achieve mastery, insert the missed words as additional items in the games in next week's lessons. Retest those children individually for the missed items before they take the next mastery test.)

Extensions

Read a Book as a Reward

 (Read *A Day with Firefighters* or another book about firefighters to children as a reward for their hard work.)

Preparation: Word containers for the Super Words Center. You may wish to remove some of the words from earlier lessons the children have mastered.

Introduce the Super Words Center

(Prepare the word containers for the Super Words Center. You may wish to remove some of the words from earlier lessons the children have mastered.)

(Add the new Picture Vocabulary Cards to words from the previous weeks. Show children one of the word containers. As you introduce each part of the game, role-play with two to three children as a demonstration.)

You will play a game called *What's My Word?* in the Super Words Center.

Let's think about how we work with our words in the Super Words Center.

You will work with a partner in the Super Words Center. Whom will you work with? *A partner.*

First you will draw a word out of the container. What do you do first? (Idea: *Draw a word out of the container.*) Don't show your partner the word card. (Demonstrate.)

Next you will tell your partner three clues that tell about the word card. What do you do next? (Idea: *I tell my partner three clues that tell about the word card.* Demonstrate.)

After each clue, your partner can make a guess. If your partner is correct, say "Yes." If your partner is not correct, say "No" and give another clue. (Demonstrate.)

Let your partner make three guesses. If your partner guesses correctly on any of the guesses, your partner gets a point. If your partner does not guess correctly, tell him or her your word and show him or her the word card. Give yourself a point. Then give your partner a turn. (Demonstrate.)

What do you do next? *Give my partner a turn.*

(This game need not be played for points.)

A Day with a Mail Carrier

author: Jan Kottke

Preparation: You will need a copy of *A Day with a Mail Carrier* for each day's lesson.

Post a copy of the Vocabulary Tally Sheet, BLM A, with this week's Picture Vocabulary Cards attached.

Each child will need one copy of the Homework Sheet, BLM 22a.

🎯 Target Vocabulary

Tier II	Tier III
doorbell	nonfiction
load	photograph
mailbox	
mail carrier	
mail cart	
post office	

*Expanded Target Vocabulary Word

DAY 1

Introduce Book

Remember that we are reading books about different kinds of workers. All these books are true. When an author writes books about things that are true, those books are called nonfiction books. What kind of books are about true things? *Nonfiction books.* What workers did we read about last week? *Firefighters.*

This week's book is called *A Day with a Mail Carrier.* What's the title of this week's book? *A Day with a Mail Carrier.*

This book was written by Jan Kottke [kott-key]. Who's the author of *A Day with a Mail Carrier*? *Jan Kottke.*

The pictures for this book were taken with a camera. They are called photographs. What do you call pictures taken with a camera? *Photographs.* What kind of illustrations does *A Day with a Mail Carrier* have? *Photographs.*

The cover of a book usually gives us some hints of what the book is about. Let's look at the front cover of *A Day with a Mail Carrier.* What do you see in the photograph? (Ideas: *A mail carrier; letters; a mail cart; a mail slot on the store; the mail carrier is wearing a uniform.*)

Take a Picture Walk

(Encourage children to use target words in their answers.) We're going to take a picture walk through this book. When we take a picture walk through a nonfiction book about workers, we look carefully at the pictures and think about what we see.

Page 5. Who do you think the man is? (Idea: *A mail carrier.*) Where is he standing? (Idea: *In the doorway of the mail truck.*) How many mail carriers do you see? *One.*

Page 7. What is the man holding? (Idea: *Letters that have been mailed.*) What do you think the mail carrier is doing with the letters? (Ideas: *Putting them into different slots; sorting the mail.*) What do you think the mail carrier is going to do with the pile of letters in his hand? (Ideas: *Put them in the slots; sort them.*)

Page 9. What is the mail carrier loading up into the truck? (Ideas: *Letters; packages.*) Do you think the letters the mail carrier had in the last picture are now in the truck? (Ideas: *Yes, because there is a lot of mail in the truck; no, the letters might be going somewhere else.*)

Page 11. What is the mail carrier doing? (Idea: *He is loading the mail into a mail cart.*) What do you think the mail carrier is getting ready to do? (Idea: *He is going to deliver the mail.*) Do you think the mail carrier is going to load up all the mail in the truck into his mail cart? Tell why or why not. (Idea: *No, there is too much mail in the truck to fit inside the mail cart.*)

Page 13. What do you think the mail carrier is doing? (Idea: *He is delivering mail to a house; he is putting mail into a mail box.*) What color is the mail box? *White.*

Page 15. What do you see in the picture? (Idea: *A mailbox.*) What numbers are on the mailbox? *4,4,3.* What does the red part of the mailbox look like? (Idea: *A flag.*)

Page 17. Who is in the picture? *A mail carrier.* Where is the mail carrier? (Ideas: *At a house; at the front door.*) What is the mail carrier doing? (Idea: *He is ringing the doorbell.*)

Page 19. Who is the mail carrier talking to? (Ideas: *A little girl and her mom; a little girl and a lady.*) What is the mail carrier giving to the little girl? (Ideas: *A letter; the mail.*)

Page 21. How do you think the mail carrier is feeling? (Ideas: *He is feeling happy; he likes his job; he is having a good day.*) How do you know? (Idea: *He has a big smile on his face.*)

Read the Book Aloud
(Read the story to children with minimal interruptions.)

Tomorrow we will read the book again, and I will ask you some questions.

Present the Target Vocabulary
 Doorbell

In this book, the mail carrier pushes the doorbell at somebody's house. A doorbell is a button you push to let someone know you are at the door. When you push the button, a bell rings inside the house to let the people inside know that you are there. **Doorbell.** Say the word. *Doorbell.*

Doorbell is a naming word. It names a thing. What kind of word is **doorbell?** *A naming word.*

A doorbell is a button you push to let someone know you are at the door. Say the word that means "a button you push to let someone know you are at the door." *Doorbell.*

(Correct any incorrect responses, and repeat the item at the end of the sequence.)

Let's think about some times you might use a doorbell. If you would use a doorbell, say "doorbell." If not, don't say anything.

- You have arrived at your friend's home and want him to know you are there. *Doorbell.*
- Your mom sent you to your next-door neighbor's house with some apples from your tree. *Doorbell.*
- You are at your home.
- You are delivering a package to the house across the street. *Doorbell.*
- You are turning on the lawn sprinkler.

- You are knocking on the door of the apartment across the hall.

What naming word means "a button you push to let someone know you are at the door"? *Doorbell.*

 Load

In the book, the mail carrier has to load the mail into his truck. That means he has to put the mail into the truck. **Load.** Say the word. *Load.*

Load is an action word. It tells what someone does. What kind of word is **load?** *An action word.*

When you load things, you put them into or onto something. Say the word that means "put things into or onto something." *Load.*

Let's think about some times when you might load something. I'll tell about a time. If you think you would load something, say "load." If not, don't say anything.

- You walk to your friend's house.
- You put the food into the bag at the grocery store. *Load.*
- You eat dinner at a restaurant.
- You put the recycling box into the trunk of your car. *Load.*
- You watched the animals at the zoo.
- The front-end loader shoveled dirt into the dump truck. *Load.*

What action word means "put things into or onto something"? *Load.*

 Mailbox

In the book, cards and letters are put into the mailbox. **Mailbox.** Say the word. *Mailbox.*

Mailbox is a naming word. It names a thing. What kind of word is **mailbox?** *A naming word.*

A mailbox is a place where cards and letters are left by a mail carrier. Say the word that means "a place where cards and letters are left by a mail carrier." *Mailbox.*

Let's think about some places where you would see a mailbox. I'll name a place. If it is a place where there would be a mailbox, say "mailbox." If not, don't say anything.

- In front of someone's house. *Mailbox.*
- In the middle of the lake.

- At your uncle's house. *Mailbox.*
- At the park.
- On the moon.
- At your grandparents' apartment. *Mailbox.*

What naming word means "a place where cards and letters are left by a mail carrier"? *Mailbox.*

◎← Mail *carrier*

In the book, the mail carrier is a person who sorts and delivers mail to people and their houses. **Mail carrier.** Say the words. *Mail carrier.*

Mail carrier is a group of naming words. It names a person. What kind of group of words is **mail carrier?** *Naming words.*

A mail carrier is a person who sorts and delivers mail to people and their homes. Say the group of words that means "a person who sorts and delivers mail to people and their homes." *Mail carrier.*

Let's think about some things a mail carrier would do at work. I'll say a thing someone does at work. If it is something a mail carrier would do, say "mail carrier." If not, don't say anything.

- Deliver a letter. *Mail carrier.*
- Dish out ice cream.
- Sort the mail. *Mail carrier.*
- Fight a forest fire.
- Cut down trees.
- Deliver important letters. *Mail carrier.*

What group of naming words means "a person who sorts and delivers mail to people and their homes"? *Mail carrier.*

Present Vocabulary Tally Sheet
(See Lesson 1, page 3, for instructions.)

Assign Homework
(Homework Sheet, BLM 22a. See the Introduction for homework instructions.)

DAY 2

Preparation: Picture Vocabulary Cards for *doorbell, load, mailbox, mail carrier.*

Read and Discuss Story

(Read story to children. Ask the following questions at the specified points. Encourage them to use target words in their answers.)

Page 4. What is the name of the mail carrier? *Dominic.* What is his job? *To bring mail to people.*

Page 6. Why do you think the mail carrier has to start his day sorting mail? (Ideas: *He has to get ready; he needs his mail so that he can deliver it; if no one sorts the mail it would be too difficult to deliver.*) What do you think the mail carrier was doing before he came to sort mail? (Ideas: *He got ready for work; put on his uniform; drove to work; talked with other mail carriers; read the newspaper.*)

Page 8. Why does the mail carrier have to load the mail into his truck? (Idea: *There is too much mail to carry by hand; he has to drive a long way away to deliver the mail; the mail is in a safe spot when it is in the truck.*) Where do you think all that mail is going? (Ideas: *To people's homes; to stores and businesses.*) How can you tell that there is a lot of mail in the truck? (Ideas: *There are many bins of mail; it looks like it is almost falling out of the boxes; the mail looks very heavy.*) Why do you think this is a good truck to be a mail truck? (Ideas: *It has a big door to make loading easy; there is a lot of space inside; there are good lights that are easy to see; the mail is safe inside the truck.*)

Page 10. Where do you think the mail cart came from? (Idea: *From the back of the truck.*) Why do you think the mail carrier is putting mail into the mail cart? (Ideas: *It makes it easier to deliver mail with a cart; he doesn't have to carry the mail; he can walk with the cart and doesn't have to drive the truck; he doesn't need to take all the mail with him.*) Why do you think there is another jacket hanging in the back of the mail truck? (Ideas: *In case the one he is wearing now gets dirty or ripped; it may be a warmer or cooler jacket; it might be a rain jacket.*)

Page 12. What kinds of things does the mail carrier put in the mailbox? (Idea: *Cards and letters.*) Why do you think mailboxes are good ideas? (Ideas: *Mail carriers don't have to go right to the home; they protect the mail from wind, rain and snow; there is lots of space to put the mail.*)

Page 14. Why is the flag on the mailbox a good idea? (Ideas: *It tells the mail carrier that there is a letter inside to be mailed; if the person doesn't have any mail the mail carrier still knows that he or she needs to stop; the mail carrier doesn't have to stop and look inside every box to see if there is a letter to be mailed.*) What would be important to remember about the flag? (Idea: *You need to remember to put the flag up to let the mail carrier know there is a letter to be mailed; once the mail carrier takes the letter he or she needs to put the flag down.*)

Page 16. Why would the mail carrier ring the doorbell if he has some important letters? (Ideas: *He does not want the letters to go missing or be stolen; he has to deliver the letter to a person; someone needs to sign a paper saying they got the letter.*) What do you think he would do if nobody were home? (Ideas: *He might try again the next day; leave a note.*) Why is the doorbell a good way to let the person inside know you are there? (Ideas: *It rings on the inside of the home; people know that when the doorbell rings, someone is at the door.*)

Page 18. Why would the mail carrier hand people their mail? (Ideas: *He wants to be friendly and considerate.*)

Page 20. What two things does this mail carrier like? (*He likes bringing mail to people and being a mail carrier.*)

Let's think about *A Day with a Mail Carrier.* What is this book about? (Idea: *A mail carrier.*) The main idea of a nonfiction book is the most important thing we learn when we read the book. What do we call the most important thing we learn when we read a nonfiction book? *The main idea.* What do you think is the most important thing we learned when we read *A Day with a Mail Carrier*? (Idea: *Mail carriers work hard to get people their mail.*)

(**Note:** At first, children will probably give details relating to the story—mail carriers sort mail; they drive mail trucks; they deliver mail to people's

houses. If the children give these responses, ask questions such as:) Do you think that's easy to do? Why do you think the mail carriers do these things? So what is the main idea of the book *A Day with a Mail Carrier*?

Review Vocabulary

(Display the Picture Vocabulary Cards. Point to each card as you say the word. Ask children to repeat each word after you.) These pictures show **doorbell, load, mailbox,** and **mail carrier.**

- What word means "a button you push to let someone know you are at the door"? *Doorbell.*
- What word means "put things into or onto something"? *Load.*
- What word means "a place where cards and letters are left by a mail carrier"? *Mailbox.*
- What words mean "the person who sorts and delivers the mail"? *Mail carrier.*

Extend Vocabulary

 Load

In *A Day with a Mail Carrier,* we learned that **load** means "put things into or onto something." Say the word that means "put things into or onto something." *Load.*

Raise your hand if you can tell us a sentence that uses **load** as an action word meaning "put things into or onto something." (Call on several children. If they don't use complete sentences, restate their examples as sentences. Have the class repeat the sentences.)

Here's a new way to use the word **load.**

- I needed four **loads** of dirt for my backyard. Say the sentence.
- I carried two **loads** of leaves to the compost pile. Say the sentence.
- The train carried a **load** of grain. Say the sentence.

In these sentences, load is a naming word that means what you can carry at one time. What word means "what you can carry at one time"? *Load.*

Raise your hand if you can tell us a sentence that uses **load** as naming word meaning "what you can carry at one time." (Call on several children. If they don't use complete sentences, restate their examples as sentences. Have the class repeat the sentences.

Present Target Vocabulary

 Mail *cart*

In the book, a mail cart is a wheeled wagon used to carry smaller loads of mail. **Mail cart.** Say the words. *Mail cart.*

Mail cart is a group of naming words. It names a thing. What kind of group of words is **mail cart?** *Naming words.*

A mail cart is a wheeled wagon used to carry small loads of mail. What group of words means "a wheeled wagon used to carry small loads of mail"? *Mail cart.*

I'll tell about some times when someone might use a mail cart. If the person would use a mail cart, say "mail cart." If not, don't say anything.

- To take the mailed packages to the house on Third Street. *Mail cart.*
- To take a horse to the horse show.
- To take a boat out of the water.
- To take more letters than you could carry. *Mail cart.*
- To deliver the mail on your street. *Mail cart.*
- To bring **all** of the mail to your city.

What naming word means "a wheeled wagon used to carry small loads of mail"? *Mail cart.*

 Post office

In the book, the mail carrier starts his day in the post office. That means he started his day in a building where the mail is sorted and stamps are sold. **Post office.** Say the word. *Post office.*

Post office is a group of naming words. It names a place. What kind of group of words is **post office?** *Naming words.*

A post office is a building where the mail is sorted and stamps are sold. Say the group of words that means "a building where the mail is sorted and stamps are sold." *Post office.*

Let's think about some times when someone might visit a post office. I'll tell about a time. If

you think that person would go to a post office, say "post office." If not, don't say anything.

- To go see your favorite animal.
- To mail a letter. *Post office.*
- To drop off a library book.
- To buy some stamps. *Post office.*
- To visit as a class and watch the mail get sorted. *Post office.*
- To send a package to your uncle. *Post office.*

What group of naming words means "a building where the mail is sorted and stamps are sold"? *Post office.*

DAY 3

Preparation: Prepare a sheet of chart paper with a web and *Mail Carrier* in the center circle. Record children's responses by recording the underlined words (and any other relevant information identified during the discussion) on the web. Draw lines to indicate the connections between the various parts of the web. A sample web is provided in the Appendix.

Make Connections (Build a Web)

(Encourage children to use target words in their answers. Model use as necessary.)

Today I'll show you the photographs taken for *A Day with a Mail Carrier.* As I show you the photographs, I'll call on several of you to tell more about mail carriers.

Get ready to tell me what you know about where mail carriers work when they are not delivering mail to people's homes. What do you call the place where mail carriers work when they're not delivering mail to people's homes? <u>A post office</u>. (Add a circle to the web for post office.)

(Read the text on pages 4, 6, and 8.) What things might be at a post office? (Ideas: <u>clothes</u>; <u>mail trucks</u>; <u>letters</u>; <u>packages</u>. Add circles to the web for clothes and mail truck.)

(Point to the post office.) What else would you see at the post office? (Ideas: A <u>computer</u>; a <u>scale</u>; <u>flag</u>; <u>stamps</u>; <u>money</u>; a <u>notice board</u>; <u>sorting shelves</u>; <u>mail bins</u>.)

(Repeat this process for *clothes* and *mail truck*, showing the appropriate photographs in the book.)

Pages 11–15. Tell me more about the work mail carriers do. (Add the work circle to the web.) What things do mail carriers do when they're at work away from the post office? (Ideas: *Unload the mail truck; load the mail cart; deliver mail; put mail into mailboxes; pick up letters that are to be mailed from mailboxes; put down the red flag on mailboxes; drive the mail truck.*)

Pages 17–21. If the mail carrier does not put your mail in your mailbox, how else might it be delivered? (Ideas: *Mail carrier might hand the letters to me; you might have a box at the post office.*)

Preparation: Write the following list of key words on the board or on a piece of chart paper: *mail carrier, post office, load, mail cart, letters, mailbox, people.*

You will need a blank sheet of chart paper. You will need the Picture Vocabulary Cards for *doorbell, loads, mailbox, mail carrier, mail cart* and *post office.*

Note: This lesson offers you two options: Making connections by building a web or a class summary writing activity.

Summarize the Book

Today we are going to summarize what we learned in the book *A Day with a Mail Carrier.* I will write the summary on this piece of chart paper. Later, we will read the summary together.

When we summarize, we use our own words to tell about the most important things in the book. What do we do when we summarize? *We use our own words to tell about the most important things in the book.*

Key words help us tell about the important ideas in our own words. (Point to the list of key words.) This is the list of key words that will help us write our summary. (Read each word to the children. Ask the children to repeat each word after you read it.)

(**Note:** You should write the summary in paragraph form. Explain to children that you indent the first line because the summary will be a paragraph.)

(Show the illustration on page 4.) What is the name of the mail carrier? *Dominic.* I'm going to start the summary with a sentence about Dominic. Dominic is a mail carrier. (Write the sentence on the chart. Touch under each word as you and children read the sentence aloud. Cross *mail carrier* off of the list of key words.)

(Show the illustration on page 6.) Where does Dominic work? *At the post office.* The next sentence in our summary will be about where Dominic works. Raise your hand if you can tell us a sentence about where Dominic works. (Idea: *He works at the post office.* Add the new sentence to the summary.) Let's read the second sentence of our summary together. (Touch under each word as you and children read the sentence aloud. Cross *post office* off of the list of key words.)

(Repeat this process for each of the key words. Show the illustrations on the following pages before each sentence is written: page 9 (*loads*), page 11 (*mail cart*), page 13 (*letters* and *mailbox*), page 19 (*people*).)

(Show the illustration on page 21.) The last sentence we are going to write will tell how Dominic feels about being a mail carrier. Raise your hand if you can tell us a sentence about how Dominic feels about being a mail carrier. (Idea: *Dominic likes being a mail carrier.* Add the new sentence to the summary.)

(Once the summary is finished, touch under each word as you and children read the summary aloud together.)

Sample Summary:

Dominic is a mail carrier. He works at the post office. He loads the mail into the mail truck. Later he puts the mail in his mail cart. Next he puts letters in people's mailboxes. Sometimes he hands letters to people. Dominic likes being a mail carrier.

We did a great job of writing a summary.

Play the Choosing Game

Today you will play the Choosing Game. Let's think about the six words we have learned; **doorbell, load, mailbox, mail carrier, mail cart,** and **post office.** (Display the Picture Vocabulary Cards.) I will say a sentence that has two of our words in it. You will have to choose the correct word for that sentence. Let's practice. (Display the word cards for the two words in each sentence as you say the sentence.)

- A person who delivers mail is called a **mail carrier** or **mail cart?** *Mail carrier.*
- When mail carriers deliver mail they deliver the mail to a **mailbox** or a **load?** *Mailbox.*
- A mail carrier has a **doorbell** or a **mail cart?** *A mail cart.*

If you tell me the correct answer, you will win one point. If you can't tell me the correct answer, I get the point.

[T] Now you're ready to play the game. (Draw a T-chart on the board for keeping score. Children earn one point for each correct answer. If they make an error, correct them as you normally would, and record one point for yourself. Repeat missed words at the end of the game. Display the word cards for the two words in each sentence as you say the sentence.)

- If a mail carrier carried some of the mail from her mail truck would she use a **mailbox** or a **mail cart?** *A mail cart.*
- Would a **doorbell** or a **load** let someone know there was a person at the front door? *A doorbell.*
- Which is a place: a **post office** or a **mail cart?** *A post office.*
- A mail carrier delivers mail to a **post office** or a **mailbox?** *A mailbox.*

(Count the points and declare a winner.) You did a great job of playing the Choosing Game.

Preparation: *Mail Carriers Help Us* booklet.

Introduce Mail Carrier Booklet

(Give each child a copy of *Mail Carriers Help Us.*) My turn to read the title of the booklet. You touch under each word as I read it. Mail Carriers Help Us. What is the title? *Mail Carriers Help Us.*

(Hold up the booklet.) Open the booklet to page 1. (Point to the picture.) Who is this? *A mail carrier.* Touch the words under the picture. My turn to read the words. You touch each word as I read it. Meet Ann. She is a mail carrier. Let's read the words together. *Meet Ann. She is a mail carrier.* Your turn. Read the words by yourselves. *Meet Ann. She is a mail carrier.*

(Repeat the procedure for the remaining pages in the booklet.)

(Assign each child a partner. Allow sufficient time for each child to read the book to his or her partner. Circulate as children read, offering praise and assistance.)

(Children should color the illustrations in *Mail Carriers Help Us.*)

Play the Choosing Game (Cumulative Review)

Let's play the Choosing Game. I will say a sentence that has two of our words in it. You will have to choose the correct word for that sentence. (Display the Picture Vocabulary Cards for *doorbell, load, mailbox, mail carrier, mail cart,* and *post office,* for two words in each sentence as you say the sentence.)

[T] Now you're ready to play the Choosing Game. (Draw a T-chart on the board for keeping score. Children earn one point for each correct answer. If they make an error, correct them as you normally would, and record one point for yourself. Repeat missed words at the end of the game.)

- If a person delivers mail would she be a **mail carrier** or a **post office?** *A mail carrier.*
- If you went to the place where mail carriers work when they're not delivering mail would you be at a **mailbox** or a **post office?** *A post office.*
- If you are carrying something to put into the truck do you have a **load** or a **post office?** *A load.*
- Would a mail carrier use a **mail cart** or a **load?** *A mail cart.*
- Which would sound like a bell; a **mail carrier** or a **doorbell?** *A doorbell.*
- What would a mail carrier put mail into; a **load** or a **mailbox?** *A mailbox.*
- On the back of the truck is there a **load** or a **mail cart** of wood? *A load.*

Now you will have to listen very carefully, because I'm not going to show you the word cards. **(This part of the game includes review words collected from previous lessons.)**

- Is the mail carrier **polite** or **frustrated** to ring the doorbell when he has some important letters? *Polite.*
- Is the mail carrier **clumsy** or **comfortable** to stop and say hello to people? *Comfortable.*
- Does the mail carrier not mean to **disturb** or **explore** people when he rings the doorbell? *Disturb.*
- Is the mail carrier **allowed** or **continued** to hand people their mail? *Allowed.*
- Would it be best for the mail carrier to be **frost** or **gentle** with the mail? *Gentle.*
- Would the mail truck **hibernate** or **protect** the mail while the mail carrier was away? *Protect.*
- Would a **mailbox** or a **cave** be the best place to leave mail? *Mailbox.*
- Were there a **few** letters or a **load** of letters in the back of the mail truck? *A load.*

(Tally the points and declare a winner.) You did a great job of playing the Choosing Game.

Preparation: Happy Face Game Test Sheet, BLM B.

Chart titled *Reading Goals* that was started in Week 21.

Read the Mail Carriers Help Us Booklet

(Assign each child a partner.) Today you'll read your booklet about mail carriers to your partner. **(Allow sufficient time for each child to read the booklet to his or her partner. Circulate as the children read, offering praise and assistance.)**

(Ask children to look at the back of their booklets about mail carriers.) This part of the booklet is for people who can help you find other books to read. It tells those people about other books that are like *A Day with a Mail Carrier.* It also tells them about a place where you can find other books. Where are some places that you could go to find other books about mail carriers or other workers in our community? **(Ideas:** *To the school library; to the public library; to a bookstore.***)**

(You may wish to read aloud and discuss the information on the back cover.)

There's one more important thing on the back cover of your book. Touch the box that is at the bottom of the page. The words above the box say "My reading goal." What do the words say? *My reading goal.*

A goal is something that you want to succeed at doing. What is a goal? *Something that you want to succeed at doing.* A reading goal is something that you want to succeed at doing with your reading.

Let's see if we can add some other reading goals to our class chart. What are some other reading goals that someone might have when they read their book? **(Accept reasonable responses. Help children put their ideas into goal statements. Add to the list of statements on the chart. Ask children to choose a goal and copy it into the box. Children may also make up an original goal that is not on the list. If children are unable to copy the goals or to write a goal of their own,** you or a helper may wish to scribe their goal statements for them before the booklets are sent home.)

Assess Vocabulary

 (Give each child a copy of the Happy Face Game Test Sheet, BLM B.)

Today you're going to play the Happy Face Game. When you play the Happy Face Game, it shows me how well you know the hard words you are learning.

If I say something that is true, color in the happy face. What will you do if I say something that is true? *Color in the happy face.*

If I say something that is false, color in the sad face. What will you do if I say something that is false? *Color in the sad face.*

Listen carefully to each item that I say. Don't let me trick you!

Item 1: If you are a **mail carrier** you deliver mail. (*True.*)

Item 2: A **mailbox** is used to hold water. (*False.*)

Item 3: A **post office** is where mail carriers sort the mail. (*True.*)

Item 4: A **mail cart** makes it easier for a mail carrier to deliver mail. (*True.*)

Item 5: A **doorbell** is used to sort mail. (*False.*)

Item 6: **Load** means what you can carry at one time. (*True.*)

Item 7: A **mail carrier** delivers mail to a **mailbox.** (*True.*)

Item 8: If you are **persistent** about becoming a good reader you will keep on trying. (*True.*)

Item 9: If you are a **mail carrier** you work at a **fire station.** (*False.*)

Item 10: **Chores** are jobs that you don't do very often. (*False.*)

You did a great job of playing the Happy Face Game!

(Score children's work. A child must score 9 out of 10 to be at the mastery level. If a child does

not achieve mastery, insert the missed words as additional items in the games in next week's lessons. Retest those children individually for the missed items before they take the next mastery test.)

Extensions

Read a Book as a Reward

 (Read *A Day with a Mail Carrier,* or another book about the post office and mail carriers, to children as a reward for their hard work.)

Preparation: Word containers for the Super Words Center. You may wish to remove some of the words from earlier lessons the children have mastered.

Introduce the Super Words Center

(Add the new Picture Vocabulary Cards to the words from previous weeks. Show children one of the word containers. Role-play with two to three children as you introduce each part of the game.)

You will play a game called *2 in 1* in the Super Words Center.

Let's think about how we work with our words in the Super Words Center.

You will work with a partner in the Super Words Center. Whom will you work with? *A partner.*

First you will draw two words out of the container. What do you do first? (Idea: *Draw two words out of the container.*) Show your partner both of the words. (Demonstrate.)

Next you will say a sentence that uses both of your words. What do you do next? (Idea: *I will say a sentence that uses both of my words.*) (Demonstrate.)

If you can use both of your words in one sentence, give yourself a point. Then give your partner a turn. (Demonstrate.)

What do you do next? *Give my partner a turn.*

Preparation: You will need a copy of *A Day with Paramedics* for each day's lesson.

Post a copy of the Vocabulary Tally Sheet, BLM A, with this week's Picture Vocabulary Cards attached.

Each child will need one copy of the Homework Sheet, BLM 23a.

A Day with Paramedics
author: Jan Kottke

Target Vocabulary

Tier II	Tier III
ambulance	nonfiction
emergency	photograph
kit	
mask	
paramedics	
stretcher	
treats	

*Expanded Target Vocabulary Word

DAY 1

Introduce Book

Remember that we are reading books about different kinds of workers. All these books are true. When an author writes books about things that are true, those books are called nonfiction books. What kind of books are about true things? *Nonfiction books.* What workers have we read about so far? (Ideas: *Firefighters; mail carriers.*)

This week's book is called *A Day with Paramedics.* What's the title of this week's book? *A Day with Paramedics.*

This book was written by Jan Kottke [kott-key]. Who's the author of *A Day with Paramedics*? *Jan Kottke.*

The pictures for this book were taken with a camera. They are called photographs. What do you call pictures taken with a camera? *Photographs.* What kind of illustrations does *A Day with Paramedics* have? *Photographs.*

The cover of a book usually gives us some hints of what the book is about. Let's look at the front cover of *A Day with Paramedics.* What do you see in the photograph? (Ideas: *Two paramedics; a man and a woman; an ambulance; a hospital; the paramedics are wearing uniforms.*)

Take a Picture Walk

(Encourage children to use target words in their answers.) We're going to take a picture walk through this book. When we take a picture walk through a nonfiction book about workers, we look carefully at the pictures and think about what we see.

Page 5. Who do you think these people are? (Idea: *Paramedics.*) Where are they standing? (Ideas: *Beside an ambulance; in front of the hospital.*) How many paramedics are there? *Two.*

Page 7. Why do you think the man is talking on the radio? (Ideas: *To find out where they need to go; to find out what they have to do next.*) Why do you think they are sitting in the truck? (Ideas: *They are ready to go; they are driving.*)

Page 9. Why do you think the picture is blurry? (Ideas: *It makes the ambulance look like it is moving really quickly; it makes the lights look as though they are flashing.*)

Page 11. Where are the paramedics standing? (*They are at the back of the ambulance.*) What do you think they are doing? (Ideas: *They are pulling things out of the ambulance; they are getting ready to help someone; they are getting the things they may need.*) Why do you think there is writing and pictures on the back of the paramedics' jackets? (Idea: *So people know they are paramedics just by looking at them.*)

Page 13. Who is the person on the ground? (Ideas: *A woman; someone who needs help; someone who is sick.*) What is the paramedic trying to put on the woman's face? (Idea: *A mask; a thing to help her breathe.*) What is the other paramedic doing? (Ideas: *He is getting the bed ready; he is giving his partner room to work; he is getting ready to move the woman.*)

Page 15. How would you feel if you were the person being loaded into the ambulance? (Ideas: *Safe; relieved; worried; sick; scared; I would know I was being well taken care of.*) Where do you think the paramedics are taking the woman? (Idea: *To the hospital.*)

Page 17. Why do you think there is only one paramedic in the back helping the woman? (Idea: *The other paramedic is driving the ambulance.*) What do you think the paramedic is doing to the woman? (Ideas: *She is checking the woman's heartbeat; she is checking the woman's blood pressure; she is trying to find out what is wrong with the woman.*)

Page 19. Where do you thing the paramedics are now? (Idea: *At the hospital.*) Who do you think the woman is in the white coat? (Ideas: *The doctor; a nurse.*)

Page 21. What do you think happened to the paramedics' patient? (Idea: *She was taken into the hospital.*) What do you think the paramedics are going to do next? (Ideas: *They are going to get ready for the next emergency.*) How do you think the paramedics feel? (Ideas: *Happy; relieved; ready to help the next person.*) Tell why they are feeling this way.

Read the Book Aloud
(Read the story to children with minimal interruptions.)

Tomorrow we will read the book again, and I will ask you some questions.

Present Target Vocabulary
◎⚊ Ambulance

In the book, the paramedics drive an ambulance. An ambulance is a truck made to carry sick or hurt people to the hospital. **Ambulance.** Say the word. *Ambulance.*

Ambulance is a naming word. It names a thing. What kind of word is **ambulance?** *A naming word.*

An ambulance is a truck made to carry sick or hurt people to the hospital. Say the word that means "a truck made to carry sick or hurt people to the hospital." *Ambulance.*

(Correct any incorrect responses, and repeat the item at the end of the sequence.)

Let's think of a time you might need an ambulance. If it is a time you would need an ambulance, say "ambulance." If not, don't say anything."

- You broke your leg at the store. *Ambulance.*
- You got a small scratch on your knee.
- You see a car accident. *Ambulance.*
- You want a hot dog from the hot dog stand.
- Someone tells you to call an ambulance. *Ambulance.*
- You woke up with a toothache.

What naming word means "a truck made to carry sick or hurt people to the hospital"? *Ambulance.*

◎⚊ Emergency

In the book, paramedics were waiting for an emergency. An emergency is a serious problem that needs attention right away. **Emergency.** Say the word. *Emergency.*

Emergency is a naming word. It names a thing. What kind of word is **emergency?** *A naming word.*

An emergency is a serious problem that needs attention right away. Say the word that means "a serious problem that needs attention right away." *Emergency.*

Let's think about some problems that might be an emergency. If the problem I name is an emergency, say "emergency." If not, don't say anything.

- There is a fire in the neighbor's house. *Emergency.*
- Jim did not do his homework last night.
- Someone fell down and is really hurt. *Emergency.*
- There is a bad car accident in front of your house. *Emergency.*
- I cannot find my hat.
- The water park is closing in five minutes.

What naming word means "a serious problem that needs attention right away"? *Emergency.*

◎⚊ Kit

In the book, an emergency kit was used to help the woman who was sick. A kit is a group of items that are kept together for a reason. **Kit.** Say the word. *Kit.*

Kit is a naming word. It names a thing. What kind of word is **kit?** *A naming word.*

A kit is a group of items that are kept together for a reason. The paramedics would keep the items they need to help sick people during an emergency together in a kit. Say the word that means "a group of items that are kept together for a reason." *Kit.*

Let's think about some different kinds of kits. If you think the items belong to a kit, say "kit." If not, don't say anything.

- Wrench, hammer, pliers, screwdrivers. *Kit.*
- Band aids, needles, disinfectant, tweezers. *Kit.*
- Grass, bicycle, airplane, toy store, zoo.
- Your teacher, a dog, a car, a building.
- Pencil, ruler, crayons, paper, erasers. *Kit.*

What naming word means "a group of items that are kept together for a reason"? *Kit.*

⊙← Mask

In the book, the paramedics put a mask on the sick woman. A mask is a covering for the face. **Mask.** Say the word. *Mask.*

Mask is a naming word. It names a thing. What kind of word is **mask?** *A naming word.*

A mask is a covering for the face. Say the word that means "a covering for the face." *Mask.*

Let's think about some times when a mask might be used. I'll tell about a time. If you think you would use a mask, say "mask." If not, don't say anything.

- There is a strong gas smell. *Mask.*
- I put something over my face because I didn't want anyone to see who I was. *Mask.*
- Mom and I took the car through a car wash.
- A diver was diving for treasure. *Mask.*
- You needed something special to help you breathe. *Mask.*
- You had a hamburger for supper.

What naming word means "a covering for the face"? *Mask.*

Present Vocabulary Tally Sheet
(See Lesson 1, page 3, for instructions.)

Assign Homework
(Homework Sheet, BLM 23a. See the Introduction for homework instructions.)

Preparation: Picture Vocabulary Cards for *ambulance, emergency, kit, mask.*

Read and Discuss Story

(Read story to children. Ask the following questions at the specified points. Encourage them to use target words in their answers.)

Page 4. What kind of people do paramedics help? (Ideas: *Sick or hurt people.*) Where do paramedics work? (Ideas: *In the ambulance; all over the city; at the hospital.*)

Page 6. How do the paramedics know when someone needs help? (Idea: *A call is made to the paramedics on the radio.*) What do you think the paramedics were doing before the call on the radio came in? (Ideas: *Resting; waiting for the next call; driving around the city; helping other people.*)

Page 8. What do the paramedics need to do when they are called to an emergency? (Ideas: *Get there as quickly as they can; drive fast; turn on the flashing lights; turn on a siren to let people know there is an emergency.*) Why do you think the ambulance has so many lights on it? (Idea: *So that people can get out of its way.*) What other thing would an ambulance have that would let people know there is an emergency? (Ideas: *A siren.*)

Page 10. Why do the paramedics need to have an emergency kit with them? (Ideas: *The things they need to help people are in the kit; they are not sure what kinds of things they will need.*) What are they pulling out of the ambulance? *A stretcher.* What do you think the stretcher might be for? (Ideas: *To put the sick person on; to take the sick person to the hospital; to move the person safely.*)

Page 12. What is the first thing Beatrice does when she sees the sick woman? *She puts a mask on the woman to help her breathe.* Where do you think the mask came from? (Idea: *From the emergency kit.*)

Pages 14–16. Why do you think the paramedics are putting the sick woman into the ambulance? (Ideas: *It is easier to treat her in the ambulance; they are going to take her to the hospital.*) If the paramedics are taking the women to the hospital, why is Beatrice still trying to help the woman? (Idea: *Beatrice may be able to treat the sick woman before they get to the hospital; she needs to try and find out what is wrong with the sick woman; she wants to help the woman.*)

Page 18. Why do you think the doctor would meet the paramedics and the sick woman at the hospital? (Idea: *The doctor wants to see the sick woman right away; the doctor can see the patient and find out what is wrong; the doctor can decide where in the hospital the sick woman needs to go.*) Why do you think it would be helpful for the doctor to talk with the paramedics? (Ideas: *The doctor could ask the paramedics important questions; Beatrice was treating the woman on the way to the hospital and knows more about the woman than the doctor.*)

Page 20. Why do the paramedics like what they do? (Idea: *They like helping people.*)

Let's think about *A Day with Paramedics.* What is this book about? (Idea: *Paramedics.*) The main idea of a nonfiction book is the most important thing we learn when we read the book. What do we call the most important thing we learn when we read a nonfiction book? *The main idea.* What do you think is the most important thing we learned when we read *A Day with Paramedics*? (Idea: *Paramedics work hard to help sick or hurt people.*)

(**Note:** At first, children will probably give details relating to the story—paramedics drive ambulances; they wait for emergencies; they take people to the hospital. If the children give these responses ask questions such as:) Do you think that the work paramedics do is easy? Why do you think the paramedics do these things? So what is the main idea of the book *A Day with Paramedics*?

Review Vocabulary

(Display the Picture Vocabulary Cards. Point to each card as you say the word. Ask children to repeat each word after you.) These pictures show **ambulance, emergency, kit,** and **mask.**

- What word means "a covering for the face"? *Mask.*
- What word means "a group of items that are kept together for a reason"? *Kit.*
- What word means "a serious problem that needs attention right away"? *Emergency.*
- What word means "a truck made to carry sick or hurt people to the hospital"? *Ambulance.*

Extend Vocabulary

 Mask

In *A Day with Paramedics,* we learned that **mask** means "a covering for the face." Say the word that means "a covering for the face." *Mask.*

Raise your hand if you can tell us a sentence that uses **mask** as a naming word meaning "a covering for the face." (Call on several children. If they don't use complete sentences, restate their examples as sentences. Have the class repeat the sentences.)

Here's a new way to use the word **mask.**

- We had to **mask** the book with thick paper to protect the cover. Say the sentence.
- I have to **mask** the rocky area with green cloth so you can't see it. Say the sentence.
- I used special tape to **mask** the cracks. Say the sentence.

In these sentences, mask is an action word that means to cover or hide something. What word means "to cover or hide something"? *Mask.*

Raise your hand if you can tell us a sentence that uses **mask** as an action word meaning "to cover or hide something." (Call on several children. If they don't use complete sentences, restate their examples as sentences. Have the class repeat the sentences.

Present Target Vocabulary

◎← Paramedics

In the book, paramedics are the people who drive ambulances and help people who are sick or hurt. **Paramedics.** Say the word. *Paramedics.*

Paramedics is a naming word. It names people. What kind of word is **paramedics?** *A naming word.*

Paramedics are the people who drive ambulances and help people who are sick or hurt. What word means "people who drive ambulances and help people who are sick or hurt"? *Paramedics.*

I'll tell about some times when someone might need the help of a paramedic. If the person would need a paramedic, say "paramedic." If not, don't say anything.

- Terry fell off her bike and got a small scrape on her knee.
- My cat is stuck up high in a tree.
- On the ski slope, David broke his leg. *Paramedic.*
- A boy was hit by a car while crossing the street. *Paramedic.*
- A man had a heart attack at the store. *Paramedic.*
- My head aches from working on a computer for so long.

What naming word means "people who drive ambulances and help people who are sick or hurt"? *Paramedics.*

◎← Stretcher

In the book, the paramedics used a stretcher to move the sick woman. A stretcher is a flat bed on which a sick or hurt person can be carried. **Stretcher.** Say the word. *Stretcher.*

Stretcher is a naming word. It names a thing. What kind of word is **stretcher?** *A naming word.*

A stretcher is a flat bed on which a sick or hurt person can be carried. Say the word that means "a flat bed on which a sick or hurt person can be carried." *Stretcher.*

Let's think about some times when someone might use a stretcher. I'll tell about a time. If you think that person might use a stretcher, say "stretcher." If not, don't say anything.

- The firefighters needed to get a hurt man out of a burning building. *Stretcher.*
- Brad needed something to help him float in the water.
- A woman broke her neck in a car accident. *Stretcher.*
- The paramedics had to remove a sick person from the 18th floor. *Stretcher.*
- I couldn't reach the can of tomato soup on the top shelf.
- You need something to help you stretch the rubber band around the box.

What naming word means "a flat bed on which a sick or hurt person can be carried"? *Stretcher.*

◎← Treats

In the book, the paramedic treats the sick woman. **Treats** means "cares for someone who is sick or hurt." **Treats.** Say the word. *Treats.*

Treats is an action word. It describes something someone does. What kind of word is **treats?** *An action word.*

Treats means cares for someone who is sick or hurt. What word means "cares for someone who is sick or hurt"? *Treats.*

I'll tell about some times when a person might treat someone. If the person treats someone, say "treats." If not, don't say anything.

- The dentist made my tooth feel better. *Treats.*
- The farmer grew a lot of corn.
- Doctor Dan put in stitches to sew up the cut on my foot. *Treats.*
- The photographer took a perfect picture of us.
- I went to the hospital and the nurse fixed my sore arm. *Treats.*
- Sue can't wait for someone to help her with this project.

What action word means "cares for someone who is sick or hurt"? *Treats.*

Preparation: Prepare a sheet of chart paper with a web and *Paramedic* in the center. Record children's responses by recording the underlined words (and any other relevant information identified during the discussion) on the web. Draw lines to indicate connections between the various parts of the web. A sample web is provided in the Appendix.

Make Connections (Build a Web)

Today I'll show you the photographs taken for *A Day with Paramedics.* As I show you the pictures, I'll call on one of you to tell more about paramedics.

Get ready to tell me what you know about where paramedics work when they are helping sick or hurt people. What do paramedics drive to get from one emergency to another? *An ambulance.* (Add a circle to the web for ambulance.)

Pages 5–8. (Read the text on pages 6 and 8.) What things might be on or inside an ambulance? (Ideas: *Paramedic's clothes; lights; radio; horns; sirens; emergency kit.*) (Add a circle to the web for *clothes* and *emergency kit.*)

(Point to the ambulance circle.) What else would you see on or inside an ambulance? (Ideas: *Signs on the ambulance; computer; stretcher; masks; emergency kit; and air tanks.*) (Encourage children to use target words when appropriate. Model use as necessary.)

(Repeat this process for *clothes* and *emergency kit,* showing the appropriate photographs in the book.)

Pages 9–13. Tell me more about the work paramedics do. (Add the work circle to the web.) What things do paramedics do when they're at work helping sick and hurt people? (Ideas: *Wait for a radio call; drive really fast to the next emergency; organize all the things they need; help people who are sick and hurt; put masks on people to help them breathe.*)

Pages 15–19. What things do paramedics do once they load the sick or hurt person onto

a stretcher? (Ideas: *Put the person into the ambulance; take the person to the hospital; one person drives the ambulance; check the person's pulse; check their blood pressure; treat the person; tell the doctor what is wrong with the person.*)

Page 21. After the sick or hurt person is in the hospital, what do paramedics do? (Idea: *They get ready for the next emergency.*)

Play the Choosing Game

Today you will play the Choosing Game. Let's think about the seven words we have learned: **ambulance, emergency, kit, mask, paramedics, stretcher,** and **treats.** (Display the Picture Vocabulary Cards.)

I will say a sentence that has two target words in it. You will have to choose the correct word for that sentence. Let's practice. (Display the word cards for the two words in each sentence as you say the sentence.)

- People who help sick and hurt people are called **paramedics** or **ambulances?** *Paramedics.*
- When paramedics get a call to help a sick or hurt person it is an **emergency** or a **kit?** *An emergency.*
- Do paramedics use a **mask** or a **stretcher** to load the sick or hurt person into the ambulance? *A stretcher.*

If you tell me the correct answer, you will win one point. If you can't tell me the correct answer, I get the point.

Now you're ready to play the game. (Draw a T-chart on the board for keeping score. Children earn one point for each correct answer. If they make an error, correct them as you normally would, and record one point for yourself. Repeat missed words at the end of the game. Display the Picture Vocabulary Cards for the two words in each sentence as you say the sentence.)

- If paramedics were ready to go to an emergency would they ride in a **stretcher** or an **ambulance?** *An ambulance.*
- Do paramedics drive fast to a **mask** or an **emergency?** *An emergency.*

- Does a **kit** or a **stretcher** help paramedics move a sick or hurt person? *A stretcher.*
- Are people who help sick and hurt people **mail carriers** or **paramedics**? *Paramedics.*
- Paramedics put a **kit** or a **mask** on a person to help them breathe better? *A mask.*

(Count the points and declare a winner.) You did a great job of playing the *Choosing Game.*

DAY 4

Preparation: Paramedics Booklet.

Introduce Paramedics Booklet

(Give each child a copy of the Paramedics Booklet.) My turn to read the title of the booklet. You touch under each word as I read it. Paramedics Help Sick and Hurt People. What is the title? *Paramedics Help Sick and Hurt People.*

(Hold up the booklet.) Open the booklet to page 1. (Point to the picture.) Who are these people? *Paramedics.* Touch the words under the picture in your booklet. My turn to read the words. You touch each word as I read it. Matt and Pat are paramedics. Let's read the words together. *Matt and Pat are paramedics.* Your turn. Read the words by yourselves. *Matt and Pat are paramedics.* (Repeat the procedure for the remaining pages in the booklet.)

(Children should color the illustrations in their Paramedics booklet.)

Play the Choosing Game (Cumulative Review)

 Let's play the Choosing Game. I will say a sentence that has two target words in it. You will have to choose the correct word for that sentence. (Display the Picture Vocabulary Cards for *ambulance, emergency, kit, mask, paramedics, stretcher,* and *treats* for two words in each sentence as you say the sentence.)

Now you're ready to play the Choosing Game. (Draw a T-chart on the board for keeping score. Children earn one point for each correct answer. If they make an error, correct them as you normally would, and record one

point for yourself. Repeat missed words at the end of the game.)

- If a person helped sick and hurt people would they be a **paramedic** or an **ambulance**? *A paramedic.*
- If you saw paramedics moving a sick person would they be using a **mask** or a **stretcher**? *A stretcher.*
- When a call comes in on the radio does it mean there is an **ambulance** or an **emergency**? *An emergency.*
- Would a paramedic drive a **kit** or an **ambulance**? *An ambulance.*
- Would paramedics put a **mask** or a **kit** on a person's face to help them breathe better? *A mask.*
- Do paramedics have some of the things they need in a **kit** or an **emergency**? *A kit.*
- Does the paramedic **treat** or **stretcher** the person on the way to the hospital? *Treat.*
- If you wanted to protect the cover of your book you would **mask** or **ambulance** it with paper? *Mask.*

Now you will have to listen very carefully, because I'm not going to show you the word cards. (This part of the game includes review words collected from previous lessons.)

- Would you see paramedics in an **ambulance** or in a **cave**? *An ambulance.*
- Are paramedics **rough** or **gentle** with the people they help? *Gentle.*
- When there is an emergency can you hear the ambulance's **siren** or **odor**? *Siren.*
- Does the man on the radio give **chores** or **directions** to the paramedics on how to get to the next emergency? *Directions.*
- Is the ambulance **tempting** or **allowed** to drive really fast? *Allowed.*
- Would a person who was really hurt be **desperate** or **disgraced** to get help from a paramedic? *Desperate.*
- Is it **dangerous** or **impressions** for an ambulance to drive really fast to the next emergency? *Dangerous.*
- Do paramedics **pester** or **rescue** people every day and bring them to safety? *Rescue.*

(Tally the points and declare a winner.) You did a great job of playing the Choosing Game.

Preparation: Paramedics booklet.
Chart titled *Reading Goals* that was started in Week 21.
Happy Face Game Test Sheet, BLM B.

Read Paramedics Booklet

(Assign each child a partner.) Today you'll read your booklet about paramedics to your partner. (Allow sufficient time for each child to read the booklet to his or her partner. Circulate as children read, offering praise and assistance.)

(Ask children to look at the back of their booklet about paramedics.) This part of the booklet is for people who can help you find other books to read. It tells those people about other books that are like *A Day with Paramedics.* It also tells them about a place where you can find other books. Where are some places that you could go to find other books about paramedics or other workers in our community? (Ideas: *To the school library; to the public library; to a bookstore.*)

(You may wish to read and discuss the information on the back cover.)

There's one more important thing on the back cover of your book. Touch the box that is at the bottom of the page. The words above the box say "My reading goal." What do the words say? *My reading goal.*

A goal is something that you want to succeed at doing. What is a goal? *Something that you want to succeed at doing.* A reading goal is something that you want to succeed at doing with your reading.

Let's see if we can add some other reading goals to our class chart. What are some other reading goals that someone might have when they read their book? (Accept reasonable responses. Help children put their ideas into goal statements. Add to the list of statements on the chart. Ask children to choose a goal and copy it into the box. Children may also make up an original goal that is not on the list. If children are unable to copy the goals or to write a goal of their own,

you or a helper may wish to scribe their goal statements for them before the booklets are sent home.)

Assess Vocabulary

 (Give each child a copy of the Happy Face Game Test Sheet, BLM B.)

Today you're going to play the Happy Face Game. When you play the Happy Face Game, it shows me how well you know the hard words you are learning.

If I say something that is true, color in the happy face. What will you do if I say something that is true? *Color in the happy face.*

If I say something that is false, color in the sad face. What will you do if I say something that is false? *Color in the sad face.*

Listen carefully to each item that I say. Don't let me trick you!

Item 1: If you are a **paramedic** you help sick or hurt people. (*True.*)

Item 2: An **ambulance** is used to help fight fires. (*False.*)

Item 3: **Paramedics** have to drive really fast to get to an **emergency.** (*True.*)

Item 4: When **paramedics** put a **mask** on a sick person, it helps them breathe better. (*True.*)

Item 5: A **firefighter** would use a **mail cart** to take the mail to a **mailbox.** (*False.*)

Item 6: If you went to visit your friend, you would ring the **doorbell** to let him or her know that you were there. (*True.*)

Item 7: A **kit** helps **paramedics** drive the **ambulance.** (*False.*)

Item 8: A **mail carrier** would drive a **fire engine** to deliver the mail. (*False.*)

Item 9: A **stretcher** helps **paramedics** move sick people. (*True.*)

Item 10: **Scrawl** and **sprawl** are rhyming words. (*True.*)

You did a great job of playing the Happy Face Game!

(Score children's work. A child must score 9 out of 10 to be at the mastery level. If a child does not achieve mastery, insert the missed words as additional items in the games in next week's lessons. Retest those children individually for the missed items before they take the next mastery test.)

Extensions

Read a Book as a Reward

(Read *A Day with Paramedics* or another book about paramedics to children as a reward for their hard work.)

Preparation: Word containers for the Super Words Center. You may wish to remove some of the words from earlier lessons the children have mastered.

Introduce the Super Words Center

(Add the new Picture Vocabulary Cards to the words from previous weeks. Show children one of the word containers. Role-play with two to three children as you introduce each part of the game.)

Let's review how to play the game called *2 in 1* in the Super Words Center.

Let's think about how we work with our words in the Super Words Center.

You will work with a partner in the Super Words Center. Whom will you work with? *A partner.*

First you will draw two words out of the container. What do you do first? (Idea: *Draw two words out of the container.*) Show your partner both of the words. (Demonstrate.)

Next you will say a sentence that uses both of your words. What do you do next? (Idea: *I will say a sentence that uses both of my words.*) (Demonstrate.)

If you can use both of your words in one sentence, give yourself a point. Then give your partner a turn. (Demonstrate.)

What do you do next? *Give my partner a turn.*

Preparation: You will need a copy of *A Day with Police Officers* for each day's lesson.

Post a copy of the Vocabulary Tally Sheet, BLM A, with this week's Picture Vocabulary Cards attached.

Each child will need one copy of the Homework Sheet, BLM 24a.

DAY 1

Introduce Book

Remember that we are reading books about different kinds of workers. All these books are true. When an author writes books about things that are true, those books are called nonfiction books. What kind of books are about true things? *Nonfiction books.* What workers have we read about so far? (Ideas: *Firefighters; a mail carrier; paramedics.*)

This week's book is called *A Day with Police Officers.* What's the title of this week's book? *A Day with Police Officers.*

This book was written by Jan Kottke [kott-key]. Who's the author of *A Day with Police Officers*? *Jan Kottke.*

The pictures for this book were taken with a camera. They are called photographs. What do you call pictures taken with a camera? *Photographs.* What kind of illustrations does *A Day with Police Officers* have? *Photographs.*

The cover of a book usually gives us some hints of what the book is about. Let's look at the front cover of *A Day with Police Officers.* What do you see in the photograph? (Ideas: *Seven police officers; officers wearing different uniforms; a police station.*)

Take a Picture Walk

(Encourage children to use target words in their answers.) We're going to take a picture walk through this book. When we take a picture walk through a nonfiction book about workers, we look carefully at the pictures and think about what we see.

A Day with Police Officers
author: Jan Kottke

🎯 **Target Vocabulary**

Tier II	Tier III
ticket	nonfiction
law	photograph
parade	
clues	
*police officers	
*police station	

*Expanded Target Vocabulary Word

Page 5. Who do you think the men and women are? (Idea: *Police officers.*) Where are they standing? (Ideas: *In front of some police cars; on the street.*) How many police officers are there? *Six.*

Page 7. Why do you think the police officer in the white shirt is talking to the other police officers? (Ideas: *He is giving them instructions; he is telling them what they are going to do today; he needs to tell the police officers important information.*) What do you think the police officers are going to do after they finish their meeting? (Ideas: *Go to their police cars, start their day; do what they were asked to do by the police officer in the white shirt.*)

Page 9. What is the police officer doing? (Ideas: *He is writing the lady a ticket for doing something wrong; he is giving the lady directions; he is helping the lady; he is checking the lady's car insurance.*)

Page 11. What are the police officers riding? *Horses.* Why do you think the police officers are riding horses? (Ideas: *They are going to be in a parade; they are watching the traffic; they are making sure that people are not doing bad things.*) Why do you think these police officers are wearing helmets? (Idea: *So that their head is protected in case they fall off the horse.*)

Page 13. What do you think this police officer is driving? (Idea: *A boat.*) What makes you think the police officer is driving a boat? (Ideas: *It looks like a boat; there is an anchor under the window of the boat; there is water all around the* boat.) How many police officers can you see on the boat? *Two.*

Page 15. How does this police officer move around the city? *On a bicycle.* Why do you think this officer would be on a bicycle? (Ideas: *He can be in places where police cars cannot go; he can move quickly in smaller areas; he can move faster when there is traffic.*)

Page 17. Who is in the picture? *A police officer.* Where is the police officer? (Idea: *In the middle of the road.*) Why do you think the police officer is in the middle of the road? (Ideas: *He is directing traffic; he is helping the cars move faster and more safely; he is making sure people do not break the law.*)

Page 19. Who is in the picture with the police officer? *A dog.* Why do you think there is a dog in this picture? (Ideas: *It is the police officer's partner; dogs are used to help with certain kinds of police work; the dog is very well trained and the two work together.*)

Page 21. How many people are in the picture? *Six.* What do you think the police officer is talking to the children about? (Ideas: *Being safe; watching out for strangers; obeying the law; being a good person.*)

Read the Book Aloud
(Read the story to children with minimal interruptions.)

Tomorrow we will read the book again, and I will ask you some questions.

Present Target Vocabulary
 Ticket

In the book, we learned that a ticket is a piece of paper given to a driver who breaks the law. Sometimes when a police officer gives you a ticket, you have to pay a fine. You all know that a fine is "money paid as a punishment for doing something wrong." What do you call "money paid as a punishment for doing something wrong"? *A fine.* **Ticket.** Say the word. *Ticket.*

Ticket is a naming word. It names a thing. What kind of word is **ticket?** *A naming word.*

A ticket is a piece of paper given to a driver who breaks the law. Say the word that means "a piece of paper given to a driver who breaks the law." *Ticket.*

Let's think about some times when someone might get a ticket. If you think that person should get a ticket, say "ticket." If not, don't say anything.

- You are riding your bicycle.
- A person is driving too fast. *Ticket.*
- Bob drove through a red light. *Ticket.*
- You didn't get your homework finished.
- You didn't eat all of your lunch.
- Sally didn't stop at the stop sign at the crosswalk. *Ticket.*

What naming word means "a piece of paper given to a driver who breaks the law"? *Ticket.*

 Law

In the book, when people drive too fast they are breaking the law. The law means a rule people must follow. **Law.** Say the word. *Law.*

Law is a naming word. It names a thing. What kind of word is **law?** *A naming word.*

Law means a rule people must follow. Say the word that means "a rule people must follow." *Law.*

Let's think about some examples of the law. If the example I give is an example of the law, say "law." If not, don't say anything.

- You cannot rob a bank. *Law.*
- Eating homemade apple pie.
- Taking your dog for a walk.
- You must drive slowly when you are near a school. *Law.*
- Helping a friend.
- You must wear a seatbelt when you are in a car. *Law.*

What naming word means "a rule people must follow"? *Law.*

 Parade

In the book, police officers ride their horses in a parade. A parade is a group of people that marches, rides, or drives together down a street. **Parade.** Say the word. *Parade.*

Parade is a naming word. It names a thing. What kind of word is **parade?** *A naming word.*

A parade is a group of people that marches, rides, or drives together down a street. Say the word that means "a group of people that marches, rides, or drives together down a street." *Parade.*

Let's think about some people and things you might see in a parade. If the person or thing I name is in a parade, say "parade." If not, don't say anything.

- A marching band. *Parade.*
- A live whale.
- Clowns. *Parade.*
- Vacuum cleaners.
- Horses and riders. *Parade.*
- Fire engines. *Parade.*

What naming word means "a group of people that marches, rides, or drives together down a street"? *Parade.*

Tell me about something you've seen in a parade. (Call on several children. Encourage them to start their answers with the words, "In the parade I saw _____.")

 Clues

In this book, the police dog helps find clues. These clues are facts that help police figure out when someone has done something wrong. **Clues.** Say the word. *Clues.*

Clues is a naming word. It names things. What kind of word is **clues?** *A naming word.*

Clues are facts that help people solve a mystery or a puzzle. Say the word that means "facts that help people solve a mystery or a puzzle." *Clues.*

(Correct any incorrect responses, and repeat the item at the end of the sequence.)

Let's think of a time you might need clues. I'll tell about a time. If it is a time you would need clues, say "clues." If not, don't say anything.

- You want to find out the teacher's favorite color. *Clues.*
- You want to find out who your teacher will be next year. *Clues.*
- You know where the lost dog is.

- You want to figure out the answer to a riddle. *Clues.*
- You know where your friend is hiding.
- You want to find out which student has the missing blue book. *Clues.*

What naming word means "facts that help people solve a mystery or a puzzle"? *Clues.*

Present Vocabulary Tally Sheet
(See Lesson 1, page 3, for instructions.)

Assign Homework
(Homework Sheet, BLM 24a. See the Introduction for homework instructions.)

DAY 2

Preparation: Picture Vocabulary Cards for *ticket, law, parade, clues.*

Read and Discuss Story

 (Read story to children. Ask the following questions at the specified points. Encourage them to use target words in their answers.)

Page 4. What do police officers do? (Ideas: *Help people and keep people safe.*) How do police officers help people and keep them safe? (Ideas: *They solve crimes; they teach children; they work with the community; they are helpful when you need to ask questions.*)

Page 6. Where do police officers start their day? (*At the police station.*) Why do you think all police officers gather at the police station? (Ideas: *One person can give out instructions; it is nice to see other police officers you work with; at the station they can put on their uniforms.*)

Page 8. What does a police officer do if someone drives too fast? (Idea: *The police officer writes a ticket.*) Do you think people like to get tickets from police officers? Tell why or why not. (Ideas: *No, because people have to pay a fine when they get a ticket.*) What did the lady driving the black car do? (Idea: *She was driving too fast.*)

Page 10. Why are the police officers in the parade on horses? (Idea: *To make sure that* *people march safely.*) What are some of the advantages of being a police officer up on a horse? (Idea: *The police officer sits high and can see a long way away; they can move very quickly if they need to; they can move through people or traffic very quickly.*) What are some of the ways you can tell the people on the horses are police officers? (Ideas: *Their clothes; badges; it says "police" on the flag; in some cities police are the only people to ride horses in the city.*)

Page 12. Why is it important to have police officers patrol the water with boats? (Ideas: *They make sure people are being safe on the water; they make sure that people aren't breaking the law.*)

Page 14. Why do you think a police officer on a bike is helpful when patrolling the park? (Ideas: *They can go where police cars can't; they are quick and quiet and they can go almost anywhere.*) What about this police officer is different from other police officers? (Ideas: *He rides a bike instead of riding in a car; he wears a helmet; he isn't wearing a jacket.*)

Page 16. How do you know this man is a police officer? (Idea: *He is in uniform; his vest says "police"; he has a badge; he is telling drivers what to do.*) Why do you think a police officer needs to be at this spot? (Ideas: *There is too much traffic; he makes sure people are crossing the street safely; there has been an accident; there is no power to the signal lights; it is during a busy time of day.*)

Page 18. Who is Buster? *A police dog.* Why would Buster be better at finding certain clues than a police officer? (Ideas: *Dogs have a better sense of smell; they are trained to look for certain things that people cannot find.*)

Page 20. Why do you think people would thank police officers for keeping them safe? (Ideas: *People like to feel safe; you can have more fun when you are safe; police officers are there to help people.*)

Let's think about the *A Day with Police Officers.* What is this book about? *Police officers.* The main idea of a nonfiction book is the most important thing we learn when we read the book. What do we call the most important thing we

learn when we read a nonfiction book? *The main idea.*

What do you think is the most important thing we learned when we read *A Day with Police Officers*? (Idea: *Police officers work hard to help people and keep people safe.*)

(**Note:** At first, children will probably give details relating to the story—police officers write tickets; they make sure people don't break the law; they make sure people cross the street safely. If children give these responses ask questions such as:) Do you think that it is easy to do a police officer's work? Why do you think police officers do these things? So what is the main idea of *A Day with Police Officers*?

Review Vocabulary

(Display the Picture Vocabulary Cards. Point to each card as you say the word. Ask children to repeat each word after you.) These pictures show **ticket, law, parade,** and **clues.**

- What word means "a piece of paper given to a driver who breaks the law"? *Ticket.*
- What word means "a rule people must follow"? *Law.*
- What word means "a group of people that marches, rides, or drives together down a street"? *Parade.*
- What word means "facts that help people solve a mystery or a puzzle"? *Clues.*

Extend Vocabulary

◎◄ Ticket

In *A Day with Police Officers* we learned that a **ticket** is "a piece of paper given to a driver who breaks the law." Say the word that means "a piece of paper given to a driver who breaks the law." *Ticket.*

Raise your hand if you can tell us a sentence that uses **ticket** as a naming word meaning "a piece of paper given to a driver who breaks the law." (Call on several children. If they don't use complete sentences, restate their examples as sentences. Have the class repeat the sentences.)

Here's a new way to use the word **ticket.**

- I paid for a **ticket** to go see the magic show. Say the sentence.

- LaToya is waiting to get on the plane with her plane **ticket** in her hand. Say the sentence.
- Kente always buys his movie **ticket** two hours before the movie starts. Say the sentence.

In these sentences, **ticket** is a naming word that means "a small card or piece of paper that shows you have paid for something." What word means "a small card or piece of paper that shows you have paid for something"? *Ticket.*

Raise your hand if you can tell us a sentence that uses **ticket** as a naming word meaning "a small card or piece of paper that shows you have paid for something." (Call on several children. If they don't use complete sentences, restate their examples as sentences. Have the class repeat the sentences.)

Present Expanded Target Vocabulary
◎←= Police officers

In the book, police officers are people who make sure others are safe and follow the laws. **Police officers.** Say the words. *Police officers.*

Police officers are naming words. They name people. What kind of words are **police officers?** *Naming words.*

Police officers are people who make sure others are safe and follow the laws. What words mean "people who make sure others are safe and follow the laws"? *Police officers.*

I'll tell about some times when someone might see police officers. If someone would see a police officer, say "police officer." If not, don't say anything.

- James was given a ticket for driving too fast. *Police officer.*
- Emma learned about traffic safety at school from a special guest in uniform. *Police officer.*
- I met the mail carrier at the end of my driveway.
- I was told not to feed the lion my sandwich.
- The woman directing the cars told me that it was safe to cross the street. *Police officer.*

- The person gave my dog some medicine to help make him feel better.

What naming words mean "people who make sure others are safe and follow the laws"? *Police officers.*

◎←= Police station

In this book, a police station is a place where police officers start their day and do some of their work. **Police station.** Say the words. *Police station.*

Police station is a group of naming words. It names a place. What kind of group of words is **police station?** *Naming words.*

A police station is a place where police officers start their day and do some of their work. Say the group of words that means "a place where police officers start their day and do some of their work." *Police station.*

Let's think about some places that might be police stations. If the place I name is where police officers work, say "police station." If not, don't say anything.

- A place where police officers start their day. *Police station.*
- A place to fill the car up with gas.
- A place to take the garbage.
- A place where there is information about law breakers. *Police station.*
- A place to go on a swing.
- A place where police officers find out where they patrol that day. *Police station.*

What group of naming words means "a place where police officers start their day and do some of their work"? *Police station.*

Preparation: Prepare a sheet of chart paper with a web with *Police Officers* in the center circle. Record children's responses by recording the underlined words (and any other relevant information identified during the discussion) on the web. Draw lines to indicate connections between the various parts of the web. A sample web is provided in the Appendix.

Make Connections (Build a Web)

Today I'll show you the photographs taken for *A Day with Police Officers*. As I show you the pictures, I'll call on one of you to tell more about police officers.

Get ready to tell me what you know about where police officers work when they are not out patrolling. What do you call the place where police officers gather at the start of the day? *A police station.* (Add a circle to the web for police station.)

Pages 4–7. (Read the text on pages 4 and 6.) What things might be at a police station? (Ideas: *Police officers; police cars; wanted posters; information about crimes; clothes; notice boards.*) (Add circles to the web for police transportation and clothes. Explain to children that *transportation* means "how people move from place to place.")

(Point to the *police station* circle.) What else would you see at the police station? (Ideas: *Computers; jail cells; offices; desks; clothes racks; ticket books.*)

(Encourage children to use target words when appropriate. Model use as necessary.)

(Repeat this process for *police transportation* and *clothes,* showing the appropriate photographs in the book.)

Pages 9–13. Tell me more about the work police officers do. (Add the work circle to the web.) What things do police officers do when they're at work? (Ideas: *Write tickets to people who break the law; make sure people don't break the law; make sure people march safely in big parades;*

and *make sure people are being safe in the water.*)

Pages 15–19. What other things do police officers do when they're at work? (Ideas: *Patrol on bikes; make sure people in the park are safe; make sure cars move when they should; make sure people cross the street safely; and work with police dogs and find clues.*)

Page 21. How do you know police officers like their work? (Ideas: *They look happy to help people; they like to know they are keeping people safe; they get to talk to people.*)

Play the Choosing Game

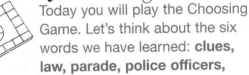

Today you will play the Choosing Game. Let's think about the six words we have learned: **clues, law, parade, police officers, police station,** and **ticket.** (Display the Picture Vocabulary Cards.)

I will say a sentence that has two target words in it. You will have to choose the correct word for that sentence. Let's practice. (Display the word cards for the two words in each sentence as you say the sentence.)

- Are people who help people and keep them safe called **police officers** or **police stations?** *Police officers.*
- If someone drives too fast, do police officers give **clues** or a **ticket?** *A ticket.*
- Do police dogs help police officers find **clues** or **laws?** *Clues.*

If you tell me the correct answer, you will win one point. If you can't tell me the correct answer, I get the point.

Now you're ready to play the game. (Draw a T-chart on the board for keeping score. Children earn one point for each correct answer. If they make an error, correct them as you normally would, and record one point for yourself. Repeat missed words at the end of the game. Display the word cards for the two words in each sentence as you say the sentence.)

- If Bill and Ted got tickets for driving too fast, would **police officers** or **clues** write the tickets? *Police officers.*
- Do police officers ride their horses in a **law** or a **parade?** *A parade.*

- Which is a place; a **police station** or a **ticket?** *A police station.*
- If someone drives too fast, are they breaking the **clues** or the **law?** *The law.*
- Was the police officer using the police dog to find **clues** or **parade?** *Clues.*

(Count the points and declare a winner.) You did a great job of playing the Choosing Game.

DAY 4

Preparation: Police Officers Booklet.

Introduce Police Officers Booklet

(Give each child a copy of the Police Officers Booklet.) My turn to read the title of the booklet. You touch under each word as I read it. Police Officers Keep People Safe. What is the title? *Police Officers Keep People Safe.*

(Hold up the booklet.) Open the booklet to page 1. (Point to the picture.) Who are these people? *Police officers.* Where are the police officers? *At the police station.*

Touch the words under the picture in your booklet. My turn to read the words. You touch each word as I read it. This is the police station. Mark and Kim are at the police station. Let's read the words together. *This is the police station. Mark and Kim are at the police station.* Your turn. Read the words by yourselves. *This is the police station. Mark and Kim are at the police station.* (Repeat the procedure for the remaining pages in the booklet.)

(Children should color the illustrations in their Police Officers booklet.)

Play the Choosing Game (Cumulative Review)

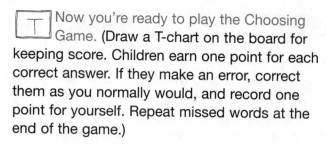

Let's play the Choosing Game. I will say a sentence that has two target words in it. You will have to choose the correct word for that sentence. (Display the Picture Vocabulary Cards for *ticket, law, parade, police officers, police station,* and *clues* for two words in each sentence as you say the sentence.)

Now you're ready to play the Choosing Game. (Draw a T-chart on the board for keeping score. Children earn one point for each correct answer. If they make an error, correct them as you normally would, and record one point for yourself. Repeat missed words at the end of the game.)

- If a person helps people and keeps them safe, would she be a **police officer** or a **police station?** *A police officer.*
- If you went to the place where police officers start their day, would you be at a **police station** or a **parade?** *A police station.*
- If you marched with a large number of people down a street, would you be in a **police station** or a **parade?** *A parade.*
- If the speed limit is 30 miles per hour and someone was driving 60 miles per hour, are they breaking the **law** or **tickets?** *The law.*
- Would a police officer give a **ticket** or a **police station** to someone who was driving too fast? *A ticket.*
- Were the police officer and the police dog looking for **clues** or **laws?** *Clues.*
- You were about to go watch a movie when someone stopped you and asked to see your **clues** or **ticket?** *Ticket.*

Now you will have to listen very carefully, because I'm not going to show you the word cards. (This part of the game includes review words collected from previous lessons.)

- Was the police officer **polite** or **dormant** when he gave the woman the ticket for driving too fast? *Polite.*
- Is the police officer on the boat there to speak **severely** or to **rescue** people from the water? *Rescue.*
- Is the police officer who is directing traffic showing cars the **directions** or **adventures** they need to go? *Directions.*
- Did the new police officer have to **remember** or **patient** to find out where he needed to patrol that day? *Remember.*
- The police dog **crept** or **soared** under the park bench to find the first clue? *Crept.*
- Was the parade **bullied** or **awesome?** *Awesome.*

- Was the police officer **clumsy** or **brave** to stand in the middle of the road and direct traffic? *Brave.*
- Is it not smart to **enormous** or **ignore** a police officer? *Ignore.*

(Tally the points and declare a winner.) You did a great job of playing the Choosing Game.

DAY 5

Preparation: Police Officers booklet.
Chart titled *Reading Goals* that was started in Week 21.
Happy Face Game Test Sheet, BLM B.

Read the Police Officers Booklet

(Assign each child a partner.) Today you'll read your booklet about police officers to your partner. (Allow sufficient time for each child to read the booklet to his or her partner. Circulate as the children read, offering praise and assistance.)

(Ask children to look at the back of their booklet about police officers.) This part of the booklet is for people who can help you find other books to read. It tells those people about other books that are like *A Day with Police Officers.* It also tells them about a place where you can find other books. Where are some places that you could go to find other books about police officers or other workers in our community? (Ideas: *To the school library; to the public library; to a bookstore.*)

(You may wish to read and discuss the information on the back cover.)

There's one more important thing on the back cover of your book. Touch the box that is at the bottom of the page. The words above the box say "My reading goal." What do the words say? *My reading goal.*

A goal is something that you want to succeed at doing. What is a goal? *Something that you want to succeed at doing.* A reading goal is something that you want to succeed at doing with your reading.

Let's see if we can add some other reading goals to our class chart. What are some other reading

goals that someone might have when they read their book? (Accept reasonable responses. Help children put their ideas into goal statements. Add to the list of statements on the chart. Ask children to choose a goal and copy it into the box. Children may also make up an original goal that is not on the list. If children are unable to copy the goals or to write a goal of their own, you or a helper may wish to scribe their goal statements for them before the booklets are sent home.)

Assess Vocabulary

 (Give each child a copy of the Happy Face Game Test Sheet, BLM B.)

Today you're going to play the Happy Face Game. When you play the Happy Face Game, it shows me how well you know the hard words you are learning.

If I say something that is true, color in the happy face. What will you do if I say something that is true? *Color in the happy face.*

If I say something that is false, color in the sad face. What will you do if I say something that is false? *Color in the sad face.*

Listen carefully to each item that I say. Don't let me trick you!

Item 1: If you are a **police officer,** you help people and keep people safe. (*True.*)

Item 2: A **police station** gives out **tickets** to people who drive too fast. (*False.*)

Item 3: Police dogs are good at finding **clues.** (*True.*)

Item 4: **Police officers** sometimes ride horses in **parades.** (*True.*)

Item 5: If there is an **emergency,** the **ambulance** will drive slowly to get there. (*False.*)

Item 6: **Police officers** give **tickets** to those people who do not follow the **law.** (*True.*)

Item 7: A **police station** is where **firefighters** work. (*False.*)

Item 8: The **kit** that **paramedics** have in the **ambulance** has items that they need to help sick and hurt people. (*True.*)

Item 9: If you needed a fire put out, you would call the **post office.** (*False.*)

Item 10: **Firefighters spray** water from **hoses** to put out fires. (*True.*)

You did a great job of playing the Happy Face Game!

(Score children's work. A child must score 9 out of 10 to be at the mastery level. If a child does not achieve mastery, insert the missed words as additional items in the games in next week's lessons. Retest those children individually for the missed items before they take the next mastery test.)

Extensions

Read a Book as a Reward

(Read *A Day with Police Officers* or another book about police officers to children as a reward for their hard work.)

Preparation: Word containers for the Super Words Center. You may wish to remove some of the words from earlier lessons the children have mastered.

Introduce the Super Words Center

(Add the new Picture Vocabulary Cards to words from the previous weeks. Show children one of the word containers. Role-play with two to three children as you introduce each part of the game.)

Let's review how to play the game called *2 in 1* in the Super Words Center.

Let's think about how we work with our words in the Super Words Center.

You will work with a partner in the Super Words Center. Whom will you work with? *A partner.*

First you will draw two words out of the container. What do you do first? (Idea: *Draw two words out of the container.*) Show your partner both of the words. (Demonstrate.)

Next you will say a sentence that uses both of your words. What do you do next? (Idea: *I will say a sentence that uses both of my words.*) (Demonstrate.)

If you can use both of your words in one sentence, give yourself a point. Then give your partner a turn. (Demonstrate.)

What do you do next? *Give my partner a turn.*

Preparation: You will need a copy of *A Busy Day at Mr. Kang's Grocery Store* for each day's lesson.

Number the pages of the story to assist you in asking comprehension questions at appropriate points.

You will need a map or globe of the world.

Post a copy of the Vocabulary Tally Sheet, BLM A, with this week's Picture Vocabulary Cards attached.

Each child will need one copy of the Homework Sheet, BLM 25a.

DAY 1

Introduce Book

Remember that we are reading books about different kinds of workers. All these books are true. When an author writes books about things that are true, those books are called nonfiction books. What kind of books are about true things? *Nonfiction books.* What workers have we read about so far? (Ideas: *Firefighters; a mail carrier; paramedics; police officers.*)

This week's book is called *A Busy Day at Mr. Kang's Grocery Store.* What's the title of this week's book? *A Busy Day at Mr. Kang's Grocery Store.*

This book was written by Alice K. Flanagan [flan-a-gun]. Who's the author of *A Busy Day at Mr. Kang's Grocery Store*? *Alice K. Flanagan.*

Christine Osinski [oh-**zin**-skee] took the photographs for this book. Who took the photographs for *A Busy Day at Mr. Kang's Grocery Store*? *Christine Osinski.*

The cover of a book usually gives us some hints of what the book is about. Let's look at the front cover of *A Busy Day at Mr. Kang's Grocery Store.* What do you see in the photograph? (Ideas: *A man smiling; a scale full of fruit; cookies in a cardboard box; bottles on a shelf; books on a shelf.*)

A Busy Day at Mr. Kang's Grocery Store
author: Alice K. Flanagan • photographer: Christine Osinski

Target Vocabulary

Tier II	Tier III
business	nonfiction
customers	photographs
kind	
generous	
*attractive	
*successful	

*Expanded Target Vocabulary Word

Take a Picture Walk

(Encourage children to use target words in their answers.) We're going to take a picture walk through this book. Remember that when we take a picture walk through a nonfiction book about workers, we look carefully at the pictures and think about what we see.

Page 3. Where do you think the man is standing? (Idea: *In front of a grocery store.*) What do you see in front of the store? (Idea: *Buckets full of flowers.*)

Pages 4–5. Who do you think the man is? (Ideas: *Mr. Kang; the owner of the grocery store.*) Wow! Look at all the different things for sale in this store!

Pages 6–7. What are some of the things that the man does at the grocery store? (Ideas*: Carries boxes of fruit; sweeps the floor.*) What do you think is in the box? (Idea: *Bananas.*)

Pages 8–9. What are some of the things for sale in the store? (Ideas: *Flowers; tomatoes; onions; garlic; cantaloupe; pineapple; avocadoes; oranges.*)

Page 10. What do you see in this photograph? (Ideas: *A cash register full of paper bills and coins; money.*)

Page 11. What is the man doing? (Idea: *Talking on the telephone.*) Who do you think a storeowner might call on the telephone? (Ideas:

Customers; people who bring food and other things for him to sell at his store; his family.)

Pages 12–13. What are some other things for sale that you see in these photographs? (Ideas: *Avocadoes; persimmons; oranges; ginger root; onions; cantaloupes; milk; juice.*) Where are the milk and juice kept? (Idea: *In the cooler; in the refrigerator.*)

Pages 14–15. What is happening here? (Idea: *A customer is buying some flowers.*) How do you think the man is feeling as he helps the customer? (Ideas: *Happy; friendly.*) Why do you think so? (Idea: *He is happy to have a customer buying something at his store.*) What else is the customer buying? (Idea: *Fruit; bananas; an orange; tomatoes; grapes; apples.*)

Pages 16–17. What do you see here? (Ideas: *Flowers; asparagus; red lettuce or cabbage; radicchio.*)

Pages 18–19. Who else do you see in the photographs on these two pages? (Idea: *A woman; two little girls.*) Who do you think these people might be? (Ideas: *Mr. Kang's wife and children.*) One of the photographs on these two pages is different than the other photographs in this book. How is it different? (Idea: *It is in black and white.*)

Pages 20–21. Where was this picture taken? (Ideas: *Outside the store; across the street from the store.*) What do you see above the store? (Ideas: *Windows.*) Do you think that anybody lives above the store? *Yes.* What makes you think so? (Idea: *There are curtains on some of the windows; plants are growing in some of the windows.*)

Page 22. What is the man pointing to? (Idea: *A map.*)

Page 23. What is the man doing? (Idea: *Moving a box of bananas.*) What other things are for sale in this grocery store? (Ideas: *Boxes; bottles; cans of food.*)

Page 29. What is the woman in this photograph holding? (Ideas: *Two paper cups; coffee.*)

Pages 30–31. When do you think this photograph was taken? (Idea: *At night.*) How do you think the storeowner is feeling? (Idea:

Happy.) What makes you think that? (Idea: *He is laughing.*)

Read the Book Aloud

(Read the story to children with minimal interruptions. Mr. Kang and his family are from Korea. You may wish to use a map or a globe to show children where Korea is located in relationship to the location of the school.)

Tomorrow we will read the story again, and I will ask you some questions.

Present Target Vocabulary
◎⚞ Business

In the story we found out that six years ago, Mr. Kang and his family "left Korea and came to America to start their own business." That means Mr. Kang owns his own store and sells things to earn money. **Business.** Say the word. *Business.*

Business is a naming word. It names a thing. What kind of word is **business?** *A naming word.*

If you own a business you own a company that makes or sells things to earn money. Say the word that means "a company that makes or sells things to earn money." *Business.*

(Correct any incorrect responses, and repeat the item at the end of the sequence.)

Let's think about some things that might be a business. I'll tell about something. If you think that thing is a business, say "business." If not, don't say anything.

- Mr. and Mrs. Shanri own The Game Store. *Business.*
- Mr. Ederer collects model airplanes.
- Mr. Kang sells groceries at his store. *Business.*
- Ms. Franklin liked to fly kites.
- We fix bicycles and sell new ones at our shop on Fifth Street. *Business.*
- Jack and Diane are two American children growing up on a farm.

What naming word means "a company that makes or sells things to earn money"? *Business.*

◎⚞ Customers

The story says Mr. Kang had to sweep the floor, arrange the fruit, and put out fresh flowers before the customers came. That means Mr. Kang had a lot to do before the people who wanted to buy things came into his store. **Customers.** Say the word. *Customers.*

Customers is a naming word. It names people. What kind of word is **customers?** *A naming word.*

Customers are the people who buy things in a store. Say the word that means "the people who buy things in a store." *Customers.*

Let's think about some people who might be customers. I'll tell about someone. If you think that person is a customer, say "customer." If not, don't say anything.

- Les went into The Game Store to buy a checkers game. *Customer.*
- Mrs. Zydeco went into the Sunrise Hair Salon to get her hair cut. *Customer.*
- The Mueller family went camping in the wilderness.
- We bought seven pounds of oranges and four pounds of apples from Mr. Kang. *Customer.*
- My Uncle Herb bought gas at the gas station. *Customer.*
- Bart shoveled the gravel in the back yard for his dad.

What naming word means "the people who buy things in a store"? *Customers.*

Generous

The story says Mr. Kang is "generous." That means he is happy to share what he has with other people. **Generous.** Say the word. *Generous.*

Generous is a describing word. It tells more about a person. What kind of word is **generous?** *A describing word.*

If you are generous, you are happy to share what you have with others. Say the word that means "happy to share what you have with others." *Generous.* **Selfish** is the opposite of **generous.** When a person is **selfish,** he or she doesn't care about others and won't share what he or she has. What word means you "don't care about others and you won't share what you have"? *Selfish.*

Let's think about some people who might be generous or who might be selfish. I'll tell about someone. If you think that person is generous, say "generous." If you think that person is selfish, say "selfish."

- Tami shared her lunch with Mel. *Generous.*
- Karl wouldn't let his little brother play with his toy cars, even though he wasn't playing with them. *Selfish.*
- Mrs. Goodfellow shared what she knows with her children. *Generous.*
- Every time someone got a compliment, Corinne wanted one too. *Selfish.*
- Peter had only twenty-five cents but he gave it to someone who had nothing at all. *Generous.*
- Mom gets a ride to work from Mr. Magrowski, even though it's a long way for him to drive. *Generous.*

What describing word means "happy to share what you have with others"? *Generous.*

Kind

The story says that Mr. Kang is "kind." That means he is friendly, helpful, and considerate. **Kind.** Say the word. **Kind.**

Kind is a describing word. It tells more about a person. What kind of word is **kind?** *A describing word.*

If you are kind, you are friendly, helpful, and considerate. You already know what **considerate** means. What word means "pays attention to what someone else needs or wants or wishes for"? *Considerate.* Say the word that means "friendly, helpful, and considerate." *Kind.*

Let's think about some people who might be kind. I'll tell about what some people did and said. If you think that person is kind, say "kind." If not, don't say anything.

- As the nurse put a bandage on Jessie's scraped knee, she smiled and said, "This should make your knee feel better." *Kind.*
- Elsa took care of the injured kitten by washing the cut, bandaging it up, and staying with the kitten all night. *Kind.*
- Mr. Williams held Amanda's hand so she would feel less afraid. *Kind.*
- She jumped out from behind the door and yelled, "Boo!"

- Martin walked all the way to the store and back to get the hat his little sister had left there. *Kind.*
- Leona saw the other child fall but she didn't go to help.

What describing word means "friendly, helpful, and considerate"? *Kind.*

Present Vocabulary Tally Sheet
(See Lesson 1, page 3, for instructions.)

Assign Homework
(Homework Sheet, BLM 25a. See the Introduction for homework instructions.)

DAY 2

Preparation: Picture Vocabulary Cards for *business, customers, kind, generous.*

Read and Discuss Story

(Read story to children. Ask the following questions at the specified points. Encourage them to use target words in their answers.)

Page 3. What kind of store does Mr. Kang own? (Idea: *A grocery store.*)

Page 5. What two things does Mr. Kang do in the morning? (Ideas: *He looks out the window; he unlocks the front door.*) What time does Mr. Kang unlock the store door? (Idea: *At eight o'clock sharp.*)

Pages 6–9. What are some of the things Mr. Kang does before the customers come? (Ideas: *Sweeps the floor; arranges the fruit; puts out fresh flowers.*)

Pages 10–11. What other things does Mr. Kang have to do? (Ideas: *Fill the cash register drawer; order supplies.*)

Pages 12–13. What does Mr. Kang do with the cartons of milk? (Ideas: *He counts and unpacks them.*) Why do you think the milk has to go in the cooler, but the fruits and vegetables can be out on the counter? (Idea: *The milk needs to be kept cold or it will spoil; fruit can be left outside and it will still be good to eat.*)

Pages 14–17. What are some of the things that a customer might want? (Ideas: *Fresh fruit; a bouquet of flowers; some vegetables.*)

Pages 18–19. Who else works in the grocery store? (Idea: *Mrs. Kang.*) How many children do they have? (Idea: *Two girls.*)

Page 21. Where does the Kang family live? (Ideas: *Upstairs; above the small store.*)

Page 22. Where did the Kang family live before they came to America? *Korea.* How many years has the Kang family been living in America? (Idea: *Six years.*) Why did they decide to come to America? (Idea: *To start their own business.*)

Pages 24–25. What are some of the things that were hard to learn? (Ideas: *A new language; new customs; going to new schools.*)

Pages 26–27. How would you describe Mr. Kang? What is he like? (Ideas: *He's a hard worker; he is generous and kind; he is considerate.*) Mr. Kang has made many new friends because he is a hard worker, is generous, and is kind. What other things do you think would make it easy for a person to make new friends? (Ideas: *Being friendly; sharing; helping others.*)

Pages 28–29. How do you know Mr. Kang's grocery store does lots of business? (Idea: *Everyone in the neighborhood comes to buy fresh fruit, flowers, or a cup of hot tea.*)

Page 30. How does Mr. Kang feel at the end of the day? (Ideas: *Tired; happy; satisfied; content.*)

Review Vocabulary
(Display the Picture Vocabulary Cards. Point to each card as you say the word. Ask children to repeat each word after you.) These pictures show **business, customers, generous,** and **kind.**

- What describing word means "friendly, helpful, and considerate"? *Kind.*
- What naming word means "the people who buy things in a store"? *Customers.*
- What describing word means "happy to share what you have with others"? *Generous.*
- What naming word means "a company that makes or sells things to earn money"? *Business.*

Extend Vocabulary

 Kind

In *A Busy Day at Mr. Kang's Grocery Store,* we learned that **kind** means "friendly, helpful, and considerate." Say the word that means "friendly, helpful, and considerate." *Kind.*

Raise your hand if you can tell us a sentence that uses **kind** as a describing word meaning "friendly, helpful, and considerate." (Call on several children. If they don't use complete sentences, restate their examples as sentences. Have the class repeat the sentences.)

Here's a new way to use the word **kind.**

- What **kind** of cat is that? Say the sentence.
- What **kind** of hat is that? Say the sentence.
- I like the **kind** of game where everyone plays on the same team. Say the sentence.

In these sentences, kind is a naming word that means sort or type. What naming word means "sort or type"? *Kind.*

Raise your hand if you can tell us a sentence that uses **kind** as naming word meaning "sort or type." (Call on several children. If they don't use complete sentences, restate their examples as sentences. Have the class repeat the sentences.)

Present Expanded Target Vocabulary

Attractive

In *A Busy Day at Mr. Kang's Grocery Store,* Mr. Kang swept the floor, arranged the fruit, and put out fresh flowers. He did all these things so his store would look nice and attract people's attention as they walked by. Another way of saying Mr. Kang's store looked nice is to say Mr. Kang's store was attractive. **Attractive.** Say the word. *Attractive.*

Attractive is a describing word. It tells more about something. What kind of word is **attractive?** *A describing word.*

When someone or something is attractive, it is nice to look at. Say the word that means "nice to look at." *Attractive.*

I'll tell about some people or places that might be attractive. If what I tell about is attractive, say "attractive." If not don't say anything.

- My grandma's garden is nice to look at. *Attractive.*
- The twins are good looking. *Attractive.*
- The troll had warts, a huge nose, and a snaggle-tooth.
- Legolas was a handsome elf. *Attractive.*
- The dog looked as though someone had given him a bad haircut.
- The mountain view was beautiful to look at. *Attractive.*
- It was so dark in the room that we couldn't even see what it looked like.

What describing word means "nice to look at"? *Attractive.*

Successful

In *A Busy Day at Mr. Kang's Grocery Store,* everyone in the neighborhood goes to Mr. Kang's store to buy fresh fruit, flowers, or a cup of tea. Mr. Kang sold lots of things and earned lots of money. Mr. Kang's business was successful. **Successful.** Say the word. *Successful.*

Successful is a describing word. It tells more about something. What kind of word is **successful?** *A describing word.*

If you are successful, you are doing well at something you want to do. If you want to learn to ride your bike, you work really hard at learning to ride. You practice and practice and practice. Then one day, you can ride your bike. You are **successful.** Say the word that means "doing well at something you want to do." *Successful.*

I'll tell about some people. If you think those people are successful, say "successful." If not, don't say anything.

- The man who owned the gas station had lots of customers. *Successful.*
- Mia won the spelling bee. *Successful.*
- No customers ever came into Mrs. Smith's bookstore.
- Marian Anderson, the singer, had thousands of people wanting to hear her sing. *Successful.*
- I learned how to cook but I wasn't good at it.
- NASA brought Apollo 13 back to Earth safely even though it was damaged. *Successful.*

What describing word means "doing well at something you want to do"? *Successful.*

Make Connections (Build a Web)

Today I'll show you the photographs taken for *A Busy Day at Mr. Kang's Grocery Store.* Mr. Kang is a grocery store owner. As I show you the pictures, I'll call on one of you to tell more about grocery store owners.

Tell me what you know about where Mr. Kang works. What do you call the place where Mr. Kang works? <u>*A grocery store.*</u> (Add a circle to the web for grocery store.)

Pages 12–15 and 23. (Read pages 12 and 13.) Mr. Kang has many things in his store that help him arrange, display, and sell things. These things are called **equipment.** (Add a circle to the web for equipment.) What equipment might you find in a grocery store? (Ideas: <u>*Coolers; shelves; counters; broom; cash register; scale.*</u>)

Mr. Kang sells many different things in his store. The things he sells are called **merchandise.** What merchandise might be in a grocery store? (Ideas: <u>*Fruit and vegetables [pineapple, bananas; grapes; oranges; cantaloupe; avocadoes; onions; ginger; mushrooms]; milk; juice; cookies; flowers; film; shampoo; soup; salad dressings; crackers.*</u>)

Pages 6–17. (Read the text as well as show the pictures.) What jobs does Mr. Kang do? (Add a circle to the web for work.) (Ideas: <u>*unlocks the door; sweeps the floor; arranges the fruit; puts out fresh flowers; fills the cash register; orders supplies.*</u>)

Pages 14–15. What else does Mr. Kang do? (Ideas: <u>*Welcomes the customers; sells them things; weighs fruit.*</u>)

(Repeat this process for *clothes*, showing the appropriate photographs in the book.)

Page 28. How do you know Mr. Kang likes his work? (Ideas: *He is happy; he keeps a really nice store; his dream of owning his own business came true.*)

Summarize the Book

Today we are going to summarize what we learned in the book *A Busy Day at Mr. Kang's Grocery Store.* I will write the summary on this piece of chart paper. Later we will read the summary together.

When we summarize, we use our own words to tell about the most important things in the book. What do we do when we summarize? *We use our own words to tell about the most important things in the book.*

Key words help us tell about the important ideas in our own words. (Point to the list of key words.) This is the list of key words that will help us write our summary. (Read each word to children. Ask children to repeat each word after you read it.)

(**Note:** You should write the summary in paragraph form. Explain to children that you indent the first line because the summary will be a paragraph.)

(Show the illustration on page 4.) This book tells about lots of people and things. We are going to write our summary about what Mr. Kang does at the grocery store. Who will our summary be about? *Mr. Kang.*

I'm going to start the summary with a sentence about Mr. Kang. (Show the illustration on pages 4 and 5.) Mr. Kang owns a grocery store. (Write the sentence on the chart. Touch under each word as you and children read the sentence aloud. Cross *grocery store* off of the list of key words.)

(Show the illustrations on pages 6 and 7.) The second sentence in our summary will tell about what Mr. Kang does in the morning before the customers come. We are writing a summary, so we are not going to tell everything that he does. Here's the second sentence of the summary: In the morning, Mr. Kang does many things to get ready for his customers. Let's read the second sentence of our summary together. (Touch under each word as you and children read the sentence aloud. Cross *customers* off of the list of key words.)

(Show the illustrations on pages 14 and 15.) The next two sentences of our summary will tell what Mr. Kang does when the customers come. We are writing a summary, so we are not going to tell everything that he does. Here's the next two sentences of the summary: When the customers come Mr. Kang welcomes them. He helps them with what they need. Let's read the next two sentences of our summary together. (Touch under each word as you and children read the sentences aloud. Cross *welcomes* off of the list of key words.)

(Show the illustration on page 18.) Who is with Mr. Kang in this illustration? *Mrs. Kang.* Raise your hand if you can tell us a sentence about what Mr. and Mrs. Kang do together at the grocery store. (Idea: *Mr. and Mrs. Kang work together at the grocery store.*) (Add the new sentence to the summary.) Let's read the next sentence of our summary together. (Touch under each word as you and children read the sentence aloud. Cross *together* off of the list of key words.)

(Show the illustration on page 26. Read the text aloud.) The next sentence in our summary will describe how Mr. Kang works when he is at the store. Raise your hand if you can tell us a sentence that describes how Mr. Kang works when he is at his store. (Idea: *Mr. Kang works hard at his store.* Add the new sentence to the summary.) Let's read the next sentence of our summary together. (Touch under each word as you and children read the sentence aloud. Cross *hard* off of the list of key words.)

(Show the illustrations on pages 30 and 31. Read the text aloud.) The last sentence we are going to write will tell how Mr. Kang feels at the end of the day. Raise your hand if you can tell us a sentence about how Mr. Kang feels in the evening. (Idea: *In the evening, Mr. Kang is tired and happy to go home to his family.* Add the new sentence to the summary.)

(Once the summary is finished, touch under each word as you and children read the summary aloud together.)

Sample summary:

Mr. Kang owns a grocery store. In the morning, Mr. Kang does many things to get ready for his customers. When the customers come, Mr. Kang welcomes them. He helps them with what they need. Mr. and Mrs. Kang work together at the grocery store. In the evening, Mr. Kang is tired and happy to go home to his family.

We did a great job of writing a summary.

Play the Choosing Game

Today, you will play the Choosing Game. Let's think about the six words we have learned: **business, customers, generous, kind, attractive,** and **successful.** (Display the Picture Vocabulary Cards.)

I will say a sentence that has two target words in it. You will have to choose the correct word for that sentence. Let's practice. (Display the word cards for the two words in each sentence as you say the sentence.)

- Are people who buy things in a store called **customers** or **business?** *Customers.*
- If something is nice to look at, is it **successful** or **attractive?** *Attractive.*
- If you are happy to share what you have with others, are you **sunrise** or **generous?** *Generous.*

If you tell me the correct answer, you will win one point. If you can't tell me the correct answer, I get the point.

Now you're ready to play the game. (Draw a T-chart on the board for keeping score. Children earn one point for each correct answer. If they make an error, correct them as you normally would, and record one point for yourself. Repeat missed words at the end of the game. Display the word cards for the two words in each sentence as you say the sentence.)

- If Al went into a toy store to buy a checkers game, would he be a **customer** or a **business?** *A customer.*
- If you own a company that makes or sells things to make money, do you own a **stretcher** or a **business?** *A business.*
- Which is a person: a **business** or a **customer?** *A customer.*
- If I sell flowers in my flower shop, do I own a **business** or a **successful?** *A business.*
- If my store is nice to look at, is it **kind** or **attractive?** *Attractive.*

(Count the points and declare a winner.) You did a great job of playing the Choosing Game.

DAY 4

Preparation: *Let's Go Shopping* Booklet.

Introduce Grocery Store Booklet

(Give each child a copy of the *Let's Go Shopping* Booklet.) My turn to read the title of the booklet. You touch under each word as I read it. Let's Go Shopping. What is the title? *Let's Go Shopping.*

(Hold up the booklet.) Open the booklet to page 1. (Point to the picture.) Who is this person? (Ideas: *Miss Rosa, a grocery store owner.*) Where is Miss Rosa? (Ideas: *At her grocery store; at her shop.*)

Touch the words under the picture in your booklet. My turn to read the words. You touch each word as I read it. This is Miss Rosa. She has a shop. Let's read the words together. *This is Miss Rosa. She has a shop.* Your turn. Read the words by yourselves. *This is Miss Rosa. She has a shop.* (Repeat the procedure for the remaining pages in the booklet.)

(Children should color the illustrations in their *Let's Go Shopping* booklet.)

Play the Choosing Game (Cumulative Review)

Let's play the Choosing Game. I will say a sentence that has two target words in it. You will have to choose the correct word for that sentence. (Display the Picture Vocabulary Cards for *business, customers, kind, generous, attractive,* and *successful* for two words in each sentence as you say the sentence.)

Now you're ready to play the Choosing Game. (Draw a T-chart on the board for keeping score. Children earn one point for each correct answer. If they make an error, correct them as you normally would, and record one point for yourself. Repeat missed words at the end of the game.)

- If a person buys things in a store, is that person a **kind** or a **customer?** *A customer.*
- If you went to a place where you could buy things, would you go to an **attractive** or a **business?** *A business.*
- If you are doing well at something you want to do, are you a **customer** or **successful?** *Successful.*
- If your store is nice to look at, is it **attractive** or **generous?** *Attractive.*
- If I ask you what type of dog you have, am I asking you what **kind** of dog or how **attractive** the dog is? *What kind.*
- If you are friendly, helpful, and considerate, are you **generous** or **kind?** *Kind.*
- If you are happy to share what you have with others, are you **generous** or in **business?** *Generous.*

Now you will have to listen very carefully, because I'm not going to show you the word cards. (This part of the game includes review words collected from previous lessons.)

- If the grocery owner paid attention to what her customers needed, wanted, or wished for, was she **uncooperative** or **considerate?** *Considerate.*
- If the pineapples in the grocery store tasted very, very good, were they **delicious** or **imaginary?** *Delicious.*

- If the bananas in the grocery store looked so good they made you really want to have one, were they **tempting** or **annoying?** *Tempting.*
- If the grocery store owner had lots of jobs to do nearly every day, did he have **chores** or **glees?** *Chores.*
- If the skin on the cantaloupe was bumpy, was it **bare** or **rough?** *Rough.*
- If the grocery store owner made up his mind he wanted his business to succeed and he wouldn't let anything stop him, was he **rude** or **determined?** *Determined.*
- If the grocery store owner was thankful for the customers who came into his store, did he **appreciate** his customers or **bother** them? *Appreciate.*
- If the customer was mad at the grocery store owner because he didn't like what the grocery store owner did, was the customer **polite** or **cross?** *Cross.*

(Tally the points and declare a winner.) You did a great job of playing the Choosing Game.

DAY 5

Preparation: *Let's Go Shopping* booklet.

Chart titled *Reading Goals* that was started in Week 21.

Happy Face Game Test Sheet, BLM B.

Read the Let's Go Shopping Booklet

(Assign each child a partner.) Today you'll read your booklet about shopping in a grocery store to your partner. (Allow sufficient time for each child to read the booklet to his or her partner. Circulate as the children read, offering praise and assistance.)

(Ask children to look at the back of their booklet about shopping for groceries.) This part of the booklet is for people who can help you find other books to read. It tells those people about other books that are like *A Busy Day at Mr. Kang's Grocery Store.* It also tells them about a place where you can find other books. Where are some places that you could go to

find other books about grocery store workers or other workers in our community? (Ideas: *To the school library; to the public library; to a bookstore.*)

(You may wish to read and discuss the information on the back cover.)

There's one more important thing on the back cover of your book. Touch the box that is at the bottom of the page. The words above the box say "My reading goal." What do the words say? *My reading goal.*

A goal is something that you want to succeed at doing. What is a goal? *Something that you want to succeed at doing.* A reading goal is something that you want to succeed at doing with your reading.

Let's see if we can add some other reading goals to our class chart. What are some other reading goals that someone might have when they read their book? (Accept reasonable responses. Help children put their ideas into goal statements. Add to the list of statements on the chart. Ask children to choose a goal and copy it into the box. Children may also make up an original goal that is not on the list. If children are unable to copy the goals or to write a goal of their own, you or a helper may wish to scribe their goal statements for them before the booklets are sent home.)

Assess Vocabulary

 (Give each child a copy of the Happy Face Game Test Sheet, BLM B.)

Today you're going to play the Happy Face Game. When you play the Happy Face Game, it shows me how well you know the hard words you are learning.

If I say something that is true, color in the happy face. What will you do if I say something that is true? *Color in the happy face.*

If I say something that is false, color in the sad face. What will you do if I say something that is false? *Color in the sad face.*

Listen carefully to each item that I say. Don't let me trick you!

Item 1: A **business** sells things that people want to buy. (*True.*)

Item 2: If you are **successful,** you can't do anything right. (*False.*)

Item 3: A **generous** person keeps everything for himself or herself. (*False.*)

Item 4: There are many different **kinds** of vegetables. (*True.*)

Item 5: **Customers** buy things in a store. (*True.*)

Item 6: You can show that you are **kind** by doing nice things for other people. (*True.*)

Item 7: If a picture is **attractive,** it is nice to look at. (*True.*)

Item 8: When a nurse **treats** you for an illness, he or she takes care of you when you are sick. (*True.*)

Item 9: If you do something **immediately,** you do it right away. (*True.*)

Item 10: When workers **load** a truck, they take things off of the truck. (*False.*)

You did a great job of playing the Happy Face Game!

(Score children's work. A child must score 9 out of 10 to be at the mastery level. If a child does not achieve mastery, insert the missed words as additional items in the games in next week's lessons. Retest those children individually for the missed items before they take the next mastery test.)

Extensions

Read a Book as a Reward

(Read *A Busy Day at Mr. Kang's Grocery Store,* or another book about grocery store workers, to children as a reward for their hard work.)

Introduce the Super Words Center

(Add the new Picture Vocabulary Cards to words from the previous weeks. Show children one of the word containers. Role-play with two to three children as you introduce each part of the game.)

Let's review how to play the game called *2 in 1* in the Super Words Center.

Let's think about how we work with our words in the Super Words Center.

You will work with a partner in the Super Words Center. Whom will you work with? *A partner.*

First you will draw two words out of the container. What do you do first? (Idea: *Draw two words out of the container.*) Show your partner both of the words. (Demonstrate.)

Next you will say a sentence that uses both of your words. What do you do next? (Idea: *I will say a sentence that uses both of my words.*) (Demonstrate.)

If you can use both of your words in one sentence, give yourself a point. Then give your partner a turn. (Demonstrate.)

What do you do next? *Give my partner a turn.*

Are You a Ladybug?
author: Judy Allen • illustrator: Tudor Humphries

Preparation: You will need a copy of *Are You a Ladybug?* for each day's lesson.

Number the pages of the story (beginning with 1 on the first page inside the cover) to assist you in asking comprehension questions at appropriate points.

Prepare a KWL chart titled *Ladybugs* on a sheet of chart paper

Post a copy of the Vocabulary Tally Sheet, BLM A, with this week's Picture Vocabulary Cards attached.

Each child will need one copy of the Homework Sheet, BLM 26a.

DAY 1

Introduce Series

For the next five weeks, we will be reading books about different animals. We will learn about five kinds of animals: ladybugs, spiders, dragonflies, snails, and ants. What animals will we read about? (Ideas: *Ladybugs; spiders; dragonflies; snails; ants.*)

All these books are true. When an author writes books about things that are true, those books are called nonfiction books. What kind of books are about true things? *Nonfiction books.*

Introduce Book

This week's book is called *Are You a Ladybug?* What's the title of this week's book? *Are You a Ladybug?*

This book was written by Judy Allen. Who's the author of *Are You a Ladybug? Judy Allen.*

Tudor Humphries made the pictures for this book. Who is the illustrator of *Are You a Ladybug? Tudor Humphries.* Who made the illustrations for this book? *Tudor Humphries.*

The cover of a book usually gives us some hints of what the book is about. Let's look at the front cover of *Are You a Ladybug?* What do you see in the illustration? (Ideas: *A ladybug walking; a ladybug flying; leaves.*)

🎯 Target Vocabulary

Tier II	Tier III
parents	nonfiction
congratulations	fact
human	
mistake	
*helpful	
*insect	

*Expanded Target Vocabulary Word

(Display the KWL chart.) Let's think about what we **know** about ladybugs. Raise your hand if you can tell us something you know about ladybugs. I'll write it down under the **K. K** stands for what we **know** about ladybugs. What does **K** stand for? *What we know about ladybugs.* (Record all children's responses under the *K* [know] section of the chart. Do not eliminate incorrect responses. They will be addressed in later lessons during the week.)

The things we know about ladybugs that are true are called **facts.** What are the true things we know about ladybugs called? *Facts.* (Point to the *K* column on the chart.) Some of the things you have told us are facts about ladybugs, and some of the things you have told us are not true. When we've finished reading *Are You a Ladybug?* we'll come back to our chart and look at it again.

Now let's think what you **want to know** about ladybugs. I'll write it down under the **W. W** stands for what we **want to know** about ladybugs. What does **W** stand for? *What we want to know about ladybugs.* (Record all children's questions under the *W* [want to know] section of the chart. If children tell about the ladybugs instead of ask questions, prompt them to ask a question.)

Take a Picture Walk

 (Encourage children to use target words in their answers.) We're going to take a picture walk through this book. When we take a picture walk through a nonfiction book, we look carefully at the pictures and tell what we see. When you look carefully at pictures, you **observe** those pictures. What do you do when you look carefully at pictures in a nonfiction book? *You observe those pictures.*

Pages 4–5. What do you observe? (Ideas: *Two ladybugs; some flowers; some leaves; some stems; a tiny bug; the ladybugs are crawling on the flowers.*)

Pages 6–7. What do you observe? (Ideas: *Leaves; a ladybug; eggs; a ladybug laying eggs; more eggs; bugs coming out of the eggs.*)

Pages 8–9. What do you observe? (Ideas: *Leaves; some funny bugs; one ladybug; the bugs are crawling on each other; the bugs are jumping on each other.*)

Page 10. What do you observe? (Ideas: *A leaf; a funny bug; three bugs crawling toward the funny bug.*)

Page 11. What do you observe? (Ideas: *A leaf; the funny bug is chasing three bugs.*)

Page 12. What do you observe? (Ideas: *A leaf; the funny bug; the funny bug looks different.*)

Page 13. What do you observe? (Ideas: *Leaves; an apple; a tree limb; two funny bugs; three other bugs.*)

Page 14. What do you observe? (Ideas: *Leaves; two funny bugs; one other bug; two funny bugs are lying on the leaf; they look different.*)

Page 15. What do you observe? (Ideas: *Two funny bugs; different-colored leaves; the funny bugs look really different now.*)

Pages 16–17. What do you observe? (Ideas: *A limb with prickles or thorns; leaves; a yellow bug is coming out of the funny bug; one yellow bug is crawling off the page.*)

Pages 18–19. What do you observe? (Ideas: *A limb with prickles or thorns; leaves; six ladybugs crawling across the limbs; the first ladybugs have light spots; the last ladybugs have dark spots.*)

Pages 20–21. What do you observe? (Ideas: *A limb with prickles or thorns; leaves; four ladybugs; one is sitting on the branch; three are flying away.*)

Page 22. What do you observe? (Ideas: *Flowers; leaves; a ladybug flying toward the flowers.*)

Page 23. What do you observe? (Ideas: *Flowers; leaves; a stem; a ladybug chasing another bug.*)

Pages 24–25. What do you observe? (Ideas: *A lady holding an umbrella; the umbrella has spots on it like a ladybug; she has a green coat; she's smiling; a man has a red tie with spots on it like a ladybug; he's wearing a dark shirt and an orange vest; a man and a woman standing next to each other; the man has a red necktie with spots on it like a ladybug.*)

Page 26. What do you observe? (Ideas: *A tree stump; grass; a child jumping off the stump; she's trying to fly like a ladybug; she has a red bow with black spots in her hair; a little ladybug flying in the sky.*)

Page 29. What do you observe? (Ideas: *A girl; leaves; roses; a rosebud with little bugs on it; one ladybug; the girl has a ladybug ribbon in her hair.*)

Read the Book Aloud

 (Read the story to children with minimal interruptions, ending with page 29.)

Tomorrow we will read the book again, and I will ask you some questions.

Present Target Vocabulary
◎ Parents

In the book, the author asks the question, "Are you a ladybug?" Then she answers the question by saying, "If you are, your parents look like this, and they eat aphids." **Parents.** Say the word. *Parents.*

Parents is a naming word. It names people or things. What kind of word is **parents?** *A naming word.*

In this book, parents are the animals that have babies. Say the word that means "animals that have babies." *Parents.*

(Correct any incorrect responses, and repeat the item at the end of the sequence.)

Let's think some animals that might have babies. I'll tell about some animals. If these animals have babies, say "parents." If not, don't say anything.

- The cow and the bull had a calf. *Parents.*
- The goose and the gander had five goslings. *Parents.*
- The young bear traveled alone.
- The doe and the buck had twin fawns. *Parents.*
- The queen bee laid thousands of eggs after she mated with the male bee. *Parents.*
- The ram and the sheep lived in the field with their three lambs. *Parents.*

What naming word means "animals that have babies"? *Parents.*

 Congratulations

In the story it says, "Congratulations, you're a ladybug!" The author was telling the ladybug it had done a good job growing up. **Congratulations.** Say the word. *Congratulations.*

Congratulations is a naming word. What kind of word is **congratulations?** *A naming word.*

If someone says congratulations, they want to tell you that you have done a good job at something. Say the word that people might say to you to tell you you've done a good job at something. *Congratulations.*

Let's think about some times when someone might say "Congratulations." I'll tell about a time. If someone might say congratulations, say "congratulations." If not, don't say anything.

- You learned to write all the letters in the alphabet. *Congratulations.*
- Your father got a new job. *Congratulations.*
- You learned to ride your bicycle. *Congratulations.*
- You left all your clothes lying on the floor in your bedroom.
- Your big brother passed his driver's test. *Congratulations.*
- You forgot your homework at school.

What naming word do people say when they want to tell someone they have done a good job at something? *Congratulations.*

 Human

In the book, the author says, "You are not a ladybug; you are a human." **Human.** Say the word. *Human.*

Human is a naming word. It names a person. What kind of word is **human?** *A naming word.*

If someone is a human, they are a person. Say the word that means "a person." *Human.*

I'll name some things. If I name a person, say "human." If not, don't say anything.

- My new baby brother. *Human.*
- An ant.
- A police officer. *Human.*
- The Billy Goats Gruff.
- Your aunt. *Human.*
- The President of the United States. *Human.*

What naming word means "a person"? *Human.*

 Mistake

In the book, it says if the young ladybug looks at its brothers and sisters, it might think they have all made a big mistake. That means it might have thought they had all done something that was wrong. **Mistake.** Say the word. *Mistake.*

Mistake is a naming word. It names a thing. What kind of word is **mistake?** *A naming word.*

A mistake is a thought or action that is wrong. Say the word that means "a thought or action that is wrong." *Mistake.*

Let's think about some times when someone might make a mistake. I'll tell about a time. If you think the person has made a mistake, say "mistake." If not, don't say anything.

- The child said one plus one was three. *Mistake.*
- My name is Fay, but my friend called me Marilyn. *Mistake.*
- The child said *d-o-g* spelled **dog.**
- Mr. Chu turned left when he should have turned right. *Mistake.*
- When I phoned my mom, she answered right away.
- My grandparents drove right to our house.

What naming word means "a thought or action that is wrong"? *Mistake.*

Present Vocabulary Tally Sheet
(See Lesson 1, page 3, for instructions.)

Assign Homework
(Homework Sheet, BLM 26a. See the Introduction for homework instructions.)

DAY 2

Preparation: Picture Vocabulary Cards for *parents, congratulations, human, mistake.*

Read and Discuss Story

(Read story to children. Ask the following questions at the specified points. Encourage them to use target words in their answers.)

Page 4. What question did the author ask? (Idea: *Are you a ladybug?*) Are you a ladybug? *No.* How do you know you're not a ladybug? (Ideas: *I don't look like the bugs on the flower and I don't eat aphids; I'm a human.*) What do you think an aphid is? (Point to the aphid on the flower near the left-hand side of the illustration.) This is an aphid. What is an aphid? (Ideas: *A bug; an insect.*)

In this book, the author is pretending you are a ladybug. She talks to you as if you are a ladybug. How does the author talk to you? (Idea: *Like I'm a ladybug.*)

Pages 6–7. When your mother lays her eggs, where are you? (Idea: *Inside one of the eggs.*) What do you do inside the egg? (Idea: *Grow.*) When do you break out of the egg? (Idea: *After I have grown big enough.*)

Pages 8–9. How many brothers and sisters do you have? (Idea: *Lots.*) Why might you think you have all made a big mistake? (Idea: *None of us are the shape of a ladybug; none of us are the color of a ladybug.*) Should you worry? *No.* What should you do? (Idea: *Just eat.*)

Pages 10–11. What do you eat first? *My own eggshell.* What do you eat next? *Lots of aphids.*

Pages 12–13. What happens as you grow bigger? (Ideas: *My skin will feel tight; my skin will split down the middle.*) Then what will you do?

(Idea: *Wriggle out of my skin; take it off; then eat more aphids.*)

Pages 14–15. How many times will you take off your skin? (Idea: *Lots of times.*) What four things will you do on the day you feel very tired? (Ideas: *Stop eating; curl up; take off my skin; wait for my new skin to grow hard.*)

Pages 16–17. Tell me what you look like when your skin splits open for the last time. (Ideas: *I'm the shape of a ladybug; I'm not the right color for a ladybug.*)

Pages 18–19. What happens to you next? (Ideas: *My color gets stronger and my black dots appear.*) What has happened to you? (Idea: *I've turned into a ladybug.*)

Page 20. What can you do now? *Fly.*

Pages 22–23. How are you feeling now that you're a ladybug? *Hungry.* What will you eat? *Aphids.*

Pages 24–26. What are you? (Ideas: *A human; a human child.*) How do you know you're a human and not a ladybug? (Ideas: *My skin will not split as I grow; I can't fly; I am not red with black dots; I have only two legs.*)

Page 28. What are some of the things you can do that ladybugs can't do? (Encourage each child to suggest something he or she can do that a ladybug can't.) Are you glad you won't ever, ever have to eat aphids?

(Display the KWL chart.) Now that we've finished reading the book *Are You a Ladybug?* let's look at our chart again. (Point to the *Know* column.) As good scientists find out more about things, they sometimes change their minds about what they know is true. Let's see if we want to change our minds about any of the items on our **Know** list. (Read each item. Ask children if that item was mentioned in the book. If it was, ask if the item is true or not true. Untrue items should be crossed out.) We're good scientists; we know how to change our minds when we learn new facts.

(Point to the *Want to Know* column.) As good scientists find out more about things, they find answers to some of their questions, and they want to ask more questions. (Read each question. Ask children if the question was answered in the book. If it was, record the answer in the *L* (Learned) column and put a check mark in front of the question.) Are there any new questions we would like to ask about ladybugs? (Record questions under the *W* column.) We're good scientists; we know how to use what we have learned to ask new questions.

Review Vocabulary

(Display the Picture Vocabulary Cards. Point to each card as you say the word. Ask children to repeat each word after you.) These pictures show **parents, congratulations, human,** and **mistake.**

- What word means "a thought or action that is wrong"? *Mistake.*
- What word means "a person"? *Human.*
- What word do people say when they want to tell someone they have done a good job at something? *Congratulations.*
- What word means "animals that have babies"? *Parents.*

Extend Vocabulary
 Parents

In the book *Are You a Ladybug?* we learned that **parents** means "animals that have babies." Say the word that means "animals that have babies." *Parents.*

Raise your hand if you can tell us a sentence that uses **parents** as a naming word meaning "animals that have babies." (Call on several children. If they don't use complete sentences, restate their examples as sentences. Have the class repeat the sentences.)

Here's a new way to use the word **parents**.

- My **parents** take good care of me every day. Say the sentence.
- Her **parents** came to school to talk to her teacher. Say the sentence.
- His **parents** are sad when he is disobedient. Say the sentence.

In these sentences, parents is a naming word that means a human mother and father. What word means "a human mother and father"? *Parents.*

Raise your hand if you can tell us a sentence that uses **parents** as a naming word meaning "a human mother and father." (Call on several children. If they don't use complete sentences, restate their examples as sentences. Have the class repeat the sentences.)

Present Expanded Target Vocabulary
 Insect

In the book, we learned about ladybugs. A ladybug is an insect. **Insect.** Say the word. *Insect.*

Insect is a naming word. It names a group of animals. What kind of word is **insect**? *A naming word.*

An insect is a small animal that has three body parts and six legs. Most insects have wings. They also have hard shells on the outside of their bodies. Say the word that means "a small animal that has three body parts and six legs." *Insect.*

I'll name some animals. If those animals are insects, say "insects." If not, don't say anything.

- A housefly. *Insect.*
- A camel.
- A kitten.
- A butterfly. *Insect.*
- A cockroach. *Insect.*
- A wasp. *Insect.*

What naming word means "a small animal that has three body parts and six legs"? *Insect.*

 Helpful

In the book, we found out ladybugs eat aphids. Aphids are pests that damage plants in our gardens. Ladybugs eat aphids. So ladybugs are **helpful.** Say the word. *Helpful.*

Helpful is a describing word. It tells more about people and animals. What kind of word is **helpful**? *A describing word.*

If you are helpful you are able to help others. Say the word that means "able to help others." *Helpful.*

I'll tell about some people or animals. If the people or animals I name are being helpful, say "helpful." If not, don't say anything.

- Ricky takes the dog for a walk so his father doesn't have to. *Helpful.*
- Honeybees make honey. *Helpful.*
- Wasps sting.
- The baby cried and cried.
- Roberta handed out the papers for the teacher. *Helpful.*
- I ate all the apples.

What describing word means "able to help others"? *Helpful.*

DAY 3

Preparation: Display KWL chart.

Read Did You Know?

Today I'll read you some facts about ladybugs that Judy Allen put in the back of her book. (Read *Did You Know?* pages 30–31 with minimal interruptions.)

Complete KWL Chart

(Review the questions children still want answered from the *W* column of the KWL chart.) Let's see if Judy Allen answered any of our questions in the *Did You Know?* part of her book.

(Read the first item on page 30, beginning with the words, "Did you know …") Did these facts answer any of our questions? (If the item did answer any of the remaining questions, put a check mark in front of the question, and write the answer in the *L* column next to the question. Repeat the question, and have children say the answer. If the item did not answer any of the remaining questions, ask the children leading questions such as:) How much does a female ladybug eat? (Idea: *seventy aphids a day.*) What did we learn about female ladybugs? (Idea: *Female ladybugs eat seventy aphids a day.*) Record the fact in the *L* column near the bottom. Do not write the fact next to any of the unanswered questions.)

(Repeat the process for the remaining 4 items. If there are any unanswered questions after you have read and discussed the *Did You Know?* pages, challenge children to find the answers in the school library, on the Internet, or at home.)

Play What's My Word?

Today you will play *What's My Word?* I'll give you three clues. After I give each clue, if you are sure you know my word, you may make a guess. If you guess correctly, you will win one point. If you make a mistake, I get the point.

Let's practice. Here's my first clue. My word is a naming word. Are you sure you know my word? If you are, you may make a guess. (If anyone wishes to guess, accept the guess. Award the point to either the class or the teacher.)

Here's my second clue. My word starts with the "h" sound. Are you sure you know my word? If you are, you may make a guess. (If anyone wishes to guess, accept the guess. Award the point to either the class or the teacher.)

Here's my third clue. My word means a person. What's my word? *Human.* (Award the point to either the class or the teacher.)

(**Note:** If a child guesses the word correctly before the last clue, give the other clues and have children decide if the answer fits those clues.)

Now you're ready to play the game. (Draw a T-chart on the board for keeping score. Children earn one point for each correct answer. If they make an error, correct them as you normally would, and record one point for yourself. Repeat missed words at the end of the game.)

- Here's my first clue. My word is a naming word. Here's my second clue. My word has an "s" sound in it. Here's my third clue. My word is something you don't like to make. What's my word? *Mistake.*
- New word. Here's my first clue. My word is a naming word. Here's my second clue. My word has a "t" sound in it. Here's my third clue. My word can tell about your mother and father or animals that have babies. What's my word? *Parents.*
- New word. Here's my first clue. My word is a naming word. Here's my second clue. My word starts with an "h" sound. Here's my third

clue. My word is something that people would like about you. What's my word? *Helpful.*

- New word. Here's my first clue. My word is a naming word. Here's my second clue. My word has a "t" sound in it. Here's my third clue. My word is something you would like people to say to you if you had done something well. What's my word? *Congratulations.*

- New word. Here's my first clue. My word is a naming word. Here's my second clue. My word has legs. Here's my third clue. My word has six legs. What's my word? *Insect.*

(Count the points and declare a winner.) You did a great job of playing *What's My Word?*

DAY 4

Preparation: *About Ladybugs* booklet. Print the following words in a column on the board: *ladybug, lays, hatch, aphids, another, skin.*

Introduce About Ladybugs Booklet

(Point to each word as you read it.) This word is **ladybug.** What word? *Ladybug.* This word is **lays.** What word? *Lays.* (Repeat process for remaining words.)

Let's read these words together. First word? *Ladybug.* Next word? *Lays.* (Repeat process for remaining words.)

Read these words by yourself. First word? *Ladybug.* Next word? *Lays.* (Repeat process for remaining words until the children can read the list accurately and confidently.)

(Use the following correction procedure if children make an error:) This word is **aphids.** What word? *Aphids.* Yes, **aphids.** (Go back to the top of the list and repeat the list until children can read it accurately and confidently.)

(Give each child a copy of the *About Ladybugs* booklet.) My turn to read each page of the booklet. You touch under each word as I read it.

Let's read the booklet together. (Have children read the story aloud with you.)

(Assign each child a partner. Allow sufficient time for each child to read the book to his or her partner. Circulate as children read, offering praise and assistance.)

(Children should color the illustrations in their *About Ladybugs* booklet. Encourage them to color the illustrations accurately.) This book is a science book. When artists color scientific illustrations they use colors that are real. (Show the children the front cover of the booklet. Point to the ladybug.) What color should this part of the ladybug be? *Red.* What color should the spots be? *Black.* Remember to use the real colors when you color the illustrations.

Play What's My Word? (Cumulative Review)

Let's play *What's My Word?* You'll have to think really hard, because my word can be any word we've learned since we read *The Ant and the Grasshopper.* I'll give you three clues. After I give each clue, if you are sure you know my word, you may make a guess. If you guess correctly, you will win one point. If you make a mistake, I get the point.

Let's practice. Here's my first clue. My words are naming words. Are you sure you know my words? If you are, you may make a guess. (If anyone wishes to guess, accept the guess. Award the point to either the class or the teacher.)

Here's my second clue. My words name a building. Are you sure you know my words? If you are, you may make a guess. (If anyone wishes to guess, accept the guess. Award the point to either the class or the teacher.)

Here's my third clue. My words mean a place where firefighters work when they're not fighting fires. What are my words? *Fire station.* (Award the point to either the class or the teacher.)

(**Note:** If a child guesses the word correctly before the last clue, give the other clues and have children decide if the answer fits those clues.)

Now you're ready to play the game. (Draw a T-chart on the board for keeping score. Children earn one point for each correct answer. If they make an error, correct them as you normally would, and record one point for yourself. Repeat missed words at the end of the game.)

- Here's my first clue. My word starts with "dis." Here's my second clue. My word is an action word. Here's my third clue. My word means "can't be seen any more." What's my word? *Disappears.*

- New word. Here's my first clue. My word is a naming word. Here's my second clue. My word starts with the "m" sound. Here's my third clue. My word means "a thought or action that is wrong." What's my word? *Mistake.*

- New word. Here's my first clue. My word is a naming word. Here's my second clue. My word ends with the "s" sound. Here's my third clue. My word is something someone might say to you if you had won a race. What's my word? *Congratulations.*

- New word. Here's my first clue. My word is a describing word. Here's my second clue. My word ends with the "ing" sound. Here's my third clue. My word means "so hungry you think you might die." What's my word? *Starving.*

- New word. Here's my first clue. My word can be used to mean two different things. Here's my second clue. My word starts with the "p" sound. Here's my third clue. My word means "a human mother and father." What's my word? *Parents.*

- New word. Here's my first clue. My word is a naming word. Here's my second clue. My word tells about an animal that has six legs. Here's my third clue. My word tells about an animal that has three body parts. What's my word? *Insect.*

- New word. Here's my first clue. I have legs. Here's my second clue. My name starts with the sound "h." Here's my third clue. I can be a police officer. What's my word? *Human.*

- New word. Here's my first clue. My word is a naming word. Here's my second clue. My word has a "p" sound in it. Here's my third clue. My word means "able to help others." What's my word? *Helpful.*

- New word. Here's my first clue. My word starts with "ex." Here's my second clue. My word is a describing word. Here's my third clue. My word means "very, very tired." What's my word? *Exhausted.*

(Count the points and declare a winner.) You did a great job of playing *What's My Word?*

DAY 5

Preparation: *About Ladybugs* booklet.

Chart titled *Reading Goals* that was started in Week 21.

Happy Face Game Test Sheet, BLM B.

Read About Ladybugs Booklet

(Assign each child a partner.) Today you'll read your booklet, *About Ladybugs,* to your partner. (Allow sufficient time for each child to read the book to his or her partner. Circulate as the children read, offering praise and assistance.)

(Ask children to look at the back of their booklet about ladybugs.) This part of the booklet is for people who can help you find other books to read. It tells those people about other books that are like *Are you a Ladybug?* It also tells them about a place where you can find other books. Where are some places that you could go to find other books about ladybugs or other insects? (Ideas: *To the school library; to the public library; to a bookstore.*)

(You may wish to read and discuss the information on the back cover.)

There's one more important thing on the back cover of your book. Touch the box that is at the bottom of the page. The words above the box say "My reading goal." What do the words say? *My reading goal.*

A goal is something that you want to succeed at doing. What is a goal? *Something that you want to succeed at doing.* A reading goal is something that you want to succeed at doing with your reading.

Let's see if we can add some other reading goals to our class chart. What are some other reading goals that someone might have when they read their book? (Accept reasonable responses. Help children put their ideas into goal statements. Add to the list of statements on the chart. Ask children to choose a goal and copy it into the box. Children may also make up an original goal that is not on the list. If children are unable to copy the goals or to write a goal of their own, you or a helper may wish to write their goal statements for them before the booklets are sent home.)

Assess Vocabulary

 (Give each child a copy of the Happy Face Game Test Sheet, BLM B.)

Today you're going to play the Happy Face Game. When you play the Happy Face Game, it shows me how well you know the hard words you are learning.

If I say something that is true, color in the happy face. What will you do if I say something that is true? *Color in the happy face.*

If I say something that is false, color in the sad face. What will you do if I say something that is false? *Color in the sad face.*

Listen carefully to each item that I say. Don't let me trick you!

Item 1: Your **parents** are your brothers and sisters. (*False.*)

Item 2: If you try to **fool** someone, you try to trick them. (*True.*)

Item 3: Your mother does not like it when you're **helpful.** (*False.*)

Item 4: You would say, **"Congratulations!"** to your friend if she fell and skinned her knee. (*False.*)

Item 5: If your teacher **demanded** that you stand quietly, she used a forceful voice. (*True.*)

Item 6: A robin is an **insect.** (*False.*)

Item 7: A lamb has **parents.** (*True.*)

Item 8: If you called your teacher by the wrong name, you would have made a **mistake.** (*True.*)

Item 9: A person who does things in a **proper** way does not do them correctly. (*False.*)

Item 10: All people are **humans.** (*True.*)

You did a great job of playing the Happy Face Game!

(Score children's work. A child must score 9 out of 10 to be at the mastery level. If a child does not achieve mastery, insert the missed words as additional items in the games in next week's lessons. Retest those children individually for the missed items before they take the next mastery test.)

Extensions

Read a Book as a Reward

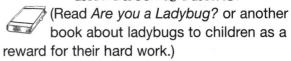 (Read *Are you a Ladybug?* or another book about ladybugs to children as a reward for their hard work.)

Preparation: Word containers for the Super Words Center.

Note: You will need to keep the cards that were removed from the center. They will be used again later in the program.

Introduce the Super Words Center

 (Put the Picture Vocabulary Cards from weeks 1 and 26 into the word cans. Make duplicates of each card to create a "Concentration" game. (You may make as many sets of duplicates as you wish to suit your class.)

(Show children one of the word containers. Demonstrate how the game is played by role-playing the game with a child. Repeat the demonstration process until the children can play the game with confidence.)

Let's think about how we work with our words in the Super Words Center.

You will work with a partner in the Super Words Center. Whom will you work with in the center? *A partner.*

There are two cards for each word in the Super Words Center. You will play a game called *Concentration.* When you play *Concentration,* you try to find two cards that match. **Match** means that both cards show the same picture and word. What does **match** mean? *Both cards show the same picture and word.*

First you will take all of the cards out of the container and place them facedown in rows on the table. What do you do first? (Idea: *Take all of the cards out and place them facedown in rows on the table.*)

Next you pick one card and turn it faceup in its spot. What do you do next? (Idea: *I pick a card and turn it faceup in its spot.*)

Then ask your partner what word the picture shows. What do you do next? (Idea: *I ask my partner what word the picture shows.*)

If your partner doesn't know the word, tell them the word. What do you do if your partner doesn't know the word? *Tell my partner the word.*

Then you will give your partner a turn. What do you do next? *Give my partner a turn.*

If your partner turns over a card that is the same as your card, he or she can take those two cards. What can your partner do? (Idea: *He or she can take both cards if he or she chooses one that is the same as my first card.*)

If your partner doesn't find one that is the same, he or she leaves both cards faceup in their spots. Then it is your turn again. Now there are two cards you can find a match for.

Whoever has the most pairs of cards when all of the cards have been taken is the winner.

(There are many ways to play *Concentration.* This is one that is fast to play. You may choose to modify the game depending on children's skill level.)

Preparation: You will
need a copy of *Are You a Spider?* for each day's lesson.

Number the pages of the story (beginning with 1 on the first page inside the cover) to assist you in asking comprehension questions at appropriate points.

Prepare a KWL chart titled *Spiders* on a sheet of chart paper

Post a copy of the Vocabulary Tally Sheet, BLM A, with this week's Picture Vocabulary Cards attached.

Each child will need one copy of the Homework Sheet, BLM 27a.

DAY 1

Introduce Book

This week's book is called *Are You a Spider?* What's the title of this week's book? *Are You a Spider?*

This book was written by Judy Allen. Who's the author of *Are You a Spider? Judy Allen.*

Tudor Humphries made the pictures for this book. Who is the illustrator of *Are You a Spider? Tudor Humphries.* Who made the illustrations for this book? *Tudor Humphries.*

The cover of a book usually gives us some hints of what the book is about. Let's look at the front cover of *Are You a Spider?* What do you see in the illustration? (Ideas: *A spider on a web; two smaller spiders; leaves and flowers.*)

(Display the KWL chart.) Let's think about what we **know** about spiders. Raise your hand if you can tell us something you know about spiders. I'll write it down under the **K. K** stands for what we **know** about spiders. What does **K** stand for? *What we know about spiders.* (Record all children's responses under the *K* (know) section of the chart. Do not eliminate incorrect responses. They will be addressed in later lessons during the week.)

Are You a Spider?
author: Judy Allen • illustrator: Tudor Humphries

Target Vocabulary

Tier II	Tier III
special	nonfiction
perfect	fact
attach	
definitely	
*enemies	
*predator	

*Expanded Target Vocabulary Word

The things we know about spiders that are true are called facts. What are the true things we know about spiders called? *Facts.*

(Point to the *K* column on the chart.) Some of the things you have told us are facts about spiders, and some of the things you have told us are not true. When we've finished reading the book *Are You a Spider?* we'll come back to our chart and look at it again.

Now let's think about what you **want to know** about spiders. I'll write it down under the **W. W** stands for what we **want to know** about spiders. What does **W** stand for? *What we want to know about spiders.* (Record all children's questions under the *W* (want to know) section of the chart. If the children tell about the spiders instead of ask questions, prompt them to ask a question.)

Take a Picture Walk

(Encourage children to use target words in their answers.) We're going to take a picture walk through this book. When we take a picture walk through a nonfiction book, we look carefully at the pictures and tell what we see. When you look carefully at pictures, you **observe** those pictures. What do you do when you look carefully at pictures in a nonfiction book? *You observe those pictures.*

Pages 4–5. What do you observe? (Ideas: *One spider; a spider web; some leaves; some stems; the sun; a beautiful sky.*)

Pages 6–7. What do you observe? (Ideas: *Leaves; a stem;* flowers; *a big spider; a lot of small baby spiders on the web and on the plants; a big spider web.*)

Pages 8–9. What do you observe? (Ideas: *A big spider with a colorful body; 8 hairy legs; two arms; a part of a spider web.*)

Pages 10–11. What do you observe? (Ideas: *Leaves; flowers; one small spider and a piece of web hanging from the spider.*)

Pages 12–13. What do you observe? (Ideas: *Leaves; flowers; three spiders on different lines of web; the spiders are upside down; the line of web is connected to two different plants.*)

Pages 14–15. What do you observe? (Ideas: *Lots of leaves; one spider; a start of a spider web; the web is connected to different plants.*)

Pages 16–17. What do you observe? (Ideas: *Plants; a spider; the spider is working on a spider web; the spider is making the round parts for the web.*)

Pages 18–19. What do you observe? (Ideas: *Plant stems with prickles or thorns; leaves; a finished spider web; a spider; two flies caught in the web—one fly has been spun into the web, the other looks like it just got caught.*)

Pages 20–21. What do you observe? (Ideas: *A large number of birds; a leaf; a small bit of spider web; the spider; the spider looks like it is trying to hide from the birds.*)

Pages 22–23. What do you observe? (Ideas: *A big wasp, the spider and the spider web; the wasp is stuck in the web.*)

Pages 24–25. What do you observe? (Ideas: *Different pictures of children; reflections of children; four mirrors; two spiders; a spider web between two mirrors.*)

Pages 26–27. What do you observe? (Ideas: *A boy with a spider on his shirt; two girls and another boy; a shadow of the kids on the wall; a light beam.*) What does the shadow look like? *A spider.*

Pages 28–29. What do you observe? (Ideas: *A boy who is watching a wasp; a spider on its web; a bug caught in the web; leaves and flowers.*)

Pages 30–31. What do you observe? (Ideas: *One big spider; four small spiders; some strings of spider web; flowers; and leaves.*)

Read the Book Aloud

(Read the story to children with minimal interruptions, ending with page 29.)

Tomorrow we will read the book again, and I will ask you some questions.

Present the Target Vocabulary

Special

In the book, the mother spider lays her eggs and wraps them in a special silk pouch. **Special.** Say the word. *Special.*

Special is a describing word. It describes a thing. What kind of word is **special?** *A describing word.*

Special means not ordinary or better than usual. Say the word that means "not ordinary" or "better than usual." *Special.*

(Correct any incorrect responses, and repeat the item at the end of the sequence.)

Let's think about some things that are special. If you think something is special, say "special." If not, don't say anything.

- It is my birthday today. *Special.*
- My dog had puppies today. *Special.*
- I can hear the phone ringing.
- I saw a truck drive on the road.
- It is pizza day at school. *Special.*
- I ate the same old sandwich for lunch.

What naming word means "not ordinary" or "better than usual"? *Special.*

Perfect

In the story, the baby spider looks perfect, with a tiny waist and eight hairy legs. **Perfect.** Say the word. *Perfect.*

Perfect is a describing word. It describes a thing. What kind of word is **perfect?** *A describing word.*

Perfect means exactly right. Say the word that means "exactly right." *Perfect.*

Let's think about some times when something is perfect. I'll tell about a time. If something is perfect, say "perfect." If not, don't say anything.

- Jennifer spelled all the words correctly on the spelling test. *Perfect.*
- There is an old car in the parking lot.
- Kevin got 10 out of 10 on the test. *Perfect.*
- You forgot to help with the laundry.
- Mark cleaned his room exactly right. *Perfect.*
- You forgot your homework at school.

What describing word means "exactly right"? *Perfect.*

◎═ Attach

In the book, the spider first must attach the threads of her web to something. Then she must attach sticky threads to the border threads. **Attach.** Say the word. *Attach.*

Attach is an action word. It tells what someone or something does. What kind of word is **attach?** *An action word.*

Attach means to join or connect things. Say the word that means "to join or connect things." *Attach.*

I'll name some things. If I name a thing that is attached, say "attached." If not, don't say anything.

- Tape holding together two pieces of paper. *Attached.*
- Light is shining through the window.
- Leaves on a limb. *Attached.*
- The hair on a dog. *Attached.*
- A garbage can on the floor.
- Milk in a milk carton.

What action word means "to join or connect things"? *Attach.*

◎═ Definitely

In the book, we learned that if you are a human child, you definitely do not have spinnerets and cannot spin silk thread. **Definitely.** Say the word. *Definitely.*

Definitely is a describing word. It tells more about what you know. What kind of word is **definitely?** *A describing word.*

Definitely means for sure. Say the word that means "for sure." *Definitely.*

I'll name some things. If you know for sure, say "definitely." If not, don't say anything.

- How to eat a cookie. *Definitely.*
- How to walk. *Definitely.*
- How many lakes there are in the world.
- How to talk. *Definitely.*
- How to laugh. *Definitely.*
- How to fly a spaceship.

What naming word means "for sure"? *Definitely.*

Present Vocabulary Tally Sheet
(See Lesson 1, page 3, for instructions.)

Assign Homework
(Homework Sheet, BLM 27a. See the Introduction for homework instructions.)

DAY 2

Preparation: Picture Vocabulary Cards for *special, perfect, attach, definitely.*

Read and Discuss Story

(Read story to children. Ask the following questions at the specified points. Encourage them to use target words in their answers.)

Pages 4–5. What question did the author ask? *Are you a spider?* Are you a spider? *No.* How do you know you're not a spider? (Ideas: *I don't look like the spider on the web; I'm not that small; I'm a human.*) In this book, the author is pretending you are a spider. She talks to you as if you are a spider. How does the author talk to you? (Idea: *Like I'm a spider.*)

Pages 6–7. When your mother lays her eggs, where are you? (Idea: *Inside one of the eggs.*) What do you do inside the egg? *Grow.* How many brothers and sisters do you have? *Lots.*

Pages 8–9. Why does the author think you look perfect? (Idea: *Spiders are supposed to have eight hairy legs, two handy claws and a tiny waist.*) *How many eyes do you have? Eight. What helps you spin webs?* (Idea: *Six spinnerets hidden under my body.*)

Pages 10–11. What is the most important thing in your life? *Silk thread.* What does the silk thread help you do? (Idea: *It helps me travel in the air.*)

Pages 12–13. What is another way you can travel? (Ideas: *Walking on the silk thread.*) If you fall what can you do? (Idea: *Wait until I stop swinging and then climb back up the thread.*)

Pages 14–15. What is a hard job you have to do? (Idea: *Build a web.*) Building a web may be hard work, but what is one good thing you get out of it? (Idea: *The web will catch flies and flies are good to eat.*)

Pages 16–17. What is the hardest part of building a web? (Ideas: *Attaching the threads that are very sticky.*) Why do you think the spider wants these threads to be sticky? (Idea: *So that flies and other bugs will get caught in the web.*)

Pages 18–19. What should you do if a fly is caught in your web? (Ideas: *I should run up and bite it.*) What does the bite do to the fly? (Idea: *It makes it go to sleep.*) What do you do if you are not really hungry right now and want to save the fly for later? (Idea: *Wrap it up in silk thread.*) What do you think you will do with this fly? (Idea: *Save it for later because I already have another fly to eat.*)

Pages 20–21. What do you need to be watchful of? *Birds.* Why don't you like birds? (Idea: *Birds like to eat spiders.*) Why is it important to keep one foot on the web? (Idea: *I want to feel the web shake if a fly gets caught in it. I have to run out and bite it before it gets away.*)

Pages 22–23. What is another thing you need to be careful of? *Wasps.* Why do you worry about wasps? (Idea: *Their sting can kill spiders.*) What is the best thing to do if a wasp gets caught in your web? (Idea: *Cut it free.*)

Pages 24–27. What are you? (Ideas: *A human; a human child.*) How do you know you're a human and not a spider? (Ideas: *I don't have eight eyes and eight legs; I don't eat flies; and I can't spin silk thread; I'm big.*)

Pages 28–29. What are some of the things you can do that spiders can't do? (Encourage each child to suggest something he or she can do that a spider can't.) Are you glad you won't ever, ever have to eat flies?

(Display the KWL chart.) Now that we've finished reading *Are You a Spider?* let's look at our chart again. (Point to the *Know* column.) As good scientists find out more about things, they sometimes change their minds about what they know is true.

Let's see if we want to change our minds about any of the items on our **Know** list. (Read each item. Ask children if that item was mentioned in the book. If it was, ask if the item is true or not true. Untrue items are crossed out.) We're good scientists; we know how to change our minds when we learn new facts.

(Point to the *Want to Know* column.) As good scientists find out more about things, they find answers to some of their questions and they want to ask more questions. (Read each question. Ask children if the question was answered in the book. If it was, record the answer in the *L* (Learned) column and put a check mark in front of the question.)

Are there any new questions we would like to ask about spiders? (Record questions under the *W* column on the chart.) We're good scientists; we know how to use what we have learned to ask new questions.

Review Vocabulary

(Display the Picture Vocabulary Cards. Point to each card as you say the word. Ask children to repeat each word after you.) These pictures show **special, perfect, attach,** and **definitely.**

- What word means "not ordinary or better than usual"? *Special.*
- What word means "to join or connect something"? *Attach.*
- What word means "exactly right"? *Perfect.*
- What word means "for sure"? *Definitely.*

Extend Vocabulary

 Special

In *Are You a Spider?* we learned that **special** means "not ordinary" or "better than usual." Say the word that means "not ordinary" or "better than usual." *Special.*

Raise your hand if you can tell us a sentence that uses **special** as a describing word meaning "not ordinary" or "better than usual." (Call on several children. If they don't use complete sentences, restate their examples as sentences. Have the class repeat the sentences.)

Here's a new way to use the word **special.**

- There was a **special** on noodles at the grocery store.
- I bought two shirts because they were on **special.**
- New cars are on **special** for today only.

In these sentences, special is a naming word that means a sale of certain things for lower prices. What word means "a sale of certain things for lower prices"? *Special.*

Raise your hand if you can tell us a sentence that uses **special** as a naming word meaning "a sale of certain things for lower prices." (Call on several children. If they don't use complete sentences, restate their examples as sentences. Have the class repeat the sentences.)

Present Expanded Target Vocabulary
◎═ Enemies

In the book, we found out that wasps and birds are dangerous to spiders. So, wasps and birds are a spider's **enemies.** Say the word. *Enemies.*

Enemies is a naming word. It names a person or animal. What kind of word is **enemies?** *A naming word.*

Enemies are animals or people who want to hurt or harm each other. Say the word that means "animals or people that want to hurt or harm each other." *Enemies.*

I'll tell about some animals. If the animals I name want to hurt or harm each other, say "enemies." If not, don't say anything.

- The fox chases the rabbit. *Enemies.*
- Two kittens play together.
- Clown fish live with the sea anemone.
- The polar bears hunted for seals. *Enemies.*
- A falcon swooped down and picked up a snake. *Enemies.*
- A gazelle runs from a hungry lion. *Enemies.*

What naming word means "animals or people that want to hurt or harm one another"? *Enemies.*

◎═ Predator

In the book, we found out that spiders catch flies for food and that birds eat spiders for food. When animals hunt other animals for food, we say the animals are predators. So, spiders and birds are both **predators. Predator.** Say the word. *Predator.*

Predator is a naming word. It names an animal. What kind of word is **predator?** *A naming word.*

A predator is an animal that hunts other animals for food. Say the word that means "an animal that hunts other animals for food." *Predator.*

I'll tell about some animals. If the animal I name is a predator, say "predator." If not, don't say anything.

- Renita's dog eats dry dog food.
- The lion chased the gazelle. *Predator.*
- The spider spun a web to catch flies. *Predator.*
- The rabbit ate lettuce from Mr. McGregor's garden.
- The snake leapt from behind the rock and bit the rabbit. *Predator.*
- The cow munched on the grass.

What naming word means "an animal that hunts other animals for food"? *Predator.*

DAY 3

Preparation: Display KWL chart.

Read Did You Know?
Today I'll read you some facts about spiders that Judy Allen put at the back of her book. (Read *Did You Know?* pages 30–31 with minimal interruptions.)

Complete KWL Chart
(Review the questions children still want answered from the *W* column of the KWL chart.) Let's see if Judy Allen answered any of our questions in the *Did You Know?* part of her book.

(Read the first item on page 30, beginning with the words, "Did you know …") Did these facts answer any of our questions? (If the item answered any of the remaining questions, put a check mark in front of the question, and write the answer in the *L* column next to the question. Repeat the question, and have children say the answer.)

(If the item did not answer any of the remaining questions, ask children leading questions such as:) What will spiders often do with a damaged web? (Idea: *They will eat it.*) What did we learn about spiders and their damaged webs? (Idea: *Spiders will often eat their damaged web.* Record the fact in the *L* column near the bottom. Do not write the fact next to any of the unanswered questions.)

(Repeat the process for the remaining three items. If there are any unanswered questions after you have read and discussed the *Did You Know?* pages, challenge children to find the answers in the school library, on the Internet, or at home.)

Play What's My Word?

Today you will play *What's My Word?* I'll give you three clues. After I give each clue, if you definitely know my word, you may make a guess. If you guess correctly, you will win one point. If you make a mistake, I get the point.

Let's practice. Here's my first clue. My word is a describing word. Are you sure you know my word? If you are, you may make a guess. (If anyone wishes to guess, accept the guess. Award the point to either the class or the teacher.)

Here's my second clue. My word starts with the "p" sound. Are you sure you know my word? If you are, you may make a guess. (If anyone wishes to guess, accept the guess. Award the point to either the class or the teacher.)

Here's my third clue. My word means "exactly right." What's my word? *Perfect.* (Award the point to either the class or the teacher.)

(**Note:** If a child guesses the word correctly before the last clue, give the other clues and have children decide if the answer fits those clues.)

Now you're ready to play the game. (Draw a T-chart on the board for keeping score. Children earn one point for each correct answer. If they make an error, correct them as you normally would, and record one point for yourself. Repeat missed words at the end of the game.)

- Here's my first clue. My word is a describing word. Here's my second clue. My word starts with an "s" sound. Here's my third clue. My word means "not ordinary" or "better than usual." It also means "a sale of certain things for lower prices." What's my word? *Special.*

- New word. Here's my first clue. My word is an action word. Here's my second clue. My word has a "t" sound in it. Here's my third clue. My word means "to join or connect something." What's my word? *Attach.*

- New word. Here's my first clue. My word is a describing word. Here's my second clue. My word has an "f" sound in it. Here's my third clue. My word means "for sure." What's my word? *Definitely.*

- New word. Here's my first clue. My word is a naming word. Here's my second clue. My word has a "d" sound in it. Here's my third clue. My word is something a small animal would be afraid of. What's my word? *Predator.*

- New word. Here's my first clue. My word is a naming word. Here's my second clue. My word names two animals. Here's my third clue. The two animals my word names want to hurt or harm each other. What's my word? *Enemies.*

(Count the points and declare a winner.) You did a great job of playing *What's My Word?*

DAY 4

Preparation: *About Spiders* booklet.
Print the following words in a column on the board: *spider, waist, claws, eyes, web, bite.*

Read the About Spiders Booklet

(Point to each word as you read it.) This word is **spider.** What word? *Spider.* This word is **waist.** What word? *Waist.* (Repeat process for remaining words.)

Let's read these words together. First word? *Spider.* Next word? *Waist.* (Repeat process for remaining words.)

Read these words by yourself. First word? *Spider.* Next word? *Waist.* (Repeat process for remaining words until children can read the list accurately and confidently.)

(Use the following correction procedure if children make an error:) This word is **claws.** What word? *Claws.* Yes, **claws.** (Go back to the top of the list and repeat the list until children can read it accurately and confidently.)

(Give each child a copy of the *About Spiders* booklet.) My turn to read each page of the booklet. You touch under each word as I read it. (After you have read page 1, have children point to each part of the spider on the illustration as you name it.)

Let's read the story together. (Have children read the story aloud with you.)

(Assign each child a partner. Allow sufficient time for each child to read the book to his or her partner. Circulate as the children read, offering praise and assistance.)

(Children should color the illustrations in their *About Spiders* booklet. Encourage them to color the illustrations accurately.) This book is a science book. When artists color scientific illustrations they use colors that are real. (Show children the front cover of the booklet. Point to the spider.) What are some colors that real spiders can be? (Ideas: *Black; brown.*) Remember to use the real colors when you color the illustrations.

Play What's My Word? (Cumulative Review)

Let's play *What's My Word?* You'll have to think really hard, because my word can be any word we've learned since we read *The Ant and the Grasshopper.* I'll give you three clues. After I give each clue, if you are sure you know my word, you may make a guess. If you guess correctly, you will win one point. If you make a mistake, I get the point.

Let's practice. Here's my first clue. My word is a describing word. Are you sure you know my word? If you are, you may make a guess. (If anyone wishes to guess, accept the guess. Award the point to either the class or the teacher.)

Here's my second clue. My word starts with the "j" sound. Are you sure you know my word? If you are, you may make a guess. (If anyone wishes to guess, accept the guess. Award the point to either the class or the teacher.)

Here's my third clue. My word describes something that is real, not fake. What's my word? *Genuine.* (Award the point to either the class or the teacher.)

(**Note:** If a child guesses the word correctly before the last clue, give the other clues and have children decide if the answer fits those clues.)

Now you're ready to play the game. (Draw a T-chart on the board for keeping score. Children earn one point for each correct answer. If they make an error, correct them as you normally would, and record one point for yourself. Repeat missed words at the end of the game.)

- Here's my first clue. My word is an action word. Here's my second clue. My word tells about something an animal does to stay alive in the winter. Here's my third clue. My word tells how animals spend the winter in a deep sleep. What's my word? *Hibernate.*
- New word. Here's my first clue. My word is a describing word. Here's my second clue. My word ends with the "ous" sound. Here's my third clue. My word describes someone who is interested in something and wants to know more about it. What's my word? *Curious.*
- New word. Here's my first clue. My word is a describing word. Here's my second clue. My word has an "f" sound in it. Here's my third clue. My word means that something is "exactly right." What's my word? *Perfect.*

- New word. Here's my first clue. My word is a naming word. Here's my second clue. My word ends with the sound "tion." Here's my third clue. My word means "the part of your mind that lets you make pictures of imaginary things or of things that didn't really happen." What's my word? *Imagination.*
- New word. Here's my first clue. My word can be used to mean two different things. Here's my second clue. My word starts with the "s" sound. Here's my third clue. Sometimes my word means that something is "on sale for a lower price." What's my word? *Special.*
- New word. Here's my first clue. My word is a naming word. Here's my second clue. My word ends in the "or" sound. Here's my third clue. My word names an animal that hunts other animals for food. What's my word? *Predator.*
- New word. Here's my first clue. My word is an action word. Here's my second clue. My word ends in the "ch" sound. Here's my third clue. My word means "to join or connect something." What's my word? *Attach.*
- New word. Here's my first clue. I am a rabbit. Here's my second clue. I am a fox. Here's my third clue. We don't like each other and want to harm each other. What's my word? *Enemies.*
- New word. Here's my first clue. My word describes what I already know. Here's my second clue. My word ends in "ly." Here's my third clue. My word means "for sure." What's my word? *Definitely.*

(Count the points and declare a winner.) You did a great job of playing *What's My Word?*

DAY 5

Preparation: *About Spiders* booklet.

Chart titled *Reading Goals* that was started in Week 21.

Happy Face Game Test Sheet, BLM B.

Read About Spiders Booklet

(Assign each child a partner.) Today you'll read your booklet, *About Spiders,* to your partner.

(Allow sufficient time for each child to read the book to his or her partner. Circulate as the children read, offering praise and assistance.)

(Ask the children to look at the back of their booklets about spiders.) This part of the booklet is for people who can help you find other books to read. It tells those people about other books that are like *Are you a Spider?* It also tells them about a place where you can find other books. Where are some places that you could go to find other books about spiders and other animals that are like spiders? (Ideas: *To the school library; to the public library; to a bookstore.*)

(You may wish to read and discuss the information on the back cover.)

There's one more important thing on the back cover of your booklet. Touch the box that is at the bottom of the page. The words above the box say "My reading goal." What do the words say? *My reading goal.*

A goal is something that you want to succeed at doing. What is a goal? *Something that you want to succeed at doing.* A reading goal is something that you want to succeed at doing with your reading.

Let's see if we can add some other reading goals to our class chart. What are some other reading goals that someone might have when they read their book? (Accept reasonable responses. Help children put their ideas into goal statements. Add to the list of statements on the chart. Ask children to choose a goal and copy it into the box. Children may also make up an original goal that is not on the list. If children are unable to copy the goals or to write a goal of their own, you or a helper may wish to scribe their goal statements for them before the booklets are sent home.)

Assess Vocabulary

 (Give each child a copy of the Happy Face Game Test Sheet, BLM B.)

Today you're going to play the Happy Face Game. When you play the Happy Face Game, it shows me how well you know the hard words you are learning.

If I say something that is true, color in the happy face. What will you do if I say something that is true? *Color in the happy face.*

If I say something that is false, color in the sad face. What will you do if I say something that is false? *Color in the sad face.*

Listen carefully to each item that I say. Don't let me trick you!

Item 1: If you don't know how to do something very well, you **definitely** know how to do it. (*False.*)

Item 2: A very long trip across the United States could be described as a **journey.** (*True.*)

Item 3: A rabbit eats only plants, so it is not a **predator.** (*True.*)

Item 4: If you are not very hungry, you might **devour** your dinner. (*False.*)

Item 5: Someone who is **persistent** does not give up easily. (*True.*)

Item 6: If you shove your toys and clothes under your bed, you have done a **perfect** job of cleaning your room. (*False.*)

Item 7: The day you were born was a very **special** day for your **parents.** (*True.*)

Item 8: If your chain falls off your bike, you don't need to **attach** it in order to ride the bike. (*False.*)

Item 9: If you did not want to hide your face you would put on a **mask.** (*False.*)

Item 10: Spiders and wasps are **enemies.** (*True.*)

You did a great job of playing the Happy Face Game!

(Score children's work. A child must score 9 out of 10 to be at the mastery level. If a child does not achieve mastery, insert the missed words as additional items in the games in next week's lessons. Retest those children individually for the missed items before they take the next mastery test.)

Extensions

Read a Book as a Reward

(Read *Are you a Spider?* or another book about spiders to children as a reward for their hard work.)

Preparation: Word containers for the Super Words Center.

Note: You will need to keep the cards that were removed from the center. They will be used again later in the program.

Introduce the Super Words Center

(Put the Picture Vocabulary Cards from weeks 2 and 27 into the word cans. Make duplicates of each card to create a "Concentration" game. You may make as many sets of duplicates as you wish to suit your class.)

(Show children one of the word containers. Demonstrate how the game is played by role-playing the game with a child. Repeat the demonstration process until the children can play the game with confidence.)

Let's think about how we work with our words in the Super Words Center.

You will work with a partner in the Super Words Center. Whom will you work with? *A partner.*

There are two cards for each word in the Super Words Center. You will play a game called *Concentration.* When you play *Concentration,* you try to find two cards that match. **Match** means that both cards show the same picture and word. What does **match** mean? *Both cards show the same picture and word.*

First you will take all of the cards out of the container and place them facedown in rows on the table. What do you do first? (Idea: *Take all of the words out and place them facedown in rows on the table.*)

Next you pick one card and turn it faceup in its spot. What do you do next? (Idea: *I pick a card and turn it faceup in its spot.*)

Then ask your partner what word the picture shows. What do you do next? (Idea: *I ask my partner what word the picture shows.*)

If your partner doesn't know the word, tell them the word. What do you do if your partner doesn't know the word? *Tell my partner the word.*

Then you will give your partner a turn. What do you do next? *Give my partner a turn.*

If your partner turns over a card that is the same as your card, he or she can take those two cards. What can your partner do? (Idea: *He or she can take both cards if he or she chooses one that is the same as my first card.*)

Are You a Dragonfly?
author: Judy Allen • illustrator: Tudor Humphries

Preparation: You will need a copy of *Are You a Dragonfly?* for each day's lesson.

- Number the pages of the story (beginning with 1 on the first page inside the cover) to assist you in asking comprehension questions at appropriate points.

- Prepare a KWL chart titled *Dragonflies* on a sheet of chart paper

- Post a copy of the Vocabulary Tally Sheet, BLM A, with this week's Picture Vocabulary Cards attached.

- Each child will need one copy of the Homework Sheet, BLM 28a.

Target Vocabulary

Tier II	Tier III
prey	nonfiction
beware	fact
bored	
hover	
*shed	
*aquatic	

*Expanded Target Vocabulary Word

The things we know about dragonflies that are true are called facts. What are the true things we know about dragonflies called? *Facts.*

(Point to the *K* column on the chart.) Some of the things you have told us are facts about dragonflies, and some of the things you have told us are not true. When we've finished reading *Are You a Dragonfly?* we'll come back to our chart and look at it again.

Now let's think what you **want to know** about dragonflies. I'll write it down under the **W**. **W** stands for what we **want to know** about dragonflies. What does **W** stand for? *What we want to know about dragonflies.* (Record all children's questions under the *W* (want to know) section of the chart. If children tell about dragonflies instead of ask questions, prompt them to ask a question.)

DAY 1

Introduce Book

This week's book is called *Are You a Dragonfly?* What's the title of this week's book? *Are You a Dragonfly?*

This book was written by Judy Allen. Who's the author of *Are You a Dragonfly? Judy Allen.*

Tudor Humphries made the pictures for this book. Who is the illustrator of *Are You a Dragonfly? Tudor Humphries.* Who made the illustrations for this book? *Tudor Humphries.*

The cover of a book usually gives us some hints of what the book is about. Let's look at the front cover of *Are You a Dragonfly?* What do you see in the illustration? (Ideas: *A big dragonfly flying among the flowers; three smaller dragonflies.*)

(Display the KWL chart.) Let's think about what we **know** about dragonflies. Raise your hand if you can tell us something you know about dragonflies. I'll write it down under the **K. K** stands for what we know about dragonflies. What does **K** stand for? *What we know about dragonflies.* (Record all children's responses under the *K* (know) section of the chart. Do not eliminate incorrect responses. They will be addressed in later lessons during the week.)

Take a Picture Walk

(Encourage children to use target words in their answers.) We're going to take a picture walk through this book. When we take a picture walk through a nonfiction book, we look carefully at the pictures and tell what we see. When you look carefully at pictures, you observe those pictures. What do you do when you look carefully at pictures in a nonfiction book? *You observe those pictures.*

Pages 4–5. What do you observe? (Ideas: *One dragonfly on a lily pad; a pond; flowers; small insects.*)

Pages 6–7. What do you observe? (Ideas: *A baby dragonfly on the stem of a plant; small water insects; water plants; two more baby dragonflies; one is going after an insect.*)

Pages 8–9. What do you observe? (Ideas: *Five dragonflies on stems of water plants; they are shedding their skin.*)

Pages 10–11. What do you observe? (Ideas: *A dragonfly on the stem of a lily pad; a beetle pouncing at the dragonfly; a duck floating on the water, looking at the dragonfly; other water creatures.*)

Pages 12–13. What do you observe? (Ideas: *It's night; the moon is up; a dragonfly is climbing a plant stem out of the water.*)

Pages 14–15. What do you observe? (Ideas: *The dragonfly is shedding its skin again.*)

Pages 16–17. What do you observe? (Ideas: *The dragonfly is removing its skin; three dragonflies are flying in different ways.*)

Pages 18–19. What do you observe? (Ideas: *The dragonfly's face; enormous eyes; birds flying around.*)

Pages 20–21. What do you observe? (Idea: *A dragonfly chasing a butterfly.*)

Pages 22–23. What do you observe? (Idea: *Four dragonflies sitting on plants.*)

Pages 24–25. What do you observe? (Ideas: *Three girls sitting by a pond; you can see their feet and their reflections in the water; lily pads; dragonflies.*)

Pages 26–27. What do you observe? (Ideas: *A flower and a dragonfly; a little girl with a diving mask looking at the dragonfly.*)

Pages 28–29. What do you observe? (Ideas: *A girl in a swimsuit and swimming mask; a large duck.*)

Pages 30–31. What do you observe? (Ideas: *Several dragonflies; some plants.*)

Read the Book Aloud

(Read the story to children with minimal interruptions, ending with page 29.)

Tomorrow we will read the book again, and I will ask you some questions.

Present the Target Vocabulary

Prey

In the book, the author tells you to creep up on your prey and grab it. **Prey.** Say the word. *Prey.*

Prey is a naming word. It names a thing. What kind of word is **prey?** *A naming word.*

Prey is an animal that is hunted by another animal for food. Say the word that means "an animal that is hunted by another animal for food." *Prey.*

(Correct any incorrect responses, and repeat the item at the end of the sequence.)

Let's think about some animals that are prey. If you think something is prey, say "prey." If not, don't say anything.

- A kitten being bothered by its brother.
- A rabbit being chased by a fox. *Prey.*
- A worm being chased by a robin. *Prey.*
- A hen gathering her chicks.
- A fly stuck in a spider web. *Prey.*
- An ant being devoured by an anteater. *Prey.*

What naming word means "an animal that is hunted by another animal for food"? *Prey.*

Beware

In the story, the baby dragonfly must beware of ducks. **Beware.** Say the word. *Beware.*

Beware is an action word. It tells you to do something. What kind of word is **beware?** *An action word.*

Beware means be careful. Say the word that means "be careful." *Beware.*

Let's think about some times when you might need to beware. I'll tell about a something. If you need to beware, say "beware." If not, don't say anything.

- Julia prepared her things for school.
- A stranger asked Madison to help him look for a lost dog. *Beware.*
- Simon went into a yard with a large dog in it. *Beware.*
- Ethan watched his fish swim in the bowl.
- Austin played near the hot stove. *Beware.*
- Amanda snuggled with her teddy bear.

What action word means "be careful"? *Beware.*

⊙⊷ Bored

In the book, the dragonfly becomes bored with life in the water and climbs out. **Bored.** Say the word. *Bored.*

Bored is a describing word. It tells how a person or animal feels. What kind of word is **bored**? *A describing word.*

If you are bored, that means that you are tired because something is not interesting to you. Say the word that means "tired because something is not interesting to you." *Bored.*

I'll name some things. If I name a thing that might make you bored, say "bored." If not, don't say anything.

- Watching an awesome fireworks display.
- Staring at a wall. *Bored.*
- Playing an exciting game of baseball.
- Watching a movie for the third time that you didn't like the first time. *Bored.*
- Listening to a dull speaker describe the movements of an ant. *Bored.*
- Watching a good cartoon on TV.

What describing word means "tired because something is not interesting to you"? *Bored.*

⊙⊷ Hover

In the book, we learned that if you are a dragonfly, you can fly fast, you can hover, or you can fly backward. **Hover.** Say the word. *Hover.*

Hover is an action word. It tells how something moves. What kind of word is **hover**? *An action word.*

Hover means stay in one place in the air. Say the word that means "stay in one place in the air." *Hover.*

I'll tell about some things. If the things are hovering, say "hover." If not, don't say anything.

- The leaf floated on the water.
- The hummingbird stayed in the air while it drank the nectar from a flower. *Hover.*
- The little girl was generous.
- A balloon floated above the room, not moving. *Hover.*
- The helicopter stayed above the trees, not moving in any direction. *Hover.*
- The cat crept across the room.

What action word means "to stay in one place in the air"? *Hover.*

Present Vocabulary Tally Sheet
(See Lesson 1, page 3, for instructions.)

Assign Homework
(Homework Sheet, BLM 28a. See the Introduction for homework instructions.)

DAY 2

Preparation: Picture Vocabulary Cards for *prey, beware, bored, hover.*

Read and Discuss Story

(Read story to children. Ask the following questions at the specified points. Encourage them to use target words in their answers.)

Pages 4–5. What question did the author ask? *Are you a dragonfly?* Are you a dragonfly? *No.* How do you know you're not a dragonfly? (Ideas: *I don't look like that dragonfly and I didn't crawl out of an egg; I am human.*) In this book, the author is pretending you are a dragonfly. She talks to you as if you are a dragonfly. How does the author talk to you? (Idea: *Like I'm a dragonfly.*) Where did your mother lay your egg? (Idea: *On the stem of a water plant.*) What were you like when you came out of your egg? (Ideas: *Very, very small; very, very hungry; I was starving; I could breathe water through the end of my tail.*)

Pages 6–7. What did you eat to help you grow? (Idea: *Tiny water creatures.*) What do you use to catch them? (Ideas: *Special grabbers; my mask.*)

Pages 8–9. Why does your skin get so tight you have to take it off? (Idea: *Because I keep eating and growing.*) *How many times do you take off your skin?* (Idea: *Lots of times.*)

Pages 10–11. What kind of food can you eat now that you're bigger? (Ideas: *Tadpoles; fish.*) What kinds of animals are **predators** to you? Remember that a predator is "an animal that hunts other animals for food." (Ideas: *Water beetles; ducks.*)

Pages 12–13. What happens after two years? (Ideas: *I get bored with life in the water.*) Why should you climb out of the water at night? (Idea: *So birds can't see me.*) What happens to your skin as it dries? (Idea: *It splits one more time.*)

Pages 14–15. What do you do after your skin splits? (Idea: *Slowly climb out of it.*) What is different about you now? (Idea: *I can breathe air through tiny holes on the sides of my body.*)

Pages 16–17. What are you? *A dragonfly.* What do you look like at first? (Idea: *Pale and crumpled.*) What will you look like soon? (Ideas: *My beautiful colors will come; my two pairs of wings will straighten out.*) What can you do now that you're a dragonfly? (Ideas: *Fly fast; hover; fly backward.*)

Pages 18–19. What kind of eyes do you have? (Idea: *Enormous.*) Why are your eyes so enormous? (Idea: *So I can see all around me all the time.*) How are your enormous eyes useful? (Ideas: *They help me find food; they help me watch for predators like birds and spiders.*)

Pages 20–21. What were you underwater? (Idea: *A fierce hunter.*) What are you in the air? (Idea: *A fierce hunter.*) Where do you hunt? (Ideas: *Over ponds, streams, and slow-flowing rivers; over marshes; in forests.*) What is your **prey**? (Ideas: *Midges; mosquitoes; flies; wasps; small butterflies.*) What do you do when you catch your prey? (Idea: *Eat it.*)

Pages 22–23. What are two kinds of dragonflies? (Idea: *Hawkers and darters.*) What does a hawker do? (Idea: *It hunts while it flies.*) What does a darter do? (Idea: *It stands still until it sees its prey. Then it darts out and grabs it.*) How is a damselfly different from you? (Ideas: *It is thinner, lighter, and slower; it picks small insects off leaves and flowers.*)

Pages 24–27. Are you a dragonfly? *No.* What are you? (Idea: *A human child.*) How do you know you're a human child and not a dragonfly? (Ideas: *I can't fly; I can't breathe underwater; I don't have a mask attached to my face.*)

Pages 28–29. What are some of the things you can do that dragonflies can't do? (Encourage each child to suggest something he or she can do that a dragonfly can't.) Are you glad you won't ever, ever be eaten by a duck?

(Display the KWL chart.) Now that we've finished reading *Are You a Dragonfly?* look at our chart again. (Point to the *Know* column.) As good scientists find out more about things, they sometimes change their minds about what they know is true.

Let's see if we want to change our minds about any of the items on our **Know** list. (Read each item. Ask children if the item was mentioned in the book. If it was, ask if the item is true or not true. Untrue items are crossed out.) We're good scientists; we know how to change our minds when we learn new facts.

(Point to the **Want to Know** column.) As good scientists find out more about things, they find answers to some of their questions and they want to ask more questions. (Read each question. Ask the children if the question was answered in the book. If it was, record the answer in the *L* (Learned) column and put a check mark in front of the question.)

Are there any new questions we would like to ask about dragonflies? (Record questions under the *W* column on the chart.) We're good scientists; we know how to use what we have learned to ask new questions.

Review Vocabulary
(Display the Picture Vocabulary Cards. Point to each card as you say the word. Ask children to repeat each word after you.) These pictures show **prey, beware, bored,** and **hover.**

- What word means "be careful"? *Beware.*
- What word means "to stay in one place in the air"? *Hover.*
- What word means "an animal that another animal hunts for food"? *Prey.*
- What word means "tired because something is not interesting to you"? *Bored.*

Extend Vocabulary
◎ Prey

In *Are You a Dragonfly?* we learned that **prey** are "animals that other animals hunt for food." Say the word that means "animals that other animals hunt for food." *Prey.*

Raise your hand if you can tell us a sentence that uses **prey** as a naming word meaning "animals that other animals hunt for food." (Call on several children. If they don't use complete sentences, restate their examples as sentences. Have the class repeat the sentences.)

Here's a new way to use the word **prey.**

- Owls **prey** on mice.
- The wolf **preys** on small animals.
- The lion **preyed** on another, slower animal.

In these sentences, prey is an action word that means to hunt and eat. What word means "to hunt and eat"? *Prey.*

Raise your hand if you can tell us a sentence that uses **prey** as an action word meaning "to hunt and eat." (Call on several children. If they don't use complete sentences, restate their examples as sentences. Have the class repeat the sentences.)

Present Expanded Target Vocabulary
 Shed

In the book, we found out that when dragonflies grow, their skin becomes tight and they crawl out of it. When the dragonfly crawls out of its skin, we say it has **shed** its skin. Say the word. *Shed.*

Shed is an action word. It tells something that a person or animal does. What kind of word is **shed?** *An action word.*

If an animal sheds, its hair or skin falls or drops off. Say the word that means an animal's "hair or skin falls or drops off." *Shed.*

I'll tell about some animals. If the animal has shed its hair or skin, say "shed." If not, don't say anything.

- The snake crawled out of its old skin. *Shed.*
- The cat dropped its toy mouse.
- There is dog hair all over my house. *Shed.*
- I found a dragonfly skin near the pond. *Shed.*
- The seagull dropped the clam onto the rocks to break it open.
- My little brother was worried when he found his lizard's skin but not his lizard. *Shed.*

What action word means "an animal's hair or skin falls or drops off"? *Shed.*

Aquatic

In the book, we found out that dragonflies are born near water, that they live in the water for the first two years, and that they hunt for food near water after they learn how to fly. The word we use to tell about those animals that live on or in the water is aquatic. **Aquatic.** Say the word. *Aquatic.*

Aquatic is a describing word. It tells about an animal or plant. What kind of word is **aquatic?** *A describing word.*

If a plant or animal is aquatic, it lives or grows on or in the water. Say the word that describes a plant or animal that "lives or grows on or in the water." *Aquatic.*

I'll name some animals and plants. If the animals or plants I name live or grow on or in the water, say "aquatic." If not, don't say anything.

- Goldfish. *Aquatic.*
- Sea turtles. *Aquatic.*
- Flowers in your garden.
- A beehive.
- Frogs. *Aquatic.*
- Pigs.

What describing word means "lives or grows on or in the water"? *Aquatic.*

DAY 3

Preparation: Display KWL chart.

Read Did You Know?

Today, I'll read you some facts about dragonflies that Judy Allen put in the back of her book. (Read *Did You Know?* pages 30–31 with minimal interruptions.)

Complete KWL Chart

(Review the questions children still want answered from the *W* column of the KWL chart.) Let's see if Judy Allen answered any of our questions in the *Did You Know?* part of her book.

(Read the first item on page 30, beginning with the words "Did you know, …") Did these facts answer any of our questions? (If the item answered any of the remaining questions, put a check mark in front of the question, and write the answer in the *L* column next to the question. Repeat the question and have children say the answer.)

(If the item did not answer any of the remaining questions, ask children leading questions such as:) How many different kinds of dragonflies are there? (Idea: *More than 4,800.*) What did we learn about the different kinds of dragonflies? (Idea: *There are more than 4,800 different kinds of dragonflies.* Record the fact in the *L* column near the bottom. Do not write the fact next to any of the unanswered questions.)

(Repeat the process for the remaining three items. If there are any unanswered questions after you have read and discussed the *Did You Know?* pages, challenge children to find the answers in the school library, on the Internet, or at home.)

Play What's My Word?

Today you will play *What's My Word?* I'll give you three clues. After I give each clue, if you definitely know my word, you may make a guess. If you guess correctly, you will win one point. If you make a mistake, I get the point.

Let's practice. Here's my first clue. My word is a naming word. Are you sure you know my word? If you are, you may make a guess. (If anyone wishes to guess, accept the guess. Award the point to either the class or the teacher.)

Here's my second clue. My word starts with the "p" sound. Are you sure you know my word? If you are, you may make a guess. (If anyone wishes to guess, accept the guess. Award the point to either the class or the teacher.)

Here's my third clue. My word means an animal that other animals hunt for food. Are you sure you know my word? If you are, you may make a guess. *Prey.* (Award the point to either the class or the teacher.)

(**Note:** If a child guesses the word correctly before the last clue, give the other clues and have children decide if the answer fits those clues.)

Now you're ready to play the game. (Draw a T-chart on the board for keeping score. Children earn one point for each correct answer. If they make an error, correct them as you normally would, and record one point for yourself. Repeat missed words at the end of the game.)

- Here's my first clue. My word is a describing word. Here's my second clue. My word ends with "e-d." Here's my third clue. My word means "tired because something is not interesting to me." What's my word? *Bored.*
- New word. Here's my first clue. My word is a describing word. Here's my second clue. My word has a "t" sound in it. Here's my third clue. My word describes a plant or animal that lives or grows in or on the water. What's my word? *Aquatic.*
- New word. Here's my first clue. My word is an action word. Here's my second clue. My word has two different meanings. Here's my third clue. My word means "to hunt and eat something." What's my word? *Prey.*
- New word. Here's my first clue. My word is an action word. Here's my second clue. My word can be done by a dog and a lizard. Here's my third clue. My word means that an animal lets something drop or fall off its body. What's my word? *Shed.*
- New word. Here's my first clue. My word is an action word. Here's my second clue. My word tells what some flying animals can do. Here's my third clue. My word means "to stay in one place in the air." What's my word? *Hover.*
- New word. Here's my first clue. My word is an action word. Here's my second clue. You might tell someone to do my word. Here's my third clue. My word means "be careful." What's my word? *Beware.*

(Count the points and declare a winner.) You did a great job of playing *What's My Word?*

DAY 4

Preparation: *About Dragonflies* booklet.

Print the following words in a column on the board: *dragonfly, dragonflies, eyes, six, when, beetles.*

Read the About Dragonflies Booklet

(Point to each word as you read it) This word is **dragonfly.** What word? *Dragonfly.* This word is **dragonflies.** What word? *Dragonflies.* (Repeat process for remaining words.)

Let's read these words together. First word? *Dragonfly.* Next word? *Dragonflies.* (Repeat process for remaining words.)

Read these words by yourself. First word? *Dragonfly.* Next word? *Dragonflies.* (Repeat process for remaining words until children can read the list accurately and confidently.)

(Use the following correction procedure if children make an error:) This word is **eyes.** What word? *Eyes.* Yes, **eyes.** (Go back to the top of the list and repeat the list until children can read it accurately and confidently.)

(Give each child a copy of the *About Dragonflies* booklet.) My turn to read each page of the booklet. You touch under each word as I read it. (After you have read page 1, have children point to each part of the dragonfly on the illustration as you name it.)

Let's read the story together. (Have children read the story aloud with you.)

(Assign each child a partner. Allow sufficient time for each child to read the book to his or her partner. Circulate as the children read, offering praise and assistance.)

(Children should color the illustrations in their *About Dragonflies* booklet. Encourage them to color the illustrations accurately.) This book is a science book. When artists color scientific illustrations they use colors that are real. (Show children the front cover of the booklet. Point to the dragonfly.) What are some colors that real dragonflies can be? (Ideas: *Brown with green*

spots; black and blue; brown.*) Remember to use the real colors when you color the illustrations.

Play What's My Word? (Cumulative Review)

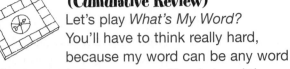

Let's play *What's My Word?* You'll have to think really hard, because my word can be any word we've learned since we read *The Ant and the Grasshopper.* I'll give you three clues. After I give each clue, if you definitely know my word, you may make a guess. If you guess correctly, you will win one point. If you make a mistake, I get the point.

Let's practice. Here's my first clue. My word is a describing word. Are you sure you know my word? If you are, you may make a guess. (If anyone wishes to guess, accept the guess. Award the point to either the class or the teacher.)

Here's my second clue. My word tells about a way you might feel. Are you sure you know my word? If you are, you may make a guess. (If anyone wishes to guess, accept the guess. Award the point to either the class or the teacher.)

Here's my third clue. My word means that you are mad because someone did something you didn't like. What's my word? *Cross.* (Award the point to either the class or the teacher.)

(**Note:** If a child guesses the word correctly before the last clue, give the other clues and have children decide if the answer fits those clues.)

Now you're ready to play the game. (Draw a T-chart on the board for keeping score. Children earn one point for each correct answer. If they make an error, correct them as you normally would, and record one point for yourself. Repeat missed words at the end of the game.)

- Here's my first clue. My word is a naming word. Here's my second clue. My word starts with the "t" sound. Here's my third clue. My word is a long, wide underground tube. What's my word? *Tunnel.*

- New word. Here's my first clue. My word is an action word. Here's my second clue. My word has the "v" sound in it. Here's my third clue. My word means "to stay in one place in the air." What's my word? *Hover.*
- New word. Here's my first clue. My word is a describing word. Here's my second clue. My word tells about the kind of person you might be. Here's my third clue. My word means "you are happy to share what you have with others." What's my word? *Generous.*
- New word. Here's my first clue. My word is a describing word. Here's my second clue. My word ends with *e-d.* Here's my third clue. My word means "tired because something is not interesting to you." What's my word? *Bored.*
- New word. Here's my first clue. My word can mean two different things. Here's my second clue. My word is an action word. Here's my third clue. My word means "to hunt and eat another animal." What's my word? *Prey.*
- New word. Here's my first clue. My word is an action word. Here's my second clue. My word is something that snakes do. Here's my third clue. My word tells how snakes move along the ground. What's my word? *Slither.*
- New word. Here's my first clue. My word is a naming word. Here's my second clue. My word has two meanings. Here's my third clue. My word means "the animal that a predator hunts and eats." What's my word? *Prey.*
- New word. Here's my first clue. My word is an action word. Here's my second clue. You might shout my word to a friend. Here's my third clue. My word means "be careful." What's my word? *Beware.*
- New word. Here's my first clue. My word describes plants and animals. Here's my second clue. My word is wet. Here's my third clue. My word describes plants or animals that live or grow on or in the water. What's my word? *Aquatic.*
- New word. Here's my first clue. My word is an action word. Here's my second clue. Dogs often do my word in the summer when it's hot. Here's my third clue. My word tells what animals do when they let their hair or skin drop or fall off. What's my word? *Shed.*

(Count the points and declare a winner.) You did a great job of playing *What's My Word?*

DAY 5

Preparation: *About Dragonflies* booklet.

Chart titled *Reading Goals* that was started in Week 21.

Happy Face Game Test Sheet, BLM B.

Read About Dragonflies Booklet

(Assign each child a partner.) Today you'll read your booklet, *About Dragonflies,* to your partner. (Allow sufficient time for each child to read the book to his or her partner. Circulate as the children read, offering praise and assistance.)

(Ask children to look at the back of their booklet about dragonflies.) This part of the booklet is for people who can help you find other books to read. It tells those people about other books that are like *Are you a Dragonfly?* It also tells them about a place where you can find other books. Where are some places that you could go to find other books about dragonflies and other flying insects? (Ideas: *To the school library; to the public library; to a bookstore.*)

(You may wish to read and discuss the information on the back cover.)

There's one more important thing on the back cover of your booklet. Touch the box that is at the bottom of the page. The words above the box say "My reading goal." What do the words say? *My reading goal.*

A goal is something that you want to succeed at doing. What is a goal? *Something that you want to succeed at doing.* A reading goal is something that you want to succeed at doing with your reading.

Let's see if we can add some other reading goals to our class chart. What are some other reading goals that someone might have when they read their book? (Accept reasonable responses. Help children put their ideas into goal statements. Add to the list of statements on the chart. Ask children to choose a goal and copy it into the box.

Children may also make up an original goal that is not on the list. If children are unable to copy the goals or to write a goal of their own, you or a helper may wish to scribe their goal statements for them before the booklets are sent home.)

Assess Vocabulary

 (Give each child a copy of the Happy Face Game Test Sheet, BLM B.)

Today you're going to play the Happy Face Game. When you play the Happy Face Game, it shows me how well you know the hard words you are learning.

If I say something that is true, color in the happy face. What will you do if I say something that is true? *Color in the happy face.*

If I say something that is false, color in the sad face. What will you do if I say something that is false? *Color in the sad face.*

Listen carefully to each item that I say. Don't let me trick you!

Item 1: A **predator preys** on other animals. (*True.*)

Item 2: A **predator** and its **prey** are not **enemies.** (*False.*)

Item 3: When a jet flies fast, we can say it **hovers.** (*False.*)

Item 4: We can say that Matthew accidentally **shed** the egg on the floor. (*False.*)

Item 5: It is nice to be around someone who is **rude.** (*False.*)

Item 6: When you see a sign that says "**Beware** of Dog," you should be very careful. (*True.*)

Item 7: Some birds, like geese and ducks, are **aquatic** animals. (*True.*)

Item 8: Animals that **burrow** make their homes in trees. (*False.*)

Item 9: Winter, spring, summer, and fall are all **seasons.** (*True.*)

Item 10: If you watch the same show over and over, you will probably become **bored.** (*True.*)

You did a great job of playing the Happy Face Game!

(Score children's work. A child must score 9 out of 10 to be at the mastery level. If a child does not achieve mastery, insert the missed words as additional items in the games in next week's lessons. Retest those children individually for the missed items before they take the next mastery test.)

Extensions

Read a Book as a Reward

 (Read *Are you a Dragonfly?* or another book about flying insects to children as a reward for their hard work.)

Preparation: Word containers for the Super Words Center.

Note: You will need to keep the cards that were removed from the center. They will be used again later in the program.

Introduce the Super Words Center

(Put the Picture Vocabulary Cards from weeks 3 and 28 into the word cans. Make duplicates of each card to create a "Concentration" game. You may make as many sets of duplicates as you wish to suit your class.)

(Show children one of the word containers. Demonstrate how the game is played by role-playing the game with a child. Repeat the demonstration process until the children can play the game with confidence.)

Let's think about how we work with our words in the Super Words Center.

You will work with a partner in the Super Words Center. Whom will you work with in the center? *A partner.*

There are two cards for each word in the Super Words Center. You will play a game called *Concentration.* When you play *Concentration,* you try to find two cards that match. **Match** means that both cards show the same picture and word. What does **match** mean? *Both cards show the same picture and word.*

First you will take all of the cards out of the container and place them facedown in rows on the table. What do you do first? (Idea: *Take all of the cards out and place them facedown in rows on the table.*)

Next you pick one card and turn it faceup in its spot. What do you do next? (Idea: *I pick a card and turn it faceup in its spot.*)

Then ask your partner what word the picture shows. What do you do next? (Idea: *I ask my partner what word the picture shows.*)

If your partner doesn't know the word, tell them the word. What do you do if your partner doesn't know the word? *Tell my partner the word.*

Then you will give your partner a turn. What do you do next? *Give my partner a turn.*

If your partner turns over a card that is the same as your card, he or she can take those two cards. What can your partner do? (Idea: *He or she can take both cards if he or she chooses one that is the same as my first card.*)

Preparation: You will need a copy of *Are You a Snail?* for each day's lesson.

Number the pages of the story (beginning with 1 on the first page inside the cover) to assist you in asking comprehension questions at appropriate points.

Prepare a KWL chart titled *Snails* on a sheet of chart paper.

Post a copy of the Vocabulary Tally Sheet, BLM A, with this week's Picture Vocabulary Cards attached.

Each child will need one copy of the Homework Sheet, BLM 29a.

Are You a Snail?
author: Judy Allen • illustrator: Tudor Humphries

Target Vocabulary

Tier II	Tier III
hatch	nonfiction
slimy	fact
damp	
stalks	
*resemble	
*conceal	

*Expanded Target Vocabulary Word

The things we know about snails that are true are called **facts.** What are the true things we know about snails called? *Facts.*

(Point to the *K* column on the chart.) Some of the things you have told us are facts about snails, and some of the things you have told us are not true. When we've finished reading *Are You a Snail?* we'll come back to our chart and look at it again.

Now let's think what you **want to know** about snails. I'll write it down under the **W. W** stands for what we **want to know** about snails. What does **W** stand for? *What we want to know about snails.* (Record <u>all</u> children's questions under the *W* (want to know) section of the chart. If the children tell about snails instead of ask questions, prompt them to ask a question.)

DAY 1

Introduce Book

This week's book is called *Are You a Snail?* What's the title of this week's book? *Are You a Snail?*

This book was written by Judy Allen. Who's the author of *Are You a Snail? Judy Allen.*

Tudor Humphries made the pictures for this book. Who is the illustrator of *Are You a Snail? Tudor Humphries.* Who made the illustrations for this book? *Tudor Humphries.*

The cover of a book usually gives us some hints of what the book is about. Let's look at the front cover of *Are You a Snail?* What do you see in the illustration? (Ideas: *A large snail; a small snail climbing a hill; plants; leaves.*)

(Display the KWL chart.) Let's think about what we **know** about snails. Raise your hand if you can tell us something you know about snails. I'll write it down under the **K. K** stands for what we **know** about snails. What does **K** stand for? *What we know about snails.* (Record <u>all</u> children's responses under the *K* (know) section of the chart. Do not eliminate incorrect responses. They will be addressed in later lessons during the week.)

Take a Picture Walk

(Encourage children to use target words in their answers.) We're going to take a picture walk through this book. When we take a picture walk through a nonfiction book, we look carefully at the pictures and tell what we see. When you look carefully at pictures, you observe those pictures. What do you do when you look carefully at pictures in a nonfiction book? *You observe those pictures.*

Pages 4–5. What do you observe? (Ideas: *A big snail on a branch of a plant; a smaller/younger snail on the leaf of another plant; eggs on the ground; plants.*)

Pages 6–7. What do you observe? (Ideas: *A large snail and a baby snail.*)

Pages 8–9. What do you observe? (Ideas: *Two snail heads; each head has things coming out of it.*)

Pages 10–11. What do you observe? (Ideas: *A snail with a large shell.*)

Pages 12–13. What do you observe? (Idea: *A snail eating a leaf in the rain.*)

Pages 14–15. What do you observe? (Ideas: *A bird holding a snail shell; the bird sleeping in its nest at night.*)

Pages 16–17. What do you observe? (Ideas: *A fox looking at a snail; it is nighttime; they are near water.*)

Pages 18–19. What do you observe? (Idea: *A snail about to get stepped on by a person wearing boots.*)

Pages 20–21. What do you observe? (Idea: *An animal that looks like a snail without its shell.*)

Pages 22–23. What do you observe? (Ideas: *It is winter turning to spring; the snail comes out of a log; it goes towards the plants.*)

Pages 24–25. What do you observe? (Ideas: *Five children standing together; one child has a snail on her shirt; another child is holding a leaf with a snail on it.*)

Pages 26–27. What do you observe? (Ideas: *A boy wearing a sweatshirt, jeans, and a backpack; the boy's shadow; a snail on the ground.*) Look at the boy's shadow closely. What does it look like? *A snail.*

Pages 28–29. What do you observe? (Ideas: *A bird sitting on a backpack; a boy watching a snail.*)

Pages 30–31. What do you observe? (Ideas: *A bird with a snail shell in its beak; a snail; the moon and a tree at night; a snail eating leaves.*)

Read the Book Aloud

 (Read the story to children with minimal interruptions, ending with page 29.)

Tomorrow we will read the book again, and I will ask you some questions.

 Hatch

In the book, the author tells you that when you hatch from your egg, you will look like your mother. **Hatch.** Say the word. *Hatch.*

Hatch is an action word. It tells what something does. What kind of word is **hatch?** *An action word.*

Hatch means to be born from an egg. Say the word that means "to be born from an egg." *Hatch.*

(Correct any incorrect responses, and repeat the item at the end of the sequence.)

Let's think about some animals that hatch. If you think something hatches, say "hatch." If not, don't say anything.

- A cat had a litter of six kittens.
- The baby chicks finally came out of their eggs. *Hatch.*
- My baby brother was born on November 16th.
- The nest was full of baby lizards after they came out of their eggs. *Hatch.*
- The fish came out of their eggs and swam after their mother. *Hatch.*
- The horse gave birth to a black foal.

What action word means "to be born from an egg"? *Hatch.*

 Slimy

In the story, we learn that snails are very slimy. **Slimy.** Say the word. *Slimy.*

Slimy is a describing word. It tells more about things. What kind of word is **slimy?** *A describing word.*

Something that is slimy is soft, wet, and slippery. Say the word that means "soft, wet, and slippery." *Slimy.*

Let's think about some things that might be slimy. I'll name some things. If the thing is slimy, say "slimy." If not, don't say anything.

- Mud. *Slimy.*
- Popcorn.
- Finger paint. *Slimy.*
- Uncooked egg. *Slimy.*
- Dry dirt.
- Newspaper.

What describing word tells you that something is "soft, wet, and slippery"? *Slimy.*

⌖ Damp

In the book, we learn that snails like damp places. **Damp.** Say the word. *Damp.*

Damp is a describing word. It tells how something feels. What kind of word is **damp?** *A describing word.*

Damp means a little bit wet or moist. Say the word that means "a little bit wet or moist." *Damp.*

I'll describe some things. If I describe a thing that is damp, say "damp." If not, don't say anything.

- A towel after drying your hands. *Damp.*
- The ocean.
- The ground after a very light rain. *Damp.*
- Your face and arms after playing outside in the heat. *Damp.*
- A clean towel in the closet.
- The sidewalk after the snow melts. *Damp.*

What describing word tells that something is "a little bit wet or moist"? *Damp.*

⌖ Stalks

In the book, we learned that if you are a snail, you have two horns and two eyes on stalks on top of your head. **Stalks.** Say the word. *Stalks.*

Stalks is a naming word. It names things. What kind of word is **stalks?** *A naming word.*

Stalks are long, thin stems that connect one part of a thing to another part. Say the word that means "long, thin stems that connect one part of a thing to another part." *Stalks.*

I'll tell about some things. If the things have stalks, say "stalks." If not, don't say anything.

- Tall flowers. *Stalks.*
- People.
- Corn growing in a field. *Stalks.*
- A snail. *Stalks.*
- A cactus with a flower on it.
- A cat.

What naming word means "long, thin stems that connect one part of a thing to another"? *Stalks.*

Present Vocabulary Tally Sheet
(See Lesson 1, page 3, for instructions.)

Assign Homework
(Homework Sheet, BLM 29a. See the Introduction for homework instructions.)

DAY 2

Preparation: Picture Vocabulary Cards for *hatch, slimy, damp, stalks, resemble, conceal.*

Read and Discuss Story

(Read story to children. Ask the following questions at the specified points. Encourage them to use target words in their answers.)

Pages 4–5. What question did the author ask? *Are you a snail?* Are you a snail? *No.* How do you know you're not a snail? (Ideas: *I don't look like that snail and my life didn't begin in an egg like that; I'm a human.*) In this book, the author is pretending you are a snail. She talks to you as if you are a snail. How does the author talk to you? (Idea: *Like I'm a snail.*)

Pages 6–7. What did you look like when you hatched? (Idea: *Like my mother, but much smaller.*) What will you do? *Grow.*

Pages 8–9. Where are your eyes? *On stalks.* What else do you have on your head? *Two horns.* What can you do with your eyes if you need to? (Idea: *Pull them down into the stalks.*) What do you feel like? *Slimy.*

Pages 10–11. What kind of shell do you have? (Ideas: *One with a beautiful pattern on it.*) How many legs do you have? *None.* How many feet do you have? *One.* What helps you slide along? (Idea: *My strong foot and my slime.*) What do you leave behind you when you move? (Idea: *A trail of silvery slime.*)

Pages 12–13. What kinds of places do you like? *Damp places.* Would you rather be out in the sun or in the rain? *In the rain.* What do you use your big, rough tongue for? (Idea: *For ripping off pieces of leaves to eat.*)

Pages 14–15. What animals prey on snails? (Ideas: *Thrushes; birds.*) What do thrushes know how to do? (Idea: *Break open a snail's shell.*) When will you be safe from thrushes? (Ideas: *At night; when they are sleeping.*)

Pages 16–17. What is another predator you should beware of? *Foxes.* When do foxes hunt? *At night.*

Pages 18–19. Are snails **prey** for humans? *No.* Why should snails beware of humans? (Ideas: *Humans might step on them; they are too slow to get out of the way.*) Why do humans not like snails? (Idea: *Snails eat their plants.*) What might humans do to keep snails from eating their plants? (Idea: *Put poison or sharp gravel around their plants.*) Why does gravel keep snails away from the plants? (Idea: *It hurts them to slide on it.*)

Pages 20–21. What animal looks like a snail without a shell? *A slug.* Is a slug a snail with its shell fallen off? *No.*

Pages 22–23. What happens to you when it gets cold outside? *I become sleepy.* What do you do in the winter to protect yourself? *Hibernate.* That's right; if you're a snail you spend the winter in a deep sleep. How does your slime protect you in the winter? (Idea: *It hardens to make a door in my shell.*) What wakes you? (Idea: *The spring warmth.*) What do you need to do after you dribble on the door of your shell? (Idea: *Find food.*)

Pages 24–27. Are you a snail? *No.* What are you? *A human child.* How do you know you're a human child and not a snail? (Ideas: *I have no shell on my back; I have no horns; my eyes are not on stalks.*)

Pages 28–29. What are some of the things you can do that snails can't do? (Encourage each child to suggest something he or she can do that a snail can't.) Are you glad you are not the least bit slimy?

(Display the KWL chart.) Now that we've finished reading *Are You a Snail?* let's look at our chart again.

(Point to the *Know* column.) As good scientists find out more about things, they sometimes change their minds about what they know is true. Let's see if we want to change our minds about any of the items on our **Know** list. (Read each item. Ask children if the item was mentioned in the book. If it was, ask if the item is true or not true. Untrue items are crossed out.) We're good scientists; we know how to change our minds when we learn new facts.

(Point to the *Want to Know* column.) As good scientists find out more about things, they find answers to some of their questions and they want to ask more questions. (Read each question. Ask children if the question was answered in the book. If it was, record the answer in the *L* (Learned) column and put a check mark in front of the question.)

Are there any new questions we would like to ask about snails? (Record questions under the *W* column on the chart.) We're good scientists; we know how to use what we have learned to ask new questions.

Review Vocabulary

(Display the Picture Vocabulary Cards. Point to each card as you say the word. Ask children to repeat each word after you.) These pictures show **hatch, slimy, damp,** and **stalks.**

- What word means "slightly wet or moist"? *Damp.*
- What word means "to be born from an egg"? *Hatch.*
- What word means "long, thin stems that connect one part of something to another part"? *Stalks.*
- What word means "soft, wet, and slippery"? *Slimy.*

Extend Vocabulary
◎— Stalks

In *Are You a Snail?* we learned that **stalks** are the "long, thin stems that connect a snail's eyes to its body." Say the word that means "long, thin stems that connect a part of something to another part." *Stalks.*

Raise your hand if you can tell us a sentence that uses **stalks** as a naming word meaning "long, thin stems that connect a part of something to another part." (Call on several children. If they don't use complete sentences, restate their examples as sentences. Have the class repeat the sentences.)

Here's a new way to use the word **stalks.**

- The cheetah carefully **stalks** its prey.
- The scientist **stalks** the insect in order to observe it.
- The fox **stalks** the rabbit through the trees.

In these sentences, **stalks** is an action word that means "quietly follows an animal in order to kill it, catch it, or observe it." What word means "quietly follows an animal in order to kill it, catch it, or observe it"? *Stalks.*

Raise your hand if you can tell us a sentence that uses **stalks** as an action word meaning "quietly follows an animal in order to kill it, catch it, or observe it." (Call on several children. If they don't use complete sentences, restate their examples as sentences. Have the class repeat the sentences.)

Present Expanded Target Vocabulary
 Resemble

In the book, we learned that when baby snails are born, they look like their mother. When a person or animal looks like one of their relatives, we say they resemble that relative. **Resemble.** Say the word. *Resemble.*

Resemble is an action word. It tells what you do. What kind of word is **resemble?** *An action word.*

Resemble means to look similar to someone or something else. Say the word that means "to look similar to someone or something else." *Resemble.*

I'll tell about some things. If they resemble someone or something else, say "resemble." If not, don't say anything.

- All of the puppies in the litter have white fur with brown spots like their mother. *Resemble.*
- When a tadpole is born, it doesn't look anything like a frog.
- You can tell that Lana and Laura are sisters just by looking at them. *Resemble.*
- This picture looks just like Uncle Joe! *Resemble.*
- This is a football and that is a basketball.
- He has his father's nose. *Resemble.*

What action word means "to look similar to someone or something else"? *Resemble.*

 Conceal

In the book, we found out that snails must hide from predators such as thrushes and foxes. When an animal hides, it conceals itself. **Conceal.** Say the word. *Conceal.*

Conceal is an action word. It tells what something or someone does. What kind of word is **conceal?** *An action word.*

Conceal means to hide something. Say the word that means "to hide something." *Conceal.*

I'll tell about some things. If the thing I mention might be concealed, say "conceal." If not, don't say anything.

- A gift for a surprise birthday party. *Conceal.*
- A small animal in the woods. *Conceal.*
- Today's lunch menu.
- The spelling words during a test. *Conceal.*
- A favorite sweater.
- An animal when its predator is near. *Conceal.*

What action word means "to hide"? *Conceal.*

DAY 3

Preparation: Display KWL chart.

Read Did You Know?

Today I'll read you some facts about snails that Judy Allen put in the back of her book. (Read *Did You Know?* pages 30–31 with minimal interruptions.)

Complete KWL Chart

(Review questions children still want answered from the *W* column of the KWL chart.) Let's see if Judy Allen answered any of our questions in the *Did You Know?* part of her book.

(Read the first item on page 30, beginning with the words "Did you know …") Did these facts answer any of our questions? (If the item answered any of the remaining questions, put a check mark in front of the question, and write the answer in the *L* column next to the question. Repeat the question, and have children say the answer. If the item did not answer any of the remaining questions, ask children leading questions such as:) What does the trail of a snail look like? (Idea: *It is broken.*) How is the trail of a snail different from the trail of a slug? (Idea: *The trail of a snail is broken, but the trail of a slug is one long line of slime.* Record the fact in the *L* column near the bottom. Do not write the fact next to any of the unanswered questions.)

(Repeat the process for the remaining 4 items. If there are any unanswered questions after you have read and discussed the *Did You Know?* pages, challenge children to find the answers in the school library, on the Internet, or at home.)

Play What's My Word?

 Today you will play *What's My Word?* I'll give you three clues. After I give each clue, if you are sure you know my word, you may make a guess. If you guess correctly, you will win one point. If you make a mistake, I get the point.

Let's practice. Here's my first clue. My word is a naming word. Are you sure you know my word? If you are, you may make a guess. (If anyone wishes to guess, accept the guess. Award the point to either the class or the teacher.)

Here's my second clue. My word ends with the "s" sound. Are you sure you know my word? If you are, you may make a guess. (If anyone wishes to guess, accept the guess. Award the point to either the class or the teacher.)

Here's my third clue. My word means "long, thin stems that attach one part of something to another part." Are you sure you know my word? If you are, you may make a guess. *Stalks.* (Award the point to either the class or the teacher.)

(**Note:** If a child guesses the word correctly before the last clue, give the other clues and have the children decide if the answer fits those clues.)

Now you're ready to play the game. (Draw a T-chart on the board for keeping score. Children earn one point for each correct answer. If they make an error, correct them as you normally would, and record one point for yourself. Repeat missed words at the end of the game.)

- Here's my first clue. My word is an action word. Here's my second clue. Fish, birds, and reptiles all do my word, but humans do not. Here's my third clue. My word means "to be born from an egg." What's my word? *Hatch.*
- New word. Here's my first clue. My word is an action word. Here's my second clue. My word has an "m" sound in it. Here's my third clue. My word means "to look similar to someone or something else." What's my word? *Resemble.*
- New word. Here's my first clue. My word is an action word. Here's my second clue. My word has two different meanings. Here's my third clue. My word means "quietly follows an animal in order to kill, catch, or observe it." What's my word? *Stalks.*
- New word. Here's my first clue. My word is a describing word. Here's my second clue. My word ends with the "ē" sound. Here's my third clue. My word describes something that is soft, wet, and slippery. What's my word? *Slimy.*
- New word. Here's my first clue. My word is an action word. Here's my second clue. My word tells what animals should do when they see a predator. Here's my third clue. My word means "to hide." What's my word? *Conceal.*
- New word. Here's my first clue. My word is a describing word. Here's my second clue. My word rhymes with something you turn on to read. Here's my third clue. My word means "slightly wet or moist." What's my word? *Damp.*

(Count the points and declare a winner.) You did a great job of playing *What's My Word?*

DAY 4

Preparation: *About Snails* booklet.
Print the following words in a column on the board: *snail, foot, from, damp, slug, winter, spring.*

Read the About Snails Booklet

(Point to each word as you read it.) This word is **snail.** What word? *Snail.* This word is **foot.**

What word? *Foot.* (Repeat process for remaining words.)

Let's read these words together. First word? *Snail.* Next word? *Foot.* (Repeat process for remaining words.)

Read these words by yourself. First word? *Snail.* Next word? *Foot.* (Repeat process for remaining words until children can read the list accurately and confidently.)

(Use the following correction procedure if children make an error:) This word is **damp.** What word? *Damp.* Yes, **damp.** (Go back to the top of the list and repeat the list until children can read it accurately and confidently.)

(Give each child a copy of the *About Snails* booklet.) My turn to read each page of the booklet. You touch under each word as I read it. (After you have read page 1, have children point to each part of the snail on the illustration as you name it.)

Let's read the story together. (Have children read the story aloud with you.)

(Assign each child a partner. Allow sufficient time for each child to read the book to his or her partner. Circulate as the children read, offering praise and assistance.)

(Children should color the illustrations in their *About Snails* booklet. Encourage them to color the illustrations accurately.) This book is a science book. When artists color scientific illustrations they use colors that are real. (Show children the front cover of the booklet. Point to the snail.) What are some colors that real snails can be? (Ideas: *Their shells are brown; the rest of them is green and brown and gray.*) Remember to use the real colors when you color the illustrations.

Play What's My Word? (Cumulative Review)

Let's play *What's My Word?* You'll have to think really hard, because my word can be any word we've learned since we read *The Ant and the Grasshopper.* I'll give you three clues. After I give each clue, if you are sure you know my word, you may make a guess. If you guess correctly,

you will win one point. If you make a mistake, I get the point.

Let's practice. Here's my first clue. My word is a naming word. Are you sure you know my word? If you are, you may make a guess. (If anyone wishes to guess, accept the guess. Award the point to either the class or the teacher.)

Here's my second clue. My word is something that you can watch. Are you sure you know my word? If you are, you may make a guess. (If anyone wishes to guess, accept the guess. Award the point to either the class or the teacher.)

Here's my third clue. My word means "a group of people that march, ride, or drive together down a street." What's my word? *Parade.* (Award the point to either the class or the teacher.)

(**Note:** If a child guesses the word correctly before the last clue, give the other clues and have children decide if the answer fits those clues.)

Now you're ready to play the game. (Draw a T-chart on the board for keeping score. Children earn one point for each correct answer. If they make an error, correct them as you normally would, and record one point for yourself. Repeat missed words at the end of the game.)

- Here's my first clue. My word is a describing word. Here's my second clue. My word starts with the "s" sound. Here's my third clue. My word describes something wet, soft, and slippery. What's my word? *Slimy.*
- New word. Here's my first clue. My word is an action word. Here's my second clue. Anything can do my word. Here's my third clue. My word means "to look similar to someone or something else." What's my word? *Resemble.*
- New word. Here's my first clue. My word is a naming word. Here's my second clue. My word starts with the "h" sound. Here's my third clue. My word means "a person." What's my word? *Human.*
- New word. Here's my first clue. My word is an action word. Here's my second clue. Birds, fish, and snakes do my word, but humans do not. Here's my third clue. My word means

"to be born from an egg." What's my word? *Hatch.*

- New word. Here's my first clue. My word can be used to mean two different things. Here's my second clue. My word is an action word. Here's my third clue. My word means "quietly follows an animal in order to kill, catch, or observe it." What's my word? *Stalks.*
- New word. Here's my first clue. My word is a naming word. Here's my second clue. Food, animals, even people can have my word. Here's my third clue. My word means "a smell." What's my word? *Odor.*
- New word. Here's my first clue. My word is a naming word. Here's my second clue. My word has two meanings. Here's my third clue. My word means "long, thin stems that connect one part of something to another part." What's my word? *Stalks.*
- New word. Here's my first clue. My word is a describing word. Here's my second clue. My word starts with the "d" sound. Here's my third clue. My word means "slightly wet or moist." What's my word? *Damp.*
- New word. Here's my first clue. My word is an action word. Here's my second clue. You can do my word to yourself or to someone or something else. Here's my third clue. My word means "to hide." What's my word? *Conceal.*
- New word. Here's my first clue. My word is a naming word. Here's my second clue. My word ends in "or." Here's my third clue. My word is the opposite of **prey.** What's my word? *Predator.*

(Count the points and declare a winner.) You did a great job of playing *What's My Word?*

Read About Snails Booklet

(Assign each child a partner.) Today you'll read your booklet, *About Snails,* to your partner. (Allow sufficient time for each child to read the book to his or her partner. Circulate as the children read, offering praise and assistance.)

(Ask children to look at the back of their booklet about snails.) This part of the booklet is for people who can help you find other books to read. It tells those people about other books that are like *Are you a Snail?* It also tells them about a place where you can find other books. Where are some places that you could go to find other books about snails and slugs? (Ideas: *To the school library; to the public library; to a bookstore.*)

(You may wish to read and discuss the information on the back cover.)

There's one more important thing on the back cover of your booklet. Touch the box that is at the bottom of the page. The words above the box say "My reading goal." What do the words say? *My reading goal.*

A goal is something that you want to succeed at doing. What is a goal? *Something that you want to succeed at doing.* A reading goal is something that you want to succeed at doing with your reading.

Let's see if we can add some other reading goals to our class chart. What are some other reading goals that someone might have when they read their book? (Accept reasonable responses. Help children put their ideas into goal statements. Add to the list of statements on the chart. Ask children to choose a goal and copy it into the box. Children may also make up an original goal that is not on the list. If children are unable to copy the goals or to write a goal of their own, you or a helper may wish to scribe their goal statements for them before the booklets are sent home.)

Assess Vocabulary

 (Give each child a copy of the Happy Face Game Test Sheet, BLM B.)

Today you're going to play the Happy Face Game. When you play the Happy Face Game, it shows me how well you know the hard words you are learning.

If I say something that is true, color in the happy face. What will you do if I say something that is true? *Color in the happy face.*

If I say something that is false, color in the sad face. What will you do if I say something that is false? *Color in the sad face.*

Listen carefully to each item that I say. Don't let me trick you!

Item 1: When you play hide-and-seek, some of the players must **conceal** themselves. (*True.*)

Item 2: A kitten **hatches** from an egg. (*False.*)

Item 3: You should take your time and move slowly in an **emergency.** (*False.*)

Item 4: Cereal is **damp** before you pour on the milk. (*False.*)

Item 5: Brothers and sisters often **resemble** each other. (*True.*)

Item 6: A **noble** person would not give you half of their lunch. (*False.*)

Item 7: Snails have two eyes on **stalks.** (*True.*)

Item 8: **Prey** sometimes **stalk** their **predators.** (*False.*)

Item 9: The trail of a snail is **slimy.** (*True.*)

Item 10: Frogs and tadpoles are **aquatic** animals. (*True.*)

You did a great job of playing the Happy Face Game!

(Score children's work. A child must score 9 out of 10 to be at the mastery level. If a child does not achieve mastery, insert the missed words as additional items in the games in next week's lessons. Retest those children individually for the missed items before they take the next mastery test.)

Extensions

Read a Book as a Reward

(Read *Are you a Snail?* or another book about snails or slugs to children as a reward for their hard work.)

Preparation: Word containers for the Super Words Center.

Note: You will need to keep the cards that were removed from the center. They will be used again later in the program.

 ### Introduce the Super Words Center

(Put the Picture Vocabulary Cards from weeks 4 and 29 into the word cans. Make duplicates of each card to create a "Concentration" game. You may make as many sets of duplicates as you wish to suit your class).

(Show children one of the word containers. Demonstrate how the game is played by role-playing the game with a child. Repeat the demonstration process until the children can play the game with confidence.)

Let's think about how we work with our words in the Super Words Center.

You will work with a partner in the Super Words Center. Whom will you work with in the center? *A partner.*

There are two cards for each word in the Super Words Center. You will play a game called *Concentration.* When you play *Concentration,* you try to find two cards that match. **Match** means that both cards show the same picture and word. What does **match** mean? *Both cards show the same picture and word.*

First you will take all of the cards out of the container and place them facedown in rows on the table. What do you do first? (Idea: *Take all of the cards out and place them facedown in rows on the table.*)

Next you pick one card and turn it faceup in its spot. What do you do next? (Idea: *I pick a card and turn it faceup in its spot.*)

Then ask your partner what word the picture shows. What do you do next? (Idea: *I ask my partner what word the picture shows.*)

If your partner doesn't know the word, tell them the word. What do you do if your partner doesn't know the word? *Tell my partner the word.*

Then you will give your partner a turn. What do you do next? *Give my partner a turn.*

If your partner turns over a card that is the same as your card, he or she can take those two cards. What can your partner do? (Idea: *He or she can take both cards if he or she chooses one that is the same as my first card.*)

Week 30

Are You an Ant?
author: Judy Allen • illustrator: Tudor Humphries

Preparation: You will need a copy of *Are You an Ant?* for each day's lesson.

Number the pages of the story (beginning with 1 on the first page inside the cover) to assist you in asking comprehension questions at appropriate points.

Prepare a KWL chart titled *Ants* on a sheet of chart paper.

Post a copy of the Vocabulary Tally Sheet, BLM A, with this week's Picture Vocabulary Cards attached.

Each child will need one copy of the Homework Sheet, BLM 30a.

Are You an Ant?
author: Judy Allen • illustrator: Tudor Humphries

🎯 Target Vocabulary

Tier II	Tier III
probably	nonfiction
storage	fact
corridor	
surface	
*colony	
*metamorphosis	

*Expanded Target Vocabulary Word

DAY 1

Introduce Book

This week's book is called *Are You an Ant?* What's the title of this week's book? *Are You an Ant?*

This book was written by Judy Allen. Who's the author of *Are You an Ant? Judy Allen.*

Tudor Humphries made the pictures for this book. Who is the illustrator of *Are You an Ant? Tudor Humphries.* Who made the illustrations for this book? *Tudor Humphries.*

The cover of a book usually gives us some hints of what the book is about. Let's look at the front cover of *Are You an Ant?* What do you see in the illustration? (Idea: *An ant on a leaf picking something up.*)

(Display the KWL chart.) Let's think about what we **know** about ants. Raise your hand if you can tell us something you know about ants. I'll write it down under the **K. K** stands for what we **know** about ants. What does **K** stand for? *What we know about ants.* (Record all children's responses under the *K* (know) section of the chart. Do not eliminate incorrect responses. They will be addressed in later lessons during the week.)

The things we know about ants that are true are called **facts.** What are the true things we know about ants called? *Facts.*

(Point to the *K* column on the chart.) Some of the things you have told us are facts about ants, and some of the things you have told us are not true. When we've finished reading *Are You an Ant?* we'll come back to our chart and look at it again.

Now let's think what you **want to know** about ants. I'll write it down under the **W. W** stands for what we **want to know** about ants. What does **W** stand for? *What we want to know about ants.* (Record all children's questions under the *W* (want to know) section of the chart. If the children tell about ants instead of ask questions, prompt them to ask a question.)

Take a Picture Walk

(Encourage children to use target words in their answers.) We're going to take a picture walk through this book. When we take a picture walk through a nonfiction book, we look carefully at the pictures and tell what we see. When you look carefully at pictures, you observe those pictures. What do you do when you look carefully at pictures in a nonfiction book? *You observe those pictures.*

Pages 4–5. What do you observe? (Ideas: *Lots of ants flying in the air; an ant on the ground in the grass, digging; wings lying on the ground by the ant.*)

Pages 6–7. What do you observe? (Ideas: *An ant lying on the ground; small worms; eggs; worms coming out of the eggs.*)

Pages 8–9. What do you observe? (Ideas: *An egg; an ant breaking out of an egg; a white ant; an ant changing from white to black; a black ant.*)

Pages 10–11. What do you observe? (Ideas: *Lots of ants; an ant home with lots of different rooms and tunnels; seeds and nuts.*)

Pages 12–13. What do you observe? (Ideas: *An ant on a leaf trying to catch a bug; an ant on another leaf looking for something; an ant coming out of the ground; two ants looking at a squished bumblebee; an ant fighting with another bug.*)

Pages 14–15. What do you observe? (Ideas: *An ant getting a crumb about to be swept up by a broom.*)

Pages 16–17. What do you observe? (Ideas: *Ants climbing up a plant with other little bugs on it; two ants throwing eggs off another leaf.*)

Pages 18–19. What do you observe? (Ideas: *An ant carrying a seed; an ant dragging a dead ladybug.*)

Pages 20–21. What do you observe? (Ideas: *Ants crawling around in the ground/tunnel; ants on the eggs.*)

Pages 22–23. What do you observe? (Ideas: *A lizard; a frog; a bird; they are all looking at a small group of ants.*)

Pages 24–25. What do you observe? (Ideas: *Three different families; each with parents and children shown in an ant house.*)

Pages 26–27. What do you observe? (Ideas: *A long line of children marching; they are marching in a parade.*)

Pages 28–29. What do you observe? (Ideas: *A bird with a boy in its beak.*)

Pages 30–31. What do you observe? (Ideas: *An ant on the ground; a flying ant; ants on leaves.*)

Read the Book Aloud

(Read the story to children with minimal interruptions, ending with page 29.)

Tomorrow we will read the book again, and I will ask you some questions.

Present Target Vocabulary

 Probably

In the book, the author says you probably won't have to march in a line with lots of others. **Probably.** Say the word. *Probably.*

Probably is a describing word. It tells about how something is done. What kind of word is **probably?** *A describing word.*

Probably means almost for sure. Say the word that means "almost for sure." *Probably.*

(Correct any incorrect responses, and repeat the item at the end of the sequence.)

Let's think about some things that would probably happen. If you think something is probably going to happen, say "probably." If not, don't say anything.

- If you study hard, you will get an A on your test. *Probably.*
- If you stay up late, you will be in a good mood in the morning.
- If a snail tries to get out of the way, it will get stepped on.
- If you throw food at the dinner table, your mom will be upset. *Probably.*
- If you work hard and do your best, you will feel proud of yourself. *Probably.*
- If a dog has a litter of puppies, the puppies will resemble each other. *Probably.*

What describing word means "almost for sure"? *Probably.*

 Storage

In the story, the ants dig storage rooms. **Storage.** Say the word. *Storage.*

Storage is a describing word. It tells more about a place. What kind of word is **storage?** *A describing word.*

Storage is a safe place to keep things until you need them. Say the word that means "a safe place to keep things until you need them." *Storage.*

Let's think about some things that might be put in a storage place. I'll name some things. If you would put this thing away in storage, say "storage." If not, don't say anything.

- Camping equipment that you would need only in the summer. *Storage.*
- Your everyday clothes.
- Special dishes that you use only when you have company. *Storage.*
- Winter clothes that you don't need to wear in the summer. *Storage.*
- Your schoolbooks.
- Extra toys that you don't play with very often. *Storage.*

What describing word means "a safe place to keep things until you need them"? *Storage.*

◎—≺ *Corridor*

In the book, some of the things the ants dig are corridors. **Corridor.** Say the word. *Corridor.*

Corridor is a naming word. It names a place. What kind of word is **corridor?** *A naming word.*

A corridor is a long hallway. Say the word that means "a long hallway." *Corridor.*

I'll describe some things. If I describe a thing that has a corridor, say "corridor." If not, don't say anything.

- A school. *Corridor.*
- A one-room apartment.
- A large office building. *Corridor.*
- A hotel. *Corridor.*
- A bus.
- A beehive.

What naming word means "a long hallway"? *Corridor.*

◎—≺ *Surface*

In the book, we learned that when the sun warms the ground, ants carry the eggs and larvae up near the surface. **Surface.** Say the word. *Surface.*

Surface is a naming word. It tells what something is. What kind of word is **surface?** *A naming word.*

The surface of something is the outside of it. Say the word that means "the outside of something." *Surface.*

I'll tell about some things. If it is on the surface, say "surface." If not, don't say anything.

- An apple core.
- An apple peel. *Surface.*
- Grass. *Surface.*
- A car's paint. *Surface.*
- A boat on the water. *Surface.*
- A shark.

What naming word means "the outside of something"? *Surface.*

Present Vocabulary Tally Sheet
(See Lesson 1, page 3, for instructions.)

Assign Homework
(Homework Sheet, BLM 30a. See the Introduction for homework instructions.)

DAY 2

Preparation: Picture Vocabulary Cards for *probably, storage, corridor, surface.*

Read and Discuss Story

(Read story to children. Ask the following questions at the specified points. Encourage them to use target words in their answers.)

Pages 4–5. What question did the author ask? *Are you an ant?* Are you an ant? *No.* How do you know you're not an ant? (Idea: *My mother is not a queen.*) In this book, the author is pretending you are an ant. She talks to you as if you are an ant. How does the author talk to you? (Idea: *Like I'm an ant.*)

Pages 6–7. Where are you before you're born? (Idea: *In one of the eggs.*) When should you hatch? (Idea: *As soon as I can.*) Do you look like an ant when you're born? *No.* What are you? *A larva.* What do you eat as a larva? *The eggs my mother laid.*

Pages 8–9. What do you become after you are a larva? (Idea: *A pupa.*) *What is a pupa like?* (Idea: *A little like an egg, only larger.*) What will you look like when you change from a pupa to an ant? (Idea: *Like an ant, only white and soft.*) What will happen to your skin? (Idea: *It will become hard and black.*)

Pages 10–11. What do you work hard to do? *Build a nest.* What does the nest have in it? (Ideas: *Storage rooms; nurseries; bedrooms; corridors.*) Do you do all this work by yourself? *No.* Who helps you? *Other worker ants.* How do you talk to each other? *By touching our feelers together.*

Pages 12–13. What kinds of things do you like to eat? (Ideas: *Seeds; bugs; wood lice; springtails.*) What do you do to your prey? (Idea: *Bite it and then spray it with acid from my tail.*) Are you a good hunter? *No.* What's an easier way for you to get food? (Idea: *Look for bugs that have been stepped on.*)

Pages 14–15. What might you find in a kitchen that is nice to eat? (Ideas: *Crumbs of food; grains of sugar.*) What must you beware of? *People.* What might people do to you? (Ideas: *Squash me; poison me; sweep the floor so I can't find food.*)

Pages 16–17. What is the best food for an ant? *Honeydew.* Where does honeydew come from? *Aphids.* What is getting honeydew from an aphid like doing? *Milking a cow.* Why should you throw ladybug eggs away if you find them near your aphids? (Idea: *Ladybugs prey on aphids.*) That's right; ladybugs hunt and eat aphids.

Pages 18–19. What are some ways you can get food home? (Ideas: *Carry it; pull it; put it in your second stomach.*) What is your crop? (Idea: *My second stomach.*) What is useful about your crop? (Idea: *I can use it to carry spare food home.*)

Pages 20–21. What do you do back at the nest? (Ideas: *Feed the queen; feed the larvae;*

take care of the eggs and larvae; take out the garbage.*) Where should you bring the eggs and larvae when it's very cold? *Deep into the nest.* Where should you take them when it's warm? *Near the surface.*

Pages 22–23. What predators do you have to beware of? (Ideas: *Lizards; birds; toads.*) Why do some birds put you under their wings? (Idea: *Because the acid in my body kills ticks.*)

Pages 24–27. Are you an ant? *No.* What are you? *A human child.* How do you know you're a human child and not an ant? (Ideas: *I don't have to take care of eggs and larvae; I don't have to milk aphids; I probably don't have to march in a line with lots of others.*)

Pages 28–29. What are some of the things you can do that ants can't do? (Encourage each child to suggest something he or she can do that an ant can't.) Are you glad a bird will never, ever put you under its wing?

(Display the KWL chart.) Now that we've finished reading *Are You an Ant?* let's look at our chart again. (Point to the *Know* column.) As good scientists find out more about things, they sometimes change their minds about what they know is true. Let's see if we want to change our minds about any of the items on our **Know** list. (Read each item. Ask children if the item was mentioned in the book. If it was, ask if the item is true or not true. Untrue items are crossed out.) We're good scientists; we know how to change our minds when we learn new facts.

(Point to the *Want to Know* column.) As good scientists find out more about things, they find answers to some of their questions and they want to ask more questions. (Read each question. Ask children if the question was answered in the book. If it was, record the answer in the L (Learned) column and put a check mark in front of the question.) Are there any new questions we would like to ask about ants? (Record questions under the *W* column on the chart.) We're good scientists; we know how to use what we have learned to ask new questions.

Review Vocabulary

(Display the Picture Vocabulary Cards. Point to each card as you say the word. Ask children to repeat each word after you.) These pictures show **probably, storage, corridor,** and **surface.**

- What word means "a safe place to put things until you need them"? *Storage.*
- What word means "a long hallway"? *Corridor.*
- What word means "the outside of something"? *Surface.*
- What word means "almost for sure"? *Probably.*

Extend Vocabulary

◎← Surface

In *Are You an Ant?* we learned that the **surface** of something is its outside. Say the word that means "the outside of something." *Surface.*

Raise your hand if you can tell us a sentence that uses **surface** as a naming word meaning "the outside of something." (Call on several children. If they don't use complete sentences, restate their examples as sentences. Have the class repeat the sentences.)

Here's a new way to use the word **surface.**

- The submarine will **surface** in four hours.
- The fish **surfaced** to eat a mosquito.
- The groundhog **surfaced** on February 2.

In these sentences, surface is an action word that means to come up from below. What word means "to come up from below"? *Surface.*

Raise your hand if you can tell us a sentence that uses **surface** as an action word meaning "to come up from below." (Call on several children. If they don't use complete sentences, restate their examples as sentences. Have the class repeat the sentences.)

Present Expanded Target Vocabulary

◎← Colony

In the book, we learned that ants live in a big family. We call this a colony. **Colony.** Say the word. *Colony.*

Colony is a naming word. It names a thing. What kind of word is **colony?** *A naming word.*

A colony is a large group of insects that lives together. Say the word that means "a large group of insects that lives together." *Colony.*

I'll tell about some things. If they are a colony, say "colony." If not, don't say anything.

- The Smith family moved to Milwaukee.
- There is a big beehive in the tree in my yard. *Colony.*
- The pack of wolves ran through the woods.
- I found two lightning bugs in the grass.
- There are several anthills on the sidewalk. *Colony.*
- I saw about a hundred ants all in one area! *Colony.*
- The cat had a litter of kittens.

What naming word means "a large group of insects that lives together"? *Colony.*

◎← Metamorphosis

In the book, we learned that an ant is born in an egg, comes out as a larva, turns into a pupa, and finally becomes an adult ant. This process is called metamorphosis. **Metamorphosis.** Say the word. *Metamorphosis.*

Metamorphosis is a naming word. It names an event. What kind of word is **metamorphosis?** *A naming word.*

Metamorphosis is the change some animals go through as they grow from an egg into an adult. Say the word that means "the change some animals go through as they grow from an egg into an adult." *Metamorphosis.*

I'll tell about some animals. If the animal went through a metamorphosis, say "metamorphosis." If not, don't say anything.

- The lamb grew into a sheep.
- The caterpillar hatched from an egg, built a cocoon around itself, and grew into a butterfly. *Metamorphosis.*
- The tadpole hatched from an egg and grew into a frog. *Metamorphosis.*
- The cub grew into a bear.
- The baby grew into a man.
- The ant hatched from an egg, grew into larva, and then grew into an ant. *Metamorphosis.*

What naming word means "the change some animals go through as they grow from an egg to an adult"? *Metamorphosis.*

DAY 3

Preparation: Display KWL chart.

Read Did You Know?

Today I'll read you some facts about ants that Judy Allen put in the back of her book. (Read *Did You Know?* pages 30–31 with minimal interruptions.)

Complete KWL Chart

(Review questions children still want answered from the *W* column of the KWL chart.) Let's see if Judy Allen answered any of our questions in the *Did You Know?* part of her book.

(Read the first item on page 30, beginning with the words "Did you know …") Did these facts answer any of our questions? (If the item answered any of the remaining questions, put a check mark in front of the question, and write the answer in the *L* column next to the question. Repeat the question, and have children say the answer. If the item did not answer any of the remaining questions, ask children leading questions such as:) How many different kinds of ants are there? *About 10,000.* What did you learn about the different kinds of ants in the world? (Idea: *There are about 10,000 different kinds of ants living all over the world.* Record the fact in the *L* column near the bottom. Do not write the fact next to any of the unanswered questions.)

(Repeat the process for the remaining 4 items. If there are any unanswered questions after you have read and discussed the *Did You Know?* pages, challenge children to find the answers in the school library, on the Internet, or at home.)

Play What's My Word?

Today you will play *What's My Word?* I'll give you three clues. After I give each clue, if you are sure you know my word, you may

make a guess. If you guess correctly, you will win one point. If you make a mistake, I get the point.

Let's practice. Here's my first clue. My word is a naming word. Are you sure you know my word? If you are, you may make a guess. (If anyone wishes to guess, accept the guess. Award the point to either the class or the teacher.)

Here's my second clue. My word begins with the "s" sound. Are you sure you know my word? If you are, you may make a guess. (If anyone wishes to guess, accept the guess. Award the point to either the class or the teacher.)

Here's my third clue. My word means "the outside of something." Are you sure you know my word? If you are, you may make a guess. *Surface.* (Award the point to either the class or the teacher.)

(**Note:** If a child guesses the word correctly before the last clue, give the other clues and have children decide if the answer fits those clues.)

Now you're ready to play the game. (Draw a T-chart on the board for keeping score. Children earn one point for each correct answer. If they make an error, correct them as you normally would, and record one point for yourself. Repeat missed words at the end of the game.)

- Here's my first clue. My word is a describing word. Here's my second clue. My word has the "b" sound in it twice. Here's my third clue. My word means "almost for sure." What's my word? *Probably.*
- New word. Here's my first clue. My word is a naming word. Here's my second clue. Some animals go through my word, but no people do. Here's my third clue. My word means "the change some animals go through as they grow from an egg to an adult." What's my word? *Metamorphosis.*
- New word. Here's my first clue. My word is a naming word. Here's my second clue. My word has the "j" sound at the end. Here's my third clue. My word means "a safe place where you put something until you need it." What's my word? *Storage.*

- New word. Here's my first clue. My word is an action word. Here's my second clue. You can do my word in water. Here's my third clue. My word means "to come up from below." What's my word? *Surface.*
- New word. Here's my first clue. My word is a naming word. Here's my second clue. My word is usually used with insects. Here's my third clue. My word means "a large group of insects that lives together." What's my word? *Colony.*
- New word. Here's my first clue. My word is a naming word. Here's my second clue. My word can be found in a school and a hotel. Here's my third clue. My word means "a long hallway." What's my word? *Corridor.*

(Count the points and declare a winner.) You did a great job of playing *What's My Word?*

DAY 4

Preparation: *About Ants* booklet.

Print the following words in two columns on the board: *queen, pupa, pupae, white, rooms, honeydew, aphids.*

Read the About Ants Booklet

(Point to each word as you read it) This word is **queen.** What word? *Queen.* This word is **pupa.** What word? *Pupa.* This word is **pupae.** It means "more than one **pupa.**" (Repeat process for remaining words.)

Let's read these words together. First word? *Queen.* Next word? *Pupa.* (Repeat process for remaining words.)

Read these words by yourself. First word? *Queen.* Next word? *Pupa.* (Repeat process for remaining words until children can read the list accurately and confidently.)

(Use the following correction procedure if children make an error:) This word is **honeydew.** What word? *Honeydew.* Yes, **honeydew.** (Go back to the top of the list and repeat the list until children can read it accurately and confidently.)

(Give each child a copy of the *About Ants* booklet.) My turn to read each page of the

booklet. You touch under each word as I read it. (After you have read page 1, have children point to each part of the ant on the illustration as you name it.)

Let's read the story together. (Have children read the story aloud with you.)

(Assign each child a partner. Allow sufficient time for each child to read the book to his or her partner. Circulate as the children read, offering praise and assistance.)

(Children should color the illustrations in their *About Ants* booklet. Encourage them to color the illustrations accurately.) This book is a science book. When artists color scientific illustrations they use colors that are real.

(Show children page 4 of the booklet. Point to the pupae.) What are these? *Pupae.* What color should pupae be? *Yellow.* (Point to the ant that is emerging from the pupa.) What color should this ant be? *White.* (Point to the first ant that has emerged.) What color should this ant be? *White.* (Point to the next ant.) What color should this ant be? *Black.* Remember to use the real colors when you color the illustrations.

Play What's My Word? (Cumulative Review)

Let's play *What's My Word?* You'll have to think really hard, because my word can be any word we've learned since we read *The Ant and the Grasshopper.* I'll give you three clues. After I give each clue, if you are sure you know my word, you may make a guess. If you guess correctly, you will win one point. If you make a mistake, I get the point.

Let's practice. Here's my first clue. My word is a naming word. Are you sure you know my word? If you are, you may make a guess. (If anyone wishes to guess, accept the guess. Award the point to either the class or the teacher.)

Here's my second clue. My word is something that you can observe. Are you sure you know my word? If you are, you may make a guess. (If anyone wishes to guess, accept the guess. Award the point to either the class or the teacher.)

Here's my third clue. My word means "a small animal that has three body parts and six legs." What's my word? *Insect.* (Award the point to either the class or the teacher.)

(**Note:** If a child guesses the word correctly before the last clue, give the other clues and have children decide if the answer fits those clues.)

Now you're ready to play the game. (Draw a T-chart on the board for keeping score. Children earn one point for each correct answer. If they make an error, correct them as you normally would, and record one point for yourself. Repeat missed words at the end of the game.)

- Here's my first clue. My word is an action word. Here's my second clue. My word has a "x" sound in it. Here's my third clue. My word means "to travel around to see what places are like." What's my word? *Explore.*
- New word. Here's my first clue. My word is a naming word. Here's my second clue. Tadpoles do my word, but humans don't. Here's my third clue. My word means "the change some animals go through as they grow from an egg to an adult." What's my word? *Metamorphosis.*
- New word. Here's my first clue. My word is a naming word. Here's my second clue. My word starts with the "k" sound. Here's my third clue. My word means "a large group of insects that lives together." What's my word? *Colony.*
- New word. Here's my first clue. My word can have two different meanings. Here's my second clue. One of my meanings is an action. Here's my third clue. My word means "to hunt and eat." What's my word? *Prey.*
- New word. Here's my first clue. My word is a describing word. Here's my second clue. My word has the "b" sound in it twice. Here's my third clue. My word means "almost for sure." What's my word? *Probably.*
- New word. Here's my first clue. My word is a naming word. Here's my second clue. My word can name a part of the ground, water, or an object. Here's my third clue. My word means "the outside of something." What's my word? *Surface.*

- New word. Here's my first clue. My word has more than one meaning. Here's my second clue. My word is an action word. Here's my third clue. My word means "to come up from below." What's my word? *Surface.*
- New word. Here's my first clue. My word is an action word. Here's my second clue. My word is something your parents might do. Here's my third clue. My word means "used a very firm voice to say what you were going to do and wouldn't give in." What's my word? *Insisted.*
- New word. Here's my first clue. My word is a naming word. Here's my second clue. My word can be found in a school, in a large office building, and in a hotel. Here's my third clue. My word means "a long hallway." What's my word? *Corridor.*
- New word. Here's my first clue. My word is a naming word. Here's my second clue. You might put your winter things in me in the summer and your summer things in me in the winter. Here's my third clue. My word is a safe place to put your things until you need them. What's my word? *Storage.*

(Count the points and declare a winner.) You did a great job of playing *What's My Word?*

DAY 5

Preparation: *About Ants* booklet.

Chart titled *Reading Goals* that was started in Week 21.

Happy Face Game Test Sheet, BLM B.

Read About Ants Booklet

(Assign each child a partner.) Today you'll read your booklet, *About Ants,* to your partner. (Allow sufficient time for each child to read the book to his or her partner. Circulate as the children read, offering praise and assistance.)

(Ask children to look at the back of their booklet about ants.) This part of the booklet is for people who can help you find other books to read. It tells those people about other books that are like *Are You an Ant?* It also tells them about a place where you can find other books. Where are some places that you could go to find other books about ants and other insects? (Ideas: *To the school library; to the public library; to a bookstore.*)

(You may wish to read and discuss the information on the back cover.)

There's one more important thing on the back cover of your booklet. Touch the box that is at the bottom of the page. The words above the box say "My reading goal." What do the words say? *My reading goal.*

A goal is something that you want to succeed at doing. What is a goal? *Something that you want to succeed at doing.* A reading goal is something that you want to succeed at doing with your reading.

Let's see if we can add some other reading goals to our class chart. What are some other reading goals that someone might have when they read their book? (Accept reasonable responses. Help children put their ideas into goal statements. Add to the list of statements on the chart. Ask children to choose a goal and copy it into the box. Children may also make up an original goal that is not on the list. If children are unable to copy the goals or to write a goal of their own, you or a helper may wish to scribe their goal statements for them before the booklets are sent home.)

Assess Vocabulary

 (Give each child a copy of the Happy Face Game Test Sheet, BLM B.)

Today you're going to play the Happy Face Game. When you play the Happy Face Game, it shows me how well you know the hard words you are learning.

If I say something that is true, color in the happy face. What will you do if I say something that is true? *Color in the happy face.*

If I say something that is false, color in the sad face. What will you do if I say something that is false? *Color in the sad face.*

Listen carefully to each item that I say. Don't let me trick you!

Item 1: The aisle of a bus is also called a

corridor. (*False.*)

Item 2: Some insects, like ants, go through a **metamorphosis** as they grow into adults. (*True.*)

Item 3: When you **harvest** your crops, you plant the seeds so they will grow. (*False.*)

Item 4: Your classroom can be called a **colony.** (*False.*)

Item 5: Boats float on the **surface** of the water. (*True.*)

Item 6: A batch of fresh, hot muffins can be very **tempting.** (*True.*)

Item 7: When a submarine **surfaces,** it comes to the top of the water. (*True.*)

Item 8: Putting your winter clothes in a **storage** box helps keep your closet neater in the summer. (*True.*)

Item 9: You would go to the **police station** if you wanted to mail a letter. (*False.*)

Item 10: A dog and a cat that are running through the house knocking things down are being **disruptive.** (*True.*)

You did a great job of playing the Happy Face Game!

(Score children's work. A child must score 9 out of 10 to be at the mastery level. If a child does not achieve mastery, insert the missed words as additional items in the games in next week's lessons. Retest those children individually for the missed items before they take the next mastery test.)

Extensions

Read a Book as a Reward

(Read *Are you an Ant?* or another book about ants or other insects to children as a reward for their hard work.)

Preparation: Word containers for the Super Words Center.

Note: You will need to keep the cards that were removed from the center. They will be used again later in the program.

Introduce the Super Words Center

(Put the Picture Vocabulary Cards from weeks 5 and 30 into the word cans. Make duplicates of each card to create a "Concentration" game. You may make as many sets of duplicates as you wish to suit your class).

(Show children one of the word containers. Demonstrate how the game is played by role-playing the game with a child. Repeat the demonstration process until the children can play the game with confidence.)

Let's think about how we work with our words in the Super Words Center.

You will work with a partner in the Super Words Center. Whom will you work with in the center? *A partner.*

There are two cards for each word in the Super Words Center. You will play a game called *Concentration.* When you play *Concentration,* you try to find two cards that match. **Match** means that both cards show the same picture and word. What does **match** mean? *Both cards show the same picture and word.*

First you will take all of the cards out of the container and place them facedown in rows on the table. What do you do first? (Idea: *Take all of the cards out and place them facedown in rows on the table.*)

Next you pick one card and turn it faceup in its spot. What do you do next? (Idea: *I pick a card and turn it faceup in its spot.*)

Then ask your partner what word the picture shows. What do you do next? (Idea: *I ask my partner what word the picture shows.*)

If your partner doesn't know the word, tell them the word. What do you do if your partner doesn't know the word? *Tell my partner the word.*

Then you will give your partner a turn. What do you do next? *Give my partner a turn.*

If your partner turns over a card that is the same as your card, he or she can take those two cards. What can your partner do? (Idea: *He or she can take both cards if he or she chooses one that is the same as my first card.*)

Appendices

Vocabulary Tally Sheet

	Weekly Tally		Weekly Tally
Picture Vocabulary Card		**Picture Vocabulary Card**	
	Weekly Tally		Weekly Tally
Picture Vocabulary Card		**Picture Vocabulary Card**	
	Weekly Tally		Weekly Tally
Picture Vocabulary Card		**Picture Vocabulary Card**	

Happy Face Game Test

Name: _____ Date: _____

Week: _____ Score: _____

Mastery Achieved: Yes   No

 1.

 2.

 3.

 4.

 5.

 6.

 7.

 8.

 9.

 10.

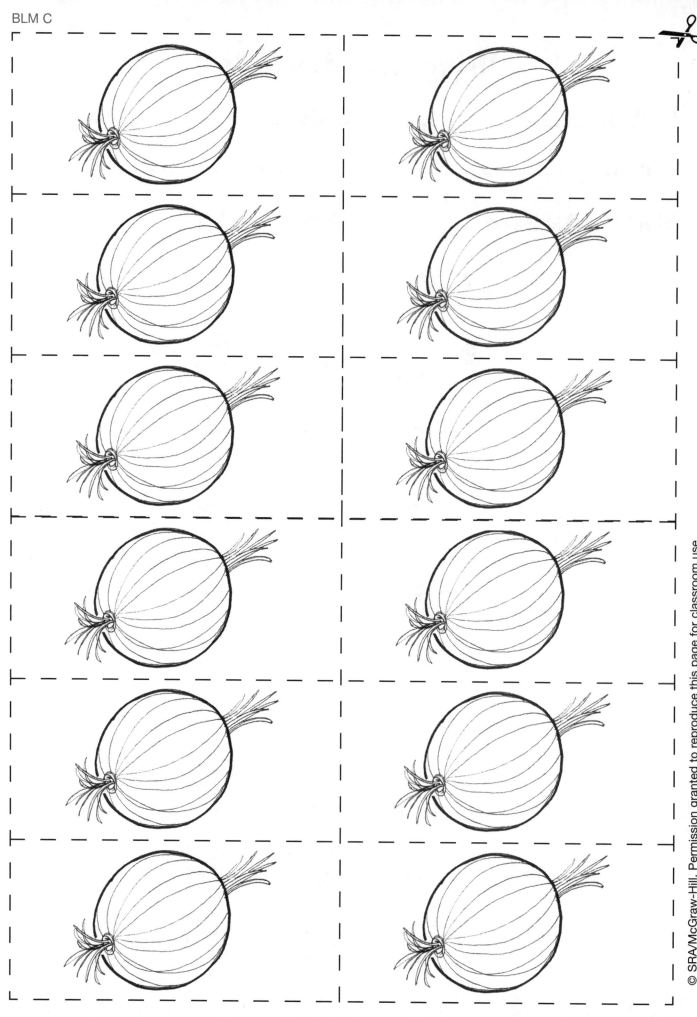

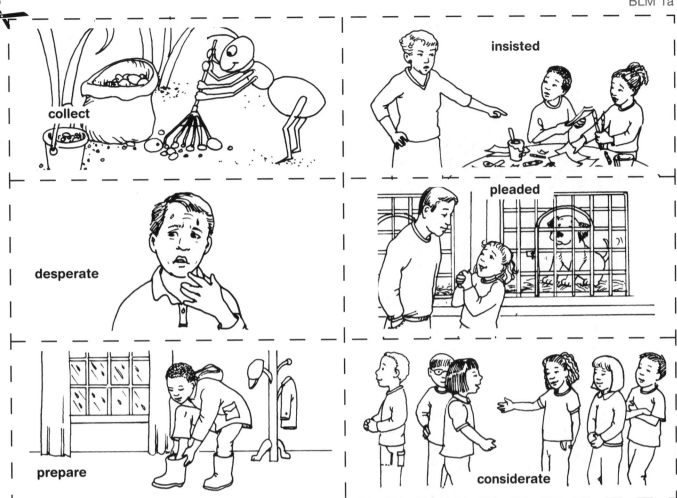

Sharing What You've Learned at School

Note: Children are not expected to be able to read the words. They are for your information.

DAY 1: (Cut the Picture Vocabulary Cards apart. Place the picture cards for *collect, pleaded, insisted,* and *prepare* in a container or small plastic bag.) (Show the child each picture card.) **What word does the picture show?** (Idea: *The picture shows an ant collecting food for winter.*)
Tell me what you know about this word. (You may wish to share what you know about the word with the child as well.)

DAY 2: (Add in 2 new words, *desperate* and *considerate.* Repeat procedure from Day 1.) **Tell me anything more that you know about this word.**

DAY 3: *Show Me, Tell Me* Game (Round One)
Let's play the *Show Me, Tell Me* game you learned at school. I'll ask you to show me how to do something. If you show me, you will win one point. If you can't show me, I get the point. Next I'll ask you to tell me. If you tell me, you will win one point. If you can't tell me, I get the point.

• **Show me how you would collect toys from the floor. Tell me what you do.** *Collect toys from the floor.*

• **Show me what you would do if you really wanted a tasty treat very badly. Tell me what you did.** *Pleaded.*
• **Show me how you would prepare to go to school in the morning. Tell me what you do.** *Prepare to go to school.*
• **Show me how you would insist that I put you to bed. Tell me what you did.** *Insisted.*
• **Show me how you would look if you liked to collect stamps. What do you like to do?** *Collect stamps.*
• **Show me how you would prepare a snack. What do you do?** *Prepare a snack.*
(If the child is enjoying this game, you may wish to add additional examples.)

DAY 4: *Show Me, Tell Me* Game (Round Two)
(Add the last two words, *desperate* and *considerate,* to the bag or container. Repeat procedure from Day 3.)

Beginning

Middle

End

Crept

Remember

Winding

Cross

Disobedient

Brave

Sharing What You've Learned at School

Note: Children are not expected to be able to read the words. They are for your information.

DAY 1: (Cut the Picture Vocabulary Cards apart. Place the picture cards for *cross, crept, remember,* and *winding* in a container or small plastic bag.)
(Show the child each picture card.) **What word does the picture show?** (Idea: *The picture shows someone who is feeling angry.*)
Tell me what you know about this word. (You may wish to share what you know about the word with the child as well.)

DAY 2: (Add in 2 new words, *brave* and *disobedient*.) (Repeat procedure from Day 1.) **Tell me anything more that you know about this word.**

DAY 3: *Show Me, Tell Me* Game (Round One)
Let's play the *Show Me, Tell Me* game you learned at school. I'll ask you to show me how to do something. If you show me, you will win one point. If you can't show me, I get the point. Next I'll ask you to tell me. If you tell me, you will win one point. If you can't tell me, I get the point.

- **Show me how I would look if you made me wait for you to get dressed for school. Tell me how you looked.** *Cross.*

- **Show me how you would get past a mean dog without him seeing you. Tell me what you did.** *I crept.*
- **Show me how a road that twists up a mountainside would look. Tell me how it looked.** *Winding.*
- **Show me how you would look if someone broke your favorite toy. Tell me how you looked.** *Cross.*
- **Show me how you would wind up a toy mouse. Tell me what you were doing.** *Winding.*
(If the child is enjoying this game, you may wish to add additional examples.)

DAY 4: *Show Me, Tell Me* Game (Round Two)
(Add the last two words, *brave* and *disobedient,* to the bag or container. Repeat procedure from Day 3.)

Beginning	Middle	End

Sharing What You've Learned at School

Note: Children are not expected to be able to read the words. They are for your information.

DAY 1: (Cut the Picture Vocabulary Cards apart. Place the picture cards for *gathering, meadow, roared,* and *angry* in a container or small plastic bag.)
(Show the child each picture card.) **What word does the picture show?** (Idea: *The picture shows someone who is feeling angry.*)
Tell me what you know about this word. (You may wish to share what you know about the word with the child as well.)

DAY 2: (Add in 2 new words, *furious* and *delicious.* Repeat procedure from Day 1.) **Tell me anything more that you know about this word.**

DAY 3: *Show Me, Tell Me* Game (Round One)
Let's play the *Show Me, Tell Me* game you learned at school. I'll ask you to show me how to do something. If you show me, you will win one point. If you can't show me, I get the point. Next I'll ask you to tell me. If you tell me, you will win one point. If you can't tell me, I get the point.

- **Show me how you would gather up your toys from the floor. Tell me what you're doing.** *Gathering toys from the floor.*

- **Show me how a lion would sound if it roared. Tell me what the lion did.** *It roared.*
- **Show me how your face would look if you felt angry when someone broke your favorite toy. Tell me how you are feeling.** *Angry.*
- **Show me how you would gather flowers in the meadow. Tell me where you gathered flowers.** *In the meadow.*
- **Show me how a vacuum cleaner would sound if it roared. Tell me what the vacuum cleaner did.** *It roared.*
- **Show me how your face would look if you felt angry when someone pushed you in line. Tell me how you are feeling.** *Angry.*

(If the child is enjoying this game, you may wish to add additional examples.)

DAY 4: *Show Me, Tell Me* Game (Round Two)
(Add the last two words, *furious* and *delicious,* to the bag or container. Repeat procedure from Day 3.)

Beginning

Middle

End

Cottage

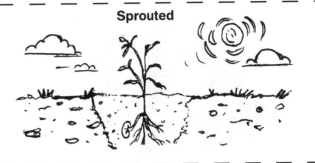

Sprouted

Uncooperative

Harvest

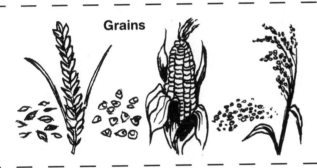

Grains

Determined

Sharing What You've Learned at School

Note: Children are not expected to be able to read the words. They are for your information.

DAY 1: (Cut the Picture Vocabulary Cards apart. Place the picture cards for *cottage, harvest, grains,* and *sprouted* in a container or small plastic bag.) (Show the child each picture card.) **What word does the picture show?** (Idea: *A cottage.*) **Tell me what you know about this word.** (You may wish to share what you know about the word with the child as well.)

DAY 2: (Add in 2 new words, *determined* and *uncooperative.* Repeat procedure from Day 1.) **Tell me anything more that you know about this word.**

DAY 3: *Show Me, Tell Me* Game (Round One) **Let's play the *Show Me, Tell Me* game you learned at school. I'll ask you to show me how to do something. If you show me, you will win one point. If you can't show me, I get the point. Next I'll ask you to tell me. If you tell me, you will win one point. If you can't tell me, I get the point.**

- **Show me the look you would have on your face if you were spending time at a cottage at the beach. Tell me the name of the place that made you look that way.** *Cottage.*

- **Show me what you would do to harvest a field of carrots. Tell me what you did.** *I harvested carrots.*
- **Show me how it would look to hold a big handful of grains. Tell me what you were holding.** *Grains.*
- **Show me how you would look if you were a seed that had just sprouted. Tell me what you did.** *I sprouted.*
- **Show me how you would look if you had a grain of sand in your eye. Tell me what you had in your eye.** *A grain of sand.*
- **Show me how you would look if you were to harvest apples from a tree. Tell me what you did.** *I harvested apples.*

(If the child is enjoying this game, you may wish to add additional examples.)

DAY 4: *Show Me, Tell Me* Game (Round Two) (Add the last two words, *determined* and *uncooperative,* to the bag or container. Repeat procedure from Day 3.)

Beginning

Middle

End

Decided

Squeaked

Disagreeable

Shouted

Muttered

I don't know.

Starving

Sharing What You've Learned at School

Note: Children are not expected to be able to read the words. They are for your information.

DAY 1: (Cut the Picture Vocabulary Cards apart. Place the picture cards for *decided, shouted, squeaked,* and *muttered* in a container or small plastic bag.) (Show the child each picture card.) **What word does the picture show?** (Idea: *Someone who shouted.*) **Tell me what you know about this word.** (You may wish to share what you know about the word with the child as well.)

DAY 2: (Add in 2 new words, *starving* and *disagreeable.* Repeat procedure from Day 1.) **Tell me anything more that you know about this word.**

DAY 3: *Whoopsy!* (Round One)
Let's play the *Whoopsy!* game you learned at school. I'll say sentences using words you learned. If the word doesn't fit in the sentence, you say "Whoopsy!" Then I'll ask you to say a sentence where the word fits. If you can do it, you get a point. If you can't do it, I get the point. If the word I use fits the sentence, don't say anything.

- **I muttered when ... I wanted everyone to hear me.** *Whoopsy!* **Can you finish the sentence so the word fits?** (Idea: *I muttered when I didn't want anyone to hear me*)
- **The mouse squeaked when ... it saw the cat.**
- **I decided what to do when ... I couldn't make up my mind.** *Whoopsy!* **Can you finish the sentence so the word fits?** (Idea: *I decided what to do when I carefully thought about it and chose to do it.*)
- **I shouted when ... I didn't want anyone to hear what I said.** *Whoopsy!* **Can you finish the sentence so the word fits?** (*Idea: I shouted when I wanted everyone to hear me.*)

(If the child is enjoying this game, you may wish to add additional examples.)

DAY 4: *Whoopsy!* (Round Two)
(Add the last two words, *starving* and *disagreeable,* to the bag or container. Repeat procedure from Day 3.)

Name _____

The Three Billy Goats Gruff

I live close to a river.
I was very hungry.
I have two brothers.
I was the first one to
cross the bridge.
Who am I?

I live close to a river.
I was very hungry.
I have two brothers.
I was the second one to
cross the bridge.
Who am I?

I was very hungry.
I wanted to cross the
river to the other side.
I have two brothers.
I knocked the troll into
the water.
Who am I?

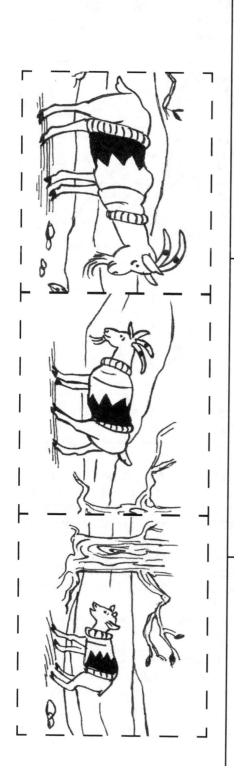

peacefully

comfortably

rough

tempting

trespassing

NO TRESPASSING

enormous

Sharing What You've Learned at School

Note: Children are not expected to be able to read the words. They are for your information.

DAY 1: (Cut the Picture Vocabulary Cards apart. Place the picture cards for *peacefully, comfortably, rough,* and *tempting* in a container or small plastic bag.) (Show the child each picture card.) **What word does the picture show?** (Idea: *The picture shows children working peacefully on a puzzle.*).
Tell me what you know about this word. (You may wish to share what you know about the word with your child as well.)

DAY 2: (Add in 2 new words, *trespassing* and *enormous.* Repeat procedure from Day 1.) **Tell me anything more that you know about this word.**

DAY 3: *Whoopsy!* **(Round One)**
Let's play the *Whoopsy!* game that you learned at school. I'll say sentences using words you learned. If the word doesn't fit in the sentence, you say "Whoopsy!" Then I'll ask you to say a sentence where the word fits. If you can do it, you get a point. If you can't do it, I get the point. If the word I use fits the sentence, don't say anything.

- **The children were playing peacefully when ... they were throwing puzzle pieces all around the room.** *Whoopsy!* (Idea: *The children were playing peacefully when they worked together to finish the puzzle.*)
- **The tempting smell of the apple pie made me want to ... run away as fast as I could.** *Whoopsy!* (Idea: *The tempting smell of the apple pie made me* want to *eat the pie right away.*)
- **My shoes fitted me comfortably when ... they gave me blisters and pinched my toes.** *Whoopsy!* (Idea: *My shoes fitted me comfortably when they didn't hurt my feet at all.*)
- **The rough voice of the storekeeper sounded ... gentle and kind.** *Whoopsy!* (Idea: *The rough voice of the storekeeper sounded harsh, not gentle or kind.*)
- **The rough skin of the cantaloupe felt ... as smooth as glass.** *Whoopsy!* (Idea: *The rough skin of the cantaloupe felt bumpy.*)

(If the child is enjoying this game, you may wish to add additional examples.)

DAY 4: *Whoopsy!* **(Round Two)**
(Add the last two words, *trespassing* and *enormous* to the bag or container. Repeat procedure from Day 3.)

Name _____

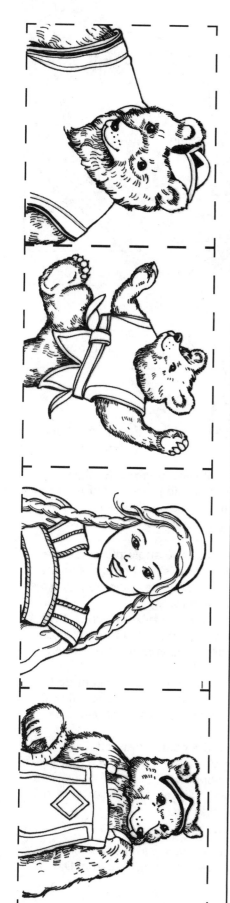

Goldilocks and the Three Bears

I like porridge.
I went upstairs in the house.
I have brown fur.
I found my pillow had been moved.
Who am I?

I went for a walk.
I walked with my family.
I saw someone had been sitting in my chair.
My chair was broken.
Who am I?

I sat on a chair.
I went upstairs in the house in the woods.
I slept in a bed.
I was trespassing.
Who am I?

Sharing What You've Learned at School

Note: Children are not expected to be able to read the words. They are for your information.

DAY 1: (Cut the Picture Vocabulary Cards apart. Place the picture cards for *noble, fine, wise,* and *exclaimed* in a container or small plastic bag. Show the child each picture card. **What word does the picture show?** (Idea: *The picture shows someone who is wise.*) **Tell me what you know about this word.** (You may wish to share what you know about the word with the child as well.)

DAY 2: (Add in 2 new words, *genuine* and *sensitive.* Repeat procedure from Day 1.) **Tell me anything more that you know about this word.**

DAY 3: *Whoopsy!* **(Round One)**
Let's play the *Whoopsy!* game that you learned at school. I'll say sentences using words you learned. If the word doesn't fit in the sentence, you say **"Whoopsy!"** Then I'll ask you to say a sentence where the word fits. If you can do it, you get a point. If you can't do it, I get the point. If the word I use fits the sentence, don't say anything.

- **Everyone said Doug was a fine young man when … he spent all of his allowance on himself.** *Whoopsy!* (Idea: *Everyone said Doug was a fine young man when he shared his allowance with others.*)
- **"What a beautiful day!"… Roger exclaimed.**
- **The lady was fined when … she crossed the street at the crosswalk.** *Whoopsy!* (Idea: *The lady was fined when she didn't cross the street in the crosswalk.*)
- **She was sensitive to fish because … she liked fish a lot.** *Whoopsy!* (Idea: *She was sensitive to fish because she got sick when she ate them.*)
- **The noble queen … was mean and selfish.** *Whoopsy!* (Idea: *The noble queen was a good person who would share what she had with others.*)
(If the child is enjoying this game, you may wish to add additional examples.)

DAY 4: *Whoopsy!* **(Round Two)**
(Add the last two words, *genuine* and *sensitive,* to the bag or container. Repeat procedure from Day 3.)

Name _____

The Princess and the Pea

I am a person.
I live in a castle.
I wanted to find a real princess.
I am the prince's mother.
Who am I?

I am a person.
I live in a castle.
I wanted to find a real princess.
I am the prince's father.
Who am I?

I am a person.
I live in a castle.
I am married.
I married the prince.
Who am I?

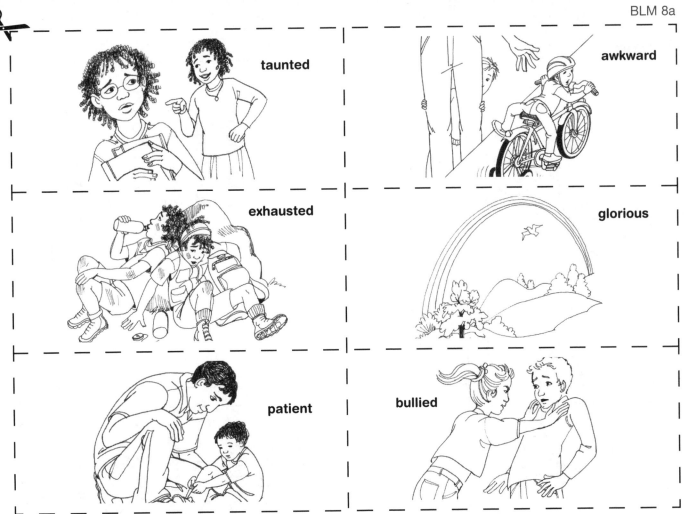

taunted

awkward

exhausted

glorious

patient

bullied

Sharing What You've Learned at School

Note: Children are not expected to be able to read the words. They are for your information.

DAY 1: (Cut the Picture Vocabulary Cards apart. Place the picture cards for *taunted, awkward, exhausted,* and *glorious* in a container or small plastic bag.) (Show the child each picture card.) **What word does the picture show?** (Idea: *A glorious rainbow.*) **Tell me what you know about this word.** (You may wish to share what you know about the word with the child as well.)

DAY 2: (Add in 2 new words *patient* and *bullied.* Repeat procedure from Day 1.) **Tell me anything more that you know about this word.**

DAY 3: *Whoopsy!* (Round One)
Let's play the *Whoopsy!* game that you learned at school. I'll say sentences using words you learned. If the word doesn't fit in the sentence, you say "Whoopsy!" Then I'll ask you to say a sentence where the word fits. If you can do it, you get a point. If you can't do it, I get the point. If the word I use fits the sentence, don't say anything.

- **Joanna was awkward when ... she danced the Mexican Hat Dance with no mistakes.** *Whoopsy!* (Idea: *Joanna was awkward when she had trouble dancing the Mexican Hat Dance.*)
- **The children taunted the little boy when ... they told him he was a good batter at baseball.** *Whoopsy!* (Idea: *The children taunted the little boy when they said he would never hit the ball.*)
- **Jamal felt awkward when ... he had to introduce his parents to his teacher.**
- **The girls were exhausted after ... they walked to the corner store.** *Whoopsy!* (Idea: *The girls were exhausted after they walked 10 miles in the thick woods.*)
- **The swan felt a glorious feeling when ... the other ducks bullied her.** *Whoopsy!* (Idea: *The swan felt a glorious feeling when she realized she was a swan.*)

(If the child is enjoying this game, you may wish to add additional examples.)

DAY 4: *Whoopsy!* (Round Two)
(Add the last two words *patient* and *bullied,* to the bag or container. Repeat procedure from Day 3.

Name _____

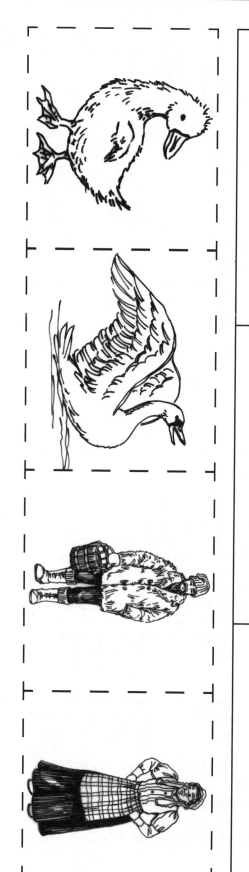

The Ugly Duckling

I am a bird.
I can swim.
I can fly.
I am white
I am beautiful.
Who am I?

I am a person.
I let the ugly duckling
come into my house.
I saved the duckling
from the ice.
My children frightened
the duckling.
Who am I?

I am a young bird.
I can fly.
I think that I am a duck.
I was bullied by
everyone.
Who am I?

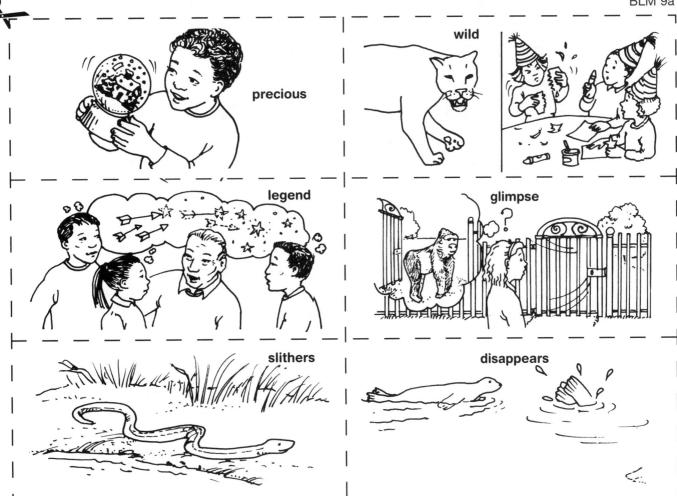

precious

wild

legend

glimpse

slithers

disappears

Sharing What You've Learned at School

Note: Children are not expected to be able to read the words. They are for your information.

DAY 1: (Cut the Picture Vocabulary Cards apart. Place the picture cards for *precious, glimpse, wild,* and *slithers* in a container or small plastic bag.) (Show the child each picture card.) **What word does the picture show?** (Idea: *The picture shows something precious.*)
Tell me what you know about this word. (You may wish to share what you know about the word with the child as well.)

DAY 2: (Add in 2 new words, *legend* and *disappears.* Repeat procedure from Day 1.) **Tell me anything more that you know about this word.**

DAY 3: *Chew the Fat* (Round One)
Let's play the *Chew the Fat* game that you learned at school. I'll say sentences with your vocabulary words in them. If I use the word correctly, say "Well done!" If I use the word incorrectly, say "Chew the fat." Then I'll ask you to finish the sentence so that it makes sense.

- **The book was precious to him because …** he didn't like the story. *Chew the fat.* **The book was precious to him because. Can you finish

the sentence so it makes sense?** (Idea: *It was very special and he loved the story.*) **Let's say the sentence together. *The book was precious to him because it was very special and he loved the story.***
- **The wild parrot lives … in the rainforests of Africa.** *Well done!*
- **Wally glimpsed the moon when … it was high in the clear sky.** *Chew the fat.* **Wally glimpsed the moon when. Can you finish the sentence so it makes sense?** (Idea: *It was low and behind some trees.*) **Let's say the sentence together. *Wally glimpsed the moon when it was low and behind some trees.***
- **Jillian slithered across the floor when she pretended to be a snake.** *Well done!*
- **Mark knew the deer was wild when … it walked up to him and let him pet it.** *Chew the fat.* **Mark knew the deer was wild when. Can you finish the sentence so it makes sense?** (Idea: *It ran away when it saw him.*) **Let's say the sentence together. *Mark knew the deer was wild when it ran away when it saw him.***

(If the child is enjoying this game, you may wish to add additional examples.)

DAY 4: *Chew the Fat* (Round Two)
(Add the last two words, *legend* and *disappears,* to the bag or container. Repeat procedure from Day 3.)

Name _____

The Loon's Necklace
(A Tsimshian Story)

An old _____ _____

not _____. He said, "Loon, please help

_____ _____"

The loon used his magic to fix the old man's

eyes. "Thank you, Loon," the _____ said.

He gave the loon his necklace _____ of

shells. The white shells _____ the loon's

neck turned into white feathers.

calm

tunnel

soared

directions

journey

protect

Sharing What You've Learned at School

Note: Children are not expected to be able to read the words. They are for your information.

DAY 1: (Cut the Picture Vocabulary Cards apart. Place the picture cards for *calm, tunnel, soared,* and *directions* in a container or small plastic bag.) (Show the child each picture card.) **What word does the picture show?** (Idea: *The picture shows a tunnel.*) **Tell me what you know about this word.** (You may wish to share what you know about the word with your child as well.)

DAY 2: (Add in 2 new words, *journey* and *protect.* Repeat procedure from Day 1.) **Tell me anything more that you know about this word.**

DAY 3: *Chew the Fat* (Round One)
Let's play the *Chew the Fat* game you learned at school. I'll say sentences with your vocabulary words in them. If I use the word correctly, say, "Well done!" If I use the word incorrectly, say, "Chew the fat." Then I'll ask you to finish the sentence so that it makes sense.

- **The hawk soared when …** it sat on its nest. *Chew the fat.* **The hawk soared when. Can you finish the sentence so it makes sense?** (Idea: *It flew high in the sky.*) **Let's say the sentence together. *The hawk soared when it flew high in the sky.***
- **The leaves on the trees were still when …** the wind was **calm.** *Well done!*

- **I followed the directions for making bread when …** I didn't read the recipe. *Chew the fat.* **I followed the directions for making bread when. Can you finish the sentence so it makes sense?** (Idea: *I did what the recipe told me to do.*) **Let's say the sentence together. *I followed the directions for making bread when I did what the recipe told me to do.***
- **My mother told me to calm down when I was** waiting politely for the party to begin. *Chew the fat.* **My mother told me to calm down when. Can you finish the sentence so it makes sense?** (Idea: *I couldn't be still while waiting for the party to begin.*) **Let's say the sentence together. *My mother told me to calm down when I couldn't be still while waiting for the party to begin.***
- **When I was in the tunnel …** I was up in the sky. *Chew the fat.* **When I was in the tunnel. Can you finish the sentence so it makes sense?** (Idea: *I was under the ground.*) **Let's say the sentence together. *When I was in the tunnel I was underground.***

(If the child is enjoying this game, you may wish to add additional examples.)

DAY 4: *Chew the Fat* (Round Two)
(Add the last two words *journey* and *protect* to the bag or container. Repeat procedure from Day 3.)

Name _____

Why Possum Has a Skinny Tail

[ ] said "I will get the [ ]." He dug a

[ ] with his [ ]. He went to the other side

of the [ ] . [ ] put some of the [ ] in

his [ ] and ran and ran. His tail got on [ ] .

The animals put out the [ ] , but his [ ] got

all skinny. And possums have had [ ] ever since.

frontier

gentle

adventures

dangerous

appreciated

imagination

Sharing What You've Learned at School

Note: Children are not expected to be able to read the words. They are for your information.

DAY 1: (Cut the Picture Vocabulary Cards apart. Place the picture cards for *gentle, frontier, dangerous,* and *adventures* in a container or small plastic bag.) (Show the child each picture card.) **What word does the picture show?** (Idea: *Something dangerous.*) **Tell me what you know about this word.**

DAY 2: (Add in 2 new words, *imagination* and *appreciated.* Repeat procedure from Day 1.) **Tell me anything more that you know about this word.**

DAY 3: *Chew the Fat* **(Round One)**
Let's play the *Chew the Fat* **game you learned at school. I'll say sentences with your vocabulary words in them. If I use the word correctly, say, "Well done!" If I use the word incorrectly, say, "Chew the fat." Then I'll ask you to finish the sentence so that it makes sense.**

- **The gentle giant … was mean to everyone.** *Chew the fat.* **The gentle giant. Can you finish the sentence so it makes sense?** (Idea: *Was kind to everyone.*) **Let's say the sentence together.** *The gentle giant was kind to everyone.*

- **It is dangerous to not wear your helmet when you ride your bicycle.** *Well done!*
- **The farmers lived on the frontier when they lived between the empty prairies and the city.** *Well done!*
- **The family had many adventures when … they stayed inside their house.** *Chew the fat.* **The family had many adventures when. Can you finish the sentence so it makes sense?** (Idea: *They traveled around the world.*) **Let's say the sentence together.** *The family had many adventures when they traveled around the world.*
- **The gentle breeze knocked branches off the tree.** *Chew the fat.* **The gentle breeze. Can you finish the sentence so it makes sense?** (Idea: *moved the leaves a little bit.*) **Let's say the sentence together.** *The gentle breeze moved the leaves a little bit.*
- **When she used the gentle soap … her skin got rough and red.** *Chew the fat.* **When she used the gentle soap. Can you finish the sentence so it makes sense?** (Idea: *Her skin felt smooth and soft.*) **Say the whole sentence.** *When she used the gentle soap her skin felt smooth and soft.*
(If the child is enjoying this game, you may wish to add additional examples.)

DAY 4: *Chew the Fat* **(Round Two)**
(Add the last two words *imagination* and *appreciate* to the bag or container. Repeat procedure from Day 3.)

Name _____

Johnny Appleseed

Johnny Appleseed was a real _____.

He had bare _____.

He wore a pot _____ his head.

He had a sack of apple _____.

He planted _____.

He gave away _____.

We _____ still _____ many

of _____ apple _____ today.

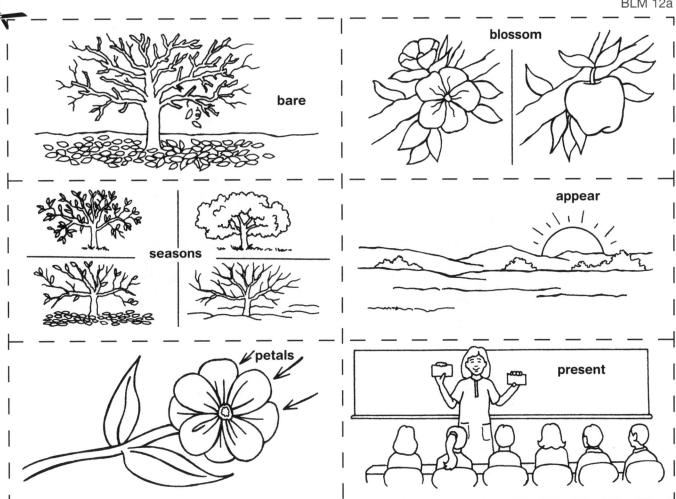

bare

blossom

seasons

appear

petals

present

Sharing What You've Learned at School

Note: Children are not expected to be able to read the words. They are for your information.

DAY 1: (Cut the Picture Vocabulary Cards apart. Place the picture cards for *bare, appear, blossom,* and *petals* in a container or small plastic bag.)
(Show the child each picture card.) **What word does the picture show?** (Idea: *The picture shows a tree that is bare.*)
Tell me what you know about this word. (You may wish to share what you know about the word with your child as well.)

DAY 2: (Add in 2 new words, *seasons* and *present.* Repeat procedure from Day 1.) **Tell me anything more that you know about this word.**

DAY 3: *Tom Foolery* (Round One)
Let's play the *Tom Foolery* game you learned at school. I'll tell you what a word means. Then I'll tell you another meaning for that word. If I tell something that's not correct, sing "Tom Foolery!" If I say something correct, don't say anything. If you say "Tom Foolery!" and you're right, you get a point. If you're wrong, I get the point.

- **Blossom** means "a flower that turns into fruit." **Blossom** also means "to get worse at things." *Tom Foolery!* Oh, you're right. **Blossom** means to get **better** at things.
- **Petals** are the outside parts of flowers. **Petals** can be white or colored different colors.
- If you **appear,** I can see you. You also say, "Appear" when your friend is looking for you and you are high on a ladder. *Tom Foolery!* Oh, you're right. I guess I was thinking of calling, "Up here!"
- If you are **gentle,** you do things in a kind, careful way. A **gentle** is also something you put in soup. *Tom Foolery!* Oh, you're right. I must have been thinking of **lentil** instead of **gentle.**
- **Bare** means "not covered." A table has nothing on it or is not covered when it is **bare.**
- **Calm** is how you feel when you are not angry, upset, or excited. **Calm** is also the name of a sea creature you dig at the seashore. *Tom Foolery!* Oh, you are very hard to fool. The sea creature you dig at the seashore is a **clam.**

(If the child is enjoying this game, you may wish to add additional examples.)

DAY 4: *Tom Foolery* (Round Two)
(Add the last two words, *seasons* and *present* to the bag or container. Repeat procedure from Day 3.)

Name _____

The Seasons

snuggle

explore

disturb

odor

wilderness

reasons

Sharing What You've Learned at School

Note: Children are not expected to be able to read the words. They are for your information.

DAY 1: (Cut the Picture Vocabulary Cards apart. Place the picture cards for *snuggle, explore, disturb,* and *odor* in a container or small plastic bag.) (Show the child each picture card.) **What word does the picture show?** (Idea: *The picture shows snuggle.*) **Tell me what you know about this word.** (You may wish to share what you know about the word with the child as well.)

DAY 2: (Add in 2 new words, *wilderness* and *reasons.* Repeat procedure from Day 1.) **Tell me anything more that you know about this word.**

DAY 3: *Tom Foolery* (Round One)
Let's play the *Tom Foolery* game you learned at school. I'll tell you what a word means. Then I'll tell you another meaning for that word. If I tell something that's not correct, sing "Tom Foolery!" If I say something correct, don't say anything. If you say, "Tom Foolery!" and you're right, you get a point. If you're wrong, I get the point.

- **Odor** means "a smell." It is also what the judge says when people are noisy in court. *Tom Foolery!* Oh, you're right. I was thinking of the word **order.** The judge says, "Order in the court!"
- **Explore** means "travel around so you can see what places are like." You also **explore** when you say something loudly when you are excited. *Tom Foolery!* Oh, you're right. I was thinking of **exclaim.** We only know the first meaning for **explore.**
- If something **disturbs** you, it bothers or worries you. **Disturb** also means "to pass out papers to everyone." *Tom Foolery!* Oh, you are very hard to fool. When you pass out papers to everyone, you **distribute** the papers.
- When you **snuggle,** you cuddle in a warm and comfortable spot, close by your father or your puppy. **Snuggle** is also what you do when you have trouble doing something. *Tom Foolery!* Oh, you're right. I must have been thinking of **struggle** instead of **snuggle.**

(If the child is enjoying this game, you may wish to add additional examples.)

DAY 4: *Tom Foolery* (Round Two)
(Add the last two words, *wilderness* and *reasons*, to the bag or container. Repeat procedure from Day 3.)

Name _____

When We Go Camping

I would like to go camping.																	

I would not like to go camping.																	

cave

den

burrow

frost

hibernate

migrate

Sharing What You've Learned at School

Note: Children are not expected to be able to read the words. They are for your information.

DAY 1: (Cut the Picture Vocabulary Cards apart. Place the picture cards for *cave, den, burrow,* and *frost* in a container or small plastic bag.)
(Show the child each picture card.) **What word does the picture show?** (Idea: *The picture shows frost on the window.*)
Tell me what you know about this word. (You may wish to share what you know about the word with your child as well.)

DAY 2: (Add in 2 new words, *hibernate* and *migrate.* Repeat procedure from Day 1.) **Tell me anything more that you know about this word.**

DAY 3: *Tom Foolery* (Round One)
Let's play the *Tom Foolery* game you learned at school. I'll tell you what a word means. Then I'll tell you another meaning for that word. If I tell something that's not correct, sing "Tom Foolery!" If I say something correct, don't say anything. If you say "Tom Foolery!" and you're right, you get a point. If you're wrong, I get the point.

- **A den is a home for wild animals like bears and beavers. Den is also the number that comes after nine.** *Tom Foolery!* **Oh, you're right. I must have been thinking of ten instead of den.**
- **A cave is a large hole in the side of a hill or mountain. A cave can also be a young cow or bull.** *Tom Foolery!* **Oh, you're right. I was thinking of calf. We only know the first meaning for cave.**
- **Many animals burrow down in the ground to make a tunnel or hole. Sometimes your parents may go to the bank to burrow money.** *Tom Foolery!* **Oh, you're right. I was thinking of borrow. You go to the bank to borrow money.**
- **A den can be a cozy room in your house where you relax and do things you enjoy. A den can also be a bang on your dad's car.** *Tom Foolery!* **Oh, you're right. I was thinking of dent. The old car has so many dents it looks like a golf ball.**

(If the child is enjoying this game, you may wish to add additional examples.)

DAY 4: *Tom Foolery* (Round Two)
(Add the last two words, *hibernate* and *migrate,* to the bag or container. Repeat procedure from Day 3.)

Name _____

says, "It's time to sleep."

limbs

awesome

dormant

chores

devour

impressions

Sharing What You've Learned at School

Note: Children are not expected to be able to read the words. They are for your information.

DAY 1: (Cut the Picture Vocabulary Cards apart. Place the picture cards for *limbs, chores, awesome,* and *devour* in a container or small plastic bag.) (Show the child each picture card.) **What word does the picture show?** (Idea: *The picture shows someone doing chores.*) **Tell me what you know about this word.** (You may wish to share what you know about the word with the child as well.)

DAY 2: (Add in 2 new words, *dormant* and *impressions.* Repeat procedure from Day 1.) **Tell me anything more that you know about this word.**

DAY 3: *Tom Foolery* (Round One)
Let's play the *Tom Foolery* game that you learned at school. I'll tell you what a word means. Then I'll tell you another meaning for that word. If I tell something that's not correct, sing, "Tom Foolery!" If I say something correct, don't say anything. If you say "Tom Foolery!" and you're right, you get a point. If you're wrong, I get the point.

- **Limbs** are the branches of a tree. **Limbs** are also baby sheep. *Tom Foolery!* Oh, you're right. I must have been thinking of **lambs** instead of **limbs.**
- **Awesome** means "amazing and hard to believe." **Awesome** is also a season we sometimes call "fall." *Tom Foolery!* Oh, you're right. I was thinking of **autumn.** We only know the first meaning for **awesome.**
- If you eat quickly and hungrily, you **devour** your food. People often devour their favorite foods.
- **Limbs** are your arms and legs. **Limbs** are also the branches on trees.
- **Chores** are the jobs you have to do nearly every day. **Chores** are also the places you go to buy things. *Tom Foolery!* Oh, you're hard to fool. I was thinking of stores. We only know the first meaning for chores.

(If the child is enjoying this game, you may wish to add additional examples.)

DAY 4: *Tom Foolery* (Round Two)
(Add the last two words, *dormant* and *impressions,* to the bag or container. Repeat procedure from Day 3.)

Name _____

_____ is fun in the winter.

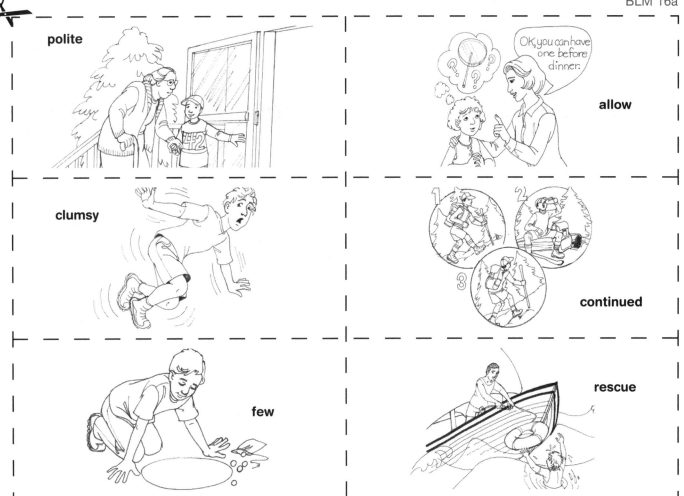

Sharing What You've Learned at School

Note: Children are not expected to be able to read the words. They are for your information.

DAY 1: (Cut apart the Picture Vocabulary Cards. Place the picture cards for *polite, continued, allow,* and *few* in a container or small plastic bag.)
(Show the child each picture card.) **What word does the picture show?** (Idea: *The picture shows someone who is being rescued.*) **Tell me what you know about this word.** (You may wish to share what you know about the word with your child as well.)

DAY 2: (Add 2 new words, *clumsy* and *rescue.* Repeat procedure from Day 1.) **Tell me anything more that you know about this word.**

DAY 3: *Hear, Say!* (Round One)
Let's play the *Hear, Say!* game that you learned at school. I'll say sentences with your vocabulary words in them. If I use the word correctly, say "That's the honest truth!" If I use the word incorrectly, say "Hear, Say!" Then I'll ask you to finish the sentence so that it makes sense.

• **A polite** girl is one who … does the right thing, has four legs, and talks like a monkey. *Hear, Say!* The first part of the sentence stays the same. I'll say the first part. **A polite** girl is one who… (Idea:

Does the right thing and acts with her best manners and actions.) **Let's say the sentence together.** *A polite girl is one who does the right thing and acts with her best manners and actions.*

• If you **allow** someone to do something, you … give them pears, or pomegranates, or parsnips to do it. *Hear, Say!* If you allow someone to do something, you… (Idea: *Give them permission to do it.*) **Let's say the sentence together.** *If you allow someone to do something, you give them permission to do it.*

• Bob **continued** as the coach of his team … for twelve years. *That's the honest truth!*

• Everyone knows that "a **few** cookies" means … some, but not many. *That's the honest truth!*

• After a long, hard hike, Jim **continued** on his way by … sitting down, unpacking his tent, and spending the night. *Hear, Say!* After a long, hard hike, Jim continued on his way by… (Idea: *Keeping on going.*) **Let's say the whole sentence together.** *After a long, hard hike, Jim continued on his way by keeping on going*

(If child is enjoying this game, you may wish to add additional examples.)

DAY 4: *Hear, Say!* (Round Two)
(Add the last two words, *clumsy* and *rescue,* to the bag or container. Repeat procedure from Day 3.)

Name _____

The Eensy-Weensy Spider: Shoe Poem

I like shoes.

I like _____ shoes.

These are shoes that I would choose.

I like _____ shoes.

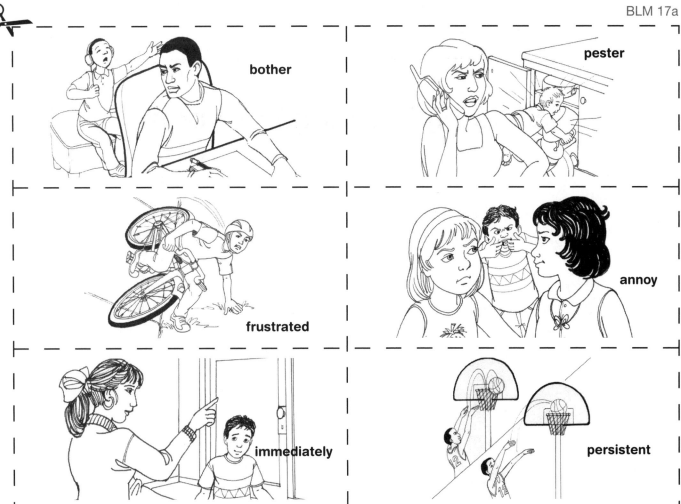

bother

pester

frustrated

annoy

immediately

persistent

Sharing What You've Learned at School

Note: Children are not expected to be able to read the words. They are for your information.

DAY 1: (Cut apart the Picture Vocabulary Cards. Place the picture cards for *bother, annoy, pester,* and *immediately* in a container or small plastic bag.) (Show the child each picture card.) **What word does the picture show?** (Idea: *The picture shows someone who is feeling annoyed.*)
Tell me what you know about this word. (You may wish to share what you know about the word with the child as well.)

DAY 2: (Add in two new words *frustrated* and *persistent*. Repeat procedure from Day 1.) **Tell me anything more that you know about this word.**

DAY 3: *Hear, Say!* **(Round One)**
Let's play the *Hear, Say!* **game that you learned at school. I'll use target words in sentences. If I use the word correctly, say "That's the honest truth!" If I use the word incorrectly, say "Hear, Say!" Then I'll ask you to finish the sentence so it is true.**

- **If you bother someone you … give them bubbles and retract them.** *Hear, Say!* **The first part of the sentence stays the same. I'll say the first part. If you bother someone you…** (Idea: *Give them*

trouble and distract them.) **Let's say the whole sentence together.** *If you bother someone you give them trouble and distract them.* **That's the honest truth!**

- **When you pester your sister … you father and ahoy her and don't mean it.** *Hear, Say!* **When you pester your sister…** (Idea: *You bother and annoy her and really mean it.*) **Let's say the whole sentence together.** *When you pester your sister you bother and annoy her and really mean it.* **That's the honest truth!**

- **Sam annoyed his mom when he … disturbed and irritated her with his loud voice.** *That's the honest truth!*

- **Mr. Smithers didn't bother to come by so … he didn't trouble himself.** *That's the honest truth!*

- **When Harold went immediately … he waited for a while before leaving.** *Hear, Say!* **When Harold went immediately…** (Idea: *He left right away.*) **Let's say the whole sentence together.** *When Harold went immediately, he left right away.*

(If the child is enjoying this game, you may wish to add additional examples.)

DAY 4: *Hear, Say!* **(Round Two)**
(Add the last two words, *frustrated* and *persistent,* to the bag or container. Repeat procedure from Day 3.)

Name _____

Shoo Fly!: Belonging Poem

Shoo fly don't bother me,

Shoo fly don't bother me,

Shoo fly don't bother me—

_____ belongs to somebody.

scrawl

chef

severely

sprawled

imaginary

disruptive

Sharing What You've Learned at School

Note: The children are not expected to be able to read the words. They are for your information.

DAY 1: (Cut the Picture Vocabulary Cards apart. Place the picture cards for *scrawl, chef, severely,* and *sprawled* in a container or small plastic bag.) (Show the child each picture card.) **What word does the picture show?** (Idea: *The picture shows someone who is a chef.*)
Tell me what you know about this word. (You may wish to share what you know about the word with your child as well.)

DAY 2: (Add in 2 new words, *imaginary* and *disruptive.* Repeat procedure from Day 1.) **Today, tell me anything more that you know about this word.**

DAY 3: *Hear, Say!* **(Round One)**
Let's play the *Hear, Say!* game. I'll say sentences with your vocabulary words in them. If I use the word correctly, say "That's the honest truth!" If I use the word incorrectly, say "Hear, Say!" Then I'll ask you to finish the sentence so that it makes sense. Now, you're ready to play the game.

• **If someone is a *chef,* she … is not a very good cook.** *Hear, Say!* **I'll say the first part. If someone is a *chef* …** (Idea: *She is a very good cook.*) **Let's say the whole sentence together.** *If someone is a chef, she is a very good cook.* **That's the honest truth!**

• **If you wrote your name in a *scrawl,* your writing is … neat and tidy.** *Hear, Say!* **I'll say the first part. If you wrote your name in a *scrawl* your writing was …** (Idea: *Messy and untidy.*) **Let's say the whole sentence together.** *If you wrote your name in a scrawl, your writing was messy and untidy.* **That's the honest truth!**

• **If the storekeeper spoke to the children *severely,* he spoke to them in a … kind voice.** *Hear, Say!* **I'll say the first part. If the storekeeper spoke to the children *severely,* he spoke to them in a …** (Idea: *Harsh voice.*) **Let's say the whole sentence together.** *If the storekeeper spoke to the children severely, he spoke to them in a harsh voice.* **That's the honest truth!**

• **If the children are *sprawled* on their chairs, they are … sitting up with their hands folded on their laps.** *Hear, Say!* **I'll say the first part. If the children are *sprawled* on their chairs, they are …** (Idea: *Sitting with their legs spread out.*) **Let's say the whole sentence together.** *If the children are sprawled on their chairs, they are sitting with their legs spread out.* **That's the honest truth!**

(If the child is enjoying this game, you may wish to add additional examples.)

DAY 4: *Hear, Say!* **(Round Two)**
(Add the last two words, *imaginary* and *disruptive* to the bag or container. Repeat procedure from Day 3.)

Appendix **35**

Name _____

Dinosaur Days

On Monday _____ came.

On Tuesday _____ came.

On Wednesday _____ came.

On Thursday _____ came.

On Friday _____ came.

On Saturday _____ came.

On Sunday _____ came.

Hadrosaurus

Apatosaurus

Triceratops

Tyrannosaurus Rex

Pteranodon

Stegosaurus

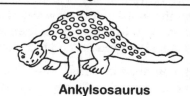
Ankylsosaurus

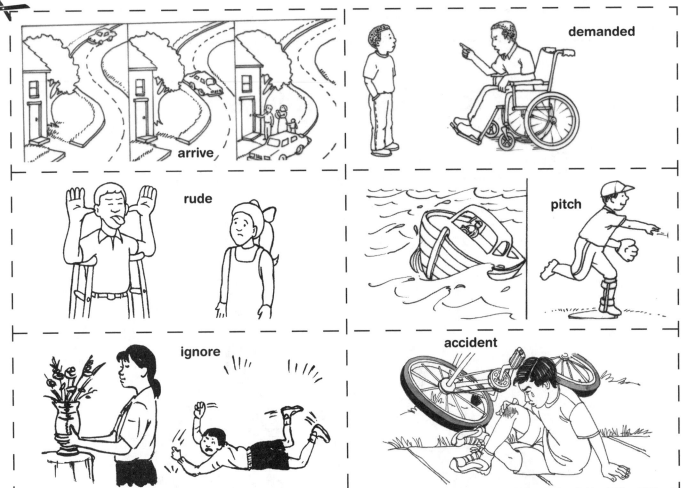

demanded

arrive

rude

pitch

ignore

accident

Sharing What You've Learned at School

Note: Children are not expected to be able to read the words. They are for your information.

DAY 1: (Cut the Picture Vocabulary Cards apart. Place the picture cards for *arrive, demanded, rude,* and *pitch* in a container or small plastic bag.)
(Show the child each picture card.) **What word does the picture show?** (Idea: *The picture shows a child pitching a ball.*)
Tell me what you know about this word. (You may wish to share what you know about the word with your child as well.)

DAY 2: (Add in 2 new words, *ignore* and *accident.* Repeat procedure from Day 1.) **Tell me anything more that you know about this word.**

DAY 3: *Hear, Say!* (Round One)
Let's play the *Hear, Say!* game that you learned at school. I'll use target words in sentences. If I use the word correctly, say "That's the honest truth!" If I use the word incorrectly, say *Hear, Say!* Then I'll ask you to finish the sentence so it is true.

• **If our friends arrive, they** … make an impression. *Hear, Say!* **I'll say the first part. If our friends arrive, they.** (Idea: *Come to a place.*) **Let's say the**

whole sentence together now. *If our friends arrive, they come to a place.* **That's the honest truth!**

• **If your cousin is rude, he … doesn't use good planners.** *Hear, Say!* **I'll say the first part. If your cousin is rude, he.** Idea: *Doesn't use good manners.* **Let's say the whole sentence together now.** *If your cousin is rude, he doesn't use good manners.* **That's the honest truth!**

• **A boat will pitch if … the waves are very small.** *Hear, Say!* **I'll say the first part. A boat will pitch if.** (Idea: *The waves are very large.*) **Let's say the whole sentence together.** *A boat will pitch if the waves are very large.* **That's the honest truth!**

• **When dad demanded I stop shouting, he ... used a force field voice.** *Hear, Say!* **I'll say the first part. When dad demanded I stop shouting, he.** (Idea: *Used a forceful voice.*) **Let's say the whole sentence together.** *When dad demanded I stop shouting, he used a forceful voice.*

(If the child is enjoying this game, you may wish to add additional examples.)

DAY 4: *Hear, Say!* (Round Two)
(Add the last two words, *ignore* and *accident,* to the bag or container. Repeat procedure from Day 3.)

Name _____

Too Many Children!

By _____

"One", said the teacher,
"Computer is for one.
With no one else to bother you,
You can have some fun."

But when she wasn't looking …

Too many children
Acting just like gluttons.
Too many children
Pushing all the buttons!

It just didn't work!

"Two", said the teacher
"Printing is for two."
"There are just enough pencils
And paper for you."

But when she wasn't looking …

Too many children
Printing with a tool.
Too many children
Wasn't very cool!

It just didn't work!

"Three", said the teacher
"Dress-up is for three."
"There aren't enough clothes
For any more, you see."

But when she wasn't looking …

Too many children
Putting on the dress.
Too many children
Causing too much stress!

It just didn't work!

"Four", said the teacher
"Building is for four."
"There's just enough space
For you on the floor."

But when she wasn't looking …

Too many children
Building with the toys.
Too many children
Making too much noise!

It just didn't work!

"Five", said the teacher
"5-4-3-2-1."
"And when I get to zero, why,
The playing time is done!"

But when she wasn't looking …

All of the children
Were sitting on the rug.
All of the children
Came and gave her a hug!

Now <u>that</u> was nice!

proper

fool

curious

notion

coward

dawn

Sharing What You've Learned at School

Note: Children are not expected to be able to read the words. They are for your information.

DAY 1: (Cut the Picture Vocabulary Cards apart. Place the picture cards for *proper, notion, fool, coward* in a container or small plastic bag.)
(Show the child each picture card.) **What word does the picture show?** (Idea: *The picture shows a child doing what is proper.*)
Tell me what you know about this word. (You may wish to share what you know about the word with the child as well.)

DAY 2: (Add in 2 new words, *curious* and *dawn.* Repeat procedure from Day 1.) **Tell me anything more that you know about this word.**

DAY 3: *Hear, Say!* (Round One)
Let's play the *Hear, Say!* game that you learned at school. I'll use target words in sentences. If I use the word correctly, say "That's the honest truth!" If I use the word incorrectly, say *Hear, Say!* Then I'll ask you to finish the sentence so it is true.

If you are a proper child, you ... have six legs. *Hear, Say!* **The first part of the sentence stays the same. If you are a proper child, you.** (Idea: *Have*

two legs.) **Let's say the whole sentence together now.** *If you are a proper child, you have two legs.* **That's the honest truth!**

If you had a notion about a game to play, you ... had no idea about what to do. *Hear, Say!* **The first part of the sentence stays the same. If you had a notion about a game to play, you.** (Idea: *Had an idea about what to do.*) **Let's say the whole sentence together now.** *If you had a notion about a game to play, you had an idea about what to do.* **That's the honest truth!**

- **When your friend made you look silly, you ... looked like a fool.** *That's the honest truth!*
- **A coward is a person who ... is more fearful than others.** *That's the honest truth!*

(If the child is enjoying this game, you may wish to add additional examples.)

DAY 4: *Hear, Say!* (Round Two)
(Add the last two words, *curious* and *dawn*, to the bag or container. Repeat procedure from Day 3.)

Name _____

Shadows: Diamante Poem

_____

_____   _____

_____   _____   _____

_____   _____

_____

My Diamond Poem by _____

Name _____

Sample Web

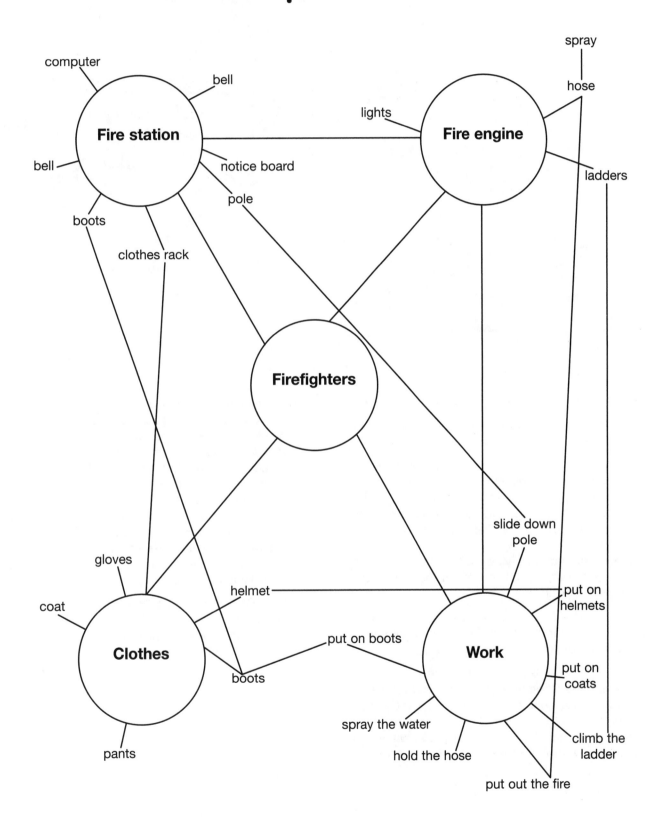

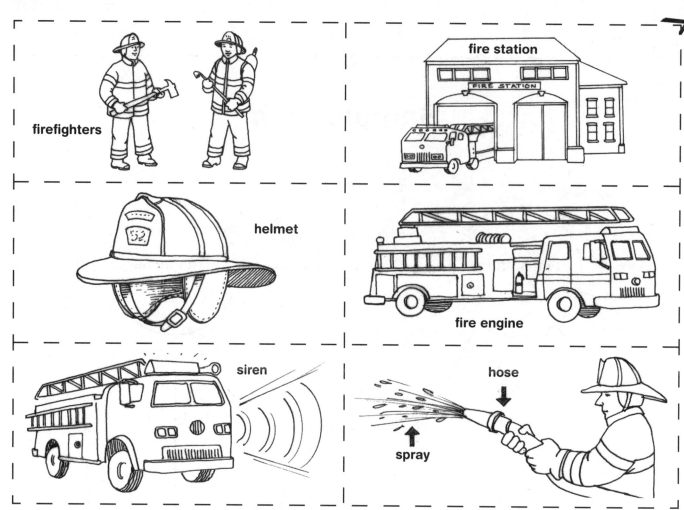

firefighters

fire station

FIRE STATION

helmet

fire engine

siren

hose

spray

Sharing What You've Learned at School

Note: Children are not expected to be able to read the words. They are for your information.

DAY 1: (Cut the Picture Vocabulary Cards apart. Place the picture cards for *firefighters, fire station, fire engine,* and *spray* in a container or small plastic bag.) (Show the child each picture card.) **What word does the picture show?** (Idea: *The picture shows a fire engine.*)

Tell me what you know about this word. (You may wish to share what you know about the word with your child as well.)

DAY 2: (Add in 3 new words, *hose, siren,* and *helmet.* Repeat procedure from Day 1.) **Tell me anything more that you know about this word.**

DAY 3: *Choosing* **Game (Round One)**
Let's play the *Choosing* game that you learned at school. I'll say sentences with two target words in them. You have to choose the correct word for the sentence. If you choose correctly, you will win one point. If you don't choose correctly, I get the point.

- **If your work was to put out fires, would you be a fire engine or a firefighter?** *A firefighter.*
- **Would a firefighter ride on a fire engine or a fire station to go to a fire?** *A fire engine.*
- **Would you find a firefighter's pole in a fire engine or a fire station?** *A fire station.*
- **If water was coming out of a shower in little drops would it be a spray or a stray?** *A spray.*
- **Which would carry ladders to a fire: a fire station or a fire engine?** *A fire engine.*

(If the child is enjoying this game, you may wish to add additional examples.)

DAY 4: *Choosing* **Game (Round Two)**
(Add the last three words, *hose, siren,* and *helmet,* to the bag or container. Repeat procedure from Day 3.)

Other books your child might enjoy:

Titles in the Hard Work series:

A Day with a Doctor
A Day with a Librarian
A Day with a Mail Carrier
A Day with Firefighters
A Day with Paramedics
A Day with Police Officers

Take your child to the public library to find more books about firefighters.

My reading goal:

7

Firefighters

1

This is a firefighter.

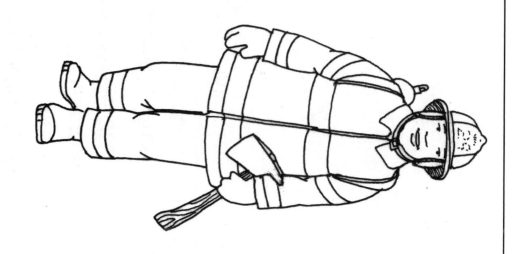

Thank you, firefighters.

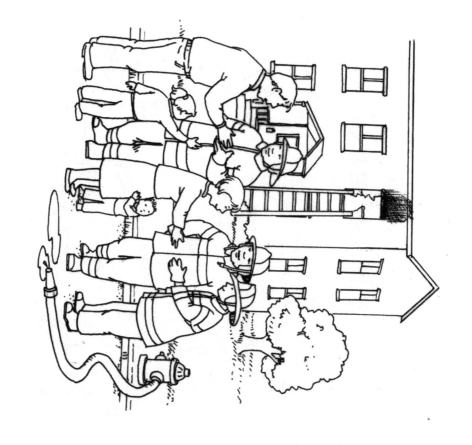

6

This is a fire engine.

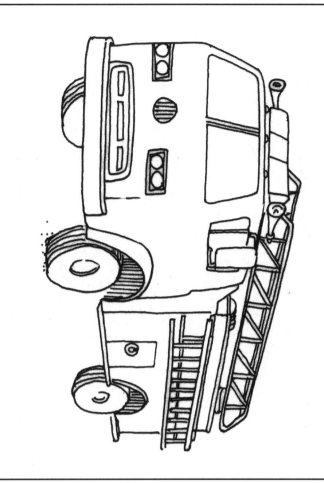

3

This is the firefighter's clothing.

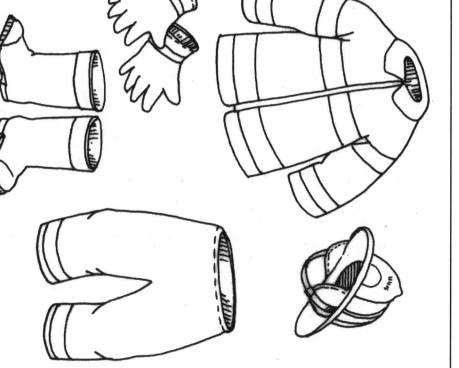

4

5

These are the firefighter's tools.

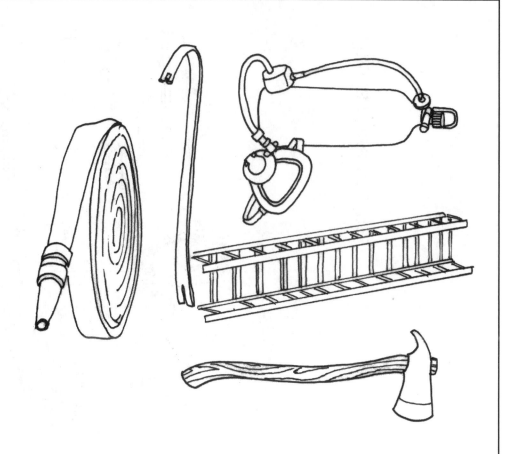

This is the fire station.

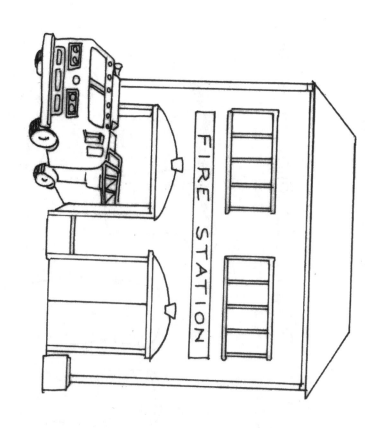

2

Name _____

Sample Web

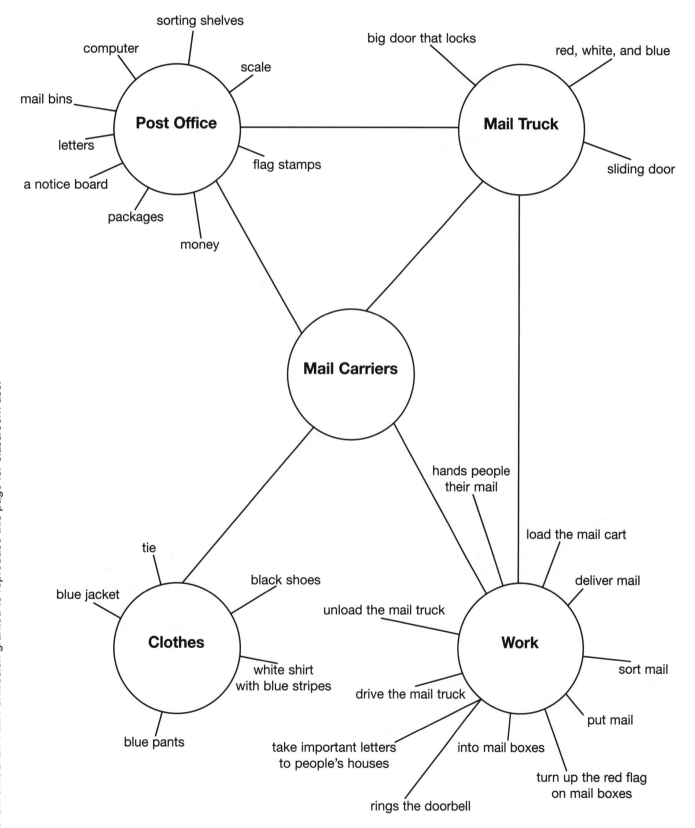

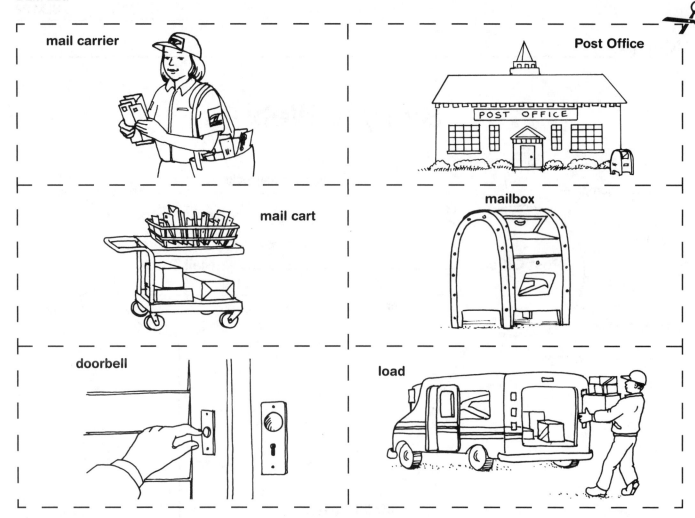

mail carrier

Post Office

mail cart

mailbox

doorbell

load

Sharing What You've Learned at School

Note: Children are not expected to be able to read the words. They are for your information.

DAY 1: (Cut the Picture Vocabulary Cards apart. Place the picture cards for *door bell, load, mail box* and *mail carrier* in a container or small plastic bag.) (Show the child each picture card.) **What word does the picture show?** (Idea: *The picture shows a doorbell.*)
Tell me what you know about this word. (You may wish to share what you know about the word with your child as well.)

DAY 2: (Add in 2 the new picture cards for *mail cart* and *post office*. Repeat procedure from Day 1.) **Tell me anything more that you know about this word.**

DAY 3: *Choosing* **Game (Round One)**
Let's play the *Choosing* game that you learned at school. I'll say sentences with two of the words you know in them. You have to choose the correct word for the sentence. If you choose correctly, you will win one point. If you don't choose correctly, I get the point.

- **If a person delivers mail would she be a mail carrier or a post office?** *A mail carrier.*
- **Would a mail carrier use a mail cart or a load?** *A mail cart.*
- **What would a mail carrier put mail into; a load or a mailbox?** *A mailbox.*
- **Is what you can carry at one time a doorbell or a load?** *A load.*
- **Which would sound like a bell; a mail carrier or a doorbell?** *A doorbell.*
- **If you are carrying something to the truck, do you have a load or a post office?** *A load.*

(If the child is enjoying this game, you may wish to add additional examples.)

DAY 4: *Choosing* **Game (Round Two)**
(Add the last two word cards, *mail cart* and *post office*, to the bag or container. Repeat procedure from Day 3.)

BLM 22b Read-Aloud Booklet

Other books your child might enjoy:

Titles in the Hard Work series:

A Day with a Doctor
A Day with a Librarian
A Day with a Mail Carrier
A Day with Firefighters
A Day with Paramedics
A Day with Police Officers

Take your child to the public library to find more books about the post office and mail carriers.

My reading goal:

7

Mail Carriers

1

Meet Ann. She is a mail carrier.

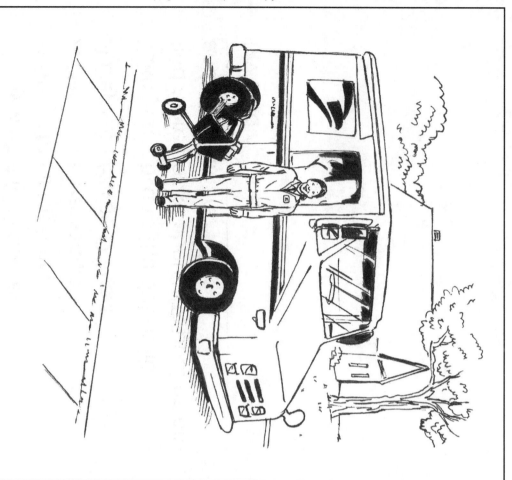

Ann has a job.

6

3

Ann loads the mail into the mail truck.

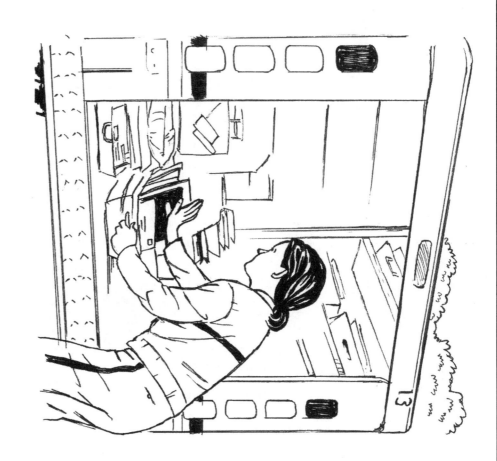

Ann loads the mail into the mail cart.

4

(Note to Teacher: This page should be photocopied on the backside of pages 3 and 4)

5

Ann has mail for the mailbox.

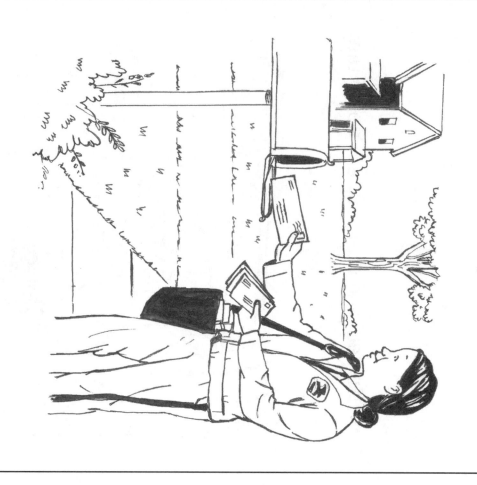

Ann's job is to give mail to me.

2

Name _____

Sample Web

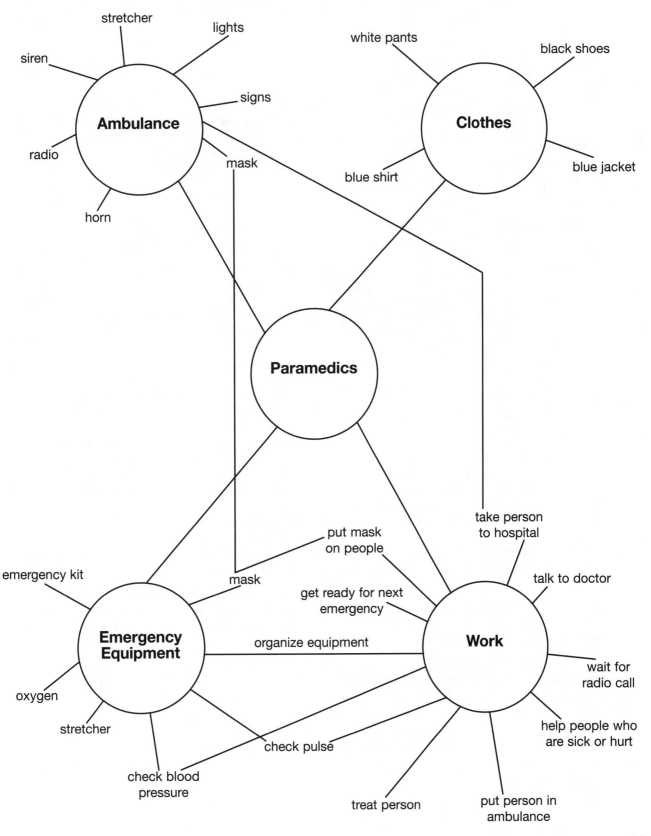

Sharing What You've Learned at School

Note: Children are not expected to be able to read the words. They are for your information.

DAY 1: (Cut the Picture Vocabulary Cards apart. Place the picture cards for *ambulance, emergency, kit,* and *mask* in a container or small plastic bag.)
(Show the child each picture card.) **What word does the picture show?** (Idea: *The picture shows an ambulance.*)
Tell me what you know about this word. (You may wish to share what you know about the word with the child as well.)

DAY 2: (Add in 3 new words, *paramedics, stretcher,* and *treats.* Repeat procedure from Day 1.) **Tell me anything more that you know about this word.**

DAY 3: *Choosing* Game (Round One)
Let's play the *Choosing* game that you learned at school. I'll say sentences with two target words in them. You have to choose the correct word for the sentence. If you choose correctly, you will win one point. If you don't choose correctly, I get the point.

- **If a person helped sick and hurt people, would they be a paramedic or an ambulance?** *A paramedic.*
- **Do paramedics have some of the things they need in a kit or an emergency?** *A kit.*
- **If you saw paramedics moving a sick person, would they be using a mask or a stretcher?** *A stretcher.*
- **Would a paramedic drive a kit or an ambulance?** *An ambulance.*

(If the child is enjoying this game, you may wish to add additional examples.)

DAY 4: *Choosing* Game (Round Two)
(Add the last three words, *emergency, mask* and *treats,* to the bag or container. Repeat procedure from Day 3.)

Other books your child might enjoy:

Titles in the Hard Work series:

A Day with a Doctor
A Day with a Librarian
A Day with a Mail Carrier
A Day with Firefighters
A Day with Paramedics
A Day with Police Officers

My reading goal:

Take your child to the public library to find more books about the paramedics and how they help people.

7

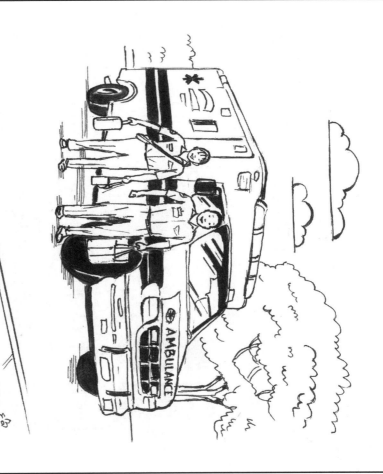

Paramedics Help Sick and Hurt People

1

Matt and Pat are paramedics.

The doctor will help Nick.

6

3

Nick has cut his arm on a rock.
His mom calls the paramedics.

Matt and Pat can help Nick.

4

(Note to Teacher: This page should be photocopied on the backside of pages 3 and 4)

1

Nick is at the hospital with Matt and Pat.

Matt and Pat are in an ambulance.

6

Name _____

Sample Web

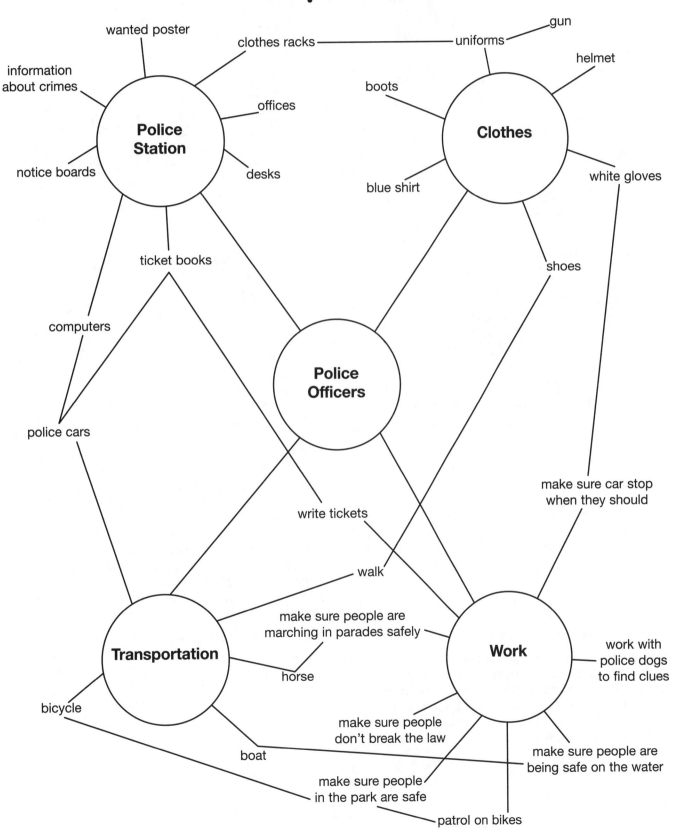

Sharing What You've Learned at School

Note: Children are not expected to be able to read the words. They are for your information.

DAY 1: (Cut the Picture Vocabulary Cards apart. Place the picture cards for *ticket, law, parade,* and *clues* in a container or small plastic bag.)
(Show the child each picture card.) **What word does the picture show?** (Idea: *The picture shows a parade.*) **Tell me what you know about this word.** (You may wish to share what you know about the word with your child as well.)

DAY 2: (Add in 2 new cards, *police officers and police station.* Repeat procedure from Day 1.) **Tell me anything more that you know about these words.**

DAY 3: *Choosing* Game (Round One)
Let's play the *Choosing* game that you learned at school. I'll say sentences with two of the words you know in them. You have to choose the correct word for the sentence. If you choose correctly, you will win one point. If you don't choose correctly, I get the point.

- **Would a police officer give a ticket or a police station to someone who was driving too fast?** *A ticket.*
- **If the speed limit is 30 and someone isdriving 60, are they breaking the law or tickets?** *The law.*
- **If you marched with a large number of people down a street, would you be in a police station or a parade?** *A parade.*
- **Were the police officer and the police dog looking for clues or law?** *Clues.*
- **If you were going to a movie, would you need a ticket or a clue?** *A ticket.*

(If the child is enjoying this game, you may wish to add additional examples.)

DAY 4: *Choosing* Game (Round Two)
(Add the last two cards, *police officers* and *police station*, to the bag or container. Repeat procedure from Day 3.)

7

Other books your child might enjoy:

Titles in the Hard Work series:

A Day with a Doctor
A Day with a Librarian
A Day with a Mail Carrier
A Day with Firefighters
A Day with Paramedics
A Day with Police Officers

Take your child to the public library to find more books about police officers and how they help people and keep people safe.

My reading goal:

Police Officers Keep People Safe

1

This is the police station. Mark and Kim are at the police station.

Thank you, Sam. We are safe.

6

3

Mark and Kim are in a police car with Al.

Mark and Kim came to help.

4

(Note to Teacher: This page should be photocopied on the backside of pages 3 and 4)

5

Sam will teach Tim and Tami to cross the street.

Al is a police dog. He helps his pals Mark and Kim.

2

Name _____

Sample Web

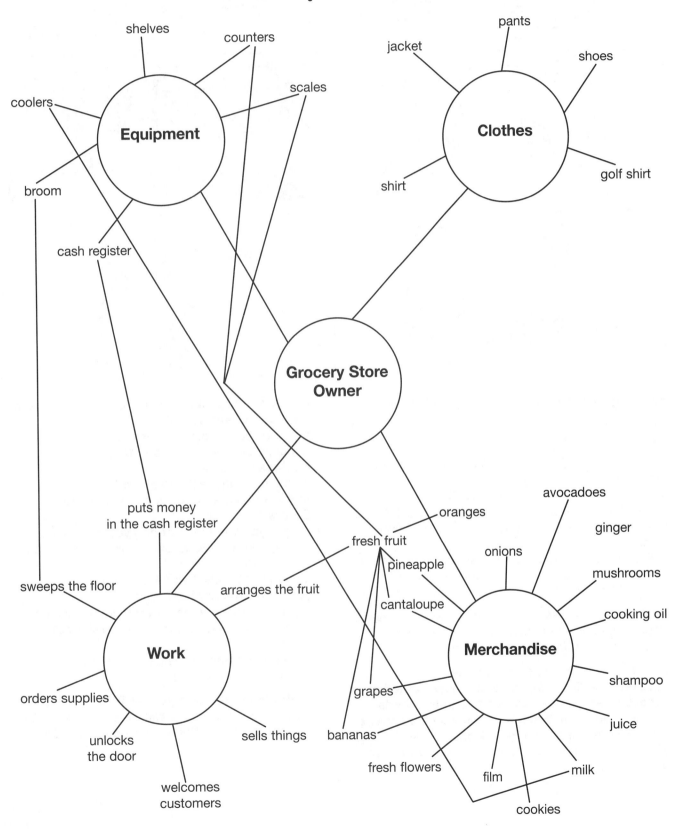

business

generous

attractive

customers

kind

successful

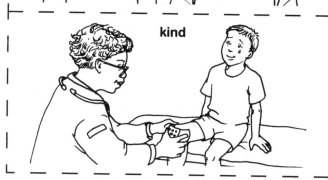

Sharing What You've Learned at School

Note: Children are not expected to be able to read the words. They are for your information.

DAY 1: (Cut the Picture Vocabulary Cards apart. Place the picture cards for *business, customers, kind,* and *generous* in a container or small plastic bag.)
(Show the child each picture card.) **What word does the picture show?** (Idea: *The picture shows customers.*)
Tell me what you know about this word. (You may wish to share what you know about the word with your child as well.)

DAY 2: (Add in 2 new words, *attractive* and *successful.* Repeat procedure from Day 1.) **Tell me anything more that you know about this word.**

DAY 3: *Choosing* **Game (Round One)**
Let's play the *Choosing* **game that you learned at school. I'll say sentences with two of the words you know in them. You have to choose the correct word for the sentence. If you choose correctly, you will win one point. If you don't choose correctly, I get the point.**

- If a person buys things in a store, is that person a **kind** or a **customer?** *A customer.*
- If you went to a place where you could buy things, would you go to an **attractive** or a **business?** *A business.*
- If you are doing well at something you want to do, are you a **customer** or **successful?** *Successful*
- If I ask you what type of dog you have, am I asking you what **kind** of dog or how **attractive** the dog is? *What kind.*
- If you are friendly, helpful, and considerate, are you **generous** or **kind?** *Kind.*
- If you are happy to share what you have with others, are you **generous** or in **business?** *Generous.*

(If the child is enjoying this game, you may wish to add additional examples.)

DAY 4: *Choosing* **Game (Round Two)**
(Add the last two words, *attractive* and *successful,* to the bag or container. Repeat procedure from Day 3.)

Other books your child might enjoy:

Titles in the Our Neighborhood series:

Call Mr. Vasquez, He'll Fix It!

Ms. Davison, Our Librarian

Riding the Ferry with Captain Cruz

The Wilsons, a House-Painting Team

Take your child to the public library to find more books about workers in your neighborhood.

My reading goal:

7

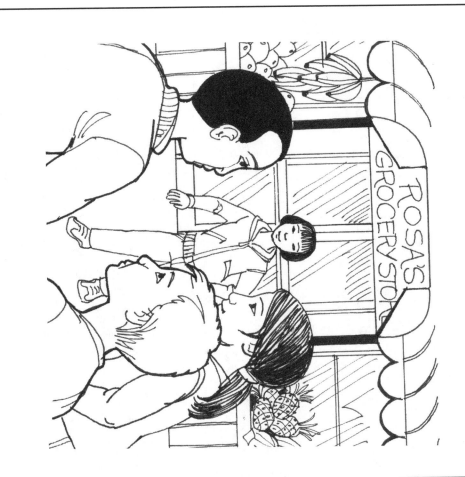

Let's Go Shopping

1

This is Miss Rosa. She has a shop.

It is lots of fun to go shopping at Rosa's shop.

6

She has meat, chops, fish, and corn in her shop.

3

Miss Rosa's dad helps her lift up the cans.

4

5

Her dad mops the shop. He likes to help.

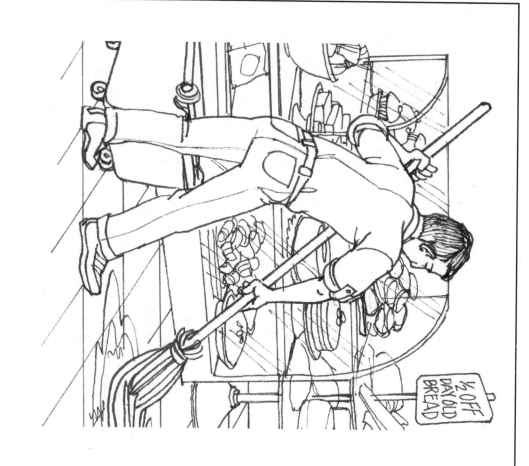

Miss Rosa has cakes in her shop.

2

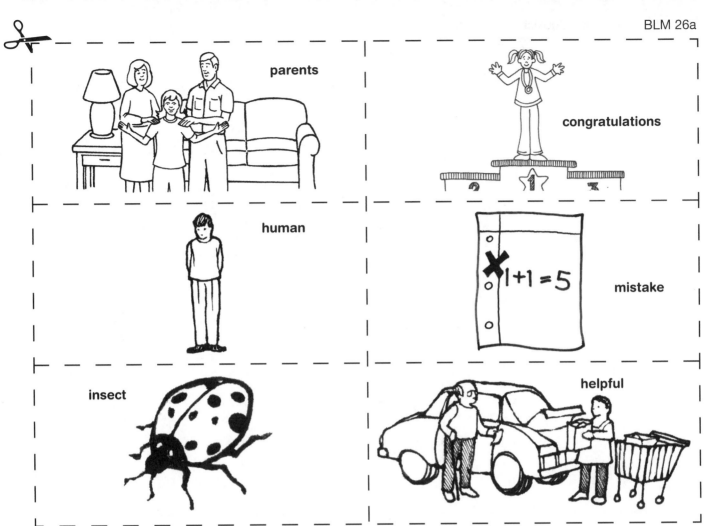

parents

congratulations

human

mistake

insect

helpful

Sharing What You've Learned at School

Note: Children are not expected to be able to read the words. They are for your information.

DAY 1: (Cut the Picture Vocabulary Cards apart. Place the picture cards for *parents, congratulations, human,* and *mistake* in a container or small plastic bag.) (Show the child each picture card.) **What word does the picture show?** (Idea: *The picture shows an insect.*) **Tell me what you know about this word.** (You may wish to share what you know about the word with your child as well.)

DAY 2: (Add in 2 new words, *helpful* and *insect.* Repeat procedure from Day 1.) **Tell me anything more that you know about this word.**

DAY 3: *What's My Word?* (Round One)
I'll give you three clues. After I give each clue, if you are sure you know my word, you may make a guess. If you guess correctly, you will win one point. If you make a mistake, I get the point.

• **First clue. My word is a naming word. Second clue. My word has an "s" sound in it. Third clue. My word is something you don't like to make. What's my word?** *Mistake.*

• **New word. First clue. My word is a naming word. Second clue. My word has a "t" sound in it. Third clue. My word means "your mother and father" or "animals that have babies." What's my word?** *Parents.*

• **New word. First clue. My word is a naming word. Second clue. My word has a "t" sound in it. Third clue. My word is something you would like people to say to you. What's my word?** *Congratulations.*

• **New word. First clue. My word is a naming word. Second clue. My word has an "h" sound in it. Third clue. All people are this. What's my word?** *Humans.*

(If the child is enjoying this game, you may wish to add additional examples.)

DAY 4: *What's My Word?* (Round Two)
(Add the last two words, *insect* and *helpful,* to the bag or container. Repeat procedure from Day 3.)

Other books your child might enjoy:

Other titles in the Are You ... ? series:

Are You an Ant?

Are You a Bee?

Are You a Butterfly?

Are You a Dragonfly?

Are You a Grasshopper?

Are You a Snail?

Are You a Spider?

Take your child to the public library to find more books about ladybugs and other insects.

My reading goal:

7

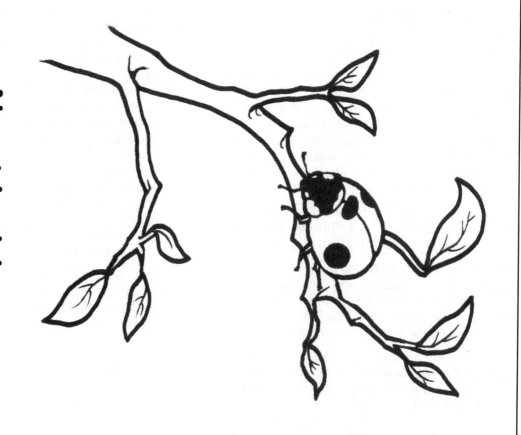

About Ladybugs

1

The ladybug lays eggs.

Now the big ladybugs eat aphids.

6

3

The little bugs eat aphids.

The little bugs get big. The bugs get another skin.

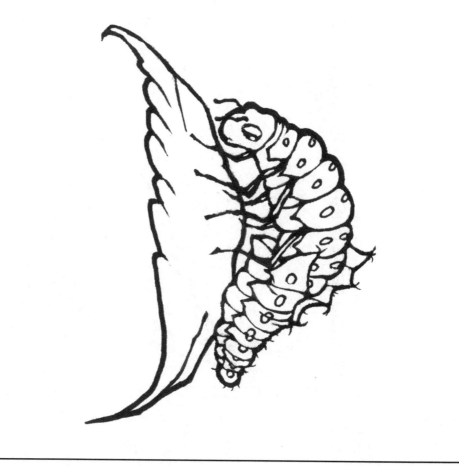

4

5

The ladybug comes out of its last skin. Then it gets dots.

The eggs hatch.

2

special

perfect

attach

definitely

enemies

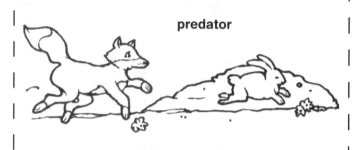

predator

Sharing What You've Learned at School

Note: Children are not expected to be able to read the words. They are for your information.

DAY 1: (Cut the Picture Vocabulary Cards apart. Place the picture cards for *special, perfect, attach,* and *definitely* in a container or small plastic bag.)
(Show the child each picture card.) **What word does the picture show?** (Idea: *The picture shows a perfect paper.*)
Tell me what you know about this word. (You may wish to share what you know about the word with the child as well.)

DAY 2: (Add in 2 new words, *enemies* and *predator.* Repeat procedure from Day 1.) **Tell me anything more that you know about this word.**

DAY 3: *What's My Word?* **(Round One)**
I'll give you three clues. After I give each clue, if you are sure you know my word, you may make a guess. If you guess correctly, you will win one point. If you make a mistake, I get the point.

- **First clue. My word is a describing word. Second clue. It has a "f" sound in it. Third clue. It means that something is exactly right. What's my word?** *Perfect.*

- **New word. First clue. My word can be used to mean two different things. Second clue. It starts with the "s" sound. Third clue. It means that something is on sale for a lower price. What's my word?** *Special.*

- **New word. First clue. My word is an action word. Second clue. It ends in the "ch" sound. Third clue. When you tape two pieces of paper together, you are doing my word. What's my word?** *Attach.*

- **New word. First clue. My word describes what I already know. Second clue. It ends in "ly." Third clue. My word means "for sure." What's my word?** *Definitely.*

(If the child is enjoying this game, you may wish to add additional examples.)

DAY 4: *What's My Word?* **(Round Two)**
(Add the last two words, *enemies* and *predator,* to the bag or container. Repeat procedure from Day 3.)

Other books your child might enjoy:

Other titles in the Are You ... ? series:

Are You an Ant?

Are You a Bee?

Are You a Butterfly?

Are You a Dragonfly?

Are You a Grasshopper?

Are You a Snail?

Are You a Spider?

Take your child to the public library to find more books about spiders and other arachnids.

My reading goal:

7

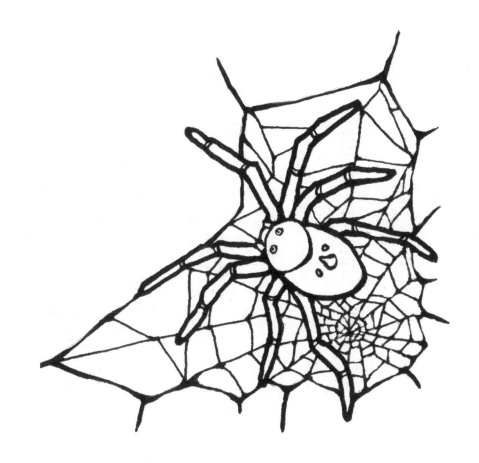

About Spiders

Here is a spider. It has a little waist, 8 legs, 2 claws, and 8 eyes.

1

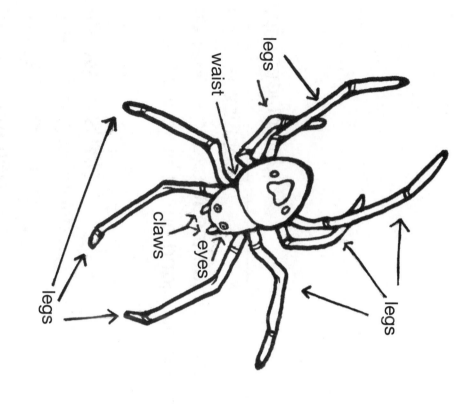

legs

waist

claws

eyes

legs

legs

Now, the spider is eating the bug.

6

3

A spider can walk on the web.

A spider can get a bug in the web.

4

5

The spider bites the bug.

The spider spins the web.

2

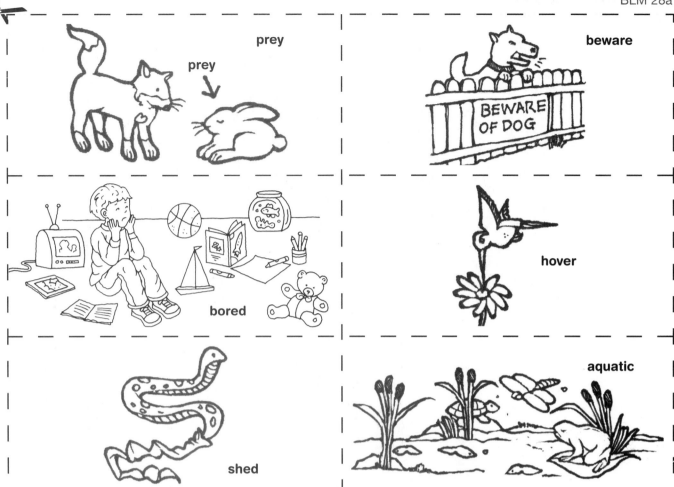

Sharing What You've Learned at School

Note: Children are not expected to be able to read the words. They are for your information.

DAY 1: (Cut the Picture Vocabulary Cards apart. Place the picture cards for *prey, beware, bored,* and *hover* in a container or small plastic bag.)
(Show the child each picture card.) **What word does the picture show?** (Idea: *The rabbit is the fox's prey.*) **Tell me what you know about this word.** (You may wish to share what you know about the word with your child as well.)

DAY 2: (Add in 2 new words, *shed* and *aquatic.* Repeat procedure from Day 1.) **Tell me anything more that you know about this word.**

DAY 3: *What's My Word?* **(Round One)**
I'll give you three clues. After I give each clue, if you are sure you know my word, you may make a guess. If you guess correctly, you will win one point. If you make a mistake, I get the point.

- **First clue. My word is an action word. Second clue. Dragonflies can do it. Third clue. It means "to stay in one place in the air." What's my word?** *Hover.*

- **New word. First clue. My word can describe how you feel. Second clue. It starts with the "b" sound. Third clue. It means "tired because something is not interesting to you." What's my word?** *Bored.*
- **New word. First clue. My word has two meanings. Second clue. It can be what an animal does. Third clue. It means "to hunt and eat an animal." What's my word?** *Prey.*
- **New word. First clue. My word tells you what to do. Second clue. It might appear on a sign. Third clue. My word means "be careful." What's my word?** *Beware.*

(If the child is enjoying this game, you may wish to add additional examples.)

DAY 4: *What's My Word?* **Game (Round Two)**
(Add the last two words, *shed* and *aquatic,* to the bag or container. Repeat procedure from Day 3.)

7

Other books your child might enjoy:

Other titles in the Are You ... ? series:

Are You an Ant?
Are You a Bee?
Are You a Butterfly?
Are You a Grasshopper?
Are You a Snail?
Are You a Spider?

Take your child to the public library
to find more books about dragonflies
and other flying insects.

My reading goal:

About Dragonflies

Here is a dragonfly. It has wings, big eyes, and six legs.

wings

legs

eyes

legs

wings

1

It can go fast. It hunts other bugs.

6

3

Little dragonflies shed their skin when they get bigger.

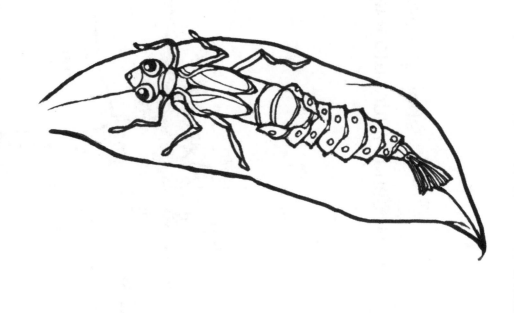

Beetles and ducks like to eat little dragonflies.

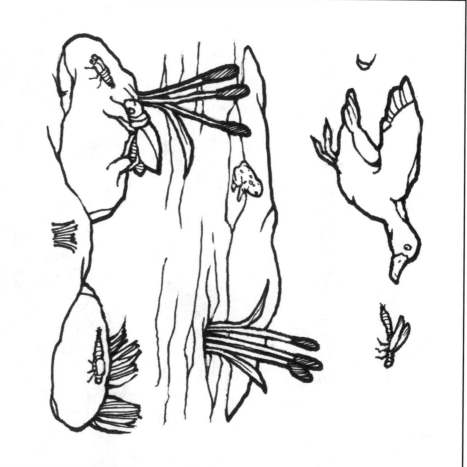

4

(Note to teacher: These pages should be photocopied on the back pages 3 and 4.)

BLM 28b Read-Aloud Booklet

5

Now, the dragonfly is big.

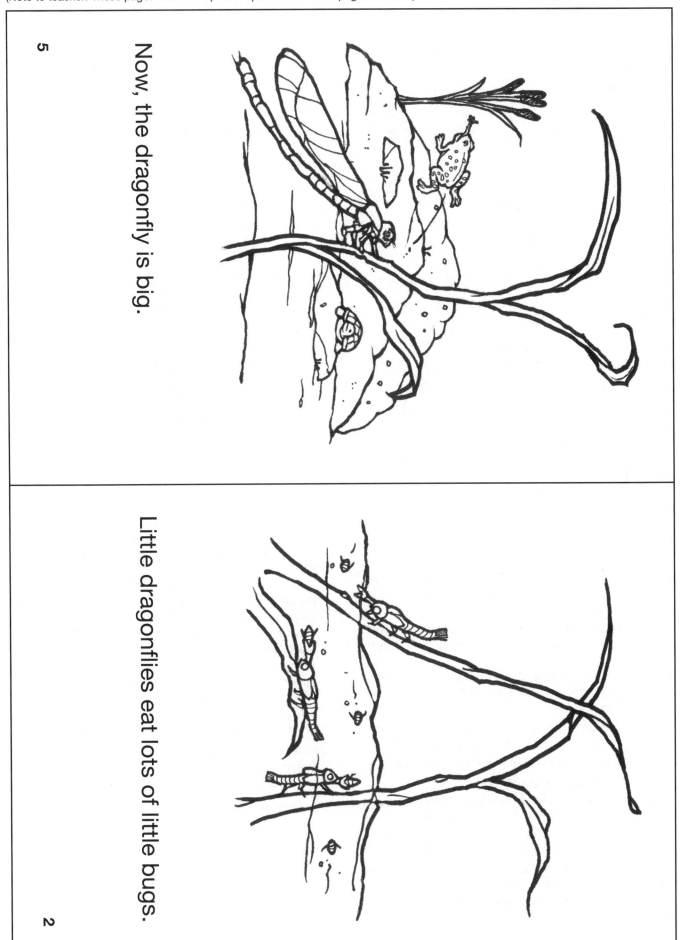

2

Little dragonflies eat lots of little bugs.

stalks

hatch

slimy

damp

resemble

conceal

Sharing What You've Learned at School

Note: Children are not expected to be able to read the words. They are for your information.

DAY 1: (Cut the Picture Vocabulary Cards apart. Place the picture cards for *hatch, slimy, damp,* and *stalks* in a container or small plastic bag.)
(Show the child each picture card.) **What word does the picture show?** (Idea: *The sidewalk is damp after the light rain.*)
Tell me what you know about this word. (You may wish to share what you know about the word with your child as well.)

DAY 2: (Add in 2 new words, *resemble* and *conceal.* Repeat procedure from Day 1.) **Today, tell me anything more that you know about this word.**

DAY 3: *What's My Word?* (Round One)
I'll give you three clues. After I give each clue, if you are sure you know my word, you may make a guess. If you guess correctly, you will win one point. If you make a mistake, I get the point.

• **First clue. My word is a describing word. Second clue. My word ends in the "p" sound. Third clue. It means "slightly wet or moist." What's my word?** *Damp.*

• **New word. First clue. My word is a describing word. Second clue. It starts with the "s" sound. Third clue. It means "soft, wet, and slippery." What's my word?** *Slimy.*
• **New word. First clue. My word is an action word. Second clue. Birds do it. Third clue. It means "to be born from an egg." What's my word?** *Hatch.*
• **New word. First clue. My word can be a naming word. Second clue. Humans don't have my word. Third clue. My word means "long, thin stems that connect one part of something to another part." What's my word?** *Stalks.*

(If the child is enjoying this game, you may wish to add additional examples.)

DAY 4: *What's My Word?* (Round Two)
Add the last two words, *conceal* and *resemble,* to the bag or container. Repeat procedure from Day 3.)

Other books your child might enjoy:

Other titles in the Are You..? series:

Are You an Ant?
Are You a Bee?
Are You a Butterfly?
Are You a Grasshopper?
Are You a Snail?
Are You a Spider?

Take your child to the public library to find more books about snails and slugs.

My reading goal:

7

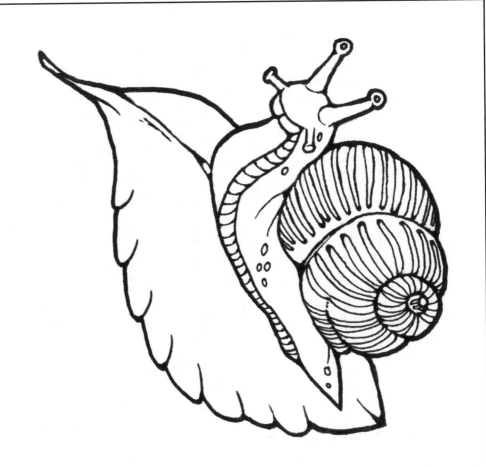

About Snails

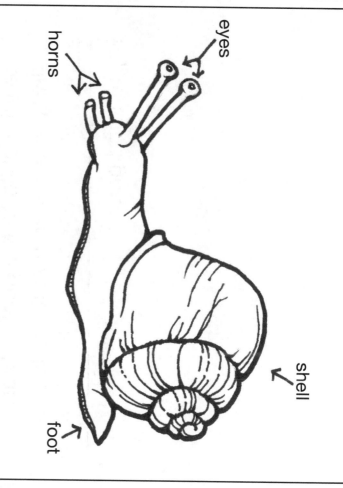

eyes

horns

shell

foot

Here is a snail. It has 2 horns and 2 eyes. It has a shell. A snail has no legs, but it has 1 foot.

1

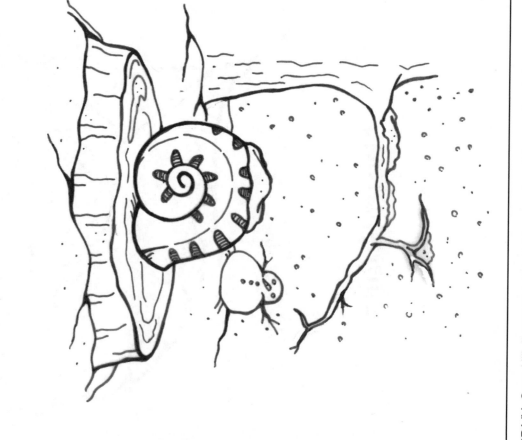

In the winter the snail sleeps in its shell. See you in the spring.

6

3

Snails like to be damp. They like the rain.

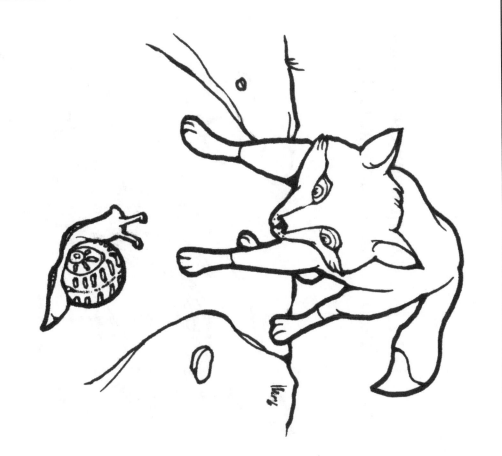

The fox would like to eat the snail.

4

(Note to Teacher: This page should be photocopied on the backside of pages 3 and 4)

5

A slug is like a snail with no shell.

A little snail comes from an egg. It will get big like its mother.

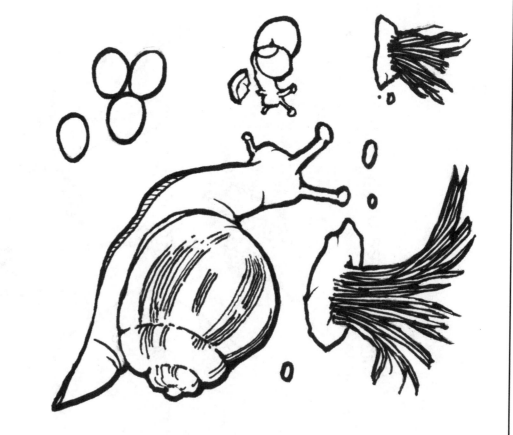

2

surface

probably

storage

corridor

colony

metamorphosis

Sharing What You've Learned at School

Note: Children are not expected to be able to read the words. They are for your information.

DAY 1: (Cut the Picture Vocabulary Cards apart. Place the picture cards for *probably, storage, corridor,* and *surface* in a container or small plastic bag.)
(Show the child each picture card.) **What word does the picture show?** (Idea: *The dolphin is surfacing from the water.*)
Tell me what you know about this word. (You may wish to share what you know about the word with the child as well.)

DAY 2: (Add in 2 new words, *colony* and *metamorphosis.*) Repeat procedure from Day 1.) **Tell me anything more that you know about this word.**

DAY 3: *What's My Word?* **(Round One)**
I'll give you three clues. After I give each clue, if you are sure you know my word, you may make a guess. If you guess correctly, you will win one point. If you make a mistake, I get the point.

- **First clue. My word is a describing word. Second clue. My word has the "b" sound in it twice. Third clue. It means "almost for sure." What's my word?** *Probably.*

- **New word. First clue. My word is a naming word. Second clue. It starts with the "d" sound. Third clue. It means "a safe place to put things until you need them." What's my word?** *Storage.*
- **New word. First clue. My word is a naming word. Second clue. It can be found in a school. Third clue. It means "a long hallway." What's my word?** *Corridor.*
- **New word. First clue. My word can be a naming word. Second clue. It has the "f" sound in it. Third clue. It means "the outside of something." What's my word?** *Surface.*

(If the child is enjoying this game, you may wish to add additional examples.)

DAY 4: *What's My Word?* **(Round Two)**
Add the last two words, *colony* and *metamorphosis,* to the bag or container. Repeat procedure from Day 3.)

Other books your child might enjoy:

Other titles in the Are You ... ? series:

Are You an Ant?
Are You a Bee?
Are You a Butterfly?
Are You a Grasshopper?
Are You a Snail?
Are You a Spider?

Take your child to the public library to find more books about ants and other insects.

My reading goal:

7

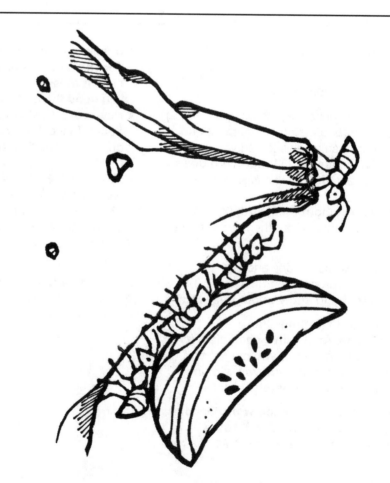

About Ants

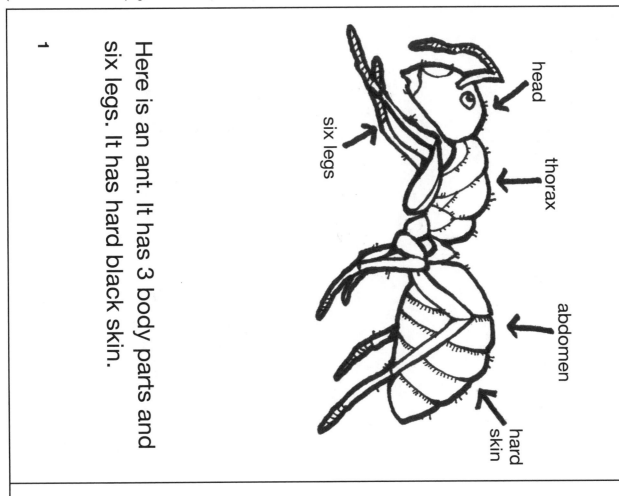

1

Here is an ant. It has 3 body parts and six legs. It has hard black skin.

6

Ants like to eat seeds and bugs. They take honeydew from aphids. It is the best.

Then the eggs are pupae. Pupae are like big eggs.

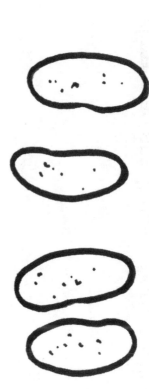

3

Soft white ants come from the pupae. They get hard black skin.

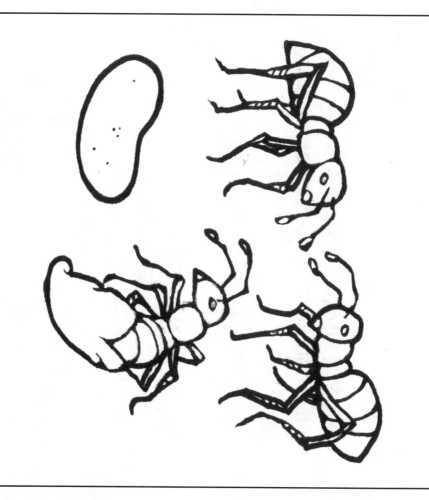

4

5

Ants like to dig and dig. They make lots and lots of rooms.

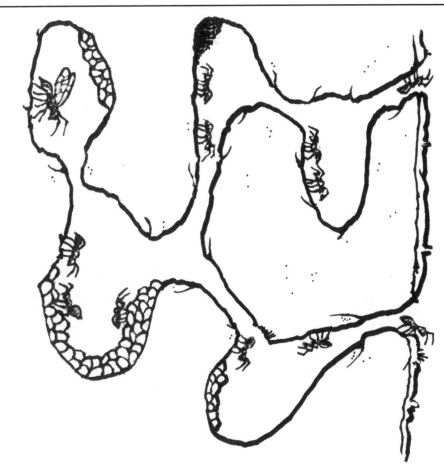

Ants start in eggs. The queen makes lots and lots of eggs.

2